Fodor's 2010

LOS S

Where
for All E

Must-Se
and Loc

Ratings

Fodor's Travel Publications New York, Toronto, London, Sydney, Auckland
www.fodors.com

FODOR'S LOS ANGELES 2010

Editors: Kelly Kealy (lead editor), Joanna Cantor

Editorial Contributor: Katherine Hamlin
Writers: Roger J. Grody, Susan MacCallum-Whitcomb, Kathy A. McDonald, Stef McDonald, Laura Randall, Kastle Waserman

Production Editor: Jennifer DePrima
Maps & Illustrations: David Lindroth and Mark Stroud, *cartographers;* Bob Blake, Rebecca Baer, *map editors*; William Wu, *information graphics*
Design: Fabrizio LaRocca, *creative director*; Guido Caroti, Siobhan O'Hare, *art directors*; Tina Malaney, Chie Ushio, Ann McBride, Jessica Walsh, *designers*; Melanie Marin, *senior picture editor*
Cover Photo: (Walk of Fame, Hollywood) Bernard Foubert/Photononstop
Production Manager: Angela L. McLean

COPYRIGHT

ISBN 978-1-4000-0850-6

ISSN 1095-3914

SPECIAL SALES

This book is available at special discounts for bulk purchases for sales promotions or premiums. Special editions, including personalized covers, excerpts of existing books, and corporate imprints, can be created in large quantities for special needs. For more information, write to Special Markets/Premium Sales, 1745 Broadway, MD 6-2, New York, New York 10019, or e-mail specialmarkets@randomhouse.com.

AN IMPORTANT TIP & AN INVITATION

Although all prices, opening times, and other details in this book are based on information supplied to us at press time, changes occur all the time in the travel world, and Fodor's cannot accept responsibility for facts that become outdated or for inadvertent errors or omissions. So **always confirm information when it matters,** especially if you're making a detour to visit a specific place. Your experiences—positive and negative—matter to us. If we have missed or misstated something, **please write to us.** We follow up on all suggestions. Contact the Los Angeles editor at editors@fodors.com or c/o Fodor's at 1745 Broadway, New York, NY 10019.

PRINTED IN THE UNITED STATES OF AMERICA

10 9 8 7 6 5 4 3 2 1

Be a Fodor's Correspondent

Your opinion matters. It matters to us. It matters to your fellow Fodor's travelers, too. And we'd like to hear it. In fact, we need to hear it.

When you share your experiences and opinions, you become an active member of the Fodor's community. That means we'll not only use your feedback to make our books better, but we'll publish your names and comments whenever possible. Throughout our guides, look for "Word of Mouth," excerpts of your unvarnished feedback.

Here's how you can help improve Fodor's for all of us.

Tell us when we're right. We rely on local writers to give you an insider's perspective. But our writers and staff editors—who are the best in the business—depend on you. Your positive feedback is a vote to renew our recommendations for the next edition.

Tell us when we're wrong. We're proud that we update most of our guides every year. But we're not perfect. Things change. Hotels cut services. Museums change hours. Charming cafés lose charm. If our writer didn't quite capture the essence of a place, tell us how you'd do it differently. If any of our descriptions are inaccurate or inadequate, we'll incorporate your changes in the next edition and will correct factual errors at fodors.com immediately.

Tell us what to include. You probably have had fantastic travel experiences that aren't yet in Fodor's. Why not share them with a community of like-minded travelers? Maybe you chanced upon a beach or bistro or B&B that you don't want to keep to yourself. Tell us why we should include it. And share your discoveries and experiences with everyone directly at fodors.com. Your input may lead us to add a new listing or highlight a place we cover with a "Highly Recommended" star or with our highest rating, "Fodor's Choice."

Give us your opinion instantly at our feedback center at www.fodors.com/feedback. You may also e-mail editors@fodors.com with the subject line "Los Angeles Editor." Or send your nominations, comments, and complaints by mail to Los Angeles Editor, Fodor's, 1745 Broadway, New York, NY 10019.

You and travelers like you are the heart of the Fodor's community. Make our community richer by sharing your experiences. Be a Fodor's correspondent.

Happy traveling!

Tim Jarrell, Publisher

CONTENTS

MAPS

ABOUT THIS BOOK

Our Ratings

Sometimes you find terrific travel experiences and sometimes they just find you. But usually the burden is on you to select the right combination of experiences. That's where our ratings come in.

As travelers we've all discovered a place so wonderful that its worthiness is obvious. And sometimes that place is so unique that superlatives don't do it justice: you just have to be there to know. These sights, properties, and experiences get our highest rating, **Fodor's Choice**, indicated by orange stars throughout this book. Black stars highlight sights and properties we deem **Highly Recommended**, places that our writers, editors, and readers praise again and again for consistency and excellence. By default, there's another category: any place we include in this book is by definition worth your time, unless we say otherwise. And we will.

Disagree with any of our choices? Care to nominate a place or suggest that we rate one more highly? Visit our feedback center at www.fodors.com/feedback.

Budget Well

Hotel and restaurant price categories from ¢ to $$$$ are defined in the opening pages of their respective chapters. For attractions, we always give standard adult admission fees; reductions are usually available for children, students, and senior citizens. Want to pay with plastic? **AE, D, DC, MC, V** following restaurant and hotel listings indicate whether American Express, Discover, Diners Club, MasterCard, and Visa are accepted.

Restaurants

Unless we state otherwise, restaurants are open for lunch and dinner daily. We mention dress only when there's a specific requirement and reservations only when they're essential or not accepted—it's always best to book ahead.

Hotels

Hotels have private bath, phone, TV, and air-conditioning and operate on the European Plan (aka EP, meaning without meals), unless we specify that they use the Continental Plan (CP, with a continental breakfast), Breakfast Plan (BP, with a full breakfast), or Modified American Plan (MAP, with breakfast and dinner) or are all-inclusive (including all meals and most activities). We always list facilities but not whether you'll be charged an extra fee to use them, so when pricing accommodations, find out what's included.

Many Listings

- ★ Fodor's Choice
- ★ Highly recommended
- ✉ Physical address
- ✥ Directions
- 📫 Mailing address
- ☎ Telephone
- 📠 Fax
- 🌐 On the Web
- E-mail
- Admission fee
- ⏲ Open/closed times
- Ⓜ Metro stations
- 💳 Credit cards

Hotels & Restaurants

- Hotel
- Number of rooms
- Facilities
- 🍽 Meal plans
- ✕ Restaurant
- Reservations
- Smoking
- BYOB
- Hotel with restaurant that warrants a visit

Outdoors

- Golf
- Camping

Other

- Family-friendly
- ⇨ See also
- Branch address
- ☞ Take note

Experience Los Angeles

WORD OF MOUTH

"One of the great things about my trip to LA was all the free guided tours I was able to take (El Pueblo de Los Angeles, Walt Disney Concert Hall, Central Library). There are so many great places to visit without spending a dime in LA. While museum admission can add up, most museums offer free admission on certain days or certain hours."

—yk

www.fodors.com/community

LOS ANGELES TODAY

Star-struck . . . excessive . . . smoggy . . . superficial. . . . There's a modicum of truth to each of the adjectives regularly applied to L.A. But Angelenos—and most objective visitors—dismiss their prevalence as signs of envy from people who hail from places less blessed with fun and sun. Pop Culture, for instance, *does* permeate life in LaLaLand: a massive economy employing millions of Southern Californians is built around it. Yet this city also boasts high-brow appeal, having amassed an impressive array of world-class museums and arts venues. Moreover, it has burgeoning neighborhoods that bear little resemblance to those featured on *The Hills* or *Entourage*. America's second-largest city has more depth than paparazzi shutters can ever capture. So set aside your preconceived notions and take a look at L.A. Today.

Downtown's Upswing

Los Angeles has been archly described as "72 suburbs in search of a city." Hence the renaissance its once-desolate Downtown is currently experiencing might come as something of a surprise. Thanks to an influx of residents (more than 15,000 of them in the past five years) long-neglected neighborhoods have been spruced up, and streets even the police deemed irredeemable have been revitalized. As if that wasn't enough, assorted new edifices have also been erected with tourists in mind. The largest of the lot is L.A. Live: a 27-acre, $2.5-billion entertainment complex adjacent to the Staples Center. The ribbon was cut on its Nokia Theatre in late 2007; while late 2008 saw the opening of Club Nokia (a smaller 2,300-seat sister venue) and the innovative Grammy Museum. Next up: a 54-story hotel tower that is expected to start welcoming guests in 2010. OK, cue the Petula Clark soundtrack.

State of the Art

SoCal's beauty-obsessed citizens aren't the only ones opting for a fresh look these days: esteemed art museums are, too. Following a trend set by the Getty Villa, which unveiled its "extreme makeover" in 2006, Anaheim's Bowers Museum and Long Beach's Museum of Latin American Art each doubled their exhibition space in 2007. The Huntington Art Gallery (a glorious mansion-cum-museum on the grounds of the Huntington Library, Art Collections, and Botanical Gardens in San Marino) emerged from its own $20-million overhaul in 2008 as a "must see" site for lovers of European art. But it's the new kid in town—the Broad Contemporary Art Museum—that is generating the biggest buzz. Set on the Los Angeles County Museum of Art campus, the three-story structure was designed by starchitect Renzo Piano and modern masters like Warhol and Hirst share wall space within its six galleries.

Food for Thought

Upscale eateries flourish here: in 2008 alone, Gordon Ramsey, José Andrés, and Michael Mina established L.A. outposts. However, the local dining scene remains relatively equalitarian. Even posh restaurants seldom require jackets, so the dress code is casual. Ditto for the menu. (In the city that invented fast food, it's no coincidence that Govind Armstrong flips gourmet burgers or that Wolfgang Puck built his reputation on pizza!) Of course, if the recession has taken a bite out of your budget, you can easily justify chowing down at McDonald's, Carl's Jr., and In-N-Out Burger because all, having started in the Five-County Area, qualify

as "indigenous cuisine." Alternately, you can savor L.A.'s international flavor by grabbing sushi from a conveyor belt in a *kaiten-zushi* restaurant, sampling *siu mai* served from a rolling cart by a Chinese matron, or ordering carne asada to go from an old-school taco truck.

Access Hollywood

Hollywood may disappoint tourists looking to overdose on glitz: after all, most of its movie makers departed for the San Fernando Valley decades ago, leaving the area to languish. Even after the much-hyped 2001 debut of the Hollywood & Highland Center (a mixed-use complex anchored by the Kodak Theater), it remained more gritty than glamorous. Yet new life is continually being pumped in. Affluent young residents are moving into lofts carved out of historic buildings; hotels are going up (among them a W Hotel slated to open in late 2009 as part of the new $600-million Hollywood & Vine development); and vintage venues like the Hollywood Palladium are being refurbished. In honor of the industry that made it famous, Madame Tussauds is also constructing a themed museum adjacent to Grauman's Chinese Theatre. Its 80-plus wax figures will be ready for their close-up in mid 2009.

Coming Clean

It isn't easy being green—especially when you're habitually held up as the poster child for air pollution—but L.A. is committed to becoming more environmentally friendly. In fact, Mayor Villaraigosa aspires to turn it into "the greenest big city in America." Measurable changes have already been made. For starters, smog levels (a standard joke among late-night monologuists) have been reduced: in part because of stricter statewide controls on greenhouse gas emissions, and in part because of ambitious civic transit projects. Metro's 2,500 buses now run on compressed natural gas, while its five subway and light rail lines are powered by electricity, making this one of the cleanest public transportations systems in the country. The "go green" agenda also extends to city-owned buildings like the Los Angeles Convention Center, which is the largest solar-generating facility of its kind on the continent.

L.A. Free Ways

Though high-profile Angelenos have elevated conspicuous consumption to an art, you can still spend time here without dropping a dime. Visiting culture vultures will be relieved to learn that the Getty Center and Getty Villa offer free admission, and that the Los Angeles County Music Center hosts complimentary tours, plus no-cost programs under the "Active Arts" banner. Frugal movie fans can get reel on Hollywood Boulevard's star-paved Walk of Fame or in the forecourt of Grauman's Chinese where celebs have been pressing hands, feet, and other body parts into cement since 1927 (time it right and you might catch a premiere too). Music buffs, meanwhile, can view memorabilia from past headliners in the free Hollywood Bowl Museum. Prefer a different kind of stargazing? There is no fee to see the Griffith Observatory's stellar exhibits or peer through its giant telescope.

—Susan MacCallum-Whitcomb

LOS ANGELES PLANNER

Weather This

Any time of the year is the right time to visit Los Angeles. From November to May, you'll find crisp, sunny, unusually smog-free days. December to April is the rainy season, but storms are usually brief, followed by brilliant skies. Nearby mountains are glorious in winter, perfect for skiing. Dining alfresco, sailing, and catching a concert under the stars—these are reserved for L.A. summers, which are virtually rainless (with an occasional air-quality alert). Prices skyrocket and reservations are essential when tourism peaks July through September.

Southern California is a temperate area, moderated by the Pacific Ocean. In addition, mountains along the north and east sides of the Los Angeles coastal basin act as buffers against the extreme summer heat and winter cold of the surrounding desert and plateau regions.

Pasadena and the San Fernando Valley are significantly hotter than Beverly Hills or Hollywood, while coastal areas can be dramatically cooler. Late spring brings "June gloom," when skies tend to be overcast until afternoon.

Getting Around

As nightmarish as the L.A. freeways can be, it is unthinkable what life would be like without them. In L.A., where the automobile is worshipped—and will be, no matter how high gas prices go—the freeways are the best way for visitors to get around town. Rent a car at the airport. If you desire a more exotic ride (e.g., Bentley, Lamborghini), specialty rental agencies can accommodate you, but be prepared to spend as much as $3,000 per day. A more modest luxury that you should never go without is a GPS system, which most rental companies offer.

With the exception of downtown high-rises, where the cost of parking is exorbitant—look for flat-rate surface lots instead—parking in L.A. is not prohibitively expensive. When driving anywhere in SoCal, avoid rush hour (before 10 AM and between 5 and 7 PM) if at all possible, and remember that even-numbered freeways run east–west, and odd-numbered ones run north–south. If you're not familiar with the city and don't have GPS in your car, make Mapquest.com your best friend.

There are, however, ways to get around Los Angeles without a car. Taxis are not as plentiful as in New York or San Francisco, but you can always find one at a major hotel. From LAX to downtown, a cab ride runs about $42 and shuttle vans cost about $16 per person. And there's no easier town in which to find a limo or town car!

To many people's surprise, modern-day L.A. does have public transit. Futuristic-looking buses rumble along all major thoroughfares (and freeways) and a burgeoning subway system (Red Line) connects downtown L.A. with Hollywood, Universal City, and the Wilshire Corridor (a "subway to the ocean," serving the Westside, is in the works). The subway is ultramodern, clean, and safe, and is complemented by grade level or elevated light rail lines that connect Pasadena (Gold Line) and Long Beach (Blue Line) to downtown. A Metro Day Pass, honored on any part of the system, costs $5 and can be purchased at any station or online. In addition, Metrolink commuter trains shuttle people in and out of L.A. from distant suburbs like Riverside, Buena Park, and Santa Clarita.

The (Entertainment) Industry

L.A. lives and breathes "the Industry," as a massive hunk of the world's film, television, and music is produced here. What is mere celebrity gossip in Baltimore is serious business in L.A. Movie premieres and award shows are to the L.A. economy as Federal Reserve interest rate meetings are to Wall Street. Much of the local economy is dedicated to the process of planning, producing, and promoting what plays in America's theaters, homes, and nightclubs. Most of the action goes on behind closed doors. If you want a closer look at the Industry, become a Method tourist! All megahits begin with an idea, and half the members of the WGA (Writers Guild of America) cultivate those ideas over coffee, frequently at Westside locations of Coffee Bean & Tea Leaf shops. If you want to lunch where studio execs and agents hammer out details with famous clients, consider the Grill on the Alley in Beverly Hills, Craft Los Angeles in Century City, or the Ivy on Robertson Boulevard, where there are always plenty of famous faces. If you want to see some real action, you'll have to tour Warner Bros. Studios in the Valley or sign up as a TV audience member with Audiences Unlimited (⇨ *see Chapter 5*).

Car Culture

Angelenos spend a disproportionate amount of time in their cars, often involuntarily during long commutes to work. But there's a beauty to the freeways—Joan Didion famously wrote about the hypnotic pull of these concrete ribbons—and the automobile has been endlessly romanticized in L.A. In fact, as many of the Beach Boys' hits (e.g., *I Get Around, Little Deuce Coupe, 409*) obsess about cars as girls. The drive-through restaurant came of age in L.A. (cult favorite In-N-Out Burger may have invented it) and funky roadside commercial architecture—towering drive-through doughnuts or hot dogs stands shaped like a giant franks—still dots the L.A. streetscape. As a tourist it's easy to get into the spirit of L.A.'s passionate car culture. A convertible may cost more to rent, but what better place to drive one? You might want to even splurge on a trendy sports car, a knockout classic, or something exotic like a Maserati. Or you might rent an ecofriendly hybrid vehicle, the choice of Cameron Diaz and Leonardo DiCaprio.

Top Festivals and Events

Tournament of Roses Every New Year's Day the world convenes in charming Pasadena to witness a parade showcasing spectacular flower-covered floats, marching bands, and equestrians. The festivities continue with the Rose Bowl college football game.

Toyota Grand Prix Long Beach may not be Monte Carlo or Le Mans, but in April exotic open-wheel cars take to the streets of this South Bay city. The world's most elite drivers participate in the race as more than 100,000 fans look on.

Cinco de Mayo Commemorating Mexico's victory over the French in 1862, this is a celebration that transcends the Latino community to involve everybody. Plenty of Mexican food, mariachi music, and folk dancing are the order of the day every May 5.

Nisei Week A multifaceted celebration in L.A.'s Little Tokyo, this August event is punctuated by the beats of traditional taiko drummers as kimono-clad dance troupes, arts-and-crafts fairs, and a tofu festival endear large crowds to the beauty of Japanese culture.

Los Angeles Film Festival This summer gathering brings filmmakers and stars from around the world to compete in what has quietly emerged as one of the most prestigious forums for independent productions.

WHAT'S WHERE

1 Downtown Los Angeles. Downtown L.A. shows off spectacular modern architecture in the swooping Walt Disney Concert Hall and the stark Cathedral of Our Lady of the Angels. The Music Center and the Museum of Contemporary Art anchor a world-class arts scene, while Olvera Street, Chinatown, and Little Tokyo reflect the city's history and diversity.

2 Hollywood. Glitzy and tarnished, good and bad, fun and sad—Hollywood is just like the entertainment business itself. They don't make many movies or TV shows here anymore, but after decades of decline the neighborhood is suddenly hot. The Walk of Fame, Grauman's Chinese Theatre, and the Hollywood Bowl keep the neighborhood's romantic past alive.

3 West Hollywood. West Hollywood's an area for urban indulgences—shopping, restaurants, nightspots—rather than sightseeing. Its main arteries are the Sunset Strip (Sunset Boulevard), shorthand for longstanding clubs and cruising past boffo billboards, and Melrose Avenue, lined with shops punk, precious, and postmodern. In WeHo, opulence and bohemianism coexist beautifully and diverse lifestyles are celebrated.

4 Beverly Hills, Century City, and the Westside. Go for the glamour, the restaurants, and the scene. This is the L.A. that gives East Coasters material for snarky jokes: plastic surgery, scads of sushi spots, and exotic cars inching along congested streets like Sunset, Wilshire, and Santa Monica boulevards. Beverly Hills' Rodeo Drive is particularly good for a look at wretched or ravishing excess. But don't forget the Westside's cultural attractions—especially the dazzling Getty Center.

5 Santa Monica, Venice, and Malibu. In Santa Monica, a lively beach scene plays out every day. A study in contrasts, real estate is breathtakingly expensive, but liberal community leaders don't scare off the homeless. Venice, just south of Santa Monica, is a more raffish mix of artists, beach punks, and yuppies, most of whom you'll see on the Venice Boardwalk. Or drive up PCH (you know, Pacific Coast Highway) to Malibu, where the rich and famous hide away in their residential "Colony." An extravagant residence of a different kind, the Getty Villa Malibu is stuffed with exquisite antiquities.

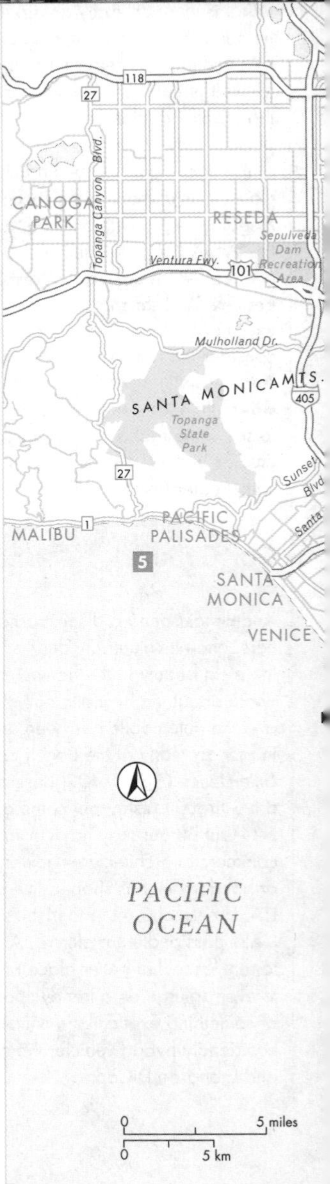

SAN GABRIEL MOUNTAINS
Mt. Wilson
Angeles Crest Hwy.
SAN FERNANDO
Foothill Fwy.
LA CAÑADA FLINTRIDGE
Golden State Fwy.
BURBANK
GLENDALE
VAN NUYS
PASADENA
HIGHLAND PARK
SHERMAN OAKS
Griffith Park
Foothill Fwy.
SAN MARINO
Sunset Blvd.
Pasadena Fwy.
Hollywood Blvd.
Santa Monica Blvd.
BEVERLY HILLS
HOLLYWOOD
ALHAMBRA
SAN GABRIEL
EL MONTE
Dodger Stadium
San Bernardino Fwy.
Monica Blvd.
DOWNTOWN
MONTEREY PARK
Santa Monica Fwy.
CULVER CITY
San Diego Fwy.
Santa Ana Fwy.
Rosemead Blvd.
Pomona Fwy.
Slauson Ave.
MARINA DEL REY
INGLEWOOD
HUNTINGTON PARK
WHITTIER
Los Angeles International Airport
Imperial Hwy.
Harbor Fwy.
DOWNEY
River Fwy.
EL SEGUNDO
Sepulveda Blvd.
Hawthorne Blvd.
Western Ave.
San Gabriel
MANHATTAN BEACH
COMPTON
Long Beach Fwy.
Riverside Fwy.
HERMOSA BEACH
TORRANCE
Pacific Coast Hwy.
San Diego Fwy.
REDONDO BEACH
LAKEWOOD
ANAHEIM
PALOS VERDES ESTATES
GARDEN GROVE
Pacific Coast Hwy.
San Diego Fwy.
RANCH PALOS VERDES
LONG BEACH
SAN PEDRO

WHAT'S WHERE

6 San Fernando Valley. Referred to simply as "the Valley," the San Fernando Valley is the undisputed center of TV and film production. It's also got a hard-to-beat rep for tackiness and soulless urban sprawl. The main sightseeing draws are tied into the Industry: Universal Studios Hollywood, studio tours at Warner Bros., and television-show tapings at NBC.

7 Pasadena Area. Like Santa Monica, Pasadena may appear to be an extension of L.A. but it's actually a separate city with a strong sense of community. (You've probably seen the main drag on TV, during the Tournament of Roses Parade on New Year's Day.) It's a quiet, genteel area to visit, with outstanding Arts and Crafts homes, good dining, and a pair of exceptional museums: the Norton Simon and the Huntington estate in adjoining San Marino.

8 Long Beach, San Pedro, and Palos Verdes. The peninsula of Palos Verdes and the port cities of San Pedro and Long Beach are far from the commotion of stars and stargazers. You'll likely come here only if you're interested in specific sights, like the Aquarium of the Pacific or the art deco Queen Mary ship in Long Beach. San Pedro is a rough fishing village beginning to attract yuppie residents, and the Palos Verdes communities are affluent enclaves.

9 Disneyland and Knott's Berry Farm. Disneyland, in Anaheim, is the top family destination, and it's expanded from the humble park of Walt Disney's vision to a mega-resort with more attractions spilling over into Disney's California Adventure. But one thing is certain—kids still consider it the happiest place on earth. Knott's Berry Farm, in nearby Buena Park, offers thrill rides, the Peanuts gang, and plenty of fried chicken and boysenberry pie.

10 Orange County and Catalina Island. For decades, Orange County was equated with Disneyland, but these days, the OC's beach communities are getting just as much attention, even if they aren't quite as glamorous as seen on TV. Coastal spots like Huntington Beach, Newport Harbor, and Laguna Beach (which offers arts festivals and nature preserves) are perfect for chilling out in a beachfront hotel. A short boat ride away is Catalina Island, with its pocket-size town and large nature preserve.

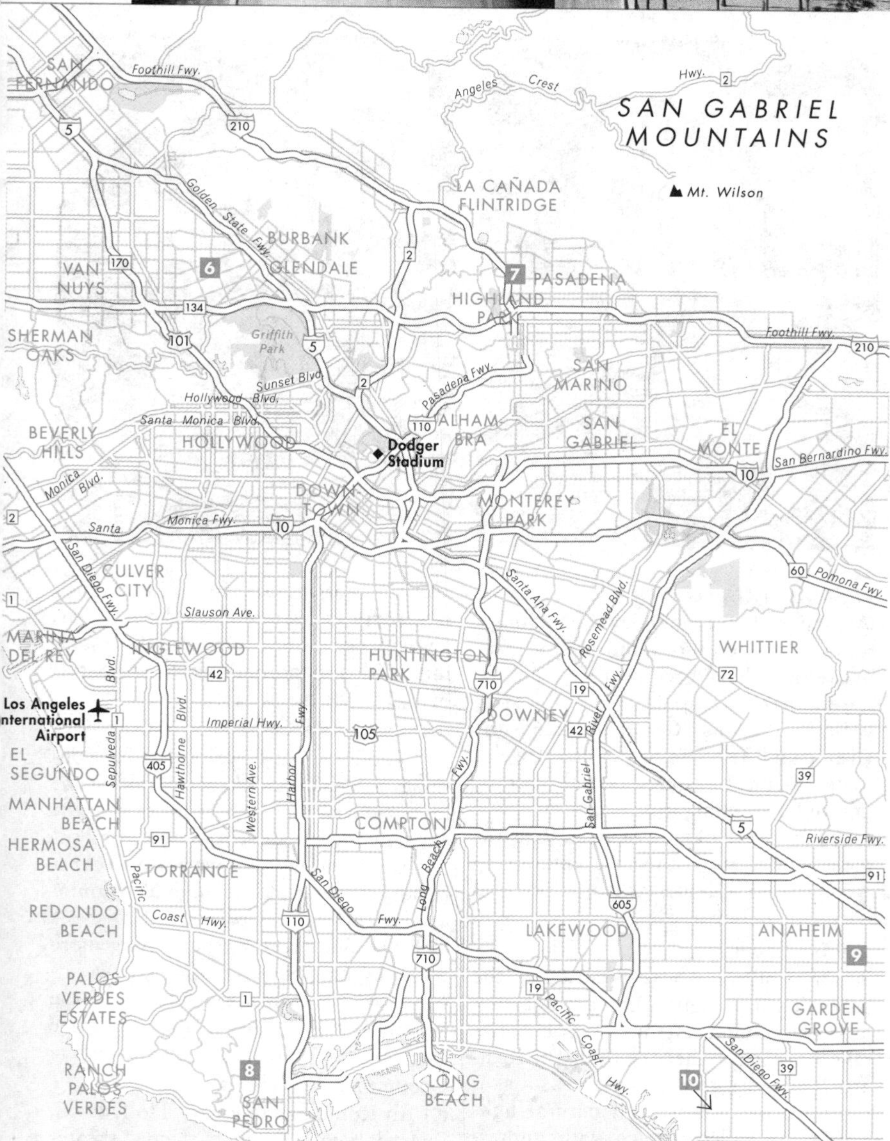
SAN GABRIEL MOUNTAINS
Mt. Wilson
Angeles Crest Hwy.
Foothill Fwy.
SAN FERNANDO
LA CAÑADA FLINTRIDGE
Golden State Fwy.
BURBANK
GLENDALE
VAN NUYS
PASADENA
HIGHLAND PARK
SHERMAN OAKS
Griffith Park
Sunset Blvd.
Hollywood Blvd.
Santa Monica Blvd.
Pasadena Fwy.
SAN MARINO
ALHAMBRA
SAN GABRIEL
EL MONTE
San Bernardino Fwy.
BEVERLY HILLS
HOLLYWOOD
Dodger Stadium
Monica Blvd.
DOWNTOWN
MONTEREY PARK
Santa Monica Fwy.
San Diego Fwy.
CULVER CITY
Santa Ana Fwy.
Rosemead Blvd.
Pomona Fwy.
Slauson Ave.
MARINA DEL REY
INGLEWOOD
HUNTINGTON PARK
WHITTIER
Los Angeles International Airport
Imperial Hwy.
DOWNEY
River Fwy.
EL SEGUNDO
Sepulveda Blvd.
Hawthorne Blvd.
Western Ave.
Harbor Fwy.
Long Beach Fwy.
San Gabriel
MANHATTAN BEACH
HERMOSA BEACH
COMPTON
Riverside Fwy.
TORRANCE
Pacific Coast Hwy.
San Diego Fwy.
REDONDO BEACH
LAKEWOOD
ANAHEIM
PALOS VERDES ESTATES
GARDEN GROVE
RANCH PALOS VERDES
SAN PEDRO
LONG BEACH
6
7
8
9
10

LOS ANGELES TOP ATTRACTIONS

Walt Disney Concert Hall

(A) Designed by Frank Gehry, the voluptuous curves of this stainless steel-clad masterpiece have become a signature of the modern metropolis. One of several venues of the Music Center, the 2,265-seat Disney Hall is home to the Los Angeles Philharmonic. It features unrivaled acoustics and a stunning pipe organ, which is as much a work of art as a musical instrument. For a truly opulent evening, pair a concert with dinner at Patina, located inside the building.

The Getty Center

(B) On a hillside above Brentwood, the $1 billion-plus Getty Center is not only a museum, but a statement that L.A. has taken its place in the art world. The Richard Meier–designed complex has a skin of travertine marble and natural light floods the galleries filled with impressionist masterpieces, Greek antiquities, and jaw-dropping exhibits of furniture and decorative arts from the French monarchy. Pedestrian plazas and gardens abound, and a sunset dinner at the restaurant, with its panoramic views, is the stuff of scrapbook memories.

Disneyland Resort

(C) "The Happiest Place on Earth," continues to delight children and all but the most cynical adults. A visit here can be enchanting, exciting, romantic, or nostalgic, depending on your age and experience. Disneyland, the original vision of Walt Disney, is now paired with Disney's California Adventure, showcasing more recent Disney characters and Hollywood-oriented attractions. Outside the theme parks, Downtown Disney supports a wide range of restaurants, bars, and clubs.

Grauman's Chinese Theatre

(D) An iconic metaphor for Hollywood, this elaborate Chinese-theme theater opened in 1927 with the premier of Cecil B. DeMille's *King of Kings*. That's when

D

E

F

G

the tradition of stars imprinting their hands or feet into the cement began with an "accidental" footprint by Norma Talmadge. More than 160 stars have contributed, and among the more unique prints are the nose of Jimmy Durante and hoofs of Trigger. The theater is adjacent to the Hollywood & Highland center.

Rodeo Drive

(E) Dominated by the exclusive names of Gucci, Versace, and Cartier, Rodeo Drive is a shoppers' paradise. Along the cobblestoned, Mediterranean-inspired Via Rodeo, you can drop a thousand dollars on python pumps or nosh on a $500 sushi dinner. Fortunately, Rodeo Drive doesn't cater exclusively to the rich and famous, and more moderate shops and restaurants are interspersed with the iconic boutiques.

The Venice Boardwalk

(F) The bohemian lifestyle of this famous boardwalk is constantly threatened by the rapid gentrification of Venice. Still, the magicians, fortune-tellers, and Muscle Beach weightlifters—this is where Hizoner, the Governor, got his start—still survive. Struggling artists sell their paintings, infiltrated by tackier purveyors of cheap watches and sunglasses. Rent a bicycle or in-line skates, grab a hot dog, and enjoy the sights and the sunset.

The Hollywood Sign

(G) With its 50-foot-tall letters, the HOLLYWOOD sign is an indelible stamp on the hills of Tinseltown visible from much of Hollywood and beyond. Originally reading HOLLYWOODLAND, it was erected on Mount Lee in 1923 to promote a real estate development (the unfamiliar appendix wasn't dropped until 1949).

GREAT ITINERARIES

L.A. Icons

Head straight for the riches of Beverly Hills. Many of the stereotypes about Angelenos are rooted here. But hey, you're a visitor, you're allowed to indulge in some gawking! Drive along Sunset Boulevard, dipping into Bel Air. Then stretch your legs with shopping, real or window, on Rodeo Drive. Gucci, Versace, and Prada may dent your nest egg, but there are also many moderate places to shop. For a fun, nostalgic look at the television industry, check out the Paley Center for Media.

A bird's-eye view of the city from the Getty Center, in Brentwood, is not far away. Wander among the stunning, travertine marble-clad pavilions and explore the gardens. And then there's the art, including exceptional European paintings and antique French furniture. But it's hard to tear your eyes from the view, especially at sunset. Dine in nearby Brentwood, West Hollywood or back in Beverly Hills—Spago, anyone?

Going Coastal

You're in L.A., so heading to the coast is a must. Before you pack your picnic, do some planning and pick a beach that suits your needs (⇨ *see Chapter 6*). The Pacific can be cold, but swimming is not the only attraction along the coast. Santa Monica Pier is nostalgic fun, complete with old-school amusement-park rides. Nearby you can rent bikes to ride along the Venice Boardwalk.

Or take that convertible up the coast to Malibu. Wander the beach or check out the revamped Getty Villa Malibu, dedicated to Greco-Roman antiquities. As with the Getty Center, the gardens and views are almost as mesmerizing as what's in the galleries. Back in Santa Monica, consider waterfront dining at the Lobster.

Downtown Bound

Pick a weekday to venture downtown—and wear comfortable shoes because unlike other parts of L.A., downtown is best explored on foot. Start at the Cathedral of Our Lady of the Angels, then proceed to Walt Disney Concert Hall and the Museum of Contemporary Art. Not far is the Grand Central Market, where you might pick up a tamale. Hop back in the car or on the convenient DASH bus for a short ride to the grand Union Station; zip across to Olvera Street for a taste of Mexican culture. Evenings downtown mean performances at Disney Hall, concerts at the state-of-the-art Nokia Theatre or games at Staples Center. For cocktails, head to the Millennium Biltmore (retro) or Downtown Standard (cutting-edge). And don't forget burgeoning Little Tokyo for sushi, or spicy fare in neighboring Chinatown.

Hurray for Hollywood

Over breakfast check the Calendar section of the *Los Angeles Times* for showtimes at old movie palaces like Grauman's Chinese or the El Capitan. (The ArcLight is another top film spot, offering plush seating and upscale snacks.) Drive or take the Metro to the Hollywood & Highland complex, and tour the Kodak Theatre, where the Academy Awards are held. You can wander the Walk of Fame, paying your respects to your favorite celluloid stars at their plaques, or drop into the Hollywood Museum. The awesome Amoeba Records shop is a mecca for music fans, and Musso & Frank Grill (Hollywood's oldest restaurant) offers classic comfort cuisine.

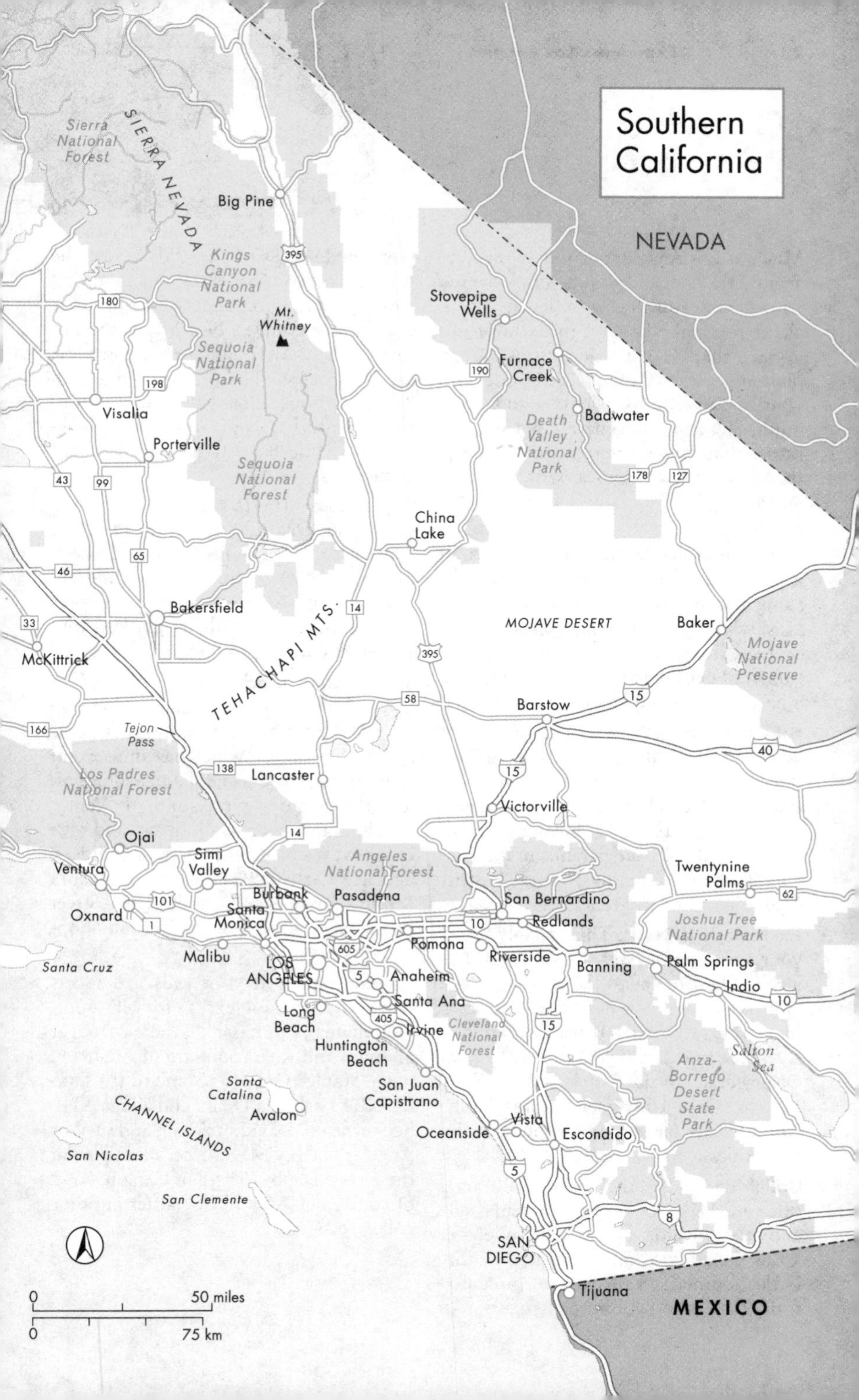

Southern California
NEVADA
MEXICO
SIERRA NEVADA
Sierra National Forest
Big Pine
395
Kings Canyon National Park
Mt. Whitney
180
Sequoia National Park
198
Visalia
Porterville
Sequoia National Forest
43
99
65
46
Bakersfield
33
McKittrick
TEHACHAPI MTS.
14
Stovepipe Wells
Furnace Creek
190
Badwater
Death Valley National Park
178
127
China Lake
MOJAVE DESERT
Baker
Mojave National Preserve
58
Barstow
15
40
166
Tejon Pass
138
Lancaster
Los Padres National Forest
Victorville
Ojai
Ventura
Simi Valley
Angeles National Forest
Twentynine Palms
62
Burbank
Pasadena
San Bernardino
101
Oxnard
Santa Monica
1
10
Redlands
Joshua Tree National Park
605
Pomona
Malibu
Riverside
Banning
Palm Springs
Santa Cruz
LOS ANGELES
5
Anaheim
Indio
Santa Ana
Long Beach
405
Irvine
Cleveland National Forest
Salton Sea
Huntington Beach
Anza-Borrego Desert State Park
Santa Catalina
San Juan Capistrano
CHANNEL ISLANDS
Avalon
Oceanside
Vista
Escondido
San Nicolas
San Clemente
8
SAN DIEGO
Tijuana
0
50 miles
0
75 km

LOS ANGELES WITH KIDS

Much of Los Angeles's economy revolves around the care and feeding of pampered young stars. Pair that with the city's penchant for make-believe and you've got a place that's a natural for kids. When planning a trip with the little ones, do your best to keep freeway time to a minimum. Stick to one general area per day rather than trying to cross the city more than once. Santa Monica, with its beach access and bike trails, is a good base for families.

Aquarium of the Pacific. One of the best aquariums in the West, this premiere Long Beach attraction is wonderful for kids, who enjoy watching frolicking seals and sea lions, learning about conservation, and petting baby sharks and rays in a hands-on marine ecosystem.

California Science Center. Filled with interactive, kid-friendly exhibits ranging from biology to seismology to astronomy and space travel, this Exposition Park museum is paired with an IMAX theater designed to wow both kids and parents. In the same park is the kid-friendly Natural History Museum of Los Angeles County.

The Disneyland Resort. This is likely top of your list (⇨ *seeChapter 8 for tips*). Ideally, it's best to spend the previous night at a nearby hotel to get an early start at the parks, rather than driving down from L.A. the same day. If you've already done Disneyland, consider Knott's Berry Farm (also in OC), Universal Studios Hollywood, or Six Flags Magic Mountain (for thrill rides).

Griffith Park. Griffith Park's 4,100 acres offer a little bit of everything. Children's activities include pony rides, a classic 1926 merry-go-round, and the Griffith Park Southern Railroad (a miniature train that takes young passengers past fabricated scenes of the Old West). The Autry National Center, commemorating cowboy and Native American culture, is also fun for families. Nearby sits the Los Angeles Zoo. Although overshadowed by San Diego's, it is an impressive venue with 80 acres of exhibits. The recently renovated Griffith Observatory and Planetarium is another of the park's "star" attractions.

Page Museum at the La Brea Tar Pits. If you'd like to squeeze in a museum, the Page Museum at La Brea Tar Pits may be best, especially if you have younger children. But look into the Getty Center, too—it's quite kid-friendly with its gardens and special children's programs.

Santa Monica Beach. Get acclimated to L.A. with a beachfront ride, picking up the oceanfront bike trail near the historic Santa Monica Pier, which has amusement rides, fishing, and a small aquarium. Follow the concrete path south to Venice Beach, grab a boardwalk snack, and take in the waves of magicians, bodybuilders, and street artists. Pedal back up to Santa Monica for an evening at the Third Street Promenade, a popular pedestrian shopping district.

Sporting Events. If your kids are sports fans, L.A. has it all (except for NFL football, that is). For baseball, there's Dodger Stadium and Angel Stadium of Anaheim, while Staples Center is home to the Lakers NBA basketball team and Kings NHL hockey team. David Beckham and the Los Angeles Galaxy MLS soccer team play at the Home Depot Center in Carson. And, of course, UCLA and USC offer big-time college events.

Exploring Los Angeles

WORD OF MOUTH

"Try to get up to Griffith Observatory at the end of a crisp clear day. Time it for just before dusk so you can see the sunset and watch the city lights start twinkling. Spectacular. Plus the Observatory itself is stunning. And it's free!"

—vivi

"A car [allows] you the freedom you need to make the most of LA. Just get used to the idea that it is not a city but a sprawl of interconnected cities."

—DalaiLlama

"We took our kids [2 & 5] to the Getty Museum. There are lots of outdoor steps and fountains that they were interested in. We (the adults) enjoyed the museum very much. It's very beautiful."

—luv2plan

www.fodors.com/community

Updated by Kastle Waserman

LOS ANGELES IS AS MUCH A FANTASY as it is a physical city. A mecca for face-lifts, film noir, shopping starlets, beach bodies, and mind-numbing traffic, it sprawls across 467 square mi; add in the surrounding five-county metropolitan area, and you've got an area of more than 34,000 square mi.

Contrary to popular myth, however, that doesn't mean you have to spend all your time in a car. In fact, getting out of your car is the only way to really get to know Los Angeles. We've divided the major sightseeing areas into 10 driving and walking tours that take you through the various entertainment-industry-centered, financial, beachfront, wealthy, and fringe neighborhoods and minicities that make up the vast L.A. area. But remember, no single locale—whether it be Malibu, Downtown, Beverly Hills, or Burbank—fully embodies Los Angeles. It's in the mix that you'll discover the city's character.

Looking at a map of sprawling Los Angeles, first-time visitors are sometimes overwhelmed. Where to begin? What to see first? And what about all those freeways? Here's some advice: relax.

Begin by setting your priorities—movie and television buffs should first head to Hollywood, Universal Studios, and a taping of a television show. Beach lovers and nature types might start out in Santa Monica or Venice or Malibu, or spend an afternoon in Griffith Park, one of the largest city parks in the country. Culture vultures should make a beeline for the twin Gettys (the center in Brentwood and the villa near Malibu), the Los Angeles County Museum of Art (LACMA), or the Norton Simon Museum. And urban explorers might begin with Downtown Los Angeles.

KNOW YOUR ROAD

Like a Boy Scout, drive by the motto "be prepared." The freeways are well marked; for non–rush hour travel they're still the best route from one end of the city to the other. Here are a couple of tips: most freeways are known by a name and a number; for example, the San Diego Freeway is I–405, the Hollywood Freeway is U.S. 101, the Ventura Freeway is a different stretch of U.S. 101, the Santa Monica Freeway is I–10, and the Harbor Freeway is I–110. It helps, too, to know which direction you're traveling; say, west toward Santa Monica or east toward Downtown Los Angeles. Distance in miles doesn't mean much, depending on the time of day you're traveling: the short 10-mi distance between the San Fernando Valley and Downtown Los Angeles might take an hour to travel during rush hour but only 20 minutes at other times.

DOWNTOWN LOS ANGELES

Once the lively heart of Los Angeles, Downtown has been a glitz-free corporate domain of high rises for the past few decades. But if there's one thing Angelenos love, it's a makeover, and now city planners have put the wheels in motion for a dramatic revitalization. Glance in every direction and you'll find construction crews building luxury lofts and retail space in hopes of attracting new residents. Two massive entertainment complexes are also in the works: the Frank Gehry–designed Grand Avenue project, to be built around the Music Center performance complex, and the L.A. Live project anchored around the Staples Center sports arena. All of this is aimed at making Downtown a one-stop destination to work, live, and play.

While all this redevelopment promises to bring throngs of new residents and visitors alike, it remains to be seen how the traffic will pan out, as Downtown currently is one of the most congested sections of Los Angeles, particularly when it becomes the site of parades, protests or film shoots, which frequently bring unexpected road closures.

In addition, longtime artist residents and businesses set up by Hispanic immigrants are fighting the powers that be and rallying their communities to stand against these sweeping changes. In the meantime, Downtown is a tale of two cities, where opposites clash. It may take a few years before the dust settles and Downtown is ready for its close-up.

WHAT TO SEE

❹ **Angels Flight Railway.** The turn-of-the-20th-century funicular, dubbed "the shortest railway in the world," operated between 1901 and 1969, when it was dismantled (but saved) to make room for an urban renewal project that saw total redevelopment of the Bunker Hill district. In 1996, 27 years later, Angels Flight returned with its two original orange-and-black wooden cable railway cars cabling people up a 298-foot incline from Hill Street (between 3rd and 4th streets) to the fountain-filled Watercourt at California Plaza. Due to a fatal accident in 2001, the railway has been closed while raising funds and undergoing a $3.3 million repair and restoration. ✉*351 S. Hill St., between 3rd and 4th Sts., Downtown* ☎*213/626–1901.*

❷ ★ **Bradbury Building.** Stunning wrought-iron railing, blond-wood and brick interior, ornate moldings, pink marble staircases, Victorian-style skylighted atrium that rises almost 50 feet, and birdcage elevators that seem to cry out for white-gloved, brass-buttoned operators: it's easy to see why the Bradbury leaves visitors awestruck. Designed in 1893 by a novice architect who drew his inspiration from a science-fiction story and a conversation with his dead brother via a Ouija board, the office building was originally the site of turn-of-the-20th-century sweatshops, but now houses a variety of business that try to keep normal working conditions despite the barrage of daily tourist visits and filmmakers. (*Blade Runner, Chinatown,* and *Wolf* were filmed here). For that reason, visits are limited to the lobby and the first-floor landing. The building is open daily 9–5 for a peek, as long as you don't wander beyond visitor-approved areas. ✉*304 S. Broadway, southeast corner Broadway and 3rd St., Downtown* ☎*213/626–1893.*

❶ **Broadway.** From the late 19th century to the 1950s—before malls and freeways—Broadway glittered with the finest shops and the highest number of luxurious theaters in the world, making it a rich, cultural haven. Though it remains the main road through Downtown's Historic District, the area has changed dramatically over the years. Currently bustling with stores and businesses catering to a mostly Mexican and Central American immigrant community, between 1st and 9th streets

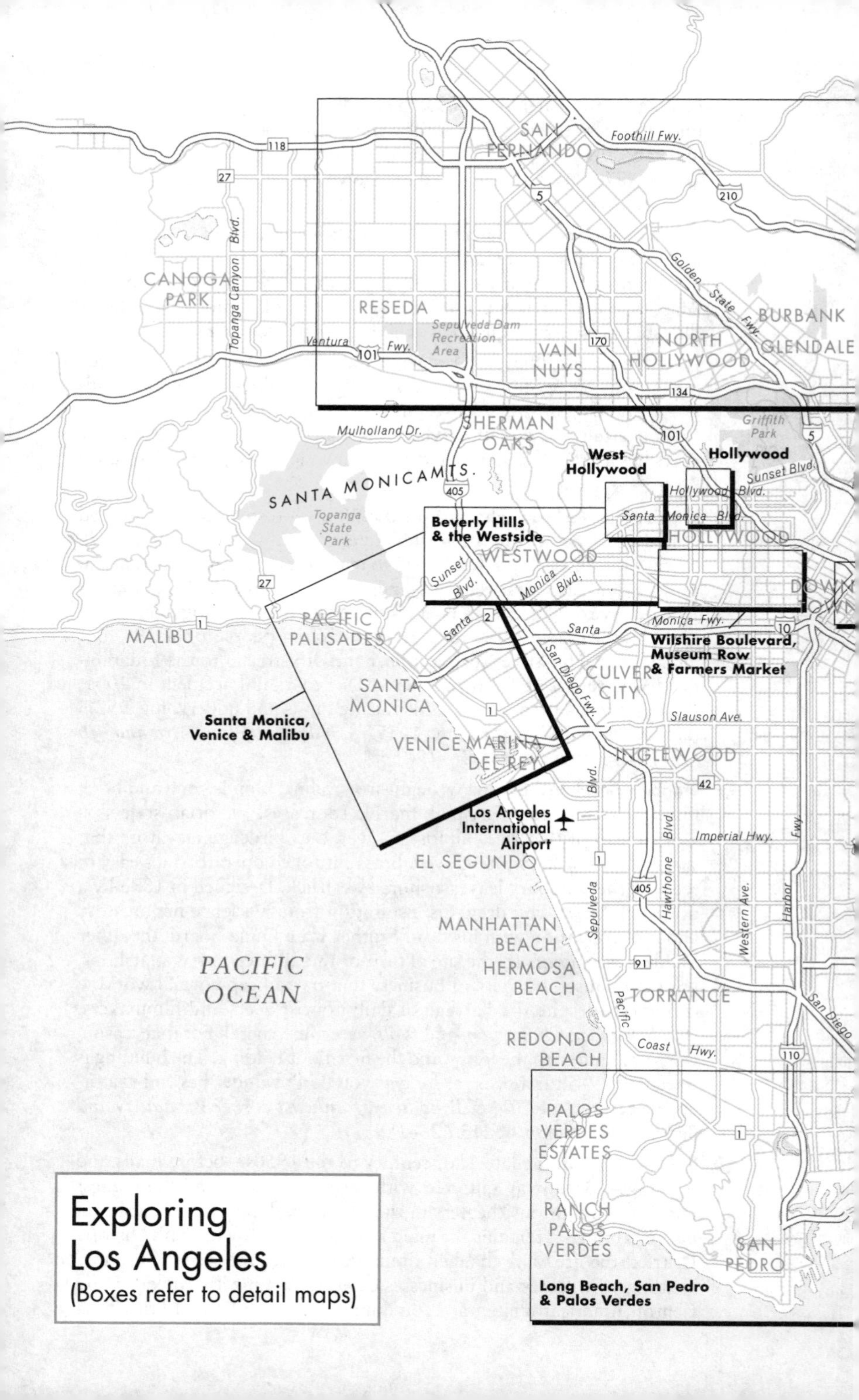

Exploring
Los Angeles
(Boxes refer to detail maps)
SAN FERNANDO
Foothill Fwy.
CANOGA PARK
Topanga Canyon Blvd.
RESEDA
Sepulveda Dam Recreation Area
VAN NUYS
NORTH HOLLYWOOD
BURBANK
GLENDALE
Golden State Fwy.
Ventura Fwy.
Mulholland Dr.
SHERMAN OAKS
Griffith Park
West Hollywood
Hollywood
Sunset Blvd.
Hollywood Blvd.
SANTA MONICA MTS.
Topanga State Park
Beverly Hills & the Westside
Santa Monica Blvd.
HOLLYWOOD
WESTWOOD
Sunset Blvd.
Monica Blvd.
DOWNTOWN
MALIBU
PACIFIC PALISADES
Santa Monica Fwy.
Wilshire Boulevard, Museum Row & Farmers Market
San Diego Fwy.
SANTA MONICA
CULVER CITY
Santa Monica, Venice & Malibu
Slauson Ave.
VENICE
MARINA DEL REY
INGLEWOOD
Los Angeles International Airport
Imperial Hwy.
EL SEGUNDO
Sepulveda Blvd.
Hawthorne Blvd.
Western Ave.
Harbor Fwy.
MANHATTAN BEACH
HERMOSA BEACH
PACIFIC OCEAN
TORRANCE
Pacific Coast Hwy.
San Diego
REDONDO BEACH
PALOS VERDES ESTATES
RANCHO PALOS VERDES
SAN PEDRO
Long Beach, San Pedro & Palos Verdes

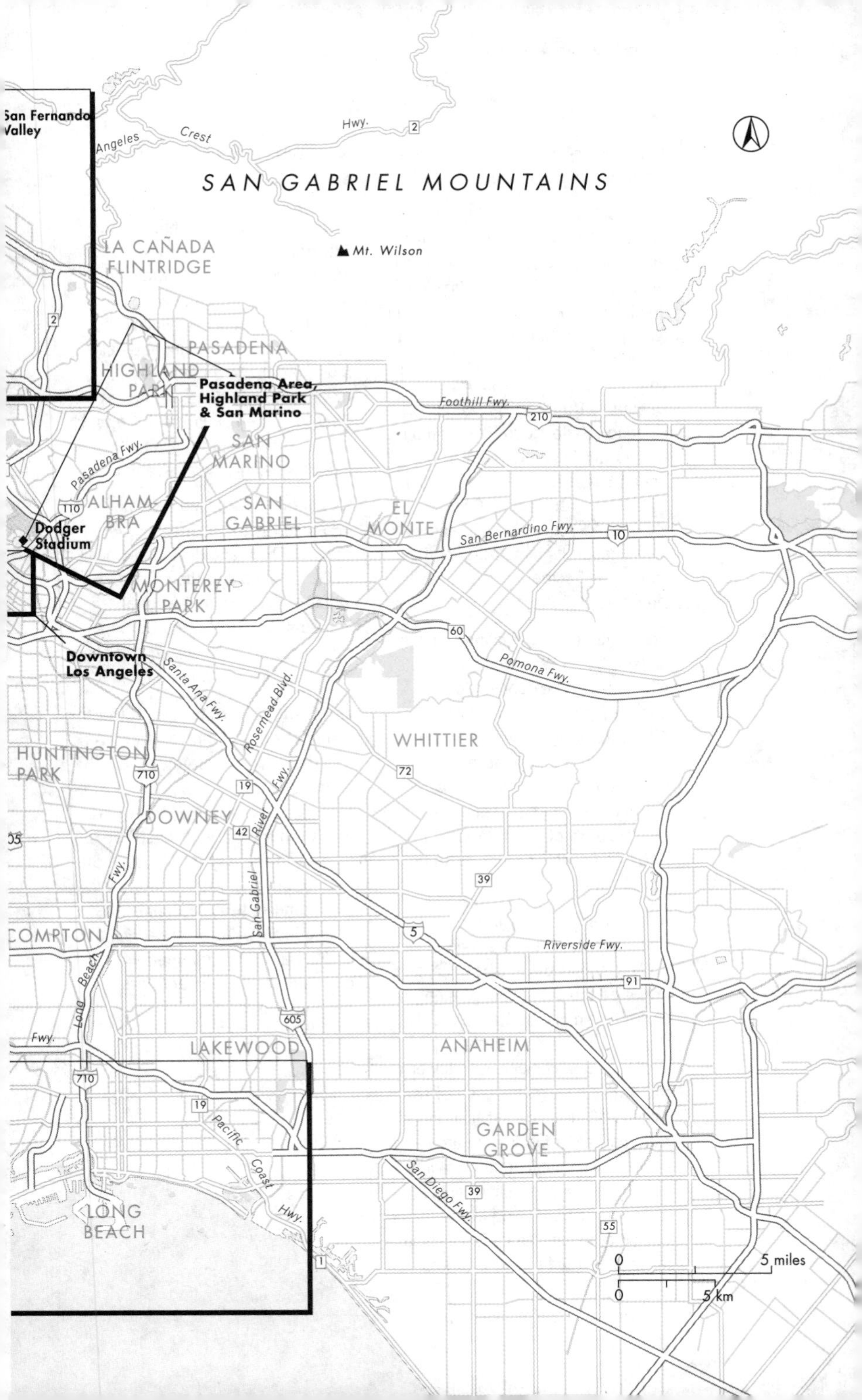

San Fernando Valley
Angeles Crest Hwy.
2
SAN GABRIEL MOUNTAINS
LA CAÑADA FLINTRIDGE
Mt. Wilson
PASADENA
HIGHLAND PARK
Pasadena Area, Highland Park & San Marino
Foothill Fwy.
210
SAN MARINO
Pasadena Fwy.
110
ALHAMBRA
SAN GABRIEL
EL MONTE
Dodger Stadium
San Bernardino Fwy.
10
MONTEREY PARK
60
Downtown Los Angeles
Pomona Fwy.
Santa Ana Fwy.
Rosemead Blvd.
WHITTIER
HUNTINGTON PARK
710
72
19
DOWNEY
42
San Gabriel River Fwy.
39
COMPTON
5
Riverside Fwy.
Long Beach Fwy.
91
605
LAKEWOOD
ANAHEIM
19
Pacific Coast Hwy.
GARDEN GROVE
San Diego Fwy.
39
LONG BEACH
55
1
0
5 miles
0
5 km

A GOOD TOUR

Numbers correspond to the Downtown Los Angeles map.

Begin a Downtown tour by heading north on **Broadway** ❶ from 8th or 9th Street. Shop workers hock cheap merchandise out of once-dazzling architectural wonders, making Broadway a demonstration of Downtown's changing times. At the southeast corner of Broadway and 3rd is the **Bradbury Building** ❷, with a fascinating interior court. (You can park behind the Bradbury Building on Spring Street for about $6.) Across the street is the **Grand Central Market** ❸—once you've made your way through its tantalizing food stalls, you'll come out the opposite side onto Hill Street.

Cross Hill Street and climb steps up a steep hill to Watercourt, a plaza with cafés and cascading fountains. (Unfortunately, the **Angels Flight Railway** ❹ won't be able to save you the hike, because it's out of service.) Next, walk toward the glass pyramidal skylight topping the **Museum of Contemporary Art (MOCA)** ❺, half a block north on Grand Avenue.

Across from MOCA glimmers the swooping stainless-steel skin of the **Walt Disney Concert Hall** ⓫, one of the performance venues along Grand that make up the **Music Center** ⓬. Heading north, you'll spot the stark concrete bell tower of the **Cathedral of Our Lady of the Angels** ⓭. The concert hall and the cathedral are a fascinating architectural odd couple, one all silvery curves, the other all sharp angles. It's well worth stepping inside the cathedral to see the delicate alabaster used instead of stained glass.

Now walk south on Grand to 5th Street, where you'll find two of Downtown's historical and architectural treasures: the **Millennium Biltmore Hotel** ❻, an atmospheric 1920s stunner, and the **Richard J. Riordan Central Library** ❼, also from the 1920s and now smartly renovated for the digital age. Take a breather behind the library in the tranquil Maguire Gardens. Across 5th Street are the **Bunker Hill Steps** ❾, a monumental stairway with a stream spilling down its center.

Return to your car, and drive north on Broadway to 1st Street. Make a right turn here and drive a few blocks to **Little Tokyo** and the expanded **Japanese American National Museum** ⓳. **The Geffen Contemporary** ⓲ art museum, an arm of MOCA, is a block north on Central.

From Little Tokyo, turn right (north) from 1st onto Alameda Street. As you pass over the freeway, you'll come to the next stop, **Union Station** ⓱, on the right. Street parking is limited, so your best bet is to park in the pay lot at Union Station (about $5). After a look inside this grand railway terminal, cross Alameda to **Olvera Street** ⓰, a pedestrian zone crammed with craft and food stalls and lots of cheerful kitsch.

2

Driving from Union Station, turn right on Alameda and then immediately left on Cesar Chavez Avenue for three blocks. At Broadway, turn right to **Chinatown.** Reverse your route on Broadway from Chinatown; cross back over the freeway, and at Temple Street make a left. Look to the right as you drive down Temple to see the back of **City Hall of Los Angeles** ⓮. Head out of Downtown Los Angeles (take Los Angeles Street south to 11th Street, turn right—west—onto 11th toward Figueroa, then turn left—south—onto Figueroa Street) past **Staples Center** ⓴ with its flying saucer–esque roof to **Exposition Park,** site of three good museums: the **California Science Center** ㉑, the **Natural History Museum of Los Angeles County** ㉒, and the **California African-American Museum** ㉓. (Heading out here, though, is worthwhile only if you're planning to hit one or more of the museums.) Adjacent to Exposition Park is the **University of Southern California (USC)** ㉔, its parklike campus a distinct contrast to its grittier surroundings. The school's got its share of snarky nicknames (e.g., the University of Spoiled Children) but there's no arguing with its strong academics and fierce athletics . . . not to mention that marching band. Return to Downtown at night for a performance at the Music Center or East West Players in Little Tokyo, and after the show take in the bright lights of the big city at BonaVista, the revolving rooftop lounge atop the **Westin Bonaventure Hotel & Suites** ❿ or take your chances of getting a rooftop seat at the **Downtown L.A. Standard** ❽ hotel.

■ TIP→ **A convenient and inexpensive minibus service—DASH, or Downtown Area Short Hop—has several routes that travel past most of the sights on this tour, stopping every two blocks or so. Each ride costs 25¢, so you can hop on and off without spending a fortune. Special (limited) routes operate on weekends. Call DASH (☎ 808–2273 from all Los Angeles area codes 🌐 www.ladottransit.com/dash) for routes and hours of operation.**

TIMING

Weekdays are the best time to experience Downtown, when the area is bustling with activity and restaurants are open for lunch. On weekends you may be able to find street parking, but with the exception of Chinatown and Olvera Street, most of Downtown is considerably quiet on weekends and most restaurants and café areas are closed. Seeing everything included on this tour in one day will require running shoes, stamina, and careful timing. Spread it over two days if possible. Try to plan your visits around specific areas you can walk to in one circuit. Parking lots run $6–$12 so if you're on a budget, you don't want to be moving your car around too much. Also allow plenty of extra time; the entertainment industry loves to use Downtown for its movie backdrops so it's not uncommon for film crews to take over entire blocks for shooting and jam up traffic in every direction. Minus a few nightspots, Downtown is best (and safest) to visit during the day. Keep in mind that some museums are closed Monday.

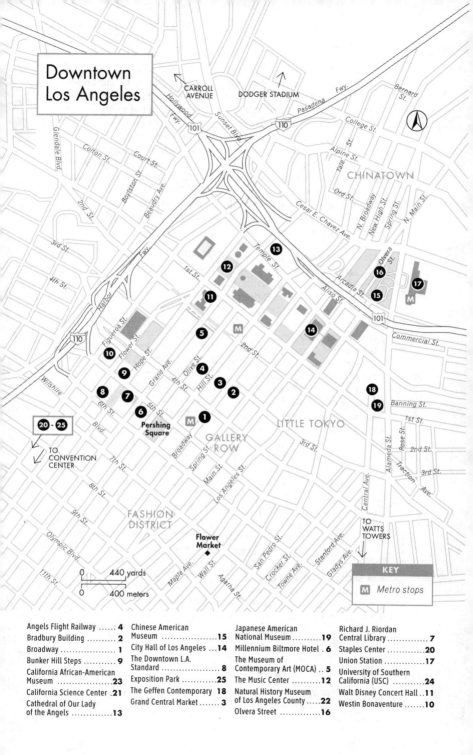

Downtown Los Angeles

- Angels Flight Railway **4**
- Bradbury Building **2**
- Broadway **1**
- Bunker Hill Steps **9**
- California African-American Museum **23**
- California Science Center .**21**
- Cathedral of Our Lady of the Angels **13**
- Chinese American Museum **15**
- City Hall of Los Angeles ...**14**
- The Downtown L.A. Standard **8**
- Exposition Park **25**
- The Geffen Contemporary **18**
- Grand Central Market **3**
- Japanese American National Museum **19**
- Millennium Biltmore Hotel . **6**
- The Museum of Contemporary Art (MOCA) .. **5**
- The Music Center **12**
- Natural History Museum of Los Angeles County **22**
- Olvera Street **16**
- Richard J. Riordan Central Library **7**
- Staples Center **20**
- Union Station **17**
- University of Southern California (USC) **24**
- Walt Disney Concert Hall ..**11**
- Westin Bonaventure **10**

you'll find mariachi and *banda* music blaring from electronics-store speakers, street-food vendors hawking sliced papaya sprinkled with chili powder, and fancy dresses for a young girl's *Quinceañera* (15th birthday). But to see the glory of its golden years, you merely have to look "up," above the storefront signs, to see the marvelous architecture and theater marquees of the majestic buildings they reside in. Thanks to preservation efforts by the Los Angeles Conservancy, classic film screenings and walking tours are available to give visitors and locals access to many of the once glorious beaux arts and art deco theater buildings.

WALKING WITH EXPERTS

The **Los Angeles Conservancy** (☎ *213/623–2489* 🌐 *www.laconservancy.org*) regularly conducts Saturday-morning walking tours of Downtown architectural landmarks and districts. Tours begin at 10 AM, last about 2½ hours, and are offered rain or shine. Call for schedule and fees.

The **Million Dollar Theater** (✉ *307 S. Broadway, Downtown* ☎ *877/677–4386*) opened in 1918 as part of Sid Grauman's famed chain of movie theaters. This Spanish Baroque–style venue had the special feature of having its own organ. Film stars such as Gloria Swanson, Rudolph Valentino, and a young Judy Garland frequently made appearances. In the '40s, the venue swung with jazz and big band performers including Billie Holiday. Later incarnations included Spanish-language variety shows and headline acts from Mexico and a Brazilian Christian Church that made alterations to the original interior, including painting the walls white. The lofts above were meant to house the entertainment community, but so far its most famous resident was Nicolas Cage, who lived in the penthouse suite in the early '90s. Though the theater is now closed to the public (with the exception of special events), it's worth a stop if you're walking past to inspect the lavish exterior with entertainment figures carved into the molding.

Opened in 1926, the opulent **Orpheum Theatre** (✉ *842 S. Broadway, Downtown* 🌐 *www.laorpheum.com*) played host to live attractions including burlesque dancers, comedians, jazz greats like Lena Horne, Ella Fitzgerald, and Duke Ellington, and later on rock-and-roll performers such as Little Richard. After massive renovation and restoration work, the Orpheum now books a variety of concerts and special events. It's worth the ticket price just to see the interior of the beautiful venue with its stunning white marble lobby that ushers you into a majestic auditorium with fleur-de-lis sidewall panels, modern seating refurbished in vintage styling, exquisite detailed moldings that run floor to ceiling, and two dazzling oversize chandeliers that hang overhead, the cherries on top of an extravagant sundae. A thick red velvet and golden-trimmed curtain signals "Showtime," and a white Wurlitzer pipe organ (one of the last remaining organs of its kind from the silent movie era) is at the ready, as the original 1926 Orpheum rooftop neon sign again shines brightly over a new era for this theater.

The Palace Theatre (✉ *630 S. Broadway, Downtown*), built in 1911, is loosely styled after an Italian Renaissance palazzo. Though only the entrance is viewable through the locked gates, you can see the multicolor terra-cotta swags, flowers, fairies, and theatrical masks. Now the oldest remaining Orpheum Theatre in the country, the Palace still hosts occasional shows and is available for rental.

The Los Angeles Theatre (✉ *615 S. Broadway, Downtown* 🌐 *www.losangelestheatre.com*), built in 1931, opened with the premiere of Charlie Chaplin's *City Lights*. Full of glorious French Baroque–inspired decor, the six-story lobby is awe-inspiring with its dramatic staircase, enormous fountain, grandiose chandeliers, and ornate gold detailing. Officially closed to the public, you can still witness the old Hollywood glamour by catching a special movie screening.

9 **Bunker Hill Steps.** Threading a peaceful path through Downtown's urban towers, a fountain stream spills down the center of this monumental staircase designed by Lawrence Halprin. Its quiet beauty is reminiscent of Rome's Spanish Steps (albeit more narrow). The stream originates at the top of the stairs where Robert Graham's nude female sculpture *Source Figure* stands atop a cylindrical base. The figure's hands are open, as if to offer water to the city. If you're not inclined to walk up, hop on the escalator parallel to the stairs. Halfway up there's a coffeehouse where you can fortify yourself before tackling the remaining climb. ✉ *5th St. between Grand Ave. and Figueroa St., Downtown.*

23 **California African-American Museum.** Works by 20th-century African-American artists and contemporary works of the African diasporas are the backbone of this museum's permanent collection. Its exhibits document the African-American experience from Emancipation and Reconstruction through the 20th century, especially as expressed by artists in California and elsewhere in the West. Special musical as well as educational and cultural events are offered the first Sunday of every month. ✉ *600 State Dr., Exposition Park* ☎ *213/744–7432* 🌐 *www.caamuseum.org* 🎫 *Free, parking $8* ⏲ *Tues.–Sat. 10–5, Sun. 11–5.*

21 **California Science Center.** You're bound to see excited kids running up to the dozens of interactive exhibits here that illustrate the relevance of science to everyday life, from bacteria to airplanes. Clustered in different "Worlds," this center provides opportunities to examine such topics as structures and communications, where you can be an architect and design your own building and learn how to make it earthquake-proof, to "Life" itself where Tess, the 50-foot animatronic star of the exhibit "Body Works," dramatically demonstrates how the body's organs work together. Air and Space Exhibits show out what it takes to go to outer space with Gemini 11, real capsule flown into space by Pete Conrad and Dick Gordon in September 1966. An IMAX theater shows large-format releases. ✉ *700 State Dr., Exposition Park* ☎ *213/744–7400 or 323/724–3623* 🌐 *www.casciencectr.org* 🎫 *Free, except for IMAX, prices vary; parking $8* ⏲ *Daily 10–5.*

OFF THE BEATEN PATH

Carroll Avenue. Looking like a street lifted out of another era, the 1300 block of Carroll Avenue in Angelino Heights has the city's highest concentration of Victorian houses. Home after home of what could only be described as life-size versions of childhood dollhouses line this street. Designated a historical monument, it's no surprise the homes here are often rented for film shoots. Look for the Sessions House (No. 1330) and the Haunted House (No. 1345)—the latter seen in Michael Jackson's *Thriller* video. To get to Carroll Avenue from Downtown, take Temple Street west to Edgeware Road, turn right onto Edgeware, and go over the freeway. Carroll Avenue is on the left.

13 **Cathedral of Our Lady of the Angels.** Controversy surrounded Spanish architect José Rafael Moneo's unconventional, costly, austere design for the seat of the Archdiocese of Los Angeles. But judging from the swarms of visitors and the standing-room-only holiday masses, the church has carved out a niche for itself in Downtown's daily life. Opened in 2002, the ocher-concrete cathedral looms up by the Hollywood Freeway. The plaza in front is relatively austere, glaringly bright on sunny days; a children's play garden with bronze animals helps relieve the stark space. Imposing bronze entry doors, designed by local artist Robert Graham, are decorated with multicultural icons and New World images of the Virgin Mary. The canyonlike interior of the church is spare, polished, and airy. By day, sunlight illuminates the sanctuary through translucent curtain walls of thin Spanish alabaster, a departure from the usual stained glass. Artist John Nava used residents from his hometown of Ojai, California, as models for some of the 135 figures in the tapestries that line the nave walls. Make sure to go underground to wander the bright, somewhat incongruous, mazelike white-marble corridors of the mausoleum. Free guided tours start at the entrance fountain at 1 on weekdays. There's plenty of underground visitor parking; the vehicle entrance is on Hill Street. ■ TIP→ **The café in the plaza has become one of Downtown's favorite lunch spots, as you can pick up a fresh, reasonably priced meal to eat at one of the outdoor tables.** ✉ *555 W. Temple St., Downtown* ☎ *213/680–5200* 🌐 *www.olacathedral.org* 🎫 *Free, parking $3 every 20 min, $14 maximum* ⏲ *Weekdays 6:30–6, Sat. 9–6, Sun. 7–6.*

Fodor's Choice ★

Chinatown. Smaller in size than San Francisco's Chinatown, this Downtown sector near Union Station still represents a slice of Southeast Asian life. Bordered by Yale, Bernard, Ord, and Alameda streets, Chinatown has its main action on North Broadway where the sidewalks are usually jammed with tourists, locals, and of course, Asian residents hustling from shop to shop picking up goods, spices, and trinkets from the many small business shops and miniplazas that line the street. Though some longtime establishments closed in recent years, the area still pulses its founding culture. During Chinese New Year, giant dragons snake down the street. And of course there are the many restaurants and quick-bite cafés specializing in Chinese feasts. One Asian holdout, the **Empress Pavilion** (✉ *988 N. Hill St.* ☎ *213/617–9898*), buzzes with activity as one of Chinatown's best restaurants. An influx of local artists has added a spark to the neighborhood by taking up available spaces and opening galleries along **Chung King Road,** a faded pedestrian passage behind the West Plaza shopping center between Hill and Yale. Also look for galleries along a little side street called **Gin Ling Way** on the east side of Broadway. Most galleries open when they have a show, or in the afternoon and early evenings from Wednesday through Saturday.

15 **Chinese American Museum.** In the El Pueblo Plaza adjacent to Olvera Street, you might think this museum should feature Mexican-American

CLOSE UP

A Guide to SoCal Freeway Driving

Pick a lane. The car-pool lane, the "fast lane," the truck lane, the merge lane—this isn't your typical freeway. First of all, keep out of the two far right lanes. The California Department of Motor Vehicles restricts buses and trucks to these two truck lanes, which run slower than the regular speed of traffic. To drive at least the speed limit, get yourself in the middle lane. If you're ready to bend the rules a bit, the fourth lane moves about 5 mi over the speed limit. Newbies should stay out of the far left lane. Speeds here range from 75 to 90 mph, and besides that, you've got to deal with car-pool-lane mergers.

And what about that car-pool lane—also known as the diamond lane? Use it if you have two or more people in your car and it's moving faster than the speed of traffic; if Bus 187 to Pasadena is in it, don't.

Speed, with caution—but we didn't tell you that. Sure, you shouldn't go faster than the posted 65 or 55 mph. Easy to say, hard to do—especially when everyone else seems to be doing it and getting away with it. If you want to keep up with the speed of traffic and avoid the prize of a speeding ticket, 70 to 74 mph is a good target range. If, however, you notice that you're passing lots of cars—slow down!

Can't we all just be friends? Here's how to avoid causing road rage: don't tailgate. Don't flail your arms in frustration. Don't glare at the driver of the car you finally have a chance to pass. And above all, don't fly the finger. Road rage is a real hazard.

Use your signal correctly. Here, signaling is a must. Because of all the different lanes, people may try to merge into the same spot as you from three lanes away. Protect yourself and your space by always using your signal. And don't forget to turn your signal off when the lane change is complete.

Get a freeway map. The small, laminated maps that just cover the jumble of freeways are indispensable if you merge onto the wrong freeway, get lost, or get stuck in traffic and want to find an alternative route. Nearly every gas station sells them; you can get a decent one for a few bucks.

Don't pull over on the freeway. Short of a real emergency, never, ever, pull over and stop on a freeway. So you took the wrong ramp and need to huddle with your map—take the next exit and find a safe, well-lighted public space to stop your car and get your bearings.

—Sarah Sper

CHINATOWN BUSTS A MOVE

Gallery openings and hip artists are bringing in a new, stylish, and younger crowd to Chinatown, and a few choice bars are getting in on the action, too, by offering a nightlife scene without the "guestlist only" snobbery of Hollywood. You can get a taste of the scene in the Central Plaza of New Chinatown by checking out three bars all within stumbling distance of each other: **The Grand Star** (✉ *943 N. Broadway* ☎ *213/626-2285*) is a cozy barfly-friendly hideaway with karaoke for those who feel inspired to kick out a little Elvis or Sinatra after a few cold ones. **Hop Louie** (✉ *950 Mei Ling Way* ☎ *213/628-4244*), a restaurant and watering hole, offers an elaborate setting of a five-tier pagoda constructed in 1941 that feels part sports bar and part classic Chinatown. **Mountain Bar** (✉ *473 Gin Ling Way* ☎ *213/625-7500*) is tucked away in what could be mistaken for a lonely alleyway off Hill Street. The laid-back vibe and cool red decor add up to a friendly local dive that offers hipsters a quiet lounge to kick back for a drink, with live music upstairs.

art. But in actuality, it's in the last surviving structure of the L.A.'s original Chinatown, although it illustrates a commonality with the Hispanic experience documenting what it's like to come to America with hopes, dreams, and radically different cultural traditions. Three floors of exhibits offer a range of displays that trace the culture of immigrants who first came to Los Angeles, set up shops, and paved the way for what is now the vibrant and varied Chinatown district. Rotating exhibits feature the work of Chinese-American fine artists. ✉ *425 N. Los Angeles St.* ☎ *213/485-8567* 🌐 *www.camla.org* 💵 *$3 suggested donation* 🕑 *Tues.–Sun. 10–3.*

⓮ **City Hall of Los Angeles.** An icon of the Los Angeles cityscape, this gorgeous 1928 landmark building has seen its fair share of stardom—from the opening scenes of the TV series Dragnet to serving as the "Daily Planet" building in the original Adventures of Superman. During an extensive renovation in the late '90s, the original Lindburg Beacon was put back in action atop the hall's 13th-story tower. The revolving spotlight, inaugurated by President Calvin Coolidge from the White House via a telegraph key, was used from 1928 to 1941 to guide pilots into the Los Angeles airport. There are free weekday tours of the beautifully detailed building at 10 and 11, which sometimes include a visit to the observation deck. Reservations are strongly recommended. ✉ *200 N. Spring St., Downtown* ☎ *213/978-1995.*

❽ **Downtown L.A. Standard.** Housed in the former Superior Oil Headquarters, the Standard's interior flaunts a cool steel design bursting with bright pop art furniture that would make Andy Warhol proud. Take the elevator right to the top for a spectacular view from the rooftop lounge. The pool gives an impression you're swimming on top of the world. Playful perks like circular waterbed pod couches, unicorn bush sculptures, and S-shaped tanning chairs provide a party setting. By night, nearby skyscrapers serve as video projections screens for hipsters to groove to. The place is pumping at night with an in-house DJ and an influx of L.A.'s beautiful people. If you want a taste of the action, it's best to call ahead to see if you can get in. Otherwise, it's worth a visit for a breakfast or lunch in the bright-yellow '60s-style diner 24-hour to take in the ambience without having to push through the party crowd. ✉*550 S. Flower St.* ☎*213/892–8080* 🌐*www.standardhotel.com.*

25 **Exposition Park.** Originally developed in 1880 as an open-air farmers' market, this 114-acre public space hosted Olympic festivities in 1932 and 1984 in conjunction with the adjacent Memorial Coliseum and Sports Arena. The park includes a lovely sunken rose garden and three museums, the **California African-American Museum, California Science Center,** and the **Natural History Museum of Los Angeles County.** Unfortunately, though, the park and neighborhood become sketchy at night, so it's wise to leave once the museums close. ✉*Between Exposition and Martin Luther King Jr. Blvds., Exposition Park.*

OFF THE BEATEN PATH

Fashion District. For visiting fashionistas, the name "Fashion District" may seem alluring. But be warned. The term "fashion" here is subject to interpretation. While designers troll this 90-block garment district for wholesale deals on fabrics, you'll need a merchant's license to access most showcase buildings. If shopping is your M.O., bring your bargain-hunting instincts and your patience to **Santee Alley** (✉*Santee St. and Maple Ave. from Olympic Blvd. to 12th St.*) where vendors are crammed side by side selling everything from faux designer sunglasses and handbags to sweatshirts, jewelry, and cell phones. Shop owners crammed into the little strip cater to their large clientele of bargain-hunting Latino families by blasting Spanish and hip-hop music from boom boxes perched at store entrances, making for a vibrant but ear-blistering scene.

The whole Fashion District area can be overwhelming in its expansiveness. If you don't know what direction to turn, the **LA Fashion District Business Improvement District (BID)** (☎*213/488–1153* 🌐*www.fashiondistrict.org*) can provide maps, info, and assistance. If you really want to know where to locate the high-fashion finds in this insider-driven district, take a tour with shopping pro Christine Silvestri of Urban Shopping Adventures (☎*213/683–9715* 🌐*www.urbanshoppingadventures.com*) who offers a three-hour walking–shopping tour Monday–Saturday $36 or a customized, hourly rate VIP tour. Or plan your visit on the last Friday of the month, when you can quench your taste for high-fashion by hitting the mega sample sales in the **California Market Center** (✉*110 E. 9th St.* ☎*213/630–3600*), a trade market housing 1,500 showrooms, and the neighboring **New Mart** (✉*127 E. 9th St.* ☎*213/627–0671* 🌐*www.newmart.net*), where cutting-edge designers sell off one-of-a-kind pieces, overstocks, and prototypes for the next big trends. This sale is cash only and quite popular.

Project Runway hopefuls may also want to walk a few blocks over to the **Fashion Institute for Design and Merchandising** (FIDM ✉*919 S. Grand Ave.* ☎*213/624–1201*) where future fashion and interior designers, graphic artists, and entertainment industry stylists get their start. The school has a scholarship store with discounted clothing, fabric, and special occasion wear, a gallery of rotating exhibits from Oscar gowns to vintage perfume bottles, and a museum shop with jewelry, books, fashion-related novelties, and FIDM alumni designs. The gallery is dark between exhibits for installation. Call ahead.

> **WORD OF MOUTH**
>
> "Grand Central Market is wonderful for a quick bite–lots of ethnic foods and vendors from which to choose. Ana Maria's tacos were fab; the second day we went back I tried the tacos at Tomas as the lineup of locals was 3 deep. Both places were excellent. Now I rue the day I have to step into Taco Bell again." —klam_chowder

2

18 ★ **The Geffen Contemporary.** Originally opened in 1982 as a temporary exhibit hall while the **Museum of Contemporary Art (MOCA)** was under construction at California Plaza, this large flexible space, designed by architect Frank Gehry, charmed visitors with its antiestablishment character and lively exhibits. Thanks to its hit reception, it remains one of two satellite museums of the MOCA (the other is outside the Pacific Design Center in W. Hollywood). Named the Geffen Contemporary, after receiving a $5 million gift from the David Geffen Foundation, this museum houses a sampling of MOCA's permanent collection and usually one or two offbeat exhibits that provoke grins from even the stuffiest museumgoer. Call before you visit as the museum sometimes closes for installations. ✉ *152 N. Central Ave., Downtown* ☎ *213/626–6222* 🌐 *www.moca-la.org* 🎟 *$10, free with MOCA admission on same day and on Thurs. 5–8* PM ⏲ *Mon. and Fri. 11–5, Thurs. 11–8, weekends 11–6.*

3 **Grand Central Market.** Handmade white-corn tamales, warm olive bread, dried figs, Mexican fruit drinks . . . hungry yet? This mouthwatering gathering place is the city's largest and most active food market. The spot bustles nonstop with locals and visitors surveying the butcher shop's display of everything from lambs' heads to pigs' tails; produce stalls are piled high with locally grown avocados and heirloom tomatoes. Stop by **Del Rey,** at stall A7, for a remarkable selection of rare chilies and spices. Even if you don't plan to buy anything, the market is a great place to browse and people-watch. ✉ *317 S. Broadway, Downtown* ☎ *213/624–2378* 🌐 *www.grandcentralsquare.com* 🎟 *Free* ⏲ *Daily 9–6.*

19 **Japanese American National Museum.** What was it like to grow up on a sugar plantation in Hawaii? How difficult was life for Japanese-Americans interned in concentration camps during World War II? These questions are addressed by changing exhibits at this museum in Little Tokyo. Insightful volunteer docents are on hand to share their own stories and experiences. The museum occupies an 85,000-square-foot adjacent pavilion as well as its original site in a renovated 1925 Buddhist temple. Exhibits for 2009 include: "Glorious Excess" featuring the work of Linkin Park musician/artist Mike Shinoda January–March, and a Kokeshi doll exhibition June–September. ✉ *369 E. 1st St., at Central Ave., next to Geffen Contemporary, Downtown* ☎ *213/625–0414* 🌐 *www.janm.org* 🎟 *$9, free Thurs. 5–8 and 3rd Thurs. of month* ⏲ *Tues., Wed., and Fri.–Sun. 11–5.*

L.A. Live / Nokia Theater. As an entertainment, sports, and residential complex adjacent to the Staples Center and Convention Center, the site includes Club Nokia, an intimate performance venue; the Conga Room, a Latin-focused nightclub that boasts ownership by Jimmy Smits, Jennifer Lopez, and Paul Rodriquez; the Lucky Strikes, hipster bowling lanes complete with a café, a bar, and billiard tables; and the Grammy Museum, a permanent home for the Grammy Awards and an exhibition space on the music industry's history and creative process plus more than 10 restaurants and eateries. ✉ *777 Chick Hearn Court, Downtown* ☎ *213/763–6030* 🌐 *www.nokiatheatrelalive.com.*

Little Tokyo. Originally the neighborhood of Los Angeles's Japanese community, this Downtown spot has been deserted by many of its founding immigrants. However, the area has recently begun to blossom again thanks to the next generation of Japanese-Americans setting up small businesses here mixed with an influx of foot-traffic coming in from neighboring redevelopment projects and newly built condos. Bounded by 1st, San Pedro, 3rd, and Central streets, Little Tokyo has dozens of sushi bars, tempura restaurants, karaoke bars, and trinket shops selling Transformer robots, lanterns, and Hello Kitty tchotchkes. On 1st Street you'll find the only strip of intact buildings from the early 1900s. Look down when you get near San Pedro Street, and you'll see the art installation "Omoide no Shotokyo" ("Remembering Old Little Tokyo"). Embedded in the sidewalk are brass inscriptions naming the original businesses, quoted reminiscences from Little Tokyo residents, and steel time lines of Japanese-American history up to World War II. Nisei Week (a nisei is a second-generation Japanese) is celebrated here every August with traditional drums, dancing, a carnival, and a huge parade. The **Japanese American Cultural and Community Center** (✉ *244 S. San Pedro St., Downtown* ☎ *213/628–2725* 🌐 *www.jaccc.org*) books traditional and contemporary cultural events. Call ahead or check the Web site for a schedule. Through the center's basement you can reach the James Irvine Garden, a serene sunken garden where local plants mix with bamboo, Japanese wisteria, and Japanese maples.

❻ **Millennium Biltmore Hotel.** The "wow" factor hits you as soon as you walk in the door. Dripping in Italian Renaissance style, the Biltmore's ornate details, frescoes, and golden columns are truly luxe. You might get a crick in your neck from admiring the magnificence of the ceilings alone. Opened in 1923, a creation of the architecture firm Schultze and Weaver, which also built New York City's Waldorf-Astoria, the Biltmore is a registered historical landmark and has served presidents, royalty, and celebrities alike. The Academy Awards were held here in the 1930s and '40s, and the hotel has also been seen in many films and TV shows, including *Chinatown.* These days, the hotel really kicks into high glamour for the holidays with special dinners, a Victorian Christmas Tea, and unparalleled New Year's bash. ✉ *506 S. Grand Ave., Downtown* ☎ *213/624–1011* 🌐 *www.thebiltmore.com.*

❺ **The Museum of Contemporary Art (MOCA).** The MOCA's permanent collection of American and European art from 1940 to the present divides itself between three spaces: this linear red-sandstone building at California Plaza, the **Geffen Contemporary,** in nearby Little Tokyo, and the

Fodor's Choice ★

satellite gallery at W. Hollywood's **Pacific Design Center.** Likewise, its exhibitions are split between the established and the cutting-edge. Heavy hitters such as Mark Rothko, Franz Kline, Susan Rothenberg, Diane Arbus, and Robert Frank are part of the permanent collection thatis rotated into the museum exhibits at different times, while at least 20 theme shows are featured annually. It's a good idea to check the schedule in advance, since some shows sell out, especially on weekends. The museum occasionally closes for exhibit installation. *✉250 S. Grand Ave., Downtown ☎213/626–6222 🌐www.moca.org 🎫$8, free on same day with Geffen Contemporary admission and on Thurs. ⏲Mon. and Fri. 11–5, Thurs. 11–8, weekends 11–6.*

ART CRAWL

Artists, scenesters, hipsters, and locals come down from their lofts the second Thursday of every month to check out the **Downtown Art Walk,** a free-for-all gallery opening where art dealers clustered around "Gallery Row," which runs along Main and Spring streets between 2nd and 9th streets, open up and showcase their wares in a party-hopping environment (☎*213/842–8574* ⏲*Noon–9*). For self-guided tour maps of participating galleries, check the official Web site (🌐*www.Downtownartwalk.com*).

12 ★ **The Music Center.** L.A.'s major performing arts venue since its opening in 1964, the Music Center is also now Downtown's centerpiece. Home to the Los Angeles Philharmonic, the Los Angeles Opera, the Center Theater Group, and the Los Angeles Master Chorale, the Music Center is also a former site of the Academy Awards.

11 Fodor's Choice ★ The center's crown jewel is the **Walt Disney Concert Hall.** Designed by Frank Gehry, the Hall opened in 2003 and instantly became a stunning icon of the city. The gorgeous stainless-steel-clad structure soars lyrically upward, seeming to defy the laws of engineering. A combination of matte and mirror steel panels gives the building texture that is illuminated by night to give the voluptuous curves a stunning glow. Inside, the Hall continues to inspire awe with a billowing ceiling of Douglas fir over head, and an enormous pine-clad organ centerpiece with branches said to have been inspired when Gehry looked at a box of McDonald's french fries and decided to put the wooden pipes out front and the metal pipes in back. The carpet, named "Lily," is a wild collage of petals inspired by Lillian Disney's love of flowers, as is the "Rose for Lily" fountain—made entirely of bits of Delftware, Mrs. Disney's favorite collectible—located in the tranquil outdoor public garden. Docent-led and audio tours of the Hall are available for $15. But note, entry to the performance space is subject to rehearsal schedules. Your chances are better in summer when the Philharmonic moves to the Hollywood Bowl. ■ TIP→ **With the high tour price not offering much more than a stroll around the venue, you're better off putting your money toward a ticket to an actual performance in this magnificent space.** Additional children's performances, lectures, and experimental works are held in surrounding smaller theater spaces: the indoor BP Hall, two outdoor mini-amphitheaters, and CalArts's intimate 266-seat REDCAT Theatre.

The largest of the center's four theaters is the **Dorothy Chandler Pavilion,** named after the philanthropic wife of former *Los Angeles Times* publisher Norman Chandler. The **Ahmanson,** at the north end, is a flexible venue for major musicals and plays. In between these two sits the round **Mark Taper Forum,** a surprisingly intimate 700-seat theater, closed for construction until mid-2008. Activity isn't limited to merely ticketed events; free tours of the Music Center are available by volunteer docents who provide a wealth of architectural and behind-the-scenes information while escorting you through elaborate, art-punctuated VIP areas. ✉ *135 N. Grand Ave., at 1st St., Downtown* ☎ *213/972–7211, 213/972–4399 for tour information* 🌐 *www.musiccenter.org* 🎫 *Free* ⏲ *Free tours Tues.–Sat. 10:30* AM*–12:30* PM.

NEED A BREAK? **For a quick bite and great people-watching in the heart of the culturally inspired Music Center Plaza, the Pinot Grill (☎ *213/972–3190*) offers a selection of entrées at $10–$25. Open weekends and daily via the take-out window for lunch and dinner. Or refuel with a quick snack from the neighboring Spotlight Café (☎ 213/972–7525) and grab a seat on an area bench; you'll have a prime spot to watch Active Arts events, outdoor public singing or dancing sessions.**

22 **Natural History Museum of Los Angeles County.** With more than 35 million specimens, this is the third-largest museum of its type in the United States (after the Field Museum in Chicago and the American Museum of Natural History in New York). Since 1913, the museum has shown a rich collection of prehistoric fossils and extensive bird, insect, and marine-life exhibits. Brilliant stones shimmer in the Gem & Mineral Hall. An elaborate diorama exhibit shows North American and African mammals in detailed replicas of their natural habitats. Exhibits typifying various cultural groups include pre-Columbian artifacts and a display of crafts from the South Pacific. The Ralph M. Parsons Discovery Center & Insect Zoo encourages kids to do hands-on exploration of the Museum's collections. The museum also features its first public paleontological preparation laboratory. This innovative lab features "Thomas," a nearly 70% complete, 65 million-year-old T. rex excavated during field expeditions in southeastern Montana. Note: Select exhibits may be temporarily relocated to different areas as the museum conducts ongoing renovations. ✉ *900 Exposition Blvd., Exposition Park* ☎ *213/763–3466* 🌐 *www.nhm.org* 🎫 *$9, free 1st Tues. of month* ⏲ *Weekdays 9:30–5, weekends 10–5.*

16 ★ **Olvera Street.** This busy pedestrian block tantalizes with piñatas, mariachis, and fragrant Mexican food. As the major draw of the oldest section of the city, known as **El Pueblo de Los Angeles,** Olvera Street has come to represent the rich Mexican heritage of L.A. It had a close shave with disintegration in the early 20th century, until the socialite Christine Sterling walked through in 1926. Jolted by the historic area's decay, Sterling fought to preserve key buildings and led the transformation of the street into a Mexican-American marketplace.

Today this character remains; vendors sell puppets, leather goods, sandals, serapes (woolen shawls), and handicrafts from stalls that line the center of the narrow street. The quality of what you'll find ranges from Tijuana-style "junkola" (donkey-shaped salt and pepper shakers) to well-made glassware and pottery. Then there are those paintings on black velvet: tacky or hip? Up to you.

On weekends, the restaurants are packed as musicians play in the central plaza. The weekends that fall around two Mexican holidays, Cinco de Mayo (May 5) and Independence Day (September 16), also draw huge crowds. ■ TIP→ **To see Olvera Street at its quietest, visit late on a weekday afternoon, when long shadows heighten the romantic feeling of the passageway.** For information, stop by the **Olvera Street Visitors Center** (✉ *622 N. Main St., Downtown* ☎ *213/628–1274* 🌐 *www.olvera-street.com*), in the Sepulveda House, a Victorian built in 1887 as a hotel and boardinghouse. The center is open weekdays 9–4, weekends 10–3. Free 50-minute walking tours leave here at 10, 11, and noon Tuesday–Saturday. Tours 🌐 *www.lasangelitas.org*.

MARIACHI MAGIC

Given the enormous Latino population of L.A., there are fiestas (parties) for almost every family event: weddings, graduations, births, and the mother of all Hispanic parties—the *Quinceañera* (a girl's 15th birthday party). Any party of any notoriety must include a well-dressed, fine-tuned Mariachi band with impeccably trimmed moustaches and shiny silver buttons cascading down their pant legs. These bands often gather on the weekend in and around Mariachi Plaza and Olvera Street and are available for hire for your local fiesta or patio table dinner. *Órale!*

Pelanconi House (✉ *W-17 Olvera St., Downtown*), built in 1855, was the first brick building in Los Angeles. It has been home to La Golondrina restaurant since 1930. **Avila Adobe** (✉ *E-10 Olvera St., Downtown*) was built as an 18-room home in 1818; today only a seven-room wing still stands. The remains have been converted to a museum space representing the oldest residential building still standing in Los Angeles. This graceful, simple structure features 3-foot-thick walls made of adobe brick over cottonwood timbers, a traditional interior courtyard, and 1840s-era furnishings. Open daily 9–3.

Another landmark, the **Italian Hall building** (✉ *650 N. Main St., Downtown*), isn't open to the public, but it's noteworthy because its south wall bears an infamous mural. Famed Mexican muralist David Alfaro Siqueiros shocked his patrons in the 1930s by depicting an oppressed worker of Latin America being crucified on a cross topped by a menacing American eagle. The anti-imperialist mural was promptly whitewashed but was later restored by the Getty Museum.

At the beginning of Olvera Street is the **Plaza,** a wonderful Mexican-style park with plenty of benches and walkways, shaded by a huge Moreton Bay fig tree. On weekends, mariachis and folkloric dance groups often perform. Two annual events particularly worth seeing: the Blessing of the Animals and Las Posadas. On the Saturday before Easter, Angelenos bring their pets (not just dogs and cats but horses, pigs, cows, birds, hamsters) to be blessed by a priest. For Las Posadas (every night between December 16 and 24), merchants and visitors parade up and down the street, led by children dressed as angels, to commemorate Mary and Joseph's search for shelter on Christmas Eve.

NEED A BREAK?

Dining choices on Olvera Street range from fast-food stands to comfortable sit-down restaurants. The most authentic Mexican food is at La Luz del Dia (✉ *W-1 Olvera St., Downtown* ☎ *213/628-7495*), which has traditional favorites such as chiles rellenos and pickled cactus, as well as handmade tortillas patted out in a practiced rhythm by the women behind the counter. Another delicious option, La Golondrina (✉ *W-17 Olvera St., Downtown* ☎ *213/628-4349*), midblock, has a delightful patio.

Pershing Square. The city's cultures come together in one of the oldest parks, named in honor of WWI general John J. Pershing. Opened in 1866, the park was renovated in the 1990s by architect Ricardo Legorreta and landscape architect Laurie Olin with colorful walls, fountains, and towers. Although the massive block-and-sphere architecture looks somewhat dated, Pershing remains an icon of Downtown L.A. Nearby office workers and visitors still utilize the area for a stroll or lunch break. From mid-November to mid-January, the place perks up with holiday events and the outdoor ice rink. ✉ *Bordered by 5th, 6th, Hill, and Olive Sts.* ☎ *213/847-4970* 🌐 *www.laparks.org/pershingsquare/pershing.htm* 🎫 *Free* 🕒 *Daily.*

7 **Richard J. Riordan Central Library.** Still known locally as the Central Library, this facility was renamed to honor the former mayor of Los Angeles. Major fires in the 1980s closed the library for six years, but today, at twice its former size, it's the third-largest public library in the nation. The original building, designed by Bertram Goodhue, was restored to its 1926 condition, with the pyramid tower and a torch symbolizing the Light of Learning crowning the building.

The mega-size of this library can be overwhelming with several floors and departments catering to your every literary wish. You can stop at a computer kiosk to search for a particular title or simply walk around to explore the interior design. The Cook rotunda on the second floor features murals by Dean Cornwell depicting the history of California, and the Tom Bradley Wing, named for another mayor, has a soaring eight-story atrium. The library offers frequent events and special exhibits, plus a small café to refuel. Out-of-towners may apply for a visitor's card by showing a valid ID to check out books. Don't ignore the gift shop, which is loaded with unique items for readers and writers. ✉ *630 W. 5th St., at Flower St., Downtown* ☎ *213/228-7000, 213/228-7168 for tour information* 🌐 *www.lapl.org* 🎫 *Free* 🕒 *Mon.–Thurs. 10–8, Fri. and Sat. 10–6, Sun. 1–5; docent tours weekdays at 12:30, Sat. at 11 and 2, and Sun. at 2. A self-guided tour map is also available on library's Web site.*

NEED A BREAK?

Overlooking the Maguire Garden just behind the Central Library, Café Pinot (✉ *700 W. 5th St., Downtown* ☎ *213/239-6500*) is the perfect pit stop for a tranquil meal and some artistic inspiration. Take a seat outside and look out on the stunning environmental art space setting, which features words and mathematical formulas in languages from around the world inscribed

along the step risers and sculptural pool. The grotto fountain pays tribute to the right to knowledge. A complimentary shuttle runs to the Music Center for evening performances.

(20) **Staples Center.** Home to the Lakers, the Clippers, the Sparks, and ice hockey team the Los Angeles Kings, the Staples Center also hosts ice shows, tennis, and superstar performers like Bruce Springsteen, Rod Stewart, and Madonna. This extravagant stadium treats its guests to high style, good sound quality, and comfortable seating. Though not open for visit except for events, the saucer-shaped building has made a permanent impression on the Downtown cityscape and now serves as an anchor for the enormous entertainment and convention complex on the surrounding blocks known as L.A. Live, set to fully open in 2010. ✉ *1111 S. Figueroa St., Downtown* ☎ *213/742–7340* 🌐 *www.staplescenter.com.*

BRIGHT LIGHTS, BIG CITY

To see L.A.'s true colors, hop aboard the Neon Cruises of classic signs from Downtown to Hollywood. You'll board a British-style double-decker bus and get a dazzling view of the city after dark while being regaled with funny trivia. The tours are presented by the Museum of Neon Art, which is currently closed for relocation. However, occasionally exhibits in temporary spaces "keep the lights on" to bring appreciation to the art of neon. Call or check the Web site for exhibit dates and locations (☎ *213/489–9918* 🌐 *www.neonmona.org*). Tour prices are $35–$75.

(17) ★ **Union Station.** Evoking an era when travel and style went hand in hand, Union Station will transport you to another destination, and another time. Built in 1939 and designed by City Hall architects John and Donald Parkinson, it combines Spanish colonial revival and art deco styles that have retained their classic warmth and quality. The waiting hall's commanding scale and enormous chandeliers have provided the setting for countless films, TV shows, and music videos. Once the key entry point into Los Angeles prior to LAX, Union Station is worth a visit even if you don't plan to go anywhere but merely want to wallow in the ambience of one of the country's last great rail stations. The indoor restaurant, **Traxx,** offers a glamorous vintage setting for lunch and dinner. ✉ *800 N. Alameda St., Downtown.*

(24) **University of Southern California (USC).** There's more to this private university than mascot Tommy Trojan and the legendary marching band. Its parklike inner-city campus dates to 1880, its film school is George Lucas's alma mater, and it fosters a fanatical crosstown rivalry with UCLA. Free docent-led campus tours are available weekdays as well as a self-guided tour map for potential students or film buffs who just want to walk in Lucas's footsteps. ✉ *Guest Relations, 615 Childs Way, University Park* ✣ *Adjacent to Exposition Park* ☎ *213/740–6605* 🌐 *www.usc.edu/visit* ⏲ *Call for tour schedule and reservations.*

OFF THE BEATEN PATH

Watts Towers of Simon Rodia. The jewel of rough South L.A. is the legacy of Simon Rodia, a tile setter who emigrated from Italy to California and erected one of the world's greatest folk-art structures. From 1921 until 1954, without any help, this eccentric man built the three main cement towers, using pipes, bed frames, and anything else he could find. He embellished them with bits of colorful glass, broken pottery, and more than 70,000 seashells. The towers still stand preserved, now the centerpiece of a state historic park and cultural center, part of an effort by Watts neighborhood leaders to overcome the area's gangland/riot-zone history—but it's still best to use your street smarts while visiting. ✉ *1727 E. 107th St., Watts* ✥ *Take I–110 to I–105 east; exit north at S. Central Ave., and turn right onto 108th St., left onto Willowbrook Ave.* ☎ *213/847–4646* 🎫 *$7, includes tour* ⏲ *Gallery Tues.–Sat. 10–4, Sun. noon–4; tours Fri. 11–3, Sat. 10:30–3, Sun. 12:30–3.*

10 **Westin Bonaventure Hotel & Suites.** In 1976 John Portman designed these five shimmering cylinders in the sky, with nary a 90-degree angle. Sheathed in mirrored glass, the now-dated building once looked like a science-fiction fantasy; this emblem of postmodern architecture has been featured countless TV shows and movies. Take a ride in the soaring glass elevator that carried Arnold Schwarzenegger in *True Lies*. For a truly panoramic view of L.A., be sure to have a meal in the Bona Vista Lounge on the 34th floor, which features floor-to-ceiling windows and rotates 360 degrees as you dine. ✉ *404 S. Figueroa St., Downtown* ☎ *213/624–1000* 🌐 *www.westin.com/bonaventure.*

HOLLYWOOD

The Tinseltown mythology of Los Angeles was born in Hollywood. But reputation aside, it's a workaday neighborhood without the glitz and glamour of places like Beverly Hills. Still, like Downtown, Hollywood is undergoing an extreme makeover designed to lure hipsters and big money back into the fold. New sleek clubs and restaurants seem to pop up every month drawing in celebrities, scenesters, and starry-eyed newcomers to create a colorful nighttime landscape (and some parking headaches).

Many daytime attractions can be found on foot around the recently relocated home of the Academy Awards at the Kodak Theater, part of the Hollywood & Highland entertainment complex. The adjacent Grauman's Chinese Theater delivers silver screen magic with its cinematic facade and ornate interiors from a bygone era. A shining example of a successful Hollywood revival can be seen and experienced just across Hollywood Boulevard at the 1926 El Capitan Theater, which offers live stage shows and a Wurlitzer organ before selected movie engagements. Walk the renowned Hollywood Walk of Stars to find your favorite celebrities and you'll encounter derelict diversions literally screaming for your attention (and dollar), numerous panhandlers, and an occasional costumed superhero not sanctified by Marvel comics. At Sunset and Vine, a developer-interpreted revival with sushi, stars, and swank condos promises to continue the sporadic renovations of the area. In summer, visit the crown jewel of Hollywood, the Hollywood Bowl, which features shows by the Los Angeles Philharmonic.

WHAT TO SEE

4 **Arclight/Cinerama Dome.** Film buffs and preservationists breathed a sigh of relief when the Arclight complex opened its doors and rewrote the book on cushy movie going. With plush stadium seating, reserved seats for some showings, state-of-the-art sound, an usher who welcomes you and introduces the film, and snack bars that cook up their own fresh caramel corn, the Arclight justifies its high ticket prices ($11–$14, depending on the hour you go). Built next to the restored geodesic Cinerama Dome, a curved-screen architectural icon, the complex also caters to film lovers with special director's Q&A nights as well as exhibits of movie costumes and photography throughout the lobby. Even though there are 14 other theaters in the complex, many films sell out quickly. Your best chance at prime seating is to order tickets online and to choose a seat in advance. A printed receipt allows you to walk directly into the theater and avoid the lines. Weekend nights have an especially hip buzz as film enthusiasts and industry power couples linger in the soaring lobby. Parking is $2 in the adjacent garage with a movie ticket purchase and validation. ✉ *6360 Sunset Blvd., at Vine St., Hollywood* ☎ *323/464–4226* 🌐 *www.arclightcinemas.com.*

OFF THE BEATEN PATH

Barnsdall Park/Hollyhock House. The panoramic view of Hollywood alone is worth a trip to this hilltop cultural center. After many years of closure as the buildings were repaired and retrofitted following the 1994 Northridge earthquake, this arts center is coming back into its own. On the grounds is the famous Hollyhock House, designed by architect Frank Lloyd Wright between 1919 and 1923. It was commissioned by philanthropist Aline Barnsdall to be the centerpiece of an arts community on the hill, complete with theaters and an actors' dorm. While Barnsdall's project didn't turn out quite the way she planned, the park now hosts the L.A. Municipal Art Gallery and Theatre, which provides exhibit space for visual and performance artists; affordable art classes for children and adults are also taught here. A film chronicling the Hollyhock House runs daily in the lobby of the Municipal Art Gallery—but better yet, join a docent tour of the building. Wright dubbed this style "California Romanza" (romanza is a musical term meaning "to make one's own form"). Stylized depictions of Barnsdall's favorite flower, the hollyhock, appear throughout the house in its cement columns, roofline, and furniture. The leaded-glass windows are expertly placed to make the most of both the surrounding gardens and the city views. ✉ *4800 Hollywood Blvd., Los Feliz* ☎ *323/644–6269* 🌐 *www.hollyhockhouse.net* 🎟 *Gallery free, Hollyhock House tour $7* ⏲ *Museum Thurs.–Sun. noon–5, Fri. noon–8:30; Hollyhock tours Wed.–Sun. hourly 12:30–3:30.*

7 **Capitol Records Tower.** According to legend, singer Nat King Cole and songwriter Johnny Mercer suggested that the record company's headquarters should be shaped to look like a stack of 45s, and their comment produced this lasting symbol of '50s chic. Or so the story goes. Architect Welton Becket claimed he just wanted to design a structure that economized space, and in so doing, he created the world's first cylindrical office building. On its south wall, L.A. artist Richard Wyatt's mural *Hollywood Jazz, 1945–1972* immortalizes musical greats

A GOOD TOUR

Numbers correspond to the Hollywood map.

Start by driving up into the Hollywood Hills on Beachwood Drive (off Franklin Avenue, just east of Gower Street) for an up-close look at the **Hollywood sign** ❶. Follow the small sign pointing the way to the LAFD Helispot. Turn left onto Rodgerton Drive, which twists and turns higher into the hills. At Deronda Drive, turn right and drive to the end. The HOLLYWOOD sign looms to the left. Retrace your route down the hill and back to Beachwood for the drive into Hollywood.

Make a right (west) at Franklin Avenue, and prepare to turn left at the next light, Gower Street. Stay on Gower, driving through the section known as **Gower Gulch,** where small B-picture "Poverty Row" studios once stood.

At Gower and Santa Monica Boulevard, look for the entrance to **Hollywood Forever Cemetery** ❷, half a block east on Santa Monica. Here you can pay your respects to Rudolph Valentino or two of the Ramones if you're so inclined. If you visit the cemetery, retrace your route back to Gower Street and turn left to drive along the western edge of the cemetery flanking Gower. Abutting the cemetery's southern edge is **Paramount Pictures** ❸. The famous gate Norma Desmond (Gloria Swanson) was driven through at the end of *Sunset Boulevard* is no longer accessible to the public, but a replica marks the entrance on Melrose Avenue: turn left from Gower Street to reach the gate.

Next, drive west (right off Gower) on Melrose for three blocks to Vine Street, turn right, and continue to the world-famous intersection of **Hollywood and Vine** ❺. Across the street is the **Capitol Records Tower** ❼, which resembles a stack of 45 rpm records. A few steps east of the intersection on Hollywood Boulevard stands the ornate, restored Pantages Theatre.

Drive west along Hollywood Boulevard. Stop along the way to look at the bronze stars that make up the **Hollywood Walk of Fame** ❻ or to visit the tourist kitsch of **Hollywood Wax Museum, Guinness World of Records,** or **Ripley's Believe It or Not Museum**—all shrines to Hollywood camp.

At Hollywood Boulevard and Las Palmas Avenue is Hollywood's first movie palace, the striking **Egyptian Theatre** ❾. Farther west, on Highland Avenue just south of Hollywood Boulevard, is the **Hollywood Museum** ❿. Continue west on Hollywood Boulevard until you see the giant, Babylonian-meets-stucco theme, hotel-retail-entertainment complex **Hollywood & Highland** ⓫, which includes the 3,300-seat Kodak Theatre, home of the Academy Awards.

Next to Hollywood & Highland is the world-famous **Grauman's Chinese Theatre** ⓬, a monument to Hollywood history. From the theater, cross Hollywood Boulevard and loop back east past the **Hollywood Roosevelt Hotel** ⓭, a spot that's both historic and trendy. Several blocks north of the boulevard on Highland Avenue is the **Hollywood Heritage Museum** ⓮, and the **Hollywood Bowl** ⓯, the beloved outdoor concert venue.

Arclight/Cinerama Dome ... **4**
Capitol Records Tower **7**
Egyptian Theatre **9**
Grauman's Chinese Theatre **12**
Griffith Observatory **8**
Guitar Center & Rockwalk **16**
Hollywood & Highland **11**
Hollywood and Vine **5**
Hollywood Bowl **15**
Hollywood Forever Cemetery **2**
Hollywood Heritage Museum **14**
Hollywood Museum **10**
Hollywood Roosevelt Hotel **13**
Hollywood Sign **1**
Hollywood Walk of Fame ... **6**
Kodak Theatre **11**
Paramount Pictures **3**

Duke Ellington, Billie Holiday, Ella Fitzgerald, and Miles Davis. Of course pop icons the Beatles, who are on display in stunning photos near the Vine Street entrance, are Capitol's most treasured offering. John Lennon's star on the Hollywood Walk of Fame lies in the sidewalk out front and is often the scene of gatherings on his birthday. The recording studios are underneath the parking lot; all kinds of major artists, including Frank Sinatra, the Beatles, and Radiohead, have filled the echo chambers with sound. At the top of the tower, a blinking light spells out "Hollywood" in Morse code. Due to tightened security, the building is not open to the public. ✉*1750 N. Vine St., Hollywood.*

ROCK ON TOUR

If the stars you want to see are the ones that rock your world, hop on the Esotouric Tour bus and find out "Where the Action Was." This three-hour tour co-hosted by local pop music critics and sponsored by Amoeba Records (with rockin' swag bags) takes you on a ride to celebrated nightclubs, record label offices, recording studios and landmarks in subculture history. Schedule rotates with other offbeat Esotouric offerings including true crime tours (the Black Dahlia) and literary LA (Raymond Chandler, Charles Bukowski). Visit the Web site for schedule (🌐*www.esotouric.com)*, tours \$55–\$65 run 3–4 hours.

OFF THE BEATEN PATH

Chemosphere House. Shaped like a flying saucer from a 1960s film, the Chemosphere House sits perched high up off Mulholland overlooking the Valley. Design by the late architect John Lautner, who studied under Frank Lloyd Wright, this house is held together with special glues used at the request of the original owner, who worked with a chemical company. Now owned by the publisher Benedikt Taschen, the Chemosphere is an awesome sight for architecture fans of the mod era. Directions: go north up Laurel Canyon, east on Mulholland, right on Torreyson Drive. Turn left up the narrow unmarked road where the Chemosphere House sits at the top—but remember: it remains a residence, so don't cause a disruption. ✉*7776 Torreyson Dr.*

9 **Egyptian Theatre.** Hieroglypics in Hollywood? Why not? Impresario Sid Grauman built Hollywood's first movie palace in 1922; the Egyptian-theme theater hosted many premieres in its early heyday. In 1992 it closed—with an uncertain future. Six years later it reopened with its Tinseltown shine restored. The nonprofit American Cinematheque now hosts special screenings and discussions with notable filmmakers, and on weekends you can watch a documentary about Hollywood history (*Forever Hollywood,* \$7). Walk past giant palm trees to the theater's forecourt and entrance. Backstage tours of the theater are available once a month. Films, primarily classics and independents, are shown in the evening. ✉*6712 Hollywood Blvd.* ☎*323/466–3456* 🌐*www.egyptiantheatre.com* 🎟*\$10; call for tour reservations and times.*

NEED A BREAK?

During Hollywood's heyday, the Pig 'n Whistle (✉*6714 Hollywood Blvd., Hollywood* ☎*323/463–0000*) was the place to stop for a bite before or after seeing a movie in the Egyptian Theatre, next door. After extensive res-

CLOSE UP

Griffith Park

With so much of Los Angeles paved in cement and asphalt, 4,100-acre Griffith Park stands out as a special place. It's the largest municipal park and urban wilderness area in the United States. On warm weekends, there are parties, barbecues, mariachi bands, and strolling vendors selling fresh fruit. Joggers, cyclists, and walkers course its roadways, and golfers play its four municipal courses. Within the park there are three tennis courts, horse stables, a collection of vintage locomotive and railroad cars called Travel Town, and pony rides. L.A.'s oldest **merry-go-round** (☎ *323/665–3051*) continues to spin here, playing a fabulous Stinson calliope. It's open weekends 11–5, and it costs $2. There's also the 6,100-seat **Greek Theatre** (✉ *2700 North Vermont* ☎ *323/665–5857* 🌐 *www.greektheatrela.com*), where Tina Turner and the Gipsy Kings have performed.

The park was named after Col. Griffith J. Griffith, a mining tycoon who donated 3,000 acres of land to the city for the park in 1896. The park has been used as a film and television location since the early days of motion pictures. One early Hollywood producer advised, "A tree is a tree, a rock is a rock, shoot it in Griffith Park."

One of the park's most famous filming sites is the **Griffith Observatory and Planetarium.** Overlooking Hollywood and Downtown, this art deco landmark off Vermont Avenue was immortalized in *Rebel Without a Cause.*

The silver-screen cowboy Gene Autry created the **Autry National Center** (✉ *4700 Western Heritage Way, at Zoo Dr.* ☎ *323/667–2000* 🌐 *www.autry-museum.org*), an impressive museum that traces the history of the American West and Western moviemaking. Open Tuesday–Sunday 10–5. Admission is $9, free second Tuesday of month.

Not far from the museum, at the junction of the Ventura Freeway (Highway 134) and the Golden State Freeway (I–5), is the 80-acre **Los Angeles Zoo** (☎ *323/644–4200* 🌐 *www.lazoo.org* 🎫 $12). You'll need good walking shoes for this as distances are compounded by plenty of construction detours. You'll see tigers, lions, and bears along with a few endangered species such as the California condor and a trio of trio of Sumatran tiger cubs born in June 2007.

After a major fire in May 2007, many hiking and equestrian trails were closed (for safety reasons, for replanting, and for the natural wildlife). The park went into a state of uncertainty, with many of the access roads closed to the public. All trails have since reopened except the Bird Sanctuary Trail, which is undergoing a major recovery effort.

Griffith Park is accessible in several places: off Los Feliz Boulevard at Western Canyon Avenue, Vermont Avenue, Crystal Springs Drive, and Riverside Drive; from the Ventura/134 Freeway at Victory Boulevard, Zoo Drive, or Forest Lawn Drive; from the Golden State Freeway (I–5) at Los Feliz Boulevard and Zoo Drive. The park is open from 5 AM to 10 PM. Information (☎ *323/644–6661*) and for emergencies, call the **ranger station** (☎ *323/913–7390*) on Crystal Springs Drive, near the merry-go-round.

toration, the historic restaurant is back, with overstuffed booths, dramatic paneled ceilings, and attentive service.

12 ★ **Grauman's Chinese Theatre.** A place that inspires the phrase "only in Hollywood," this fantasy of Chinese pagodas and temples has become a shrine to stardom. Although you have to buy a movie ticket to appreciate the interior trappings, the courtyard is open to the public. Here you'll find those oh-so-famous cement hand- and footprints. This tradition is said to have begun at the theater's opening in 1927, with the premiere of Cecil B. DeMille's *King of Kings,* when actress Norma Talmadge just happened to step into wet cement. Now more than 160 celebrities have contributed imprints for posterity, including some oddball specimens, such as ones of Whoopi Goldberg's dredlocks and Betty Grable's legs. Recent inductees include the cast and director of *Ocean's Thirteen,* the Harry Potter kids, and Will Smith.

The main theater itself is worth visiting, if only to see a film in the same seats as hundreds of celebrities who have attended big premieres here. You could also take a tour for $12 that takes you around the theaters and the VIP lounge. If it's movies you want, six more theaters are next to the Hollywood & Highland complex with every modern moviegoing comfort. You may have to wade through the crowd of tourists and performance artists on the sidewalk for the front box office, but there's easy access to the upper theaters from the Highland parking garage through the elevators near the Kodak Theater. ✉ *6925 Hollywood Blvd., Hollywood* ☎ *323/464–8111, 323/463–9576 for tours* 🌐 *www.manntheatres.com.*

8 **Griffith Observatory.** High on a hillside overlooking the city, the Griffith Observatory is one of the most celebrated icons of Los Angeles, and now, after a massive expansion and cosmic makeover, its interior is as rich as its exterior featuring sleek exhibits with dramatic lighting and graphics. A lower level was dug deep into the hillside for the expansion. In true L.A. style, the Leonard Nimoy Event Horizon Theater presents guest speakers and shows on current topics and discoveries. The planetarium now features a new dome, laser digital projection system, theatrical lighting, and stellar sound system. Shows are $7. Not to be outdone, the café serves delicious food thanks to "chef to the stars" Wolfgang Puck. You might recognize the observatory and grounds from such movies as *Rebel Without a Cause* and *The Rocketeer.* ✉ *2800 E. Observatory Rd., Griffith Park* ☎ *213/473–0800* 🌐 *www.griffithobservatory.org* ⏲ *Tues.–Fri. noon–10* PM, *weekends 10–10.*

Guinness World of Records. Saluting those who have gone the extra mile to earn placement in the *Guinness Book of Records,* this for-profit museum exhibits replicas and photographs of endearing record breakers that include such oddities as the most-tattooed human and the world's heaviest man. An interactive simulation theater allows guests to sit in moving, vibrating seats while viewing a film to actually "experience" the force of a record being broken, and educational monitors give a hands-on approach to trivia pursuit. For world record buffs and freak show fans mainly. ✉ *6764 Hollywood Blvd., Hollywood* ☎ *323/463–6433* 🌐 *www.guinnessattractions.com* 🎟 *$15.95* ⏲ *9:30* AM*–midnight daily.*

16 **Guitar Center and Hollywood RockWalk.** For those about to rock, this store salutes you. Musicians and the fans who love them will want to stop by the Guitar Center on Sunset, where you can try out any musical instrument your heart desires as well as view memorabilia donated by some of the store's star customers—Led Zeppelin's set list, Jeff Beck's yellow Strat guitar, and KISS members' platform boots are memorable highlights.

A place that has provided equipment for virtually every band to have come out of Los Angeles since the 1960s, the store pays tribute to its rock star clientele with a "RockWalk," out front. The concrete slabs are imprinted with the talented hands of Van Halen, Bonnie Raitt, Chuck Berry, Dick Dale, Def Leppard, Carlos Santana, KISS, and others. Two standouts are Joey Ramone's upside-down hand and Lemmy of Motörhead's "middle finger salute." Inductees are celebrated with a ceremony that's open to the public—check the Web site for details. ✉*7425 Sunset Blvd., Hollywood* ☎*323/874–1060* 🌐*www.rockwalk.com* 🎫*Free* 🕙*10–7 daily.*

11 ★ **Hollywood and Highland.** Now an extremely busy tourist attraction (read: not a lot of locals), this hotel-retail-entertainment complex was a dramatic play to bring glitz, foot traffic, and commerce back to Hollywood. The design pays tribute to the city's film legacy with a grand staircase leading up to a pair of white stucco 33-foot-high elephants, a nod to the 1916 movie *Intolerance.* (Something tells us that the reference is lost on most visitors.) **TIP→ Pause at the entrance arch, Babylon Court, which frames the HOLLYWOOD sign in the hills above for a picture-perfect view.** There are plenty of clothing stores and eateries—and you may find yourself ducking into these for a respite from the crowds and street artists. On the sidewalk below you could encounter everything from a sidewalk evangelist to a guy dressed as Spiderman posing for pictures. In the summer and during Christmas vacation special music programs and free entertainment keep strollers entertained. A Metro Red Line station provides easy access to and from other parts of the city, and there's plenty of underground parking accessible from Highland Avenue. ✉*Hollywood Blvd. and Highland Ave., Hollywood* ☎*323/467–6412 visitor center* 🌐*www.hollywoodandhighland.com* 🎫*Parking $2 with validation* 🕙*Mon.–Sat. 10–10, Sun. 10–7.*

5 **Hollywood and Vine.** The mere mention of this intersection inspires images of a street corner bustling with movie stars, hopefuls, and moguls arriving on foot or in Duesenbergs and Rolls-Royces. In the old days this was the hub of the radio and movie industry: film stars like Gable and Garbo hustled in and out of their agents' office buildings at these fabled cross streets. Now that glamour has dimmed and the area only comes alive after dark as a place for theater and nightlife. The **Pantages Theatre** (✉*6233 Hollywood Blvd.*) brings in Broadway shows such as the *Lion King, Hairspray,* and a production of *Wicked* unique to L.A. Across the street is the opulent **Henry Fonda Music Box Theatre** (✉*6126 Hollywood Blvd.* 🌐*www.henryfondatheater.com*), built in the 1920s with an open-air palazzo. Pop-music concerts and small theater productions are both put on here. Just north on Vine, the **Avalon Theater** (✉*1735 N. Vine St.* 🌐*www.avalonhollywood.com*) hosts rock

concerts and dance nights in the space where the 1950s TV show *This Is Your Life* was recorded. Even the Red Line Metro station here keeps up the Hollywood theme, with a *Wizard of Oz*–style yellow brick road and giant movie projectors decorating the station.

NEED A BREAK?

Stop at Dakota at the Hollywood Roosevelt Hotel (✉ *7000 Hollywood Blvd.* ☎ *323/466–7000*) for breakfast, lunch, or dinner. Deep brown leather booths and handsome lights fastened around the hotel's columns provide a swank, yet somehow cozy retreat from the sticky sidewalks of Hollywood Boulevard just outside the leaded 15-foot windows of this historical Hollywood landmark hotel.

15 **Hollywood Bowl.** Classic Hollywood doesn't get better than this. Summer-evening concerts have been a tradition since 1922 at this amphitheater cradled in the Hollywood Hills. The Bowl is the summer home of the Los Angeles Philharmonic, but the musical fare also includes pop and jazz. A new much larger shell arrived in 2004, improving the acoustics and allowing the occasional dance and theater performance on stage with the orchestra. Evoking the 1929 shell structure, the new shell ripples out in a series of concentric rings. The 17,000-plus seating capacity ranges from boxes (where alfresco preconcert meals are catered) to concrete bleachers in the rear. Since most of the box seats are reserved for season ticket holders, a great alternative are the ideally located Super Seats with comfortable armrests and great sight lines. Come early for a picnic in the grounds.

Before the concert, or during the day, visit the **Hollywood Bowl Museum** (☎ *323/850–2058* ⏲ *Tues.–Fri. 10–5*) for a time-capsule version of the Bowl's history. The microphone used during Frank Sinatra's 1943 performance is just one of the pieces of rare memorabilia on display. Throughout the gallery, drawers open to reveal vintage programs or letters written by fans tracing their fondest memories of going to the Bowl. Headphones let you listen to recordings of such great Bowl performers as Amelita Galli-Curci, Ella Fitzgerald, and Paul McCartney, and videos give you a tantalizing look at performances by everyone from the Beatles to Esa-Pekka Salonen. Be sure to pick up a map and take the "Bowl Walk" to explore the park-like grounds of this beautiful setting. ✉ *2301 N. Highland Ave., Hollywood* ☎ *323/850–2000* 🌐 *www.hollywoodbowl.com, www.laphil.com* 🎟 *Tickets $1–$125, museum free* ⏲ *Museum Tues.–Sat. 10–4:30; July–mid-Sept. concert nights, 10 AM–showtime; grounds daily dawn–dusk, call for performance schedule.*

2 ★ **Hollywood Forever Cemetery.** Leave it to Hollywood to have a graveyard that feels more V.I.P. than R.I.P. With its revived grounds and media-genic approach, this celebrity-filled cemetery (formerly the Hollywood Memorial Park) is well worth a visit. The lush gardens, lakes, and spectacular views of the Hollywood sign and Griffith Park Observatory (whose founder, Griffith J. Griffith, is buried here) make it a good spot for an afternoon walk; you can pick up a map of the grounds in the gift shop. Among the graves are those of Cecil B. DeMille, Douglas Fairbanks Sr., and Mel Blanc, voice of many Warner Bros. cartoon characters, whose headstone reads, "That's all, folks!"

Film and music fans flock here to find their recently departed idols, including King Kong's love Fay Wray and punk rockers Johnny Ramone and Dee Dee Ramone (buried under his given name Douglas Glenn Colvin). The large Grecian tomb in the center of the lake belongs to philanthropist William A. Clark Jr., founder of the Los Angeles Philharmonic. Inside the Cathedral Mausoleum is Rudolph Valentino's crypt, stained red from many lipstick kisses. For years, a mysterious "Lady in Black" visited Valentino's tomb on the anniversary of his death.

2

In summer, the cemetery hosts events including Shakespeare in the Cemetery and film screenings starring Valentino and other interred residents on the mausoleum's outer wall, and the grounds become quite a party scene. At Halloween-time the cemetery hosts Dia De Los Muertos, a colorful Mexican festival celebrating the dead with colorful costumes, art, and music. The cemetery also has a kiosk in the main office with video memorials and digital scrapbooks of those buried here. Note: When planning a visit, even for a festive event, maintain respect to the gravesites. Many families of the departed have voiced concerns of unruly visitors. The cemetery also still performs burials here and proper etiquette is expected. ✉*6000 Santa Monica Blvd., Hollywood* ☎*323/469–1181* 🌐*www.hollywoodforever.com* *$10 Shakespeare, $10 movies, $5 Day of the Dead* ⏲*Daily 8–5.*

14 **Hollywood Heritage Museum.** A must for Cecil B. DeMille fans, this unassuming building across from the Hollywood Bowl is a trove of memorabilia from the earliest days of Hollywood filmmaking, including a thorough history of DeMille's career. Large sections of the original stone statue props from *The Ten Commandments* lay like fallen giants among smaller items in glass cases around the perimeter of this modest museum. A documentary tracking Hollywood's golden era is worth taking in. The building itself is the restored Lasky–DeMille Barn, designated a California State Historic Landmark in 1956. ✉*2100 N. Highland Ave., Hollywood* ☎*323/874–2276* 🌐*www.hollywoodheritage.org* *$5* ⏲*Thurs.–Sun. noon–4.*

OFF THE BEATEN PATH

Hollywood High School. Grease is the word! This stellar high school has seen a who's who of Hollywood royalty in its classrooms and many productions shot in its halls. The school's most memorable starring role was in *Grease* with Sandy and Danny dancing their way across the grassy playground during a true L.A. heat wave. Surely no other high school has such a shining alumni list. Such names as Carol Burnett, Carole Lombard, John Ritter, Lana Turner, and Sarah Jessica Parker called HHS their alma mater. While you cannot enter the school grounds, it's easy to imagine the precelebs struggling over an algebra equation or being asked out to the prom. You can also see the star-studded mural *Diversity in Entertainment,* by famed local painter Eloy Torrez. ✉*1521 N. Highland Ave., Hollywood.*

10 Fodor's Choice ★ **Hollywood Museum.** Lovers of Hollywood's glamorous past will be singing "Hooray for Hollywood" when they stop by this gem of cinema history. It's inside the Max Factor Building, purchased in 1928. Factor's famous makeup was made on the top floors and a glamorous salon was hosted on the ground floor. After its renovation, this art deco landmark

now holds more than 10,000 bits of film memorabilia. The extensive exhibits inside include those dedicated to Marilyn Monroe and Bob Hope and to costumes and set props from such films as *Moulin Rouge, The Silence of the Lambs,* and *Planet of the Apes.* There's an impressive gallery of photos showing movie stars frolicking at such venues as the Brown Derby, Ciro's, the Trocadero, and the Mocambo. Hallway walls are covered with the stunning autograph collection of ultimate fan Joe Ackerman; aspiring filmmakers will want to check out an exhibit of early film equipment. The museum's showpiece, however, is the Max Factor exhibit, where separate dressing rooms are dedicated to Factor's "color harmony": creating distinct looks for "brownettes" (Factor's term), redheads, and of course, bombshell blondes. You can practically smell the peroxide of Marilyn Monroe getting her trademark platinum look here. You can also spy the actual makeup cases owned by Lucille Ball, Lana Turner, Ginger Rogers, Bette Davis, Rita Hayworth, and others who made the makeup as glamorous as the starlets who wore it. ✉ *1660 N. Highland Ave., Hollywood* ☎ *323/464–7776* 🌐 *www.thehollywoodmuseum.com* 🎟 *$15* ⏲ *Wed.–Sun. 10–5.*

⓭ **Hollywood Roosevelt Hotel.** In the hotel world, the Roosevelt's something of a comeback kid. This historical landmark opened in 1927 and hosted the first Academy Awards that same year. It was a glamour magnet during Hollywood's golden age, but its reputation then slumped until the late '90s. New owners, a substantial face-lift, and some hip club promoters turned it around. These days, you're likely to need an insider connection to get into the celeb-filled club or the Tropicana poolside bar, where you can peek at the underwater mural by David Hockney. Though the new management tries to play down the ghost stories of the hotel's past—including sightings of Montgomery Clift, Clark Gable, and Carole Lombard—they did put a replica of the famous "Marilyn Mirror" in every room, modeled after the original, which sparked reports of the actress's ghostly reflection. ✉ *7000 Hollywood Blvd., Hollywood* ☎ *323/466–7000* 🌐 *www.hollywoodroosevelt.com.*

❶ ★ **HOLLYWOOD Sign.** With letters 50 feet tall, Hollywood's trademark sign can be spotted from miles away. The sign, which originally read HOLLYWOODLAND, was erected on Mt. Lee in the Hollywood Hills in 1923 to promote a real-estate development. In 1949 the "land" portion of the sign was taken down. By 1973, the sign had earned landmark status, but since the letters were made of wood, its longevity came into question. A makeover project was launched and the letters were auctioned off (rocker Alice Cooper bought the O, singing cowboy Gene Autry sponsored an L) to make way for a new sign made of sheet metal. Inevitably, the sign has drawn pranksters who have altered it over the years, albeit temporarily, to spell out HOLLYWEED (in the 1970s, to commemorate lenient marijuana laws), GO NAVY (before a Rose Bowl game), and PEROTWOOD (during the 1992 presidential election). A fence and surveillance equipment have since been installed to deter intruders. Use caution if driving up to the sign on residential streets since many cars speed around the blind corners. 🌐 *www.hollywoodsign.org.*

❻ ★ **Hollywood Walk of Fame.** Along Hollywood Boulevard runs a trail of affirmations for entertainment-industry overachievers. On this mile-long stretch of sidewalk, inspired by the concrete handprints in front of Grauman's Chinese Theatre, names are embossed in brass, each at the center of a pink star embedded in dark-gray terrazzo. They're not all screen deities; many stars commemorate people who worked in a technical field. The first eight stars were unveiled in 1960 at the northwest corner of Highland Avenue and Hollywood Boulevard: Olive Borden, Ronald Colman, Louise Fazenda, Preston Foster, Burt Lancaster, Edward Sedgwick, Ernest Torrence, and Joanne Woodward (some of these names have stood the test of time better than others). Since then, more than 1,600 others have been immortalized, though that honor doesn't come cheap—upon selection by a special committee, the personality in question (or more likely his or her movie studio or record company) pays about $15,000 for the privilege. To aid you in spotting celebrities you're looking for, stars are identified by one of five icons: a motion-picture camera, a radio microphone, a television set, a record, or a theatrical mask. Contact the **Hollywood Chamber of Commerce** (✉ *7018 Hollywood Blvd.* ☎ *323/469–8311* 🌐 *www.hollywoodchamber.net*) for celebrity-star locations and information on future star installations.

Hollywood Wax Museum. Desperately looking for stars? You can spot celebrities past (Mary Pickford, Elvis Presley, and Clark Gable) and present (Angelina Jolie, Russell Crowe, Keanu Reeves, and Nicolas Cage), or at least their waxy likenesses (squinting helps), here in this for-profit museum that pays tribute to Hollywood's favorites. A short film on Oscar winners is shown daily. The lighting is purposely kept low to give the wax figures a more lifelike appearance, but some look downright spooky. Be especially cautious when entering the Horror Chamber, where figures of serial slashers and horror favorites from *Nightmare on Elm Street, Friday the 13th,* and *Texas Chainsaw Massacre* are animated to leap out to greet you. The creepiness is especially evident at night, when fewer visitors are around. Since this isn't Madame Tussaud's, set your expectations low and you might score some joyfully silly photos for your scrapbook. ✉ *6767 Hollywood Blvd., Hollywood* ☎ *323/462–8860* 🌐 *www.hollywoodwax.com* 🎟 *$15.95* ⏲ *Sun.–Thurs. 10 AM–midnight, Fri. and Sat. 10 AM–1 AM.*

NEED A BREAK?

Musso & Frank Grill (✉ *6667 Hollywood Blvd., at N. Las Palmas Ave.* ☎ *323/467–5123*), open since 1919, is the last remaining Old Hollywood watering hole. Come for dinner or just stop in for a martini and soak up some atmosphere. Expect high prices and some unjustified attitude. On the lighter and weirder side, the **Snow White Cafe** (✉ *6769 Hollywood Blvd., at Highland Ave.* ☎ *323/465–4444*), supposedly created by some of the original Disney animators and filled with murals of the film's characters, is a good stop for a quick bite.

Ivar Street. William Faulkner wrote *Absalom, Absalom!* while he lived at the old **Knickerbocker Hotel** (✉ *1714 N. Ivar St., Hollywood*), and Nathanael West wrote *The Day of the Locust* in his apartment at the **Parva Sed-Apta** (✉ *1817 N. Ivar St., Hollywood*).

WALK OF FAME LOCATIONS

Here are the sites of a few of the stars along the Walk of Fame. Seeking out a particular star? Hit the directory on the Hollywood Chamber of Commerce's Web site, www.hollywoodchamber.net.

Marlon Brando: 1765 Vine St.

David Bowie: 7021 Hollywood Blvd.

Carol Burnett: 6439 Hollywood Blvd.

Charlie Chaplin: 6751 Hollywood Blvd.

Tom Cruise: 6912 Hollywood Blvd.

Bette Davis: 6225 Hollywood Blvd.

Clark Gable: 1608 Vine St.

Cary Grant: 1610 Vine St.

Ella Fitzgerald: 6738 Hollywood Blvd.

Tom Hanks: 7000 Hollywood Blvd.

Audrey Hepburn: 1652 Vine St.

Alfred Hitchcock: 6506 Hollywood Blvd.

Nicole Kidman: 6801 Hollywood Blvd.

Marilyn Monroe: 6774 Hollywood Blvd.

Jack Nicholson: 6925 Hollywood Blvd.

Mary-Kate and Ashley Olsen: 6801 Hollywood Blvd.

⓫ ★ **Kodak Theatre.** Follow the path of red-carpet Hollywood royalty to the home of the Academy Awards. While taking a half-hour tour of this famous setting isn't cheap, it's a worthwhile expense for movie buffs who just can't get enough insider information. The tour guides share plenty of behind-the-scenes tidbits about Oscar ceremonies as they take you through the theater. You'll get to step into the VIP George Eastman Lounge, where celebrities mingle on the big night and get a bird's-eye view from the balcony seating. (Be sure to ask how Oscar got his name.) The interior design was inspired by European opera houses, but underneath all the trimmings, the space has some of the finest technical systems in the world. Although you may not make it in for the Oscar show itself, you can always come here for a musical or concert performance by the likes of Alicia Keys or the Dixie Chicks. ✉ *6801 Hollywood Blvd., Hollywood* ☎ *323/308–6300* 🌐 *www.kodaktheatre.com* 🎫 *Tours $15 daily 10:30–2:30.*

❸ Fodor's Choice ★ **Paramount Pictures.** With a history dating to the early 1920s, this studio was home to some of Hollywood's most luminous stars, including Rudolph Valentino, Mae West, Mary Pickford, and Lucille Ball, who filmed episodes of *I Love Lucy* here. The lot still churns out memorable movies and TV shows, including *Forrest Gump, Titanic,* and *Star Trek*. You can take a studio tour (reservations required) led by friendly guides who walk and trolley you around the back lots. As well as gleaning some gossipy history (see the lawn where Lucy and Desi broke up), you'll spot the sets of TV and film shoots in progress, including such hits as *Entertainment Tonight, Dr. Phil,* and *Everybody Hates Chris*. You can also be part of the audience for live TV tapings. Tickets are free; call for listings and times. ✉ *5555 Melrose Ave., Hollywood*

CLOSE UP

L.A. on the Fast Track

Once upon a time, Los Angeles had an enviable public transportation system known as the Pacific Electric Red Cars, trolleys that made it possible to get around this sprawling city without an automobile. In the mid-1900s, the last of the Red Cars disappeared, and Los Angeles lost itself in the car culture. Make no mistake, the car culture is here to stay; an afternoon in rush-hour traffic will drive that point home. But for the last few years, a sleek new rail system has emerged. You can now take a subway through parts of Downtown Los Angeles, Hollywood, Pasadena, and North Hollywood.

The Metro Red Line subway, which is the most useful for exploring parts of the city, starts at Downtown's Union Station, then curves northwest to Hollywood and on to Universal City and North Hollywood. The Blue and Green light rail lines are geared for commuters. The latest addition, the Gold Line, goes from Union Station up to Pasadena.

Though it takes some planning, using the Metro can spare you time you might otherwise spend stuck in traffic—if the stations are convenient, that is. For nuts-and-bolts information on riding the Metro Rail, see ⇨ Travel Smart Los Angeles. If you're worried about being caught in the subway during an earthquake, keep in mind that stations and tunnels were built with reinforced steel and were engineered to withstand a magnitude-8 earthquake.

The Metro Rail stations are worth exploring themselves, and you can sign up for a free docent-led **MTA art tour** (☎ *213/922–2738* 🌐 *www.mta.net or* 🌐 *www.metro.net/about%5Fus/metroart/ma_docent.htm*), which departs from the Hollywood & Highland and Union Stations at 10 AM the first weekend of each month. You'll receive a free day pass to ride the rails as you visit the colorful murals, sculptures, and architectural elements of each station, designed to carry out themes of Los Angeles history. The Universal City station is next to the site of the Campo de Caheunga, where Mexico relinquished control of California to the United States in 1847, and the station features a time line of the area's past done in the traditional style of colorful Mexican folk art.

The North Hollywood station also celebrates local history: native Gabrielino culture, many immigrant communities, Amelia Earhart (a local), Western wear designer Nudie, and the history of transportation in Los Angeles County. The station at Hollywood Boulevard and Highland plays off Tinseltown fantasies, encouraging travelers to look beyond the subway station.

The Hollywood and Vine station has recycled film reels on the ceiling, original Paramount Pictures film projectors from the 1930s, and floor paving that looks like the yellow brick road from *The Wizard of Oz.* There are imposing, glass-clad columns juxtaposed with rock formations at the Vermont and Beverly station. The old Red Car trolley makes a guest appearance in the Hollywood and Western station.

☎323/956–1777 ⊕*www.paramount.com/paramount.php* 🎟*Tours weekdays by reservation only, $35.*

Ripley's Believe It or Not. "Odditorium" is a good name for it—while the ticket price may be a bit steep for these slighted faded relics of the bizarre and sometimes creepy— where else can you see a bikini made of human hair, a sculpture of Marilyn Monroe made of shredded money, a "killing kit" from 1850, and animal freaks of nature? You're asked to "believe it or not," and many of the curiosities may fail a strict authenticity test, but it still offers some goofy fun. ✉*6780 Hollywood Blvd., Hollywood* ☎*323/466–6335* ⊕*www.ripleys.com* 🎟*$14.99* ⏲*10 AM–midnight daily.*

OFF THE BEATEN PATH

Los Feliz, Silver Lake & Echo Park. Over the past few years, these neighborhoods east of Hollywood have become an intriguing mix of subcultures. Low rents drew artists and musicians to Los Feliz, then farther southeast to Silver Lake and, lately, Echo Park. Funky, independent boutiques, galleries, and cafés have followed in their wake. Los Feliz is the most gentrified, Echo Park the least. Silver Lake's namesake is a lovely oasis, and the neighborhood also has a cluster of modernist homes designed by Richard Neutra and R. M. Schindler. Echo Park's **Echo Lake** has a sprawling lotus bed; its slender **Sunset Art Park,** at 1478 Sunset Boulevard, gives a glimpse of "drive-by art."

Musicians can brush up on their skills with $25 lessons at the **Silver Lake Conservancy of Music** (✉*3920 W. Sunset* ☎*323/665–3363* ⊕*www.silverlakeconservatory.com*) founded by Flea of the Red Hot Chili Peppers. For a blast of the neighborhoods' creative and gay energy, visit during late summer's **Sunset Junction Street Fair** (⊕*www.sunsetjunction.org*), with concerts by alternative bands. There's also an annual **Silver Lake Film Festival** (⊕*www.silverlakefilmfestival.org*), which showcases up-and-coming independent filmmakers. Both of these annual events bring together a crowd drawn from the arts, Latino, and gay communities. The easiest way to reach these neighborhoods is to drive east on Sunset Boulevard, then head north up Hillhurst or Vermont Avenue to Los Feliz, or continue southeast on Sunset to Silver Lake and Echo Park.

WILSHIRE BOULEVARD, MUSEUM ROW, AND FARMERS MARKET

The three-block stretch of Wilshire Boulevard known as Museum Row, east of Fairfax Avenue, racks up five intriguing museums and a prehistoric tar pit to boot. Only a few blocks away are the historic Farmers Market and The Grove shopping mall, a great place to people-watch over breakfast. Wilshire Boulevard itself is something of a cultural monument—it begins its grand 16-mi sweep to the sea in Downtown Los Angeles. Along the way it passes through once-grand but now run-down neighborhoods near MacArthur Park; Mid-Wilshire, holding some of the city's first high-rise office buildings; the elegant old-money enclave of Hancock Park along with Miracle Mile and Museum Row; the showy city of Beverly Hills; and the high-price high-rise condo corridor in Westwood, before ending its march at the cliffs above the

Pacific Ocean. The drive from Downtown to the ocean can be traffic clogged; Wilshire is a major thoroughfare and tends to be busy all day long. **TIP→Finding parking along Wilshire Boulevard can present a challenge any time of the day; you'll find advice on the information phone lines of most attractions.** For avid urban explorers, the most interesting stretch historically is the boulevard's eastern portion, from Fairfax Avenue to Downtown.

WHAT TO SEE

8 **Architecture and Design Museum (A+D).** Unique buildings are what make Los Angeles a captivating city, so it's no wonder a museum dedicated to celebrating design would open here. Nestled into Museum Row with exhibits themed around residential and commercial structures, interior landscaping, product design, and their creators, the museum features rotating exhibits that range from hanging panels of photographs to designers' models in this one-room, exposed-ceiling, warehouse-style space that's sure to inspire flights of fancy beyond generic stucco. The museum occasionally closes for installations, so call ahead. ✉ *5900 Wilshire Blvd., Miracle Mile* ☎ *323/932–9393* 🌐 *www.aplusd.org* 🎟 *$5* 🕐 *Tues.–Fri. 10–6, weekends 11–5.*

6 **Craft and Folk Art Museum (CAFAM).** A small but important cultural landmark in the city, CAFAM pioneered support for traditional folk arts. These days, the two-story space takes on a global scope, embracing international contemporary crafts, social movements, and long-established artisan work. The gallery space mounts rotating exhibitions where you might see anything from costumes of carnival celebrations around the world to Mennonite quilts. The courtyard area provides a tranquil space for periodic exhibits and opening receptions. Be sure to take a look around the ground-level gift shop for unique collection of handcrafts, jewelry, ceramics, books, and textiles. ✉ *5814 Wilshire Blvd., Miracle Mile* ☎ *323/937–4230* 🌐 *www.cafam.org* 🎟 *$5* 🕐 *Tues., Wed., Fri. 11–5, Thurs. 11–7, weekends noon–6* 🎟 *Free 1st Wed. of month.*

1 **Farmers Market and The Grove.** The saying "Meet me at 3rd and Fairfax" became a standard line for generations of Angelenos who ate, shopped, and spotted the stars who drifted over from the studios for a breath of unpretentious air. Starting back in 1934 when two entrepreneurs convinced oil magnate E.B. Gilmore to open a vacant field for a bare-bones market, this spot became a humble shop for farmers selling produce out of their trucks. From this seat-of-the-pants situation grew a European-style open-air market and local institution at the corner of 3rd Street and Fairfax Avenue.

Fodor's Choice ★

Now the market includes 110 stalls and more than 20 counter-order restaurants, plus the landmark 1941 Clock Tower. In 2002 a massive expansion called The Grove opened; this highly conceptualized outdoor mall has a pseudo-European facade, with cobblestones, marble mosaics, and pavilions. Los Angeles history gets a nod with the electric steel-wheeled Red Car trolley, which shuttles two blocks through the Farmers Market and The Grove. If you hate crowds, try visiting The Grove before noon for the most comfortable shopping experience. By afternoon, it bulges with shoppers and teens hitting the movie theaters

A GOOD TOUR

Numbers correspond to the Wilshire Boulevard, Museum Row, and Farmers Market map.

Start the day with coffee and fresh-baked pastries at the **Farmers Market** ❶, a few blocks north of Wilshire Boulevard at 3rd Street and Fairfax Avenue. Drive south on Fairfax Avenue to the **Miracle Mile** ❷ district of Wilshire Boulevard. The black-and-gold art deco building on the northeast corner is a former May Company department store that now houses satellite exhibition galleries of the Los Angeles County Museum of Art (LACMA). Turn left onto Wilshire and proceed to Ogden Drive or a block farther to Spaulding Avenue, where you can park the car and set out on foot to explore the museums.

The large complex of contemporary buildings surrounded by a park on the corner of Wilshire and Ogden Drive is the **Los Angeles County Museum of Art (LACMA)** ❸, the largest art museum west of Chicago. Also in the park are the prehistoric **La Brea Tar Pits** ❹, where many of the fossils displayed at the adjacent **Page Museum at the La Brea Tar Pits** ❺ were found. Across Wilshire is the **Architecture and Design Museum** ❽ and the **Craft and Folk Art Museum (CAFAM)** ❻ and, back at the corner of Wilshire and Fairfax, the **Petersen Automotive Museum** ❼, which surveys the history of the car in Los Angeles.

From Museum Row and Miracle Mile, a drive east along Wilshire Boulevard to Downtown gives you a mini-tour of a historical and cultural cross section of Los Angeles. At Highland Avenue you enter the old-money enclave that is the **Hancock Park** neighborhood. At Western Avenue the **Wiltern Theater** ❾ stands across the street from the intersection's Metro station. The frequency of Korean-language signs in this area is a clue that you're now driving along the edge of **Koreatown.** If you'd like one more look at cool architecture, continue on Wilshire until it crosses Vermont Avenue toward Downtown Los Angeles, and you'll pass the magnificent **Bullock's Wilshire** building. Otherwise, stick around Koreatown for some Korean barbecue.

TIMING

The museums open between 10 and noon, so plan your tour around the opening time of the museum you wish to visit first. LACMA is open Monday but closed Wednesday and has extended hours into the evening, closing at 8 (9 on Friday). The other museums are closed on Monday (except the Page). If you're on a tight budget, keep tabs on museum free days; for instance, on the second Tuesday of the month LACMA admission to all but ticketed exhibits is free. Set aside a day to do this entire tour: an hour or two for the Farmers Market and The Grove, four hours for the museums, and an hour for the Wilshire Boulevard sights.

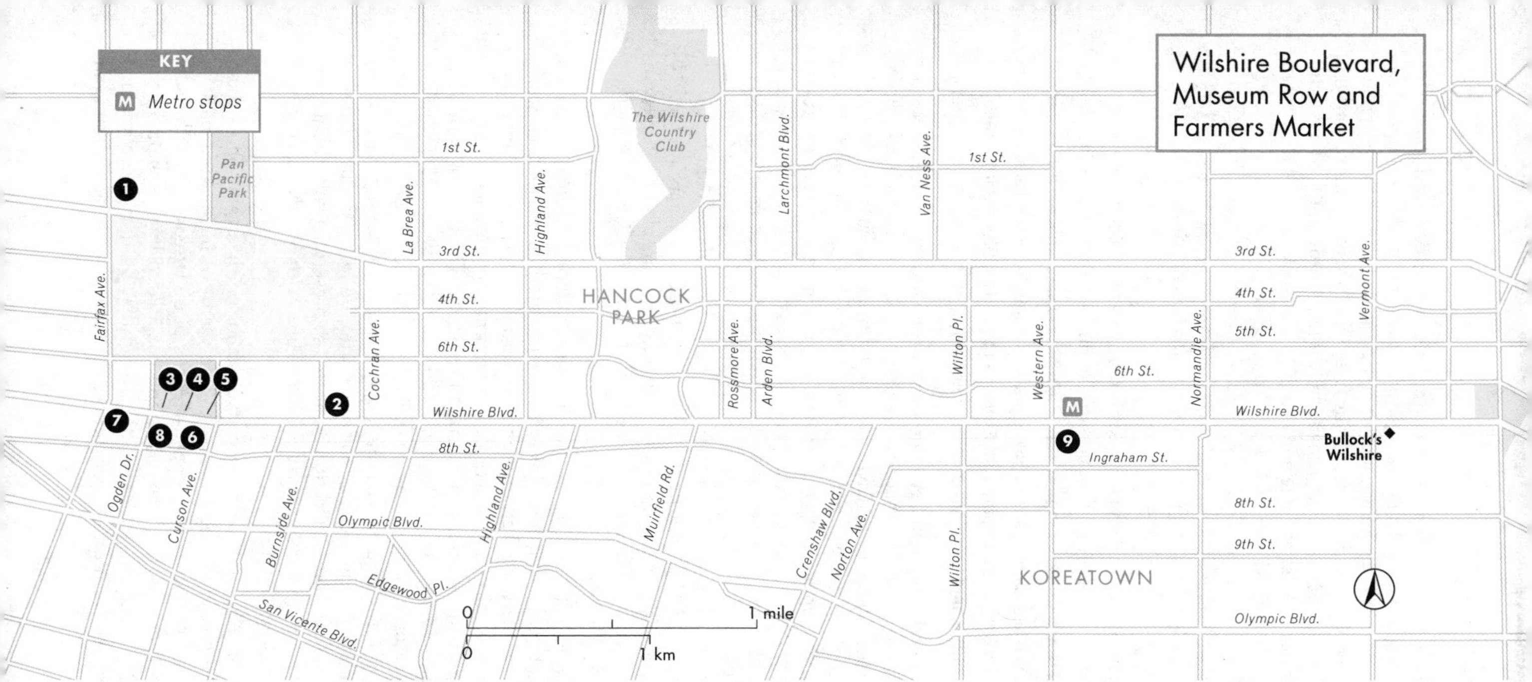

A&D Museum 8

Craft and Folk Art Museum (CAFAM) 6

Farmers Market and The Grove 1

La Brea Tar Pits 4

Los Angeles County Museum of Art (LACMA) 3

Miracle Mile 2

Page Museum at the La Brea Tar Pits 5

Petersen Automotive Museum 7

Wiltern Theater 9

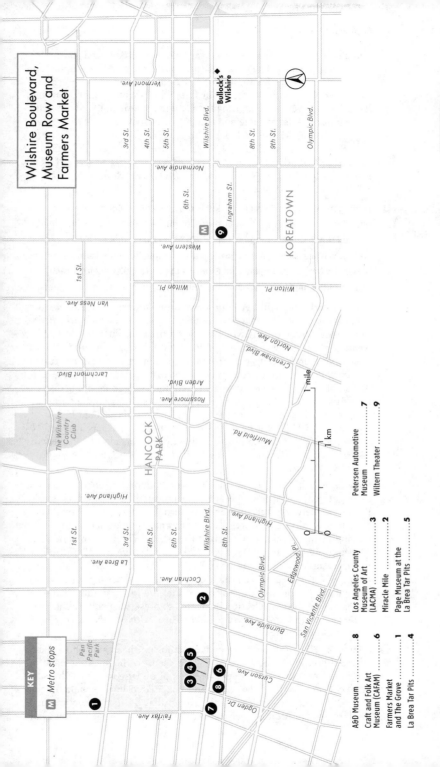

and chain stores such as Banana Republic, Crate & Barrel, Barnes & Noble, and J. Crew. The parking structure on the east side handles the cars by monitoring the number of spaces available as you go up each level, combined with the first hour free, which helps to make parking less of a pain. ■ TIP→**The Grove really dazzles around Christmas, with an enormous Christmas tree and a nightly faux snowfall until New Year's Day.** ✉ *Farmers Market, 6333 W. 3rd St.; The Grove, 189 The Grove Dr., Fairfax District* ☎ *323/933–9211 Farmers Market, The Grove* ☎ *323/900–8080* 🌐 *www.farmersmarketla.com* ⏲ *Farmers Market weekdays 9–9, Sat. 9–8, Sun. 10–7; The Grove Mon.–Thurs. 10–9, Fri. and Sat. 10–10, Sun. 11–8.*

NEED A BREAK?

Feeling peckish? The Farmers Market is the place to be. Snag a snack at one of the fruit stands or fresh bakeries, or for something more substantial, hit the French Crepe Company (☎ *323/934–3113*) for made-on-the-spot crepes, waffles, salads, and sandwiches. In the middle of the Farmers Market is also the long-standing favorite Gumbo Pot (☎ *323/933–0358*), which steams with Cajun goodies—gumbos, jambalaya, corn bread, and beignets.

Hancock Park. Highland Avenue marks the western perimeter of the neighborhood called Hancock Park (which is east of the park of the same name, home of LACMA and the La Brea Tar Pits). In the 1920s, wealthy families came here to build English Tudor–style homes with East Coast landscaping that defied local climate and history. Today Hancock Park is a quiet, relatively suburban neighborhood whose residents frequently venture out to the **Larchmont Village** shopping district to browse a collection of bookstores, antiques shops, and a Saturday farmers' market. Neighbors are still up in arms about the **"House of Davids"** (✉ *304 S. Muirfield, at 3rd St.*), whose owner has installed 18 white statues of Michelangelo's *David* around his circular driveway. ✉ *Bordered by Wilshire and Beverly Blvds., Highland Ave., and Wilton Pl., Mid-Wilshire.*

Koreatown. Although L.A.'s sizable Korean population is scattered throughout the city, it's especially concentrated here, along Olympic Boulevard between Vermont and Western avenues, where you'll find Korean specialty food stores and restaurants among many shops displaying furniture, electronics, and other items. The **Korean American Museum** (✉ *3727 W. 6th St., Suite 400, Miracle Mile* ☎ *213/388–4229* 🌐 *www.kamuseum.org* 🎟 *Free* ⏲ *Wed.–Fri. 11–6, Sat. 11–3. Subject to periodic closings; call ahead*) highlights the cultural heritage of Korean-Americans. On the fourth floor of an office building, the museum is a modest but devoted collection dedicated to preserving cultural history. ✉ *Bordered by Vermont and Western Aves., 8th St., and Pico Blvd., west of Downtown.*

4 ★ **La Brea Tar Pits.** Do your children have dinos on the brain? Show them where dinosaurs come from by taking them to the stickiest park in town. About 40,000 years ago, deposits of oil rose to the earth's surface, collected in shallow pools, and coagulated into asphalt. In the early 20th century, geologists discovered that all that goo contained the largest collection of Pleistocene, or Ice Age, fossils ever found at

one location: more than 600 species of birds, mammals, plants, reptiles, and insects. Roughly 100 tons of fossil bones have been removed in excavations over the last seven decades, making this one of the world's most famous fossil sites. You can see most of the pits through chain-link fences. (They can be a little smelly, but your kids are sure to love it.) Pit 91 is the site of ongoing excavation; tours are available, and you can volunteer to help with the excavations in summer. There are several pits scattered around Hancock Park and the surrounding neighborhood; construction in the area has often had to accommodate them, and in nearby streets and along sidewalks, little bits of tar occasionally ooze up, unstoppable. The nearby ⇨**Page Museum at the La Brea Tar Pits** displays fossils from the tar pits. ✉*Hancock Park, Miracle Mile* 🌐*www.tarpits.org* 🎫*Free.*

❸ Fodor's Choice ★ **Los Angeles County Museum of Art (LACMA).** Serving as the focal point of the museum district along Wilshire Boulevard, LACMA's vast, encyclopedic collection of more than 100,000 objects dating from ancient times to the present is widely considered one of the most comprehensive in the western United States. Since opening in 1965 the museum has grown from three buildings to seven, stretching across a 20-acre campus. As part of an ambitious 10-year facelift plan that is becoming a work of art on its own, entitled "Transformation," the museum is on a mission to integrate the seven buildings and outdoor spaces into a coherent whole. Phase one began with the opening of the impressive Broad Contemporary Art Museum (BCAM) in early 2008. With three vast floors, BCAM's purpose is to more fully integrate contemporary art into LACMA's program and explore the interplay art of current times with that of the past.

The museum space is now making better use of its courtyard space, before merely a long walk from one building to the next, the setting now makes use of the adjacent park to provide tranquil places to sit and "take it all in," and an installment of Chris Burden's "Urban Light" project, that consists of 202 antique cast-iron lampposts from around Los Angeles, showcases the way the city designed street lamps to reflect the identity of each area. The playful exhibit beckons young and old alike to walk through their maze of towering light.

With rotating displays from its permanent collection, at any time it's possible to see items from LACMA's abundant holdings of works by leading Latin American artists including Diego Rivera and Frida Kahlo, prominent Southern California artists, collections of Islamic and European art, paintings by Henri Matisse and Rene Magritte, as well as works by Paul Klee and Wassily Kandinsky who taught at Germany's Bauhaus school in the 1920s, art representing the ancient civilizations of Egypt, the Near East, Greece and Rome, plus a vast costume and textiles collection dating back to the 16th century. American Art, as well as art from Latin America and special exhibitions are on view in the "Art of Americas" building.

The Pavilion for Japanese Art showcases scrolls, screens, drawings, paintings, textiles, and decorative arts from Japan; it's a particularly peaceful space, with natural light and a fountain on the ground floor that fills the building with the sound of flowing water. The Bing Center holds a research library, resource center, and film theater.

The Boone's Children's Gallery on the soon-to-be "transformed" LACMA West end maintains an art-making mission through classes, interactive displays, and brightly colored decor.

The museum organizes special exhibitions and host major traveling shows. **TIP→ Temporary exhibits sometimes require tickets purchased in advance, so check the calendar ahead of time.** *✉5905 Wilshire Blvd., Miracle Mile ☎323/857–6000 🌐www.lacma.org 🎟$12, free 2nd Tues. of month, after 5 policy: "pay what you wish" ⏲Mon., Tues., and Thurs. noon–8, Fri. noon–9, weekends 11–8.*

NEED A BREAK?

For a pop art–style meal, detour up Fairfax to Swingers (*✉8020 Beverly Blvd. ☎323/653–5858*). Andy Warhol cow-print wallpaper, tartan vinyl booths, and rock-and-roll waitresses dressed in short skirts give an updated hipster take on the average coffee shop. The menu ranges from greasy-spoon standbys such as burgers and fries to organic and vegan selections.

2 **Miracle Mile.** The strip of Wilshire Boulevard between La Brea and Fairfax avenues was vacant land in the 1920s, when a developer bought the parcel to build a shopping and business district that catered to automobile traffic. Nobody thought the venture could be successful, but the auto age was just emerging, and the strip became known as Miracle Mile. It was the world's first linear Downtown, with building designs incorporating wide store windows to attract attention from passing cars. The area went into a decline in the 1950s and '60s, when high-rises began to break up its cohesiveness, but it's now enjoying a comeback as Los Angeles' art deco architecture has come to be appreciated, preserved, and restored. The exemplary architecture includes **El Rey Theater** (*✉5515 Wilshire Blvd., Miracle Mile ☎323/936–6400*), now a regular concert hall.

5 **Page Museum at the La Brea Tar Pits.** This member of the Natural History Museum family is sunk, bunkerlike, half underground. A bas-relief around four sides depicts life in the Pleistocene era, and the museum has more than 3 million Ice Age fossils. Exhibits include reconstructed, life-size skeletons of mammoths, wolves, sloths, eagles, and condors. The fishbowl-like, glass-enclosed laboratory is a real attention getter—here you can watch paleontologists as they clean, identify, catalog, and piece together bits of fossils excavated from the nearby asphalt deposits. *The La Brea Story,* a short documentary film, is shown every 15–30 minutes. A hologram magically puts flesh on 9,000-year-old "La Brea Woman." *✉5801 Wilshire Blvd., Miracle Mile ☎323/934–7243 🌐www.tarpits.org 🎟$7, free 1st Tues. of month ⏲Weekdays 9:30–5, weekends 10–5.*

7 **Petersen Automotive Museum.** You don't have to be a gearhead to appreciate this building full of antique and unusual cars. The Petersen is likely to be one of the coolest museums in town with its take on some of the most unusual creations on wheels and rotating exhibits of the icons who drove them. Lifelike dioramas and street scenes spread through the ground floor help to establish a local context for the history of the automobile.

Fodor's Choice ★

The second floor may include displays of Hollywood-celebrity and movie cars, "muscle" cars (like a 1969 Dodge Daytona 440 Magnum), alternative-powered cars, motorcycles, and a showcase of the Ferrari. You'll also learn about the origins of our modern-day car-insurance system, as well as the history of L.A.'s formidable freeway network. A children's interactive Discovery Center illustrates the mechanics of the automobile and fun child-inspired creations; there are also a gift shop and a research library. ✉*6060 Wilshire Blvd., Miracle Mile* ☎*323/930–2277* 🌐*www.petersen.org* 🎟*$10* ⏲*Tues.–Sun. 10–6.*

WEST HOLLYWOOD

West Hollywood is not a place to see things (like museums or movie studios) as much as it is a place to do things—like go to a nightclub, eat at a world-famous restaurant, or attend an art gallery opening. Since the end of Prohibition, the Sunset Strip has been Hollywood's nighttime playground, where stars headed to such glamorous nightclubs as the Trocadero, the Mocambo, and Ciro's. Las Vegas eclipsed the Strip's glitter in the 1950s, but in the next decade the music industry moved into town, and rock clubs like the Whisky A Go-Go took root. While the trendiest nightclubs are orbiting elsewhere, today's Sunset Strip is still going strong, with clubgoers lining up outside well-established spots like the House of Blues. But hedonism isn't all that drives West Hollywood. Also thriving is an important interior-design and art-gallery trade.

In the 1980s, a coalition of seniors, gays, and lesbians spearheaded a grassroots effort to bring cityhood to West Hollywood, which was still an unincorporated part of Los Angeles County. The coalition succeeded in 1984, and today West Hollywood has emerged as one of the most progressive cities in southern California. It's also one of the most gay-friendly cities anywhere, with one-third of its population estimated to be either gay or lesbian. Its annual Gay Pride Parade is one of the largest in the nation, drawing tens of thousands of participants each June.

WHAT TO SEE

6 **Avenues of Art and Design.** Established in 1996, the area defined by Melrose Avenue and Robertson and Beverly boulevards becomes its own little district: the Avenues of Art and Design. More than 300 businesses including more than 30 art galleries; 100 antiques, contemporary furniture, and interior design stores; and 40 restaurants are clustered here. Although most galleries in this pedestrian-friendly area are very high-end, it doesn't cost anything to window shop, explore the latest trends, and admire the exquisite craftsmanship. For one Saturday in June, the Avenues of Art and Design hosts the annual Art & Design Walk to give shoppers a chance to let loose in some of the hottest boutiques like John Varvatos, Phyllis Morris, James Perse, and Williams-Sonoma Home. (Bonus: The area is also good for celebrity sightings.) ☎*310/289–2525 or 800/368–6020* 🌐*www.avenuesartdesign.com.*

NEED A BREAK?

If the buzz of L.A. gives you a hankering for a pick-me-up, stop into Urth Café (✉*8565 Melrose Ave.* ☎*310/659–0628*). It's pumping with crowds of the beautiful people refueling on organic eats of sandwiches, salads, fresh

Avenues of Art and Design 6
Chateau Marmont 2
Los Angeles Museum of the Holocaust 8
Melrose Ave. 9
Pacific Design Center 5
Santa Monica Boulevard 7
Sunset Boulevard 1
Sunset Plaza 4
Sunset Strip 3

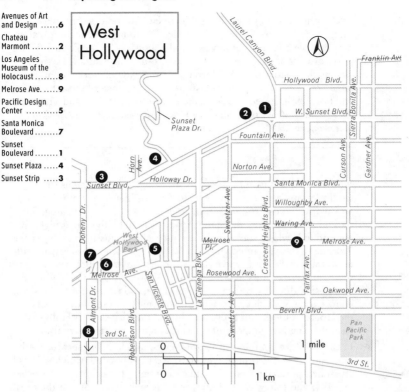

juices, and desserts. The outdoor patio is a great place to take in the scene. It's also a good place to spot celebrities.

❷ **Chateau Marmont.** If we had a dollar for every time a celebrity interview was conducted alongside the Marmont pool. . . . This secluded hotel, hidden in greenery off the Sunset Strip, has earned its stripes as a popular hideaway for industry actors, musicians, and writers. The ambience is chic without being frosty; most important, the hotel cultivates a sense of privacy. Stars such as Jim Morrison, Robert De Niro, Boris Karloff, Marilyn Monroe, and Dustin Hoffman liked this hotel so much that they moved in for long periods of time. In 1982 actor John Belushi checked out permanently here, of a drug overdose. Though most areas are strictly for guests, you can visit the main-floor lounge or outdoor patio for a meal or a cocktail. ✉*8221 Sunset Blvd., West Hollywood* ☎*323/656–1010* 🌐*www.chateaumarmont.com.*

❽ **Los Angeles Museum of the Holocaust.** This museum, dedicated solely to the Holocaust, has struggled to maintain a permanent home and is often confused with the Museum of Tolerance (further west on Wilshire). Now next to the Jewish Federation, it uses its extensive collections of photos and artifacts to evoke European Jewish life in the 20th century. In one chilling moment, you must step through a replica train car that signals the fate of millions of Jews: the concentration camps. The museum also

2

A GOOD DRIVE

Numbers correspond to the West Hollywood map.

Begin a driving-loop tour of West Hollywood by heading west along **Sunset Boulevard** ❶ from Fairfax Avenue. Keep going west on Sunset, and as you enter the "Strip," the first block past Crescent Heights Boulevard, look up the hill to the right for a glimpse of the famous **Chateau Marmont** ❷ hotel. While cruising down the boulevard, look up at the billboards, or "vanity boards," advertising the latest in everything from jeans to entertainment.

About three blocks west of the Chateau Marmont, you'll pass the landmark art deco masterpiece the Sunset Tower Hotel, on the left. Built in 1929 and now back on the map after a revamp, the hotel counted many celebrities among its residents, including Clark Gable and Marilyn Monroe. Next up are two famous nightclubs on the **Sunset Strip** ❸: the Delta-inspired House of Blues, on the left, and the Comedy Store, on the right. (The legendary Ciro's nightclub used to occupy the Comedy Store spot.) Look to the left for the all-white Mondrian Hotel; its poolside SkyBar lounge still attracts a buzz.

Sunset Plaza ❹ is a good place to get out of the car and take a stroll, do some high-end window-shopping, or pass the time people-watching from a sidewalk café. Look for parking in the lot behind the shops, off Sunset Plaza Drive. The club scene picks up again along this stretch of Sunset, with the Viper Room, the Whisky A Go-Go, which has rocked since the '60s, and the Roxy, a Strip mainstay since 1972.

Doheny Drive marks the division between West Hollywood and Beverly Hills. From Sunset, turn left on Doheny to drive south to **Santa Monica Boulevard** ❼. At Santa Monica, turn left to continue the loop tour. From roughly Robertson Boulevard to La Cienega Boulevard, Santa Monica Boulevard is the commercial core of West Hollywood's large gay and lesbian community. (It also used to be part of Route 66.) A right turn at San Vicente Boulevard will bring you West Hollywood's most visible landmark, the **Pacific Design Center** ❺. There's public parking available at the PDC, and you can get out and walk back a block to Santa Monica Boulevard or head west on **Melrose Avenue** ❾. This walkable section of town is known as the **Avenues of Art and Design** ❻, because of its many design studios and art galleries.

Plan to return to West Hollywood in the evening to check out the club scene along Sunset and Santa Monica boulevards.

TIMING

Traffic on Sunset and Santa Monica boulevards is heavy most of the time, especially at night and on weekends. Weekday afternoons are generally the easiest driving times. For street parking, bring plenty of quarters; parking on residential streets is by permit only.

documents resistance movements and the founding of Israel. A groundbreaking ceremony was held in January 2008 for the museum's new permanent home in Pan Pacific Park, with acclaimed architect Hagy Belzberg (Walt Disney Concert Hall interior) signed on for the building's design, which is slated to open in 2010. ✉ *6435 Wilshire Blvd., West Hollywood* ☎ *323/651–3704* 🌐 *www.lamuseumoftheholocaust.org* ⏲ *Mon.–Thurs. 10–4, Fri. 10–2, Sun. noon–4* 🎫 *Free.*

❾ **Melrose Avenue.** Back when alternative music was, well, alternative (and not Top 40), Melrose drew a colorful crowd of underground punks and heavy metal peacocks scouring the anti-conformist clothing shops and record stores along the "strip" between Fairfax and Poinsettia. Today, Melrose's hip factor has been tempered with mainstream additions such as Urban Outfitters and Coffee Bean & Tea Leaf. You'll find a good selection of vintage wear at resale shops Slow and Aardvarks' Odd Ark, or pre–Hot Topic alt-rock gear at Posers or Shrine, then get your designer fix by traveling farther west to higher-end shops such as Fred Segal, Paul Smith, Marc Jacobs, Agent Provocateur, and Betsey Johnson. Don't bother trying to hit the stores here early: shops usually don't start opening until noon.

NEED A BREAK?

Pair a shopping high with a sugar rush at Boule Pâtisserie (✉ *408 N. La Cienega Blvd., between Melrose Ave. and Beverly Blvd.* ☎ *310/289–9977*), a streamlined, Paris-influenced pastry place from acclaimed pastry chef Michelle Myers. The mouthwatering, handmade chocolates, sweets, and ice creams include unusual flavors, like chocolates laced with Scotch bonnet chilies and caramel cardamom sorbet. Or take your sweet tooth over to Sweet Lady Jane (✉ *8360 Melrose Ave., at N. Kings Rd.* ☎ *323/653–7145*), where you can eat a sandwich or lemon bar while watching people jockey for the beautifully decorated cakes.

❺ **Pacific Design Center.** Cesar Pelli designed these two architecturally intriguing buildings, one sheathed in blue glass (known as the Blue Whale), the other in green (the Green Whale). Together, they house 150 design showrooms, making this the largest interior design complex in the western United States. Though focused on the professional trade (meaning only pro decorators can shop the showrooms), the PDC has become more open over the past few years, with public events and some showroom access. Construction started on the new red building in the fall of 2007 with plans to open sometime at the end of 2010. The Downtown Museum of Contemporary Art has a small satellite **MOCA Gallery** (☎ *310/289–5233* 🌐 *www.moca.org*) here that showcases current artists and designers and hosts exhibit-related talks. Three cafés on the premises are also open to the public. ✉ *8687 Melrose Ave., West Hollywood* ☎ *310/657–0800* 🌐 *www.pacificdesigncenter.com* ⏲ *Weekdays 9–5.*

❼ **Santa Monica Boulevard.** For many gay and lesbian visitors, Santa Monica Boulevard is the Main Street of modern gay America. From La Cienega Boulevard on the east to Doheny on the west, it's the commercial core of West Hollywood's gay community, with restaurants and cafés, bars and clubs, bookstores, and other establishments catering largely to gays and lesbians. Twice a year, during June's Gay Pride Parade and on Halloween, in October, the boulevard becomes an open-air festival. **TIP→Santa Monica Boulevard is also prone to bad traffic, so if you need to get out of a jam, try Pico or Olympic boulevards, which run roughly parallel a bit farther south.**

❶ **Sunset Boulevard.** One of the most fabled avenues in the world, Sunset Boulevard began humbly enough in the 18th century as a route from El Pueblo de Los Angeles (today's Downtown L.A.) to the ranches in the west and then to the Pacific Ocean. Now as it winds its way across the L.A. basin to the ocean, it cuts through gritty urban neighborhoods and what used to be the working center of Hollywood's movie industry. In West Hollywood, it becomes the sexy and seductive Sunset Strip, then slips quietly into the tony environs of Beverly Hills and Bel Air, twisting and winding past gated estates. Continuing on past UCLA in Westwood, through Brentwood and Pacific Palisades, Sunset finally descends to the beach, the edge of the continent, and the setting sun.

❹ **Sunset Plaza.** With a profusion of sidewalk cafés, Sunset Plaza is one of the best people-watching spots in town. Sunny weekends reach the highest pitch, when people flock to this stretch of Sunset Boulevard for brunch or lunch and to browse in the shops, which tend to be expensive and showy. There's free parking in the lot behind the shops. ✉ *8600 block of Sunset Blvd., 2 blocks west of La Cienega Blvd., West Hollywood.*

NEED A BREAK?

For a truly rocking meal, stop by the laid-back, low-lighted Duke's (✉ *8909 W. Sunset Blvd., at N. San Vicente Blvd.* ☎ *310/652–3100*) coffee shop, where autographed rock posters and glossies cover the walls. The menu here suits tight budgets, and the packed table arrangements increase your odds of rubbing elbows with a celebrity or a hung-over local musician indulging in the greasy-spoon comfort food. Just remember, it's not polite to ask for autographs while they're eating. Note that Duke's closes at 3:30 PM on weekends. News junkies should hit the Newsroom (✉ *120 N. Robertson Blvd., at Beverly Blvd.* ☎ *310/652–4444*), which streams current event headlines nonstop on several TVs hung around the café. It's also got a magazine stand and Internet access to distract you while you wait for a table (which could take a while during peak hours). The menu's health-focused, with smoothies and vegetarian choices.

❸ ★ **Sunset Strip.** For 60 years the Hollywood's night owls have headed for the 1¾-mi stretch of Sunset Boulevard between Crescent Heights Boulevard on the east and Doheny Drive on the west, known as the Sunset Strip. In the 1930s and '40s, stars such as Tyrone Power, Errol Flynn, Norma Shearer, and Rita Hayworth came for wild evenings of dancing and drinking at nightclubs like Trocadero, Ciro's, and Mocambo. By the '60s and '70s, the Strip had become the center of rock and roll for acts like Johnny Rivers, the Byrds, and the Doors. The '80s punk riot gave way to hair metal lead by Mötley Crüe and Guns N' Roses on the stages of the **Whisky A Go-Go** (✉ *8901 Sunset Blvd., West Hollywood* ☎ *310/652–4202* 🌐 *www.whiskyagogo.com*) and the **Roxy** (✉ *9009 Sunset Blvd., West Hollywood* ☎ *310/276–2222* 🌐 *www.theroxyonsunset.com*).

Nowadays it's the **Viper Room** (✉8852 *Sunset Blvd., West Hollywood* ☎*310/358–1880* 🌐*www.viperroom.com*), the **House of Blues** (✉8430 *Sunset Blvd., West Hollywood* ☎*323/848–5100* 🌐*www.hob.com*), and the **Key Club** (✉9039 *Sunset Blvd., West Hollywood* ☎*310/274–5800* 🌐*www.keyclub.com*), where you'll find on-the-cusp actors, rock stars, club-hopping regulars, and out-of-towners all mingling over drinks and live music. Parking and traffic around the Strip can be tough on weekends, expect to pay around $10–$25 to park, which can take a bite out of your partying budget, but the time and money may be worth it if you plan to make the rounds—most clubs are within walking distance of each other.

WORD OF MOUTH

"My star-struck relatives always like a drive down the Sunset Strip so they can ogle Chateau Marmont (where stars of yore OD'ed and stars of now stay) and Sunset Plaza–just a strip of fancy shops and restaurants, but lots of outdoor tables where they can look for celebrities they rarely see."
–thursday

BEVERLY HILLS AND CENTURY CITY

If you only have a day to see L.A., see Beverly Hills. Love it or hate it, it delivers on a dramatic, cinematic scale of wealth and excess. Beverly Hills is the town's biggest movie star, and she always lets those willing to part with a few bills into her year-round party. Just remember to bring your sunscreen, sunglasses, and money for parking.

Boutiques and restaurants line the palm tree–fringed sidewalks. People tend to stroll, not rush. Shopping ranges from the accessible and familiar (Pottery Barn) to the unique, expensive, and architecturally stunning (Prada on Rodeo Drive). It's hard not to imagine yourself in a film since this locale has basically become a backlot itself.

Just a few blocks west on Santa Monica Boulevard is Beverly Hills's buttoned-down brother, Century City. If Beverly Hills is about spending money, Century City is about making it. This district of glass office towers is home to entertainment companies, law firms, and investment corporations. Two of Hollywood's key talent agencies, CAA and ICM, moved to Century City in 2007. It's a peculiarly precise place, with angular fountains, master-planned boulevards, and pedestrian bridges make it worth a drive down its famous "Avenue of the Stars" if only to imagine yourself amongst them. The Century City Mall is worth a visit, having received a Hollywood-style makeover that beautifully updated this open-air space, generous food court, and movie theaters, making a visit to your regular mall shops seem ever-so-glamorous.

WHAT TO SEE

❷ **Beverly Hills Hotel and Bungalows.** The iconic "Pink Palace" has been steeped in Hollywood lore since 1912. Greta Garbo, Howard Hughes, and other movie-industry guests kept low profiles when staying at this pastel landmark. If you can't afford the rooms but still want to savor some star treatment, indulge in a lunch in the Polo Lounge where film luminaries have cut high-powered deals (note: reservations are a must), or book a treatment at the in-house Spa by La Prairie and combine it with a stroll through the hotel's neatly manicured grounds. By night, pose like you're waiting to be discovered over drinks at the new Bar Nineteen 12. ✉*9641 Sunset Blvd., 1 mi west of Doheny Dr.* ☎*310/276–2251* 🌐*www.thebeverlyhillshotel.com.*

ONE LUMP OR TWO?

For the white glove treatment, take in a spot of tea at the Greystone Mansion. Afternoon tea on the terrace is served one Saturday a month May–August. The fee is $43 per person for nonresidents. Reservations are highly recommended by calling ☎*310/550–4753*. Tea starts promptly at 4 PM. What could be more civilized?

5 **Beverly Wilshire, a Four Seasons Hotel.** Anchoring the south end of Rodeo Drive at Wilshire Boulevard, this hotel may be best known for its exterior: it's the place where Richard Gere ensconced himself with Julia Roberts in the movie *Pretty Woman.* But inside, this hotel has been an opulent house of luxury since opening in 1928. A renovation in 2006, along with a name change, pushes it further up the ladder as a preferred address of the rich and famous with recent additions such as a new 8,000-square-foot spa, the new Pool Bar & Café, and luxurious poolside cabanas. To dip a toe in its glamorousness, book a dinner at the sleek Wolfgang Puck restaurant CUT or lunch at the Blvd. ✉*9500 Wilshire Blvd., Beverly Hills* ☎*310/275–5200* 🌐*www.fourseasons.com/beverlywilshire*

NEED A BREAK?

A longtime refuge from California's lean cuisine, Nate 'n' Al's (✉*414 N. Beverly Dr., at Brighton Way, Beverly Hills* ☎*310/274–0101*) serves up steaming classic pastrami, matzo ball soup, and potato latkes. Or stop at the Farm (✉*439 N. Beverly Dr.* ☎*310/273–5578*) and grab a seat at one of the sidewalk tables. The restaurant is known for dishes such as ahi tuna appetizer, a lobster club with applewood-smoked bacon, and a luscious brownie sundae. Reserve a table on the patio, sit back with an endless glass of iced tea with mint, and take in the view; you'll have a good chance of a celeb sighting here.

Century City. A sprawling 280 acres of office buildings, a shopping center, hotels, an entertainment complex, and housing, this complex was built in the 1960s on what used to be the backlot of Twentieth Century Fox. (The studio is not open to the public.) The focal point of this complex is a pair of silvery triangular towers known as **Century City Towers** (✉*Ave. of the Stars and Constellation Blvd.*). The **Westfield Century City** (✉*10250 Santa Monica Blvd.* ☎*310/277–3898*) is an open-air shopping center with a sparkling white exterior that makes strolling store-to-store (through places like BCBG, Apple, Banana Republic, Kenneth Cole, and Macy's) feel like a jaunt down the catwalk.

1 **Greystone Mansion.** L.A.'s answer to the châteaus of Europe, this 1927 neo-Gothic mansion was owned by oilman Edward Doheny (Doheny Drive is named after him). Now owned by the city of Beverly Hills, it

A GOOD TOUR

Numbers correspond to the Beverly Hills and the Westside map.

Begin a tour of Beverly Hills with a drive into the hills above Sunset Boulevard for a look at **Greystone Mansion** ❶, on Loma Vista Drive. Less than a mile west on Sunset is the landmark **Beverly Hills Hotel** ❷, otherwise known as the Pink Palace. Snap your postcard picture here, then duck around behind the hotel to Elden Way, where you'll find the **Virginia Robinson Gardens** ❸, the oldest estate in Beverly Hills and now open to the public for walking tours.

Across the street from the Beverly Hills Hotel is the pretty little triangular park named for the cowboy-philosopher Will Rogers, who was once honorary mayor of Beverly Hills. Turn south here onto **Rodeo Drive** ❹ (pronounced ro-*day*-o). You'll pass through a residential neighborhood before hitting the shopping stretch of Rodeo south of Santa Monica Boulevard. Find a parking space, slide on your sunglasses (the better to subtly people-watch, my dear), and flex your credit card. At Rodeo Drive and Dayton Way you'll see the aluminum sculpture *Torso,* by Robert Graham; installed in summer 2003, it ushered in the Walk of Style, the fashionista equivalent of Hollywood's Walk of Fame. Across Wilshire, the **Beverly Wilshire, a Four Seasons Hotel** ❺ serves as a temporary residence for the rich, famous, and cultured. The **Paley Center for Media** ❻ stands a block east of Rodeo, on Beverly Drive. A few blocks west of Beverly Hills is the high-rise office-tower and shopping-center complex known as **Century City.**

TIMING

After a drive along Sunset Boulevard and a foray or two up into the hills for a look at the opulent homes, plan to arrive in the Golden Triangle of Beverly Hills at midday. Most stores open by 10 or 11, with limited hours on Sunday. (Some close on Sunday or Monday.) Park your car in one of several municipal lots (the first one or two hours are free at most of them), and spend as long as you like strolling along Rodeo Drive. The major routes in and out of Beverly Hills—Wilshire and Santa Monica boulevards—get very congested during rush hours.

sits on 18½ landscaped acres and has been used in such films as *The Witches of Eastwick* and *Indecent Proposal.* Though you can't actually enter the mansion itself, the gardens are open for self-guided tours, and you can get an idea of the exquisite interior by peeking through the windows. Picnics are permitted in specified areas during hours of operation, and, sporadically, concerts are held in the mansion's courtyard on summer afternoons. The grounds close for period special events; call to check hours prior to your visit during these months. ✉ *905 Loma Vista Dr., Beverly Hills* ☎ *310/550–4796* 🌐 *www.greystonemansion.org* 🎟 *Free* ⏲ *Daily 10–5.*

❻ ★ **Paley Center for Media.** Formerly the Museum of Television and Radio, this institution changed its name in 2007 with a look toward a future that encompasses all media in the ever-evolving world of entertainment and information. Reruns are taken to a curated level in this sleek stone-

Beverly Hills and the Westside

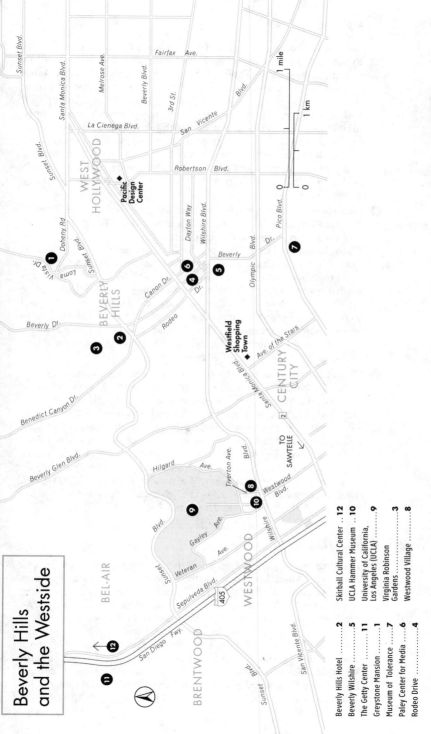

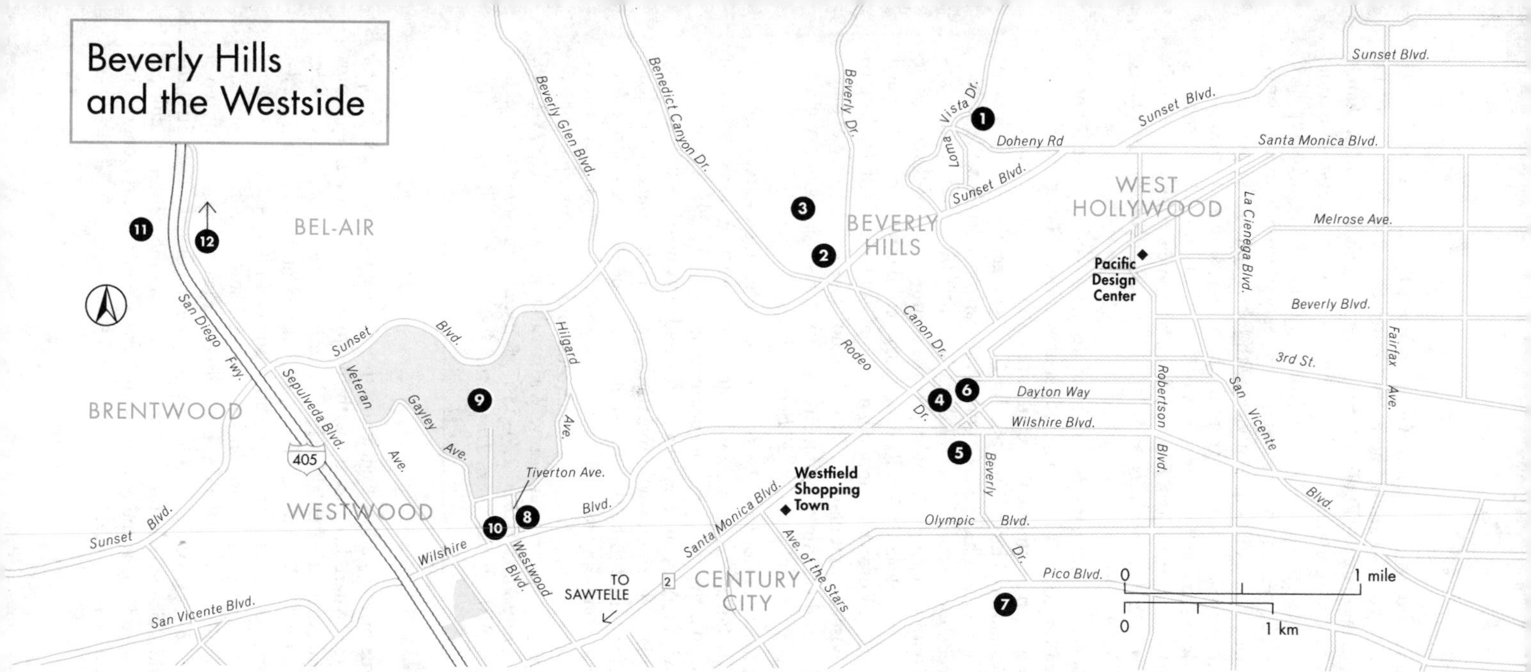

Beverly Hills Hotel 2
Beverly Wilshire 5
The Getty Center 11
Greystone Mansion 1
Museum of Tolerance 7
Paley Center for Media 6
Rodeo Drive 4
Skirball Cultural Center .. 12
UCLA Hammer Museum .. 10
University of California, Los Angeles (UCLA) 9
Virginia Robinson Gardens 3
Westwood Village 8

and-glass building, designed by Getty architect Richard Meier. A sister to the New York location, the Paley Center carries a duplicate of its collection: more than 100,000 programs spanning eight decades. Search for your favorite commercials and television shows on easy-to-use computers. A radio program listening room provides cozy seats supplied with headphones playing snippets of a variety of programming from a toast to Dean Martin to an interview with John Lennon. Frequent seminars with movers 'n' shakers from the film, television and radio world are big draws, as well as screenings of documentaries and short films. Free parking is available in the lot off Santa Monica Boulevard. ✉ *465 N. Beverly Dr., Beverly Hills* ☎ *310/786–1000* 🌐 *www.paleycenter.org* ⏲ *Wed.–Sun. noon–5.*

❹ **Rodeo Drive.** The ultimate shopping indulgence—Rodeo Drive is one of Southern California's bona fide tourist attractions. The art of window-shopping is prime among the retail elite: Tiffany & Co., Gucci, Jimmy Choo, Valentino, Harry Winston, Prada . . . you get the picture. Several nearby restaurants have patios where you can sip a drink while watching career shoppers in their size 2 threads saunter by with shopping bags stuffed with superfluous delights. At the southern end of Rodeo Drive (at Wilshire Boulevard), **Via Rodeo,** a curvy cobblestone street designed to resemble a European shopping area, makes the perfect backdrop to strike a pose for that glamour shot. The holidays bring a special magic to Rodeo and the surrounding streets with twinkling lights, swinging music, and colorful banners. ✉ *Beverly Hills.*

Fodor's Choice ★

❸ **Virginia Robinson Gardens.** A paean to park life, this estate, the oldest in Beverly Hills, was owned by department store heir Harry Robinson and his wife, Virginia, who bequeathed it to Los Angeles County. The classic Mediterranean-style villa is surrounded by nearly 6 sloping acres of lush planted grounds with five theme gardens. Its collection of King palms is reported to be the largest grove outside the tree's native Australia. Fountains and falls flow through a grove of citrus and camellias. Call in advance to schedule a docent-led tour. Home and garden may be viewed by appointment only. Wear walking shoes. ✉ *1008 Elden Way, Beverly Hills* ☎ *310/276–5367* 🌐 *www.robinson-gardens.com* 🎟 *Tours: $10.* ⏲ *Tues.–Fri. 10* AM *and 1* PM.

THE WESTSIDE

For some privileged Los Angelenos, the city begins west of La Cienega Boulevard, where keeping up with the Joneses becomes an epic pursuit. Chic, attractive neighborhoods with coveted postal codes—Bel Air, Brentwood, Westwood, West Los Angeles, and Pacific Palisades—are home to power couples pushing power kids in power strollers. But conspicuous consumption has changed since the flashy '80s and dot-com '90s. Now the status game involves prestigious schools, yoga studios, holiday locales, and airspace rights to coastal views. Still, the Westside is rich in culture—and not just entertainment-industry culture. It's home to UCLA, the monumental Getty Center, and the engrossing Museum of Tolerance.

WHAT TO SEE

11 Fodor's Choice ★ **The Getty Center.** With its curving walls and isolated hilltop perch, the Getty Center resembles a pristine fortified city of its own. You may have been lured up by the beautiful views of L.A. (on a clear day stretching all the way to the Pacific Ocean), but the architecture, uncommon gardens, and fascinating art collections will be more than enough to capture and hold your attention. When the sun is out, the complex's rough-cut travertine marble skin seems to soak up the light. You'll need to do some advance planning, since parking reservations are sometimes required during vacation periods, but the experience is well worth the effort.

J. Paul Getty, the billionaire oil magnate and art collector, began collecting Greek and Roman antiquities and French decorative arts in the 1930s. He opened the J. Paul Getty Museum at his Malibu estate in 1954, and in the 1970s, he built a re-creation of an ancient Roman village to house his initial collection. When Getty died in 1976, the museum received an endowment of $700 million that grew to a reported $4.2 billion. The Malibu villa, reopened in 2006, is devoted to the antiquities. The Getty Center, designed by Richard Meier, opened in 1998 and pulled together the rest of the collections, along with the museum's affiliated research, conservation, and philanthropic institutes.

Getting to the center involves a bit of anticipatory lead-up. At the base of the hill, a pavilion disguises the underground parking structure. From there you either walk or take a smooth, computer-driven tram up the steep slope, checking out the Bel Air estates across the humming 405 freeway. The five pavilions that house the museum surround a central courtyard and are bridged by walkways. From the courtyard, plazas, and walkways, you can survey the city from the San Gabriel Mountains to the ocean.

In a ravine separating the museum and the Getty Research Institute, conceptual artist Robert Irwin created the playful **Central Garden** in stark contrast to Meier's mathematical architectural geometry. The garden's design is what Hollywood feuds are made of: Meier couldn't control Irwin's vision, and the two men sniped at each other during construction, with Irwin stirring the pot with every loose twist his garden path took. The result is a refreshing garden walk whose focal point is an azalea maze (some insist the Mickey Mouse shape is on purpose) in a reflecting pool.

Inside the pavilions are the galleries for the permanent collections of European paintings, drawings, sculpture, illuminated manuscripts, and decorative arts, as well as American and European photographs. The Getty's collection of French furniture and decorative arts, especially from the early years of Louis XIV (1643–1715) to the end of the reign of Louis XVI (1774–92), is renowned for its quality and condition; you can see a pair of completely reconstructed salons. In the paintings galleries, a computerized system of louvered skylights allows natural light to filter in, creating a closer approximation of the conditions in which the artists painted. Notable among the paintings are Rembrandt's *The Abduction of Europa,* Van Gogh's *Irises,* Monet's *Wheatstack, Snow Effects,* and *Morning,* and James Ensor's *Christ's Entry into Brussels.*

A GOOD TOUR

Numbers correspond to the Beverly Hills and the Westside map.

The major sights on the Westside are spread out, so choosing a starting point is arbitrary; the best strategy is to select one of the major attractions as a destination and plan your visit accordingly. A visit to the **Museum of Tolerance** ❼ in the morning, for example, can be easily followed with lunch and shopping in Beverly Hills or Century City. Afterward you might drive through **Westwood Village** ❽, home to the **University of California, Los Angeles** ❾ campus and the Fowler Museum of Cultural History, stopping at the **UCLA Hammer Museum** ❿. The vast **Getty Center** ⓫ offers the trifecta of art, architecture, and sweeping views at its hilltop perch in Brentwood. A visit here could easily eat up a few hours as you wander around the grounds, have a bite at the café (the food's a cut above the average museum fare), and explore the galleries. About 2 mi north on Sepulveda Boulevard is the **Skirball Cultural Center** ⓬, which has a gallery exhibition on Jewish life.

For a less destination-oriented tour of the posh Westside, simply follow Wilshire Boulevard west out of low-rise Beverly Hills as it turns into a canyon of million-dollar condos. Once past the San Diego Freeway (I–405), detour to the right onto San Vicente Boulevard and the upscale urban-village center of Brentwood. At the Santa Monica city line, turn right on 26th Street and follow it as it turns into Allenford Avenue. The route will loop you around to Sunset Boulevard. A left turn here will take you to Pacific Palisades and the ocean. A right leads back toward Beverly Hills and West Hollywood, past the Getty Center and Bel Air mansions, all but invisible behind high walls and lush landscaping.

TIMING

Advance reservations are not essential but are recommended for visits to the Museum of Tolerance, closed Saturday, and the Getty Center, closed Monday—so plan accordingly. Each museum merits at least a half day. If the Getty Center's on your list, try to get there relatively early, so that you can park close to the main complex. (Using the satellite parking lots means you'll have to take an extra tram ride.) In the evening and on weekends, the restaurants, cafés, and streets of Westwood Village and Brentwood's commercial district on San Vicente Boulevard come alive. The afternoon rush hour can be maddening in this area. To avoid hours-long traffic snarls, it's best to plan your visits for the morning hours 10–noon or Sunday, when high-rolling partiers are sleeping in.

If you want to start with a quick overview, pick up the brochure in the entrance hall that guides you to 15 highlights of the collection. There's also an instructive audio tour ($5) with commentaries by art historians. Art information rooms with multimedia computer stations contain more details about the collections. The Getty also presents lectures, films, concerts, and special programs for kids and families. The complex includes an upscale restaurant and downstairs cafeteria with panoramic window views, and two outdoor coffee bar cafes. ■ TIP→ **On-site parking is subject to availability and usually fills up by late afternoon**

on holidays and summer weekends, so try to come early in the day. You may also take public transportation (MTA Bus 561 or Santa Monica Big Blue Bus 14). ✉ *1200 Getty Center Dr., Brentwood* ☎ *310/440–7300* 🌐 *www.getty.edu* *Free, parking $8* ⏲ *Tues.–Fri. 10–5:30, Sat. 10–9, Sun. 10–5:30.*

> **WORD OF MOUTH**
>
> "As for places to go, the Getty Museum, off the 405 freeway at Getty Drive is a must. It's architecturally beautiful and the gardens are absolutely wonderful. It's not the type of museum that you have to just focus on the art works as we Angelenos like to be outside which is why the outside spaces and views are so breathtaking. Now, in February, there could be a little rain, but it shouldn't be any big deal. We're outside all year here." —Guenmai

7 ★ **Museum of Tolerance.** Using interactive technology, this important museum (part of the Simon Wiesenthal Center) challenges visitors to confront bigotry and racism. One of the most affecting sections covers the Holocaust, with film footage of deportation scenes and simulated sets of concentration camps. Each visitor is issued a "passport" bearing the name of a child whose life was dramatically changed by the German Nazi rule and by World War II; as you go through the exhibit, you learn the fate of that child. Anne Frank artifacts are part of the museum's permanent collection as is Wiesenthal's Vienna office, set exactly as the famous "Nazi hunter" had it while performing his research that brought more than 1,000 war criminals to justice. Interactive exhibits include the "Millennium Machine," which engages visitors in finding solutions to human rights abuses around the world, Globalhate.com, which examines hate on the Internet by exposing problematic sites via touch screen computer terminals, and the "Point of View Diner," a re-creation of a 1950s diner, red booths and all, that "serves" a menu of controversial topics on video jukeboxes. Recent renovations brought a new youth action floor and revamped 300-seat theater space. To ensure a visit to this popular museum, make reservations in advance (especially for Friday, Sunday, and holidays) and plan to spend at least three hours there. Testimony from Holocaust survivors is offered at specified times. Museum entry stops at least two hours before the actual closing time. A photo ID is required for admission and all visitors must go through a security search. ✉ *9786 W. Pico Blvd., just south of Beverly Hills* ☎ *310/553–8403* 🌐 *www.museumoftolerance.com* *$15* ⏲ *Weekdays 10–5, Sun. 11–5, early close at 3 PM Fri. Nov.–Mar.*

12 **Skirball Cultural Center.** With a mission of exhibiting the connections "between four thousand years of Jewish heritage and the vitality of American democratic ideals," this Jewish cultural institution sits, grand in scale, atop the Santa Monica Mountains. Within it traces Jewish life including immigration to resettlement into America in a rotating exhibit "Visions and Values: Jewish Life from Antiquity to America." Twelve galleries use artifacts, building reconstructions, and multimedia installations. Highlights include a large collection of Judaica and a two-thirds-size replica of the torch of the Statue of Liberty. The Center also hosts special lectures and performances that examine the culture of our times.

CLOSE UP

Stargazing 101

OK, here's the situation: You're in Du-Par's coffee shop in Studio City, and George Clooney is in the next booth, downing a short stack. This may not be the best time to run up and ask for an autograph and a quick pic, but when is a good moment? And . . . wait! George is about to pay the check and split. You decide to jump at the chance. Remain calm. Use common courtesy and hang on to your sense of decorum. Remember to be polite, brief, and have the pen and paper ready if an autograph is part of your mission. When introducing yourself, mention that you're "visiting from . . ." It will buy you a lot of leeway.

JUST ANOTHER DAY . . .

When in L.A., it's tempting to buy star maps—however, they're notoriously inaccurate and out of date. Instead, think like a resident. Plenty of stars go about their daily routines on the streets of Beverly Hills, so keep your eyes peeled. The Farm of Beverly Hills, on Beverly Boulevard, is a favorite lunch haunt, as is the Lobby Lounge at the Regent Beverly Wilshire hotel. The Grill on the Alley gets busy around Oscar time. Also try restaurants around the studios. For most stars, a day of shooting or preproduction is their day at the office, and they want to get out a little at lunch. Try Lucy's El Adobe Café, across the street from Paramount or French 75 in Burbank.

HIT THE TRAIL

Stars spend the first half of the day doing lunch and the second part of the day working it off. Gyms are out and hiking is in, so put on your sneakers and head for the hills. Fryman Canyon, off Laurel Canyon, is TV-star turf and gives stunning views of the San Fernando Valley. The Lake Hollywood Reservoir has a surprisingly bucolic 3.2-mi waterside walk with the HOLLYWOOD sign as a backdrop. Just remember: Avoid hiking after sunset and never hike alone.

Dog parks are also low-key places celebs like to go to relax and spend quality time with their furry pals. Even if you don't have dog, you can join the many who go to stroll the parklike settings. Try Runyon Canyon Park on Franklin and Fuller Avenue, Laurel Canyon Dog Park, 8260 Mulholland Drive just west of Laurel Canyon, or Barrington Dog Park, 333 S. Barrington Avenue in West L.A.Love the Nightlife?

L.A. is famous for its after-dark scenes. You may have heard much about the Sunset Strip, Bar Marmont, and the nomadic clubs with the tattooed bouncers waiting to step in as the next Vin Diesel. Trying to predict the latest hot spot, though, is like trying to predict the next earthquake—nearly impossible. But if you're feeling brave enough to take on the guest-list wielding doorman, some hot spots to try are Joseph's Café, 1775 N. Ivar Avenue, Monday mock-metal nights with Steel Panther at the Key Club, and poolside at the Roosevelt Hotel's Tropicana bar.

Keep in mind even if you do get into the right place, your chances of brushing elbows with a celeb are still slim; many clubs have private VIP rooms for the exclusive inner circle.

AROUND TOWN

Stylists may get a lot of credit (or blame) these days for red carpet looks, but stars still go shopping. Hot spots include Montana Avenue in Santa Monica, Fred Segal on Melrose

Seeing stars in person can be one of the delights of visiting L.A.

Avenue, and Westfield Shoppingtown Century City (known locally as the Century City mall).

Stars are fans, too, and if you can snag tickets to a Lakers game, chances are you won't be down front sitting next to Jack Nicholson but if you bring binoculars, you might get a glimpse of him cheering on the home team.

GIVE THEM A HAND

When all else fails, head for the one place stars must make an appearance: the studio. Many TV shows need a live audience to clap and laugh so you'll be helping them out as you see the stars in their "natural habitat." Book well in advance to attend a taping and plan to spend about three to four hours there. It will give you a new appreciation for the half-hour final product. Hide a snack in your pocket, and make sure you have a government-issued photo ID—you'll need it to get in. **Audiences Unlimited** (*www.tvtickets.com*) is the best source for tickets to many television shows. For tickets and information about *The Tonight Show with Jay Leno,* contact NBC (*818/840-3537*).

If you happen to be in town when one of your favorite celebrities is getting a star on the Walk of Fame, you've got a guaranteed celeb-spotting and the public is welcome to watch the ceremony from the sidelines. Check the Hollywood Chamber of Commerce Web site for upcoming inductions. *www.hollywoodchamber.net/upcoming_ceremonies*

The latest big draw is the new Noah's Ark interactive gallery where a life-size animals roam as unique and stunning works of art created by Chris Green. Children are invited to become "Noah" as they join the animals in generating a rainstorm, boarding the Ark, and discovering how to live in harmony with each other as they recreate this famous story using their own imagination. ✉ *2701 N. Sepulveda Blvd., north of Brentwood* ☎ *310/440–4500* 🌐 *www.skirball.org* 🎟 *$10, Thurs. free* ⏲ *Tues.–Fri. noon–5, weekends 10–5.*

10 **UCLA Hammer Museum.** The bold murals and installations at this museum have been known to bring traffic on Wilshire Boulevard to a crawl. In the heart of Westwood, the Hammer emphasizes the here and now, luring in new museumgoers with splashy, eye-catching displays in the museum's glass entryway. Focused on art and artists of our time, the museum forms a bridge between the city's artistic expression and the forward educational spirit of adjacent UCLA. Selections from Armand Hammer's permanent collection are also incorporated, including works by Claude Monet, Vincent van Gogh, and John Singer Sargent's powerful portrait of Dr. Pozzi. The 295-seat Billy Wilder Theater opened in 2006 and features selections from UCLA's Film & Television Archive to host unique public programs. ✉ *10899 Wilshire Blvd., Westwood* ☎ *310/443–7000* 🌐 *www.hammer.ucla.edu* 🎟 *$7, free Thurs.; 3-hr parking $3 with validation* ⏲ *Tues., Wed., Fri., and Sat. 11–7, Thurs. 11–9, Sun. 11–5.*

9 **University of California, Los Angeles (UCLA).** With spectacular buildings such as a Romanesque library, the parklike UCLA campus makes for a fine stroll through one of California's most prestigious universities. In the heart of the north campus, the **Franklin Murphy Sculpture Garden** contains more than 70 works of artists such as Henry Moore and Gaston Lachaise. The **Mildred Mathias Botanic Garden,** which contains some 5,000 species of plants from all over the world in a 7-acre outdoor garden, is in the southeast section of the campus and is accessible from Tiverton Avenue. West of the main-campus bookstore, the **Morgan Center Hall of Fame** displays the sports memorabilia and trophies of the university's athletic departments. Many visitors head straight to the **Fowler Museum at UCLA** (☎ *310/825–4361* 🌐 *www.fowler.ucla.edu*), which presents exhibits on the world's diverse cultures and visual arts, especially those of Africa, Asia, the Pacific, and Native and Latin America. Museum admission is free; use parking lot 4 off Sunset Boulevard ($8). The Fowler Museum is open Wednesday–Sunday noon–5, Thursday until 8 PM.

Campus maps and information are available at drive-by kiosks at major entrances daily, and free 90-minute walking tours of the campus are given on weekdays at 10:15 and 2:15 and Saturday at 10:15. Call 310/825–8764 for reservations, which are required several days to two weeks in advance. The campus has cafés, plus bookstores selling UCLA Bruins paraphernalia. The main-entrance gate is on Westwood Boulevard. Campus parking costs $8. ✉ *Bordered by Le Conte, Hilgard, and Gayley Aves. and Sunset Blvd., Westwood* 🌐 *www.ucla.edu.*

8 **Westwood Village.** Laid out in the 1930s as a master-planned shopping district next to the UCLA campus, Westwood Village has lost some of its luster as locals opt for one-stop shopping centers and multiplexes. But the Village offers some terrific movie theaters, like the Mann Village, and casual eateries; on weekends, it still teems with students. ■ **TIP→Look for the long line of students outside Diddy Riese Cookies at 926 Broxton Avenue, which bakes up L.A.'s best (and cheap) cookies and mile-high ice cream sandwiches.** Westwood is also the site of a cemetery with one of the world's most famous graves. Tucked behind one of the behemoth office buildings on Wilshire Boulevard is **Westwood Village Memorial Park** (⊠ *1218 Glendon Ave.*). Marilyn Monroe is buried in a simply marked crypt on the north wall. For 25 years after her death, her former husband Joe DiMaggio had six red roses placed on her crypt three times a week. Also buried here are Truman Capote and Natalie Wood; Jack Lemmon and Billy Wilder are posthumous neighbors.

SANTA MONICA, VENICE, AND MALIBU

Hugging the Santa Monica Bay in an arch, the desirable communities of Malibu, Santa Monica, and Venice move from the ultrarich, ultracasual Malibu to the bohemian/seedy Venice. What they have in common, however, is cleaner air, mild temperatures, horrific traffic, and an emphasis on the beach-focused lifestyle that many people consider the hallmark of Southern California.

Santa Monica—which, because of its liberal populace, has been dubbed the People's Republic of Santa Monica—is a pedestrian-friendly little city, about 8.3 square mi, with a dynamic population of artists and writers, entertainment folk, educators, and retired people, all attracted by the cooler, sometimes-foggy climate. Mature trees, Mediterranean-style architecture, and strict zoning have helped create a sense of place often missing from L.A.'s residential neighborhoods. This character comes with a price: real estate costs are astronomical.

Venice was a turn-of-the-20th-century fantasy that never quite came true. Abbot Kinney, a wealthy Los Angeles businessman, envisioned this little piece of real estate as a romantic replica of Venice, Italy. He developed an incredible 16 mi of canals, floated gondolas on them, and built scaled-down versions of the Doge's Palace and other Venetian landmarks. Some canals were rebuilt in 1996, but they don't reflect the old-world connection quite as well as they could. Figures. Ever since Kinney first planned his project, it was plagued by ongoing engineering problems and drifted into disrepair. Three small canals and bridges do remain and can be viewed from the southeast corner of Pacific Avenue and Venice Boulevard. Another great glimpse of the canals can be caught when walking along Dell Avenue from Washington Street north to Venice.

North of Santa Monica, up the Pacific Coast Highway, past rock slides, Rollerbladers, and cliffside estates, is Malibu. Home to blockbuster names like Spielberg, Hanks, and Streisand, this ecologically fragile 23-mi stretch of coastline can feel like a world of its own, with its slopes slipping dramatically into the ocean. In the public imagination Malibu is synonymous with beaches and wealth—but in the past couple of years there's been some friction between these two signature elements. Some property owners, such as billionaire music producer David Geffen, have come under attack for blocking public access to the beaches in front of their homes. ■ **TIP→ All beaches are technically public, though; if you stay below the mean high-tide mark you're in the clear.** And everyone is welcome (with reservations) to the reimagined yet still intimate seaside Getty Villa and its collection of Greek, Etruscan, and Roman art and artifacts.

WHAT TO SEE

12 **Adamson House and Malibu Lagoon Museum.** With spectacular views of Surfrider Beach and lush garden grounds, this house epitomizes all the reasons to live in Malibu. Built in 1929 by the Rindge family, who owned much of the Malibu area in the early part of the 20th century, they knew even then this was an ideal setting to settle down. Malibu was quite isolated then, with all visitors and supplies arriving by boat at the nearby Malibu Pier (and it can still be isolated these days when rock slides close the highway). Built in 1929, the house reflects a Moorish Spanish–style. The Rindges had an enviable Malibu lifestyle, decades before the area was trendy. The house, covered with magnificent tile work in rich blues, greens, yellows, and oranges from the now-defunct Malibu Potteries, is right on the beach—high chain-link fences keep out curious beachgoers. Even an outside dog shower, near the servants' door, is a tiled delight. Docent-led tours provide insights on family life here as well as the history of Malibu and its real estate. Signs posted around the grounds outside direct you on a self-guided tour, but you can't go inside the house without a guide. Garden tours take place on Friday at 10 AM. There's pay parking in the adjacent county lot or in the lot at PCH and Cross Creek Road. ✉ *23200 Pacific Coast Hwy., Malibu* ☎ *310/456–8432* 🌐 *www.adamsonhouse.org* 🎟 *$5* 🕑 *Wed.–Sat. 11–3; last tour departs at 2.*

5 **Bergamot Station.** Named after a stop on the Red Trolley line that once shuttled between Downtown and the Santa Monica Pier, Bergamot Station is now a depot for intriguing art. The industrial facades house more than a dozen art galleries, shops, a café, and a museum. The galleries cover many kinds of media: photography, jewelry, and paintings from somber to lurid. Inside one of the many cavernous, steel-beamed warehouses that make up this unique area, the **Santa Monica Museum of Art** (☎ *310/586–6488* 🌐 *www.smmoa.org*) showcases exhibits of emerging artists. Open Tuesday–Friday 11–6, Saturday 11–8, with a $5 suggested donation. The museum also presents evening salons with artists, performers, and speakers. ✉ *2525 Michigan Ave., Santa Monica* ☎ *310/453–7535* 🌐 *www.bergamotstation.com* 🕑 *Galleries generally Tues.–Fri. 10–6, Sat. 11–5:30.*

6 **California Heritage Museum.** The real star of this collection is the 1894 Victorian house the museum occupies. The interior has been beautifully restored to represent four decades of design. Rotating exhibits focus California decorative and folk art including paintings, furniture, photography, sculpture, and a solid collection of California tiles and

A GOOD DRIVE

Numbers correspond to the Santa Monica, Venice, and Malibu map.

Look for the arched neon sign at the foot of Colorado Avenue marking the entrance to the **Santa Monica Pier** ❶, the city's number one landmark, built in 1906. Park on the pier and take a turn through **Pacific Park** ❷, an amusement park. The wide swath of sand on the north side of the pier is Santa Monica Beach, on hot summer weekends one of the most crowded beaches in southern California. From the pier, walk to Ocean Avenue, where **Palisades Park** ❸ provides panoramic ocean views. Three blocks inland is the **Third Street Promenade** ❹, a popular outdoor mall. If this whets your shopping appetite, head up a few blocks to Montana Avenue, another street thick with boutiques, particularly past 9th Street.

Retrieve your car and drive two blocks inland on Colorado to Main Street. Turn right and continue to Ocean Park Boulevard. There you'll find the **California Heritage Museum** ❻. The next several blocks south along Main Street are great for browsing.

Next stop: **Venice Boardwalk** ❼. Walk up Main Street through the trendy shopping district until you hit Rose Avenue. Ahead on the left you'll spot an enormous pair of binoculars, the front of the Frank Gehry–designed Chiat-Day Mojo office building. Turn right toward the sea. The main attraction of this dead end is the classic/odd boardwalk.

For the drive to Malibu, retrace your route along Main Street. At Pico Boulevard, turn west, toward the ocean, and then right on Ocean Avenue.

When you pass the pier, prepare to turn left down the California Incline (the incline is at the end of Palisades Park at Wilshire Boulevard) to Pacific Coast Highway (Highway 1), also known as PCH. About 5 mi north is the spectacular **Getty Villa Malibu** ❾. Another 6 mi or so will bring you into Malibu proper. Park in the lot adjacent to the **Malibu Pier** ❿ and take a stroll out to the end for a view of the coast. Back on land, take a walk on **Malibu Lagoon State Beach** ⓫, also known as Surfrider Beach. On the highway side of the beach is the Moorish **Adamson House and Malibu Lagoon Museum** ⓬, a tiled beauty with a great Pacific view.

TIMING

If you've got the time, break your coastal visit into two excursions: Santa Monica and Venice on one excursion, and Malibu on the other. The best way to "do" L.A.'s coastal communities is to park your car and walk, cycle, or skate along the 3-mi beachside bike path. For this, of course, a sunny day is best; on all but the hottest days, when literally millions of Angelenos flock to the beaches, try to get started in the late morning. Places like Santa Monica Pier, Main Street, and the Venice Boardwalk are more interesting to observe as the day progresses. Try to avoid the boardwalk, beach, and back streets of Santa Monica and Venice at night, when the crowds dissipate. Avoid driving to Malibu during rush hour, when traffic along PCH moves at a snail's pace.

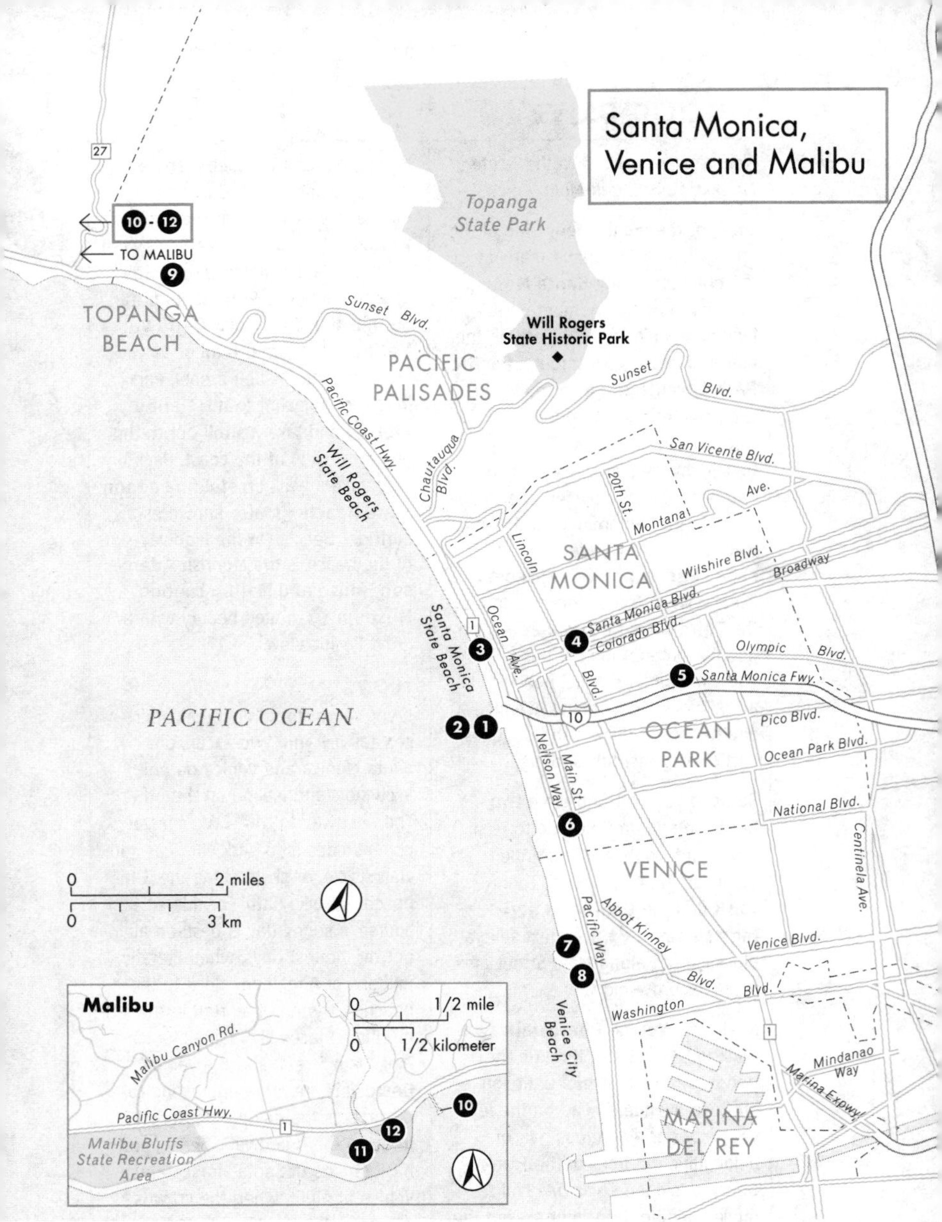

Adamson House and Malibu Lagoon Museum ... 12
Bergamot Station 5
California Heritage Museum 6
Getty Villa Malibu 9
Malibu Lagoon State Beach 11
Malibu Pier 10
Muscle Beach 8
Pacific Park 2
Palisades Park 3
Santa Monica Pier 1
Third Street Promenade 4
Venice Boardwalk 7

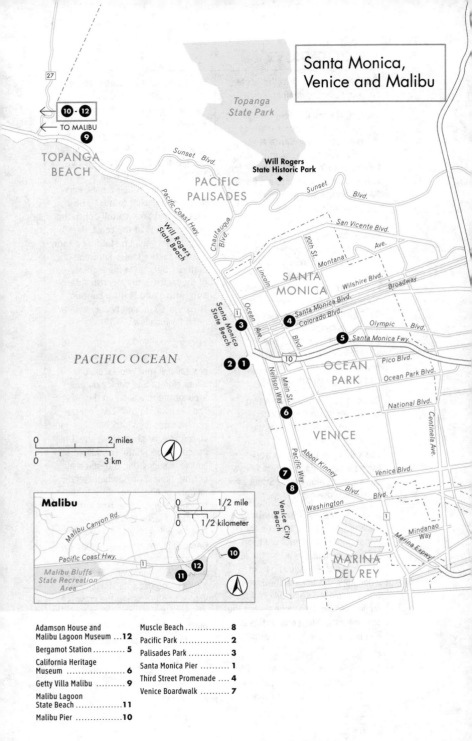

CLOSE UP

The Heart of Screenland

Culver City. Located halfway between Hollywood and the coast, Culver City shares a glamorous history of its own. Known as "Screenland," the area boasts two film studios. The first, **Culver City Studios** (✉ *9336 W. Washington Blvd., Culver City* ☎ *310/202–1234* 🌐 *www.ci.culver-city.ca.us/*) is best known as the location where *Gone With the Wind* was filmed in addition to classics including *Citizen Kane* and the Desilu Productions TV hits of the '50s including *The Andy Griffith Show, Lassie,* and *Batman*. This studio does not offer tours to the public. **Sony Studios** (✉ *10202 W. Washington, Culver City* ☎ *310/244–4000* 🌐 *www.sonypicturesstudios.com*), where movie magic from *Wizard of Oz* to *Spiderman* was made, offers two-hour walking tours ($25, reservation recommended) to dive into their rich TV and blockbuster film history. If game shows are your thing, you can also watch be a part of the studio audience for *Jeopardy!* or *Wheel of Fortune* (for tickets call ☎ *800/482–9840*). The area of Culver City itself has seen revitalization in recent years as visitors discover the charming district of the area's "downtown." In its heart is the **Culver Hotel** (✉ *9400 Culver Blvd., Culver City* ☎ *310/838–7963* 🌐 *www.culverhotel.com*), built in 1924 and now preserved as a Historical Landmark; it will catch your eye with its old world glory and lobby entrance with its sweeping dark wood and high ceiling that's a seductive as the many classic film stars that took up residency here over the years including Greta Garbo, Joan Crawford, John Wayne, Clark Gable, Buster Keaton, Ronald Reagan, and cast members from *Wizard of Oz* and *Gone With the Wind* as they filmed in the nearby studio. The surrounding area is loaded with shops, cafés, the art deco–style **Pacific Movie Theatre** (☎ *310/360–9565*), and a vibrant art gallery scene. One museum with its own unique spin is the **Museum of Jurassic Technology** (✉ *9341 Venice Blvd., Culver City* ☎ *310/836–6131* 🌐 *www.mjt.org* 🎟 *$5 suggested donation* ⏲ *Thurs. 2–8, Fri.–Sun. noon–6*), with an oddball assortment of natural (and partly fictional) "art" pieces such as fruit stone carvings, theater models, string figures, finds from mobile home parks, and a tribute room filled with paintings of dogs from the Soviet Space Program, all housed in a low-lighted haunted house–style atmosphere that makes you feel as if the Addams' Family butler will come to greet you at any moment. If you feel inclined to stay awhile, head up to the second floor to the small, samovar-equipped tearoom for a free cuppa to allow your brain to process all that you've seen.

pottery. ✉ *2612 Main St., Santa Monica* ☎ *310/392–8537* 🌐 *www.californiaheritagemuseum.org* 🎟 *$5* ⏲ *Wed.–Sun. 11–4.*

❾ **Getty Villa Malibu.** Feeding off the cultures of ancient Rome, Greece, and Etruria, the remodeled Getty Villa opened in 2006 with much fanfare—and some controversy concerning the acquisition and rightful ownership of some of the Italian artifacts on display. The antiquities are astounding, but on a first visit even they take a backseat to their environment. This megamansion sits on some of the most valuable coastal property in the world. Modeled after an Italian country home,

Fodor's Choice ★

the Villa dei Papiri in Herculaneum, the Getty Villa includes beautifully manicured gardens, reflecting pools, and statuary. The largest and most lovely garden, the Outer Peristyle, gives you glorious views over a rectangular reflecting pool and geometric hedges to the Pacific. The new structures blend thoughtfully into the rolling terrain and significantly improve the public spaces, such as the new outdoor amphitheater, gift store, café, and entry arcade. Talks and educational programs are offered at an indoor theater. TIP→ **An advance timed entry ticket is required for admission. Tickets are free and may be ordered from the Web site or by phone.** ✉ *17985 Pacific Coast Hwy., Pacific Palisades* ☎ *310/440–7300* 🌐 *www.getty.edu* 🎫 *Free, tickets required. Parking $10, cash only* ⏲ *Thurs.–Mon. 10–5.*

11 **Malibu Lagoon State Beach.** Bird-watchers, take note: in this 5-acre marshy area you could spot egrets, blue herons, avocets, and gulls. (You'll need to stay on the boardwalks so as not to disturb their habitats.) The path leads out to a rocky stretch of beach and makes for a pleasant stroll. You're also likely to spot a variety of marine life. Look for the signs to help identify these sometimes exotic-looking creatures. The lagoon is open 24 hours and is particularly enjoyable in the early morning and at sunset. The parking lot has limited hours but street-side parking is usually available at off-peak times. ✉ *23200 Pacific Coast Hwy., Malibu.*

NEED A BREAK?

The Sunset Restaurant and Bar (✉ ***Off Pacific Coast Hwy., just north of Zuma Beach, 6800 Westward Beach Rd., Malibu*** ☎ ***310/589–1007*****) is as close to the beach as you can get without getting sand in your drink. This local secret serves up breathtaking views of the surf, dolphins, surfers, and celebrity locals taking a break on the protected patio. Stop in for a cocktail at the friendly bar or a light meal of chicken tempura sticks or unique salad mixes.**

10 **Malibu Pier.** This 780-foot fishing dock is a great place to drink in the sunset, take in some coastal views, or to watch local fishermen reel up a catch. A pier has jutted out here since the early 1900s; storms destroyed the last one in 1995, and it was rebuilt in 2001. In 2004 private developers worked with the state and refurbished the pier, yielding a bait shop, water-sport rentals, and a surfing museum. ✉ *Pacific Coast Hwy. at Cross Creek Rd.* 🌐 *www.parks.ca.gov.*

OFF THE BEATEN PATH

Marina del Rey. Located just south of Venice, this condo-laden, chain restaurant–lined development is a good place to grab brunch (but watch for price gougers), take a stroll or ride bikes along the waterfront. A number of places, such as **Hornblower Cruises and Events** (✉ *13755 Fiji Way* ☎ *888/467–6256* 🌐 *www.hornblower.com*) in Fisherman's Village, rent boats for romantic dinner or party cruises around the marina. There are a few man-made beaches, but you're better off hitting the larger (and cleaner) beaches up the coast.

8 **Muscle Beach.** Bronzed young men bench-pressing five girls at once, weight lifters doing tricks on the sand—Muscle Beach fired up the country's imagination from the get-go. There are actually two spots known as Muscle Beach. The original Muscle Beach, just south of the Santa Monica Pier, is where bodybuilders Jack LaLanne and Vic and Armand Tanny used to work out in the 1950s. When it was closed in

BIKE THE COAST

Whether you're the next Lance Armstrong or an occasional cyclist, the coastal areas of LA provide plenty of opportunities to see the sights and get some exercise in.

The casual rider can take the beach-side bike path, the Strand, which starts as far north as Temescal Canyon and stretches around the harbor at Marina del Ray, south toward Hermosa Beach and beyond. The bike path is in good condition but can get busy on weekends so watch for nonchalant pedestrians, skateboarders, and cycle-cops eager to issue tickets to those who ignore the "Get-off and Walk" signs.

Major streets with bike lanes include Venice Boulevard and San Vicente (from Santa Monica to Brentwood). Hardcore enthusiasts can find more challenging rides around Palos Verdes or up Pacific Coast Highway (PCH), which offers a spectacular route with side diversions up a number of winding canyon roads that are as lengthy and steep as any in the Pyrenees. It's not unusual to see members of the pro peloton gliding past in January as they train for the Tour of California.

1959, the bodybuilders moved south along the beach to Venice, to a city-run facility known as "the Pen," and the Venice Beach spot inherited the Muscle Beach moniker. The spot is probably best known now as a place where a young Arnold Schwarzenegger first came to flex his muscles in the late '60s and began his rise to fame. The area now hosts a variety of sports and gymnastic events and the occasional "beach babe" beauty contests that always draws a crowd. ✉ *1800 Ocean Front Walk, Venice.*

❷ **Pacific Park.** Built on Santa Monica Pier, extending over the bay, this small amusement area harks back to the days of the grand Pacific Ocean Park (1957–67). Its attractions include a tame coaster, a large Ferris wheel, and a handful of rides that wildly satisfy the under-six crowd. **TIP→This isn't squeaky-clean Disneyland, so expect real-world litter and watch your personal belongings. Since the pier is riddled with nails and splinters, opt for sneakers over flip-flops.** ✉ *380 Santa Monica Pier, Santa Monica* ☎ *310/260–8744* 🌐 *www.pacpark.com* 🎟 *Rides $2–$6, all-day pass $20* ⏲ *Hrs vary, weather permitting. Call or check Web site for schedule.*

❸ **Palisades Park.** The ribbon of green that runs along the top of the cliffs from Colorado Avenue to just north of San Vicente Boulevard offers picture perfect views of the ocean. The beautiful setting is ideal to join the regular joggers and strollers who frequent the walkway, if you don't mind hurdling the occasional homeless person, as they also find this to be an appealing area to camp out.

❶ **Santa Monica Pier.** Souvenir shops, a psychic adviser, carnival games, arcades, eateries, and **Pacific Park** are all part the festive atmosphere of this truncated pier at the foot of Colorado Boulevard below Palisades Park. The pier's trademark 46-horse Looff Carousel is the Pier's hallmark, built in 1922, has appeared in several films, including *The*

Sting. Free concerts are held on the pier in summer. ✉*Colorado Ave. and the ocean, Santa Monica* ☎*310/458–8900* 🌐*www.santamonicapier.org* 🎫*Rides $2.50* ⏲*Carousel hours vary depending on season and weather conditions, so call ahead.*

THE DAWN OF DOGTOWN

Pacific Ocean Park was meant to be Disneyland on the water. But in 1967, the failed park closed. In true L.A. fashion, a gang of surfers, outcasts, and X-treme athletes took the art of riding a board to the concrete ruins of the park—thus skateboard culture was born. These surf punks established a subculture where broken bones were badges of honor in a neighborhood known as "Dogtown," now immortalized in the films *Dogtown and Z-Boys* and *Lords of Dogtown* as the place where extreme skateboarding was born.

Santa Monica Pier Aquarium. From sharks to colorful fish to a crowd-drawing touch tanks, the aquariums are carefully watched over by informed staff members ready to provide information on their oceanic residents. Run by beach conservation group Heal the Bay, this live marine life menagerie features a collection of several large aquarium tanks maintained by the "Aquadoption" program. A theater room runs education films throughout the day, and a Kid's Corner provides books, games and a puppet-show. Don't miss this chance learn about the area's ecology and staggering evidence of how pollution is affecting the ocean and the animals and plants who live there. Look for it tucked under the eastern end of the Santa Monica Pier bridge along Ocean Front Walk, just follow the colorful seascape murals that cover the outside walls. ✉*1600 Ocean Front Walk, Santa Monica* ☎*310/393–6149* 🌐*www.healthebay.org/smpa* 🎫*$2 minimum donation* ⏲*Tues.–Fri. 2–5, weekends 12:30–5.*

❹ ★ **Third Street Promenade.** Stretch your legs along this pedestrians-only three-block stretch of 3rd Street, just a whiff away from the Pacific, lined with jacaranda trees, ivy-topiary dinosaur fountains, strings of lights, and branches of nearly every major U.S. retail chain. Outdoor cafés, street vendors, movie theaters, and a rich nightlife make this a main gathering spot for locals, visitors, as well as street musicians and performance artists. Plan a night just to take it all in or take an afternoon for a long people-watching stroll. There's plenty of parking in city structures on the streets flanking the promenade. ✉*3rd St. between Wilshire Blvd. and Broadway, Santa Monica* 🌐*www.thirdstreetpromenade.com.*

❼ Fodor's Choice ★ **Venice Boardwalk.** "Boardwalk" may be something of a misnomer—it's really a five-block section of paved walkway—but this L.A. mainstay delivers year-round action. Bicyclists zip along and bikini-clad Rollerbladers attract crowds as they put on impromptu demonstrations, vying for attention with magicians, fortune-tellers, a chain-saw juggler, and sand mermaids. At the adjacent Muscle Beach, bulging bodybuilders with an exhibitionist streak pump iron at an outdoor gym. Pick up some cheap sunglasses, grab a hot dog, and enjoy the boardwalk's show. You can rent in-line skates, roller skates, and bicycles (some with baby seats) at the south end of the boardwalk (officially known as Ocean Front Walk), along Washington Street near the Venice Pier.

OFF THE BEATEN PATH

Will Rogers State Historic Park. The humorist, actor, and rambling cowboy Will Rogers lived on this site in the 1920s and 1930s. His ranch house, a folksy blend of Navajo rugs and Mission-style furniture, has become a museum featuring Rogers memorabilia. A short film presented in the visitor center highlights his roping technique and homey words of wisdom. Rogers was a polo enthusiast, and in the 1930s, His ranch house reopened in 2006 for docent-led tours. Featuring Rogers' stuffed practice calf and the high ceiling he raised so he could practice his famed roping style indoors, this house also holds and impression array of Navajo rugs, saddles, and Mission-style furniture. Rogers was a polo enthusiast, and in the 1930s, his front-yard polo field attracted such friends as Douglas Fairbanks Sr. for weekend games. The tradition continues, with free weekend games scheduled April–October, weather permitting. The park's broad lawns are excellent for picnicking, and there's hiking on miles of eucalyptus-lined trails. From the Pacific Coast Highway, turn inland at Sunset Boulevard. Follow Sunset for about 5 mi to the park entrance. ✉ *1501 Will Rogers State Park Rd., Pacific Palisades* ☎ *310/454–8212* 💰 *Free, parking $7* ⏲ *Parking daily 8–dusk, house tours Tues.–Fri. 11, 1, 2, Sat.–Sun. 10–4.*

THE SAN FERNANDO VALLEY

The San Fernando Valley gets a bad rap. Mocked in the infamous Frank Zappa song and Nicolas Cage film, both of the same name, "Valley Girl," this area of suburban bliss is located just over the hill of the notably "more cool" areas of Downtown, Hollywood, and the Westside. There are even some Angelenos who swear, with a sneer, that they will never set foot in "the Valley." But despite all the snickering, the Valley is home to many of the sets and artists that have made Los Angeles famous: Disney, Warner Bros., Universal Studios, NBC, and, ahem, a large chunk of pornography. In fact, nearly 70% of all entertainment productions in L.A. happen here. That means that some very rich entertainment executives regularly undergo sweltering summer temperatures, smog, and bumper-to-bumper traffic to go there everyday on their trek from their Westside and Malibu compounds to their less glamorous workplaces.

So what's in store for you? Well, besides the somewhat tired Universal Studios Hollywood, there's an archetypal urban sprawl. You might start wondering if there's a center to this maze of minimalls, gas stations, and mid-century tract homes. Nope. Instead, there are a dozen or so neighborhoods with names like Encino, Van Nuys, and Burbank, each with its own character if you look hard enough. One small jewel of the valley, Studio City, is rich with film history dating to 1920s silent movies. Its pedestrian-friendly strip along Ventura Boulevard has some of the tallest palms in L.A. and many interesting boutiques, antiques stores, and great nonchain outdoor cafés. But with so much to see on "the other side of the hill," your visit to the Valley is most likely best spent focusing on the entertainment industry aspect rather than searching for the diamond in the rough.

CLOSE UP

Main Street, CA

When you want to trade urban sprawl and traffic for boutique shopping, handmade sweets, and a good ol' fashioned community vibe, park your car and stroll down to Main Street. Start at the **California Heritage Museum** (see expanded listing), then head over to the **Victorian Baker Café** (✉ *2640 Main St., Santa Monica* ☎ *310/392-4956* 🌐 *www.thevictorian.com*), for a sweet sugar rush with their cakes, muffins, and scones served up in a festive atmosphere filled with locals on the deck of a large, beautifully restored Victorian house. Head farther down and you'll come across the gift shop, **Clever on Main** (✉ *2823 Main St., Santa Monica* ☎ *310/396-8108* 🌐 *www.cleveronmain.com*), a boutique that stocks flea-market-like finds with a fashionable edge. Farther down is the must-see store for all Francophiles, **Paris 1900** (✉ *2703 Main St., Santa Monica* ☎ *310/396-0405* 🌐 *www.paris1900.com*), featuring all things Paris-themed such as note cards, baubles, jewelry, linens, antique lace, and wedding dresses. It's open by appointment only, so call ahead.

Next door is the head-turning **Jadis** (✉ *2701 Main St., Santa Monica* ☎ *310/396-3477*) storefront featuring an odd collection of movie props and gizmos that usually draws a crowd to the window. It will cost you a dollar just to browse, but you'll be rewarded with an up-close look at everything from antique cameras to chemistry sets and other curious knickknacks used in big name movies. Across the street, stop in **Ritual Adornments** (✉ 2708 Main St. ☎ *310/452-4044*) for an eyeful of amazing beads and pendant-worthy stones and settings. A couple of blocks down is **Patagonia** (✉ *2936 Main St., Santa Monica* ☎ *310/314-1776* 🌐 *www.patagonia.com*), the stop for ecofriendly action clothes to wear your pro-green stance on your sleeve. After full afternoon of shopping, refuel at one of the many eateries such at the **World Café** (✉ *2820 Main St., Santa Monica* ☎ *310/392-1661* 🌐 *www.worldcafela.com*) that sparkles with tiny lights around its cozy indoor setting and lively outdoor patio. For a full directory of Main Streets offerings, visit 🌐 *www.mainstreetsm.com.*

TIMING The Valley is surrounded by mountains, and the major routes to and from it go through mountain passes. During rush hour, traffic jams on the Hollywood Freeway (U.S. 101/Highway 170), San Diego Freeway (I–405), and Ventura Freeway (U.S. 101/Highway 134) can be brutal, so avoid trips to or from the Valley at those times. Expect to spend most of a day at Universal Studios Hollywood and CityWalk; studio tours at NBC and Warner Bros. last up to two hours.

WHAT TO SEE

OFF THE BEATEN PATH

Americana at Brand. What would at trip to LA be without shopping? While Hollywood and Beverly Hills offer their share of temptations, a new outdoor complex in Glendale is offering some competition for your dollars in this once low-key neighborhood. From the developers who created The Grove, this similar experience offers 75 shops ranging from designer brand names like Armani and BCBG to more trendy H&M and Ed Hardy. You can also refuel on substance from Katsuya sushi to

Starbuck's. While you're there, you can stake out some of the residential space above the shops. But be prepared to break the bank, condos start at $2 million. ✉ *889 Americana Way, Glendale* ☎ *818/637–8982* 🌐 *www.americanaatbrand.com* ⏱ *Mon.–Thurs. 10–9, Fri. and Sat. 10–10, Sun. 11–8.*

❶ **Disney Studios.** Although tours of this film studio are not available, a peek from Riverside Drive shows you that Disney's innovations go beyond the big and small screens to fanciful touches of architecture (note the little Mickey Mouse heads mounted on the surrounding fence). On the Michael Eisner Building, designed by architect Michael Graves, giant figures of the Seven Dwarfs support the roof's gable. The Animation Building, meanwhile, has a cartoonish spin with an 85-foot-tall "Sorcerer's Apprentice" hat, red-and-white stripes, and the word ANIMATION in tall letters. You can see the colorful complex from the Ventura Freeway (Highway 134). ✉ *500 S. Buena Vista, Burbank.*

❷ **NBC Television Studios.** In the entertainment sector of Burbank, the NBC studios is home to some of TVs most popular talk shows, soap operas, and news broadcasts. An hour-long tour gives you behind-the-scenes access to shows including the *Tonight Show with Jay Leno, Days of Our Lives,* the *Ellen DeGeneres Show, Access Hollywood, and LA studios for the Today Show and other news programs.* If you'd like to be part of a live studio audience, free tickets are available for tapings of the various NBC shows. ✉ *3000 W. Alameda Ave., Burbank* ☎ *818/840–3537* 🎫 *Tours $8.50.*

NEED A BREAK?

Only in L.A. could a Bob's Big Boy (✉ *4211 W. Riverside Dr., at W. Alameda Ave., Burbank* ☎ *818/843–9334*) be classified a historical landmark. Built in 1949, this Big Boy stands as the best example of streamlined coffeeshop architecture in L.A. Its signature Big Boy Combo plate stacks a double-decker burger with fries and a salad, preferably with the rich blue cheese dressing. The best time to come is on Friday night in summer, when local car clubs flood the diner's parking lot to show off their restored hot rods. Weekends from 5 PM to 10 PM are car-hop nights, when waitresses will serve your burger and malt on 1950s-style window trays.

NoHo Arts District. Don't let the name fool you—this West Coast enclave bears little resemblance to its New York namesake. In fact, the name *NoHo* was spawned when the city, desperate to reinvent this depressed area, abbreviated the region's North Hollywood name. A square mile at the intersection of Lankershim and Magnolia in North Hollywood, the NoHo Arts District has slowly tried to transform itself into a cultural hot spot that includes several theaters showcasing aspiring young actors, dance schools, a comedy club, art galleries, boutiques, and restaurants. The results are mixed at best. The month of May brings the annual Theater and Arts Festival: free live theater performances, arts exhibits from an eclectic range of southern California's visual artists, music, an arts and crafts marketplace, dance showcases, and a children's area are all part of the fun. ✉ *Intersection of Lankershim and Magnolia Blvds., North Hollywood* 🌐 *www.nohoartsdistrict.com.*

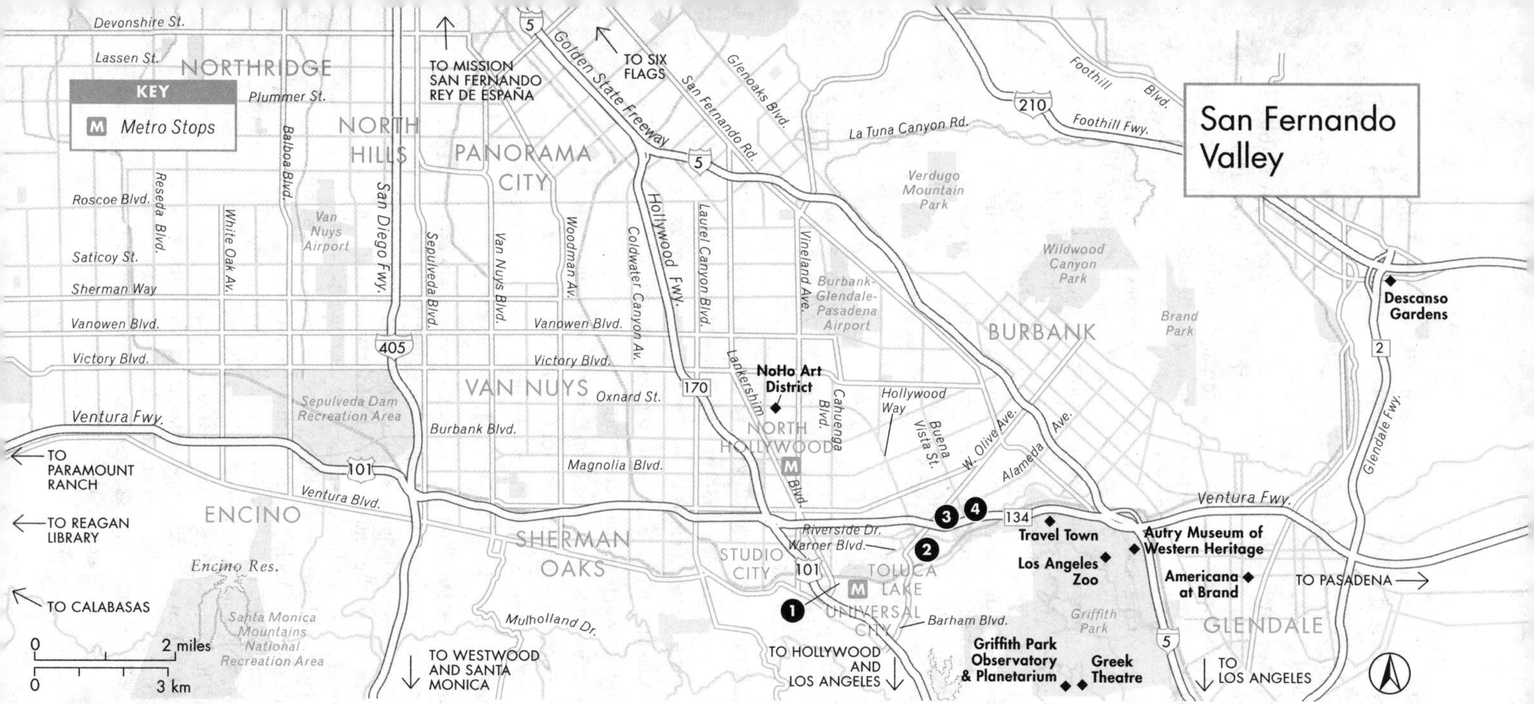

Disney Studios 1

NBC Television Studios 2

Universal Studios Hollywood 3

Warner Bros. Studios 4

CLOSE UP

Laurel Canyon and Mulholland Drive

The hills that separate Hollywood from the Valley are more than a symbolic dividing line between the city slickers and the suburbanites; the hills have a community in their own right and a reputation as a bohemian artists' hideaway for those who have been fortunate enough to make a living at their creative pursuits. The 2002 movie *Laurel Canyon* provided one view of the lifestyle of one kind of Canyon dweller—freethinking entertainment-industry movers and shakers who seek a peaceful refuge in their tree-shaded homes. By day they're churning out business deals and working on projects; by night they're living it up with private parties high above the bustle of the city streets.

Though you may not get to see all the goings-on inside these homes, you can use your imagination as you take a drive through Laurel Canyon and pass estates and party pads dating back to the silent film era, such as that of Clara Bow, on to music icons of the '60s and '70s (including Brian Wilson and Frank Zappa).

Canyon Country Store (✉ *2108 Laurel Canyon Blvd.* ☎ *323/654–8091*), at the Canyon's halfway point, is an institution of hippie-esque good vibes filled with household essentials and specialty foods that include vegetarian items and British imports. If you stop for dinner at **Pace** (✉ *2100 Laurel Canyon Blvd.* ☎ *323/654–8583*), below the store, there's a good chance of spotting a movie star on a low-key date. This cozy, soft-lighted setting is a perfect spot for a romantic dinner nestled among the canyon hills and lots of Hollywood history. Because the restaurant is popular with the locals, make weekend reservations at least a few days in advance.

A few steps away from Pace is the house once occupied by Jim Morrison. Take a drive up Lookout Mountain and you'll find yourself on the grounds that inspired resident Joni Mitchell to pen "Ladies of the Canyon." If you have time to cruise Mulholland Drive, you'll get breathtaking views that can help take you away from the city's relentless pulse.

2

★ **The Ronald Reagan Presidential Library and Museum.** On 100 acres high up in the hills of Simi Valley is the final resting place of President Ronald Reagan along with an extensive museum that chronicles his early days as a Hollywood movie star, the two terms he served as governor of California, and his journey to the presidency. A massive new pavilion shelters the Air Force One plane that flew Reagan and six other presidents 1973–2001. Give yourself a good three hours to get through it all; a guided tour is your best bet. Don't forget to step outside to take time to enjoy the spectacular views and pay your respects at Reagan's gravesite. The library holds more than 50 million pages of presidential papers, photographs, film, video, audio, and books. It takes at least an hour to drive here from Downtown L.A. ✉ *40 Presidential Dr., Simi Valley* ☎ *800/410–8354* 🌐 *www.reaganfoundation.org* 🎫 *$12* ⏲ *Daily 10–5.*

Santa Monica Mountains National Recreation Area. The line that forms the boundary of the San Fernando Valley is one of the most famous thoroughfares in this vast metropolis. **Mulholland Drive** cuts through the

Santa Monica Mountains National Recreation Area, a vast parkland that stretches along the top and west slopes of the Santa Monica Mountains from Hollywood to the Ventura County line. Driving the length of the hilltop road is slow and can be treacherous, but the rewards are sensational views of valley and city on each side and expensive homes along the way. The park incorporates several local and state parks, including Will Rogers and Malibu Lagoon. Large scenic portions of these oak-studded hills were owned at one time by such Hollywood stars as Ronald Reagan and Bob Hope. They provided location sites for many movies; the grassy rolling hillside continues to serve a stand-in for the Wild West. Sets at the **Paramount Ranch** backlot (✉*2813 Cornell Rd., Agoura Hills*) have been preserved and continue to be used as location sites. Rangers regularly conduct tours of the Paramount Ranch, where you can see sets used by *M*A*S*H* and *Dr. Quinn, Medicine Woman.* This expansive area provides plenty of hiking and picnicking trails. Pick up a map in the ranger's station. To reach Mulholland Drive from Hollywood, go via Outpost Drive off Franklin Avenue or Cahuenga Boulevard west via Highland Avenue north. Note that it changes from Mulholland Drive to Mulholland Highway when you cross Calabasas. It ends at the coast north of Zuma Beach near Ventura. Keep an eye out for riders on horses as well as deer, raccoons, or a rare mountain lion along the way. Note: The visitor center is outside of the park area. ✉*401 W. Hillcrest Dr., Thousand Oaks* ☎*805/370–2301* 🎫*Free* ⏲*Daily 9–5.*

❸ ★ **Universal Studios Hollywood.** While most first-time Los Angeles visitors consider this to be a must-see stop, bear in mind there many other attractions that define Hollywood without the steep prices and tourist traps found here. Despite the amusement park clichés, hard-core sightseeing and entertainment junkies will make this required visiting. **■ TIP→If you get here when the park opens, you'll likely save yourself from long waits in line—arriving early pays off.**

The first-timer favorite is the tram tour, during which you can experience the parting of the Red Sea; duck from spitting creatures in Jurassic Park; visit the *Desperate Housewives* neighborhood and Dr. Seuss's "Whoville"; see the airplane wreckage of War of the Worlds and the still-creepy Psycho house; be attacked by the ravenous killer shark of *Jaws* fame; and survive an all-too-real simulation of an earthquake that measures 8.3 on the Richter scale, complete with collapsing earth. The trams have audio-visual monitors that play video clips of the TV shows and movies shot on the sets you pass by as this guided trip circles the 415-acre complex all day long. **■ TIP→This tram ride is usually the best place to start, since it's on the lower level of the park, which gets really crowded in the afternoon.**

Many attractions are based on Universal films and television shows, designed to give you a thrill in one form or another. Take your pick from the bone-rattling roller coaster *Revenge of the Mummy—The Ride,* the virtual world of *Terminator 2: 3D*, visit a jungle full of dinosaurs in *Jurassic Park—The Ride,* which includes an 84-foot water drop, or experience a simulated warehouse fire in *Backdraft* that is so real you can feel the heat.

Shrek 4-D reunites the film's celebrity voices to pick up where the movie left off in a 15-minute trailer of 3-D animation shown in an action simulation theater. Fear Factor Live and the House of Horrors are guaranteed to provide screams, while the Animal Actors show provides milder entertainment courtesy of some talented furry friends. The newest attraction based on the Simpsons animated series, opened in summer 2008, takes you on a journey like no other through their Springfield neighborhood in a ride that only the beloved, albeit cantankerous, Krusty the Klown could dream up.

WHEN TO PASS ON A PASS

Face it, admission to Universal Studios is high enough. Still, you may be tempted to get the $99 pass that takes you to the front of the line. Try to resist this splurge. Once inside you can see that most of the lines move quickly or are nonexistent. Pass on the premium and spend it on a decent lunch outside the park.

2

Throughout the park you'll wander through prop-style settings of a French Village or a travel back in time to the good ol' '50s, as costumed characters mingle with guests and pose for photos. Aside from the park, CityWalk is a separate venue, where you'll find a slew of shops, restaurants, nightclubs, and movie theaters, including IMAX 3-D. The old favorite King Kong attraction was lost in a fire in summer 2008, but the rest of the park was spared. ✉ *100 Universal City Plaza, Universal City* ☎ *818/622–3801* 🌐 *www.universalstudioshollywood.com* 🎟 *$67, parking $10* 🕐 *Contact park for seasonal hrs.*

❹ **Warner Bros. Studios.** If you're looking for a more authentic behind-the-scenes look at how films and TV shows are made, head to this major studio center. There aren't many bells and whistles here, but you'll get a much better idea of production work than you will at Universal Studios. You start with a short film on Warner Bros. movies and TV shows, then hop into a tram for a ride through the sets and soundstages of such favorites as *Friends, Gilmore Girls, ER, Casablanca,* and *Rebel Without A Cause.* You'll see the bungalows where icons such as Marlon Brando and Bettie Davis spent time between shots, and the current production offices for Clint Eastwood and George Clooney. You might even spot a celeb or see a shoot in action—tours change from day to day depending on the productions taking place on the lot. Reservations are required. Call at least one week in advance and ask about provisions for people with disabilities; children under 8 are not admitted. Tours are given at least every hour, more frequently from May to September. A five-hour deluxe tour is available for $150, which includes a VIP lunch and allows visitors to spend more time on the sets, thus more ops for behind-the-scenes peeks and star spotting. ✉ *3400 W. Riverside Dr., Burbank* ☎ *818/972–8687* 🌐 *www.wbsf.com* 🎟 *$39* 🕐 *Weekdays 8:30–4:30.*

OFF THE BEATEN PATH

Six Flags Magic Mountain. True thrill seekers looking for "monster" rides and breathtaking roller coasters come to this anti-Disney amusement park for several of the biggest, fastest, and scariest in the world. The aptly named Scream, for instance, drops you 150 feet and tears through a 128-foot vertical loop. *Superman: The Escape* is a 41-story coaster that hurtles you from 0 to 100 mph in less than seven seconds. On Riddler's Revenge, the world's tallest and fastest stand-up roller coaster, you stand for a mile-long 65-mph total panic attack. Batman the Ride puts you on ski lift-style trains suspended from a track above to provide a zero-gravity, nothing-under-your-feet, flying experience as you sail through hairpin turns and vertical loops. In 2008, the Park's popular coaster, X, was transformed reopened as X2, complete with sleeker trains and a one-of-a-kind tunnel and light show. Beloved children's icon *Thomas The Tank Engine* and his friends entertains kids at *Thomas Town* or take them to meet their favorite Looney Tunes characters in Bugs Bunny World. Shows, dining, parades younger kids rides and those scream-inducing roller coasters make it a full day on this massive park (be sure to wear your walking shoes and brace yourself for some of the hilly areas).

Weekends are peak times here, so be prepared to stand in line for the more popular rides. (In warm weather, be sure you have sunscreen and water.) Save $20 and pass the long lines upon arrival by purchasing and printing your tickets ahead of time from the Web site. This place is also popular with teenagers so be prepared to pass plenty of loud packs, or just send your own here to have a day away from the parents. If your trip falls during one of L.A.'s heat waves and you need a place to cool down (and don't mind communal pools), you can hop over to its sister theme park, Six Flags Hurricane Harbor, right next door, and for $16.99 take a slippery cool trip down its massive waterslides. Rumor has it Six Flags is possibly selling and closing the park in the near future to make way for condos and homes in this desirable location—so call ahead. ✉ *26101 Magic Mountain Pkwy., off I–5, 25 mi northwest of Universal Studios and 36 mi outside L.A., Valencia* ☎ *661/255–4100* 🌐 *www.sixflags.com* 🎟 *$60, parking $15* 🕒 *Mid-Mar.–mid-Sept., daily; mid-Sept.–early Mar., weekends; call for hrs.*

PASADENA AREA

Although seemingly absorbed into the general Los Angeles sprawl, Pasadena is a separate and distinct city. Noted for its Tournament of Roses, seen around the world each New Year's Day, the city brims with noteworthy spots, from its gorgeous Craftsman homes to its exceptional museums, particularly the Norton Simon and the Huntington Library, Art Collections, and Botanical Gardens.

Between Downtown Los Angeles and Pasadena, the Pasadena Freeway follows the curves of the arroyo (creek bed). This was the main road north during the early days of Los Angeles, when horses and buggies made their way through the countryside to the small town of Pasadena. In 1939 the road became the Arroyo Seco Parkway, the first freeway in Los Angeles, later renamed the Pasadena Freeway. The freeway remains a pleasant drive in non–rush hour traffic, with old sycamores winding up the arroyo in a pleasant contrast to the more common 10-lane freeways of Los Angeles.

To reach Pasadena from Downtown Los Angeles, drive north on the Pasadena Freeway (I–110). From Hollywood and the San Fernando Valley use the Ventura Freeway (Highway 134, east), which cuts through Glendale, skirting the foothills, before arriving in Pasadena.

WHAT TO SEE

❼ **Castle Green.** One block south of Colorado Boulevard stands the one-time social center of Pasadena's elite. This Moorish building is the only remaining section of a turn-of-the-20th-century hotel complex. Today the often-filmed tower (see The *Sting*, *Edward Scissorhands*, *The Last Samurai*, *The Prestige*) is residential; local painter R. Kenton Nelson can often be spotted at work in his turret art studio along Raymond Avenue. The building is not open to the public on a daily basis, but it does organize seasonal tours on the first Sunday of December and June. ✉*99 S. Raymond Ave., Pasadena* ☎*626/577–6765* 🌐*www.castlegreen.com.*

OFF THE BEATEN PATH

Descanso Gardens. Getting its name from the Spanish word for "rest," this lovely oasis is a truly tranquil setting, shaded by massive oak trees. Known for being a smaller, mellower version of the nearby Huntington, Descanso Gardens features denser foliage, quaint dirt paths, and some hilly climbs that can make for good exercise. Once part of the vast Spanish Rancho San Rafael, these 160 acres were purchased by E. Manchester Boddy, publisher of the *Los Angeles Daily News,* in 1937. He developed the area into acres of lushly planted gardens and slopes covered in native chaparral as well as an elegant 22-room mansion, which now serves as a museum. A forest of California live oak trees makes a dramatic backdrop for thousands of camellias, azaleas, and a breathtaking 5-acre International Rosarium holding 1,700 varieties of antique and modern roses. The Japanese Tea House operates on weekends between February and November: its Zen garden is a nice spot to stop for refreshments and reflection. There are also a tram, a gift shop, and a café. (Be advised the café and teahouse are independently owned and sometimes keep different hours from the gardens.) ✉*1418 Descanso Dr., La Cañada/Flintridge* ☎*818/949–4200* 🌐*www.descansogardens.org* 🎟*$8* 🕒*Daily 9–5.*

❷ **Fenyes Mansion.** With its elegant dark wood paneling and floors, curved staircases, and a theatrical stage in the parlor, it's easy to envision how this 1905 mansion along Pasadena's Millionaire's Row once served as gathering place for the city's elite. Most rooms on the ground and second floors are still fitted with original furniture; you can peek into these roped-off spaces, now home to mannequins dressed in period clothing, to get a sense of what life was like a century ago. Docent-led tours are available, which give an extensive history of the home and its owners, many of whom can be seen in the mansion's impressionist paintings. Also be sure to take a moment to visit the adjacent Historical Center Gallery with rotating exhibits dedicated to the art and culture of Pasadena. ✉*470 W. Walnut St., Pasadena* ☎*626/577–1660* 🌐*www.pasadenahistory.org* 🎟*Tours $4–$8; museum $5* 🕒*Wed.–Sun. noon–5. Hrs for tour vary. Call ahead.*

❸ ★ **Gamble House.** Built by Charles and Henry Greene in 1908, this is a spectacular example of American Arts and Crafts bungalow architecture.

A GOOD TOUR

Numbers correspond to the Pasadena Area, Highland Park and San Marino map.

A good place to start a short driving tour of Pasadena is on Orange Grove Boulevard, aka Millionaire's Row, where wealthy Easterners built grand mansions. One example is the **Tournament House (Wrigley Mansion)** ❶, an Italian Renaissance wedding cake of a house with grounds and gardens reminiscent of the neighborhood's glory days. To get there, take the Orange Grove exit off the Ventura Freeway (Highway 134); turn right at Orange Grove and travel five blocks. From the Pasadena Freeway (Highway 110), stay on the freeway until it ends at Arroyo Parkway. From Arroyo Parkway turn left at California Boulevard and then right at Orange Grove.

From the Wrigley Mansion, travel north on Orange Grove to Walnut Street and the **Fenyes Mansion** ❷, now headquarters of the Pasadena Historical Society. Continue on Orange Grove to Arroyo Terrace, where a left turn will take you into an architectural wonderland. Greene and Greene, the renowned Pasadena architects, designed all of the houses on Arroyo Terrace, as well as others in the area. To view their Craftsman masterpiece, the three-story, shingled **Gamble House** ❸, turn right on Westmoreland Place. Also in this section is the Frank Lloyd Wright–designed Millard House ("La Miniatura"), on Prospect Crescent (from Westmoreland, turn left onto Rosemont Avenue, right on Prospect Terrace, and right onto Prospect Crescent to No. 645). The famous **Rose Bowl** ❹ is nestled in a gully just to the west off Arroyo Boulevard. Leave this area via Rosemont Avenue, driving away from the hills to the south. From Rosemont, turn right onto Orange Grove Boulevard. Then, at Colorado Boulevard, turn left. Immediately on the left is the contemporary, austere **Norton Simon Museum** ❺, a familiar backdrop to so many viewers of the annual New Year's Day Tournament of Roses Parade. Inside are outstanding collections of Impressionist and Asian art—if you're a fan of Degas's work, don't miss this museum. Just west, paralleling the modern freeway bridge, Colorado crosses the historic concrete-arched Colorado Street Bridge, built in 1913.

East of the Norton Simon Museum, you'll enter **Old Town Pasadena** ❻. You'll want to walk around this section of Pasadena, heading east on Colorado. Parking's easy to find; look for signposted lots, often behind the main line of shops. Take a right on South Raymond Avenue and walk a block and a half down to the **Castle Green** ❼, a former grand hotel and architectural gem. For a look at domed Pasadena City Hall, turn left from Colorado Boulevard onto Fair Oaks Avenue, then right on Holly Street. Garfield Avenue will bring you back to Colorado. The next intersection is Los Robles Avenue. One-half block north on Los Robles, the **Pacific Asia Museum** ❽ literally sticks out by virtue of its pagoda-style roofline. Back on Los Robles, head north and make a quick right onto East Union Street to find the stark **Pasadena Museum of California Art** ❾. This is a small but interesting spot, well worth a quick dip into the native art scene.

Castle Green **7**
Fenyes Mansion **2**
Gamble House **3**
Huntington Library, Art Collections, and Botanical Gardens........ **10**
Kidspace Chilldren's Museum **11**
Norton Simon Museum **5**
Old Town Pasadena **6**
Pacific Asia Museum **8**
Pasadena Museum of California Art **9**
Rose Bowl **4**
Tournament House (Wrigley Mansion).........**1**

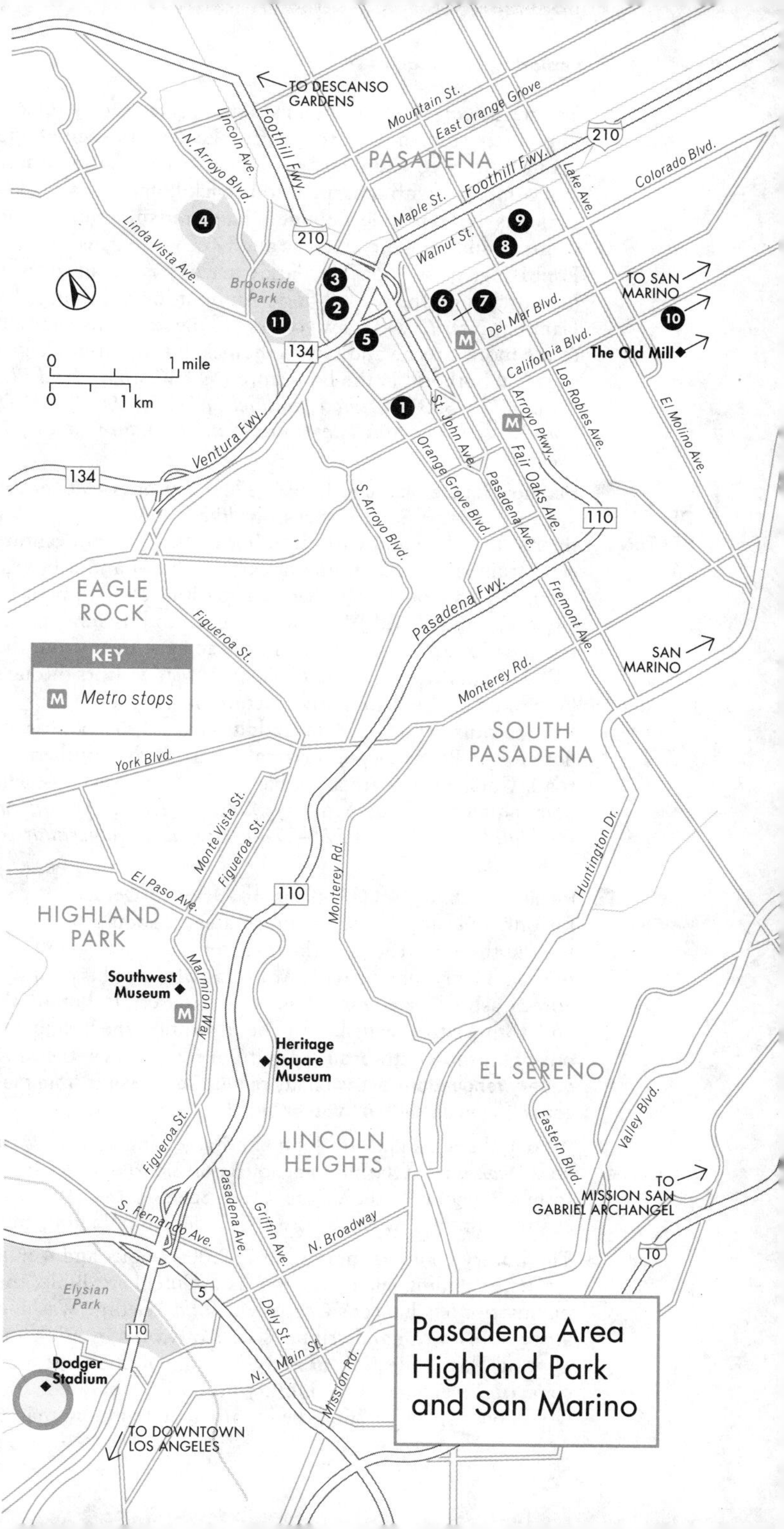

The term *bungalow* can be misleading, since the Gamble House is a huge three-story home. To wealthy Easterners such as the Gambles (as in Procter & Gamble), this type of vacation home seemed informal compared with their mansions back home. What makes admirers swoon is the incredible amount of handcraftsmanship, including a teak staircase and cabinetry, Greene and Greene–designed furniture, and an Emil Lange glass door. The dark exterior has broad eaves, with sleeping porches on the second floor. An hour-long, docent-led tour of the Gamble's interior will draw your eye to the exquisite details. If you want to see more Greene and Greene homes, buy a self-guided tour map of the neighborhood in the bookstore. ✉ *4 Westmoreland Pl., Pasadena* ☎ *626/793–3334* 🌐 *www.gamblehouse.org* 🎟 *$10* 🕙 *Thurs.–Sun. noon–3; tickets go on sale Thurs.–Sat. at 10, Sun. at 11:30. 1-hr tour every 20 min.*

OFF THE BEATEN PATH

Heritage Square Museum. Looking like a prop street set up by a film studio, Heritage Square sticks out like a row of bright dollhouses in the modest Highland Park neighborhood. Five 19th-century residences, a train station, a church, a carriage barn, and a boxcar that was originally part of the Southern Pacific Railroad, all built between the Civil War and World War I, were moved to this small park from various locations in southern California to save them from the wrecking ball. Docents dressed in period costume lead visitors through the lavish homes, giving an informative picture of what life in Los Angeles was like a century ago. The latest addition is a 1907 boxcar, now parked next to the Palms Depot, originally part of the Southern Pacific Railroad. Guided tours are available for $10 on weekends. They are also open on most holiday Mondays. ✉ *3800 Homer St., off Ave. 43 exit, Highland Park* ☎ *323/225–2700* 🌐 *www.heritagesquare.org* 🎟 *$10* 🕙 *Fri.–Sun. 11:30–4.*

10 Fodor's Choice ★

Huntington Library, Art Collections, and Botanical Gardens. If you have time for only one stop in the Pasadena area, it should be the Huntington, built in the early 1900s as the home of railroad tycoon Henry E. Huntington. Henry and his wife, Arabella (who was his aunt by marriage), voraciously collected rare books and manuscripts, botanical specimens, and 18th-century British art. The institution they established became one of the most extraordinary cultural complexes in the world. **Ongoing gallery renovations occasionally require some works from the permanent collection to be shifted to other buildings for display.**

Among the highlights are John Constable's intimate *View on the Stour near Dedham* and the monumental *Sarah Siddons as the Tragic Muse,* by Joshua Reynolds. In the Virginia Steele Scott Gallery of American Art you can see paintings by Mary Cassatt, Frederic Remington, and more.

The library contains more than 700,000 books and 4 million manuscripts, including such treasures as a Gutenberg Bible, the Ellesmere manuscript of Chaucer's *Canterbury Tales,* George Washington's genealogy in his own handwriting, scores of works by William Blake, and a world-class collection of early editions of Shakespeare. You'll find some of these items in the Library Hall with more than 200 important works on display. In 2006 the library acquired more than 60,000 rare books and reference volumes from the Cambridge, Massachusetts–based Bundy Library, making the Huntington the source of one of the biggest history of science collections in the world.

> **WORD OF MOUTH**
>
> ". . . Two thumbs waayyy up for the Huntington. . . . Because of its 'four-in-one' feature (the extraordinary gardens, the art collections, the library, and the tearoom), I rate it as one of the top 5 museums in all of the U.S. (maybe in the world, in terms of my own enjoyment, in one day)." —rex

Although the art collections are increasingly impressive here, don't resist being lured outside into the stunning Botanical Gardens. From the main buildings, lawns and towering trees stretch out toward specialty areas. The 10-acre Desert Garden, for instance, has one of the world's largest groups of mature cacti and other succulents, arranged by continent. Visit this garden on a cool morning or in the late afternoon, or a hot midday walk may be a little too authentic. In the Japanese Garden, an arched bridge curves over a pond; the area also has stone ornaments, a Japanese house, a bonsai court, and a Zen rock garden. There are collections of azaleas and 1,500 varieties of camellias. The 3-acre rose garden is displayed chronologically, so the development leading to modern varieties of roses can be observed; on the grounds is the charming **Rose Garden Tea Room,** where traditional afternoon tea is served. (Reservations required for English tea.) There are also herb, palm, and jungle gardens, plus the Shakespeare Garden, which blooms with plants mentioned in Shakespeare's works.

The Rose Hills Foundation Conservatory for Botanical Science, a massive greenhouse–style center with dozens of kid-friendly, hands-on exhibits illustrate plant diversity in various environments. (These rooms are quite warm and humid, especially the central rotunda, which displays rain-forest plants.) The new Bing Children's Garden is a tiny tot's wonderland filled with opportunities for children to explore the ancient elements of water, fire, air, and earth. A classical Chinese Garden "Liu Fang Yuan" (or Garden of Flowing Fragrance) opened in spring 2008, the largest of its kind outside China. Work on this will continue for the next several years. A 1¼-hour guided tour of the botanical gardens is led by docents at posted times, and a free brochure with map and highlights is available in the entrance pavilion. ✉ *1151 Oxford Rd., San Marino* ☎ *626/405–2100* 🌐 *www.huntington.org* 🎟 *$15 weekdays, $20 weekends, free 1st Thurs. of month* ⏲ *Tues.–Fri. noon–4:30, weekends 10:30–4:30.*

OFF THE BEATEN PATH

The Old Mill (El Molino Viejo). Built in 1816 as a gristmill for the San Gabriel Mission, the mill is one of the last remaining examples in Southern California of Spanish Mission architecture. The thick adobe walls and textured ceiling rafters give the interior a sense of quiet strength. Be sure to step into the back room, now a gallery with rotating quarterly exhibits in alliance with the California Art Club. Outside, a chipped section of the mill's exterior reveals the layers of brick, ground seashell paste, and oxblood used to hold the structure together. The surrounding gardens are reason enough to visit, with a flower-decked arbor and old sycamores and oaks. In summer the California Philharmonic ensemble performs in the garden. ✉ *1120 Old Mill Rd., San Marino* ☎ *626/449–5458* 🌐 *www.old-mill.org* 🎫 *Free* ⏲ *Tues.–Sun. 1–4.*

11 **Kidspace Children's Museum.** Looking like a Looney Tunes cartoon, this activity-focused, kid-centric playground with oversize replicas of familiar objects offers lessons along with some fun. Imaginative exhibits invite kids to interact, while parents can gain tidbits of knowledge on earthquakes, animals, and insects. In the towering leaf, climb inside a sunny atrium; kids assume the role of ants on their daring ascent, while outside they can run and climb the grounds along a running river, or take on a tricycle race on the "Trike Tracks." It's a place practically built to wear out the little ones out and give parents a much needed break. ✉ *480 N. Arroyo Blvd., Pasadena* ☎ *626/449–9144* 🌐 *www.kidspacemuseum.org* 🎫 *$9* ⏲ *Tues.–Fri. 9:30–5, weekends 10–5.*

OFF THE BEATEN PATH

Southwest Museum. Readily spotted from the Pasadena Freeway (Highway 110), this huge Mission Revival building, now added to the National Register of Historic Places, stands halfway up Mt. Washington. The Southwest Museum and Library holds one of the nation's largest archive collections related to the American Indian. In addition, it has extensive display of pre-Hispanic, Spanish colonial, Latino, and Western American art and artifacts. Note: The museum is undergoing a massive repair and renovation makeover through 2011, so it is currently only open on weekends. ✉ *234 Museum Dr., Highland Park* ☎ *323/221–2164* 🌐 *www.southwestmuseum.org* 🎫 *Free* ⏲ *Weekends noon–5.*

5 Fodor's Choice ★ **Norton Simon Museum.** Long familiar to television viewers of the New Year's Day Rose Parade, this low-profile brown building is more than just a background for the passing floats. It's one of the finest small museums anywhere, with an excellent collection that spans more than 2,000 years of Western and Asian art. It all began in the 1950s when Norton Simon (Hunt-Wesson Foods, McCalls Corporation, and Canada Dry) started collecting the works of Degas, Renoir, Gauguin, and Cézanne. His collection grew to include old masters, impressionists, and modern works from Europe and Indian and Southeast Asian art. After he retired, Simon reorganized the failing Pasadena Art Institute and continued to assemble one of the world's finest collections.

Today the Norton Simon Museum is richest in works by Rembrandt, Goya, Picasso, and, most of all, Degas: this is one of the only two U.S. institutions to hold the complete set of the artist's model bronzes (the other is New York's Metropolitan Museum of Art). Renaissance, baroque, and rococo masterpieces include Raphael's profoundly spiritual *Madonna with Child with Book* (1503), Rembrandt's *Portrait of a Bearded Man in a Wide-Brimmed Hat* (1633), and a magical Tiepolo ceiling, *The Triumph of Virtue and Nobility Over Ignorance* (1740–50). The museum's collections of Impressionist (Van Gogh, Matisse, Cézanne, Monet, Renoir) and Cubist (Braque, Gris) works are extensive. Several Rodin sculptures are placed throughout the museum. Head down to the bottom floor to see rotating exhibits and phenomenal Southeast Asian and Indian sculptures and artifacts, where graceful pieces like a Ban Chiang blackware vessel date to well before 1000

BC. Don't miss a living artwork outdoors: the garden, conceived by noted southern California landscape designer Nancy Goslee Power. The tranquil pond was inspired by Monet's gardens at Giverny. ✉ *411 W. Colorado Blvd., Pasadena* ☎ *626/449–6840* 🌐 *www.nortonsimon.org* 🎟 *$8, free first Fri. of month 6–9* PM ⏲ *Wed., Thurs., and Sat.–Mon. noon–6, Fri. noon–9.*

2

6 ★ **Old Town Pasadena.** Once the victim of decay, the area was revitalized in the 1990s as a blend of restored 19th-century brick buildings with a contemporary overlay. A phalanx of chain stores has muscled in, but there are still some homegrown shops and plenty of tempting cafés and restaurants. In the evening and on weekends, streets are packed with people, and Old Town crackles with energy. The 12-block historic district is anchored along Colorado Boulevard between Pasadena Avenue and Arroyo Parkway.

NEED A BREAK?

Stop in Leonidas Chocolate Cafe (✉ *49 W. Colorado Blvd.* ☎ *626/577-7121*) for a cup of joe enriched with delectable Belgian chocolate. The "white hot cocoa," made with white chocolate, is creamy heaven. Or, to cool off, follow the intoxicating aroma of freshly pressed waffle cones to Tutti Gelati (✉ *62 W. Union St., No. 1* ☎ *626/440-9800*), an Italian gelateria behind Crate & Barrel on Colorado Boulevard. Flavors include zabaglione, *stracciatella* (chocolate chip), and hazelnut; many ingredients come directly from Milan, and everything is made on the premises.

8 **Pacific Asia Museum.** Devoted to the arts and culture of Asia and the Pacific Islands, this manageably sized museum displays changing exhibits drawn from its permanent collection of 17,000 works and artifacts. It's not the place for blockbuster shows—instead, you'll find modest displays of ceramics, calligraphy, textiles, traditional robes, and the like. The building itself is worth a look: it's inspired by Han Dynasty structures and surrounds a koi fishpond. ✉ *46 N. Los Robles Ave., Pasadena* ☎ *626/449–2742* 🌐 *www.pacificasiamuseum.org* 🎟 *$7, free 4th Fri. of month* ⏲ *Wed.–Sun. 10–6.*

9 **Pasadena Museum of California Art.** The first thing you see when you approach this museum is the graffiti-riddled parking structure. Was it vandalized by local taggers? Nope—it's the handiwork of artist George Kenny Scharf as part of this museum's dedication to all forms of Californian art, architecture, and design from 1850 to the present. The regularly changing exhibits are focused and thoughtfully presented; you might find anything from early California landscapes to contemporary works on car culture. Subject to closures for installations; call ahead. ✉ *490 E. Union St., Pasadena* ☎ *626/568–3665* 🌐 *www.pmcaonline.org* 🎟 *$7, free 1st Fri. of month* ⏲ *Wed.–Sun. noon–5.*

4 **Rose Bowl.** With an enormous rose, the city of Pasadena's logo, adorned on its exterior, it's hard to miss this 100,000-seat stadium, host of many Super Bowls and home to the UCLA Bruins. Set in Brookside Park at the wide bottom of an arroyo, the facility is closed except during games and special events such as the monthly Rose Bowl Flea Market, which is considered the granddaddy of West Coast flea markets. If you

want the best selection of items, show up early. People start arriving here at the crack of dawn, but note you will also pay a higher entry fee for having first dibs on the selection. The best bargaining takes place at the end of the day when vendors would rather settle for a few less dollars then have to lug their goods homes. ✉ *1001 Rose Bowl Dr. at Rosemont Ave., Pasadena* ☎ *626/577–3100* 🌐 *www.rosebowlstadium.com for flea market, www.rgcshows.com for shows* 🎫 *$7 from 9* AM *on, $10 for 8–9* AM *entrance, $15 for 7–8* AM *entrance* ⏲ *Flea market 2nd Sun. of month 9–3.*

OFF THE BEATEN PATH

Mission San Gabriel Archangel. Wondering where the Mission District got its name? Here's the answer. Established in 1771 as the fourth of 21 missions founded in California, this massive adobe complex was dedicated by Father Junípero Serra to St. Gabriel. Within the next 50 years, the San Gabriel Archangel became the wealthiest of all California missions. In 1833 the Mexican government confiscated the mission, allowing it to decline. The U.S. government returned the mission to the church in 1855, but by this time the Franciscans had departed. In 1908 the Claretian Missionaries took charge and poured much care into preserving the rich history. The cemetery here, the first in L.A. County, is said to contain approximately 6,000 Gabrieleno Indians. Tranquil grounds are lushly planted and filled with remnants of what life was like nearly two decades ago. The museum underwent a renovation in 2006 to further preserve the 1812 structure that originally served as the living space for the mission fathers. Public mass is held at the mission Sunday morning at 7 and 9:30. If you're lucky, you'll hear the six bells that ring out during special services—a truly arresting experience. You can take a self-guided tour of the grounds here by purchasing a map in the gift shop or come for History Day the first Saturday of the Month. Docent led tours are also available by appointment. ✉ *428 S. Mission Dr., San Gabriel* ☎ *626/457–3048* 🌐 *www.sangabrielmission.org* 🎫 *$5* ⏲ *Daily 9–4:30.*

❶ **Tournament House (Wrigley Mansion).** Chewing-gum magnate William Wrigley purchased this white Italian Renaissance–style house in 1914. Upon his wife's death in 1958, Wrigley donated the house to the city of Pasadena under the stipulation that it be used at the headquarters for the Tournament of Roses. The mansion features a green-tile roof and manicured rose garden with 1,500 floral varieties. The interior still provides a glimpse of the over-the-top style of the area in the early 20th century. Tours of the house last about an hour; fans of the Rose Parade will see the various crowns and tiaras worn by former Rose Queens, plus Rose Bowl related trophies and memorabilia. ✉ *391 S. Orange Grove Blvd., Pasadena* ☎ *626/449–4100* 🌐 *www.tournamentofroses.com* 🎫 *Free* ⏲ *Tours every Thurs. 2–4.*

LONG BEACH, SAN PEDRO, AND PALOS VERDES

The coastline south of Venice mellows into a string of low-key beach communities. Those around the bulge of the Palos Verdes Peninsula—including Redondo Beach, Palos Verdes Estates, and Rancho Palos Verdes—are collectively called the South Bay. Pacific Coast Highway dips inland, skimming above San Pedro and continuing to Long Beach at the tail end of Los Angeles County.

The hilly Palos Verdes Peninsula, an expensive, gentrified residential area, is edged with rocky cliffs and tide pools. Point Vicente, in Rancho Palos Verdes, is a good place for whale-watching during the gray whale migrations from January through March. The communities are zoned for horses, so you'll often see riders along the streets (they have the right of way). San Pedro, L.A.'s working harbor, is an old seaport community full of small 1920s-era white clapboards. Greek and Yugoslav markets and restaurants abound here, underlining the town's strong Mediterranean flavor. San Pedro and neighboring Wilmington are connected to Downtown Los Angeles by a narrow, 16-mi-long stretch of land, less than ½ mi wide in most places, annexed in the late 19th century to preserve Los Angeles's transportation and shipping interests. ■ TIP→ **Unfortunately, gang activity sometimes flares up in San Pedro, especially around Cabrillo Beach, so avoid walking around here at night.**

Long Beach, long stuck in limbo between Los Angeles and Orange County in the minds of visitors, is steadily rebuilding its place in the Southern California scheme. Founded as a seaside resort in the 19th century, the city boomed in the early 20th century as oil discoveries drew in Midwesterners and Dust Bowlers. Bust followed boom and the city took on a somewhat raw, industrial, neglected feel. But a long-term redevelopment plan begun in the 1970s has finally come to fruition, turning the city back to its resort roots.

WHAT TO SEE

❷ ★ **Aquarium of the Pacific.** Sea lions, nurse sharks, and octopuses, oh my!—this aquarium focuses primarily on ocean life from the Pacific Ocean, with a detour into Australian birds. The main exhibits include lively sea lions, a crowded tank of various sharks, and ethereal sea dragons, which the aquarium has successfully bred in captivity. Most impressive is the multimedia attraction, *Whales: A Journey With Giants*. This panoramic film shows in the aquarium's Great Hall, and when the entire core of the aquarium goes dark, you suddenly feel as if you're swimming with the giants. Ask for showtimes at the information desk. For a nonaquatic experience, head over to Lorikeet Forest, a walk-in aviary full of the friendliest parrots from down under. Buy a cup of nectar and smile as you become a human bird perch. Since these birds spend most of their day feeding, you're guaranteed a noisy—and possibly messy—encounter. (A sink, soap, and towels are strategically placed at the exhibit exit.) If you're a true animal lover, book an up-close-and-personal Animal Encounters Tour ($90) to learn about and assist in care and feeding of the animals; or find out how aquarium functions with the extensive Behind the Scenes Tour ($34.95). ✉ *100 Aquarium Way, Long Beach* ☎ *562/590–3100* 🌐 *www.aquariumofpacific.org* 🎫 *$23.95* ⏲ *Daily 9–6.*

WORD OF MOUTH

"You might check out the Cabrillo Marine Aquarium. It is smaller in scale but for little kids it is the perfect size (admission is free but they do accept donations). It is located right on the water (Cabrillo Coast Park) where you can walk on the trails to tide-pools, salt marshes, and of course the beach. Bring a picnic lunch and make a day of it (there is a playground there as well)."
—overyonder

9 **Cabrillo Marine Aquarium.** Dedicated to the marine life that flourishes off the southern California coast, this Frank Gehry–designed center gives an intimate and instructive look at local sea creatures. Head to the Exploration Center and S. Mark Taper Foundation Courtyard for kid-friendly interactive exhibits and activity stations. Especially fun is the "Crawl In" aquarium, where you can be surrounded by fish without getting wet. **TIP→ From March through July the aquarium organizes a legendary grunion program, when you can see the small, silvery fish as they come ashore at night to spawn on the beach.** After visiting the museum, you can stop for a picnic or beach stroll along Cabrillo Beach. ✉ *3720 Stephen M. White Dr., San Pedro* ☎ *310/548–7562* 🌐 *www.cabrilloaq.org* 🎫 *$5 suggested donation, parking available in adjacent lot at reduced rate of $1 for museumgoers* ⏲ *Tues.–Fri. noon–5, weekends 10–5.*

OFF THE BEATEN PATH

General Phineas Banning Residence Museum and Banning Park. General Phineas Banning, an early entrepreneur in Los Angeles, is credited with developing the Los Angeles Harbor into a viable economic entity and naming the area Wilmington (he was from Delaware). Part of his estate has been preserved in this 20-acre park. (The picnicking possibilities here are excellent.) A 100-year-old wisteria, near the arbor, blooms in spring. You can see the interior of the house on an hour-long, docent-led tour that take you through each room and fills you in on how Banning conducted business from his home office, peered over his land from the top tower, entertained his guests, and kept his family in the most luxurious creature comforts of the day. The nearby gift shop offers crafts and decorative boutique items. ✉ *401 E. M St., Wilmington* ☎ *310/548–7777* 🌐 *www.banningmuseum.org* 🎫 *Suggested donation for tours $5* ⏲ *Guided tours Tues.–Thurs. 12:30, 1:30, and 2:30, weekends 12:30, 1:30, 2:30, and 3:30.*

5 **Long Beach Museum of Art.** This museum fills a charming 1912 shingle-clad Arts and Crafts estate and an adjacent gallery with a small but captivating collection of Californian modernist works and landscapes. You might find it hard to tear yourself away from the stunning ocean view from the terrace, though. But don't overlook the Children's Art Gallery; it has some especially lively pieces. ✉ *2300 E. Ocean Blvd., Long Beach* ☎ *562/439–2119* 🌐 *www.lbma.org* 🎫 *$7, free Fri.* ⏲ *Tues.–Sun. 11–5.*

A GOOD TOUR

Numbers correspond to the Long Beach, San Pedro, and Palos Verdes map.

Because a single drive around these three areas would encompass more than 100 mi, it's best to approach the area on two separate trips; both include a visit to an aquarium. If you're new here, Long Beach will likely be the more appealing pick.

Begin a tour of Long Beach at what is still the city's most famous attraction, the art deco ship the **Queen Mary** ❶. Then take the Queens Way Bridge back across the bay to the **Aquarium of the Pacific** ❷. From here, stops along Shoreline Drive at **Rainbow Harbor** ❸ or the colorfully painted waterfront shopping center, Shoreline Village, give the best views of the harbor and the Long Beach skyline. At Ocean Boulevard, Shoreline Drive turns into Alamitos Avenue. Continue on Alamitos to the corner of 7th Street and the **Museum of Latin American Art (MoLAA)** ❹. Return to Ocean Boulevard and turn east. Just past the commercial district lie the **Long Beach Museum of Art** ❺ and grand old homes dating from the early 1900s. From Ocean Boulevard, turn onto Livingston Drive and then 2nd Street to drive through Belmont Shores before arriving at Alamitos Bay and **Naples** ❻, a picturesque enclave of canals and marinas, and the place to take a gondola ride.

For an overview of Palos Verdes and San Pedro, begin at the Point Vicente Lighthouse, at Palos Verdes Drive and Hawthorne Boulevard. The lighthouse has stood here since 1926 and it's also a great spot for whale-watching between January and March. Nearby is Point Vicente Park, where you'll have a postcard view of the ocean. From there, take a leisurely coastline drive south on Palos Verdes Drive. Two miles down, on your left, you'll see the all-glass **Wayfarers Chapel** ❼. Continue south and you'll hit San Pedro and Los Angeles Harbor. Follow the signs to Cabrillo Beach, where you'll find the **Cabrillo Marine Aquarium** ❾. From here it's a quick hop over to **Ports O' Call** ❽ for a bite to eat and a stroll around this vibrant port.

TIMING

In Long Beach, guided tours of the *Queen Mary* last about an hour. If you've planned in advance, you could end the day with a sunset gondola cruise on the canals in Naples. If you have kids in tow, expect to stay at least an hour at either the Long Beach or San Pedro aquariums. Don't forget to factor in 15 to 20 minutes' driving time between attractions, and remember that the museums and the Cabrillo Marine Aquarium are closed on Monday. If you're here anytime from January through March, you might be able to squeeze in some whale-watching during the gray whale migration.

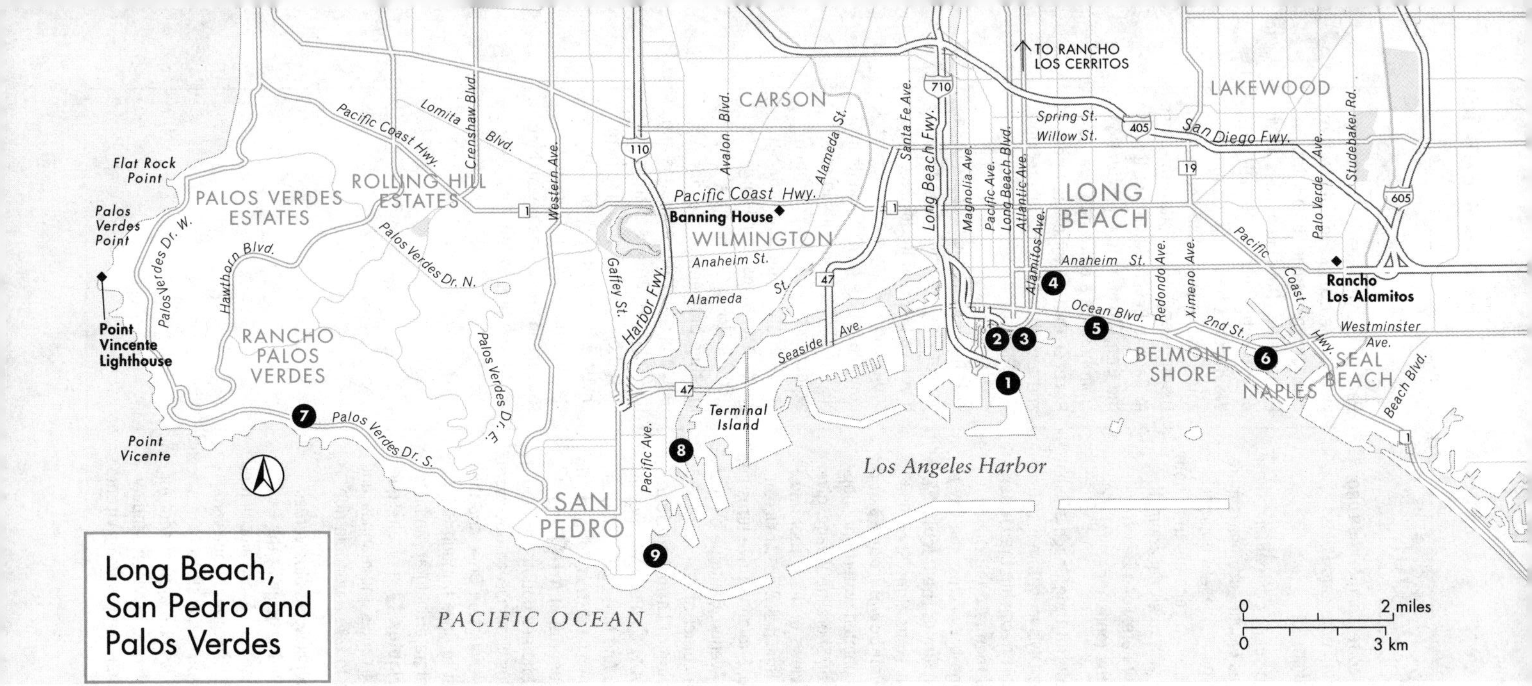

Long Beach, San Pedro and Palos Verdes

Aquarium of the Pacific 2
Cabrillo Marine Aquarium 9
Long Beach Museum of Art 5
Museum of Latin American Art (MoLAA) 4
Naples 6
Ports O'Call 8
Queen Mary 1
Rainbow Harbor 3
Wayfarers Chapel 7

NEED A BREAK?

Stroll seaside to the Long Beach Museum of Art and grab a water-view table under a yellow umbrella at Claire's at the Museum (✉ ***2300 E. Ocean Blvd.*** ☎ ***562/439–2119 Ext. 237*****). Here you can grab a bite to eat or indulge in one of the signature desserts. Plan your visit in time for sunset on the weekends when the café closes at 5 PM and you'll have a front row view of the stunning, fire-red skies across the bay.**

2

❹ **Museum of Latin American Art (MoLAA).** After three years of massive renovation work, this museum—the only one of its kind on the West Coast devoted exclusively to contemporary art from Mexico and Central and South America—expanded its exhibit space to 55,000 square feet and added a sculpture garden, a new gift store, a film-screening room, a research library, and art lab for classes. The result is an elegant space with splashes of bold color that reflects the vibrant Latin American culture. Rotating exhibits of large canvas fine art and sculptures reflect a diverse range of emotions and statements. Name markers also provide information on each artist's country of origin. The museum gift store features carved masks, textiles, and other work by local and Latin American artists. Admission includes an informative audio tour. ✉ *628 Alamitos Ave., Long Beach* ☎ *562/437–1689* 🌐 *www.molaa.org* 🎫 *$9, free Sun.* 🕑 *Wed.–Sun. 11–5.*

❻ **Naples.** If you can't quite make it to Italy, say, "buongiorno" to Naples in Long Beach! Consisting of three small islands in man-made Alamitos Bay, Naples features rows of quaint (but high-price) homes, each boasting its own eclectic architecture: vintage Victorians, Craftsman bungalows, and Mission Revivals. No cars in these front driveways, just boats ranging from lofty yachts to pedal rafts. To reach the area, park near Bay Shore Avenue and 2nd Street and walk across the bridge to meander amongst the streets with Italian names. To make your experience "molto buono," take a tour on a gondola through the canals by making a reservation (at least a week in advance) with **Gondola Getaway** (✉ *5437 E. Ocean Blvd., Naples, Long Beach* ☎ *562/433–9595* 🌐 *www.gondo.net*). The one-hour rides, upon authentic Venetian boats, take you through Naples in pure Italian style as the gondoliers treat you to a smooth water journey using the one oar "rowing" technique. You'll greet passing gondolas with a friendly "Ciao!" They may even sing you an Italian love song as the rides are quite popular with romantic couples, but groups of up to 16 people can be accommodated. Bread, salami, and cheese are served—you bring the wine. Rides cost $75 per couple, $20 each additional person, and run from 11 AM to 11 PM.

❽ **Ports O' Call.** The cluster of buildings aims its restaurants and gift shops squarely at tourists, but locals can be lured here, too, especially for the harbor cruises. It's a great place to catch a boat for a whale-watching cruise or a trip out to Catalina. A stroll down this lively strip, along the Port of Los Angeles' Main Channel, leads you to the **Maritime Museum** (✉ *Berth 84, at end of 6th St., San Pedro* ☎ *310/548–7618* 🌐 *www.lamaritimemuseum.org* 🎫 *$3* 🕑 *Tues.–Sat. 10–5, Sun. noon–5*), which displays more than 700 ship and boat models and a large collection of navigational gear. ✉ *1100 Nagoya Way, Berth 77, San Pedro* ☎ *310/548–8076.*

1 ***Queen Mary.*** There's a saying among staff members that the more you get to know the *Queen Mary,* the more you realize that she has an endearing personality to match her wealth of history. The beautifully preserved ocean liner was launched in 1934 and made 1,001 transatlantic crossings before finally berthing in Long Beach in 1967. It has gone through many periods of renovations since, but in 1993, the RMS Foundation took over ownership and restored its original art deco style. Private investors "Save the Queen" took over in early 2008 with plans to oversee ongoing renovations.

On board, you can take one of five tours, such as the informative Behind the Scenes walk or the downright spooky Ghost and Legends tour. (Spirits have been spotted in the pool and engine room.) You could stay for dinner at one of the ship's restaurants, partake in the utterly English tradition of afternoon tea ($35–$40, monthly themes, call for reservations ☎ *562/499–1772*), or even spend the night in one of the wood-paneled rooms. The ship's neighbor, a geodesic dome originally built to house Howard Hughes's *Spruce Goose* aircraft, now serves as a terminal for Carnival Cruise Lines, making the *Queen Mary* the perfect pit stop before or after a cruise. And anchored next to the *Queen* is the *Scorpion,* a Russian submarine you can tour for a look at Cold War history. ✉ *1126 Queens Hwy., Long Beach* ☎ *562/435–3511* 🌐 *www.queenmary.com* 🎟 *Tours $24.95–$31.95, includes a self-guided audio tour* ⏲ *Call for times and frequency of guided tours.*

3 **Rainbow Harbor.** In the quest to generate some commercial gold, this segment of the waterfront has been developed to complement Long Beach's other harbor attractions. The brightly painted clusters of restaurants, boutiques, and souvenir stores that make up **Shoreline Village** (✉ *Shoreline Dr. and Shoreline Village Rd., Long Beach* ☎ *562/435–2668*) cap the area to the east. You can rent surreys, bikes, sailboats, or Jet Skis here; the Pelican Pier Pavilion has a small carousel and arcade games. The **Pike at Rainbow Harbor** is a stucco-clad collection of uninspired shops and restaurants found in malls across America. Depending on the season and day of the week, Rainbow Harbor is also the place to catch the city's AquaBus water shuttle to the *Queen Mary.* ✉ *Shoreline Dr. between Aquarium of Pacific and Shoreline Village, Long Beach* 🌐 *www.thepikeatlongbeach.com.*

OFF THE BEATEN PATH

Rancho Los Alamitos Historic Ranch and Gardens. One of the country's oldest adobe one-story domestic buildings still standing, this landmark was built circa 1800, when the Spanish flag still flew over California. Docents lead guided tours of the ranch house and barnyard; there is a working blacksmith shop in the barn and a stable of farm animals that include draft horses, sheep, and goats, plus four acres of lush, colorful gardens to wonder through. Take note, however, that the barns area is undergoing major restoration through 2010, some areas may be closed and most livestock will be boarded off site during construction. Call ahead for updates. ✉ *6400 E. Bixby Hill Rd., enter at guard gate at Palo Verde and Anaheim Sts., Long Beach* ☎ *562/431–3541* 🌐 *www.rancholosalamitos.com* 🎟 *Donation suggested* ⏲ *Wed.–Sun. 1–5; free 90-min tour every ½ hr 1–4.*

7 ★ **Wayfarers Chapel.** A look at this stunning, all-glass Swedenborgian church is practically guaranteed to fill you with awe. Built in 1949 by architect Lloyd Wright (son of Frank Lloyd Wright), it intentionally blends in with the trees and lush garden setting on the Palos Verdes Peninsula. The flower-filled garden includes a number of plants that are mentioned in the Bible. On a clear day you can see straight across the ocean to Catalina Island. Little wonder the church is a very popular wedding destination; you'll see tributes to this in the dedication bricks along the Walk of Honor. ✉ *5755 Palos Verdes Dr. S, Rancho Palos Verdes* ☎ *310/377–1650* 🌐 *www.wayfarerschapel.org* ⏲ *Daily 8–5.*

Where to Eat

WORD OF MOUTH

"The Restaurant at the Getty Center is very good, and a most-memorable setting. Make a reservation if you're there on a Saturday, go up to the Museum late late afternoon and stay for a sunset dinner. On other days the restaurant is only open for lunch."

—clarkgriswold

www.fodors.com/community

By Roger J. Grody

CELEBRITY IS BIG BUSINESS IN LOS ANGELES, so it's no accident the concept of the celebrity chef—emerging from the kitchen to schmooze with an even more famous clientele—is a key part of the local dining scene. Wolfgang Puck, the city's most illustrious celebrity chef, can still be found exchanging air kisses with Oscar-winning guests at Spago, but a new generation of culinary stars—David Myers (Sona, Comme Ça), Suzanne Goin (Lucques, A.O.C.), Neal Fraser (Grace, BLD), Gino Angelini (Angelini Osteria, La Terza)—have taken center stage and some talented twentysomething understudies are waiting in the wings. Suddenly, transcontinental superstars Mario Batali (Pizzeria Mozza, Osteria Mozza), Tom Colicchio (Craft), and Laurent Tourondel (BLT Steak) are giving L.A.'s dining scene a taste of the Big Apple, while Todd English collaborates with *Desperate Housewives* star Eva Longoria Parker in Latin-theme Beso. San Francisco-based chef Michael Mina arrives on the Sunset Strip with his flashy XIV, and Great Britain's colorful Gordon Ramsay expands his global empire with West Hollywood's Gordon Ramsay at the London. Longtime local favorite Michel Richard has returned to Hollywood with Citrus at Social, and his fellow Washington, D.C., celebrity chef José Andrés shows off contemporary Spanish cuisine at the Bazaar by José Andrés, adjacent to Bevely Hills.

The culinary riches are hardly limited to Beverly Hills, with West Hollywood and Santa Monica now grabbing much of the spotlight. Furthermore, long-forgotten Hollywood and Downtown L.A. are experiencing dramatic renaissances that have captured the imagination of pioneering restaurateurs. Even smaller communities like Culver City and South Pasadena are emerging as important dining destinations. Casual L.A. doesn't rival New York in terms of luxe dining rooms, but its strategic location contributes to an imaginative native cuisine that takes full advantage of California's bountiful countryside. The availability of fresh seasonal ingredients from regional farms is the bedrock of California cuisine and a growing emphasis on organic and sustainable practices further enhances the role of local growers, ranchers, and fishermen. Artisanal producers dominate L.A.'s farmers' markets, where home cooks browse shoulder-to-shoulder with acclaimed chefs. (*See* Chapter 7 for a rundown on local markets.)

As a bona fide capital of the Pacific Rim, L.A. absorbs exotic culinary influences from its diverse Asian communities. In suburban San Gabriel Valley, dim sum palaces rival those in Hong Kong, while West L.A. has become one of the best places for sushi outside of Tokyo. High-end sushi bars, serving both traditional and cutting-edge fare, are now being joined by pub-like izakayas showcasing other styles of Japanese cuisine. And suddenly, Korean cooking has stepped out of Koreatown to become a sizzling-hot mainstream favorite. A gateway to Latin America, L.A.'s varied Latino communities add further depth to the local food scene. French-trained chefs incorporate ingredients and techniques from El Salvador, Colombia, and Peru, while discovering that Mexico's diverse regional traditions hold promising secrets for culinary innovation.

Reservations

Keep in mind that they're nearly always advisable and are absolutely essential at many of the city's trendier venues. While making your reservation, inquire about parking. You'll find most places, except small mom-and-pop establishments, provide valet parking at dinner for reasonable rates (often under $5 plus tip).

Dress

Dining out in Los Angeles tends to be a casual affair, and even at some of the most expensive restaurants you're likely to see customers in jeans (although this is not necessarily considered in good taste). It's extremely rare for L.A. restaurants to actually require a jacket and tie, but all of the city's more formal establishments appreciate a gentleman who dons a jacket—let your good judgment be your guide.

Smoking

Smokers should keep in mind that California law forbids smoking in all enclosed areas, including bars. Smoking is not necessarily permitted even on patios, so call ahead to find out a restaurant's policy.

Health and Safety

All restaurants in Los Angeles County—everything from hole-in-the-wall take-out joints to opulent dining rooms—are required to post the letter grade (A, B, or C) on the premises that reflects the score received from Los Angeles County health officials, who regularly inspect kitchen and storage facilities. Establishments that fail are closed until the deficiencies are corrected.

WHAT IT COSTS

¢	$	$$	$$$	$$$$
Restaurants				
under $7	$7–$12	$12–$22	$22–$32	over $32

Prices are per person for a main course or equivalent combination of smaller plates (e.g., tapas, sushi), excluding 8.25% sales tax.

Dining Hours

Despite its veneer of decadence, L.A. is not a particularly late-night city for eating. (The reenergized Hollywood dining scene is emerging as a notable exception.) The peak dinner times are from 7 to 9, and most restaurants won't take reservations after 10 PM. Unless otherwise noted, the restaurants listed in this guide are open daily for lunch and dinner. Generally speaking, restaurants are closed either Sunday or Monday; a few are shuttered both days. Most places—even the upscale spots—are open for lunch on weekdays, since plenty of Hollywood megadeals are conceived at that time.

Wine

L.A. is an extremely wine-friendly city. Although some profit-conscious restaurateurs resist, most are happy to assess a relatively modest corkage fee (typically $10 to $25 per bottle, sometimes less) for diners who bring their own wine. However, you should avoid bringing anything you would expect to find on the restaurant's wine list or anything too ordinary. Courtesy also demands that you offer the sommelier or your server a taste of what you've brought.

BEST BETS FOR L.A. DINING

With thousands of restaurants to choose from, how will you decide where to eat? Fodor's writers and editors have selected their favorite restaurants by price, cuisine, and experience in the Best Bets lists below. You can also search by neighborhood—just peruse the following pages to find specific details about a restaurant in the full reviews later in the chapter.

Fodor's Choice★

Angelini Osteria $$, p. 130
A.O.C. $$, p. 129
The Apple Pan ¢, p. 151
Asanebo $$$, p. 154
Citrus at Social $$$, p. 121
CUT $$$$, p. 117
The Dining Room $$$$, p. 157
Gordon Ramsay at The London $$$$, p. 132
Mélisse $$$$, p. 148
Mimosa $$, p. 133
Mori Sushi $$$, p. 152
Patina $$$$, p. 138
Philippe the Original ¢, p. 138
Pizzeria Mozza $$, p. 120
Providence $$$$, p. 126
Saddle Peak Lodge $$$, p. 153
Sona $$$$, p. 134
Spago Beverly Hills $$$$, p. 119
Urasawa $$$$, p. 120
Valentino $$$, p. 149
Yujean Kang's Gourment Chinese Cuisine $$, p. 159

By Price

¢

The Apple Pan, p. 151
Philippe the Original, p. 138

$

Bombay Café, p. 151
La Serenata Gourmet, p. 152

$$

Angelini Osteria, p. 130
A.O.C., p. 129
Beacon, p. 141
Café Bizou, p. 153
Fraîche, p. 144
Mimosa, p. 133
Ocean Star, p. 156
Osteria Mozza, p. 126
Pecorino, p. 139
Pizzeria Mozza, p. 120
Yujean Kang's Gourmet Chinese Cuisine, p. 159

$$$

All' Angelo, p. 121
Asanebo, p. 154
The Bazaar by José Andrés, p. 116
Citrus at Social, p. 121
Comme Ça, p. 131
Craft, p. 120
The Foundry, p. 131
XIV, p. 132
Hatfield's, p. 132
Hokusai, p. 118
La Cachette, p. 120
Lucques, p. 133
Matsuhisa, p. 119
Mori Sushi, p. 152
Saddle Peak Lodge, p. 153
Traxx, p. 138
Valentino, p. 149
Water Grill, p. 138
Wa Sushi & Bistro, p. 134

$$$$

Campanile, p. 131
CUT, p. 117
The Dining Room, p. 157
Gordon Ramsay at The London, p. 132
Mélisse, p. 148
Ortolan, p. 134
Patina, p. 138
Providence, p. 126
Sona, p. 134
Spago Beverly Hills, p. 119
Urasawa, p. 120

By Cuisine

AMERICAN

Apple Pan ¢, p. 151
Philippe the Original ¢, p. 138

CHINESE

Ocean Star $$, p. 156
Yujean Kang's Gourmet Chinese Cuisine $$, p. 159

FRENCH

Café Bizou $$, p. 153
Comme Ça $$$, p. 131
La Cachette $$$, p. 120
Mélisse $$$$, p. 148
Mimosa $$, p. 133
Ortolan $$$$, p. 134
Patina $$$$, p. 138

INDIAN

Bombay Café $, p. 151

ITALIAN

All' Angelo $$, p. 121
Angelini Osteria $$, p. 130
Osteria Mozza $$, p. 126
Pecorino $$, p. 139
Pizzeria Mozza $$, p. 120
Valentino $$$, p. 149

JAPANESE

Asanebo $$$, p. 154
Hokusai $$$, p. 118
Matsuhisa $$$, p. 119
Mori Sushi $$$, p. 152
Urasawa $$$$, p. 120
Wa Sushi & Bistro $$$, p. 134

KOREAN

Gyenari $$, p. 144

MEDITERRANEAN

A.O.C. $$, p. 129
Campanile $$$$, p. 131
Fraîche $$, p. 144

MEXICAN

La Serenata Gourmet $, p. 152
Monte Alban $, p. 152

NEW AMERICAN

Citrus at Social $$$$, p. 121
Craft $$$, p. 120
The Dining Room $$$$, p. 157
The Foundry $$$, p. 131
XIV $$$, p. 132
Hatfield's $$$, p. 132
Lucques $$$, p. 133
Saddle Peak Lodge $$$, p. 153
Sona $$$$, p. 134
Spago Beverly Hills $$$$, p. 119
Traxx $$$, p. 138

SEAFOOD

Providence $$$$, p. 126
Water Grill $$$, p. 138

SPANISH

Bar Pintxo $, p. 146
The Bazaar by José Andrés $$$, p. 116
Cobras & Matadors $$, p. 131

STEAKHOUSE

BLT Steak $$$$, p. 130
CUT $$$$, p. 117
Nic & Stef's Steakhouse $$$, p. 136

VIETNAMESE

Crustacean $$$, p. 116
Gingergrass $, p. 129

By Experience

BAR SCENE

The Foundry $$$, p. 131
Fraîche $$, p. 144
Blue Velvet $$$, p. 135

Nobu Malibu $$$, p. 145

BRUNCH

The Belvedere $$$$, p. 116
Hotel Bel-Air $$$$, p. 139
Campanile $$$$, p. 131

CELEB-SPOTTING

Craft $$$, p. 120
CUT $$$$, p. 117
The Grill on the Alley $$$, p. 118
Nobu Malibu $$$, p. 145
Spago Beverly Hills $$$$, p. 119
Matsushisa $$$, p. 119

CHILD-FRIENDLY

Fred 62 ¢, p. 127
Philippe the Original ¢, p. 138

GOOD FOR GROUPS

A.O.C. $$, p. 129
Beacon $$, p. 141
Craft $$$, p. 120
XIV $$$, p. 132
Gordon Ramsay at The London $$$$, p. 132
Ocean Star $$, p. 156

GREAT VIEW

Beau Rivage $$, p. 145
Blue Velvet $$$, p. 135
Encounter $$, p. 145
Gladstone's Malibu $$$, p. 145

HISTORIC

Campanile $$$$, p. 131
Cicada $$$, p. 135
Engine Co. No. 28 $$, p. 135
Musso & Frank Grill $$, p. 125
Philippe the Original ¢, p. 138
Traxx $$$, p. 138

LATE-NIGHT DINING

Canter's ¢, p. 131
XIV $$$, p. 132
Fred 62 ¢, p. 127
Kate Mantilini $$, p. 118
25 Degrees $, p. 127

MOST ROMANTIC

Cicada $$$, p. 135
La Cachette $$$, p. 120
Mélisse $$$, p. 148
Patina $$$$, p. 138
Saddle Peak Lodge $$$, p. 153

BEVERLY HILLS, CENTURY CITY, AND HOLLYWOOD

BEVERLY HILLS

$–$$ AMERICAN ✕**Barney Greengrass.** Unlike your corner lox-and-bagel joint, this *haute* deli on the fifth floor of Barneys department store has an appropriately runway-ready aesthetic: limestone floors, mahogany furniture, and a wall of windows. On the outdoor terrace, at tables shaded by large umbrellas, you can savor flawless smoked salmon, sturgeon, and whitefish flown in fresh from New York. The deli closes at 6 PM. ✉*Barneys, 9570 Wilshire Blvd., Beverly Hills* ☎*310/777–5877* ▭*AE, DC, MC, V.*

$$$–$$$$ SPANISH ★ ✕**The Bazaar by José Andrés.** Celebrity Spanish chef José Andrés conquers L.A. with a multifaceted concept that includes two dining rooms (one old-school, one modern, each with a tapas bar), a cocktail bar stocked with liquid nitrogen, and a flashy pâtisserie. There are even roaming pushcarts dispensing foie gras wrapped in cotton candy. Half of the menu is dedicated to traditional Spanish tapas: creamy chicken croquetas, bacalao (salt cod) fritters with honey aïoli, and plates of chorizo or prized jamón Ibérico. The other half involves some wild inventions of molecular gastronomy inspired by Andrés' former mentor Ferran Adrià of world-famous El Bulli restaurant. Among the latter are "liquid" olives (created through a technique called spherification), and an ethereal version of the traditional tortilla Española in which an egg is cooked very slowly at 63 degrees, just short of coagulation. A splendid list of Spanish wines is offered, and for dessert, items like beet meringue with pistachios and chocolate lollipops await. ✉*SLS Hotel at Beverly Hills, 465 S. La Cienega Blvd., Beverly Hills* ☎*310/246–5555* 🌐*www.thebazaar.com* ✍*Reservations essential* ▭*AE, D, DC, MC, V.*

$$$$ AMERICAN ✕**The Belvedere.** In the entertainment industry's A-list hotel, the Peninsula, you're sure to be rubbing elbows with power brokers. The refined cooking here elevates the opulent Belvedere far above the usual hotel dining room. You may want to start with the signature house-smoked salmon with scallion pancakes and chive crème fraîche and caviar, then indulge in grilled Alaskan halibut with pomegranate gastrique, osso bucco, or Kansas City strip steak. At lunch, deal makers convene over whimsical small bites (e.g., tuna and hamachi lollipops with mango-sesame sauce), salads, and glamburgers like sautéed salmon with pinot noir–cured onions. Of course, the execs who favor this place are prone to special ordering—and the staff graciously obliges. ✉*9882 S. Santa Monica Blvd., Beverly Hills* ☎*310/788–2306* 🌐*www.peninsula.com* ▭*AE, D, DC, MC, V.*

$$$–$$$$ VIETNAMESE ✕**Crustacean.** A perennially hot scene, this head-turning venue of San Francisco's An family is a surreal reproduction of colonial Vietnam. Exotic fish swim in a floor-to-ceiling aquarium and through a glass-topped "river," sunk into the marble floor, which meanders toward the bar. The French-influenced Southeast Asian menu includes lemongrass-scented bouillabaisse and filet mignon with ponzu glaze. Colossal tiger prawns and whole Dungeness crab simmered in sake, chardonnay, and cognac parade out of the "secret kitchen" (a kitchen-within-a-kitchen to which access is strictly limited to An family members, thereby protecting treasured recipes). ✉*9646 Santa Monica Blvd., Beverly Hills*

☎310/205–8990 🌐*www.anfamily.com* *Reservations essential* *AE, D, DC, MC, V* *Closed Sun. No lunch weekends.*

$$$$ STEAKHOUSE Fodor's Choice ★ ✕ **CUT.** In a true collision of artistic titans, celebrity chef Wolfgang Puck presents his take on steak house cuisine in a space designed by Getty Center architect Richard Meier. Its contemporary lines and cold surfaces recall little of the home comforts of this beloved culinary tradition. And like Meier's design, Puck's fare doesn't dwell much on the past, and a thoroughly modern crab Louis is the closest thing to nostalgia on the menu. Playful dishes like bone marrow flan take center stage before delving into genuine Japanese Kobe beef or a perfect dry-aged hunk of Nebraskan sirloin that proves the Austrian-born superchef understands our quintessentially American love affair. ✉*Regent Beverly Wilshire, 9500 Wilshire Blvd., Beverly Hills* ☎*310/276–8500* 🌐*www.wolfgangpuck.com* *Reservations essential* *AE, D, DC, MC, V* *Closed Sun. No lunch.*

$–$$ ITALIAN ✕ **Da Pasquale.** In the land of Gucci, an affordable meal is harder to spot than a pair of sensible shoes. And that's one reason to visit Da Pasquale. An even better reason is the wonderful thin-crust pizza topped with ingredients like fresh tomato, garlic, and basil or three cheeses and prosciutto. The kitchen also excels at familiar pastas and roasted chicken. Despite talent-agency regulars, the homey Old Napoli interior and friendly staff make everybody feel welcome. ✉*9749 S. Santa Monica Blvd.,Beverly Hills* ☎*310/859–3884* 🌐*www.dapasqualecaffe.com* *AE, MC, V* *Closed Sun. and Mon. No lunch Sat.*

$$–$$$ ITALIAN ✕ **Enoteca Drago.** High-flying Sicilian chef Celestino Drago scores with this sleek but unpretentious version of an *enoteca* (a wine bar serving small snacks). It's an ideal spot for skipping through an Italian wine list—more than 50 wines are available by the glass—and enjoying a menu made up of small plates such as stuffed olives, an assortment of cheeses and *salumi,* ricotta-stuffed zucchini flowers, or *crudo* (Italy's answer to ceviche) from the raw bar. Although the miniature mushroom-filled ravioli bathed in foie gras–truffle sauce is a bit luxurious for an enoteca, it's one of the city's best pasta dishes. Larger portions and pizzas are also available here, but the essence of an enoteca is preserved. ✉*410 N. Cañon Dr., Beverly Hills* ☎*310/786–8236* 🌐*www.celestinodrago.com* *Reservations essential* *AE, DC, MC, V.*

$$$$ BRAZILIAN ✕ **Fogo de Chão.** *Churrascarias* (Brazilian steak houses) are suddenly the norm in L.A. and Fogo de Chão is one of the best, with an elegant spin on the traditional meat fest. Start at the buffet, helping yourself to salads and sides. Back at your table, use the marker to signal for service; turn it to green and servers dressed as gauchos speed over with beautifully barbecued meats, carving them onto your plate from swordlike spits. There are about 15 different kinds of beef, chicken, lamb, and pork to try—when you're ready to admit defeat, turn the marker to red. The dining room itself recalls a fine steak house with a hint of Vegas: white linen–topped tables, wooden wine racks, massive murals, and fountains. ✉*133 N. La Cienega Blvd., Beverly Hills* ☎*310/289–7755* 🌐*www.fogodechao.com* *Reservations essential* *AE, D, DC, MC, V* *No lunch weekends.*

3

$$$–$$$$ AMERICAN

The Grill on the Alley. Beverly Hills restaurants can take you many places, from Provence to Polynesia, but in this case it's just up the Golden State Freeway to a traditional San Francisco–style grill with dark-wood paneling and brass trim. This clubby chophouse, where movie industry execs power-lunch creates tasty, simple American fare, including steaks, chicken potpies, and Cobb salad. If you've really made it in Hollywood, you've got your usual booth at The Grill. ✉ *9560 Dayton Way, Beverly Hills* ☎ *310/276–0615* 🌐 *www.thegrill.com* *Reservations essential* 💳 *AE, DC, MC, V* ⏲ *No lunch Sun.*

$$–$$$ JAPANESE ★

Hokusai. The superb, artfully crafted sushi (served with a houseblended soy sauce) is just part of the story at Hokusai, whose menu reflects a pronounced Gallic influence. You are just as likely to find sautéed foie gras, a slow-braised Kobe beef cheek stew resembling French daube or filet mignon in classic truffle–infused Périgueux sauce next to an order of melt-in-your-mouth toro sashimi with Maui onions. The intimate candlelit space, with sleek bar and black linen-topped tables, is artsy and seductive. Hokusai's staff demonstrates a refreshing desire to please, unlike some other Beverly Hills hot spots. ✉ *8400 Wilshire Blvd., Beverly Hills* ☎ *323/782–9717* 🌐 *www.hokusairestaurant.com* *Reservations essential* 💳 *AE, DC, MC, V* ⏲ *Closed Sun. No lunch Sat.*

$$–$$$ AMERICAN

Kate Mantilini. Casual but cool, this is a good place to remember for breakfast on weekends or for a late-night snack (open until midnight on weekends). The lengthy menu lines up all-American staples like New England clam chowder, macaroni and cheese, meat loaf, and a white chili made with white beans and chicken. Despite its truck stop/diner–style comfort food, the cavernous ultramodern space exudes a hip urban vibe and prices are much more Beverly Hills than *Smallville.* ✉ *9101 Wilshire Blvd., Beverly Hills* ☎ *310/278–3699* 🌐 *www.gardensonglendon.com* 💳 *AE, DC, MC, V.*

$$ JAPANESE

Luckyfish. In Japan, kaiten sushi—a system in which plates are plucked off conveyor belts at inexpensive sushi bars—appeals to businesspeople short on time and students short on cash. At Luckyfish, the concept is enhanced with a hip, trend-conscious setting and crisp table service, but the essence of the experience, which showcases a wide selection of value-oriented sushi, sashimi and rolls, remains intact. The quality of the preassembled dishes—here each plate is embedded with a microchip to ensure nothing stays on the meandering belt too long—is surprisingly high, and cooked items like seared toro and skewers of Kobe beef are prepared upon request. ✉ *338 N. Cañon Dr., Beverly Hills* ☎ 310/274–9800 🌐 *www.luckyfishsushi.com* 💳 *AE, D, DC, MC, V* ⏲ *No lunch Sun.*

$$$$ STEAK

Mastro's Steakhouse. With a prime Beverly Hills location and classic steak house menu, this Arizona import is proving to be a popular alternative to the big chains yet retains far more tradition than some trendier newcomers. Starters include a shrimp cocktail dramatically presented in a cloud of dry ice. Massive steaks, swimming in butter, are served on the bone for maximum flavor. The downstairs dining room is appropriately sleek and studied, but Rat Pack–era gentlemen and their conspicuously younger companions sometimes let loose at a piano bar upstairs. ✉ *246 N. Cañon Dr., Beverly Hills* ☎ *310/888–8782* 🌐 *www.*

mastrosrestaurants.com ✍*Reservations essential* ▭*AE, D, DC, MC, V* ⊙*No lunch.*

TOP 5
Ocean Star for a sea of dim sum.
Patina, inside stunning Walt Disney Concert Hall.
Philippe the Original for the classic French Dip sandwich.
Spago Beverly Hills, stellar food *and* clientele.
Urasawa for a once-in-a-lifetime Japanese feast.

$$$–$$$$ JAPANESE ★ ✕ **Matsuhisa.** Freshness and innovation are the hallmarks of this flagship restaurant of Nobu Matsuhisa's empire. The prolific chef-restaurateur had planned on closing it in favor of his newer, more glamorous Nobu up the street, but ultimately bowed to clamoring protests from loyal patrons.The surprisingly modest-looking place draws celebrities and serious sushi buffs alike. Here you'll encounter such dishes as caviar-capped tuna stuffed with black truffles, squid "pasta" with garlic sauce, sea urchin wrapped in a *shiso* leaf, and monkfish liver pâté wrapped in gold leaf. Reflecting his past stint in Peru, Matsuhisa incorporates intriguing Latin ingredients into traditional Japanese cuisine. Regulars ask for the omakase, assured of an amazing culinary experience, and then steel themselves for a big tab. ✉*129 N. La Cienega Blvd., Beverly Hills* ☎*310/659–9639* 🌐*www.nobumatsuhisa.com* ✍*Reservations essential* ▭*AE, DC, MC, V* ⊙*No lunch weekends.*

$$$$ NEW AMERICAN Fodor's Choice ★ ✕ **Spago Beverly Hills.** The famed flagship restaurant of Wolfgang Puck, Mr. Celebrity Chef himself, is justifiably a modern L.A. classic. The illustrious restaurant centers on a buzzing outdoor courtyard shaded by 100-year-old olive trees. From an elegantly appointed table inside, you can glimpse the exhibition kitchen and, on rare occasions, the affable owner greeting his famous friends (these days, compliments to the chef are directed to Lee Hefter). The people-watching here is worth the price of admission, but the clientele is surprisingly inclusive, from the biggest Hollywood stars to Midwestern tourists to foodies more preoccupied with vintages of Burgundy than with faces from the cover of *People.* Foie gras has disappeared, but the daily-changing menu might offer a four-cheese pizza topped with truffles, *côte de boeuf* with Armagnac-peppercorn sauce, Cantonese-style duck, and some traditional Austrian specialties. Acclaimed pastry chef Sherry Yard works magic with everything from an ethereal apricot soufflé to Austrian *kaiserschmarrn* (crème fraîche pancakes with fruit). ✉*176 N. Cañon Dr., Beverly Hills* ☎*310/385–0880* 🌐*www.wolfgangpuck.com* ✍*Reservations essential* ▭*AE, D, DC, MC, V* ⊙*No lunch Sun.*

$$–$$$ INDIAN ✕ **Tanzore.** The design and menu of a venerable traditional Indian restaurant has been dramatically transformed to create a totally new experience. Now lighter contemporary fare prepared with seasonal California ingredients—like coriander-crusted tuna with avocado raita (a yogurt-based condiment) and tandoori sea bass—dominates the menu, while its colorful spaces encompass sleek blond wood surfaces, water features, a showy glass-ensconced wine cellar, and ultrahip lounge. ✉*50 N. La Cienega Blvd., Beverly Hills* ☎*310/652–3894* 🌐*www.tanzore.com* ✍*Reservations essential* ▭*AE, D, DC, MC, V* ⊙*Closed Mon.*

$$$$ JAPANESE Fodor's Choice ★ ✕**Urasawa.** Shortly after celebrated sushi chef Masa Takayama packed his knives for the Big Apple, his soft-spoken protégé Hiroyuki Urasawa settled into the master's former digs. The understated sushi bar has few precious seats, resulting in incredibly personalized service. At a minimum of $350 per person for a strictly *omakase* (chef's choice) meal, Urasawa remains the priciest restaurant in town, but the endless parade of masterfully crafted, exquisitely presented dishes renders few regrets. The maple sushi bar, sanded daily to a satinlike finish, is the scene of a mostly traditional cuisine with magnificent ingredients. You might be served velvety bluefin toro paired with beluga caviar, slivers of foie gras to self-cook *shabu-shabu* style, or egg custard layered with *uni* (sea urchin), glittering with gold leaf. This is also the place to come during *fugu* season, when the legendary, potentially deadly blowfish is artfully served to adventurous diners. ✉*2 Rodeo, 218 N. Rodeo Dr., Beverly Hills* ☎*310/247–8939* ✍*Reservations essential* ▭*AE, DC, MC, V* ⊙*Closed Sun. No lunch.*

CENTURY CITY

$$$–$$$$ NEW AMERICAN ★ ✕**Craft Los Angeles.** Prominent New York chef Tom Colicchio (star judge of TV's Top Chef) spreads his burgeoning empire with this sleek Southern California outpost. Thanks to Century City's growing legions of Hollywood agents and lawyers, Craft has emerged as a major industry hangout. In its open, airy dining room vaguely reminiscent of an elegant special events tent, deals are brokered over lunches featuring seasonal, artisanal ingredients. In the evening, Craft is ideal for groups sharing plates from Colicchio's signature à la carte menu that changes daily to encompass the likes of roasted Peruvian octopus in saffron sauce, sweet corn agnolotti, and succulent veal sweetbreads with plums. Boutique produce goes into a plethora of side dishes, and desserts may include a salted chocolate tart or intriguing olive oil sorbet. The endless, nondescriptive menu can be frustrating and some dishes miss the mark—but just as many sparkle. ✉*10100 Constellation Blvd., Century City* ☎*310/279–4180* 🌐*www.craftrestaurant.com* ✍*Reservations essential* ▭*AE, D, DC, MC, V* ⊙*No lunch weekends.*

$$$–$$$$ FRENCH ★ ✕**La Cachette.** Owner-chef Jean-François Meteigner, regarded as one of the city's top French chefs (he developed a following while cooking at the revered, now-defunct L'Orangerie), continues to pamper a loyal clientele at La Cachette. Here he combines traditional Gallic fare—foie gras, Provençal bouillabaisse, rack of lamb—with a lighter, more modern cuisine reflected in dishes like seared sea scallops in a harissa-lobster emulsion with couscous. A dressy (well, by L.A. standards) crowd makes sure that this elegant, flower-filled *cachette* (little hiding place) doesn't stay hidden. ✉*10506 Santa Monica Blvd., Century City* ☎*310/470–4992* 🌐*www.lacachetterestaurant.com* ✍*Reservations essential* ▭*AE, D, DC, MC, V* ⊙*Closed Sun. No lunch weekends.*

$$ ITALIAN Fodor's Choice ★ ✕**Pizzeria Mozza.** The other, more casual half of Silverton & Batali's partnership (the first being Osteria Mozza), this casual venue gives newfound eminence to the humble "pizza joint." With traditional Mediterranean items like white anchovies, lardo, squash blossoms, and Gorgonzola, Mozza's pies—thin-crusted delights with golden, blistered edges—are much more Campania than California, and virtually every

one is a winner. Antipasti include simple salads, bone marrow al forno and platters of salumi. All sing with vibrant flavors thanks to superb market-fresh ingredients, and daily specials include crisp duck legs with lentils and lasagna. Like the menu, the wine list is both interesting and affordable. ☒*641 N. Highland Ave., Hollywood* ☎*323/297–0101* *Reservations essential* ▭*AE, MC, V.*

> **WORD OF MOUTH**
>
> "I've found the trick to avoiding long waits at Pizzeria Mozza is to go at off hours. Try arriving at 3, 4 or 5 PM—you'll be seated fairly quickly. If you need to eat at a more conventional hour, definitely make reservations. They start taking them one month before the day you want to dine. If you can get a seat at the pizza bar, it's really fun to watch them making the pizzas." —Erin74

HOLLYWOOD

$$ ITALIAN ★ ✕ **All' Angelo.** Addressing the realities of the current economy, owner Stefano Ongaro has transformed his chic *ristorante* into a more affordable, approachable trattoria. The Murano sconces are still up, but the tables have been stripped of linen and the vibe is more relaxed and casual. The kitchen specializes in risotto, house-made pastas like osso buco–filled agnolotti and entrées such as short ribs with polenta and a calamari-and frisée salad from the Adriatic Coast. The restaurant's signature antique meat-slicing machine turns out magnificent plates of prosciutto and salami. ☒*7166 Melrose Ave., Hollywood* ☎*323/933–9540* ⊕*www.allangelo.com* *Reservations essential* ▭*AE, MC, V* ⊙*Closed Sun. No lunch Mon.–Thurs. or Sat.*

$$–$$$ AMERICAN ✕ **Ammo.** This hip canteen proves that the designers and photographers (aka the regulars here) have good taste in food as well as fashion. Lunch might be French lentil salad; a prosciutto, mozzarella, and arugula sandwich; or a really great burger. Start dinner with one of the kitchen's market-fresh salads, then follow up with a duck confit pizza, parsley puree, a solid burger, or a grilled hanger steak. The crisp, minimal setting is cool but not chilly. ☒*1155 N. Highland Ave., Hollywood* ☎*323/871–2666* ⊕*www.ammocafe.com* ▭*AE, MC, V.*

$$$$ LATIN AMERICAN ✕ **Beso.** Celebrity chef Todd English takes on Hollywood, collaborating with television star Eva Longoria Parker at this stylish, Latin-themed restaurant with a name that means "kiss" in Spanish. Glittering chandeliers dangle over a dramatic scene: young hipsters sipping mojitos at a marble bar, and tourists sliding into cozy booths with a view of the prominent exhibition kitchen. Begin with one of the inventive appetizers, such as the soft shell crab taco with caper aïoli, or the artichoke guacamole, or addictive crispy lamb ribs with peanut-chipotle sauce. For the main course, move on to a steak with chimichurri sauce, paella, or scallops with a mild mole. Churros with chocolate and dulce de leche dipping sauces make an ideal finale. Beso is pure Hollywood, but because it doesn't take itself too seriously, it adds plenty of fun to the legendary neighborhood. ☒*6350 Hollywood Blvd., Hollywood* ☎*323/467–7991* ⊕*www.besohollywood.com* *Reservations essential* ▭*AE, D, MC, V* ⊙*Closed Sun. No lunch.*

$$$$ NEW AMERICAN ✕ **Citrus at Social.** New York–based restaurateur Jeffrey Chodorow (Asia de Cuba) has refurbished the historic Hollywood Athletic Club—once

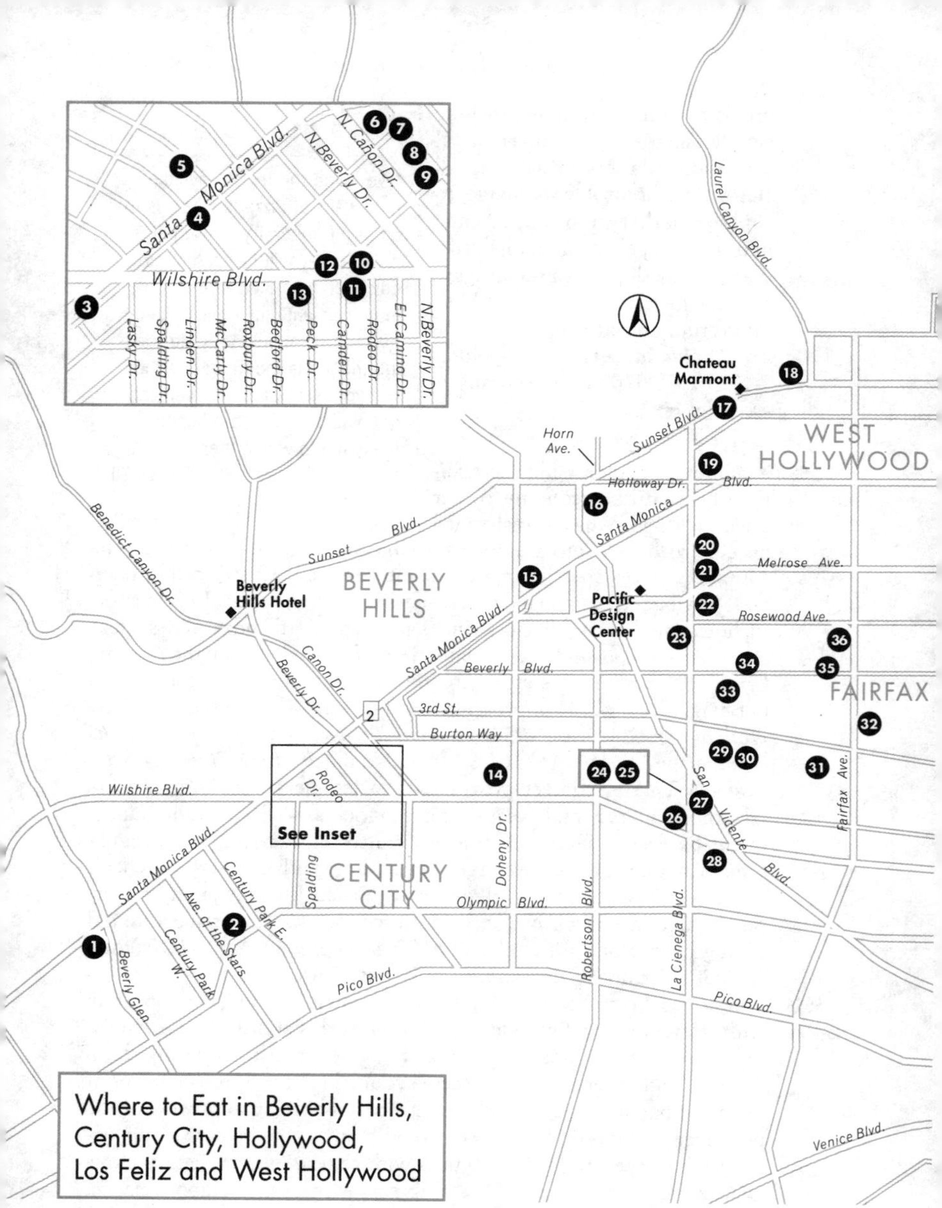

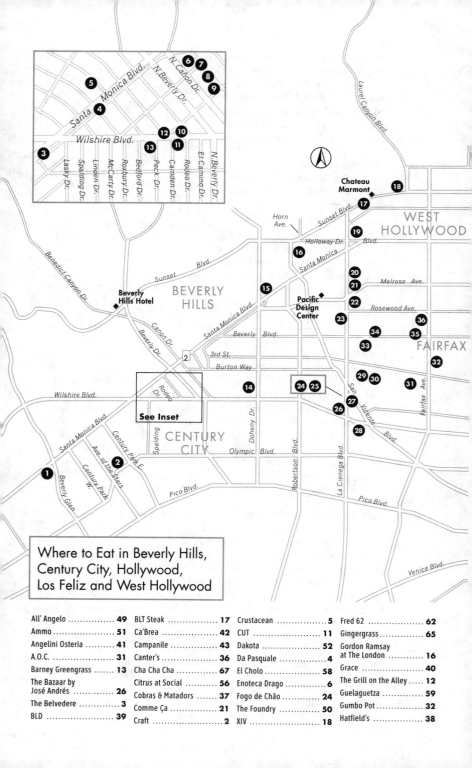

Where to Eat in Beverly Hills, Century City, Hollywood, Los Feliz and West Hollywood

All' Angelo 49
Ammo 51
Angelini Osteria 41
A.O.C. 31
Barney Greengrass 13
The Bazaar by José Andrés 26
The Belvedere 3
BLD 39
BLT Steak 17
Ca'Brea 42
Campanile 43
Canter's 36
Cha Cha Cha 67
Citrus at Social 56
Cobras & Matadors 37
Comme Ça 21
Craft 2
Crustacean 5
CUT 11
Dakota 52
Da Pasquale 4
El Cholo 58
Enoteca Drago 6
Fogo de Chão 24
The Foundry 50
XIV 18
Fred 62 62
Gingergrass 65
Gordon Ramsay at The London 16
Grace 40
The Grill on the Alley 12
Guelaguetza 59
Gumbo Pot 32
Hatfield's 38

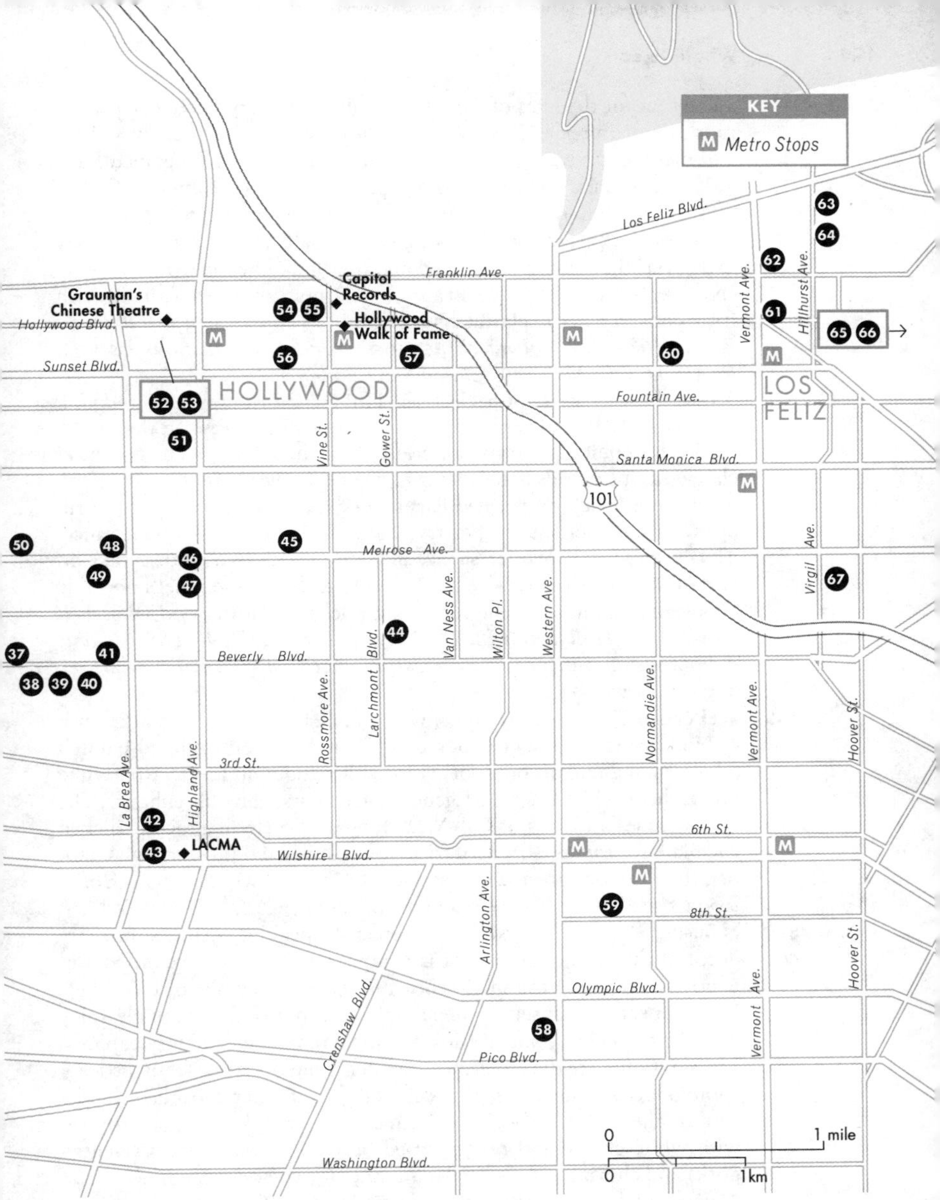

Hokusai 28
House of Chan Dara 44
Jar 34
Kate Mantilini 14
Koi 20
La Cachette 1
LAMILL Coffee Boutique .. 66
Loteria! Grill Hollywood .. 55
Luckyfish 7
Lucques 22
Mandarette 33
Mastro's Steakhouse 8
Matsuhisa 25
Mimosa 35
Musso & Frank Grill 54
Nobu Los Angeles 21
Ortolan 29
Osteria Mozza 46
The Palm 15
Pink's Hot Dogs 48
Pizzeria Mozza 47
Providence 45
Roscoe's House of Chicken 'n' Waffles 57
Sofi 30
Sona 23
Spago Beverly Hills 9
Tanzore 27
Trattoria Farfalla 64
25 Degrees 53
Urasawa 10
Vermont 61
Wa Sushi Bistro 19
Yuca's Hut 63
Zankou Chicken 60

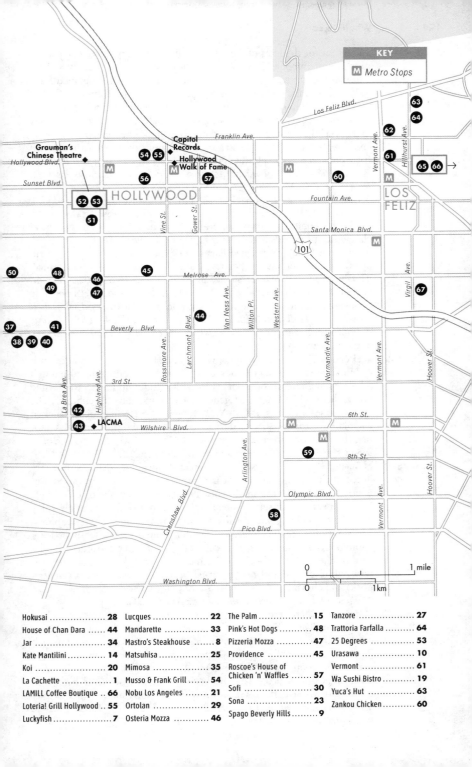

a hangout for the likes of Chaplin, Gable, and Barrymore. The restaurant now features a sleek modernist look with a cheery citrus palette and menu conceived by super-chef Michel Richard, who gained fame at L.A.'s landmark Citrus before departing for Washington, D.C. The affable Frenchman is rarely here, but the kitchen reflects his playfulness in dishes like "beluga pearls," which are actually Israeli couscous served in a caviar tin—tinted with squid ink, they look like the real deal—layered over lobster. They also do a soulful 72-hour short rib with ultrarich frites cooked twice in clarified butter. ✉*6525 Sunset Blvd., Hollywood* ☎*323/462–5222* 🌐*www.citrusatsocial.com* ✍*Reservations essential* 💳*AE, D, DC, MC, V* ⏲*Closed Sun. No lunch.*

$$$–$$$$ STEAK ✕**Dakota.** After years of neglect, the Hollywood Roosevelt Hotel got a face-lift in 2005 and is once again a fashionable address on the Boulevard. This contemporary steak house, though, is far from a superficial change, as it succeeds in balancing hipness with the spirit of an American institution. Snack on truffled Parmesan fries, tuck into a grass-fed rib eye with salsa verde sauce, or try Scottish salmon in a red wine sauce. The decor—lots of leather, suede, and dark wood—is a modern take on Old Hollywood, but service has been expanded to the hotel's poolside Tropicana Bar, a hot scene for young celebs. ✉*Hollywood Roosevelt Hotel, 7000 Hollywood Blvd., Hollywood* ☎*323/769–8888* 🌐*www.dakota-restaurant.com* ✍*Reservations essential* 💳*AE, D, DC, MC, V* ⏲*No lunch.*

$–$$ MEXICAN ✕**El Cholo.** The first of what's now a small chain, this landmark south of Hollywood has been packing them in since the '20s. A hand-painted adobe ceiling and an outdoor patio with a fountain create a partylike atmosphere, which the bar's legendary margaritas can only enhance. The fare includes all kinds of Cal–Mex standards, including tacos, chicken enchiladas, *carnitas* (shredded fried pork), and, from July through October, their famous green-corn tamales. ✉*1121 S. Western Ave., Hollywood* ☎*323/734–2773* 🌐*www.elcholo.com* 💳*AE, DC, MC, V.*

$–$$ MEXICAN ✕**Guelaguetza.** Catering to a largely Spanish-speaking clientele, the spare decor at this in-the-know spot is compensated by a festive mood and exotic scents filling the small, cheerful space. Surely one of L.A.'s best Mexican eateries, it serves the complex but not overpoweringly spicy cooking of Oaxaca, one of Mexico's most renowned culinary capitals. The standouts are the moles, whose intense flavors come from intricate combinations of nuts, seeds, spices, chiles, and bitter chocolate. But be sure to check out barbecued-goat tacos or pizzalike *clayudas* topped with white cheese and *tasajo* (dried beef) or *cecina* (chili-marinated pork) and chorizo. ✉*3337½ W. 8th St., Hollywood* ☎*213/427–0601* 🌐*www.guelaguetzarestaurant.com* 💳*AE, D, DC, MC, V.*

$–$$ THAI ✕**House of Chan Dara.** Known for its head-turning waitresses and its rock-and-roll/showbiz crowd, this casual eatery is on the edge of charming Larchmont Village, the commercial district serving ritzy Hancock Park. Try any of the noodle dishes, especially those with crab and shrimp. Also on the extensive menu are *satay* (skewered meats with a tangy peanut sauce); Thai barbecued chicken, pork, or beef; and deep-fried whole catfish. Finish up with an exotic mango cheesecake. ✉*310 N. Larchmont Blvd., Hollywood* ☎*323/467–1052* 🌐*www.houseofchandara.com* 💳*AE, D, DC, MC, V.*

CLOSE UP

The Hotel Dining Room Revival

Some of L.A.'s best restaurants hold forth in hotels, and locals vie for tables along with the guests.

From the Cambodian silks to the French porcelain, **Jaan** (☎ *310/278–3344* 🌐 *www.raffles.com*), at the Raffles L'Ermitage Hotel in Beverly Hills, swaddles you in luxe surroundings. Its inventive contemporary cuisine incorporates luxury ingredients—Kobe beef, black truffles, caviar—from around the world.

Catch (☎ *310/581–7714* 🌐 *www.catchsantamonica.com*), at Santa Monica's Hotel Casa del Mar, showcases sushi, crudo, and refined French-inspired seafood dishes in an oceanfront room famous for its sunsets. At the nearby Viceroy Santa Monica, **Whist** (☎ *310/451–8711* 🌐 *www.viceroysantamonica.com*) serves market-driven contemporary fare in a dramatic dining room with rows of vintage English china, or at poolside cabanas.

The Tower Bar (☎ *323/848–6677* 🌐 *www.sunsettowerhotel.com*), at Sunset Towers, is a seductive hideaway evoking its glamorous Hollywood history. **Simon LA** (☎ *310/278–5444* 🌐 *www.simonlarestaurant.om*) in West Hollywood's Sofitel Los Angeles, "rock 'n' roll chef" Kerry Simon puts a hip spin on nostalgic American comfort foods. Celebrated Italian chef Gino Angelini didn't hesitate locating his sophisticated West Hollywood restaurant, **La Terza** (☎ *323/782–8384* 🌐 *www.laterzarestaurant.com*), at the Orlando Hotel.

CUT (☎ *310/276–8500* 🌐 *www.wolfgangpuck.com*), Wolfgang Puck's latest venture, is a strikingly modern steak house hidden in the stately Italian Renaissance–style Regent Beverly Wilshire.

Pasadena's Langham, Huntington Hotel & Spa is packed with amenities, but the cuisine at **The Dining Room** (☎ *626/577–2867* 🌐 *www.langhamhotels.com*) is reason enough to go.

—Roger J. Grody

3

¢–$$ MEXICAN **✕Lotería! Grill Hollywood.** After drawing an almost cult-like following from a stand in the Farmers Market, Lotería! takes on Hollywood with a sleek sit-down restaurant with essentially the same time-tested menu. Start with banana squash and corn soup or chicharron de queso (a crunchy, paper-thin sheet of addictive griddle-toasted cheese) with guacamole while sipping on tequila you've selected from a long list. Then tuck into tacos or burritos stuffed with epazote-spiced mushrooms and cheese, meatballs in tomato-chipotle sauce, or cochinita pibil (Yucatán-style pork). And after halibut in a spicy chile sauce, nothing soothes the palate like homemade Mexican ice cream. ✉ *6627 Hollywood Blvd., Hollywood* ☎ *323/465–2500* 🌐 *www.loteriagrill.com* 💳 *AE, D, MC, V.*

$$–$$$ AMERICAN **✕Musso & Frank Grill.** Liver and onions, lamb chops, goulash, shrimp Louis salad, gruff waiters—you'll find all the old favorites here in Hollywood's oldest restaurant. A film-industry hangout since it opened in 1919, Musso & Frank still attracts the working studio set to its maroon faux-leather booths, along with tourists and locals nostalgic

for Hollywood's golden era. Great breakfasts are served all day, but the kitchen's famous "flannel cakes" (pancakes) are served only until 3 PM. ☒*6667 Hollywood Blvd., Hollywood* ☎*323/467–7788* ▭*AE, DC, MC, V* ⊙*Closed Sun. and Mon.*

$$–$$$ ITALIAN ★ **Osteria Mozza.** Born from the immensely popular collaboration between celebrated bread maker Nancy Silverton (founder of L.A.'s La Brea Bakery and Campanile) and Iron Chef Mario Batali, Osteria Mozza features candlelit, linen-clad tables surrounding a central marble-topped mozzarella bar, ideal for solo diners. From that bar come several presentations of velvety burrata cheese and perfectly dressed salads, while the kitchen turns out an oversize raviolo oozing ricotta and egg in brown butter sauce, blissful sweetbreads piccata and grilled whole orata (Mediterranean sea bream), capped off with Italian cheeses and unique rosemary–olive oil cakes. If you can't score a reservation here, treat yourself to the partners' pizzeria next door. ☒*6602 Melrose Ave., Hollywood* ☎*323/297–0100* ⊕*www.mozza-la.com* *Reservations essential* ▭*AE, MC, V* ⊙ *No lunch.*

¢ AMERICAN **Pink's Hot Dogs.** Orson Welles ate 18 of these hot dogs in one sitting, and you, too, will be tempted to order more than one. The chili dogs are the main draw, but the menu has expanded to include a Martha Stewart Dog (a 10-inch frank topped with mustard, relish, onions, tomatoes, sauerkraut, bacon, and sour cream). Since 1939 Angelenos and tourists alike have been lining up to plunk down some modest change for one of the greatest guilty pleasures in L.A. Pink's is open until 3 AM on weekends. ☒*709 N. La Brea Ave., Hollywood* ☎*323/931–4223* ⊕*www.pinkshollywood.com* *Reservations not accepted* ▭*No credit cards.*

$$$$ SEAFOOD Fodor's Choice ★ **Providence.** Chef-owner Michael Cimarusti has elevated Providence to the ranks of America's finest seafood restaurants. Activity in the elegant dining room, dappled by subtle nautical accents, is smoothly overseen by co-owner–general manager Donato Poto as well-heeled patrons work their way through elaborate tasting menus. Obsessed with quality and freshness, the meticulous chef maintains a network of specialty purveyors, some of whom tip him off to their catch before it even hits the dock. This exquisite seafood then gets the Cimarusti treatment of French technique, traditional American themes, and Asian accents. Pastry chef Adrian Vasquez' exquisite desserts are not to be missed; consider a three- to eight-course dessert tasting menu. ☒*5955 Melrose Ave., Hollywood* ☎*323/460–4170* ▭*AE, DC, MC, V* ⊙*No lunch Mon.–Thurs. and weekends.*

$ SOUTHERN **Roscoe's House of Chicken 'n Waffles.** Don't be put off by the name of this casual eatery, which honors a late-night combo popularized in Harlam jazz clubs. Roscoe's is *the* place for real down-home Southern cooking. Just ask the patrons, who drive from all over L.A. for Roscoe's bargain-price fried chicken, wonderful waffles (which, by the way, turn out to be a great partner for fried chicken), buttery chicken livers, and grits. Although Roscoe's has the intimate feel of a smoky jazz club, those musicians hanging out here are just taking five. ☒*1514 N. Gower St., Hollywood* ☎*323/466–7453* ⊕*www.roscoeschickenandwaffles.com* *Reservations not accepted* ▭*AE, D, DC, MC, V.*

$–$$ AMERICAN **25 Degrees.** Named after the difference in temperature between a medium-rare and well-done burger, this upscale burger joint sits in one of Hollywood's hippest hotels. The action at 25 Degrees revolves around a counter constructed of rich oak instead of Formica, and cabernet is favored over cola. Order the #1 (caramelized onions, Gorgonzola and Crescenza cheeses, bacon, arugula, and Thousand Island) or create your own masterpiece from a selection of premium meats, artisanal cheeses, and house-made condiments. A long list of half-bottles makes wine pairings easy for solo diners. They're open 24 hours—and mercifully do offer other items, including a good fried egg sandwich, if you're not sure about burgers for breakfast. ✉ *Hollywood Roosevelt Hotel, 7000 Hollywood Blvd., Hollywood* ☎ *323/785–7244* 🌐 *www.25degreesrestaurant.com* *Reservations not accepted* *AE, D, DC, MC, V.*

A MOVEABLE FEAST

In L.A., you can find tacos everywhere, from trendy high-end dining rooms to obscure neighborhood dives. For a taste of the real deal—and a celebration of genuine urban entrepreneurism—patronize one of the city's several thousand taco trucks that set up shop curbside. These are the city's finest kitchens on wheels.

¢–$ MIDDLE EASTERN **Zankou Chicken.** Forget the Colonel. Zankou's aromatic, Armenian-style rotisserie chicken with perfectly crisp, golden skin is one of L.A.'s truly great budget meals. It's served with pita bread, veggies, hummus, and unforgettable garlic sauce. If this doesn't do it for you, try the kebabs, falafel, or sensational *shawarma* (spit-roasted lamb or chicken) plates. ✉ *5065 W. Sunset Blvd., Hollywood* ☎ *323/665–7845* 🌐 *www.zankouchicken.com* *Reservations not accepted* *No credit cards.*

LOS FELIZ AND SILVER LAKE

LOS FELIZ

$–$$ CARIBBEAN **Cha Cha Cha.** Left-of-center Cha Cha Cha attracts an eclectic crowd. It's hip without being pretentious or overly trendy. A giant map on the wall suggests the restaurant's Caribbean influences. You can sit in the small dining room or on the enclosed tropical-à-la-Carmen-Miranda patio. Standard options include empanadas, Jamaican jerk chicken or pork, curried shrimp, fried plantain chips, and paella. Sangría is the drink of choice. ✉ *656 N. Virgil Ave., Los Feliz* ☎ *323/664–7723* 🌐 *www.theoriginalchachacha.com* *AE, D, DC, MC, V.*

¢–$ AMERICAN **Fred 62.** A tongue-in-cheek take on the American diner created by funky L.A. chef-restaurateur Fred Eric. The usual burgers and shakes are joined by choices like grilled salmon, Southern-style brisket and a "Poorest Boy" sandwich (crispy fried chicken, onions, and rémoulade on a French roll). Toasters sit on every table and breakfasts range from tofu scrambles to "Hunka Hunka Burnin' Love" (pancakes made with peanut butter, chocolate chips, and banana). Like the neighborhood itself, nobody is out of place here, with everybody from button-down businesspeople to tattooed musicians showing up at some point during its 24/7 cycle. ✉ *1850 N. Vermont Ave., Los Feliz* ☎ *323/667–0062* 🌐 *www.fred62.com* *Reservations not accepted* *AE, DC, MC, V.*

CLOSE UP

Local Chains Worth Stopping For

It's said that the drive-in burger joint was invented in L.A., probably to meet the demands of an ever-mobile car culture. What's certain is that the fast food in L.A. tastes better than fast food elsewhere. For burgers—the original signature food of the metropolis—there are a couple chains worth noting. Cars line up at all hours at **In-N-Out Burger** (🌐 *www.in-n-out.com*; many locations), still a family-owned operation (and very possibly America's original drive-thru) whose terrific made-to-order burgers are revered by Angelenos. Visitors may recognize the chain as the infamous spot where Paris Hilton got nabbed for drunk driving, but locals are more concerned with getting their burger fix off the "secret" menu with variations like "Animal style" (mustard-grilled patty with grilled onions and extra spread) or a "4x4" (four burger patties and four cheese slices for heavy eaters). The company's Web site lists explanations for other popular secret menu items.

Tommy's sells a delightfully sloppy chili burger; the original location (✉ *2575 Beverly Blvd., Los Angeles* ☎ *213/389-9060*) is a no-frills culinary landmark. For rotisserie chicken that will make you forget the Colonel forever, head to **Zankou Chicken** (✉ *5065 Sunset Blvd., Hollywood* ☎ *323/665-7845* 🌐 *www.zankouchicken.com*), a small chain noted for its golden crispy-skinned birds, potent garlic sauce, and Armenian specialties. Homesick New Yorkers will appreciate **Jerry's Famous Deli** (✉ *10925 Weyburn Ave., Westwood* ☎ *310/208-3354* 🌐 *www.jerrysfamousdeli.com*), where the massive menu includes all the classic deli favorites. With a lively bar scene, good barbecued ribs, contemporary takes on old favorites, and even sushi, the more upscale **Houston's** (✉ *202 Wilshire Blvd., Santa Monica* ☎ *310/576-7558* 🌐 *www.hillstone.com*) is a popular local hangout. And **Señor Fish** (✉ *422 E. 1st St., Downtown* ☎ *213/625-0566* 🌐 *www.senor-fish.com*) is known for its healthy Mexican seafood specialties, such as scallop burritos and ceviche tostadas.

$$ ITALIAN ✕ **Trattoria Farfalla.** This reliable, brick-walled trattoria brought Los Feliz out of the spaghetti-and-meatballs mode in the '80s and has remained a favorite ever since, thanks in part to its fair prices. Regulars tend to order the Caesar salad on a pizza-crust bed, roasted herbed free-range chicken, and penne *alla Norma* (studded with rich, smoky eggplant). For lighter snacks, check out Vinoteca Farfalla next door, the owners' popular wine bar. ✉ *1978 N. Hillhurst Ave., Los Feliz* ☎ *323/661–7365* 🌐 *www.farfallatrattoria.com* 💳 *AE, D, DC, MC, V* ⏲ *No lunch Sun.*

$$–$$$ NEW AMERICAN ✕ **vermont.** This stylish eatery kicked off a renaissance on its colorful namesake street. Vaulted ceilings, Persian rugs, and fresh flowers make the interior graceful and inviting. The modern menu starts with the likes of crab cakes with mustard–lemon aïoli, or duck salad with ginger–soy vinaigrette, then moves on to crispy whitefish with basil sauce, flat iron steak with a fiery peppercorn sauce, and vegetarian risotto. Well-suited for quiet business lunches, vermont becomes lively during dinner. An alluring lounge adjoins the restaurant attracting everyone from Armani-

clad studio suits to bohemian artists. ✉ *1714 N. Vermont Ave., Los Feliz* ☎ *323/661–6163* 🌐 *www.vermontrestaurantonline.com* 💳 *AE, D, DC, MC, V* ⏲ *No lunch weekends.*

¢ MEXICAN **Yuca's Hut.** Blink and you'll miss this place, whose reputation far exceeds its size (it may be the tiniest place to have ever won a James Beard award). It's known for carne asada, carnitas, and *cochinita pibil* (Yucatán–style roasted pork) tacos and burritos. This is a fast-food restaurant in the finest tradition—independent, family-owned, and sticking to what it does best. The liquor store next door sells lots of Coronas to Hut customers soaking up the sun on the makeshift parking-lot patio. There's no chance of satisfying a late-night craving, though; it closes at 6 PM. ✉ *2056 N. Hillhurst Ave., Los Feliz* ☎ *323/662–1214* *Reservations not accepted* 💳 *No credit cards* ⏲ *Closed Sun.*

3

SILVER LAKE

$–$$ VIETNAMESE **Gingergrass.** Traditional Vietnamese favorites emerge from this café's open kitchen, sometimes with a California twist. With a minimalist decor marked by tropical wood banquettes, Silver Lake's bohemian past and über-trendy present converge at Gingergrass. Consider classic crispy-skinned imperial rolls (filled with chicken, veggies, or crab and shrimp, served with lettuce and mint for wrapping), variations on *pho* (Vietnam's ubiquitous noodle soup), and Cal-light versions of *bánh mì* (baguette sandwiches that fuse French and Southeast Asian traditions), along with a refreshing basil-lime elixir. ✉ *2396 Glendale Blvd., Silver Lake* ☎ *323/644–1600* 🌐 *www.gingergrass.com* *Reservations not accepted* 💳 *AE, D, MC, V.*

$$ CONTEMPORARY **LAMILL Coffee Boutique.** With a sleek, neoclassical design and menu designed by Providence chef Michael Cimarusti and his acclaimed pastry chef Adrian Vasquez, this is no ordinary neighborhood coffeehouse. For coffee connoisseurs, LAMILL features the finest beans from around the world, brewed in a French press or through a siphon apparatus that looks like it was salvaged from the laboratory of a mad scientist. For foodies, house-cured Tasmanian sea trout with wasabi crème fraîche, steak frites or chai-spiced duck with vadouvan (a garlicky Indian masala) and black olive-rosemary honey are followed by exquisitely presented desserts like chocolate lollipops and an exotic Asian twist on s'mores. ✉ *1636 Silver Lake Blvd., Silver Lake* ☎ 323/663–4441 🌐 *www.lamillcoffee.com* 💳 *AE, D, DC, MC, V.*

WEST HOLLYWOOD

$$–$$$ MEDITERRANEAN Fodor's Choice ★ **A.O.C.** Since it opened in 2002, this restaurant and wine bar has revolutionized dining in L.A., pioneering the small-plate format that has now swept the city. The space is dominated by a long, candle-laden bar serving more than 50 wines by the glass. There's also a charcuterie bar, an L.A. rarity. The tapaslike menu is perfectly calibrated for the wine list; you could pick duck confit, fried oysters with celery root rémoulade, an indulgent slab of pork *rillettes* (a sort of pâté), or just plunge into one of the city's best cheese selections. Named for the acronym for Appellation d'Origine Contrôlée, the regulatory system that ensures the quality of local wines and cheeses in France, A.O.C. upholds the standard of excellence. ✉ *8022 W. 3rd St., West Hollywood*

☎323/653–6359 🌐*www.aocwinebar.com* ✍*Reservations essential* 💳*AE, DC, MC, V* ⏲*No lunch.*

> **WORD OF MOUTH**
>
> "The word 'casual' always throws me here—just about EVERY restaurant in California is casual."
>
> —rjw_lgb_ca

$$$ ITALIAN Fodor'sChoice ★ ✕**Angelini Osteria.** You might not guess it from the modest, rather congested dining room, but this is one of L.A.'s most celebrated Italian restaurants. The key is chef-owner Gino Angelini's thoughtful use of superb ingredients, evident in dishes such as a salad of lobster, apples and pomegranate; and pumpkin tortelli with butter, sage, and asparagus. An awesome lasagna verde, inspired by Angelini's grandmother, is not to be missed. Whole branzino, crusted in sea salt, and boldly flavored rustic specials (e.g., tender veal kidneys, rich oxtail stew) consistently impress. An intelligent selection of mostly Italian wines complements the menu, and desserts like the open-face marmalade tart are baked fresh daily. ✉*7313 Beverly Blvd., West Hollywood* ☎*323/297–0070* 🌐*www.angelinoosteria.com* 💳*AE, MC, V* ⏲*Closed Mon. No lunch weekends.*

$$–$$$ AMERICAN ✕**BLD.** Chef Neal Fraser leaves his high-end cuisine behind at Grace, just down the street, to concentrate on simple, approachable fare at this casual yet sophisticated eatery open morning to night. With its versatile menu, you can enjoy a frittata or ricotta–blueberry pancakes in the morning, snack on an excellent selection of cheeses and charcuterie between meals, enjoy a Cuban sandwich or all-American burger for lunch, or tuck into a steak at dinner. Prices are reasonable, too, which helps explain the line at the door. ✉*7450 Beverly Blvd., West Hollywood* ☎*323/930–9744* 🌐*www.bldrestaurant.com* ✍*Reservations not accepted* 💳*AE, MC, V.*

$$$$ STEAK ✕**BLT Steak.** Laurent Tourondel is a French chef in love with the classic American steak house. His restaurant BLT (Bistro Laurent Tourondel) Steak now occupies the Sunset Strip building formerly home to legendary industry hangout Le Dôme; the space is now more casual and sparingly decorated, with a hip vibe and a vague bistro essence. Certified Angus beef is the main attraction here, following samplings from a raw bar, respectable crab cakes, or kampachi sashimi spiked with yuzu and kumquats. Pass on the domestic Wagyu (which lacks the consistency of the Japanese product) and hanger steak (too chewy). Instead, enjoy a big red wine with the bone-in rib eye or fillet with a béarnaise sauce worthy of a real French bistro, and finish with a killer peanut butter-chocolate mousse. ✉*8270 Sunset Blvd., West Hollywood* ☎*310/360–1950* 🌐*www.bltrestaurants.com* ✍*Reservations essential* 💳*AE, D, DC, MC, V* ⏲*No lunch.*

$$–$$$ ITALIAN ✕**Ca' Brea.** Starters steal the show at this reliable spot—try baked goat cheese wrapped in pancetta and served atop a Popeye-size mound of spinach. Among the entrées, look for the osso buco or the lamb chops with black-truffle and mustard sauce. A 2007 renovation after a fire resulted in warm blend of stone, brick, and Venetian plaster. ✉*346 S. La Brea Ave., West Hollywood* ☎*323/938–2863* 🌐*www.cabrearestaurant.com* 💳*AE, DC, MC, V* ⏲*Closed Sun. No lunch Sat.*

$$$–$$$$ MEDITERRANEAN ★ **Campanile.** Chef-owner Mark Peel has mastered the mix of robust Mediterranean flavors with homey Americana. The 1926 building (which once housed the offices of Charlie Chaplin) exudes a lovely Renaissance charm and Campanile is one of L.A.'s most acclaimed and beloved restaurants. Appetizers may include butternut squash risotto topped with white truffles, while pan-seared black cod with white bean–eggplant puree and prime rib with tapenade are likely to appear as entrées. Thursday night, grilled cheese sandwiches are a huge draw, as the beloved five-and-dime classic is morphed into exotic creations. For an ultimate L.A. experience, come for weekend brunch on the enclosed patio. *624 S. La Brea Ave., West Hollywood 323/938–1447 www.campanilerestaurant.com Reservations essential AE, D, DC, MC, V No dinner Sun.*

¢–$ DELI **Canter's.** This granddaddy of L.A. delicatessens (it opened in 1928) cures its own corned beef and pastrami and has an in-house bakery. It's not the best deli in town, or the friendliest, but it's a true L.A. classic and open 24/7. Next door is the Kibitz Room, where there's live music every night. *419 N. Fairfax Ave., Fairfax District 323/651–2030 www.cantersdeli.com Reservations not accepted DC, MC, V.*

$$–$$$ SPANISH **Cobras & Matadors.** A bustling storefront spot whose cramped tables and long bar channel the aura of a Madrid side street, Cobras & Matadors hits the mark with quality ingredients and value-oriented pricing. Among the numerous appetizers and tapas are traditional gazpacho, Galician-style grilled octopus with salsa verde, and bacalao (salted cod) cakes with garlicky aïoli. Larger plates may include roast game hen with Catalan sweet-and-sour sauce or paella. There's no wine list here, but no corkage fee either—bring a bottle from your own cellar or buy one from the owner's wine shop next door, where the intriguing inventory leans heavily toward Spanish vino. *7615 Beverly Blvd., West Hollywood 323/932–6178 AE, MC, V No lunch.*

$$$ FRENCH ★ **Comme Ça.** This brasserie from Sona chef David Myers, with polished service and a menu with something for everyone, is styled for those craving a decidedly French joie de vivre. Simple tables covered in butcher paper offset elegant antique mirrors, and a long chalkboard doubles as a wall. Comme Ça can't help but encourage an affair with food and wine. Savor specialties like tarte flambée, steak frites, and perfectly roasted chicken for two. Drain a carafe of Côtes du Rhône with French cheeses before concluding with profiteroles or brioche pudding while you longingly imagine yourself in Montparnasse (at least your dollar stretches further here). *8479 Melrose Ave., West Hollywood 323/782–1178 www.commecarestaurant.com Reservations essential AE, D, DC, MC, V.*

$$$ NEW AMERICAN ★ **The Foundry.** Ex–Patina chef Eric Greenspan is a bear of a young man whose passion is reflected in every aspect of his Streamline Moderne–inspired restaurant, from the live music in the lounge to his work station on the dining room side of an open kitchen, allowing him direct access to guests—and immediate feedback. After sending out starters like miso-glazed pork belly or rich lobster gratin, Greenspan impresses with crispy skate wing with saffron–green apple puree or a glammed up rendition of beef short ribs. For a more relaxed environment, head to the covered patio, warmed by a fireplace. *7465 Melrose Ave., West Hollywood*

☎323/651–0915 🌐*www.thefoundryonmelrose.com* ✍*Reservations essential* ▭*AE, D, DC, MC, V* ⏲*Closed Mon. No lunch.*

$$$$ NEW AMERICAN ★ ✕**XIV.** Superchef Michael Mina and partners give an old Sunset Strip nightclub a glitzy makeover by über-designer Philippe Starck; it combines stainless steel, marble, and polished wood to arrive at a 21st-century urban château. Here diners select from a menu of intriguing, globally inspired but classically prepared small plates to create indulgent tasting menus. Consider dishes like crispy nuggets of pork belly with cashew puree, or duck breast paired with foie gras and lavender-honey jus. Generally just a few bites each, dishes are elegantly presented. Inventively composed cheese courses and desserts make lasting final impressions. A vegetarian counterpart is available for every menu selection. Truly ambitious diners opt for a taste of all 35 items, a culinary marathon priced at $250. ✉*8117 Sunset Blvd., West Hollywood* ☎*323/656–1414* 🌐*www.xivla.com* ✍*Reservations essential* ▭*AE, DC, MC, V* ⏲*No lunch.*

$$$$ FRENCH Fodor'sChoice ★ ✕**Gordon Ramsay at The London.** The foul-mouthed celebrity chef from Fox's Hell's Kitchen shows why he ranks among the world's finest chefs as his dining empire expands from London, Tokyo, and Dubai to this chic West Hollywood boutique hotel. Two pastel-color dining rooms with city views flank a formidable white marble bar, creating a space that feels trendy yet surprisingly unpretentious. A menu of small plates accommodates both light suppers and indulgent feasts alike. Highlights include a terrine of foie gras with black truffle, apple, and a Pedro Ximénez reduction, Kobe beef short rib, and tiger prawn ravioli with fennel puree and lobster sauce. To maximize the experience, consider one of the flexible tasting menus ($85 or $100), artfully crafted by Ramsay's local culinary team and orchestrated by a polished, gracious serving staff. ✉*The London, 1020 N. San Vicente Blvd., West Hollywood* ☎*323/358–7788* 🌐*www.gordonramsay.com* ✍*Reservations essential* ▭*AE, D, DC, MC, V.*

$$$–$$$$ NEW AMERICAN ✕**Grace.** Chef/owner Neal Fraser offers a modern American cuisine with an emphasis on local artisan ingredients. He mixes textures and contrasting flavors in dishes like risotto with pumpkin, sea urchin and sweet shrimp; a hunk of braised pork belly atop purple sticky rice with figs; and wild boar tenderloin in violet mustard sauce. Upscale interpretations of nostalgic favorites (e.g., maple–caramel doughnuts, cookies and milk) highlight the compelling dessert menu. ✉*7360 Beverly Blvd., West Hollywood* ☎*323/934–4400* 🌐*www.gracerestaurant.com* ✍*Reservations essential* ▭*AE, MC, V* ⏲*Closed Mon. No lunch.*

¢–$ CAJUN ✕**Gumbo Pot.** Well it's not exactly "down by the bayou," but this order-at-the-counter outdoor café does serve a mean gumbo rich in shrimp, chicken, and andouille sausage. It's also the place for New Orleans–style po'boy and *muffaletta* sandwiches, jambalaya, and *beignets* (the Big Easy's take on doughnuts). ✉*Farmers Market, 6333 W. 3rd St., West Hollywood* ☎*323/933–0358* 🌐*www.thegumbopotla.com* ✍*Reservations not accepted* ▭*AE, D, MC, V.*

$$$–$$$$ NEW AMERICAN ★ ✕**Hatfield's.** The true spirit of California cuisine is celebrated in this spare but elegant dining room with a wraparound patio. Chef Quinn Hatfield turns out market-driven dishes like Arctic char in a leek froth,

and date- and mint-crusted rack of lamb following a whimsical, not-to-be-missed California–style *croque madame* (hamachi and proscuitto sandwiched between buttery brioche toast, topped with a sunny-side-up quail egg). Sweet tooths are sated by Quinn's wife, Karen, whose creations include chocolate–peanut butter truffle cake or sugar- and spice-dusted beignets paired with a frothy shot of milkshake. ✉ *7458 Beverly Blvd., West Hollywood* ☎ *323/935–2977* 🌐 *www.hatfieldsrestaurant.com* ✍ *Reservations essential* 💳 *AE, MC, V* ⏲ *Closed Sun. No lunch.*

3

$$$–$$$$
AMERICAN

✕ **Jar.** A contemporary glaze of style layered over a retro, woodsy warmth frames the classic American cooking of chef Suzanne Tracht. The menu at this bastion of comfort cuisine represents a hit parade of all-American favorites, executed with a refined touch. After crab deviled eggs or devilish pork belly with port wine sauce, consider a 24-ounce porterhouse, rack of lamb, or a massive slab of tender pot roast that's a world apart from the one Mom used to make. Homey desserts like rich chocolate pudding or banana cream pie summon a sweet ending. ✉ *8225 Beverly Blvd., West Hollywood* ☎ *323/655–6566* 🌐 *www.thejar.com* 💳 *AE, DC, MC, V* ⏲ *No lunch Mon.–Sat.*

$$$–$$$$
JAPANESE

✕ **Koi.** Celebs and trendoids vastly outnumber sushi purists here. The sexy, understatedly exotic design includes several intimate spaces, both indoors and out—surely a dose of positive feng shui. A buzzing crowd indulges in well-executed dishes such as crispy rice topped with spicy tuna, Kobe beef carpaccio with crispy shiitake mushrooms and yuzu vinaigrette, and sesame-crusted lobster tail. ✉ *730 N. La Cienega Blvd., West Hollywood* ☎ *310/659–9449* 🌐 *www.koirestaurant.com* ✍ *Reservations essential* 💳 *AE, D, DC, MC, V* ⏲ *No lunch.*

$$$–$$$$
NEW AMERICAN
★

✕ **Lucques.** Formerly silent-film star Harold Lloyd's carriage house, this brick building has morphed into a chic restaurant that has elevated chef/co-owner Suzanne Goin to national prominence. In her veggie-intense contemporary American cooking, Goin uses finesse to balance tradition and invention. Consider the Italian heirloom pumpkin soup with sage and chestnut cream, Alaskan black cod with acorn squash and chorizo–golden raisin vinaigrette, and short ribs with horseradish cream. Finish with the likes of acacia honey panna cotta with blood orange granita. ✉ *8474 Melrose Ave., West Hollywood* ☎ *323/655–6277* 🌐 *www.lucques.com* ✍ *Reservations essential* 💳 *AE, MC, V* ⏲ *No lunch Sun. and Mon.*

$–$$
CHINESE

✕ **Mandarette.** Clad in warm wood and copper finishes, this inviting café began as a casual spin-off of the Mandarin in Beverly Hills, but the casual concept has outlasted its high-end originator. Start with cucumber salad with spicy peanut dressing, scallion pancakes, or curried chicken dumplings before indulging in *kung pao* scallops or crispy sesame beef. ✉ *8386 Beverly Blvd., West Hollywood* ☎ *323/655–6115* 🌐 *www.mandarettecafe.com* 💳 *AE, DC, MC, V.*

$$–$$$
FRENCH
Fodor's Choice
★

✕ **Mimosa.** If you're craving a perfect Provençal meal, turn to chef Jean-Pierre Bosc's menu. There's *salade Lyonnaise,* served with a poached egg, a nifty tomato tarte Tatin, probably L.A.'s best bouillabaisse, soulful coq au vin and hearty steak frites. The atmosphere is that of a classic bistro—balanced against a hint of elegance—with mustard walls, cozy banquettes, and crocks of cornichons and olives delivered to every table on arrival. ✉8009 Beverly Blvd., West Hollywood ☎323/655–8895 🌐www.mimosarestaurant.com 💳AE, DC, MC, V ⏲Closed Sun. and Mon. No lunch.

$$$$ FRENCH ★ **Ortolan.** Despite a minor galaxy of crystal chandeliers, Ortolan attempts to take the pretentiousness out of haute cuisine. Here designer jeans outnumber designer suits. But chef Christophe Émé—whose career has exposed him to a constellation of Michelin stars—maintains impeccable standards in the kitchen with dishes such as Napa Valley escargots with lettuce emulsion and Parmesan crust, lobster spaghetti with sea urchin sauce, and what may be the silkiest foie gras in the city. Many creations are dramatically presented on stone slabs or in unique vessels. The one thing even Émé can't get you is the namesake game bird; it's endangered. ✉*8338 W. 3rd St., West Hollywood* ☎*323/653–3300* 🌐*www.ortolanrestaurant.com* *Reservations essential* 💳*AE, MC, V* ⏲*Closed Sun. and Mon. No lunch.*

$$$–$$$$ STEAK **The Palm.** All the New York elements are present at this West Coast replay of the famous Manhattan steak house—mahogany booths, tin ceilings, a boisterous atmosphere, and New York–style, no-nonsense waiters rushing you through your cheesecake (flown in from the Bronx). This is where you'll find the biggest and best lobster, good steaks, prime rib, chops, great French-fried onion rings, and paper-thin potato slices. When writers sell a screenplay, they celebrate with a Palm lobster. ✉*9001 Santa Monica Blvd., West Hollywood* ☎*310/550–8811* 🌐*www.thepalm.com* 💳*AE, D, DC, MC, V* *Reservations essential* ⏲*No lunch weekends.*

$$–$$$ GREEK **Sofi.** Hidden from bustling, increasing hip 3rd Street, this friendly little taverna offers all the Greek classics: dolmades, *taramasalata* (a creamy, salty dip made from fish roe), spanakopita, and souvlaki. The smart, casual dining room is more than comfortable, but consider sitting outside on the lovely bougainvillea-shaded garden patio. All that's missing is a view of the Aegean Sea. ✉*8030¾ W. 3rd St., West Hollywood* ☎*323/651–0346* 🌐*www.sofirestaurant.com* 💳*AE, D, DC, MC, V.*

$$$$ NEW AMERICAN Fodor's Choice ★ **Sona.** Young, intense David Myers—one of the city's most exciting and unpredictable chefs—dazzles his fashionable followers here. A slab of polished granite topped with an exquisite orchid arrangement anchors the sleek dining room. If you're willing to spend the money, the prix-fixe tasting menus ($95 for six courses; $145 for nine) are the way to go, since they allow you to try many of Myers's distinctive dishes. An occasional item is too precious, but the successful dishes win out. Highlights might include seared foie gras paired with kumquat puree and licorice root ice cream, duck with chestnut agnolotti and red wine reduction, and a fromage blanc soufflé. ✉*401 N. La Cienega Blvd., West Hollywood* ☎*310/659–7708* 🌐*www.sonarestaurant.com* *Reservations essential* 💳*AE, D, DC, MC, V* ⏲*Closed Sun. and Mon. No lunch.*

$$$–$$$$ JAPANESE ★ **Wa Sushi & Bistro.** Founded by three alums from trendsetting Matsuhisa, Wa offers a more personalized experience with comparable high-quality sushi and intriguing Japanese cooking. Particularly enticing are dishes enhanced with French-inspired sauces. For instance, Chilean sea bass is layered with foie gras and bathed in a port reduction, while Santa

Barbara prawns crowned with uni are dosed with a perfect beurre blanc prepared on a rickety range behind the sushi bar. Although casual, Wa's second-story hillside location allows for seductive city views from a small handful of tables dressed up with linen and candles. ✉ *1106 N. La Cienega Blvd., West Hollywood* ☎ *310/854–7285* *Reservations essential* *AE, D, DC, MC, V* *Closed Mon. No lunch.*

DOWNTOWN

$$ NEW AMERICAN — **Blue Velvet.** Carved out of an abandoned Holiday Inn in an ecoconscious apartment building, this hip poolside restaurant reflects the dynamic changes occurring in downtown L.A. Featuring striking views of the new $2.5 billion L.A. Live project, a lively lounge, and a contemporary menu from a daring kitchen, cosmopolitan Blue Velvet oozes sex appeal. The mostly small-plate menu offers crispy Kurobuta pork belly with squash puree, hamachi sashimi with apple sauce, and hanger steak with onion rings, all enhanced with organic herbs from a rooftop garden, making Blue Velvet one cool green scene. ✉ *750 Garland Ave., Downtown* ☎ *213/239–0061* *www.bluevelvetrestaurant.com* *Reservations essential* *AE, MC, V* *No lunch weekends.*

$$$–$$$$ ITALIAN — **Cicada.** Certainly one of the most romantic and architecturally dramatic dining venues in L.A., Cicada occupies the ground floor of the 1928 art deco Oviatt Building. The glass doors are Lalique, carved maple columns soar two stories to a gold leaf ceiling, and from the mezzanine a glamorous bar overlooks the spacious dining room. With dishes like tuna carpaccio with lemon-ginger sauce, and lamb chops with rosemary-mirin sauce, "Modern Italian" best describes a menu that is a bit overshadowed by the ambience. ✉ *617 S. Olive St., Downtown* ☎ *213/488–9488* *www.cicadarestaurant.com* *Reservations essential, jacket required* *AE, D, DC, MC, V* *Closed Mon. No lunch.*

$$$ LATIN AMERICAN — **Ciudad.** The sunny interior here, with its bold, vaguely primeval murals, perfectly complements the new-wave culinary tour of the Americas offered by celebrity chefs Mary Sue Milliken and Susan Feniger. Kick off the evening with a Brazilian *caipirinha* or Cuban *mojito*; then tuck into starters (a few together can compose a meal) like rabbit-and-Serrano ham croquetas, Argentine empanadas or Peruvian ceviche. Entrées include tamarind-glazed salmon and a Moorish-spiced Andalucian skirt steak. Every Tuesday night, a choice of Spanish paellas is offered on the patio, along with the bar's killer sangría. ✉ *445 S. Figueroa St., Downtown* ☎ *213/486–5171* *www.ciudad-la.com* *AE, D, MC, V* *No lunch weekends.*

$$–$$$ AMERICAN — **Engine Co. No. 28.** A lovingly restored 1912 fire station, where everything—even the original brass sliding pole—has been preserved, now rushes out solid, old-fashioned comfort food. The long bar is a popular hangout for downtown workers delaying their rush-hour commute. The kitchen does a fine job with crab cakes, chili, macaroni and cheese, and thick slabs of terrific meat loaf. Specials showcase recipes inspired by firehouse cooking across the country. ✉ *644 S. Figueroa St., Downtown* ☎ *213/624–6996* *www.engineco.com* *AE, DC, MC, V* *No lunch weekends.*

CLOSE UP

Snacking at the Market

The landmark Los Angeles Farmers Market, at the corner of 3rd Street and Fairfax Avenue, is crammed with delicious food from all corners of the globe. Most spots are fast-food–style eateries sharing a common seating area—good for people-watching. An authentic *croque monsieur* sandwich, as well as crepes both savory and sweet, is available at **the French Crepe Company** (☎ *323/934–3113* 🌐 *www.frenchcrepe.com*). You can find more French specialties like coq au vin or beef bourguignon at the cozy, sit-down **Monsieur Marcel** (☎ *323/939–7792* 🌐 *www.mrmarcel.com*) wine bar and bistro. For a taste of the Mediterranean, stop by **Ulysses Voyage** (☎ *323/939–9728* 🌐 *www.ulyssesvoyage.com*), another full-service charmer, for classic spanakopita and moussaka. Some of the city's best tacos, wrapped in freshly made tortillas, are found at **Loteria! Grill** (☎ *323/930–2211* 🌐 *www.loteriagrill.com*), and folks line up for the bold flavors of Louisiana—including decent jambalaya and one of the few authentic New Orleans–style muffuletta sandwiches in L.A.—at **the Gumbo Pot** (☎ *323/933–0358* 🌐 *www.thegumbopotla.com*). **Bob's Coffee & Doughnuts** (☎ *323/933–8929*) is legendary for its raspberry-filled bismarcks, and some of L.A.'s most beloved pies are peddled at **Du-par's** (☎ *323/933–8446*).

The original spirit of the Farmers Market has been preserved despite the aggressive development of some adjoining commercial property. At **The Grove** shopping center next door, restaurants include **Morels** (☎ *323/965–9595*), a French bistro and steak house with a winning patio, and **La Piazza** (☎ *323/933–5050* 🌐 *www.lapiazzaonline.com*), where thin-crusted pizzas are the best bet. Also adjacent to the Farmers Market is **Wood Ranch BBQ & Grill** (☎ *323/937–6800* 🌐 *www.woodranch.com*), where hordes of devotees line up at the door for heaping portions of ribs.

$–$$ DELI ✕ **Langer's Deli.** With fluorescent lighting and Formica tables, Langer's has the look of a no-frills Jewish deli back in New York. The draw here is the hand-cut pastrami, which is relatively lean, peppery, and robust in flavor—those who swear it's the best in town have a strong case. Some regulars opt for the legendary #19 (pastrami with Swiss and coleslaw piled high on twice-baked rye), but purists prefer it straight up with Russian dressing. The neighborhood is rough around the edges, but the nearby metro station brings plenty of businesspeople here from the heart of downtown. ✉ *704 S. Alvarado St., Downtown* ☎ *213/483–8050* 🌐 *www.langersdeli.com* ✍ *Reservations not accepted* 💳 *MC, V* ⏲ *Closed Sun. No dinner.*

$$$–$$$$ STEAK ✕ **Nick & Stef's Steakhouse.** The contemporary beef palace of restaurateurs Joachim and Christine Splichal, named after their twin boys, has been so successful they've replicated the concept in other cities. Despite a sleek modern aesthetic, elements of the traditional steak house—comfortable booths, crisp white linen, wood accents—remain. The premium steaks come from a glassed-in, on-site aging chamber; build up your order by choosing from a diverse array of sauces, starches, and vegetables

Where to Eat in Downtown Los Angeles

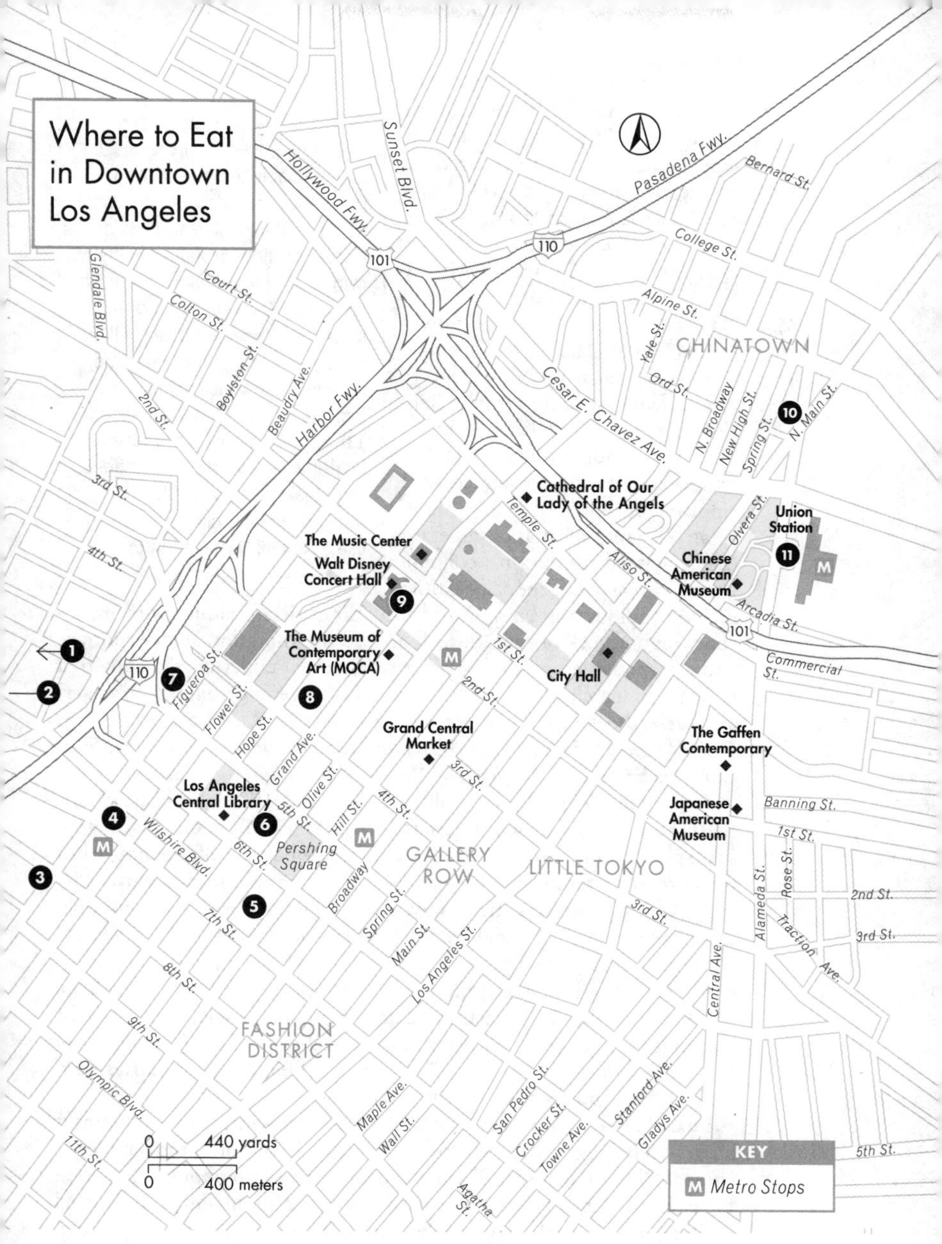

Blue Velvet 2
Cicada 5
Ciudad 7
Engine Co. No. 28 4
Langer's Deli 1
Nick & Stef's Steakhouse 8
Patina 9
Philippe The Original 10
Traxx 11
Water Grill 6
Zucca 3

that give honored steak-house traditions a little sex appeal. The wine list, deep in California reds, is predictably strong. ✉ *330 S. Hope St., Downtown* ☎ *213/680–0330* 🌐 *www.patinagroup.com* ✍ *Reservations essential* ▭ *AE, MC, V* ⏲ *No lunch weekends.*

> **FLAVOR OF THE MONTH**
>
> L.A.—arguably the most fickle city in America—is all about popular trends, and its dining scene is no less susceptible to sudden shifts of favor than the fashion world or the box office. The vegetarian restaurants stereotyped in *Annie Hall* are largely extinct and the "raw food" movement, in which animal-free ingredients are not heated above 118 degrees, hasn't really taken hold. These days, the contemporary steak house (e.g., **CUT, BOA**) rules, along with hip sushi bars like **Katsuya, Nobu,** and **Koi.**

$$$$ FRENCH Fodor's Choice ★ ✕ **Patina.** In a bold move, chef-owner Joachim Splichal moved his flagship restaurant from Hollywood to downtown's striking Frank Gehry–designed Walt Disney Concert Hall. His gamble paid off—the contemporary space, surrounded by a rippled "curtain" of rich walnut, is an elegant, dramatic stage for the acclaimed restaurant's contemporary French cuisine. Specialties include copious amounts of foie gras, caramelized halibut with mushroom ragout, rack of venison with braised chestnuts and quince chutney, and a formidable *côte de boeuf* for two, carved tableside. Finish with a hard-to-match cheese tray (orchestrated by a genuine *maître fromager*) and sensual desserts. ✉ *Walt Disney Concert Hall, 141 S. Grand Ave., Downtown* ☎ *213/972–3331* 🌐 *www.patinagroup.com* ✍ *Reservations essential* ▭ *AE, D, DC, MC, V* ⏲ *Closed Mon. No lunch weekends.*

¢–$ AMERICAN Fodor's Choice ★ ✕ **Philippe the Original.** L.A.'s oldest restaurant (1908), Philippe claims the French dip sandwich originated here. You can get one made with beef, pork, ham, lamb, or turkey on a freshly baked roll; the house hot mustard is as famous as the sandwiches. Its reputation is earned by maintaining traditions, from sawdust on the floor to long communal tables where customers debate the Dodgers or local politics. The home cooking—orders are taken at the counter where some of the motherly servers have managed their long lines for decades—includes huge breakfasts, chili, pickled eggs, and an enormous pie selection. The best bargain: a cup of java for just 10¢ including tax. ✉ *1001 N. Alameda St., Downtown* ☎ *213/628–3781* 🌐 *www.philippes.com* ✍ *Reservations not accepted* ▭ *No credit cards.*

$$$ AMERICAN ★ ✕ **Traxx.** Hidden inside historic Union Station, this intimate restaurant is an art deco delight. Its linen-topped tables spill out onto the main concourse. Chef-owner Tara Thomas's menu gussies up popular favorites; for example, crab cakes come with chipotle rémoulade, while seared scallops are dressed up with a pistachio crust and an Asian-inspired sauce. The jacaranda-shaded courtyard is a local secret. A well-stocked bar, occupying what was originally the station's telephone room, is just across the concourse. ✉ *Union Station, 800 N. Alameda St., Downtown* ☎ *213/625–1999* 🌐 *www.traxxrestaurant.com* ▭ *AE, D, MC, V* ⏲ *Closed Sun. No lunch weekends.*

$$$–$$$$ SEAFOOD ★ ✕ **Water Grill.** There's a bustling, enticing rhythm here as platters of glistening shellfish get whisked from the oyster bar to the cozy candlelit booths. Chef David LeFevre's menu shows off his slow-cooking skills.

Entrées such as olive oil–poached salmon with a mushroom vinaigrette and sumac–coated Australian barramundi with calamari–strewn Israeli couscous and Castelvetrano olives exemplify his light, sophisticated touch. Excellent desserts and a fine wine list round out this top-notch dining experience. ✉*544 S. Grand Ave., Downtown* ☎*213/891–0900* 🌐*www.watergrill.com* *Reservations essential* 💳*AE, D, DC, MC, V* ⏲*No lunch weekends.*

$$–$$$ ITALIAN ✕**Zucca.** Here superchef-restaurateur Joachim Splichal turns his attention to Italian cuisine, leavening sophistication with earthy flavors. The Murano glass chandeliers and mural of a Venetian carnival scene energize a seductive but noisy dining room. You can opt for dishes like pumpkin tortelloni—*zucca,* after all, is squash in Italian—with butter-sage sauce, osso buco, and a whole Mediterranean-style *branzino* (sea bass). Hit this spot for good pretheater dining. ✉*801 S. Figueroa St., Downtown* ☎*213/614–7800* *Reservations essential* 💳*AE, D, DC, MC, V* ⏲*No lunch weekends.*

3

COASTAL AND WESTERN LOS ANGELES

BEL AIR

$$$$ NEW AMERICAN ✕**Hotel Bel-Air.** This secluded hotel's restaurant spills into a lush garden, with a terrace overlooking a pond dotted with swans. A meal at this special-occasion spot will make you feel like a Hollywood insider (read: keep an eye out for celebs). But the restaurant's not just a pretty face; look for seasonal appetizers such as sautéed blue prawn with truffled macaroni and cheese or griddled duck liver cake with green lentils (fading from fashion but still available upon request is the restaurant's signature tortilla soup). Entrées might include fresh Dover sole meunière and seared scallops with cider-glazed pork belly. For a memorable feast, "Table One"—a chef's table adjacent to the kitchen—awaits a pampered party. The hotel also hosts a superlative high tea, and Sunday brunch on the terrace can be magical. ✉*701 Stone Canyon Rd., Bel Air* ☎*310/472–5234* 🌐*www.hotelbelair.com* *Reservations essential* 💳*AE, D, DC, MC, V.*

$$$$ AMERICAN ✕**Vibrato Grill, Jazz, etc.** Co-owned by trumpeter Herb Albert, Vibrato takes a high-road approach to a jazz club: this is a stylish, acoustically perfect venue where every table has a line of sight to the stage. The kitchen is as notable as the music; it turns out contemporary American fare such as white sea bass with parsley *pistov,* mac-and-cheese with bacon-brioche crust, and USDA Prime steaks. Art on the walls was painted by the Grammy-winning owner himself. ✉*2930 Beverly Glen Circle, Bel Air* ☎*310/474–9400* 🌐*www.vibratogrilljazz.com* *Reservations essential* 💳*AE, MC, V* ⏲*Closed Mon. No lunch.*

BRENTWOOD

$$–$$$ ITALIAN ★ ✕**Pecorino.** San Vicente Boulevard is lined with trendy trattorias, but Pecorino presents a delightful compromise between old-world charm and modern L.A. sensibilities. Wrought-iron chandeliers hang from a beamed ceiling above a room dressed up with white-linen tablecloths and red velvet curtains while the pleasures of the namesake sheep's milk cheese are explored in simply sauced pastas and Abruzzo–style lamb

CLOSE UP

Good Morning, L.A.

In L.A., many a big-screen megahit has been conceived over a breakfast of yogurt and granola or huevos rancheros. At **Hugo's** (✉ *8401 Santa Monica Blvd., West Hollywood* ☎ *323/654–3993* 🌐 *www.hugosrestaurant.com*), one of the city's top morning destinations, breakfast specialties include pumpkin pancakes and "Pasta Mama" (pasta scrambled with eggs, garlic, and Parmesan cheese). A favorite of Hollywood heavy-hitters is **Gardens** (✉ *Four Seasons Hotel, 300 S. Doheny Dr., Beverly Hills* ☎ *310/273–2222* 🌐 *www.fourseasons.com*), where an occasional dollop of caviar turns up on the breakfast menu. Meanwhile, those still waiting for their big breaks might be found at **the Griddle Café** (✉ *7916 Sunset Blvd., Hollywood* ☎ *323/874–0377* 🌐 *www.thegriddlecafe.com*) tucking into "Black Magic" flapjacks (filled with Oreo crumbs). But for a thoroughly unpretentious L.A. AM experience, head over to the Westside's **John O'Groats** (✉ *10516 W. Pico Blvd., West L.A.* ☎ *310/204–0692* 🌐 *www.ogroatsrestaurant.com*), where the good old-fashioned American breakfasts are accompanied by signature homemade biscuits.

In Pasadena, folks line up outside **Marston's** (✉ *151 E. Walnut St.* ☎ *626/796–2459* 🌐 *www.marstonsrestaurant.com*), a cozy bungalow. Over in Century City a modest café called **Clementine** (✉ *1751 Ensley Ave.* ☎ *310/552–1080* 🌐 *www.clementineonline.com*) reels in fans with fresh scones and buttermilk-biscuit egg-and-ham sandwiches. In Beverly Hills, New York expats huddle at **Nate 'n Al** (✉ *414 N. Beverly Dr.* ☎ *310/274–0101*) over matzo brei or corned beef hash, while French expats and Francophiles gather at **Anisette Brasserie** (✉ *225 Santa Monica Blvd., Santa Monica* ☎ *310/395–3200* 🌐 *www.anisettebrasserie.com*) for omelets and *viennoiserie* in Santa Monica. And for an authentic Japanese breakfast, head to **Azalea Restaurant & Bar** (✉ *120 S. Los Angles St.* ☎ *213/253–9235*) at Little Tokyo's Kyoto Grand Hotel and Gardens.

casserole. A huge baked onion filled with eggplant, raisins, and pine nuts is a terrific vegetarian beginning; a plate of pecorino cheeses from every corner of Italy is a perfect finish. ✉ *11604 San Vicente Blvd., Brentwood* ☎ *310/571–3800* 🌐 *www.pecorinorestaurant.com* ✍ *Reservations essential* 💳 *AE, D, MC, V* ⏲ *No lunch Sun.*

$$–$$$ ITALIAN ✕ **Vincenti.** A big exhibition kitchen with a mammoth, revolving rotisserie is the heart of this restaurant, fusing modernism and elegance. Off the spit come roasted pork, veal, venison, or whole spit-roasted fish such as orata (Mediterranean sea bream) and Dover sole. A rustic sausage plate or prosciutto paired with creamy *burrata* cheese are fine ways to begin, and pasta courses (like bucatini with house-cured *guanciale*) are always skillfully prepared. ✉ *11930 San Vicente Blvd., Brentwood* ☎ *310/207–0127* 🌐 *www.vincentiristorante.com* ✍ *Reservations essential* 💳 *AE, MC, V* ⏲ *Closed Sun. No lunch Sat. and Mon.–Thurs.*

DINING BY DESIGN

Architecture buffs needn't go hungry in L.A. **The Restaurant at the Getty Center** (✉ *1200 Getty Center Dr., Brentwood* ☎ *310/440–6810* 🌐 *www.getty.edu*) places sophisticated fare in the midst of Richard Meier's travertine-clad museum, and acclaimed **Patina** sits inside Frank Gehry's stainless steel–plated Walt Disney Concert Hall. **Cicada,** in the Oviatt Building (an art deco masterpiece), serves modern Italian cuisine, while contemporary American fare is offered at **Encounter,** whose iconic Theme Building at LAX was designed by pioneering African-American architect Paul Williams.

$$$–$$$$ JAPANESE ✕ **Katsuya.** Katsuya indulges Angelenos' sushi bars mania, catering to a beautiful, trend-conscious clientele. This place ups the ante with a seductive, ultramodern look created by celebrated designer Philippe Starck, in which walls are lined with backlit murals of a geisha's face—glossy lips kiss the room's clientele from one wall, while kohl-rimmed eyes peer out from behind the sushi bar on another. Unlike some of its peers, however, the food here is not simply an afterthought. Highly regarded sushi chef Katsuya Uechi turns out spicy tuna atop crispy rice, whimsical wonton cones filled with scoops of mousselike crab and tuna tartare, and larger plates like baked miso-marinated black cod. Don't neglect the plates from the *robata* bar, where skewers of veggies, seafood, and meats are grilled over hot coals. ✉ *11777 San Vicente Blvd., Brentwood* ☎ *310/207–8744* 🌐 *www.sbeent.com* ✍ *Reservations essential* 💳 *AE, MC, V* ⏲ *No lunch weekends.*

CULVER CITY

$$ ASIAN ★ ✕ **Beacon.** Trendsetting chef Kazuto Matsusaka (his résume includes Spago, Chinois on Main, and Buddha Bar in Paris) has opened this unpretentious restaurant in Culver City. Here he specializes in a Pacific Rim cuisine that's refreshingly grounded and restrained. His alluring menu offers crispy fried oysters wrapped in lettuce with a tartar sauce, a pastrylike "pizza" layered with wasabi mayo and ahi tuna, grilled hangar steak, delicate miso-glazed black cod, and lilikoi (passion fruit) cheesecake. The expansive space is casual and fun (if a bit noisy), fueling the revitalization of this sleepy Westside community. ✉ *3280 Helms*

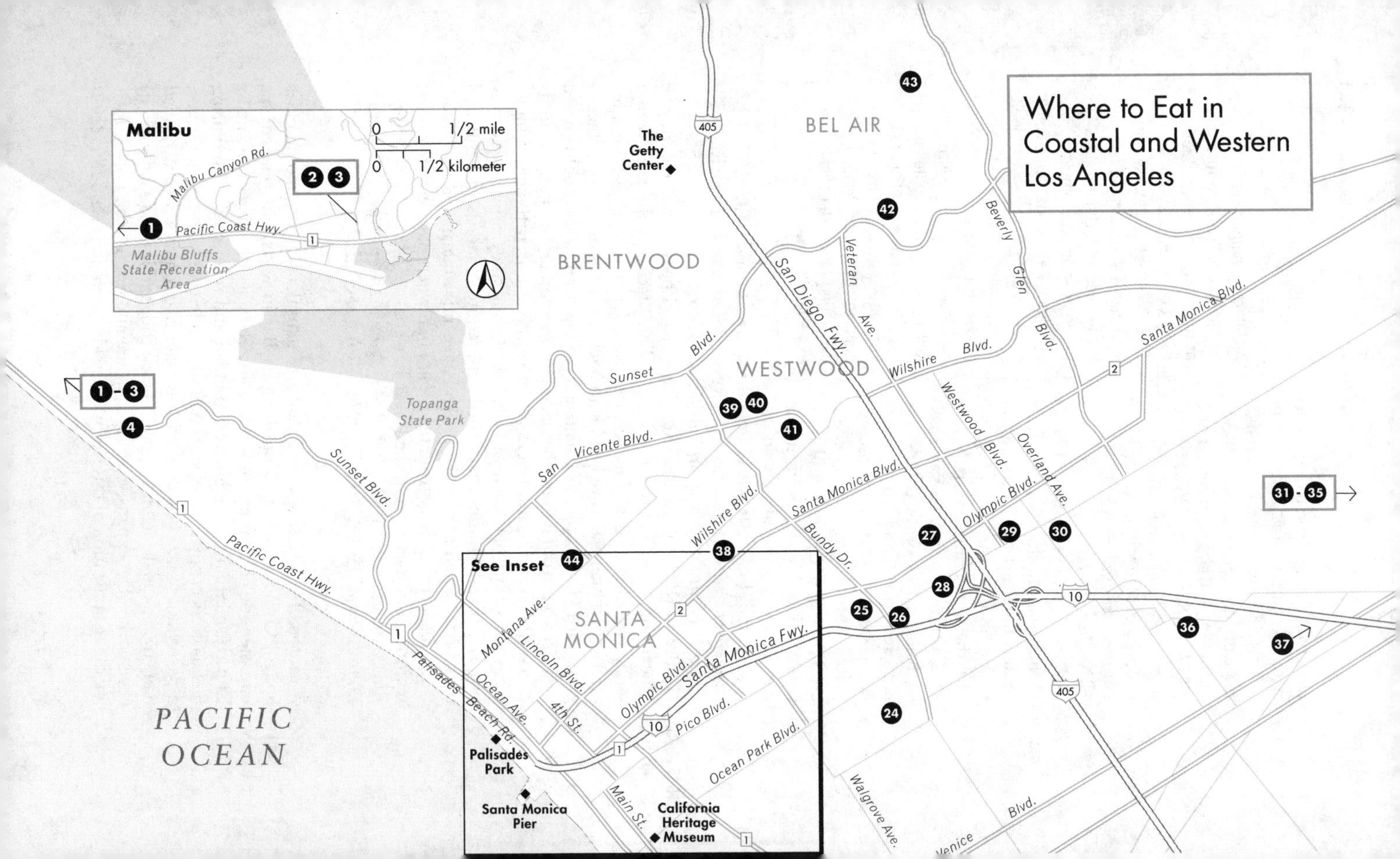

Where to Eat in Coastal and Western Los Angeles
Malibu
0 1/2 mile
0 1/2 kilometer
Malibu Canyon Rd.
Pacific Coast Hwy.
Malibu Bluffs State Recreation Area
The Getty Center
BEL AIR
BRENTWOOD
WESTWOOD
SANTA MONICA
Topanga State Park
PACIFIC OCEAN
San Diego Fwy.
Veteran Ave.
Beverly Glen Blvd.
Sunset Blvd.
Wilshire Blvd.
Santa Monica Blvd.
San Vicente Blvd.
Westwood Blvd.
Overland Ave.
Olympic Blvd.
Bundy Dr.
Santa Monica Fwy.
Pico Blvd.
Ocean Park Blvd.
Walgrove Ave.
Venice Blvd.
Montana Ave.
Lincoln Blvd.
Ocean Ave.
4th St.
Main St.
Palisades Beach Rd.
Palisades Park
Santa Monica Pier
California Heritage Museum
See Inset

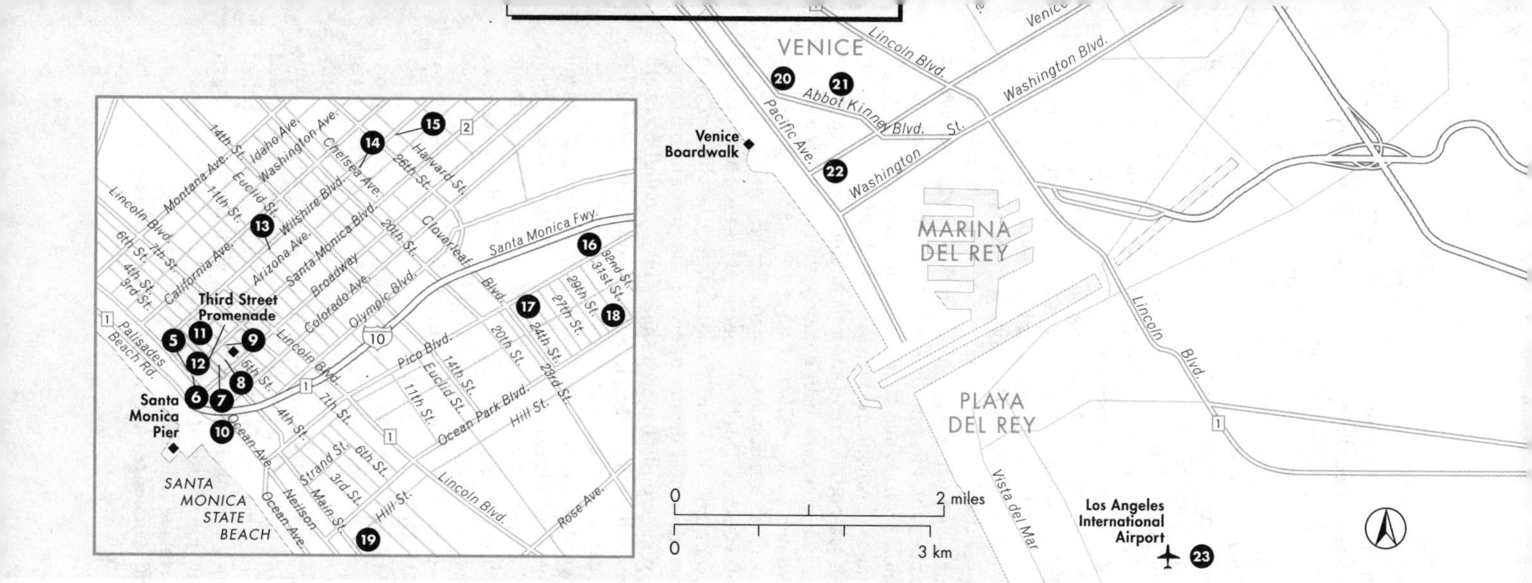

Anisette Brasserie **12**	The Counter **18**	Hotel Bel-Air **42**	The Lobster **10**	Tra di Noi **2**
The Apple Pan **30**	Cucina Paradiso **36**	James' Beach **22**	Mélisse **13**	Typhoon **24**
Bar Pintxo **11**	Drago **15**	JiRaffe **9**	Monte Alban **38**	Valentino **16**
Beacon **31**	Encounter **23**	Joe's Restaurant **21**	Mori Sushi **28**	Versailles **37**
Beau Rivage **1**	Father's Office **44**	Josie **17**	Mr. Cecil's California Ribs **26**	Vibrato Grill, Jazz, etc. **43**
BOA Steakhouse **5**	Fraîche **35**	Katsuya **40**	Nobu Malibu **3**	Vincenti **39**
Bombay Cafe **25**	Gladstone's Malibu **4**	Kiriko **27**	Ocean Avenue Seafood **6**	Wilshire **14**
Border Grill **8**	Gyenari **34**	La Serenata Gourmet **29**	Pecorino **41**	
Broadway Deli **7**	Honey's Kettle Fried Chicken **33**	Lilly's French Café & Bar **20**	Tender Greens **32**	
Chinois on Main **19**				

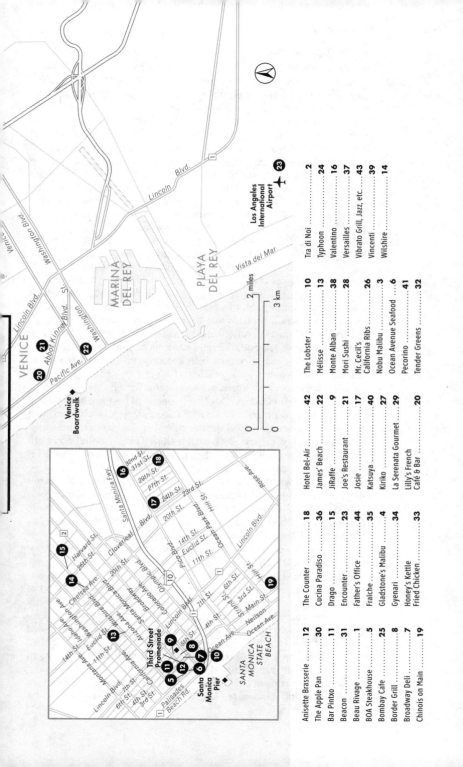

Ave., Culver City ☎*310/838–7500* 🌐*www.beacon-la.com* ✍*Reservations essential* ▭*AE, DC, MC, V* ⏲*No dinner Mon. No lunch Sun.*

$$–$$$ MEDITERRANEAN ★ ✕ **Fraîche.** Further fueling the transformation of unglamorous Culver City into a not-to-be-missed dining destination is this smart-looking restaurant where Gino Angelini (Angelini Osteria) protégé Jason Travi celebrates flavors from both the French and Italian countryside. Ebullient patrons begin with platters of fruits de mer, boudin noir with Dijon-crème fraîche, or porcini salad before moving on to pastas, lamb spezzatino (stew), or steak frites. The soul-warming fare is enhanced by 50-plus wines under $50 and desserts designed by Travi's wife, Miho. The casually sophisticated stone-clad dining room, with tables spilling onto the sidewalk, suits varied occasions. ✉*9411 Culver Blvd., Culver City* ☎*310/839–6800* 🌐*www.fraicherestaurant.com* ✍*Reservations essential* ▭*AE, D, DC, MC, V* ⏲*No lunch weekends.*

$$–$$$$ KOREAN ✕ **Gyenari.** Korean cuisine is emerging from L.A.'s Koreatown to the delight of a dining public craving a healthy, interactive experience, and Gyenari is among a flurry of new mainstream Korean restaurants. Named for a flower that blooms just once a year—a mural featuring the blossom dominates a whole wall—this is a sleek, stylish restaurant whose custom-made tables feature down-draft burners (excellent for fanning away smokiness). While California influences appear, you'll find traditional japchae cellophane noodles, mandoo (dumplings), an ample selection of seafood, the requisite kimchi, and marinated meats ranging from Wagyu beef to pork belly comprise the reasonably authentic menu. ✉*9540 Washington Blvd., Culver City* ☎*310/838–3131* 🌐*www.gyenari.com* ✍*Reservations essential* ▭*AE, MC, V.*

¢–$ SOUTHERN ✕ **Honey's Kettle Fried Chicken.** This family-operated business has updated the old-fashioned practice of kettle-cooking, frying its chicken with intense heat in stainless steel drums, allowing the juices to be sealed beneath a crackly, generously battered skin. This is soulful Southern goodness, and for folks who appreciate this kind of food—it's a bit greasy, but you can say that about any respectable fried chicken—Honey's is well worth a visit. In addition to the golden bird, the menu offers a satisfying fried catfish, hot cakes, and some of the fluffiest biscuits in town. Hang out on the patio with a glass of homemade lemonade and observe the hipsters filing into the high-end eateries that surround unpretentious Honey's. ✉ *9537 Culver Blvd., Culver City* ☎*310/202–5453* 🌐*www.honeyskettle.com* ✍*Reservations not accepted* ▭*AE, D, DC, MC, V.*

$ AMERICAN ✕ **Tender Greens.** Here, in the center of Culver City's burgeoning restaurant district, veterans from posh hotel kitchens turn out the kind of fast food your mom, accountant, and nutritionist would unanimously approve of—emphasizing health and value without compromising quality. After you stand in line for a bit, locally produced greens are tossed in front of you in a big metallic bowl, plated with perfectly grilled meats or fish. Enjoy your ahi tuna Niçoise or chipotle barbecue chicken salad with creamy lime dressing on the sidewalk patio with a glass of Sancerre or homemade lemonade. ✉*9523 Culver Blvd., Culver City* ☎*310/842–8300* 🌐*www.tendergreensfood.com* ✍*Reservations not accepted* ▭*AE, MC, V.*

LOS ANGELES INTERNATIONAL AIRPORT

$$–$$$ NEW AMERICAN ✕ **Encounter.** If you're flying to L.A., you can begin or end your trip with a stop by the dramatic Theme Building for a meal with a runway view. Designers from Walt Disney Imagineering whipped up the intergalactic atmosphere. Choices such as tuna tartare, Peking-style duck, and roasted chicken with a mustard cream sauce certainly beat airplane fare. The place, with its colorful, futuristic design and close encounters with rumbling 747s, is a delight for kids and kids-at-heart. ✉*209 World Way, LAX* ☎*310/215–5151* 🌐*www.encounterlax.com* ▭*AE, MC, V* ⏲*No dinner Mon.–Wed.*

MALIBU

$$–$$$ MEDITERRANEAN ✕ **Beau Rivage.** One of the few Malibu restaurants with a view of the beach and ocean, this romantic Mediterranean villa–style dining room has copper domes and lush landscaping. The expansive menu includes filet mignon with a three-mustard sauce, salmon steak with a Champagne-raspberry sauce, and a strong lineup of pastas, risotto, and gnocchi. In contrast to trendier Malibu haunts, the staff here is warm and welcoming. ✉*26025 Pacific Coast Hwy., Malibu* ☎*310/456–5733* 🌐*www.beaurivagerestaurant.com* ✍*Reservations essential* ▭*AE, D, DC, MC, V* ⏲*Closed Tues. No lunch weekdays.*

$$$–$$$$ JAPANESE ✕ **Nobu Malibu.** At famous chef-restaurateur Nobu Matsuhisa's coastal outpost, the casually chic clientele swarm over morsels of the world's finest fish. In addition to stellar sushi, Nobu serves many of the same ingenious specialties offered at his original Matsuhisa in Beverly Hills or glitzy Nobu in West Hollywood. You'll find exotic species of fish artfully accented with equally exotic South American peppers, ultratender Kobe beef, and a broth perfumed with rare matsutake mushrooms. Elaborate omakase dinners start at $90. ✉*3835 Cross Creek Rd., Malibu* ☎*310/317–9140* 🌐*www.noburestaurants.com* ✍*Reservations essential* ▭*AE, DC, MC, V* ⏲*No lunch.*

$$–$$$ ITALIAN ✕ **Tra di Noi.** The name means "among us," and Malibu natives are trying to keep this simple *ristorante* just that—a local secret. A Tuscan villa-inspired hideaway, the homey Tra di Noi draws everyone from movie stars to well-heeled neighborhood regulars. Nothing too fancy or *nuovo* on the menu, just generous salads, hearty lasagna and other freshly made pastas, short ribs braised in Chianti, and a whole two-pound branzino with herb sauce. An Italian buffet is laid out for Sunday brunch. ✉*3835 Cross Creek Rd., Malibu* ☎*310/456–0169* ▭*AE, MC, V.*

PACIFIC PALISADES

$$$ SEAFOOD ✕ **Gladstone's Malibu.** Gladstone's is one of the most popular restaurants along the Southern California coast; its demand has even spawned a sister restaurant in Universal Studios' CityWalk (though the lack of beachfront makes it far less attractive). The food is notable mostly for its oversize portions: giant bowls of crab chowder, lobsters up to 6 pounds, and the famous mile-high chocolate cake, which can easily feed a small regiment. But the real reason to visit Gladstone's is the glorious vista of sea, sky, and beach. It's also a good breakfast spot. ✉*17300 Pacific Coast Hwy., at Sunset Blvd., Pacific Palisades* ☎*310/454–3474* 🌐*www.gladstones.com* ▭*AE, D, DC, MC, V.*

SANTA MONICA

$$–$$$ FRENCH ✕**Anisette Brasserie.** Parisian-born chef Alain Giraud, famous for some of L.A.'s most elaborate tasting menus, now turns his attention to the energy of a casual brasserie. The soaring space is decked out with imported vintage floor tiles, antique mirrors and sconces—an authenticity reinforced by the waiters' accents. A buzzing, eclectic crowd of tourists, expats, and nearby residents tuck into familiar brasserie favorites such as onion soup gratinée, platters of fruits de mer from the raw bar, duck confit, and daube, a braised beef cheek stew in a soulful red wine reduction. A classic zinc bar was also brought from France and the scene there looks like it might have been lifted from a brasserie on Boulevard Saint-Michel. For lunch, there are frisée salads and croque monsieur sandwiches. ✉*225 Santa Monica Blvd., Santa Monica* ☎*310/395–3200* 🌐*www.anisettebrasserie.com* ▭*AE, DC, MC, V.*

$–$$ SPANISH ✕**Bar Pintxo.** Inspired by his trips to Spain, chef Joe Miller (Joe's restaurant in Venice) opened this lively, warmly appointed tapas bar. In the Basque region, tapas are called pintxos, and this narrow, Americanized slice of the Iberian Peninsula carries the spirit of the genuine article, despite having a view of the Pacific—the Bay of Biscay would be more appropriate—and being occupied by SoCal surfer dudes and struggling screenwriters taking advantage of the good values. Sip a glass of Albariño or sangría while snacking on croquetas de pollo y jamón, morcilla (blood sausage), or paprika-laden chorizo with fried quail eggs. A bowl of Andalusian gazpacho is perfect on a hot California evening. ✉*109 Santa Monica Blvd., Santa Monica* ☎*310/458–2012* ✍*Reservations not accepted* ▭*AE, D, MC, V.*

$$$–$$$$ STEAK ✕**BOA Steakhouse.** This is not your father's steak house; businesspeople and somber mahogany have been swapped out for a fun-loving crowd bathed in multicolor lights from avant-garde fixtures. But you can still start with a prawn cocktail or a traditional Caesar salad prepared tableside before slicing your Laguiole knife into a dry-aged prime New York strip or rib eye (genuine Japanese Wagyu and certified organic beef are also available). Although the steaks are delicious without any frills, you could opt for an embellishment such as a blue cheese rub or cabernet reduction sauce. ✉*101 Santa Monica Blvd., Santa Monica* ☎*310/899–4466* 🌐*www.boasteak.com* ✍*Reservations essential* ▭*AE, D, DC, MC, V.*

$$–$$$ MEXICAN ✕**Border Grill.** Massive, colorful murals—a bit primeval—are a perfect complement to modern interpretations of this busy restaurant's ancient Mayan dishes such as *cochinita pibil* (achiote-marinated pork). Other favorites include a wild-mushroom quesadilla, vinegar-and-pepper-grilled turkey, and daily ceviche specials. Celebrity chef-owners Mary Sue Milliken and Susan Feniger display a passion for Mexican cuisine here, but they do mellow the dishes to suit a broad audience. ✉*1445 4th St., Santa Monica* ☎*310/451–1655* 🌐*www.bordergrill.com* ▭*AE, D, DC, MC, V.*

$–$$ AMERICAN ✕**Broadway Deli.** The name tells just half the story. This lively, cavernous place is a cross between a European brasserie and an upscale diner. The huge menu goes way beyond corned beef and pastrami sandwiches to include pizzas, an ostrich burger, shepherd's pie, even duck enchiladas.

Breads are baked on-site, and there's a kids' menu. ✉*1457 3rd St. Promenade, Santa Monica* ☎*310/451–0616* 🌐*www.broadwaydeli.com* ✍*Reservations not accepted* ▭*AE, MC, V.*

$$$–$$$$ ASIAN ✕ **Chinois on Main.** A once-revolutionary outpost in Wolfgang Puck's repertoire, this is still one of L.A.'s most crowded—and noisy—restaurants. The jazzy interior is just as loud as the clientele. Although the menu has expanded, the restaurant's happy marriage of Asian and French cuisines shows best in its signature dishes such as Chinois chicken salad, Shanghai lobster with spicy ginger-curry sauce, and Cantonese duck with fresh plum sauce. ✉*2709 Main St., Santa Monica* ☎*310/392–9025* 🌐*www.wolfgangpuck.com* ✍*Reservations essential* ▭*AE, D, DC, MC, V* ⏲*No lunch Sat.–Tues.*

3

$ BURGERS ✕ **The Counter.** Angelenos still adore the venerable Apple Pan, but they've also embraced its upscale, contemporary burger-joint counterpart. Here—by checking off your preferences on a sushi bar–style order sheet—you can select beef, turkey, or veggie patties, then specify your preferred cheeses, toppings, one of 18 different sauces (anything from honey-mustard to peanut), and bun (or, for carb counters, a "burger-in-a-bowl"). Even with the slick surroundings and wild combinations, this emerging chain is a nostalgic reminder of L.A.'s ongoing love affair with the burger. ✉*2901 Ocean Park Blvd., Santa Monica* ☎*310/399–8383* 🌐*www.thecounterburger.com* ✍*Reservations not accepted* ▭*AE, MC, V.*

$$–$$$ ITALIAN ✕ **Drago.** Native Sicilian Celestino Drago's home-style fare is carefully prepared and attentively served in stark designer surroundings. White walls and white linen–covered tables line both sides of a floating service station dressed up with a towering arrangement of fresh flowers. The menu adds sophisticated finishes to rustic foundations in dishes such as pappardelle tossed in a pheasant and morel mushroom sauce, squid-ink risotto, or pan-roasted rabbit in sweet-and-sour sauce. ✉*2628 Wilshire Blvd., Santa Monica* ☎*310/828–1585* 🌐*www.celestinodrago.com* ▭*AE, MC, V* ⏲*No lunch weekends.*

$–$$ AMERICAN ✕ **Father's Office.** With a facade distinguished only by a vintage neon sign, Father's Office is a congested, gentrified pub famous for hand-crafted beers and what is widely regarded as L.A.'s best burger. Topped with Gruyère and Maytag blue cheeses, arugula, caramelized onions, and applewood-smoked bacon compote, the "Office Burger" is a guilty pleasure worth waiting in line for (which is usually required). Other options include steak frites and Spanish tapas, with side orders of addictive sweet potato fries served in a miniature shopping cart with aïoli—don't even think of asking for ketchup, because FO enforces a strict no-substitutions policy. So popular is the Office Burger that chef-owner Sang Yoon has recently opened a second location in Culver City. Note: Because Father's Office is a bar, it's strictly 21 and over. ✉*1018 Montana Ave., Santa Monica* ☎*310/393–2337* 🌐*www.fathersoffice.com* ✍*Reservations not accepted* ▭*AE, D, MC, V* ⏲*No lunch weekdays.*

$$$–$$$$ NEW AMERICAN ✕ **JiRaffe.** The two-story California bistro with ceiling-high windows and polished dark-wood accents is as handsome as the menu is tasteful. Chef-owner Raphael Lunetta, who is also an accomplished surfer, turns out seasonal appetizers such as a delicate roasted-tomato tart or a roasted-beet salad with caramelized walnuts and dried Bing cherries.

They're worthy preludes to main dishes like a truly memorable crispy-skinned salmon with parsnip puree, braised fennel, and sweet balsamic reduction. ✉*502 Santa Monica Blvd., Santa Monica* ☎*310/917–6671* 🌐*www.jirafferestaurant.com* ✍*Reservations essential* ▭*AE, DC, MC, V* ⏲*No lunch.*

$$$–$$$$ AMERICAN ✕**Josie.** Done in understated taupe hues with generously spaced tables, this cosmopolitan establishment feels like it belongs in San Francisco instead of laid-back L.A. The kitchen, however, blends that sophistication with inspirations from the Great Outdoors, resulting in "campfire trout" cooked in a cast-iron skillet, venison ragout, and signature buffalo burger with truffle fries. ✉*2424 Pico Blvd., Santa Monica* ☎*310/581–9888* 🌐*www.josierestaurant.com* ✍*Reservations essential* ▭*AE, MC, V* ⏲*No lunch.*

$$–$$$ SEAFOOD ✕**The Lobster.** Anchoring the beach end of the festive Santa Monica Pier, the Lobster usually teems with locals and tourists alike, who come here for the jubilant scene, the great view, and the comfort seafood of chef Allyson Thurber. Start with lobster cocktail with tarragon-lemon aïoli, lobster clam chowder, or lobster salad with sweet corn pancakes. For entrées, the theme continues with both Maine and Pacific spiny varieties—but dishes like king salmon in herb sauce are equally satisfying. Weather permitting, request a table on the terrace, both for the views and an escape from the high-decibel interior. ✉*1602 Ocean Ave., Santa Monica* ☎*310/458–9294* 🌐*www.thelobster.com* ✍*Reservations essential* ▭*AE, D, DC, MC, V.*

$$$$ FRENCH Fodor'sChoice ★ ✕**Mélisse.** In a city where informality reigns, this is one of L.A.'s more dressy—but not stuffy—restaurants. The dining room is contemporary yet elegant, with well-spaced tables topped with flowers and Limoges china. The garden room loosens up with a stone fountain and a retractable roof. Chef-owner Josiah Citrin enriches his modern French cooking with seasonal California produce. Consider seared sweet corn ravioli in brown butter–truffle froth, lobster Thermidor, venison with *poivrade* sauce, or duck in a Banyuls reduction. The cheese cart is packed with domestic and European selections. ✉*1104 Wilshire Blvd., Santa Monica* ☎*310/395–0881* 🌐*www.melisse.com* ✍*Reservations essential* ▭*AE, D, DC, MC, V* ⏲*Closed Sun. and Mon. No lunch.*

$$$–$$$$ SEAFOOD ✕**Ocean Avenue Seafood.** Operating since 1946, this cavernous restaurant isn't right on the water, but the Pacific is just across the street—ask for a table by the window for an ocean view. Low ceilings, dim lighting, well-spaced tables, and attentive service create a close-knit mood. There are plenty of lobster dishes, but other options from the daily-changing menu include paella, sesame-crusted big eye tuna, grilled Channel Island swordfish with pineapple salsa, wild salmon in pinot noir–cherry sauce, and prime steaks. The oyster bar offers a dizzying selection. ✉*1401 Ocean Ave., Santa Monica* ☎*310/394–5669* 🌐*www.oceanave.com* ▭*AE, D, DC, MC, V.*

$$–$$$ ASIAN ✕**Typhoon.** Owner Brian Vidor, who traveled the world as a rock musician and naturalist, brings home some of his favorite gastronomic experiences to this restaurant. If you can tear your attention away from the windows overlooking the Santa Monica Airport flight paths, the exhibition kitchen, and the mirrored weather map above a crowded

bar, you can embark on a culinary grand tour of Asia. You'll find sashimi from Japan, samosas from India, and curries from Thailand. For even more adventure—or bragging rights—you can order stir-fried crickets, Manchurian mountain ants, or Singapore-style scorpions, all beautifully seasoned. ☒*3221 Donald Douglas Loop S, Santa Monica* ☎*310/390–6565* ⊕*www.typhoon.biz* *Reservations essential* ▭*AE, D, DC, MC, V* ⊙*No lunch Sat.*

$$$–$$$$ ITALIAN Fodor's Choice ★ ✕**Valentino.** Renowned as one of the country's top Italian restaurants, Valentino has a truly awe-inspiring wine list. With nearly 2,800 labels consuming 130 pages, backed by a cellar overflowing with nearly 100,000 bottles, this restaurant is nothing short of heaven for serious oenophiles. In the 1970s, suave owner Piero Selvaggio introduced L.A. to his exquisite modern Italian cuisine, and he continues to impress guests with dishes like a timballo of wild mushrooms with rich Parmigiano-Reggiano–saffron *fonduta*, squid ink–tinted risotto with Maine lobster, a memorable osso buco, and sautéed branzino with lemon emulsion. A welcome addition to this exalted venue is its more casual vin bar for wine tasting, crudo, and carpaccio. ☒*3115 Pico Blvd., Santa Monica* ☎*310/829–4313* ⊕*www.valentinorestaurantgroup.com* *Reservations essential* ▭*AE, DC, MC, V* ⊙*Closed Sun. No lunch Sat. and Mon.–Thurs.*

SANDWICH CITY

Angelenos love sandwich variety; a Vietnamese *bánh mì* from **Gingergrass**, a genuine New Orleans–style *muffaletta* from the **Gumbo Pot**, or a classic French Dip from **Philippe the Original. Porto's Bakery** (☒*315 N. Brand Blvd., Glendale* ☎*818/956–5996*) serves up one of the best Cuban *media noche* sandwiches. On Thursday nights at **Campanile**, you can bite into a quail Sloppy Joe or French croque monsieur. And Wolfgang Puck's **Sidebar** (☒*Beverly Wilshire, 9500 Wilshire Blvd.* ☎*310/275–5200*) pairs killer Kobe beef "sliders" with cocktails.

$$$–$$$$ NEW AMERICAN ✕**Wilshire.** The woodsy patio at Wilshire is one of the most coveted spaces on the L.A. dining circuit—its candlelight, firelight, and gurgling fountain reel in a hip crowd beneath a cloud of canvas. A passion for organic market-fresh ingredients is reflected in dishes like sunchoke-apple soup with blue cheese croutons and leg of lamb with cumin-scented bean puree. The eclectic wine list is first-rate, and there's a lively bar scene here, too. ☒*2454 Wilshire Blvd., Santa Monica* ☎*310/586–1707* ⊕*www.wilshirerestaurant.com* *Reservations essential* ▭*AE, D, DC, MC, V* ⊙*Closed Sun. No lunch weekends.*

VENICE

$$–$$$ AMERICAN ✕**James' Beach.** With a menu that's more old-school than those at its neighbors in now-trendy Venice, this coastal hot spot seems just right for a seaside lunch or supper, inside or out on the patio. The menu focuses on American classics like meat loaf, chicken potpie, and fried chicken, but you can also find tuna tartare and shrimp tacos. If you're so inclined, sip your dessert wine between shots at the billiard table in a bungalow behind the patio. It's open until 1 AM Thursday–Saturday. ☒*60 N. Venice Blvd., Venice* ☎*310/823–5396* ⊕*www.jamesbeach.com* ▭*AE, D, DC, MC, V* ⊙*No lunch Mon. and Tues.*

CLOSE UP

A Table Outdoors

It's November or March, but the request is still possible: "We'd like a table outdoors." Thanks to L.A.'s weather, you can eat outside nearly year-round, and there are dozens of alfresco options from Malibu to Pasadena. Some restaurants give you an ocean view, some evoke Provençal herb gardens, and others line up sidewalk tables for great people-watching. If an outdoor table is your goal, be sure to specify one when making reservations.

Begonias, burbling fountains, and candlelighted tables fill the patio at **Il Cielo** (*9018 Burton Way, Beverly Hills 310/276–9990 www.ilcielo.com*). On a moonlight night, it's romantic enough to elicit the unthinkable from a confirmed bachelor.

For stunning coastal views, head to **Geoffrey's** (*27400 Pacific Coast Hwy., Malibu 310/457–1519 www.geoffreysmalibu.com*), where you'll be sandwiched between surf and stars. The olive tree–shaded patio at **Dominick's** (*8715 Beverly Blvd., West Hollywood 310/652–2335 www.dominicksrestaurant.com*) draws a new generation of wannabe Rat Packers.

A hip, retro vibe permeates the air at **blue on blue** (*Avalon Hotel, 9400 W. Olympic Blvd., Beverly Hills 310/277–5221 www.avalonbeverlyhills.com*), where cabanas surround an hourglass-shaped pool.

The best tables at **Michael's** (*1147 3rd St., Santa Monica 310/451–0843 www.michaelssantamonica.com*), an early landmark of California cuisine, are in its enchanting garden. At **Chez Mimi** (*246 26th St., Santa Monica 310/393–0558 www.chezmimirestaurant.com*), simple French fare is served on a brick patio with vine-covered trellises and trees entwined with lights.

For a true star-gazing experience, consider **the Ivy** (*113 N. Robertson Blvd., adjacent to Beverly Hills 310/274–8303*), whose picket-fence-enclosed patio is often filled with famous faces. To watch bustling Old Pasadena pass before you, head to **Mi Piace** (*25 E. Colorado Blvd. 626/795–3131 www.mipiace.com*), a popular Italian spot. Sushi is paired with spectacular skyline views on the wraparound veranda at **Takami** (*811 Wilshire Blvd., Downtown 213/236–9600 www.takamisushi.com*), a penthouse restaurant rising 21 stories above the city.

—Roger J. Grody

$$$ AMERICAN

Joe's Restaurant. In what was originally a turn-of-the-20th-century beach house, Joe Miller has created the definitive neighborhood restaurant with a citywide reputation. His imaginative French-influenced California cooking focuses on fresh ingredients. Start with tuna tartare or porcini ravioli in mushroom-Parmesan broth, and continue with Berkshire pork *crépinette* (a type of sausage) or potato-crusted red snapper in port wine sauce. For dessert, try the baked Alaska or unique house-made ice creams. Lunch is a terrific value—all entrées are $18 or less and come with soup or salad. *1023 Abbott Kinney Blvd., Venice 310/399–5811 www.joesrestaurant.com AE, D, DC, MC, V Closed Mon.*

$$–$$$ FRENCH ✕**Lilly's French Café & Bar.** Forget haute cuisine—Lilly's celebrates the robust flavors of French bistro cooking. Start with *flamiche* (a northern French goat cheese and leek tart) or that bistro staple, escargots with garlic-herb butter. Then go on to duck breast with wild cherry sauce or entrecôte with Béarnaise sauce and finish with profiteroles or a lemon tart. The daily prix-fixe lunch is a great value: soup or salad plus a gorgeous sandwich or omelet for about $12. No reservations are accepted for lunch, but be sure to call ahead for dinner. ✉*1031 Abbot Kinney Blvd., Venice* ☎*310/314–0004* 🌐*www.lillysfrenchcafe.com* 💳*AE, MC, V.*

WORD OF MOUTH

"I've been going [to the Apple Pan] since I was a kid, and now bring my kid here. . . . Sometimes it's nice when nothing changes, especially in L.A., where everything does." —Shannon

3

WEST LOS ANGELES

¢ AMERICAN Fodor's Choice ★ ✕**The Apple Pan.** A burger-insider haunt since 1947, this unassuming joint with a horseshoe-shaped counter—no tables here—turns out one heck of a good burger topped with Tillamook cheddar, plus a hickory burger with barbecue sauce. You'll also find great fries and, of course, an apple pie indulgent enough to christen the restaurant (although many regulars argue that the banana cream deserves the honor). Be prepared to wait, but the veteran countermen turn the stools at a quick pace. ✉*10801 W. Pico Blvd., West L.A.* ☎*310/475–3585* *Reservations not accepted* 💳*No credit cards* *Closed Mon.*

$–$$ INDIAN ★ ✕**Bombay Café.** Some of the menu items at Bombay Cafe are strictly authentic, others have been lightened up a bit to suit Southern California sensibilities, and a few are truly innovative (e.g., California tandoori salad with lemon-cilantro dressing, green apple-cranberry chutney, ginger margarita). Regulars (and there are many) swear by the chili-laden lamb *frankies* (burritolike snacks sold by vendors on the beaches of Bombay), *sev puri* (wafers topped with onions, potatoes, and chutneys), and Sindhi chicken, a complex poached-then-sautéed recipe with an exotically seasoned crust. ✉*12021 Pico Blvd., West L.A.* ☎*310/473–3388* 🌐*www.bombaycafe-la.com* 💳*MC, V.*

$$–$$$ ITALIAN ✕**Cucina Paradiso.** With its linen-draped tables, attentive service, and marble-topped wine bar, this eager-to-please trattoria feels homey and approachable. The menu bears out that impression with choices like garlicky scampi, pancetta-mascarpone risotto, osso buco, and a terrific filet mignon in Gorgonzola cream. During autumn's truffle season, a luxurious perfume wafts through the dining room as dishes are generously topped with shavings of the prized fungus. ✉*3387 Motor Ave., West L.A.* ☎*310/839–2500* 🌐*www.cucinaparadiso.net* *Reservations essential* 💳*AE, D, DC, MC, V* *No lunch weekends.*

$$$–$$$$ JAPANESE ✕**Kiriko.** Here in "Little Tokyo West," this understated restaurant with contemporary art and rough-timbered sushi bar distinguishes itself from the competition. Friendly chef-owner Ken Namba might send out beautifully marbled salmon, smoked in-house and crowned with caviar, or lightly seared toro topped with a tiny dollop of minced hot peppers. An omakase feast could include sea urchin risotto and

dramatically plated live Pacific lobster succeeded by a parade of beautifully presented, but never overwrought, sushi. Regulars finish with house-made honey-sesame ice cream while contemplating their next visit. ✉ *Olympic Collection, 11301 Olympic Blvd., #102, West L.A.* ☎ *310/478–7769* 🌐 *www.kirikosushi.com* ✍ *Reservations essential* 💳 *AE, MC, V* ⏲ *Closed Mon. No lunch weekends.*

$–$$ MEXICAN ★ ✕ **La Serenata Gourmet.** With uncomfortable chairs and crowds from the nearby Westside Pavilion boosting decibel levels, this branch of the East L.A. original isn't ideal for leisurely conversation. But the restaurant scores big points for its boldly flavored Mexican cuisine. Pork dishes and moles are delicious, but seafood is the real star—there are chubby *gorditas* (cornmeal pockets stuffed with shrimp), juicy shrimp enchiladas in tomatillo sauce, and simply grilled fish, with cilantro or garlic sauce, that sings with flavor. If your experience with Mexican food has been on the Tex-Mex end of the spectrum, come here to broaden your taste bud horizons. ✉ *10924 W. Pico Blvd., West L.A.* ☎ *310/441–9667* 🌐 *www.laserenataonline.com* 💳 *AE, D, DC, MC, V.*

$–$$ MEXICAN ✕ **Monte Alban.** This family-owned café serves the subtle cooking of one of Mexico's most respected culinary regions, Oaxaca. Flavors here are intense without being fiery. Try their version of chiles rellenos (bright green chili peppers stuffed with chicken, raisins, and groundnuts); any of the complex moles with chicken, pork, or salmon; or extra-tender stewed goat. For dessert, there's fried, sliced sweet plantain topped with crème fraîche that's delicioso. ✉ *11927 Santa Monica Blvd., West L.A.* ☎ *310/444–7736* 💳 *AE, D, MC, V.*

$$$–$$$$ JAPANESE Fodor's Choice ★ ✕ **Mori Sushi.** Only a small fish logo identifies the facade of this restaurant, but many consider it the best sushi bar in L.A. and Morihiro Onodera one of the great sushi masters in America. The austere whitewashed space stands in contrast to the chef's artful presentations of pristine morsels of seafood, all served on ceramic plates he makes himself. Allow him to compose an entire meal for you—this can be an expensive proposition—and he'll send out eye-popping presentations of sushi or sashimi accented with touches of rare sea salts, yuzu, and freshly ground wasabi, as well as intricately conceived salads, house-made tofu, and soups. ✉ *11500 Pico Blvd., West L.A.* ☎ *310/479–3939* 🌐 *www.morisushi.org* 💳 *AE, MC, V* ⏲ *Closed Sun. No lunch Sat.*

$–$$ SOUTHERN ✕ **Mr. Cecil's California Ribs.** A rib-loving movie-studio exec opened this eatery in a tiny, circular hatbox of a building. The meaty, tender St. Louis–style ribs are particularly outstanding, with a spirited but not overpowering sauce. Aficionados of pecan pie should also beat a path here. Bonus: it's the only rib joint in town where you can order a bottle of Château Lafite Rothschild. ✉ *12244 W. Pico Blvd., West L.A.* ☎ *310/442–1550* 🌐 *www.mrcecilscaribs.com* 💳 *AE, MC, V.*

$–$$ CUBAN ✕ **Versailles.** Despite its no-frills dining room in which noise echos off Formica surfaces and art is an afterthought, people line up outside the door for Versailles's respectable, bargain-price Cuban food. Most are crazy about the citrusy *mojo*-marinated chicken seasoned with loads of garlic. Others prefer oxtail, *ropa vieja* (shredded beef), or paella. ✉ *10319 Venice Blvd., West L.A.* ☎ *310/558–3168* 🌐 *www.versaillescuban.com* ✍ *Reservations not accepted* 💳 *AE, MC, V.*

SAN FERNANDO VALLEY

BURBANK

$$ FRENCH ✕ **Bistro Provence.** The contemporary, French-inspired cooking of chef-owner Miki Zivkovic is a highlight of the Burbank dining scene. While the restaurant's shopping center location may be less than glamorous, its wood-clad candlelighted interior is warm and inviting. From the prix-fixe menu—at about $30, it's among the best deals in town—you might select fennel-*crusted* ahi with Niçoise salad followed by beef bourguignonne or lamb pot-au-feu, and finish with profiteroles. Like a genuine bistro, this is an unpretentious neighborhood spot. ✉*345 N. Pass Ave., Burbank* ☎*818/840–9050* ✍*Reservations essential* ▭*AE, D, DC, MC, V* ⊙*Closed Sun. No lunch Sat.*

> **CHILLING OUT**
>
> In L.A. you can find deliciously multicultural takes on ice cream. **Al Gelato** (*✉806 S. Robertson Blvd., south of Beverly Hills ☎ 310/659–8069*) is favored for its Italian classics like hazelnut and *stracciatella*. Endearing hole-in-the-wall **Mateo's** (*✉4222 W. Pico Blvd., Mid-City ☎ 323/931–5500*) serves Oaxacan-style ice creams and sorbets (e.g., cactus fruit, tamarindo). For a Middle Eastern scoop, hit **Mashti Malone's** (*✉1525 N. La Brea Ave., Hollywood ☎ 323/874–0144 🌐www.mashtimalone.com*) for ginger-rosewater ice cream.

CALABASAS

$$$$ AMERICAN Fodor'sChoice ★ ✕ **Saddle Peak Lodge.** When you've had enough big-city attitude, head for this romantic retreat in the Santa Monica Mountains—it feels a thousand miles from L.A. What was once a bordello is now a restaurant oozing with rustic elegance. Mounted stag and moose heads watch over roaring fireplaces and mountain views. They also hint at the lodge's specialty: game. Bring out the knives for wood-fired rack of venison, seared New Zealand elk tenderloin with a ragout of bacon and cherries, Nilgai Texas antelope, and buffalo short ribs. The sprawling terrace is an idyllic spot for Sunday brunch. ✉*419 Cold Canyon Rd., Calabasas* ☎*818/222–3888* 🌐*www.saddlepeaklodge.com* ✍*Reservations essential* ▭*AE, DC, MC, V* ⊙*Closed Mon. and Tues. No lunch Wed.–Fri.*

NORTH HOLLYWOOD

$$ ITALIAN ✕ **Ca' del Sole.** With antique wood hutches, copper moldings, and a fireplace, this studio-area establishment draws a diverse clientele in search of thinly sliced octopus drizzled in extra virgin olive oil, soulful spaghetti carbonara, pumpkin-filled *mezzelune* (half moon–shaped ravioli), and classic osso buco. The wine list is moderately priced and, weather permitting, you can sit in the walled patio that, despite its proximity to L.A. traffic, feels wonderfully escapist. ✉*4100 Cahuenga Blvd., North Hollywood* ☎*818/985–4669* 🌐*www.cadelsole.com* ▭*AE, DC, MC, V* ⊙*No lunch Sat.*

SHERMAN OAKS

$$ FRENCH ★ ✕ **Café Bizou.** Housed in an old bungalow that complements its casual brand of elegance, Café Bizou is *the* place for fine California-French bistro fare at bargain prices. Sauces are classic, soups are rich (try the luscious lobster bisque), and combinations are creative. Among the

Art's Delicatessen 4
Asanebo 5
Bistro Provence 6
Ca' del Sole 7
Café Bizou 2
Pinot Bistro 3
Saddle Peak Lodge 1

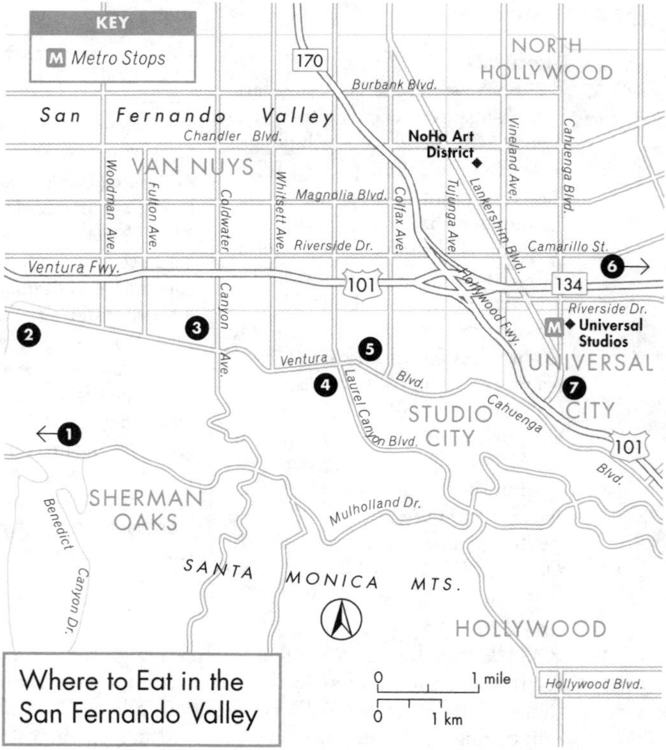

Where to Eat in the San Fernando Valley

best starters is the homemade ravioli, stuffed with lobster and salmon puree, and a winning entrée is the sesame seed–coated salmon layered over potato-pancake triangles. Those who bring their own bottle pay a mere $2 corkage fee. ✉*14016 Ventura Blvd., Sherman Oaks* ☎*818/788–3536* 🌐*www.cafebizou.com* ✍*Reservations essential* ▭*AE, D, DC, MC, V.*

STUDIO CITY

$–$$ DELI ✕**Art's Delicatessen.** One of the best kosher-style delis in the city, Art's serves mammoth corned beef and pastrami sandwiches to hungry hordes from the nearby studios. Matzo-ball and sweet-and-sour cabbage soups, chopped liver, and knishes reel in regulars. This is one of the few delis with valet parking. ✉*12224 Ventura Blvd., Studio City* ☎*818/762–1221* 🌐*www.artsdeli.com* ✍*Reservations not accepted* ▭*AE, D, DC, MC, V.*

$$$–$$$$ JAPANESE Fodor's Choice ★ ✕**Asanebo.** Don't let its nondescript minimal location deter you: Asanebo is one of L.A.'s finest Japanese restaurants—and still relatively undiscovered. Once strictly a sashimi bar, this congested but inviting establishment introduced top-quality sushi to satisfy increasing local demand and also offers a wealth of innovative dishes. From a simple morsel of pristine fish dusted with sea salt to intricate cooked items, Asanebo continues to impress. The affable chefs will introduce you to

memorable specialties such as a caviar-topped lobster cocktail and succulent seared toro drizzled with a light garlic cream. ✉*11941 Ventura Blvd., Studio City* ☎*818/760–3348* ✍*Reservations essential* 💳*AE, D, DC, MC, V* ⏲*Closed Mon. No lunch weekends.*

$$–$$$ FRENCH ✕**Pinot Bistro.** This was the first—and possibly still the best—of Joachim Splichal's chain of Pinot restaurants. The main dining room is standard SoCal, but the bar area is a lovely re-creation of a Parisian bistro, with mustard walls, polished wood, and black-and-white-tile floors. The menu pairs bistro mainstays such as *movles marinière* and cassoulet along with grilled items worthy of a top steak house enhanced with a lineup of sauces from béarnaise to truffle butter. For dessert, don't miss the chocolate croissant bread pudding with a bourbon sauce. ✉*9160412969 Ventura Blvd., Studio City* ☎*818/990–0500* 🌐*www.patinagroup.com* 💳*AE, D, DC, MC, V* ⏲*No lunch weekends.*

PASADENA, GLENDALE, AND SAN GABRIEL VALLEY

GLENDALE

$$–$$$ MIDDLE EASTERN ✕**Carousel.** One of L.A.'s flashiest Middle Eastern restaurants, Carousel is a sprawling place displaying colorful frescos and exotic hookahs. Belly dancers take it up another notch, but the real draw is an extensive menu of Armenian, Lebonese, and Greek specialties. Knowing regulars concentrate on *meze* (appetizers) such as *fatayer* (cheese-filled phyllo pastries) and *muhammara* (walnut-chili paste with pomegranate juice). If you're not as stuffed as the grape leaves you just consumed, continue with platters of kebabs before concluding with baklava and potent coffee. ✉*304 N. Brand Blvd., Glendale* ☎*818/246 –7775* 🌐*www.carouselrestaurant.com* 💳*AE, D, DC, MC, V* ⏲*Closed Mon.*

$$ NEW AMERICAN ✕**Palate Food + Wine.** Chef/owner Octavio Becerra has carved an intimate restaurant out of a historic warehouse building, creating a dining experience that's casual yet sophisticated. His small plate menu, which changes frequently, showcases approachable cuisine crafted from artisanal ingredients. Even the butter is churned in-house. Comforting (and addictive) salmon, chicken, or pork rillettes arrive in miniature mason jars; a generous "porkfolio" charcuterie plate is accompanied by vegetables pickled on-site; and flash-fried squash blossoms filled with ricotta are paired with house-made aïoli. Becerra's take on salade lyonnaise revives bistro memories while unglamorous items like pork trotters and lamb belly earn a new image. A cave accommodates 50 multinational cheeses supported by a wine list loaded with intriguing small producers. A few steps behind the exhibition kitchen are a retail wine shop, wine bar and library. ✉*933 S. Brand Blvd., Glendale* ☎*818/662–9463* 🌐*www.palatefoodwine.com* ✍*Reservations essential* ⏲*Closed Sun. No lunch.* 💳*AE, MC, V.*

¢–$ CUBAN ✕**Porto's Bakery.** What began as a small family business catering to L.A.'s Cuban-American community has evolved into a multimillion-dollar entrepreneurial phenomenon with a diverse multicultural clientele. It's very popular, so plan on waiting in line. In addition to some magnificent cakes, the cases are filled with European pastries, from French Napoleons to German strudels. A café accommodates customers looking for a cup of café con leche or Cuban snacks like media noches (pressed sandwiches with ham, cheese, pork and pickles), ham croquetas or papas rellenas (potato balls filled with seasoned ground beef). Although it doesn't stay open past 7 PM, Porto's offers Cuban dinner plates, such as ropa vieja (shredded beef in tomato-based sauce) with plantains. ✉*315 N. Brand Blvd., Glendale* ☎*818/956–5996* 🌐*www.portosbakery.com* ✍*Reservations not accepted* 💳*No credit cards* ⏲*No dinner Sun.*

WORD OF MOUTH

"Monterey Park is where the Chinese foodies go. Ocean Star is the 'star' of a number of restaurants there. Marvelous dim sum."

—easytraveler

MONTEREY PARK

$–$$ CHINESE

✕ **Lake Spring Shanghai Restaurant.** There are countless good Chinese restaurants in the San Gabriel Valley, but Lake Spring stands out; in fact, it's one of the most renowned Shanghai-style eateries in America. Unlike many of its frenetic, no-frills neighbors, Lake Spring's dining room exudes a refreshing calm. Devotees come for the tender, slow-cooked pork rump; spinach-tinted jade shrimp; cured pork with bamboo-shoot casserole; and plump scallops in garlic sauce. ✉*219 E. Garvey Ave., Monterey Park* ☎*626/280–3571* 💳*MC, V.*

$$–$$$ CHINESE ★

✕ **Ocean Star.** Reminiscent of Hong Kong's dim sum palaces, this stronghold of Chinese seafood is so vast—it seats 800—that the staff resorts to walkie-talkies. It's known for the quality and freshness of its fish and shellfish, and you're free to select your meal from one of the many aquariums lining the marble walls. Try the boiled-live shrimp with soy-chili dipping sauce, huge scallops served in their shell, king crabs with black-bean sauce, any of the whole steamed fish, or pricey delicacies like shark's fin soup. The best way to experience Ocean Star is to bring a whole dim sum posse for lunch. ✉*145 N. Atlantic Blvd., Monterey Park* ☎*626/308–2128* 🌐*www.oceansf.com* 💳*AE, DC, MC, V.*

PASADENA

$–$$ INDIAN

✕ **All India Cafe.** Reflecting the eclectic scene of Old Pasadena is this authentic Indian eatery. Ingredients are fresh, and flavors are bold without depending on overpowering spiciness. Start with the *bhel puri,* a savory puffed rice-and-potatoes dish. In addition to meat curries and tikkas, there are many vegetarian selections and some hard-to-find items such as the burritolike frankies, a favorite Bombay street food. The prices are as palatable as the meals: a full lunch still costs less than $10. ✉*39 Fair Oaks Ave., Pasadena* ☎*626/440–0309* 🌐*www.allindiacafe.com* 💳*AE, MC, V.*

$$$–$$$$ FRENCH

✕ **Bistro 45.** One of Pasadena's most stylish and sophisticated dining spots, Bistro 45 blends traditional French themes with modern concepts to create fanciful California hybrids that delight locals and visitors alike. Seared ahi tuna with a black-and-white-sesame crust, and duck with orange-ginger sauce incorporate Pacific Rim accents. The art deco bungalow has been tailored into a sleek environment. Oenophiles, take note: in addition to having one of the best wine lists in town, owner Robert Simon regularly hosts lavish winemaker dinners. ✉*45 S. Mentor Ave., Pasadena* ☎*626/795–2478* 🌐*www.bistro45.*

GOURMET TO-GO

Angelenos are always on the run and getting food to go. Desperate housewives cheat all the time at luxurious **Bistro Garden at Coldwater** (✉ *12950 Ventura Blvd., Studio City* ☎ *818/501–0202* 🌐 *www.bistrogarden.com*), where they take home chocolate soufflés or pack a picnic basket for the Hollywood Bowl. **The Cheese Store of Silver Lake** (✉ *3926-28 W. Sunset Blvd., Silver Lake* ☎ *323/644–7511* 🌐 *www.cheesestoresl.com*) is stocked with cheese, salumi, and baked goods—have them pack a box for a Dodgers game. The prepared dishes at **Joan's on Third** (✉ *8350 W. 3rd St., south of West Hollywood* ☎ *323/655–2285* 🌐 *www.joansonthird.com*) range from pesto-crusted salmon to Korean short ribs. Just down the street, **Little Next Door** (✉ *8142 W. 3rd St., south of West Hollywood* ☎ *323/951–1010* 🌐 *www.thelittledoor.com*), the take-out market/deli companion to the Mediterranean-inspired restaurant, the Little Door, dishes out Moroccan-spiced crab cakes and ratatouille. **Porta Via Italian Foods** (✉ *1 W. California Blvd., Pasadena* ☎ *626/793–9000* 🌐 *www.portavia-foods.com*) dispenses hand-crafted salumi, pastas, and Italian cheeses.

com ⚠ *Reservations essential* ▭ *AE, D, DC, MC, V* ⊙ *Closed Mon. No lunch weekends.*

$$$–$$$$ NEW AMERICAN ✕ **Derek's Bistro.** Complete with a romantic fireplace and a tranquil patio, this casually elegant restaurant pioneered contemporary American cuisine in what was once strictly meat-and-potatoes territory. Dinner might start with seared foie gras with caramelized mangos or ethereal deep-fried Gorgonzola-stuffed baby artichokes, followed by wild salmon in a thyme beurre blanc or a rosy rack of lamb. Sate your sweet tooth with warm brioche bread pudding with crème anglaise or a refreshing Grand Marnier granita. ✉ *181 E. Glenarm St., Pasadena* ☎ *626/799–5252* 🌐 *www.dereks.com* ▭ *AE, D, MC, V* ⊙ *Closed Mon. No lunch Fri.*

$$$$ AMERICAN Fodor'sChoice ★ ✕ **The Dining Room.** Until the arrival of charismatic chef Craig Strong, there wasn't much to say about this high-price hotel restaurant. But Strong brought with him global inspirations and a culinary finesse beyond his years. A perfectionist (he insists, for instance, on importing butter from Normandy), Strong continually surprises with dishes such as lemongrass-scented spicy coconut milk–Dungeness crab soup, brandade-stuffed squash blossoms, and sautéed duck breast and leg confit with potato-basil mousseline and huckleberry sauce. The chef relishes the opportunity to personalize his cuisine, so consider springing for a customized tasting menu. Langham Hotels, taking over the property from Ritz-Carlton, has remained committed to the restaurant, contributing an updated look and an enhanced wine list. ✉ *The Langham, Huntington Hotel & Spa, 1401 S. Oak Knoll Ave., Pasadena* ☎ *626/577–2867* 🌐 *www.langhamhotels.com* ▭ *AE, D, DC, MC, V* ⊙ *Closed Sun. and Mon. No lunch.*

$$$–$$$$ ECLECTIC ✕ **Parkway Grill.** This ever-popular, influential restaurant (once referred to as the Spago of Pasadena) sports all-American fixtures like brick walls, a carved-wood bar, and a prominent fireplace. The food wanders farther afield, incorporating influences from Italian to Southwestern

- All India Cafe **5**
- Briganti **13**
- Bistro 45 .... **8**
- Carousel **1**
- Derek's Bistro **12**
- The Dining Room **11**
- Lake Spring Shanghai Restaurant **15**
- Ocean Star **16**
- Parkway Grill **7**
- Pie 'N Burger .. **10**
- Porto's Bakery **2**
- Saladang Song **6**
- Shiro **14**
- Smitty's Grill **9**
- Trattoria Tre Venezie **3**
- Yujean Kang's Gourmet Chinese Cuisine **4**

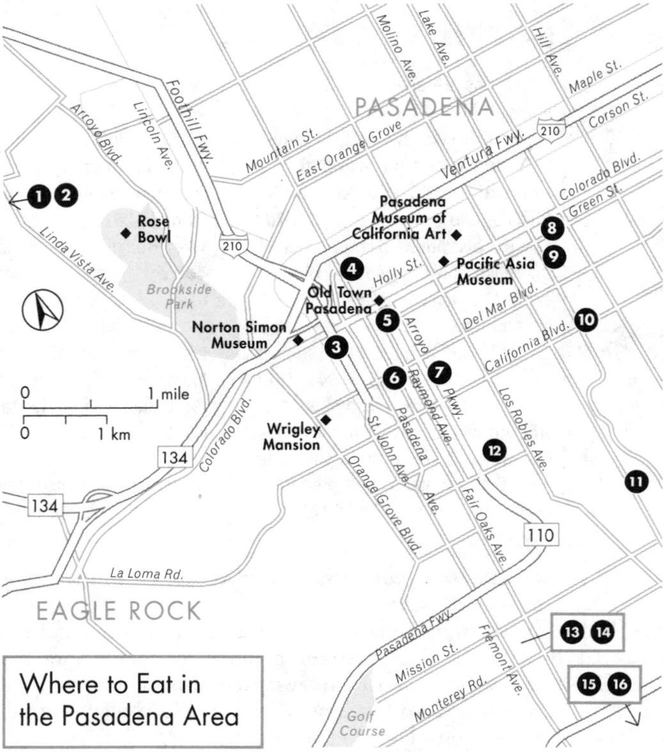

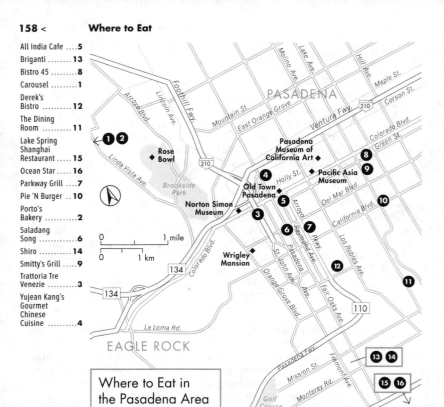

Where to Eat in the Pasadena Area

to Japanese. In one sitting you might have black bean soup or a tiger shrimp corn dog with Thai aïoli, then filet mignon or whole fried catfish with yuzu–ponzu sauce, and s'mores for dessert. ✉*510 S. Arroyo Pkwy., Pasadena* ☎*626/795–1001* 🌐*www.theparkwaygrill.com* ✍*Reservations essential* ▭*AE, MC, V* ⏲*No lunch weekends.*

¢–$ AMERICAN ✕**Pie 'N Burger.** A legendary Caltech hangout, this place serves up a burger the locals justifiably worship, plus potpies, a bargain lover's steak, traditional fountain drinks, and good pies (especially peach, pecan, or peanut butter). There are only a few tables, but you'll be treated right at a long counter filled with astrophysicists. ✉*913 E. California Blvd., Pasadena* ☎*626/795–1123* 🌐*www.pienburger.com* ✍*Reservations not accepted* ▭*No credit cards.*

$–$$ THAI ✕**Saladang Song.** The owners of Saladang, a standard Thai restaurant next door, concoct a more interesting menu here, going well beyond the usual satays and pad thai. It's a striking Thai-tech pavilion surrounded by outdoor tables and towering, ornamental pierced-steel panels that put this eatery in its own graciously hermetic world. For lunch or dinner, consider the spicy fish cakes or salmon with curry sauce. Or for a rarer treat, come for a Thai breakfast, with *kao-tom-gui* (rice soup with or without various meats and seafood) and *joak* (the Thai-style rice porridge), with sweet potato, taro, and pumpkin. ✉*383 S. Fair Oaks Ave., Pasadena* ☎*626/793–5200* ▭*AE, D, MC, V.*

$$–$$$ AMERICAN **Smitty's Grill.** Straightforward American fare is what Smitty's is all about. Black-and-white photos of Joltin' Joe, Ike, and a young Liz Taylor crowd the walls. You can depend on the steaks (half the price of a high-end steak house yet nearly as satisfying), but you'll also find respectable mac and cheese, barbecued ribs, cornmeal-encrusted rainbow trout, and corn bread baked in an iron skillet. If you're not in the mood for a fancy meal but don't feel like slumming it, Smitty's is the ideal compromise. *110 S. Lake Ave., Pasadena 626/792–9999 www.smittysgrill.com Reservations essential AE, MC, V No lunch weekends.*

$$$ ITALIAN **Trattoria Tre Venezie.** Much more than a neighborhood trattoria, this unexpected ristorante excels in specialties from a trio of Italy's northernmost regions along the Austrian border, collectively referred to as Tre Venezie. Sparked with unusual ingredients and sauces, the menu can challenge your preconceptions about Italian food. Start with *jota* (a traditional sweet-and-sour soup) before enjoying the signature smoked pork chop with sauerkraut and a light Gorgonzola sauce. *119 W. Green St., Pasadena 626/795–4455 AE, DC, MC, V Closed Mon. No lunch Tues. or weekends.*

$$–$$$ CHINESE Fodor's Choice ★ **Yujean Kang's Gourmet Chinese Cuisine.** Forget any and all preconceived notions of what Chinese food should look and taste like—Kang's cuisine is nouvelle Chinese. Start with tender slices of veal on a bed of enoki mushrooms, topped with a tangle of quick-fried shoestring yams; or sea bass with kumquats and passion-fruit sauce. Even familiar dishes, such as the crispy sesame beef, result in nearly revelatory culinary experiences. And don't shy away from desserts like sweet bean-curd crepes or delicate mandarin orange cheesecake, which are elegantly light. *67 N. Raymond Ave., Pasadena 626/585–0855 www.yujeankangs.com AE, D, DC, MC, V.*

SOUTH PASADENA

$$–$$$ ITALIAN **Briganti.** Part of a wave of new dining spots shaking up sleepy South Pas, this inviting downtown favorite has a space split between a narrow dining room and covered patio. At simply appointed white linen–covered tables, locals feast on remarkably light gnocchi, deftly prepared risotto and excellent pastas in sauces that are more refined than one might expect at a suburban trattoria. High quality market-driven ingredients prevail and the kitchen ups the ante with a truffle-studded menu. *1423 Mission St., South Pasadena 626/441–4663 www.brigantisouthpas.com AE, D, MC, V No lunch weekends.*

$$–$$$ ASIAN **Shiro.** Chef Hideo Yamashiro made quite a splash when he first began serving sizzling whole catfish with a tangy soy-citrus ponzu sauce, and his contemporary cuisine balancing Asian and French traditions remains exciting and fresh. Beyond the signature catfish you'll find lobster- and scallop-filled spring rolls with spicy yuzu sauce, John Dory and shrimp in curry-Champagne sauce, and duck with juniper berry sauce. For a sweet conclusion, try the passion fruit mousse. *1505 Mission St., South Pasadena 626/799–4774 www.restaurantshiro.com Reservations essential AE, DC, MC, V Closed Mon. and Tues. No lunch.*

Where to Stay

WORD OF MOUTH

"If you want to be a pedestrian, heed the advice to stay at the Beverly Wilshire which is very pedestrian-friendly! Great nearby streets for strolling either to shop, window shop or . . . enjoying the architecture and the landscaping. Beverly Hills is unlike the typical LA landscape and is a very walkable place!"

—socialworker

"My advice for bumping into stars, is to stay at the Chateau Marmont. It has gotten pricey, but it is worth it for a couple of nights, I think. You can hang out at the pool, and mingle in the lobby, and poke around the bungalows, and even have a key to the pool area you can get to off Sunset."

—Kailani

www.fodors.com/community

WHERE TO STAY PLANNER

Amenities and Extras

Most hotels have air-conditioning, cable TV, and in-room irons and ironing boards. Those in the moderate and expensive price ranges often have voice mail, coffeemakers, bathrobes, and hair dryers as well. Most also have at least dial-up Internet service in guest rooms, with a 24-hour use fee (though at a number of hotels it's free). High-speed wireless access (Wi-Fi) is now common even at budget properties. Southern California's emphasis on being in shape means most hotels have fitness facilities; if the one on-site is not to your liking, ask for a reference to a nearby sports club or gym.

If a particular amenity is important to you, ask for it; many hotels will provide extras upon request. Also double-check your bill at checkout. These days, hotels are fond of tacked-on charges such as a "minibar restocking fee" or cleaning charges for smokers. If a charge seems unreasonable, ask to remedy it at checkout. If you're traveling with pets, note that pet policies do change and some hotels require substantial cleaning fees. A cautionary note to smokers: some hotels are entirely smoke-free, meaning even smoking outdoors is frowned upon or prohibited.

Prices

Tax rates for the area will add 10% to 15.5% to your bill depending on where in Los Angeles County you stay; some hoteliers tack on energy, service or occupancy surcharges. Because you'll need a car no matter where you stay in Los Angeles, parking is another expense to consider. Though a few hotels have free parking, most charge for the privilege—and some resorts only have valet parking, with fees as high as $35 per night.

When looking for a hotel, don't write off the pricier establishments immediately. Price categories are determined by "rack rates"—the list price of a hotel room, which is usually discounted. Specials abound, particularly downtown on the weekends. Many hotels have packages that include breakfast, theater tickets, spa services, or exotic rental cars. Pricing is very competitive, so always check out the hotel Web site in advance for current special offers.

Finally, when making reservations, particularly last-minute ones, check the hotel's Web site for exclusive Internet specials or call the hotel directly.

Word of Mouth

'This seems to be a pattern, closing the chain hotels in and around L.A., renovating, and opening as a boutique hotel . . . A good thing for those looking for a nicer more upsacale hotel, but a bad thing for the wallet." —emdl

WHAT IT COSTS

¢	$	$$	$$$	$$$$
Hotels				
under $75	$75–$125	$125–$200	$200–$325	over $325

The lodgings we list are the top selections of their type in each price category. Price categories are assigned based on the range between the least and most expensive standard double rooms in nonholiday high season, on the European Plan (no meals) unless otherwise noted. Taxes (10%–15.5%) are extra. In listings, we always name the facilities available, but we don't specify whether they cost extra. When pricing accommodations, always ask what's included.

Updated by Kathy A. McDonald

WHAT'S NEW ATTRACTS THE MOST ATTENTION IN LOS ANGELES. Remakes and nip-and-tucks are not just a Hollywood tradition: L.A.'s hotels have seen their share of redo's in recent years with the trend toward luxury and more expensive stays. While chain properties and family-owned budget motels are still found, increasing competition means that many a derelict or forgotten spot has been made over.

Several notable new properties opened in 2009. The superposh digs, dining, and spa at the Montage Beverly Hills, the sister property of the Montage Laguna Beach, are definitely impressive. The SLS Hotel at Beverly Hills bursts with eye-catching design by Philippe Starck, while nightlife impresario Sam Nazarian helps create the happening party scene. In Westwood, the Hotel Palomar sensibly incorporates ecoconscious principles like energy conservation with comfort. Close to the beach and Santa Monica Pier, the Hotel Shangri-La reopened after a thorough makeover that included the addition of a pool, rooftop bar, and lounge for the perfect sunset moment.

Even established hotels get updates: in BelAir, the genteel Ho tel Bel-Air added a suitably exclusive spa to its picturesque grounds. The Mondrian is still a hot spot, now with leaner design. And the AnDaz in West Hollywood showcases a new concept in hotel lobbies—the front desk has been replaced with a welcoming lounge and host.

In Los Angeles, the outdoors is always in because of Southern California's great weather. Many hoteliers have moved socializing alfresco. Dine or drink outside year-round in designer-made outdoor living rooms, whether under striped cabanas at Santa Monica's Viceroy or poolside at the Beverly Hilton's outdoor living room with cocktails by Trader Vic's. The patio of Fig, the Fairmont Miramar's indoor-outdoor restaurant, keeps it fresh with seasonal, locally grown produce.

With so many lodging selections, Los Angeles hoteliers need to keep up with the Hiltons (so to speak). Virtually all in the $$$ and $$$$ categories have high-speed Internet access in guest rooms and business centers. Some, such as Shutters in Santa Monica and the Beverly Wilshire, have wireless Internet access throughout the property and even poolside. Other high-tech must-haves: flat-screen TVs and iPod home bases. Luxury bedding, pillow-top mattresses, and fine linens are part of most stays: at the Sofitel, you can even order up the mattress and bedding to take home.

On the horizon: a spiffy new Ritz-Carlton and Marriott Marquis downtown will be part of the L.A. Live complex; Terranea—a full service, 102-acre resort on the Palos Verdes Peninsula—is due to open soon after this writing; and a W Hotel is receiving its finishing touches in the heart of Hollywood's nightlife at Hollywood & Vine.

BEST BETS FOR L.A. LODGING

Fodor's offers a selective listing of lodging experiences at every price range. Here, we've compiled our top recommendations by price and experience. The very best properties are designated in the listings with the Fodor's Choice logo.

Fodor's Choice★

By Price

$

$$

$$$

$$$$

By Experience

BEST DESIGN

BEST SPAS

ECOFRIENDLY

GREAT POOLS

HOT SCENE

MOST KID-FRIENDLY

WHERE TO STAY

	NEIGHBORHOOD VIBE	PROS	CONS
Beverly Hills and Century City	Pricey and posh high-end hotels with resort-style amenities as well as stylish boutiques.	Great shopping, celeb-spotting, numerous restaurants all near quiet residential areas.	Expect spendy stays with few budget options.
Hollywood and West Hollywood	Trendy and design orientated; kickin' nightlife.	Heart of the action for nightclubs and see-and-be-seen spots.	At capacity weekends and holidays, few deals, and parking issues are ongoing.
Downtown	Office towers, civic and cultural institutions with a growing residential scene.	Pedestrian friendly, home to Disney Hall and MOCA, diverse clientele at restaurants and bars.	Large homeless population, some sketchy areas at night.
Bel Air, Westwood, Malibu, and Santa Monica	Upscale and very chic—the most coveted neighborhoods for L.A.'s moneyed elite.	Ocean breezes, the best of everything, miles of public beaches.	Ocean-view rooms command highest rates in Los Angeles. Limited low-budget choices.
Venice and Marina del Rey	Venice is arty, fun, and hip. Marina is casual but crowded with high-rise apartments.	Fresh air, seaside, low-key vibe. Numerous restaurants and bars.	Heavy traffic and congestion; expect gridlock summer weekends. Boardwalk a bit freaky at night.
Manhattan Beach, Hermosa Beach, Redondo Beach	Outdoorsy, sporty types flock to these beaches and the slower-paced lifestyle.	Cleanest beaches and water, low-rise buildings, casual dining and sports bars.	Limited diversity, far from most cultural institutions.
San Fernando Valley	Vast valley suburbs means very safe neighborhoods and typical suburban amenities.	Family-friendly. There are few density issues and endless dining choices.	As dull as any suburb. The action is on the other side of the hill.
Pasadena Area	Conservative, mid-Western style suburb with historic mansions and leafy streets.	Super-safe, numerous high-tech corporate headquarters, art museums, and cultural institutions.	Scorching hot and smoggy in summer; far from beaches but close to mountains.
Long Beach	Up-and-coming, dining and shopping in Belmont Shore. Downtown rather corporate and touristy.	Diverse neighborhoods but close to the ocean without the Westside's spendiness. Long Beach airport a great travel alternative.	Near the industrial seaport: traffic and pollution issues from nearby refineries and heavy trucking.

4

BEVERLY HILLS, CENTURY CITY, HOLLYWOOD, AND WEST HOLLYWOOD

BEVERLY HILLS AND VICINITY

$$$ **Avalon.** Combining space-age architectural details like large lobby plate-glass windows and terazzo floors with tech-savvy substance make this a comfortably cosmopolitan boutique hotel. Rooms at the three-building property incorporate '50s retro design, with classic pieces from George Nelson and Charles Eames; there are also Frette linens, chenille throws, and a menu of spa treatments that can be ordered in-room. For extended stays, the Avalon also has stylish apartments that come with all hotel services, including twice-daily housekeeping. Weather permitting, things get busy poolside and in the fun private cabanas. **Pros:** stylish, Beverly Hills location at a reasonable rate, in-house restaurant, blue on blue, earns critical raves. **Cons:** poolside social scene can be rowdy. ✉ *9400 W. Olympic Blvd., Beverly Hills* ☎ *310/277–5221 or 800/670–6183* 🌐 *www.avalonbeverlyhills.com* *76 rooms, 10 suites* *In-room: safe, refrigerator, DVD, Internet, Wi-Fi. In-hotel: restaurant, room service, bar, pool, gym, laundry facilities, laundry service, Wi-Fi, parking (paid), some pets allowed, no-smoking rooms* *AE, DC, MC, V.*

$$ **Best Western Carlyle Inn.** A gussied-up Best Western, the Carlyle is adjacent to Beverly Hills and Century City in a predominately Jewish neighborhood. Popular with an older crowd, rooms are on the small side, enlivened by bold gold and brown patterned bedcovers. Bathrooms are efficient shower-and-tub combinations and sparkling clean. Exposed outdoor walkways lead to rooms at this five-story pocket hotel. **Pros:** full breakfast available inside or out, walk to kosher markets and restaurants. **Cons:** smallish rooms and street noise from busy Robertson and nearby Pico Blvds. Weekends often sell out—book ahead. ✉ *1119 S. Robertson Blvd., Beverly Hills* ☎ *310/275–4445 or 800/322–7595* 🌐 *www.carlyle-inn.com* *32 rooms* *In-room: safe, refrigerator, Wi-Fi. In-hotel: gym, Internet terminal, Wi-Fi, parking (paid), no-smoking rooms* *AE, D, DC, MC, V* *BP.*

$$$$ **Beverly Hills Hotel.** Remarkably still at the top of her game, the "Pink Palace" continues to attract Hollywood's elite after 98 years. Celebrity guests favor the private bungalows; most others come for the "royal" treatment by staff. Standard rooms are also nothing to sniff at, with original artwork, butler service, Frette linens and duvets, walk-in closets, and huge marble bathrooms. Swiss skin-care company La Prairie runs the hotel's swanky day spa, which specializes in de-aging treatments. The Polo Lounge remains an iconic Hollywood meeting place. Bar Nineteen 12 is a most contemporary addition. Canine guests are also pampered here; 24-hour dog-walking service is available. **Pros:** multiple recreation choices pool, spa, and tennis, legendary, retro 20-seat Fountain Coffee room. **Cons:** average and pricey fare at the Polo Lounge. ✉ *9641 Sunset Blvd., Beverly Hills* ☎ *310/276–2251 or 800/283–8885* 🌐 *www.beverlyhillshotel.com* *145 rooms, 38 suites, 21 bungalows* *In-room: safe, kitchen (some), refrigerator, DVD, Internet, Wi-Fi. In-hotel: 4 restaurants, room service, bars, tennis courts, pool, gym, spa,*

laundry service, Wi-Fi, parking (paid), some pets allowed, no-smoking rooms ▭*AE, DC, MC, V.*

$$ **Beverly Hills Plaza Hotel.** With a precious courtyard surrounding the pool, the well-maintained, all-suite Beverly Hills Plaza has a look that would be right at home in the south of France. A combination of two former apartment buildings, the property borders a golf course and busy Wilshire Boulevard at the edge of Beverly Hills. Warm tones of beige, gold, and cream paired with the outdoor gardens complete with a waterfall and koi pond make for a relaxed atmosphere. You'll find bathrobes, hair dryers, movies, and coffeemakers in the roomy suites; VCRs can be rented at the front desk. **Pros:** european ambience, amiable staff, new lobby in 2008. **Cons:** lowest-priced suites are accessible via stairs only, no services or restaurants close-by, so car or public transport a must. ✉*10300 Wilshire Blvd., Beverly Hills* ☎*310/275–5575 or 800/800–1234* 🌐*www.beverlyhillsplazahotel.com* *116 suites* *In-room: safe, refrigerator, kitchen (some), Internet. In-hotel: restaurant, room service, bar, pool, gym, laundry service, Internet terminal, parking (paid), no-smoking rooms* ▭*AE, D, DC, MC, V.*

4

$$$ **Beverly Hilton.** Home of the Golden Globe Awards, the Beverly Hilton is as polished as its glitzy address after some pricey renovation. Tower rooms have spectacular views of Beverly Hills and sizeable balconies. In-room bathrooms, though compact, feel expansive thanks to an opaque glass wall that faces the room and a pocket door. Walls are creamy white; furnishings include versatile, leather-top, oval-shaped work desks that swivel to the side. Flat-screen TVs and CD players are standard in every room. The venerable Trader Vic's is now an indoor-outdoor poolside lounge—don't worry, you can still have classic Mai Tais and ogle the tacky tiki art. Circa 55 is the hotel's mid-century modern styled restaurant. Just off the almost-Olympic-size pool is the Aqua Star Spa—indulge in a spray-on tan for the true SoCal look. **Pros:** walking distance to Beverly Hills, complimentary car service for short jaunts, L.A.'s largest hotel pool. **Cons:** ongoing adjacent construction, corporate feel, unremarkable dining. ✉*9876 Wilshire Blvd., Beverly Hills* ☎*310/274–7777 or 877/414–8018* 🌐*www.beverlyhilton.com* *469 rooms, 101 suites* *In-room: safe, refrigerator, DVD (some), Internet, Wi-Fi. In-hotel: restaurant, room service, bars, pool, gym, laundry service, Internet terminal, Wi-Fi, parking (paid), some pets allowed, no-smoking rooms* ▭*AE, D, DC, MC, V.*

$$$$ **Beverly Wilshire, a Four Seasons Hotel.** Built in 1928, the Italian Renaissance–style Wilshire wing of this fabled hotel is replete with elegant details: crystal chandeliers, oak paneling, walnut doors, crown moldings, and marble. The contemporary Beverly wing, added in 1971, lacks the Wilshire wing's historic panache. Rodeo Drive beckons outside; a complimentary Rolls-Royce can drive you anywhere within 3 mi of the hotel. Paneled in leather and wood, with soaring ceilings, the Blvd is the hotel's posh dining room. At dinner, Hollywood's elite packs the coolly modern steak house CUT featuring steaks and sides by Wolfgang Puck and interiors by architect Richard Meier. Take time to unwind at the hotel's first-rate spa. **Pros:** chic location, top-notch service, and refined vibe. **Cons:** small lobby, valet parking backs up at peak times,

Fodor's Choice ★

super expensive dining choices. ✉9500 Wilshire Blvd., Beverly Hills ☎310/275–5200 or 800/427–4354 ⊕www.fourseasons.com/beverlywilshire ⇨258 rooms, 137 suites ♿In-room: safe, refrigerator, DVD, Internet, Wi-Fi. In-hotel: 2 restaurants, room service, bars, pool, gym, spa, laundry service, Internet terminal, Wi-Fi, parking (paid), some pets allowed, no-smoking rooms ▭AE, DC, MC, V.

$$$ ★ **The Crescent.** Built in 1926 as a dorm for silent film actors, the Crescent is now a sleek boutique hotel within walking distance of the Beverly Hills shopping triangle. Low couches and tables, an indoor-outdoor fireplace, French doors that open to its streetside patio restaurant, boé, and shimmering candlelight at night give the hotel's public areas a welcoming and sophisticated look. Guest rooms are small, but platform beds and built-in furniture maximize the space. Bathrooms are finished in concrete—utilitarian but also coolly cozy. High-tech amenities include flat-screen TVs, in-room iPods, and a library of the latest CDs and DVDs. **Pros:** boé's tasy cuisine and convivial happy hour, the lobby is fashionista-central. **Cons:** dorm-sized rooms, gym an additional fee and only accessed outside hotel via Sports ClubLA, no elevator. *✉403 N. Crescent Dr., Beverly Hills ☎310/247–0505 ⊕www.crescentbh.com ⇨35 rooms ♿In-room: refrigerator, Wi-Fi. In-hotel: restaurant, room service, bar, laundry service, Wi-Fi, parking (paid), no-smoking rooms ▭AE, D, MC, V.*

$$$$ Fodor's Choice ★ **Four Seasons Hotel Los Angeles at Beverly Hills.** High hedges and patio gardens make this hotel a secluded retreat that even the hum of traffic can't permeate. It's a favorite of Hollywood's elite, so don't be surprised by a well-known face poolside or in the Windows bar. (Come awards season, expect to spot an Oscar winner or two.) The staff here will make you feel pampered, as will the plush guest rooms, which have beds with Frette linens, soft robes and slippers, and French doors leading to balconies. Extras include 24-hour business services, overnight shoe shine, and a morning newspaper. For a relaxing meal or a healthy smoothie, you can dine poolside on the tropically landscaped terrace. Massages here are among the best. **Pros:** expert concierge, deferential service, celeb magnet. **Cons:** small gym, Hollywood scene in bar and restaurant means rarefied prices. *✉300 S. Doheny Dr., Beverly Hills ☎310/273–2222 or 800/332–3442 ⊕www.fourseasons.com/losangeles ⇨187 rooms, 98 suites ♿In-room: safe, kitchen (some), refrigerator, DVD, Internet, Wi-Fi. In-hotel: 2 restaurants, room service, bar, pool, gym, spa, laundry service, Internet terminal, Wi-Fi, parking (paid), some pets allowed (fee), no-smoking rooms ▭AE, DC, MC, V.*

$ **Hotel Beverly Terrace.** Centered around a cheerful pool and courtyard, rooms at the Beverly Terrace are super-compact: think train compartment-size. Bathrooms have shower stalls and are equally tiny. Plasma TVs and free Wi-Fi are among the frills. Rates are reasonable considering the upscale location on the West Hollywood–Beverly Hills border. Complimentary Continental breakfast, which visitors give high marks, is served outside by the pool. **Pros:** well-maintained and super-clean, reliable Trattori Amici restaurant on-site. **Cons:** small rooms, stairs mean limited access, busy intersection. *✉469 N. Doheny Dr., Beverly Hills ☎310/274–8141 or 800/842–6401 ⊕www.hotelbeverlyterrace.com ⇨39 rooms ♿In-room: refrigerator, Wi-Fi. In-hotel: restaurant,* *pool, Wi-Fi, parking (free), some pets allowed, no-smoking rooms* ▭*AE, D, DC, MC, V* 🍽*CP.*

$$$–$$$$ **Luxe Hotel Rodeo Drive.** Refined design rules at this boutique hotel discreetly tucked away on Rodeo Drive between Valentino and Michael Kors boutiques. Streetside rooms look out over Gucci and the extravagant Prada Epicenter store. Dark mahogany and brushed metals fill the lobby, and the compact rooms go glam with black-and-white photography, 8-foot-high mirrors, and Egyptian linens. Café Rodeo, Luxe's intimate skylight restaurant, draws a well-heeled local lunch crowd with upscale comfort food and potent martinis. Check-in includes a guest pass to the nearby Sports ClubLA at no extra charge. **Pros:** only hotel on Rodeo Drive, excellent dining room, discreet rear entrance. **Cons:** compact, Manhattan-size hotel rooms, street noise on Rodeo Drive side. ✉*360 N. Rodeo Dr., Beverly Hills* ☎*310/273–0300 or 866/589–3411* 🌐*www.luxehotelrodeodrive.com* *84 rooms, 4 suites* *In-room: safe, refrigerator, Internet, Wi-Fi. In-hotel: restaurant, room service, bar, laundry service, Internet terminal, Wi-Fi, parking (paid), no-smoking rooms* ▭*AE, D, DC, MC, V.*

$$$ **Maison 140.** Colonial chic reigns in this three-story, 1930s spot, Beverly Hills' most grandly designed boutique hotel. The look mixes French and Far East with gleaming antiques, textured wallpaper, and colorfully painted rooms. (These dramatic visuals compensate for compact rooms and bathrooms.) Refinements include down comforters and fine linens and bathrobes. Take advantage of the pool and restaurant at the sister property, the Avalon hotel, 1 mi away. Beverly Hills's golden triangle of shopping is within close walking distance. The hotel's ebony and blood-red *Bar Noir* inspires intrigue. **Pros:** ultimate boutique stay, eye-catching design, short walk to all Beverly Hills shopping. **Cons:** few amenities, room service from another hotel, 100% smoke-free. ✉*140 S. Lasky Dr., Beverly Hills* ☎*310/281–4000 or 800/670–6182* 🌐*www.maison140beverlyhills.com* *43 rooms* *In-room: safe, refrigerator, DVD, Internet, Wi-Fi. In-hotel: room service, bar, gym, laundry service, Internet terminal, Wi-Fi, parking (paid), no-smoking rooms* ▭*AE, DC, MC, V.*

$$$$ **Montage Beverly Hills.** The new kid on a very posh block, the Montage Beverly Hills, which opened in late 2008, is a five-story, Mediterranean-style palazzo dedicated to welcoming those who relish the highest-end stay. Rates match the seemingly endless list of amenities, includeing butler service for suites, a two-story spa with mineral water pool, plush bedding, and a rooftop pool and lounging area that feels like a serene oasis. Baths are mostly marble with custom-scented bath products; some rooms have small balconies to better appreciate the city and hillside views. Parq, the hotel's mosaic tiled dining room, has a stunning show kitchen and looks over the hotel's leafy and fountain-filled garden. **Pros:** a feast for the senses, architectural details include fruitwood floors and shimmery copper ceilings; the highly trained staff is most obliging. **Cons:** all this finery adds up to a hefty tab at checkout. ✉*225 N. Canon Dr., Beverly Hills* ☎*310/860–7800 or 888/860–0788* 🌐*www.montagebeverlyhills.com* *146 rooms, 55 suites* *In-room: safe, kitchen (some), refrigerator, DVD, Internet, Wi-Fi. In-hotel: 3 restaurants, room service, bars, pool, gym, spa, laundry service, Internet*

4

terminal, Wi-Fi, parking (paid), some pets allowed, no-smoking rooms ▭*AE, D, DC, MC, V.*

$$$$ **Mosaic Hotel.** Stylish, comfortable, and decked out with the latest electronics, the Mosaic is on a quiet side street that's central to Beverly Hills's business district. Iridescent mosaic tiles shimmer on the surfaces, while the teak-furnished, poolside lounging area gets an atmosphere boost with grand palms and simulated moonlight at night. Room amenities are posh: Italian linens, feather bed, and plush carpets. Hush, the lobby restaurant and bar, feels like a private club; at night, a candle wall adds a warm glow. An extra perk: guests have access to the nearby, huge Sports ClubLA for an extra fee. **Pros:** intimate and cozy, friendly service, free Wi-Fi and local shuttle service. **Cons:** small and shaded pool, mini-lobby. ✉*125 S. Spalding Dr., Beverly Hills* ☎*310/278–0303 or 800/463–4466* ⊕*www.mosaichotel.com* *44 rooms, 5 suites* *In-room: safe, refrigerator, DVD (some), Internet, Wi-Fi. In-hotel: restaurant, room service, bar, pool, gym, laundry service, parking (fee), some pets allowed, no-smoking rooms* ▭*AE, DC, MC, V.*

$$$$ Fodor's Choice ★ **Peninsula Beverly Hills.** This French Riveria–style palace is a favorite of Hollywood bold-face names, but all kinds of visitors consistently describe their stay as near perfect—though very expensive. Rooms overflow with antiques, artwork, and marble; high-tech room amenities and flat screen TV are controlled by a bedside panel. Service is exemplary and always discreet. Soak up the sun by the fifth-floor pool with its fully outfitted cabanas or sip afternoon tea in the living room under ornate chandeliers. Belvedere, the hotel's flower-filled restaurant, is a lunchtime favorite for film business types. A complimentary Rolls-Royce is available for short jaunts in Beverly Hills. **Pros:** central, walkable Beverly Hills location, stunning flowers, one of the best concierges in the city. **Cons:** serious bucks required to stay here, somewhat stuffy. ✉*9882 S. Santa Monica Blvd., Beverly Hills* ☎*310/551–2888 or 800/462–7899* ⊕*www.beverlyhills.peninsula.com* *144 rooms, 36 suites, 16 villas* *In-room: safe, refrigerator, DVD, Internet, Wi-Fi. In-hotel: restaurant, room service, bar, pool, gym, spa, concierge, laundry service, Internet terminal, Wi-Fi, parking (paid), some pets allowed, no-smoking rooms* ▭*AE, D, DC, MC, V.*

$$$$ **Raffles L'Ermitage Beverly Hills.** Every indulgence and practicality is considered here from the smooth, crisp designer sheets, soaking tubs, and oversize bath towels to the caviar and Champagne service in the lobby-adjacent, Writer's Bar. Platform beds, original art, and mirrored dressing rooms are found in the enormous, sycamore-paneled rooms. French doors open to mini-balconies, some with remarkable views of the city or the mountains. Business-minded guests appreciate the direct-dial phones with private numbers, careful lighting, four multiline phones, and combination fax-copiers. The rooftop pool area has straight-up gorgeous views and privacy screens between the teak loungers. Exclusively for hotel guests, the Amrita Spa has Asian-style beauty body treatments. Service is deferential and professional as the hotel is a favorite of the very rich and also very famous. **Pros:** squeaky clean throughout, usable work desk, free sodas in the minibar. **Cons:** subpar, pricey restaurant, small spa and pool. ✉*9291 Burton Way,*

Beverly Hills ☎*310/278–3344 or 800/768–9009* ⊕*raffles-lermitagehotel.com* ⇨*103 rooms, 16 suites* ♁*In-room: safe, refrigerator, DVD, Internet, Wi-Fi. In-hotel: restaurant, room service, bar, pool, gym, spa, laundry service, Internet terminal, Wi-Fi, parking (paid), some pets allowed, no-smoking rooms* ▭*AE, D, DC, MC, V.*

$$$–$$$$ **SLS Hotel at Beverly Hills.** Imagine dropping into Alice in Wonderland's rabbit hole: this is the colorful, textured, and tchotke-filled lobby of the SLS from design maestro Philippe Starck. Hotel guests enter into a fashionable living room that encourages socializing complete with fireplace, hidden nooks, and a communal table for dining. Visual stimulation ranges from the succulent garden in oversized pots and white leather couches out front to the elevators backed with oversized portraits. Rooms have crisp, fine linens, eggshell-shaped soaking tubs, and high-tech sound and video systems. Owned by L.A. nightlife pro Sam Nazarian, there's atmosphere, photo-ready spots (the rooftop pool is strictly for scene making) and dining by celebrated Spanish chef José Andrés. Forward thinking abounds: gym equipment is stellar, the business center has MacBooks, and the spa feels like a dreamy lounge. **Pros:** a vibrant newcomer with lofty ambitions, much thought has gone into design and cuisine. **Cons:** standard rooms are compact but you pay for the scene; pricey hotel dining. ✉*465 S. La Cienega Blvd., Beverly Hills* ☎*310/247–0400* ⊕*www.slshotels.com* ⇨*236 rooms, 61 suites* ♁*In-room: safe, DVD, Internet, Wi-Fi. In-hotel: 3 restaurants, room service, bars, pool, gym, spa, laundry service, Internet terminal, Wi-Fi, parking (paid), some pets allowed, no-smoking rooms* ▭*AE, D, DC, MC, V.*

$$$–$$$$ **Sofitel Los Angeles.** From this perch bordering busy La Cienega Boulevard, you're close to some of the city's best restaurants and nightlife including Stone Rose, the hotel's cool indoor–outdoor lounge by nightclub kingpin Rande Gerber. Simon LA, the hotel's restaurant, serves updated American classics including a decadent junk food platter dessert; the canvas-covered patio is the favored spot for breakfast. A glass-walled and dramatically lit entrance introduce Sofitel's polished style—guest rooms are tones of grays and blacks, with Hollywood Regency–style furniture, flat-screen TVs, and frosted-glass sliding doors leading to the bathrooms. Blond-wood paneling sets off the feather duvet–topped beds. **Pros:** ultracomfy beds, upper floors have great views towards the hills, geared towards business types. **Cons:** costly room service charges, small pool, Beverly Center view a downer. ✉*8555 Beverly Blvd., Beverly Hills* ☎*310/278–5444 or 800/521–7772* ⊕*www.sofitel.com* ⇨*267 rooms, 28 suites* ♁*In-room: safe, Internet, Wi-Fi. In-hotel: restaurant, room service, bar, pool, gym, spa, laundry service, Internet terminal, Wi-Fi, parking (paid), some pets allowed, no-smoking rooms* ▭*AE, DC, MC, V.*

$$ **Thompson Beverly Hills.** The Beverly Hills outpost of New York's Thompson Hotels has smoky-sexy interiors and lacquered all-black corridors are by designer Dodd Mitchell who makes the most of the '70s-era boxy-rooms, filling them with texture and reflective surfaces (slim mirrored panels on the ceiling). The all-white duvet on the low-rise platform bed contrasts with the dark wood built-ins and workspace, all of it illuminated by hanging globes. Bathrooms are shimmering mosaic

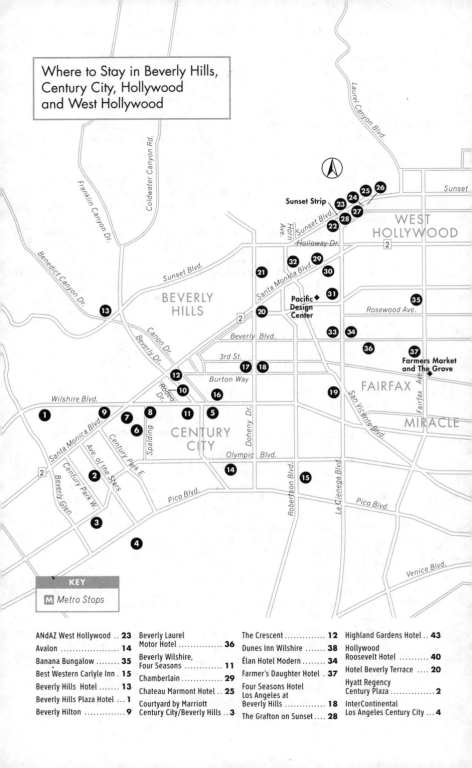

Where to Stay in Beverly Hills, Century City, Hollywood and West Hollywood

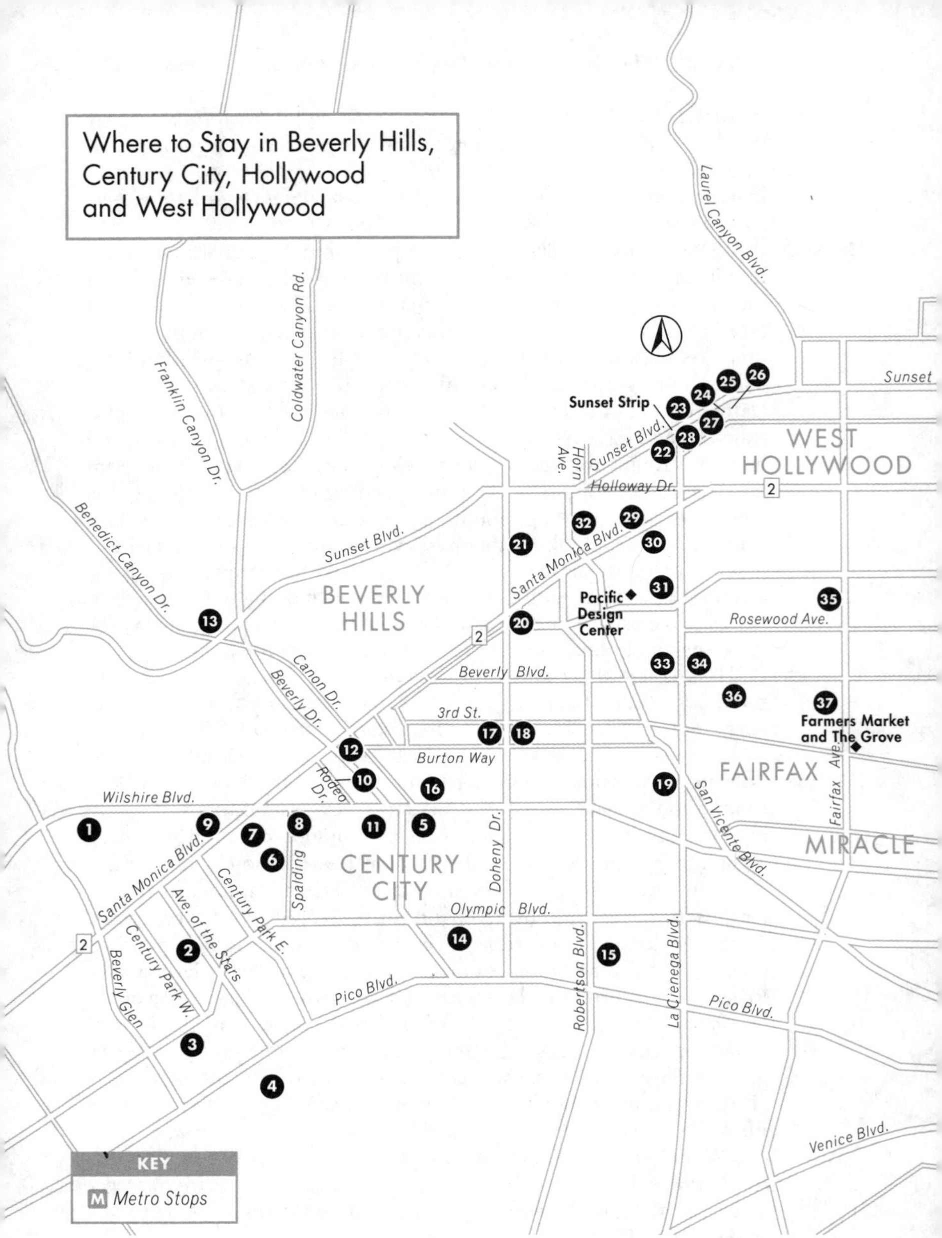

- ANdAZ West Hollywood .. **23**
- Avalon **14**
- Banana Bungalow **35**
- Best Western Carlyle Inn . **15**
- Beverly Hills Hotel **13**
- Beverly Hills Plaza Hotel ... **1**
- Beverly Hilton **9**
- Beverly Laurel Motor Hotel **36**
- Beverly Wilshire, Four Seasons **11**
- Chamberlain **29**
- Chateau Marmont Hotel .. **25**
- Courtyard by Marriott Century City/Beverly Hills .. **3**
- The Crescent **12**
- Dunes Inn Wilshire **38**
- Élan Hotel Modern **34**
- Farmer's Daughter Hotel . **37**
- Four Seasons Hotel Los Angeles at Beverly Hills **18**
- The Grafton on Sunset **28**
- Highland Gardens Hotel .. **43**
- Hollywood Roosevelt Hotel **40**
- Hotel Beverly Terrace **20**
- Hyatt Regency Century Plaza **2**
- InterContinental Los Angeles Century City ... **4**

- Le Montrose Suite Hotel .. **21**
- Le Parc Suite Hotel **31**
- London West Hollywood . **32**
- Luxe Hotel Rodeo Drive .. **10**
- Magic Castle Hotel **44**
- Maison 140 .... **6**
- Mondrian **27**
- Montage Beverly Hills **16**
- Mosaic Hotel **8**
- Orange Drive Manor Hostel **41**
- Peninsula Beverly Hills **7**
- Raffles L'Ermitage Beverly Hills **17**
- Ramada Plaza West Hollywood **30**
- Renaissance Hollywood Hotel **42**
- SLS at Beverly Hills **19**
- Sofitel Los Angeles **33**
- The Standard, Hollywood **24**
- Sunset Marquis Hotel and Villas **22**
- The Sunset Tower Hotel .. **26**
- Thompson Beverly Hills **5**
- Wilshire Plaza Hotel **39**

tile and black marble, artfully lit. Provocative images by fashion photographer Stephen Klein are found throughout. Expect the fashion crowd and those who like a darkened nightclub feel. A private rooftop pool and gym delivers drop-dead views of Beverly Hills. Within walking distance is all of Beverly Hills famed shopping and eateries (Spago is across the street). The clubby BondSt, complete with a sushi bar, provides the stylish dining. **Pros:** visually enticing interiors, famed NY eatery and party scene on the rooftop. **Cons:** compact rooms. ✉ *9360 Wilshire Blvd., Beverly Hills* ☎ *310/273–1400* 🌐 *www.thompsonhotels.com* *100 rooms, 15 suites* *In-room: safe, refrigerator, DVD, Internet, Wi-Fi. In-hotel: restaurant, room service, bar, pool, gym, laundry service, Wi-Fi, parking (paid), no-smoking rooms* 💳 *AE, D, DC,MC, V.*

> **WORD OF MOUTH**
>
> "Century City is a good location—not far from places to see and yet a little less expensive for hotels."
>
> —elnap29

CENTURY CITY

$$ **Courtyard by Marriott Century City/Beverly Hills.** Minutes from Beverly Hills, this Marriott has a convenient location adjacent to Century City's businesses and medical center. Wedged as it is into a compact lot overlooking busy Olympic Boulevard, rooms at the back of the hotel are quietest. The decor is basic, but desks have space to spread out. **Pros:** friendly hotel staff, daily breakfast buffet, close to cosmetic medical centers. **Cons:** compact, basic rooms, constant traffic out the front door, no pool. ✉ *10320 W. Olympic Blvd., Century City* ☎ *310/556–2777 or 800/321–2211* 🌐 *www.courtyard.com* *135 rooms* *In-room: refrigerator, Internet. In-hotel: restaurant, gym, Wi-Fi, laundry facilities, laundry service, Internet terminal, Wi-Fi, parking (paid), no-smoking rooms* 💳 *AE, D, DC, MC, V.*

$$$–$$$$ **Hyatt Regency Century Plaza.** A glowing, red-lighted exterior at night celebrates the Century Plaza's more than 40 years as one L.A.'s most frequented business hotels. Rooms have large bathrooms, balconies, and stunning city views. Tech gadgets include flat screen TVs, iPod stations, and electronic minibars. The two-story lobby lounge is always busy and surveys the fully furnished outdoor terrace, inviting pool and cabanas. Seafood and sushi is the specialty at the hotel's contemporary restaurant, Breeze. The Westfield Century City and its vast food court and state-of-the-art movie theaters are across the street. **Pros:** on-site power gym, Equinox Fitness Club and Spa, open to quests for an extra fee, stunning views to west, lower weekend rates. **Cons:** large, corporate hotel, isolated location in Century City. ✉ *2025 Ave. of the Stars, Century City* ☎ *310/228–1234 or 800/233–1234* 🌐 *www.centuryplaza.hyatt.com* *728 rooms, 14 suites* *In-room: safe, DVD, Internet, Wi-Fi. In-hotel: 2 restaurants, room service, 3 bars, pool, gym, spa, Internet terminal, Wi-Fi, laundry service, parking (paid), some pets allowed, no-smoking rooms* 💳 *AE, D, DC, MC, V.*

$$$ **InterContinental Los Angeles Century City.** The InterContinental is tucked away on Avenue of the Stars, overlooking 20th Century Fox Studios' back lot. The central Westside location is handy for all kinds of visits

but business types predominate. There's a decent-size balcony off every room; most have excellent views. Ask for a room facing west for brilliant sunsets (smog permitting). Desks are computer ready with convenient cordless phones. Bathrooms have marble vanities and separate shower and tub. Nightly, a talented sushi chef sets up shop in the lobby bar. Spa treatments, offered in three spa villas with deep soaking tubs and a private outdoor patio, are a soothing indulgence. **Pros:** helpful staff, intimate spa with excellent treatments, welcoming pool and hot tub. **Cons:** vast, impersonal entryway, expensive in-house dining. ✉*2151 Ave. of the Stars, Century City* ☎*310/284–6500 or 888/424–6835* 🌐*www.intercontinental.com/losangeles* *206 rooms, 157 suites* *In-room: safe, refrigerator, Internet, Wi-Fi. In-hotel: restaurant, room service, bar, pool, gym, spa, laundry service, Internet terminal, Wi-Fi, parking (paid), some pets allowed, no-smoking rooms* *AE, D, DC, MC, V.*

4

HOLLYWOOD AND VICINITY

$ **Dunes Inn–Wilshire.** Centered between downtown Los Angeles and Beverly Hills, the Dunes is a classic roadside motel with a 1960s vibe, complete with an oval pool and basic decor. Its midcity location and low price are an increasingly rare combination in metro L.A. Rooms here are modest in size (for a quieter stay, ask for those facing south, away from busy Wilshire Boulevard). **Pros:** short drive to Larchmont Boulevard eateries, multinight stays equal significant discounts, quiet neighborhood. **Cons:** tired decor, no restaurant. ✉*4300 Wilshire Blvd., Hollywood* ☎*323/938–3616 or 888/790–5264* 🌐*www.dunesla.com* *In-room: kitchen (some), refrigerator, Internet, Wi-Fi. In-hotel: pool, laundry facilities, laundry service, parking (free), no-smoking rooms* *AE, D, DC, MC, V.*

$–$$ ★ **Farmer's Daughter Hotel.** Tongue-in-cheek country style is the name of the game at this motel: rooms are upholstered in blue gingham with denim bedspreads, and farm tools serve as art. A curving blue wall secludes the interior courtyard and the hotel's clapboard-lined restaurant, Tart. Pancakes here are a local favorite. Rooms are snug but outfitted with whimsical original art and amenities such as CD and DVD players. It's a favorite of *The Price Is Right* hopefuls; the TV show tapes at the CBS studios nearby. **Pros:** great central city location; across from the cheap eats of the Farmers Market and The Grove's shopping/entertainment mix. **Cons:** pricey restaurant, roadside motel-size rooms, shaded pool, less than stellar service. ✉*115 S. Fairfax Ave., Hollywood* ☎*323/937–3930 or 800/334–1658* 🌐*www.farmersdaughterhotel.com* *64 rooms, 2 suites* *In-room: safe, refrigerator, DVD, Wi-Fi. In-hotel: restaurant, room service, pool, laundry service, Wi-Fi, parking (paid), some pets allowed, no-smoking rooms* *AE, D, DC, MC, V.*

$ **Highland Gardens Hotel.** A large, sparkling pool and a lush, if somewhat overgrown, tropical garden set this hotel apart from other budget lodgings. Spacious but basic units have either two queen-size beds, or a king bed with a queen-size sleeper sofa, plus a desk and sitting area with Formica tables. Rooms facing busy Franklin Avenue are noisy; ask for one facing the courtyard. **Pros:** quick walk to Hollywood and Metro Rail, pet friendly, low price. **Cons:** late '80s decor, street noise, no elevator. ✉*7047 Franklin Ave., Hollywood* ☎*323/850–0536 or*

800/404–5472 ⊕www.highlandgardenshotel.com 70 rooms, 48 suites In-room: kitchen (some), refrigerator, Wi-Fi. In-hotel: pool, laundry facilities, Internet terminal, Wi-Fi, parking (free), some pets allowed, no-smoking rooms AE, MC, V CP.

TOP 5

- **Four Seasons Hotel Los Angeles at Beverly Hills** for the showbiz action.
- **Peninsula Beverly Hills,** supreme elegance and service.
- **Renaissance Hollywood Hotel,** close to Hollywood's nightlife.
- **Shutters on the Beach** to be right on the sand.
- **Hotel Bel-Air** for the royal treatment.

$$$–$$$$ **Hollywood Roosevelt Hotel.** Think hip bachelor pad when considering the Roosevelt. Poolside cabana rooms have dark-wood furnishings and mirrored walls; rooms in the main building have contemporary platform beds. Although Hollywood's oldest hotel, a renovation and a pair of hot nightspots have breathed new life into this historic spot. Lobby and poolside socializing is nonstop most weekends. Spanish Colonial Revival details include Spanish tiles, painted ceilings, arches, and fountains that evoke early Hollywood glamour. The David Hockney–painted pool adds to the playful vibe. A Metro stop is one block away. **Pros:** in the heart of Hollywood's action, lively social scene, great burgers at hotel's restaurant, 25 Degrees. **Cons:** noise, attitude, and stiff parking charges. *✉7000 Hollywood Blvd., Hollywood ☎323/466–7000 or 800/950–7667 ⊕www.hollywoodroosevelt.com 305 rooms, 48 suites In-room: safe, refrigerator, Wi-Fi. In-hotel: 2 restaurants, room service, 3 bars, pool, gym, laundry service, Wi-Fi, parking (paid), no-smoking rooms AE, D, DC, MC, V.*

$$–$$$ **Magic Castle Hotel.** Close to the action (and traffic) of Hollywood, this former apartment building faces busy Franklin Avenue and is a quick walk to a nearby Red Line stop at Hollywood & Highland. There's nothing theme-y about the guest room decor, but larger rooms have kitchens with eating areas. There's a decent-size, heated pool, and the patio has lots of greenery. TIP→ **Guests at the hotel can secure dinner reservations and attend nightly magic shows at the Magic Castle, a private club for magicians and their admirers that's housed in a 1908 mansion next door.** (Jacket and tie are required for men; kids are allowed only during brunch on weekends.) **Pros:** remarkably friendly and able staff, free Wi-Fi, good value. **Cons:** traffic-y locale, no elevator, small bathrooms. *✉7025 Franklin Ave., Hollywood ☎323/851–0800 or 800/741–4915 ⊕www.magiccastlehotel.com 10 rooms, 30 suites In-room: safe, kitchen (some), refrigerator, DVD, Wi-Fi. In-hotel: pool, laundry facilities, laundry service, Wi-Fi, parking (paid), no-smoking rooms AE, D, DC, MC, V CP.*

¢ **Orange Drive Manor Hostel.** Once an elegant Hollywood mansion, the Orange Drive Manor now hosts a budget-conscious mix of student and international travelers who also like its central Hollywood location. Accommodations are sometimes rented as dorms and other times as private rooms, depending on occupancy. The rooms are spare but clean and light-filled. The hostel is near the Hollywood & Highland

CLOSE UP

Spa Specialists

L.A. hotel day spas are serene, urban sanctuaries that promise relaxation and revitalization, if you're willing to pay the price. A one-hour massage can set you back as much as $160 up to $435 (for the Four Seasons Westlake Village's tandem treatment by two massage therapists). Hotel spas tend to be on the small side in-town.

The **Spa at the Four Seasons, Beverly Hills** (✉ *300 S. Doheny Dr., Beverly Hills* ☎ *310/273–2222 or 310/786–2229*) concentrates on traditional body treatments in small, seasonally scented private quarters. Choose your own music or sounds in the deluxe treatment rooms; try the vigorous Swe-Thai massage, which combines deep tissue and limbering Thai massage. The **Peninsula Spa at the Peninsula Beverly Hills** (✉ *9882 S. Santa Monica Blvd., Beverly Hills* ☎ *310/975–2854 or 800/462–7899*) is an exclusive rooftop retreat; rarefied treatments here include massages with oils laced with pulverized precious stones.

Chill out under a fabulous rain shower—cascades vary from a cool mist to a brisk Atlantic storm, at the **Spa at the Beverly Wilshire** (✉ *9500 Wilshire Blvd., Beverly Hills* ☎ *310/385–7023 or 310/275–5200*). A super-size, mosaic-tile steam room is just one of the elegant spa's calming touches. Celeb facialist Kate Somerville's products are featured; intensive 20-minute treatments help soothe techie-neck and, for PDA users, "crampberry" spasms.

Just off the hotel's main entrance, the sleek **LeSpa at Sofitel** (✉ *8955 Beverly Blvd., Los Angeles* ☎ *310/228–6777*) has a decidedly chic, urban vibe. Robes are cushy black; spa suites offer total privacy and soaking tubs. Close to the hotel's famed pool, **the Beverly Hills Hotel Spa by La Prairie** (✉ *9641 Sunset Blvd., Beverly Hills* ☎ *310/887–2505*) is discreetly tucked away. Treatments here are all about the bling: skin treatments involving caviar, gold, and diamonds.

Off the hotel pool and spiffy gym, the boutique spa at the **Ritz-Carlton Marina del Rey** (✉ *4375 Admiralty Way, Marina del Rey* ☎ *310/574–4296*) shimmers throughout. Mosaic tiles and original art (suitably soothing) make this one of L.A.'s prettiest hotel spas. Bridal parties go for the sparkly, nail-care room.

In Santa Monica, Hollywood skin-care guru Ole Henriksen is behind the treatments at **One** (✉ *Shutters on the Beach, 1 Pico Blvd., Santa Monica* ☎ *310/587–1712*). Body treatments here, such as sea mineral scrubs, turn skin silky soft using Henriksen's all-natural tonics. L.A.'s largest hotel spa, **Spa at Four Seasons Westlake Village** (✉ *Dole Dr., Westlake Village* ☎ *818/575–3010*) at 40,000 square feet, is a resort-size beauty tricked out with many extras like private sunbathing, rain shower, steam, and indoor Jacuzzi. The 28 treatment rooms all open out to private, walled gardens. There's a special Thai massage room with a low-rise bed.

When booking a massage, specify your preference for a male or female therapist. Expect to pay a minimum of $160 for a one-hour massage or facial. You should tip at least 15% to 20%. Most reservations must be guaranteed by a credit card. Blackberry-addicts take note: cell phones and PDAs are now banned in most spas.

complex and a Metro Rail stop. A common kitchen is available for those who like DIY meals. **Pros:** steps from Hollywood Blvd., reliable, cheap, and clean. **Cons:** no amenities or air-conditioning. ✉*1764 N. Orange Dr., Hollywood* ☎*323/850–0350* 🌐*www.orangedrivehostel.com* *25 rooms* *In-room: no a/c, no phone, no TV, Wi-Fi. In-hotel: Internet terminal, Wi-Fi, parking (paid), no-smoking rooms* *AE, D, DC, MC, V.*

$$$ ★ **Renaissance Hollywood Hotel.** Part of the massive Hollywood & Highland shopping and entertainment complex, this 20-story Renaissance is at the center of Hollywood's action. Contemporary art (notably by L.A. favorites Charles and Ray Eames), retro '60s furniture, terrazzo floors, a Zen rock garden, and wood and aluminum accents greet you in the lobby. Rooms are vibrant: chairs are red, table lamps are molded blue plastic. For the ultimate party pad, book the Panorama Suite, with angled floor-to-ceiling windows, vintage Eames furniture, a grand piano, and a sunken Jacuzzi tub with a view. Spa Luce, the hotel's poolside spa, offers nontoxic products for nail services, soothing spice-tinged body treatments, and spa cuisine. **Pros:** large rooms, blackout shades, and Red Line Metro–station adjacent. **Cons:** large and corporate feeling, very touristy. ✉*1755 N. Highland Ave., Hollywood* ☎*323/856–1200 or 800/769–4774* 🌐*www.renaissancehollywood.com* *604 rooms, 33 suites* *In-room: safe, refrigerator, Internet, Wi-Fi. In-hotel: restaurant, room service, bars, pool, gym, laundry service, Internet terminal, Wi-Fi, parking (paid), no-smoking rooms* *AE, D, DC, MC, V.*

$$ **Wilshire Plaza Hotel.** A handy midcity location ensures a steady stream of tourist bookings here; the bustling lobby and café give a good first impression. Guest rooms are nothing to write home about, but they have all the necessary amenities, plus oak desks and floor-to-ceiling windows with good views. Across the street from a Red Line station, the hotel gives you easy access to downtown, Hollywood and Universal City. A limo rental service is available on-site. **Pros:** metro Rail adjacent, lively Korean neighborhood with many restaurants and bars, large rooms. **Cons:** Fodor's readers complain about service issues, rooms need updating. ✉*3515 Wilshire Blvd., Hollywood* ☎*213/381–7411 or 877/752–9264* 🌐*www.wilshireplazahotel.com* *380 rooms, 13 suites* *In-room: safe, Internet, Wi-Fi. In-hotel: restaurant, room service, bar, gym, laundry service, Internet terminal, Wi-Fi, parking (paid), no-smoking rooms* *AE, D, DC, MC, V.*

WEST HOLLYWOOD

$$$ **ANdAZ West Hollywood.** Right on the busy Sunset Strip and reopened in January 2009, the ANdAZ is a complete update of the former Hyatt West Hollywood, known as the "riot house," for its famed but badly behaved rock-and-roll guests. Enter to find standing "hosts" welcoming guests and checking them in via high-tech tablet (there's no front desk!). Sip a bit of tea or a glass of wine in the lounge and wander over to the wide-open hotel restaurant, RH, and its equally open kitchen that cooks up fresh seasonal specialties and delectable tapas. Generous-sized rooms are spare but the sensible minimalism results in ample work space with task chair, a comfy seating area, and vented windows. Bathrooms are super practical with overhead shower heads. Nicely done:

The refrigerator is stocked with free nonalcoholic drinks and healthful snacks. Check out the rooftop pool deck for jetliner city views. **Pros:** sleek new interiors with the latest gadgets like free Wi-Fi throughout and sizable flat-screen TVs; ambitious hotel dining and bar concepts; excellent gym overlooks Sunset Boulevard's nonstop action. **Cons:** traffic congestion impedes access, Sunset Strip is wildly popular weekends and holidays. ✉ *8401 Sunset Blvd.,West Hollywood* ☎ *232/656–1234 or 800/233–1234* 🌐 *www.andaz.com* *251 rooms, 1 suite* *In-room: safe, refrigerator, Internet, Wi-Fi. In-hotel: restaurant, room service, bar, pool, gym, laundry service, Internet terminal, Wi-Fi, parking (paid), some pets allowed, no-smoking rooms* *AE, D, DC, MC, V.*

¢–$ **Banana Bungalow.** Spartan but clean, the Banana Bungalow is a busy and often fully booked hostel on a major bus line. Welcoming international guests (who are eligible to stay in dorm rooms for as low as $22 per night), single travelers, and families—who utilize private rooms with queen and bunk beds—the bare-bones decor is complemented by free Wi-Fi access throughout, daily breakfast, and evening socializing on the tiki-styled patio. Although there's no pool, a TV/movie lounge with flat-screen TV, game room, and outdoor patios add up to a super casual and friendly vibe. Within walking distance are numerous diversions such as the Farmers Market and The Grove as well as Melrose Avenue's diverse shopping options. **Pros:** inexpensive stay within walking distance of many bars and restaurants, access to public transport, international visitors welcomed. **Cons:** for the budget-conscious traveler, international travelers only in dorm rooms, decor is budget basic at best. ✉ *603 N. Fairfax Ave., West Hollywood* ☎ *323/655–2002 or 877/666–2002* 🌐 *www.bananabungalowus.com* *35 rooms* *In-room: no phone, refrigerator (some), no TV (some), Wi-Fi. In-hotel: laundry facilities, Internet terminal, Wi-Fi, parking (free)* *MC, V* *CP.*

$ **Beverly Laurel Motor Hotel.** A family-run operation for more than 40 years, the Beverly Laurel stands out for its low rates and central city location bordering West Hollywood. Touring bands and up-and-coming actors stay here on their way to the big time. The ground floor is home to Swingers coffee shop, which is popular with the actors, models, and musicians who also frequent the motel. **Pros:** legendary stepping stone for actors and musicians on their way to big-time, central city location, close to Farmers Market and numerous restaurants. **Cons:** Wi-Fi fee, small shaded pool, motel-size rooms. ✉ *8018 Beverly Blvd., West Hollywood* ☎ *323/651–2441, 800/962–3824 outside CA* *323/651–5225* *52 rooms* *In-room: kitchen (some), refrigerator, Internet, Wi-Fi. In-hotel: restaurant, pool, parking (free), some pets allowed, no-smoking rooms* *AE, D, MC, V.*

$$$ **Chamberlain.** On a leafy residential side street, the Chamberlain is steps from Santa Monica Boulevard and close to the Sunset Strip, bringing in young business types, the fashion/design crowd, and 24-hour party people looking to roam WeHo and the Strip. Rooms are handsomely tailored in gray and teal, with snappy gray and white Regency-style furniture. All rooms have a fireplace and balcony. The work desks are oversize, but the bathrooms are compact (those in grand rooms have separate shower and tub). Tech extras include flat-screen TVs, cordless

4

phones, iPod docks, and CD players. Beds have pillow-top mattresses. You can soak up the sunshine next to the rooftop pool with dramatic city and Hollywood Hills views. **Pros:** excellent guests-only dining room and bar, pleasing design, close to Strip without the hassle. **Cons:** compact baths. ✉ *1000 Westmount Dr., West Hollywood* ☎ *310/657–7400 or 800/201–9652* 🌐 *www.chamberlainwesthollywood.com* *114 suites* *In-room: safe, refrigerator, DVD, Internet, Wi-Fi. In-hotel: restaurant, room service, bar, pool, gym, laundry service, Internet terminal, Wi-Fi, parking (paid), some pets allowed, no-smoking rooms* *AE, D, DC, MC, V.*

$$$$ **Chateau Marmont Hotel.** The Chateau's swank exterior disguises its lurid place in Hollywood history—many remember it as the scene of John Belushi's fatal overdose in 1982. Celebs like Johnny Depp appreciate the hotel for its secluded cottages, bungalows, and understated suites and penthouses. For those who don't grace the cover of *Vanity Fair*, service can be frosty. The interior is 1920s style, although some of the decor looks dated rather than vintage. The Wi-Fi throughout the hotel means that you can surf the Net while seated on the hotel's always busy scenic, landscaped terrace. **Pros:** walking distance to all of Sunset Strip's action, great food and vibe at Bar Marmont, guaranteed celeb spotting. **Cons:** attitude and then some from staff, ancient elevators. ✉ *8221 Sunset Blvd., West Hollywood* ☎ *323/656–1010 or 800/242–8328* 🌐 *www.chateaumarmont.com* *11 rooms, 63 suites* *In-room: safe, refrigerator, kitchen (some), DVD, Internet, Wi-Fi. In-hotel: restaurant, room service, bar, pool, gym, laundry service, Wi-Fi, parking (paid), some pets allowed, no-smoking rooms* *AE, DC, MC, V.*

$$ **Élan Hotel Modern.** Small and modest, and a favorite of international travelers, this hotel has an enviable location within walking distance of some of the city's best restaurants and the Beverly Center. Guests have been known to forgo car rentals as there's DASH service to the nearby Farmers Market; Beverly Hills is a short hop via taxi. Guest rooms are compact with mostly nondescript views. Blond wood accents and black-and-white photographs enliven the otherwise plain rooms. In the streetside lobby lounge you can have coffee while you navigate the Net or enjoy the daily afternoon wine and cheese nosh. **Pros:** friendly staff, central location with many great restaurants nearby. **Cons:** super-compact rooms, no pool. ✉ *8435 Beverly Blvd., West Hollywood Los Angeles* ☎ *323/658–6663 or 866/203–2212* 🌐 *www.elanhotel.com* *46 rooms, 3 suites* *In-room: safe, refrigerator, Internet, Wi-Fi. In-hotel: gym, laundry service, Internet terminal, Wi-Fi, parking (paid), no-smoking rooms* *AE, D, DC, MC, V* *CP.*

$$$ **The Grafton on Sunset.** It's easy to tap into the Sunset Strip energy here, especially since the hotel's hip steak house, BOA, is usually packed. Rooms are small, but large windows with plantation shutters and full-length mirrors help open the space up. Ask for a room facing the interior courtyard, both to avoid noise from the Strip and to overlook the heated pool area with its mosaic-tiled waterfall and striped lounge chairs. Hospitable touches include portable room phones that work poolside, bathrobes, nightly turndown service, CD players, iPod docking stations, and free transportation within 3 mi. **Pros:** playful amenities, snazzy

suites, heart of Strip's action. **Cons:** weekend stays higher, Strip traffic, very small standard rooms. *✉8462 W. Sunset Blvd., West Hollywood ☎323/654–4600 or 800/821–3660 🌐www.graftononsunset.com 🛏103 rooms, 5 suites ♿In-room: refrigerator, DVD, Wi-Fi. In-hotel: restaurant, room service, bar, pool, gym, laundry service, Internet terminal, Wi-Fi, parking (paid), some pets allowed, no-smoking rooms ▭AE, D, MC, V.*

$$$ **Le Montrose Suite Hotel.** Once an apartment building, this hotel plays host to those in the entertainment business. Close to Beverly Hills and Hollywood and a short drive from the Valley, it's just off the busy Sunset Strip on a quiet residential block. Loftlike suites, with sunken living room, fireplace, and private balcony, have chocolate brown walls, brightened by a geometric patterned duvet. Couches are covered in plush corduroy, and the flat-screen TV and DVD player are hidden inside a dark-wood sideboard. Bathrooms are small, with combination showers and tubs. **Pros:** rooftop pool and tennis court with stellar views, super-private and discreet industry favorite. **Cons:** no on-street parking, in the heart of W. Hollywood's congestion. *✉900 Hammond St., West Hollywood ☎310/855–1115 or 800/776–0666 🌐www.lemontrose.com 🛏132 suites ♿In-room: kitchen (some), refrigerator, DVD, Internet, Wi-Fi. In-hotel: restaurant, room service, bar, tennis court, pool, gym, bicycles, laundry service, Internet terminal, Wi-Fi, parking (paid), some pets allowed, no-smoking rooms ▭AE, D, DC, MC, V.*

$$$ **Le Parc Suite Hotel.** On a tree-lined residential street close to CBS Television City and the Pacific Design Center, this congenial low-rise hotel aims to make guests feel coddled, with extremely personalized service and a strong commitment to privacy. Even the most basic suites here are spacious (650 square feet) and well-outfitted with expensive accessories like wall-mounted plasma TVs and Frette linens. They also have sunken living rooms with fireplaces and private balconies. Secluded on the third floor, the hotel's hidden restaurant Knoll is an exceptional choice. **Pros:** private, in-house dining, great views from rooftop pool deck and lighted tennis court. **Cons:** small lobby. *✉733 W. Knoll Dr., West Hollywood ☎310/855–8888 or 800/578–4837 🌐www.leparcsuites.com 🛏154 suites ♿In-room: safe, kitchen, refrigerator, Wi-Fi. In-hotel: restaurant, room service, tennis court, pool, gym, laundry facilities, laundry service, Wi-Fi, parking (paid), some pets allowed, no-smoking rooms ▭AE, D, DC, MC, V.*

$$$$ **London West Hollywood.** Just off the Sunset Strip, cosmopolitan and chic in design, the London WeHo is a remake of 1984-built Bel Age. The large suites and rooftop pool with city-wide views remain but all else has been spiffed and brightened up with luxury textures like ultrasuede covered hallway walls, framed mirrors throughout, and glam touches like gold lame leather couches. A visual treat inside and out, though some of the custom-made pieces from British designer David Collins, like the marble topped desk and glass-walled showers, are sharp-edged and might prove perilous. Rooftops are masked with gardens and topiary—British whimsy includes a bulldog as hotel mascot. Celebrity chef Gordon Ramsay runs the restaurant and bar—his first in Los Angeles. **Pros:** perfectly designed interiors, hillside and city views in generous-sized suites all with balconies and steps from the Strip. **Cons:** too chi-chi for youngsters, lower floors have mundane views. ✉ *1020 N. San Vicente Blvd., West Hollywood* ☎ *310/854–1111 or 866/282–4560* 🌐 *www.thelondonwesthollywood.com* *200 suites* *In-room: safe, refrigerator, Internet, Wi-Fi. In-hotel: restaurant, room service, bars, pool, gym, laundry service, Internet terminal, Wi-Fi, parking (paid), some pets allowed, no-smoking rooms* 💳 *AE, D, MC, V.*

$$$$ **Mondrian.** A city club attitude pervades at the spendy Mondrian. Socializing begins in the revamped lobby bar and lounge, extends through the all-white Asia de Cuba restaurant, and then moves out onto the sparkly patio to the divans surrounding the pool. Hotel guests gain access to the Sky Bar—still a scene most weekends. Designer Benjamin Noriega completely redid the rooms, adding bamboo floors and an oversize mirror—think mod-looking glass—that swivels to reveal a flat-screen TV. Bathrooms have a convenient wall of hooks, pocket door, and rain showerhead. Sheer curtains hide the closet. Windows are now double-paned for quiet, a good thing as street noise from Sunset Boulevard is constant to the north and the pool and Sky Bar echo with party people year-round to the south. **Pros:** pool, spa, and nighttime social scene means never having to leave the property. **Cons:** $32 per night valet parking only, late-night party scene, inflated prices. ✉ *8440 Sunset Blvd., West Hollywood* ☎ *323/650–8999 or 800/697–1791* 🌐 *www.mondrianhotel.com* *54 rooms, 183 suites* *In-room: safe, refrigerator, DVD, Wi-Fi. In-hotel: restaurant, room service, bars, pool, gym, spa, laundry service, Wi-Fi, parking (paid), no-smoking rooms* 💳 *AE, D, DC, MC, V.*

$$ **Ramada Plaza West Hollywood.** Popular with Aussie and Kiwi tour groups, this Ramada outlet has a prime West Hollywood–close-to–Sunset Strip position. Although the exterior is vibrantly colorful, inside the decor shows wear and tear and the guest room air-conditioners can be noisy. However, its location and its party vibe guarantee sold-out holiday weekends. (Halloween is particularly raucous.) Parking is an extra $27 per night—unusually steep for such a modest establishment. **Pros:** free Wi-Fi, close to nightlife, friendly staff. **Cons:** street noise and sound-proofing issues, shaded pool, parking fees. ✉ *8585 Santa Monica Blvd., West Hollywood* ☎ *310/652–6400 or 800/272–6232* 🌐 *www.ramadaweho.com* *130 rooms, 45 suites* *In-room: safe, refrigerator, Wi-Fi. In-hotel: restaurant, room service, bar, pool, gym, laundry facilities, laundry service, Internet terminal, Wi-Fi, parking (paid), no-smoking rooms* 💳 *AE, D, DC, MC, V.*

$$ **The Standard, Hollywood.** Hotelier André Balazs created this playful Sunset Strip hotel out of a former retirement home. The aesthetic is '70s kitsch: pop art, shag carpets and ultrasuede sectionals fill the lobby, while the rooms have inflatable sofas, beanbag chairs, surfboard tables, and Warhol poppy-print curtains. After a decade of heavy use, rooms show the wear-and-tear, and service issues and staff attitude are commonplace. DJs spin nightly and lobby socializing begins at the front desk and extends to the blue AstroTurfed pool deck outside. **Pros:** on-site, decent 24-hour coffee shop, poolside socializing, live DJs. **Cons:** extended party scene for twentysomethings, staff big on attitude rather

than service. ✉8300 Sunset Blvd., West Hollywood ☎323/650–9090 🌐www.standardhotel.com 137 rooms, 2 suites In-room: refrigerator, Wi-Fi. In-hotel: restaurant, room service, bar, pool, laundry service, Internet terminal, Wi-Fi, parking (paid), some pets allowed, no-smoking rooms ▭AE, D, DC, MC, V.

$$$$ ★ **Sunset Marquis Hotel and Villas.** If you're in town to cut your new hit single, you'll appreciate the two on-site recording studios here. Many a rocker has called the Sunset Marquis home—check out their oversize portraits lining the walls of the hotel's exclusive Bar 1200. But even the musically challenged will appreciate this property on a quiet cul-de-sac just off the Sunset Strip. Suites and ultraprivate villas, which are set amid lush gardens, are roomy and plush (ultrasuede bed throws and flat-screen TVs abound). Windows are as soundproof as they come; blackout curtains ensure total serenity. Forty new villas are lavish with extras: kitchens, fireplaces, room-size bathrooms and on-call butlers available to handle everything from unpacking to booking spa appointments. **Pros:** superior service, discreet setting just off the Strip, clublike atmosphere. **Cons:** standard suites are somewhat small. ✉1200 N. Alta Loma Rd., West Hollywood ☎310/657–1333 or 800/858–9758 🌐www.sunsetmarquishotel.com 102 suites, 52 villas In-room: safe, kitchen (some), refrigerator, DVD, Internet, Wi-Fi. In-hotel: 2 restaurants, room service, bars, pools, gym, spa, laundry service, Internet terminal, Wi-Fi, parking (paid), no-smoking rooms ▭AE, D, DC, MC, V.

$$$ **The Sunset Tower Hotel.** A clubby style infuses the 1929 Art Deco landmark formerly known as the Argyle. The lobby sets the tone with dark wood, mauve accents, and marble floors; vintage Hollywood star photos add retro glamour to the Tower Bar where you can sink into couches and cozy upholstered corners while taking in the dramatic city views. The indoor-outdoor Terrace restaurant sits poolside and has an equally impressive vista. Guest rooms soft-pedal the look with art deco–inspired fixtures and walnut armoires. The spa and elaborate beauty salon add to the resort-in-the-city feel. **Pros:** sunset Strip's diversions right out the door, Tower Bar a favorite of Hollywood's elite, incredible city views. **Cons:** wedged into the Strip—driveway a challenge, small standard rooms. ✉8358 Sunset Blvd., West Hollywood ☎323/654–7100 or 800/225–2637 🌐www.sunsettowerhotel.com 20 rooms, 44 suites In-room: safe, refrigerator, Wi-Fi. In-hotel: 2 restaurants, room service, bar, pool, gym, spa, laundry service, Internet terminal, Wi-Fi, parking (paid), some pets allowed, no-smoking rooms ▭AE, D, DC, MC, V.

DOWNTOWN

$$ ★ **Figueroa Hotel.** On the outside, it's Spanish Revival; on the inside, this 1926, 12-story hotel is a mix of Southwestern, Mexican, and Mediterranean styles, with earth tones, hand-painted furniture, and wrought-iron beds. You can lounge around the pool and bubbling hot tub surrounded by tropical greenery under the shadow of downtown skyscrapers. (Make it even better with a soothing drink from the back patio bar.) **Pros:** a short walk to Nokia Theatre, LA Live, Convention Center; well-priced, great poolside bar. **Cons:** somewhat funky room decor;

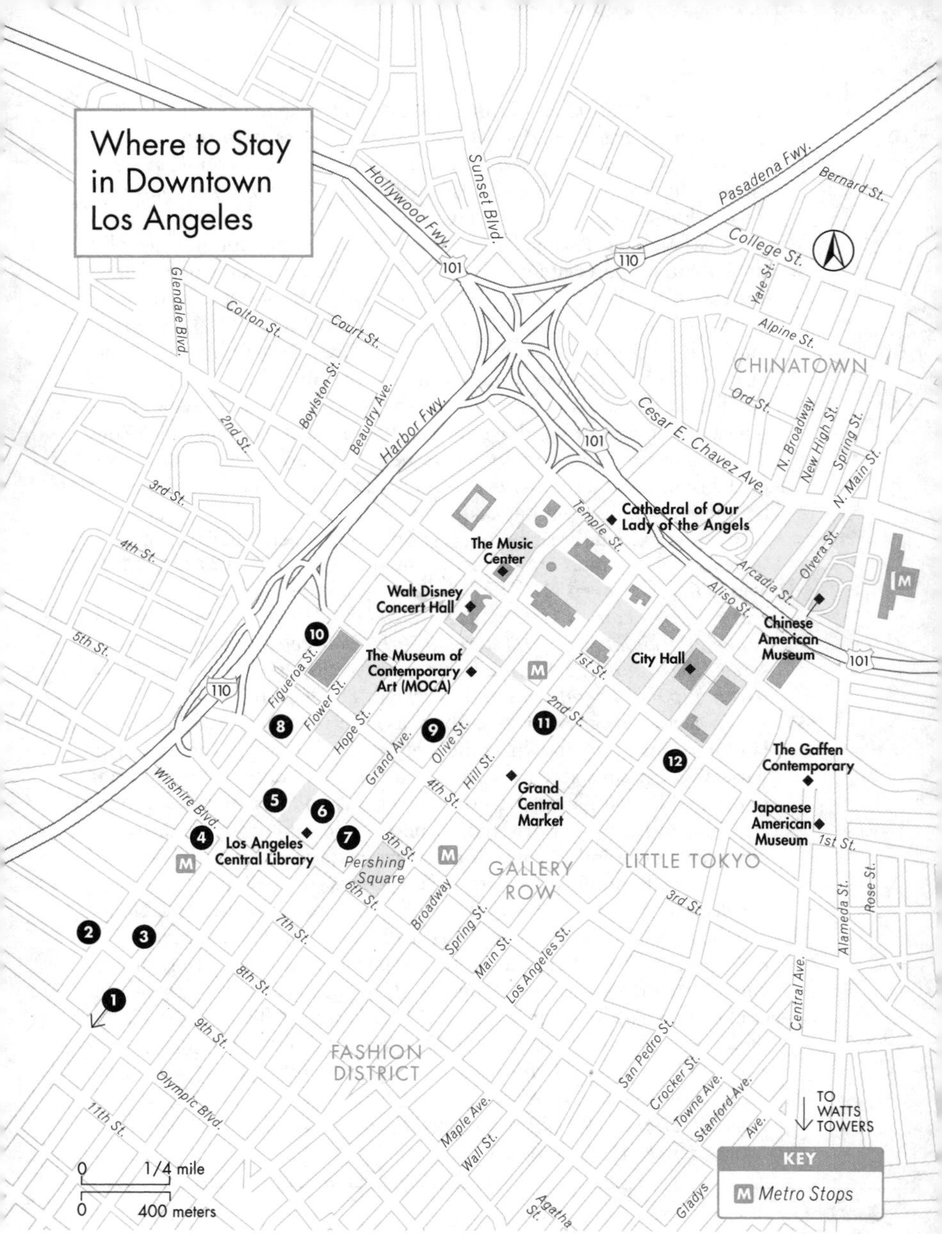

Figueroa Hotel **2**
Hilton Checkers Los Angeles **6**
Inn at 657 .... **1**
Kawada Hotel **11**
Kyoto Grand Hotel and Gardens **12**
Los Angeles Marriott Downtown **10**
Millennium Biltmore Hotel **7**
O Hotel **3**
Omni Los Angeles Hotel at California Plaza **9**
The Standard, Downtown L.A **5**
Westin Bonaventure Hotel & Suites **8**
Wilshire Grand **4**

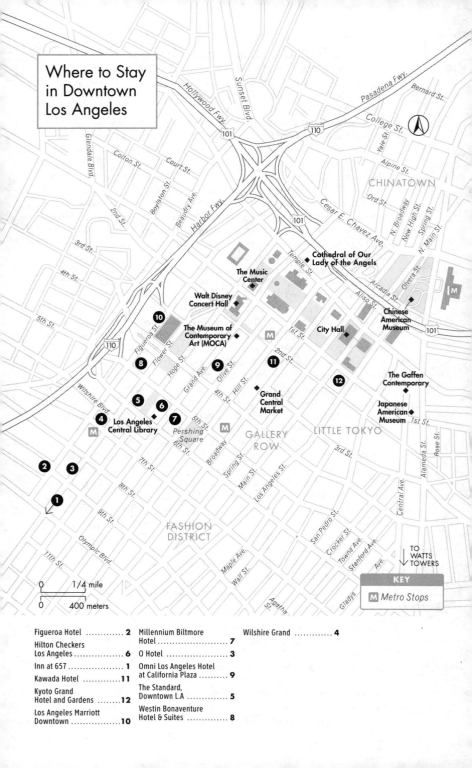

small bathrooms, gentrifying neighborhood. ✉ *939 S. Figueroa St., Downtown* ☎ *213/627–8971 or 800/421–9092* 🌐 *www.figueroahotel.com* *285 rooms, 2 suites* *In-room: refrigerator, Wi-Fi. In-hotel: restaurant, bars, pool, laundry facilities, laundry service, public Wi-Fi, parking (fee), no-smoking rooms* 💳 *AE, DC, MC, V.*

$$$$ ★ **Hilton Checkers Los Angeles.** Opened as the Mayflower Hotel in 1927, Checkers retains much of its original character; its various-size rooms all have charming period details, although they also have contemporary luxuries like pillow-top mattresses, coffeemakers, 24-hour room service, and cordless phones. The rooftop pool deck overlooks the L.A. library and nearby office towers. The plush lobby bar and lounge look like they belong in a private club, with comfortable leather chairs and a large plasma-screen TV. **Pros:** historic charm, business-friendly, rooftop pool and spa. **Cons:** no on-street parking, some rooms very compact, very urban setting. ✉ *535 S. Grand Ave., Downtown* ☎ *213/624–0000 or 800/445–8667* 🌐 *www.hiltoncheckers.com* *188 rooms, 9 suites* *In-room: Internet, Wi-Fi. In-hotel: restaurant, room service, bar, pool, gym, spa, laundry service, Wi-Fi, parking (fee), no-smoking rooms* 💳 *AE, D, DC, MC, V.*

$$ ★ **Inn at 657.** Proprietor Patsy Carter runs a homey, welcoming bed-and-breakfast near the University of Southern California. Rooms in this 1904-built Craftsman have down comforters, Oriental silks on the walls, and needlepoint rugs. The vintage dining room table seats 12; conversation is encouraged. You're also welcome to hang out with the hummingbirds in the private garden. All rooms include a hearty breakfast and free local phone calls. **Pros:** vintage home and quiet garden, homemade breakfast, you'll meet the innkeeper. **Cons:** low-tech stay, you'll have to speak to other guests, no elevator. ✉ *657 W. 23rd St., Downtown* ☎ *213/741–2200 or 800/347–7512* 🌐 *www.patsysinn657.com* *11 rooms* *In-room: Wi-Fi. In-hotel: restaurant, laundry service, Internet terminal, Wi-Fi, parking (free), no-smoking rooms* 💳 *MC, V* *BP.*

$ **Kawada Hotel.** This modest, four-story redbrick hotel near the Walt Disney Hall, Music Center, and local government buildings is at the foot of Bunker Hill. Standard guest rooms are on the small side, with equally compact bathrooms. Studios are available for stays of one month or longer. Decor is functional at best. It's a favorite of Asian tourists due to its close proximity to Little Tokyo. **Pros:** downtown's cheapest stay, walk to courthouses and Disney Hall. **Cons:** for the budget-minded, nondiscerning traveler-only. ✉ *200 S. Hill St., Downtown* ☎ *213/621–4455 or 800/752–9232* 🌐 *www.kawadahotel.com* *115 rooms, 1 suite* *In-room: kitchen (some), refrigerator, Internet. In-hotel: restaurant, bar, laundry facilities, parking (paid), no-smoking rooms* 💳 *AE, D, DC, MC, V.*

$$$ **Kyoto Grand Hotel and Garden.** Formerly the New Otani, the Kyoto Grand may have new owners and name, but its mix of Japanese culture and corporate America remains in place. The "Japanese Suites" have tatami mats, futon beds, extra-deep bathtubs, and paper screens on the windows. The American-style rooms are somewhat plain and compact. Two of the restaurants serve Japanese cuisine at authentically steep Tokyo prices. The third serves straightforward contemporary food,

including a daily lunch buffet for downtown's office crowd. The hotel is close to the Civic Center and state and federal courthouses. For those who seek a contemplative moment (or a scenic wedding spot), there's a ½-acre Japanese garden on the roof. **Pros:** on-site spa specializing in Shiatsu massage, unique Japanese garden, super-quiet. **Cons:** homeless encampments nearby (and throughout downtown); although rooms and public areas are updated, it's very old-fashioned. ✉ *120 S. Los Angeles St., Downtown* ☎ *213/629–1200 or 888/354–0831* 🌐 *www.kyotograndhotel.com* *414 rooms, 20 suites* *In-room: safe, refrigerator, Wi-Fi. In-hotel: 3 restaurants, room service, bars, gym, spa, laundry service, Internet terminal, Wi-Fi, parking (paid), no-smoking rooms* 💳 *AE, D, DC, MC, V.*

$$$ **Los Angeles Marriott Downtown.** Near the U.S. 101 and I–110 freeways and five blocks north of the Staples Center, L.A. Live, and the L.A. Convention Center, the 14-story, glass-walled Marriott is an especially good choice if you're traveling on business. Guest rooms are oversize with marble baths and huge windows. Stay plugged in at the business center, which has computers, copiers, and fax machines. Weekend rates are extra-reasonable; downtown's many cultural attractions are within walking distance. **Pros:** new luxury bedding, great city views, three screen movie theater on-site. **Cons:** corporate feel, weekday rates higher, expensive dining. ✉ *333 S. Figueroa St., Downtown* ☎ *213/617–1133 or 866/210–8879* 🌐 *www.losangelesmarriottdowntown.com* *400 rooms, 69 suites* *In-room: safe, Internet, Wi-Fi. In-hotel: 3 restaurants, room service, bars, pool, gym, laundry service, Wi-Fi, Internet terminal, parking (paid), no-smoking rooms* 💳 *AE, D, DC, MC, V.*

$$$ **Millennium Biltmore Hotel.** One of downtown L.A.'s true treasures, the gilded 1923 beaux arts masterpiece exudes ambience and history. The lobby (formerly the Music Room) was the local headquarters of JFK's presidential campaign, and the ballroom hosted some of the earliest Academy Awards. These days, the Biltmore hosts business types drawn by its central downtown location, ample meeting spaces, and services such as a well-outfitted business center that stays open 24/7. Some of the guest rooms are small by today's standards, but all have classic, formal furnishings, shuttered windows, and marble bathrooms. Bring your bathing suit for the vintage tiled indoor pool and adjacent steam room. **Pros:** historic character, famed filming location, club level rooms have many hospitable extras. **Cons:** pricey valet parking, standard rooms truly compact. ✉ *506 S. Grand Ave., Downtown* ☎ *213/624–1011 or 866/866–8086* 🌐 *www.millenniumhotels.com* *627 rooms, 56 suites* *In-room: Internet, Wi-Fi. In-hotel: 3 restaurants, room service, bars, pool, gym, laundry service, Internet terminal, Wi-Fi, parking (paid), no-smoking rooms* 💳 *AE, D, DC, MC, V.*

Fodor's Choice ★

$ **O Hotel.** A former residential hotel, the O has been completely cleaned up and redone in a minimalist, Zen-modern style. A glowing, granite-faced fireplace heats up the two-story lobby, dotted with low seating. Ergonomic work desk and chair, designer lighting and platform beds occupy the compact rooms also outfitted with flat-screen TV; stone-floored bathrooms are found behind a space-saving pocket door. Close to L.A.'s convention center, the Nokia Theatre and L.A. Live at downtown's southern edge, numerous new hot spots are also within walking distance.

Mediterranean-influenced cuisine and tapas are the specialties of O Bar & Kitchen, the on-site restaurant. Convention goers and downtown business types will appreciate the convenience, low-key vibe and amiable staff. **Pros:** boutique, European city-style hotel, ambitious restaurant cuisine, rapidly gentrifying neighborhood. **Cons:** boxy, almost monastic cell-like rooms and few views, gentrifying neighborhood means numerous homeless people and deserted streetscapes come nightfall. ✉ *819 S. Flower St., Downtown* ☎ *213/623–9904* 🌐 *www.ohotelgroup.com* *68 rooms* *In-room: safe, refrigerator, Internet. In-hotel: restaurant, room service, bar, gym, laundry service, Internet terminal, Wi-Fi, parking (paid), no-smoking rooms* ▭ *AE, D, DC, MC, V.*

$$$ **Omni Los Angeles Hotel at California Plaza.** The 17-story Omni is in downtown's cultural and business heart, just steps from the Museum of Contemporary Art and the Los Angeles Philharmonic's home, Walt Disney Concert Hall. The airy rooms have a cheery, California-casual look. Business rooms have all the necessities, including extra power strips, an oversize desk, and office supplies. Portable treadmills are available for in-room workouts. You can have breakfast or lunch on the Grand Café's pleasant outdoor terrace, which overlooks the Museum of Contemporary Art's entrance. Nightly, Noé serves flavorful Asian-influenced California cuisine; a small plates menu is available in the bar. True gourmands splurge on the nine-course tasting menu. **Pros:** western-facing rooms have stunning views including Disney Hall, a short walk to most downtown culture and courthouses, great dining at Noé. **Cons:** confusing lobby layout (pedestrian and street entrances on different floors), Olive Street super-traffic-y and not pedestrian-friendly, $30 valet parking. ✉ *251 S. Olive St., Downtown* ☎ *213/617–3300 or 888/444–6664* 🌐 *www.omnihotels.com* *439 rooms, 14 suites* *In-room: refrigerator, Wi-Fi. In-hotel: 2 restaurants, room service, bar, pool, gym, spa, laundry service, Internet terminal, Wi-Fi, parking (paid), some pets allowed, no-smoking rooms* ▭ *AE, D, DC, MC, V.*

$$$ Fodor'sChoice ★ **The Standard, Downtown LA.** Built in 1955 as Standard Oil's company's headquarters, the building was completely revamped under the sharp eye of owner André Balazs. The large guest rooms are practical and funky: all have sexy see-through showers, windows that actually open, and platform beds. Some bathrooms have extra-large tubs. The indoor-outdoor rooftop lounge has a preening social scene and stunning setting, but be prepared for some attitude at the door. **Pros:** on-site Rudy's barbershop for grooming, 24/7 coffee shop for dining, rooftop pool and lounge for fun. **Cons:** disruptive party scene weekends and holidays, street noise, hipper-than-thou attitude at the door. ✉ *550 S. Flower St., Downtown* ☎ *213/892–8080* 🌐 *www.standardhotel.com* *205 rooms, 2 suites* *In-room: safe, refrigerator, DVD, Wi-Fi. In-hotel: restaurant, room service, bars, pool, gym, laundry service, Internet terminal, Wi-Fi, parking (paid), some pets allowed, no-smoking rooms* ▭ *AE, D, DC, MC, V.*

$$–$$$ **Westin Bonaventure Hotel & Suites.** L.A.'s largest hotel has five towers, each mirrored, cylindrical, and 35 stories tall. Inside the futuristic lobby are fountains, an indoor lake, an indoor track, and 12 glass elevators. Although these days, the hotel's cold, concrete and tile lobby

feels a bit dated. Color-coded hotel floors and numerous signs help newcomers navigate the hotel. Standard rooms are on the small side, but the suites are expansive and come with practical extras such as two-line speaker phones and ergonomic office chairs. All rooms have floor-to-ceiling windows, many with terrific views. **Pros:** numerous restaurants including Korean barbecue, shiatsu or chair massage at the Asian-theme spa, revolving rooftop lounge a classic. **Cons:** lacking personal touch, mazelike lobby and public areas. ✉ *404 S. Figueroa St., Downtown* ☎ *213/624–1000 or 866/716–8132* 🌐 *www.westin.com* *1,354 rooms, 135 suites* *In-room: safe, refrigerator, Internet, Wi-Fi. In-hotel: 17 restaurants, room service, bars, pool, gym, spa, laundry service, Internet terminal, Wi-Fi, parking (paid), some pets allowed, no-smoking rooms* *AE, D, DC, MC, V.*

$$–$$$ **Wilshire Grand Los Angeles.** Wedged in among the other high-rises at the start of Wilshire Boulevard, this sprawling 16-story hotel is two blocks from the Staples Center, the Nokia Theater, L.A. Live, and is close to the convention center and all major office towers. The location and services are the strong suits; guest rooms are small for the price, and the decor begs for an update. Dining choices include Seoul Jung, serving savory Korean barbecue. Point Moorea, the lower lobby sports bar, makes good martinis and attracts a lively happy hour scene. **Pros:** metro stop adjacent, free access to mega-size Gold's Gym nearby, walking-distance to Nokia Theatre, L.A. Live, and Staples. **Cons:** car access somewhat dicey due to traffic/one-way streets, $35 valet parking, small pool. ✉ *930 Wilshire Blvd., Downtown* ☎ *213/688–7777 or 888/773–2888* 🌐 *www.wilshiregrand.com* *865 rooms, 35 suites* *In-room: Internet, Wi-Fi. In-hotel: 4 restaurants, room service, pool, gym, laundry service, Internet terminal, Wi-Fi, parking (paid), no-smoking rooms* *AE, D, DC, MC, V.*

COASTAL AND WESTERN LOS ANGELES

BEL AIR

$$ **Hotel Angeleno.** A thoroughly up-to-date remake of the landmark 1970s mod, cylindrical tower hotel, this building conveniently sits at the crossroads of Sunset Boulevard and the I–405. Compact, triangle-shaped rooms, each with a tiny balcony, give views of Bel Air's hills or the freeway, a serpentine river of lights at night. Granite counters and stone-lined showers add a bit of luxury to the bathrooms. Instead of closets, you'll find armoires with conveniently placed hooks outside. On the 17th floor, complete with panoramic views, West is hotel's coppery, wood-accented restaurant serving robust Italian specialties. **Pros:** free shuttle to nearby Getty Center, free Wi-Fi, intriguing design throughout. **Cons:** compact rooms, small, shaded pool, somewhat isolated location. ✉ *170 N. Church La., Bel Air* ☎ *310/476–6411 or 800/264–3536* 🌐 *www.jdvhotels.com/angeleno* *206 rooms, 3 suites* *In-room: safe, refrigerator, Wi-Fi. In-hotel: restaurant, room service, bar, pool, gym, laundry service, Internet terminal, Wi-Fi, parking (paid), no-smoking rooms* *AE, D, DC, MC, V.*

$$$$ Fodor's Choice ★ **Hotel Bel-Air.** In a wooded canyon with lush gardens and a swan-filled lake, the Hotel Bel-Air's fairy-tale luxury and seclusion have made it

a favorite of discreet celebs and royalty for decades. Bungalow-style rooms feel like fine homes, with country-French, expensively upholstered furniture in silk or chenille; many have hardwood floors. Several rooms have wood-burning fireplaces (the bell captain will build a fire for you). Eight suites have private outdoor hot tubs. Complimentary tea service greets you upon arrival; enjoy it on the terrace warmed by heated tiles. A pianist plays nightly in the bar. **Pros:** ultraprivate in-town hideaway, gorgeous restaurant terrace, service par-excellence. **Cons:** very expensive dining. ✉ *701 Stone Canyon Rd., Bel Air* ☎ *310/472–1211 or 800/648–4097* 🌐 *www.hotelbelair.com* *52 rooms, 39 suites* *In-room: safe, DVD, Wi-Fi. In-hotel: restaurant, room service, bar, pool, gym, concierge, laundry service, Internet terminal, Wi-Fi, parking (paid), some pets allowed, no-smoking rooms* *AE, DC, MC, V.*

4

$$$ **Luxe Hotel Sunset Boulevard.** On 7 landscaped acres near the Getty Center, the Luxe feels like a secluded country club—but it's also next to the I–405, for easy freeway access. Guest rooms have a comfortable residential look, with a taupe-and-brown color scheme, feather duvets, flat-screen TVs, and iPod base stations on bedside tables. Book lessons with the hotel's tennis pro or head for the spa, which offers 16 kinds of massage. On Sunset, the hotel's hidden restaurant is a neighborhood favorite for lunch on the sunny patio. **Pros:** country-club feel, oversize rooms, central for Westside business meetings. **Cons:** some freeway noise, off extremely busy intersection, car almost essential. ✉ *11461 Sunset Blvd., Bel Air* ☎ *310/476–6571 or 866/589–3411* 🌐 *www.luxehotels.com* *110 rooms, 51 suites* *In-room: safe, refrigerator, Wi-Fi. In-hotel: restaurant, room service, bar, tennis court, pool, gym, spa, laundry service, Internet terminal, Wi-Fi, parking (paid), some pets allowed, no-smoking rooms* *AE, D, DC, MC, V.*

LONG BEACH

$–$$ *Queen Mary.* Experience the golden age of transatlantic travel without the seasickness: A 1936–art deco style reigns on the *Queen Mary* from the ship's mahogany paneling to the nickel-plated doors to the majestic Grand Salon. Dry-docked for more than 40 years, the on-board hotel attracts a mix of tourists and those attending events in the floating hotel's many party spaces. There are plenty of nighttime diversions, from the silver Observation Bar to a comedy club to live theater to jazz. Holidays are big on the *Queen Mary;* New Year's Eve and July 4 are famously spectacular. Sunday Brunch in the Grand Salon is a step back in time. Room stays include a self-guided tour of the venerable vessel. **Pros:** walking the historic Promenade deck, views from Long Beach out to the Pacific, art deco details. **Cons:** Wi-Fi available in the lobby only, uneven service, no soundproofing. ✉ *1126 Queens Hwy., Long Beach* ☎ *562/435–3511 or 800/437–2934* 🌐 *www.queenmary.com* *357 staterooms, 8 suites* *In-room: refrigerator (some). In-hotel: 4 restaurants, room service, bars, gym, spa, Wi-Fi, parking (paid), no-smoking rooms* *AE, DC, MC, V.*

$$$ **Renaissance Long Beach Hotel.** Set in the heart of Long Beach's business district, directly across from the Long Beach Convention Center's entrance, the Renaissance's updated lobby is mix of bold green, orange, and yellow with digital images floating on screens behind the check-

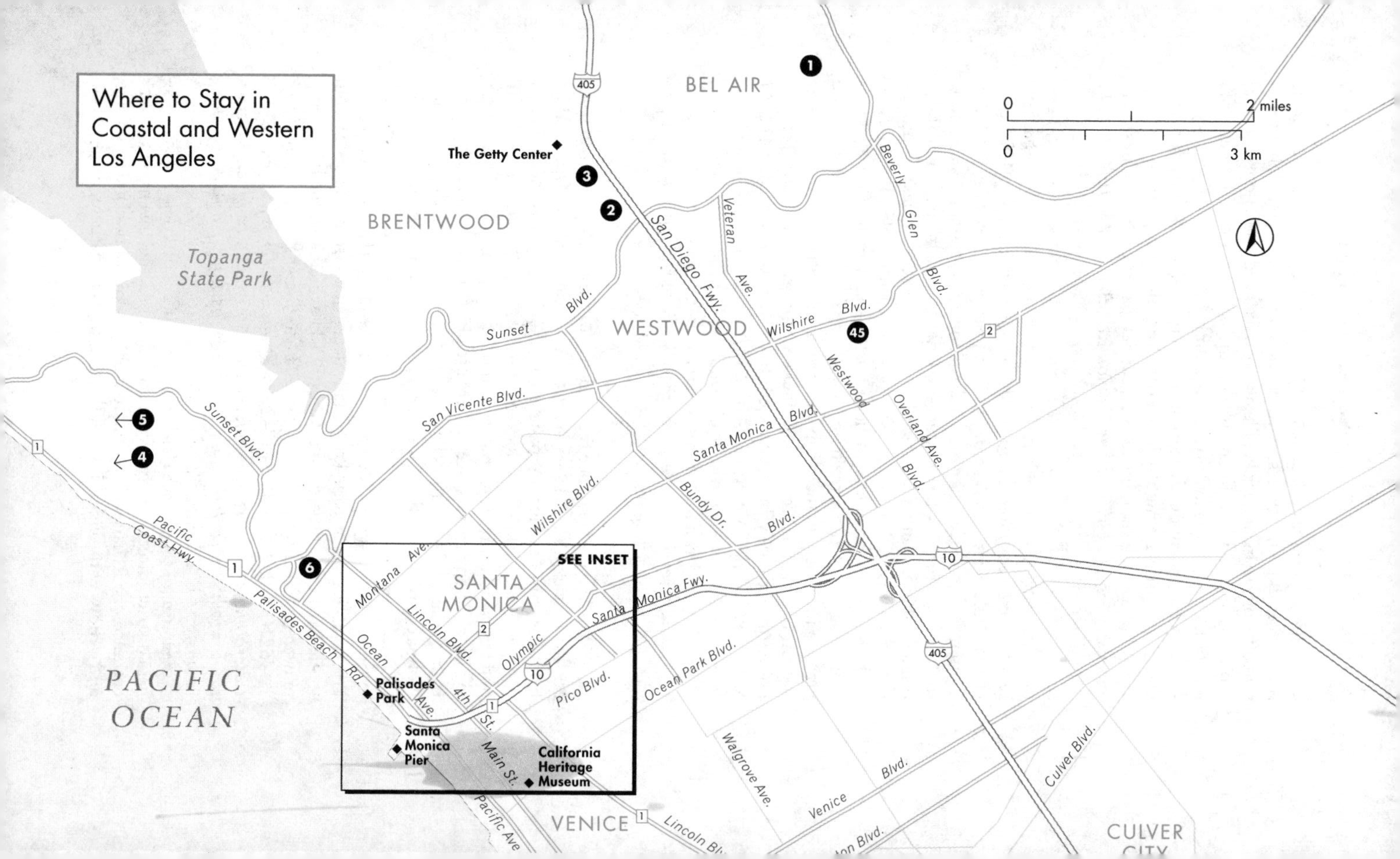
Where to Stay in Coastal and Western Los Angeles
BEL AIR
BRENTWOOD
WESTWOOD
SANTA MONICA
VENICE
CULVER CITY
Topanga State Park
PACIFIC OCEAN
The Getty Center
Palisades Park
Santa Monica Pier
California Heritage Museum
SEE INSET
0
2 miles
0
3 km
San Diego Fwy.
Santa Monica Fwy.
Sunset Blvd.
San Vicente Blvd.
Wilshire Blvd.
Santa Monica Blvd.
Veteran Ave.
Beverly Glen Blvd.
Westwood Blvd.
Overland Ave.
Bundy Dr.
Montana Ave.
Ocean Ave.
Lincoln Blvd.
Olympic Blvd.
Pico Blvd.
Ocean Park Blvd.
4th St.
Main St.
Walgrove Ave.
Venice Blvd.
Culver Blvd.
Pacific Coast Hwy.
Palisades Beach Rd.
Pacific Ave
405
10
1
2
1
2
3
4
5
6
45

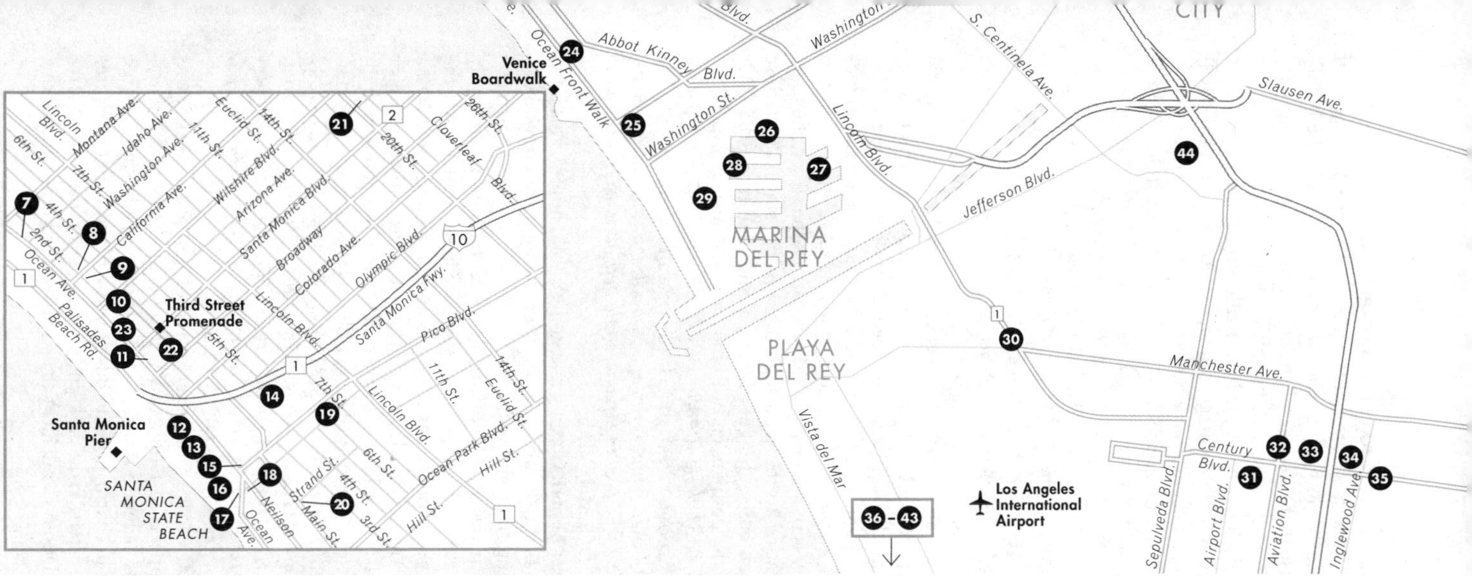

The Ambrose 21	Custom Hotel 30	Hotel Carmel 22	Los Angeles Airport Marriott 32	Marina Pacific Hotel & Suites 24	Sea Shore Motel 20
Ayres Hotel 42	Doubletree Guest Suites 14	Hotel Casa del Mar 17	Luxe Hotel Sunset Boulevard 2	Oceana 7	shade 43
Bayside Hotel 18	Fairmont Miramar Hotel Santa Monica 10	Hotel Palomar 45	Malibu Beach Inn 4	The Portofino Hotel & Yacht Club 38	Sheraton Gateway Hotel 31
Beach House at Hermosa 39	The Georgian 11	Hotel Shangri-La 23	Marina del Rey Marriott 29	Queen Mary 37	Sheraton Delfina 19
Cal Mar Hotel Suites 8	Hilton Los Angeles Airport 32	The Huntley 9	Marina del Rey Hotel & Marina 27	Radisson Los Angeles Westside 44	Shutters on the Beach 16
Casa Malibu 5	Holiday Inn LAX 34	Hyatt Summerfield Suites 40	Marina International Hotel & Bungalows 28	Renaissance Long Beach Hotel 36	Venice Beach House 25
Channel Road Inn 6	Hotel Angeleno 3	Le Merigot Beach Hotel & Spa 12		Ritz-Carlton Marina del Rey 26	Viceroy 15
Crowne Plaza Redondo Beach & Marina Hotel 41	Hotel Bel-Air 1	Loews Santa Monica Beach Hotel 13			Westin Los Angeles Airport 35

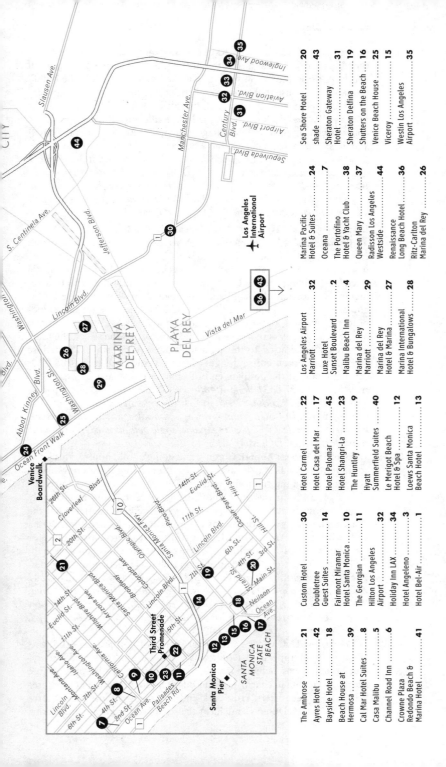

in desk. Catering primarily to convention goers and business-types, there's a morning breakfast buffet plus high-tech features such as a self check-in kiosk and Wi-Fi throughout the hotel. Tracht's is the hotel's modern chophouse that offers excellent fare in the most contemporary of settings. The heated patio with fire-pit is great spot to unwind; the pool and Jacuzzi deck overlook the busy boulevard. **Pros:** easy walk to convention center, Shoreline Village dining, and Aquarium of the Pacific. **Cons:** rooms facing south have best views, definite corporate vibe. ✉*111 E. Ocean Blvd., Long Beach* ☎*562/437–5900 or 800/468–3571* 🌐*www.renaissancehotels.com* *360 rooms, 14 suites* *In-room: Internet, Wi-Fi. In-hotel: 2 restaurants, room service, bar, pool, gym, spa, laundry service, Internet terminal, Wi-Fi, parking (paid), some pets allowed, no-smoking rooms* *AE, D, DC, MC, V.*

LOS ANGELES INTERNATIONAL AIRPORT

$ **Custom Hotel.** Close enough to LAX to see the runways, the Custom Hotel is a playful and practical redo of a 12-story, mid-century, modern tower by famed L.A. architect Welton Beckett (of Hollywood's Capitol Records' building and the Dorothy Chandler Pavilion). Playful touches include espresso at check-in, sheep-shaped chairs roaming the lobby, and a sociable pool bar with fire-pit and DJs. Practical are the soundproofed windows, ample bedside lighting and free LAX shuttle. Close to all the beach cities with a decent public park across the street, the hotel is a welcome addition to the Westside's often pricey stays. **Pros:** close to LAX and beach cities, designer interiors and high-tech, free LAX shuttle. **Cons:** at the desolate end of Lincoln Boulevard. ✉*8639 Lincoln Blvd., LAX* ☎*310/645–0400 or 877/287–8601* 🌐*www.customhotel.com* *248 rooms, 2 suites* *In-room: safe, refrigerator, DVD (some), Wi-Fi. In-hotel: room service, bar, pool, gym, laundry service, Internet terminal, Wi-Fi, parking (paid), some pets allowed, no-smoking rooms* *AE, D, DC, MC, V.*

$$–$$$ **Hilton Los Angeles Airport.** Coming and going at odd hours? This hotel could fill the bill as it ticks away 24/7 with arriving flight crews, businesspeople, and international visitors. The multilingual staff, currency exchange, 24-hour bistro, 24-hour business center, and an absurdly large 24-hour health club cover all sorts of needs no matter what the clock says. Rooms are done in basic browns and beiges and come with a large work desk. Airport shuttle adds convenience. **Pros:** lower rates for weekend stays, 24/7 everything, a world onto itself. **Cons:** immense hallways mean long treks to elevator, hotel as big as it gets in Los Angeles. ✉*5711 W. Century Blvd., LAX* ☎*310/410–4000 or 800/321–3232* 🌐*www.hilton.com* *1,234 rooms, 152 suites* *In-room: Internet, Wi-Fi. In-hotel: 3 restaurants, room service, bar, pool, gym, laundry service, Internet terminal, Wi-Fi, parking (paid), some pets allowed, no-smoking rooms* *AE, D, DC, MC, V.*

$$ **Holiday Inn LAX.** Close to the intersection of I–405 and I–105, this 12-story hotel appeals to families as well as businesspeople. Twenty-four-hour services include a shuttle to the airport and a business center. Although lacking in charm, accommodations are functional: there's free Wi-Fi and coffeemakers. **Pros:** park-and-fly packages, close to LAX, free Wi-Fi. **Cons:** McDonald's-adjacent means drive-thru noise and odors,

run-down, industrial neighborhood. ✉ *9901 La Cienega Blvd., LAX* ☎ *310/649–5151 or 800/624–0025* 🌐 *www.hilax.com* *405 rooms, 2 suites* *In-room: Internet, Wi-Fi. In-hotel: restaurant, room service, bar, pool, gym, laundry facilities, laundry service, Internet terminal, Wi-Fi, parking (paid), no-smoking rooms* *AE, D, DC, MC, V.*

$$ **Hyatt Summerfield Suites.** There's room to spread out in these extra-large one- and two-bedroom suites (check out the bonus living-room sleeper sofas). Cook in the fully outfitted kitchens or on the gas grills outside. The staff will stock your refrigerator with groceries (the service is free, but you'll have to pay for the groceries). Weeknights, the hotel welcomes you to a happy hour with complimentary drinks and snacks. **Pros:** efficiency suites for the price of one-room stays, family-friendly, prepaid weekend rates as low as $98. **Cons:** unremarkable neighborhood, car essential. ✉ *810 S. Douglas Ave., LAX* ☎ *310/725–0100 or 866/974–9288* 🌐 *www.summerfieldsuites.com* *122 suites* *In-room: kitchen, refrigerator, DVD, Internet, Wi-Fi. In-hotel: pool, gym, laundry facilities, laundry service, Wi-Fi, parking (paid), some pets allowed, no-smoking rooms* *AE, D, DC, MC, V* *BP.*

$$$ **Los Angeles Airport Marriott.** Popular with single-overnight travelers and conventioneers, this 18-story Marriott hums year-round. A well-outfitted business center with FedEx and Kinko's services caters to business needs. Rooms are on the small side but soundproof (a good thing, since many face a busy runway). Champions, the hotel's TV-filled sports bar, attracts local sports fans. **Pros:** LAX airport shuttle, popular meeting spaces, business-friendly overall: rooms have office-desks and chairs. **Cons:** wi-Fi extra, isolated airport-adjacent location. ✉ *5855 W. Century Blvd., LAX* ☎ *310/641–5700 or 800/228–9290* 🌐 *www.marriott.com* *985 rooms, 19 suites* *In-room: safe, refrigerator, Internet, Wi-Fi. In-hotel: 3 restaurants, room service, bars, pool, gym, laundry facilities, laundry service, Internet terminal, Wi-Fi, parking (paid), no-smoking rooms* *AE, D, DC, MC, V.*

$$ **Radisson Los Angeles Westside.** Just 3 mi north of LAX, the Radisson Westside is close to freeways and a good value for those who want to fly in and find a hotel right away. The updated contemporary rooms are spacious; beds have cushy duvets. Executive-floor perks include late check-out and pillow-top mattresses. **Pros:** within walking distance of Howard Hughes Promenade's numerous shops, restaurants, and cinemas; park-and-fly packages and free Internet access. **Cons:** unremarkable dining. ✉ *6161 Centinela Ave., LAX* ☎ *310/649–1776 or 888/201–1718* 🌐 *www.radisson.com/culvercityca* *365 rooms, 3 suites* *In-room: refrigerator, Internet, Wi-Fi. In-hotel: restaurant, room service, bars, pool, gym, laundry service, Internet terminal, parking (paid), some pets allowed, no-smoking rooms* *AE, D, DC, MC, V.*

$$$ ★ **Sheraton Gateway Hotel.** LAX's coolest looking hotel is so swank that guests have been known to ask to buy the black-and-white photos hanging behind the front desk. Extras for in-transit visitors include 24-hour room service, a 24-hour fitness center, a business center, and a 24-hour airport shuttle. Rooms are compact but soundproof and have helpful details such as coffeemakers, hooks for hanging garment bags, and oversize work desks. Faux animal-skin headboards and ebonized

furniture make the guest rooms feel more sophisticated than corporate. **Pros:** weekend rates significantly lower, free LAX shuttle, Shula's 347 steak house. **Cons:** convenient to airport but not much else. ✉*6101 W. Century Blvd., LAX* ☎*310/642–1111 or 888/716–8130* 🌐*www.sheratonlosangeles.com* *714 rooms, 88 suites* *In-room: Internet, Wi-Fi. In-hotel: 2 restaurants, room service, bar, pool, gym, laundry service, Internet terminal, Wi-Fi, parking (paid), some pets allowed, no-smoking rooms* 💳*AE, D, DC, MC, V.*

$$$ **Westin Los Angeles Airport.** Close to the I–405 and on the airport's hotel corridor, the jumbo Westin offers reasonable park-and-ride packages. But there are strong suits here other than convenience and the long list of amenities including two business centers. Guest rooms are spacious and have the famed Westin Heavenly bed. They also offer special pet amenities; ask ahead for the doggie bed. **Pros:** smoke-free property, free LAX shuttle, luxury bedding. **Cons:** super-size hotel, unremarkable dining, surrounding area is primarily industrial. ✉*5400 W. Century Blvd., LAX* ☎*310/216–5858 or 800/937–8461* 🌐*www.westin.com* *707 rooms, 33 suites* *In-room: safe, Internet, Wi-Fi. In-hotel: restaurant, room service, bar, gym, laundry service, Internet terminal, Wi-Fi, parking (paid), some pets allowed, no-smoking rooms* 💳*AE, D, DC, MC, V.*

HERMOSA BEACH

$$$–$$$$ ★ **Beach House at Hermosa.** Sitting right on the sand, bordering SoCal's famous beach bike and walk path, the Strand, the Beach House looks like a New England sea cottage from a century ago. Outside it's all gray shingles and overhanging white eaves, but inside you'll find contemporary amenities in split-level, loftlike rooms. Ocean-front rooms facing the Strand have terrific sunset views and small balconies. All rooms have two flat-screen TVs, four multiline phones, CD player, fireplace, wet bar, and extra soundproofing. Expect to pay more for ocean-view rooms and weekend and summer stays. Rent bikes nearby or stroll on the Hermosa Beach pier. Mornings, muffins and coffee await you in the pleasant breakfast room. Many guests book an in-room massage. **Pros:** on the beach, great outdoorsy activities, ample space. **Cons:** continental breakfast only, noise from the busy Strand, no pool. ✉*1300 The Strand, Hermosa Beach* ☎*310/374–3001 or 888/895–4559* 🌐*www.beach-house.com* *96 suites* *In-room: kitchen, refrigerator, DVD, Internet, Wi-Fi. In-hotel: room service, gym, beachfront, laundry service, Internet terminal, Wi-Fi, parking (paid), no-smoking rooms* 💳*AE, D, DC, MC, V* *CP.*

MALIBU

$$–$$$ **Casa Malibu Inn.** Catch an early-morning surf break or just hang out all day on Casa Malibu's private stretch of beach—raked smooth each morning. Directly on the sand, the comfy inn is a favorite of families, couples, and even a movie star or two. Though modest in decor and amenities, the views are unrivaled: to the south is all of exclusive Carbon Beach; north is Malibu's restored pier and Surfrider beach. The Pacific is your front yard—seabirds and dolphins your neighbors. Ask for a room with a fireplace for the complete experience. Each room is different in layout; a few are accessible only by stairs. There's no

smoking on the property—even at the beach. Guests get the use of beach chairs, towels, umbrellas, and outdoor shower. Call the hotel directly to make reservations. **Pros:** stellar location, low-key beachy vibe, close to most of Malibu's best restaurants. **Cons:** summer weekends and holidays book up six months in advance, small tidy bathrooms. ⊠*22752 Pacific Coast Hwy., Malibu* ☎*310/456–2219 or 800/831–0858* *19 rooms, 2 suites* *In-room: no a/c (some), kitchen (some), DVD, Wi-Fi. In-hotel: beachfront, laundry service, Wi-Fi, parking (free), no-smoking rooms* *AE, MC, V* *CP.*

$$$$ **Malibu Beach Inn.** Set right on exclusive and private Carbon Beach, home to all manner of the super-rich, the inn's location doesn't get any better than this. Third-floor ocean-view rooms, with wood-beamed ceilings and private balconies, are instantly calming and definitely romantic. Feather beds, inset lighting, original artwork, and custom-made furniture combine with creamy yellow walls for designer-perfect rooms and an ultrachic, residential feel. The inn's Carbon Beach Club restaurant overlooks the Pacific and nearby Malibu pier and presents California cuisine and local Malibu wines. Guests can access the Malibu Health and Fitness across the highway. Teak beach loungers, umbrellas, and towels are provided. Holidays require multinight stays. **Pros:** live like a billionaire in designer-perfect interiors right on the beach. **Cons:** noise of PCH, no pool, gym, or hot tub. Billionaire's travel budget also required. ⊠*22878 Pacific Coast Hwy., Malibu* ☎*31/456–6444* *www.malibubeachinn.com* *41 rooms, 6 suites* *In-room: safe, refrigerator, DVD, Internet, Wi-Fi. In-hotel: restaurant, room service, bar, beachfront, laundry service, Wi-Fi, parking (paid), no-smoking rooms* *AE, D, DC, MC, V.*

MANHATTAN BEACH

$$ ★ **Ayres Hotel.** The rates may be relatively modest, but the style here is grand. This hotel resembles a stone-clad château—and though it feels very "French countryside," it's actually close to I–405. Inside you'll find high ceilings, oil paintings, and formal furniture: in short, not the typical casual beachy look. The kitchen facilities in the guest rooms are a thoughtful plus. A free shuttle runs within a 3-mi area. **Pros:** free parking and breakfast, kids packages include babysitter. **Cons:** on the edge of Manhattan Beach, requires drive to the ocean. ⊠*14400 Hindry Ave., Manhattan Beach Hawthorne* ☎*310/536–0400 or 800/675–3550* *www.ayresmanhattanbeach.com* *173 rooms* *In-room: refrigerator, Internet. In-hotel: restaurant, room service, pool, laundry facilities, laundry service, Wi-Fi, parking (free), no-smoking rooms* *AE, D, DC, MC, V* *BP.*

$$$–$$$$ **shade.** Super-contemporary design makes this place feel like an adults-only playground. Rooms come with a sunken whirlpool tub surrounded by a movable shoji-like screen, a sculptural fireplace, a martini shaker, and overhead "chromatherapy" lighting that changes color via digital touch plates. Up on the roof is a sundeck and workout area; stand on tiptoe to see the ocean. The hotel's just a short walk to the shoreline, the local pier, and Manhattan Beach's lively, compact downtown. Just off the hotel's patio is the Triology Spa for tropical-style pampering. **Pros:** lively bar scene at Zinc, a quick walk to the beach and dozens

of restaurants. **Cons:** sharp-edged furniture, recommended for adults or older kids only, small dipping pool. ✉ *1221 N. Valley Dr., Manhattan Beach* ☎ *310/546–4995 or 866/742–3377* 🌐 *www.shadehotel.com* *33 rooms, 5 suites* *In-room: safe, refrigerator, DVD, Internet, Wi-Fi. In-hotel: restaurant, room service, bar, pool, gym, laundry service, Internet terminal, Wi-Fi, parking (paid), no-smoking rooms* *AE, D, DC, MC, V* *BP.*

MARINA DEL REY

$$ **Marina del Rey Hotel & Marina.** The balconies, patios, and harbor-view rooms take full advantage of the hotel's waterfront position. Cruises and charters are easily accessible from nearby slips; bike and in-line skate rentals are nearby, too. A clubby bar overlooks the Marina and is popular with local boatmen. The pool is small; more for a dip than swim. Proximity to LAX and low rates makes this hotel popular with budget travelers. New owners are working on a complete makeover pending city approvals. **Pros:** free parking and Wi-Fi, generous-size rooms, some with great Marina views. **Cons:** pending updates means tired decor, check for ongoing construction. ✉ *13534 Bali Way, Marina del Rey* ☎ *310/301–1000 or 800/882–4000* 🌐 *www.marinadelreyhotel.com* *150 rooms, 3 suites* *In-room: Wi-Fi. In-hotel: restaurant, room service, bar, pool, laundry service, Internet terminal, Wi-Fi, parking (free), no-smoking rooms* *AE, DC, MC, V.*

$$$ **Marina del Rey Marriott.** A jazzy lobby with plush couches, armchairs, and a welcoming bar is inside; outside is Glow, the hotel's popular lounge. The hotel is just across from the protected waters of the Marina and a short jaunt to Venice. There's across-the-board appeal here. Families like the heated pool and hot tub and proximity to the Venice boardwalk. Business types appreciate the two floors of meeting space. Brides go for the rooftop ballroom with stunning views. Rooms are a mix of traditional furniture, sea-theme prints, blue and gold accents, and plush, pillow-top mattresses with an avalanche of pillows. Sliding glass doors lead to French balconies: open them for sea breezes. Ask for upper-floor rooms facing the marina for the best views. **Pros:** 15 minutes to LAX, outdoor lounge for nighttime socializing, bike rentals, and quiet beach across the street. **Cons:** traffic and noise from busy Admiralty Way, small gym. ✉ *4100 Admiralty Way, Marina del Rey* ☎ *310/301–3000 or 800/228–9290* 🌐 *www.marriotthotels.com* *332 rooms, 38 suites* *In-room: safe, refrigerator, Internet, Wi-Fi. In-hotel: restaurant, room service, bar, pool, gym, laundry service, Internet terminal, Wi-Fi, parking (paid), no-smoking rooms* *AE, D, DC, MC, V.*

$–$$ **Marina International Hotel & Bungalows.** A quaint "village" look is evoked by white shutters on each window and private balconies overlooking a central courtyard and pool. Large rooms have contemporary decor and French doors; some have partial views of the water. The split-level bungalows, each with its own private entrance, are huge. TIP→ **Because it's across from a sandy beach within the marina, the hotel is a good choice for families with children.** **Pros:** free parking, across from family-friendly beach, reasonable rates. **Cons:** decline in service and decor due to a proposed renovation. ✉ *4200 Admiralty Way, Marina del Rey* ☎ *310/301–2000 or 800/529–2525* 🌐 *www.marinainternationalhotel.com* *110 rooms, 24* *bungalows* ♿*In-room: refrigerator, Wi-Fi. In-hotel: restaurant, room service, bar, pool, laundry service, Internet terminal, Wi-Fi, parking (paid), no-smoking rooms* ▭*AE, DC, MC, V.*

$$$$ ★ **Ritz-Carlton Marina del Rey.** You might have a sense of déjà vu here since this resort, overlooking L.A.'s largest marina, is a favorite location of dozens of TV and film productions. Traditionally styled rooms in warm, gold tones have French doors, marble baths, and feather beds, but the true luxury is in the spectacular, panoramic views. Book early for the popular Sunday champagne brunch at the waterside restaurant, Jer-ne. Check out the chlorine-free pool: it uses a balance of minerals to keep the water clean. Club level rooms are worth the extra fee. **Pros:** sparkling gym and spa, waterside location, resort amenities in-town. **Cons:** formal dining only (poolside eatery, summers only), $31 valet parking. ✉*4375 Admiralty Way, Marina del Rey* ☎*310/823–1700 or 800/241–3333* 🌐*www.ritzcarlton.com* *292 rooms, 12 suites* ♿*In-room: safe, refrigerator, DVD, Internet, Wi-Fi. In-hotel: restaurant, room service, bar, tennis courts, pool, gym, spa, bicycles, laundry service, Internet terminal, Wi-Fi, parking (paid), some pets allowed, no-smoking rooms* ▭*AE, D, DC, MC, V.*

REDONDO BEACH

$$$ ★ **Crowne Plaza Redondo Beach & Marina Hotel.** Redondo Beach's man-made seaside lagoon is a short walk away from this contemporary, five-story hotel. SoCal's most famed and scenic bike path borders the property. Adding to seaside resort feel: the Redondo Beach Pier restaurants, shops, and arcade are also within walking distance. Sizeable rooms are shades of beiges and browns set off by white duvets; most have balconies with a water view. A free shuttle is available to the two major shopping malls nearby. A favorite guest perk: stays include use of the on-site Gold's Gym. **Pros:** numerous resort amenities, steps from bike path, beach and pleasure pier. **Cons:** large, corporate stay, best dining off-site. ✉*300 N. Harbor Dr., Redondo Beach* ☎*310/318–8888 or 877/227–6963* 🌐*www.crowneplaza.com* *334 rooms, 5 suites* ♿*In-room: safe, refrigerator, Internet, Wi-Fi. In-hotel: restaurant, room service, bar, tennis court, pool, gym, spa, bicycles, laundry facilities, Internet terminal, Wi-Fi, laundry service, parking (paid), no-smoking rooms* ▭*AE, D, DC, MC, V.*

$$$–$$$$ **The Portofino Hotel & Yacht Club.** Open your balcony door and listen to the sounds of a free-range Sea World at the Portofino. Ocean- and channel-side rooms echo with the calls of sea birds and sea lions; harbor side rooms look over sailboats and docks. From the hotel's very private peninsula, walk or bike to the nearby seaside lagoon or rent a kayak and explore the protected harbor. Interiors are beachy but sophisticated—guest rooms are a mix of blues and yellows, set off by crisp, white bed linens. Compact, well-designed bathrooms are accented in stainless steel, with extra-plush towels and pleasing Spa Terre products. In its own building overlooking the harbor, is Baleen, the hotel's excellent restaurant—a most welcome addition to the South Bay dining scene. **Pros:** bike or walk to beach, relaxing stay, some ocean views. **Cons:** higher rates in summer and for ocean-view rooms. ✉*260 Portofino Way, Redondo Beach* ☎*310/379–8481 or 800/468–4292*

www.hotelportofino.com 161 rooms, 2 suites In-room: refrigerator, DVD, Wi-Fi. In-hotel: restaurant, room service, pool, gym, water sports, bicycles, laundry service, Internet terminal, Wi-Fi, parking (paid), no-smoking rooms AE, D, DC, MC, V.

SANTA MONICA

$$–$$$ **The Ambrose.** An air of tranquillity pervades the four-story Ambrose, which blends right into its mostly residential Santa Monica neighborhood. The decor incorporates many Asian accents, following the principles of feng shui. Management prides itself on following "green" principles—cleaning products are nontoxic and water use is reduced. Social consciousness here also means comfort—rooms have deluxe, chenille throws, Italian linens, Frette towels and robes, and a minibar with health-oriented elixirs. Windows are double-paned for quiet; upper floors have partial ocean views. Room service and the breakfast buffet include healthy choices. A biodiesel fuel-powered London taxi is on call for free short jaunts in the area. **Pros:**L.A.'s most ecoconscious hotel with nontoxic housekeeping products and recycling cans in each room. **Cons:** quiet, residential area of Santa Monica, no restaurant on-site. *1255 20th St., Santa Monica 310/315–1555 or 877/262–7673 www.ambrosehotel.com 77 rooms In-room: safe, refrigerator, DVD, Internet, Wi-Fi. In-hotel: room service, gym, bicycles, Internet terminal, Wi-Fi, laundry service, parking (free), no-smoking rooms AE, D, DC, MC, V CP.*

$–$$ **Bayside Hotel.** Tucked snugly into a narrow corner lot, the supremely casual Bayside's greatest asset is its prime spot directly across from the beach, within walkable blocks from the Third Street Promenade and Santa Monica Pier. Expect no frills. Rooms are tidy with access via exterior walkway; there's a small front office instead of lobby and the parking is free but drivers must negotiate a cramped lot. If keeping cool is a must, request one of the seven rooms with air-conditioning or one of those with unobstructed ocean views and balconies. Book early for summer weekends; the hotel typically sells out then. **Pros:** cheaper weeknight stays, beach access and views. **Cons:** homeless neighbors, some rooms without air-conditioning, basic bedding. *2001 Ocean Ave., Santa Monica 310/396–6000 or 800/525–4447 www.baysidehotel.com 45 rooms In-room: no a/c (some), kitchen (some), refrigerator (some), Wi-Fi. In-hotel: Wi-Fi, parking (free) AE, D, MC, V.*

$$ **Cal Mar Hotel Suites.** On a residential street one block from the Third Street Promenade and within a short walk to the beach, this low-profile, two-story, all-suite hotel is a comparative bargain. In summer, though, a two-night minimum stay is required. Standard and master one-bedroom suites have king or twin beds and a full-size sofa bed. Furnishings are contemporary and comfortable without much thought given to decorating, but the atmosphere is friendly and informal. Rooms wrap around an interior courtyard with pool and windows open to the street or back alley, adding up to city sounds and noise both day and night. **Pros:** lower off-season rates, full kitchens, very low-key vibe. **Cons:** street noise, no a/c—hope for ocean breezes. *220 California Ave., Santa Monica 310/395–5555 or 800/776–6007 www.calmarhotel.com 36 suites In-room: no a/c, kitchen, refrigerator, DVD, Wi-Fi.*

In-hotel: pool, laundry facilities, Wi-Fi, parking (paid), no-smoking rooms ▭*AE, MC, V.*

$$$ ★ **Channel Road Inn.** A quaint surprise in Southern California, the Channel Road Inn is every bit the country retreat B&B lovers adore, with canopy beds with fluffy duvets and a cozy living room with fireplace. Rooms are old-fashioned, but each has a private bath (one room has only a shower, and a few have hot tubs). A sumptuous home-cooked breakfast is included; enjoy it downstairs or in your room. Walk a block to the beach or borrow one of the bicycles. Unwind in the lovely rose garden or book an in-room massage. **Pros:** quiet residential neighborhood close to beach, free Wi-Fi and evening wine and hors d'oeuvres. **Cons:** no pool. ✉*219 W. Channel Rd., Santa Monica* ☎*310/459–1920* 🌐*www.channelroadinn.com* *15 rooms* *In-room: refrigerator (some), Wi-Fi. In-hotel: bicycles, Internet terminal, Wi-Fi, parking (free), no-smoking rooms* ▭*AE, MC, V* *BP.*

$$–$$$ **Doubletree Guest Suites.** Sunlight streams through the glass-enclosed atrium and spills over a patiolike sitting area in the lobby. One- and two-bedroom soundproofed suites include a separate living room with a large desk, wet bar, and sofa bed; microwaves and refrigerators are available upon request. Just off the busy Santa Monica Freeway (I–10), the hotel is within walking distance of the Third Street Promenade, beaches, and the pier. **Pros:** spacious suites appeal to families as do many diversions nearby, on the Tide Shuttle route. **Cons:** somewhat dated decor. ✉*1707 4th St., Santa Monica* ☎*310/395–3332 or 800/222–8733* 🌐*www.doubletree.com* *253 suites* *In-room: refrigerator (some), Wi-Fi. In-hotel: restaurant, room service, bar, pool, gym, laundry facilities, laundry service, Internet terminal, Wi-Fi, parking (paid), no-smoking rooms* ▭*AE, D, DC, MC, V.*

$$$$ **Fairmont Miramar Hotel Santa Monica.** A mammoth Moreton Bay fig tree dwarfs the main entrance; the modernized lobby bar opens out to a heated patio. Fig, the hotel's new restaurant, emphasizes local and fresh ingredients. Low-rise and extremely luxurious, residential-style bungalows, built between 1920 and 1946, are outfitted like minimansions, complete with butler service—a favorite of visiting VIPs. Standard rooms in the 10-story tower have no room to spare, but they do come with beautiful ocean views, alabaster light fixtures, carved wood armoires, Bose stereo systems, and down duvets. Ecoconscious efforts include free parking for hybrid vehicles and "green" meetings. **Pros:** walking distance to beach and Third Street Promenade shopping and dining. **Cons:** pricey in-house dining. ✉*101 Wilshire Blvd., Santa Monica* ☎*310/576–7777 or 800/257–7544* 🌐*www.fairmont.com/santamonica* *251 rooms, 51 suites, 32 bungalows* *In-room: safe, refrigerator, Internet, Wi-Fi. In-hotel: restaurant, room service, bar, pool, gym, spa, bicycles, laundry service, Internet terminal, Wi-Fi, parking (paid), some pets allowed, no-smoking rooms* ▭*AE, D, DC, MC, V.*

$$$–$$$$ **The Georgian.** You can't miss the Georgian: the art deco exterior is aqua, with ornate bronze grillwork and a charming oceanfront veranda. Built in 1933, the hotel retains its retro character with cream-color walls, vintage tiles, marble floors accented with sea-foam green and silver blue, and individually styled rooms with cherrywood furnishings and gold

and silver accents. Popular with visiting Europeans, the hotel's lobby echoes with foreign languages. Sit on the veranda to best appreciate the beach, ocean, and Santa Monica views or to enjoy breakfast or lunch. **Pros:** ocean-view rooms, free parking for hybrids, front terrace a great people-watching spot, free Wi-Fi. **Cons:** "Vintage" bathrooms, unremarkable views from many rooms. ✉ *1415 Ocean Ave., Santa Monica* ☎ *310/395–9945 or 800/538–8147* 🌐 *www.georgianhotel.com* *56 rooms, 28 suites* *In-room: safe, Wi-Fi. In-hotel: restaurant, room service, bar, gym, Internet terminal, Wi-Fi, laundry service, parking (paid), some pets allowed, no-smoking rooms* *AE, D, DC, MC, V.*

$$ **Hotel Carmel.** Price and location are the calling cards of this older, unpretentious hotel, favored by international travelers set on a busy corner in the heart of Santa Monica's commercial district. Basic rooms are small; some have ocean views. Continental breakfast is served next door at Interactive Café. You can stroll to the Third Street Promenade or to the beach a couple of blocks away. In summer, rooms often sell out early so make reservations months ahead. **Pros:** location, location, location. **Cons:** badly in need of updating, cleanliness and service issues. ✉ *201 Broadway, Santa Monica* ☎ *310/451–2469 or 800/445–8695* 🌐 *www.hotelcarmel.com* *96 rooms, 8 suites* *In-room: Wi-Fi. In-hotel: laundry service, parking (paid), no-smoking rooms* *AE, D, DC, MC, V* *CP.*

$$$$ ★ **Hotel Casa del Mar.** In the 1920s it was a posh beach club catering to the city's elite; now the Casa del Mar is one of SoCal's most luxurious and pricey beachfront hotels, with three extravagant two-story penthouses, a raised deck and pool, and an elegant ballroom facing the sand. Guest rooms, designed to evoke the good old days with furnishings like four-poster beds and handsome armoires, are filled with contemporary amenities like flat-screen TVs, iPod docking stations, and supremely comfortable beds with sumptuous white linens. Bathrooms are gorgeous, with sunken whirlpool tubs and glass-enclosed showers. Catch is the hotel's elegant and striking restaurant and sushi bar, specializing in what else? Seafood. **Pros:** excellent dining by chef Michael Reardon at Catch, lobby socializing, gorgeous beachfront rooms. **Cons:** no room balconies, without a doubt, one of L.A.'s most pricey stays. ✉ *1910 Ocean Front Way, Santa Monica* ☎ *310/581–5533 or 800/898–6999* 🌐 *www.hotelcasadelmar.com* *129 rooms, 4 suites* *In-room: safe, Internet, Wi-Fi. In-hotel: restaurant, room service, bar, pool, gym, spa, Wi-Fi, laundry service, parking (paid), some pets allowed, no-smoking rooms* *AE, D, DC, MC, V.*

$$$$ **Hotel Shangri-La.** Across from Santa Monica's busy Palisades Park and promenade, the 1939-built, art deco–styled Shangri-La is now in tune with the 21st century. A two-year gleaming update has preserved the original, brilliant white curved facade. Deco accents are a blend of vintage and custom-built features such as casement windows (helpfully soundproofed), maple floors, indirect lighting, nickel-plated hardware, burled wood cabinets, and polished work spaces. Wall-mounted, flat-screen TVs are new, as are the thoroughly modern baths, each outfitted with marble counter, sunken Jacuzzi tub, Euro-style toilet, ecofriendly bath products in biodegradable bottles, and gorgeous light fixtures.

There's a strong nautical theme as the Pacific Ocean is within view. Salt air and a glam seaside vibe pervade the open-air corridors—a unique feature to the hotel. Upper floor rooms facing west have stunning beach, ocean, and Malibu views. **Pros:** admirable rehabilitation of deco-styled building now with up-to-date conveniences like soundproofing, a/c, and iPod docks. **Cons:** some rooms are close to cruise-ship size. ✉ *301 Ocean Ave., Santa Monica* ☎ *310/394–2791* 🌐 *www.shangrila-hotel.com* *36 rooms, 35 suites* *In-room: safe, kitchen (some), refrigerator (some), Internet, Wi-Fi. In-hotel: restaurant, room service, bars, pool, gym, laundry service, Internet terminal, Wi-Fi, parking (paid), some pets allowed, no-smoking rooms* *AE, D, DC, MC, V.*

$$$$ **The Huntley.** A school of 300 ceramic fish crossing a lobby wall signals the Huntley's stylish but unstuffy approach. The location's terrific, close to the beach, the Third Street Promenade, and chic Montana Avenue. In the thoughtfully designed guest rooms, large framed mirrors help enlarge the space. Earth tones and tufted suede headboards keep things mellow. Work desks are ample and come with some very retro accessories: a quill pen and inkwell. Other gadgets are thoroughly of-the-moment: plasma-screen TV, Wi-Fi, and room numbers are spotlighted. Corner rooms have the best views. **Pros:** ocean views, fun social scene and great views at the Penthouse, the hotel's top floor restaurant. **Cons:** no pool. ✉ *1111 2nd St., Santa Monica* ☎ *310/394–5454* 🌐 *www.thehuntleyhotel.com* *188 rooms, 21 suites* *In-room: safe, refrigerator, DVD, Wi-Fi. In-hotel: restaurant, room service, bar, gym, laundry service, Internal terminal, Wi-Fi, parking (fee), no-smoking rooms* *AE, D, DC, MC, V.*

$$$$ ★ **Le Merigot Beach Hotel & Spa.** Steps from Santa Monica's expansive beach, Le Merigot caters to a corporate clientele (it's a JW Marriott property). Upper floors have panoramic views of the Santa Monica Pier and the Pacific; many rooms have terraces. The contemporary rooms have feather beds and fine linens, and bathrooms come with playful bath toys and votive candles. Expect a seashell (not chocolate) at turndown. A checkerboard slate courtyard, including a pool, cabanas, fountains, and outdoor living room, is the center of activity. You can book a massage at the spa for a true attitude adjustment, or enjoy Cal-French fare at the comfortable Cézanne restaurant. **Pros:** steps from the beach and pier, welcoming to international travelers, walk to Third Street Promenade. **Cons:** small shaded pool. ✉ *1740 Ocean Ave., Santa Monica* ☎ *310/395–9700 or 888/539–7899* 🌐 *www.lemerigothotel.com* *175 rooms, 15 suites* *In-room: safe, refrigerator, Internet, Wi-Fi. In-hotel: restaurant, room service, bar, pool, gym, spa, beachfront, laundry service, Internet terminal, Wi-Fi, parking (paid), some pets allowed, no-smoking rooms* *AE, D, DC, MC, V.*

$$$–$$$$ **Loews Santa Monica Beach Hotel.** Walk to the ocean side of the soaring atrium here and you'll feel like you're on a cruise ship. Huge petrified palm trees loom over the dramatic lobby. Rooms that face the seaside are definitely worth the extra cost. In all rooms you'll find sunken bathtubs, stone counters, wood armoires, and CD players. You can order lunch poolside while lounging on bright-yellow terry-cloth chaises. Ocean & Vine, the hotel's restaurant, aptly pairs small plates with

select wines and has a fun outdoor patio complete with firepits. Pets go first-class at Loews: each receives a treat upon arrival. **Pros:** resort vibe, walk to beach, pet and kid friendly. **Cons:** small spa and pool. ✉ *1700 Ocean Ave., Santa Monica* ☎ *310/458–6700 or 800/235–6397* 🌐 *www.loewshotels.com* *323 rooms, 19 suites* *In-room: safe, refrigerator, Internet, Wi-Fi. In-hotel: 2 restaurants, room service, pool, gym, spa, beachfront, bicycles, laundry service, Internet terminal, Wi-Fi, parking (paid), some pets allowed, no-smoking rooms* ▭ *AE, D, DC, MC, V.*

$$$$ **Oceana.** Generous-size suites, double-glazed, soundproofed windows, an open-air courtyard and pool, and ocean proximity add up to a delightful boutique hotel. There's a distinctly SoCal beach vibe: the welcoming residential feel begins in the glass-covered lobby where guests sit down to check-in. An all-white, designer-perfect lounge is for guests only. Menu design is by New York's famed chef Jonathan Morr. Business types like the in-room offices with extra-large work spaces and Wi-Fi throughout. Digital gadgets include iPod HomeBase and two plasma TVs in each suite. **Pros:** walkable distance to prime shopping on Montana Avenue and the Third Street Promenade, the Palisades park, or the beach. **Cons:** small pool. ✉ *849 Ocean Ave., Santa Monica* ☎ *310/393–0486 or 800/777–0758* 🌐 *www.hoteloceanasantamonica.com* *70 suites* *In-room: safe, kitchens (some), Internet, Wi-Fi. In-hotel: restaurant, room service, pool, gym, laundry service, Internet terminal, Wi-Fi, parking (paid), no-smoking rooms* ▭ *AE, D, DC, MC, V.*

$ **Sea Shore Motel.** On Santa Monica's busy Main Street, the Sea Shore is a throwback to Route 66 and to '60s-style roadside motels. The neighborhood around it is now as trendy as they come, and just two blocks from the beach and bike path. Rooms have tile floors and basic amenities. The rooftop sundeck is a prime spot come sunset, and Amelia's, the motel's sidewalk café, is popular with locals. Santa Monica's Big Blue Bus line passes out front. This hotel is popular in summer: book early. **Pros:** close to beach and great restaurants, free Wi-Fi and parking. **Cons:** street noise, motel-style decor and beds. ✉ *2637 Main St., Santa Monica* ☎ *310/392–2787* 🌐 *www.seashoremotel.com* *19 rooms, 5 suites* *In-room: kitchen (some), refrigerator, Internet, Wi-Fi. In-hotel: restaurant, laundry facilities, laundry service, Internet terminal, Wi-Fi, parking (free), some pets allowed, no-smoking rooms* ▭ *AE, D, MC, V.*

$$$ **Sheraton Delfina.** Not far from I–10 and most Westside businesses, this Sheraton appeals to business types weekdays, but international travelers and families appreciate the hotel's proximity to Santa Monica's handy, public transport, the Tide Shuttle. The soaring lobby atrium, with plump armchairs and divans, welcomes all. Rooms are done in calming ocean colors and the textured headboards look like crocodile skin—that is if crocodiles were blue. Oversize work desks are practical and ergonomic. Most rooms have balconies, and those facing west on the upper floors have expansive views of the ocean and Santa Monica Mountains. On the ground floor, banquettes, cabanas, and a teak deck surround the pool, are prime for socializing. **Pros:** five blocks from beach, spacious rooms, designer rooms. **Cons:** away from Santa Monica's main dining and shopping. ✉ *530 W. Pico Blvd., Santa Monica* ☎ *310/399–9344*

or 888/627–8532 ⊕www.sheratonsantamonica.com ⇆299 rooms, 11 suites ♨In-room: safe, refrigerator, Internet, Wi-Fi. In-hotel: restaurant, room service, bar, pool, gym, laundry facilities, laundry service, Internet terminal, Wi-Fi, parking (paid), some pets allowed, no-smoking rooms ▭AE, D, DC, MC, V.

> **WORD OF MOUTH**
>
> "We stayed at the Sheraton Delfina in Santa Monica recently and really liked it there. It is a very good value, and a great location. You can walk a couple of blocks to the beach from the hotel. We had a good meal at Lobster and the beachfront restaurant at The Shutters." —PeaceOut

$$$$ ★ **Shutters on the Beach.** Set right on the sand, this gray-shingle inn has become synonymous with in-town escapism. Guest rooms have those namesake shutter doors, pillow-top mattresses, and white built-in cabinets filled with art books and curios. Bathrooms are luxe, each with a whirlpool tub, a raft of bath goodies, and a three-nozzle, glass-walled shower. While the hotel's service gets mixed reviews from some readers, the beachfront location and show-house decor make this one of SoCal's most popular luxury hotels. **Pros:** romantic, discreet, residential vibe. **Cons:** service not as good as it should be. *⊠1 Pico Blvd., Santa Monica ☎310/458–0030 or 800/334–9000 ⊕www.shuttersonthebeach.com ⇆186 rooms, 12 suites ♨In-room: safe, DVD, Internet, Wi-Fi. In-hotel: 2 restaurants, room service, bar, pool, gym, spa, beachfront, bicycles, laundry service, Internet terminal, Wi-Fi, parking (paid), no-smoking rooms ▭AE, D, DC, MC, V.*

$$$$ **Viceroy.** Whimsy abounds at this stylized seaside escape—just look at the porcelain dogs as lamp bases and Spode china plates mounted on the walls. The compact rooms all have French balconies, and sexy mirrored walls. The mostly marble bathrooms have seated vanities and supremely refreshing aromatherapy products. Glamorous socializing takes place in the pool and cabana area amid all-white armchairs and divans. People-watch at the black-hued bar and lobby lounge. Whist, the hotel's attractive restaurant, presents a sumptuous Sunday brunch. Upper-floor, ocean-view rooms are brilliant at sunset. **Pros:** eye-catching design, lobby social scene, pedestrian-friendly area. **Cons:** super-pricey bar and dining, pool for dipping not laps. *⊠1819 Ocean Ave., Santa Monica ☎310/260–7500 or 800/622–8711 ⊕www.viceroysantamonica.com ⇆158 rooms, 4 suites ♨In-room: safe, refrigerator, DVD, Internet, Wi-Fi. In-hotel: restaurant, room service, bar, pools, gym, Internet terminal, Wi-Fi, laundry service, parking (paid), some pets allowed, no-smoking rooms ▭AE, DC, MC, V.*

VENICE

$$–$$$ **Marina Pacific Hotel & Suites.** As Venice's fortunes have changed, the surrounding neighborhood has gone upscale and multimillion-dollar mansions abound, so have the Marina Pacific's. A new top floor added spiffy rooms with glass-walled balconies; the entire hotel was repainted and refurnished. Rooms are cheerful with bold patterned bedspreads, all black furniture and flat screen TVs. Original contemporary art by Venice artists is found throughout. Within blocks are numerous art galleries, shops, and more than 25 restaurants. Stroll the scenic Venice canals and

CLOSE UP

With Children?

Most hotels in Los Angeles allow children under a certain age to stay in their parents' room at no extra charge, but others charge for them as extra adults; be sure to find out the cutoff age for children's discounts.

Hotel pools are dependable distractions for kids, but some are better than others. The **Beverly Hilton** has an almost-Olympic-size pool that's perfect for splash time. Santa Monica's **Le Merigot Beach Hotel & Spa** has a small pool and even bigger beach out the back door. Kids get all the makings for sand castles: small shovel, bucket, and sand shapes. At the **Beverly Hills Hotel** there are a lifeguard and swimming lessons and pool toys for children. Turndown for kids includes cookies, milk, and a teddy bear. On the sand, experienced swimmers can go native and use **Casa Malibu's** boogie boards or opt for board rentals from a nearby surf shop.

More economical choices include El Segundo's **Summerfield Suites** that have plenty of room, snacks, and easy access to the beach cities.

Kids' suites at **Beverly Garland's Holiday Inn** come with bunk beds and video games. Also in the Valley, the venerable **Sportsmen's Lodge** is close to Universal Studios, but a world unto itself: there's plenty of room for kids to roam safely and a family friendly coffee shop. Prior to arrival at the **Loews Santa Monica** a family concierge can suggest family-friendly vacation ideas. The hotel also offers childproofing kits and special children's menus. **Shutters on the Beach** has weekly sandcastle building lessons, boogie board and bike rentals, and keeps kid-appropriate DVDs on hand. Teens will like the **Renaissance Hollywood Hotel,** which links directly to Hollywood & Highland's shopping and Mann Theaters. The **Magic Castle Hotel,** more reasonably priced, is also close to Hollywood's action; kids can attend the famed magic show here only at Sunday brunch. And downtown amidst skyscrapers, the **Omni** welcomes kids with a special goodie bag, lends out toys and games and offers a special room service menu. The outdoor rooftop pool is sized just right.

boardwalk or rent bikes next door at a discount; racquetball and tennis courts are also close. The best rates obtained by calling hotel directly. **Pros:** completely refurbished, friendly staff. **Cons:** summer rates significantly higher although hotel repeatedly sells out, homeless encamp nearby, boardwalk is noisy and teeming summer weekends. ✉ *1697 Pacific Ave., Venice* ☎ *310/452–1111 or 800/786–7789* 🌐 *www.mphotel.com* *82 rooms, 36 suites* *In-room: safe, refrigerator, Internet, Wi-Fi. In-hotel: beachfront, laundry facilities, laundry service, Wi-Fi, parking (paid), no-smoking rooms* 💳 *AE, D, DC, MC, V* *CP.*

$$ **Venice Beach House.** A vestige of Venice's founding days, the Venice Beach House was one of the seaside enclave's first mansions. Many Craftsman-era details remain: dark woods, the glass-enclosed breakfast nook, a lattice-framed portico, and a fleet of stairs. Privacy is not why guests stay here—soundproofing standards are circa 1911. The recently added air-conditioning helps somewhat. However, historic

charm radiates and the location, steps from the beach and boardwalk, is what Southern California is all about. **Pros:** historic home with many charms, steps from beach and bike bath. **Cons:** privacy and noise issues, full prepayment required with cancellation penalties. ✉ *15 30th Ave., Venice* ☎ *310/823–1966* 🌐 *www.venicebeachhouse.com* *4 rooms without baths, 4 suites* *In-room: Internet. In-hotel: restaurant, beachfront, parking (paid), no-smoking rooms* 💳 *AE, MC, V* *CP.*

OLDIES BUT GOODIES

While Los Angeles has a well-earned and unfortunate rep for tearing down historic buildings, there still a few places where history trumps hip:

A trio of late Victorian era B&B's: **Artists Inn & Cottages** (1895), **Inn at 657** (1904), and **Venice Beach House** (1911)

The Langham, Huntington Hotel & Spa—Pasadena's grande dame (1907)

Beverly Hills Hotel—Repeated face-lifts keep this 1912-gem polished

WESTWOOD

$ **Hotel Palomar Los Angeles–Westwood.** Bold colors in the convivial lobby and smartly designed rooms set this Wilshire Boulevard Kimpton-managed hotel apart. Because of its proximity to UCLA, the Palomar also attracts those visiting the sprawling university for business and students' friends and families. An ergonomic work chair and desk space that's user-friendly plus the 24-hour business center aid efficiency; the on-demand yoga, meditation, and Pilates channels on TV, and yoga mat in-room, promote relaxation. Recycling bins and ecoconscious practices abound. Blvd. 16 is the hotel's ambitious restaurant offering market-fresh fare. Complimentary morning coffee and tea and a nightly wine hour bring guests together. Pets are pampered with many services. **Pros:** visually appealing room design, in-room luxe touches like Frette linens, friendly staff. **Cons:** isolated on a busy thoroughfare of high-rise condos, access to Westwood and nearby Beverly Hills, requires a car or use of (limited) public transport. Shaded outdoor pool. ✉ *10740 Wilshire Blvd., Westwood* ☎ *310/475–8711 or 800/472–8556* 🌐 *www.hotelpalomar-lawestwood.com* *238 rooms, 26 suites* *In-room: safe, refrigerator, DVD, Internet, Wi-Fi. In-hotel: restaurant, room service, bar, pool, gym, laundry service, Internet terminal, Wi-Fi, parking (paid), some pets allowed, no-smoking rooms* 💳 *AE, D, DC, MC, V.*

SAN FERNANDO VALLEY

BURBANK

$–$$ **Burbank Airport Marriott Hotel & Convention Center.** Across the street from the Burbank's Bob Hope Airport, this hotel is a comfortable choice for business travelers. Rooms have ergonomic office chairs, work desks, and flat-screen TVs. Lobby decor salutes the nearby studios with framed photos of stars. The reliable Daily Grill provides 24-hour room service. Need a break? A free shuttle and discounted tickets to Universal Studios are available. Ask for rooms in the East Tower, facing away from the airport, for the quietest stay. **Pros:** closest hotel to Burbank's airport with free shuttle, large gym, Daily Grill restaurant on-site. **Cons:** nearby restaurants limited to fast food outlets, airport noise. ✉*2500 Hollywood Way, Burbank* ☎*818/843–6000 or 888/236–2427* 🌐*www.marriott.com/burap* *409 rooms, 79 suites* *In-room: refrigerator (some), Internet. In-hotel: restaurant, room service, bar, pools, gym, laundry facility, laundry service, Internet terminal, Wi-Fi, parking (paid), some pets allowed, no-smoking rooms* *AE, D, DC, MC, V.*

$$ **Coast Anabelle Hotel.** This small hotel's location on Burbank's main drag is handy, especially for those on studio business since it's a straight-shot mile from NBC and 3 mi from Warner Bros. However, this setting also translates into guest reports of traffic noise and poor soundproofing. Nightly turndown, in-room coffee, a morning paper, and free Wi-Fi are part of the stay. Guest can use the pool next door at the hotel's sister property, the Safari Inn. **Pros:** studio adjacent, free Burbank airport shuttle, use of pool and pets welcome at Safari Inn next door. **Cons:** soundproofing issues, average restaurant and room decor. ✉*2011 W. Olive Ave., Burbank* ☎*818/845–7800 or 800/716–6199* 🌐*www.coasthotels.com* *40 rooms, 7 suites* *In-room: safe, refrigerator, Internet, Wi-Fi. In-hotel: restaurant, room service, bar, gym, laundry facilities, laundry service, Wi-Fi, parking (free), no-smoking rooms* *AE, DC, MC, V.*

$$$ ★ **Hotel Amarano Burbank.** Close to Burbank's TV and movie studios, the smartly designed Amarano feels like a Beverly Hills boutique hotel. The vibe is residential; the look understated (muted beiges and greens). The lobby is a welcoming living room with glass fireplace and corners for quiet conversation, cocktails or tapas. Feather beds are covered in comfy duvets; thoughtful touches include plush bathrobes and hooks for hanging garment bags. Generous work spaces have state-of-the-art lighting, and bathrooms have granite vanities, makeup mirrors, and shelves for storage. The rooftop sundeck has a brightly striped cabana and view of the nearby hills. **Pros:** boutique style in a Valley location, rooftop gym, pleasant breakfast room. **Cons:** no pool to cool off during scorching summertime; Pass Ave. street noise. ✉*322 N. Pass Ave., Burbank* ☎*818/842–8887 or 888/956–1900* 🌐*www.hotelamarano.com* *91 rooms, 10 suites* *In-room: safe, kitchen (some), refrigerator, DVD, Internet, Wi-Fi. In-hotel: restaurant, room service, bar, gym, laundry service, Internet terminal, Wi-Fi, parking (paid), some pets allowed (paid), no-smoking rooms* *AE, D, DC, MC, V.*

NORTH HOLLYWOOD

$$ **Beverly Garland's Holiday Inn.** The Hollywood connection starts in the lobby where framed photos of hotel namesake actress Beverly Garland decorate the lobby. Still family run, the lodgelike hotel, in two separate buildings near Universal Studios, evokes rustic California with its adobe walls, covered walkways and pines. Rooms have private balconies or patios; all are bright and airy with whitewashed walls and comfortable beds. Those next to the Hollywood Freeway are double-paned for soundproofing. Transportation to Universal Studios and a nearby Metro stop is free. A sweet bonus: special kids' suites have bunk beds and access to video games. **Pros:** large pool and play area, unpretentious and friendly feel, on-site Wi-Fi café. **Cons:** small bathrooms, touristy, $13 self-parking lot charge. ✉*4222 Vineland Ave., North Hollywood*

Artists' Inn & Cottage 10
Beverly Garland's Holiday Inn 5
Burbank Airport Marriot Hotel & Convention Center 13
Coast Anabelle Hotel 12
El Patio Inn 4
Four Seasons West Lake Village 1
Hilton Pasadena Hotel 8
Hilton Woodland Hills 2
Hotel Amarono Burbank 11
The Langham, Huntington Hotel & Spa 9
Sheraton Universal 6
Sportsmen's Lodge 3
Westin Pasadena 7

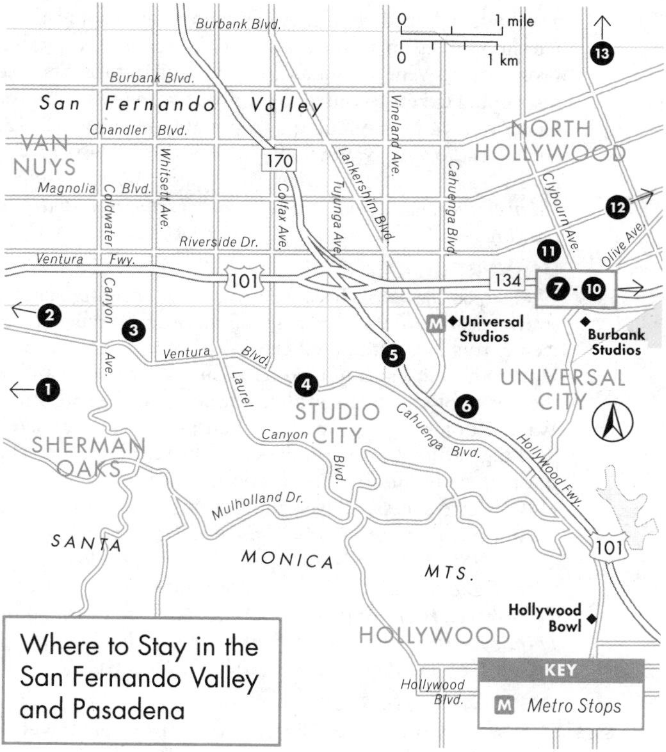

818/980–8000 or 800/238–3759 www.beverlygarland.com 245 rooms, 10 suites In-room: refrigerator (some), DVD (some), Internet, Wi-Fi. In-hotel: restaurant, room service, bar, tennis courts, pool, gym, laundry facilities, laundry service, Wi-Fi, parking (paid), no-smoking rooms AE, D, DC, MC, V.

STUDIO CITY

¢–$ **El Patio Inn.** Behind a classic hacineda-style adobe and neon-lit facade, El Patio Inn is a throwback to 1960s-era roadside motels. Located within sight of Universal Studios, this budget basic stay has decent-sized bathrooms, some cable TV, and queen beds. Location and free parking are the reasons to stay; look for Hollywood hopefuls who often book for multiple nights. **Pros:** close to Universal Studios and a Metro line stop, Ventura Boulevard has an endless supply of restaurants, low rates. **Cons:** no pool, service matches the low rates, zero amenities. *11466 Ventura Blvd., Studio City 818/508–5828 www.elpatioinn.com 24 rooms In-room: safe (some), refrigerator, Internet. In-hotel: parking (free) MC, V.*

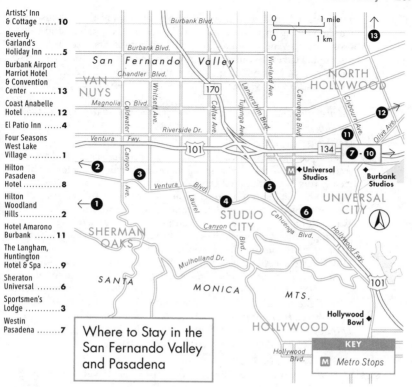

$$ **Sportsmen's Lodge.** Under new ownership and management, the sprawling five-story hotel is midway through an update, with new room decor and much-needed sprucing up. The Olympic-size pool and patio with outdoor bar (summers only) remain, as do the extra wide halls

and high-ceilinged rooms. Americana abounds and the in-house coffee shop serves up all the classics with breakfast a notable good value. **Pros:** close to Ventura Boulevard's plentiful restaurants, free shuttle, and discounted tickets to Universal Hollywood, garden view rooms quietest. **Cons:** renovations ongoing and possibly intrusive. ✉ *12825 Ventura Blvd., Studio City* ☎ *818/769–4700 or 800/821–8511* 🌐 *www.slhotel.com* *177 rooms, 13 suites* *In-room: Wi-Fi. In-hotel: restaurant, room service, bars, pool, gym, laundry facilities, laundry service, Wi-Fi, parking (paid), no-smoking rooms* 💳 *AE, D, DC, MC, V.*

UNIVERSAL CITY

$$$ **Sheraton Universal.** Because of its large meeting spaces and veteran staff, this Sheraton buzzes year-round. Business types come for the high-tech extras like automated check-in, convenient in-room coffeemaker with to-go cup, and numerous business services. Families appreciate the big pool and free shuttle to adjacent Universal Studios and CityWalk. Rooms are in cool blues and grays with flat screen TVs, iPod docking stations, oversize desks, and swiveling office chairs; contemporarily styled lobby. **Pros:** woodsy location straddling Hollywood Hills, Metro access, all new room furnishings. **Cons:** average, in-house restaurant, touristy. ✉ *333 Universal Hollywood Dr., Universal City* ☎ *818/980–1212 or 800/325–3535* 🌐 *www.sheraton.com/universal* *436 rooms, 25 suites* *In-room: safe, DVD (some), Internet, Wi-Fi. In-hotel: restaurant, room service, bar, pool, gym, laundry facilities, laundry service, Internet terminal, Wi-Fi, parking (paid), some pets allowed, no-smoking rooms* 💳 *AE, D, DC, MC, V.*

WESTLAKE VILLAGE

$$$$ **Four Seasons Westlake Village.** Midway between downtown Los Angeles and Santa Barbara, L.A.'s newest Four Seasons, set in an office park next to the 101 freeway, overflows with marble and stone—from the massive boulders dredged from Thailand's River Kwai that dot the landscaped grounds to the polished onyx of the sushi bar. Views from the lobby lounge and restaurants overlook the cascading, rocky waterfall—designed to block out freeway views and noise. Rooms are expensively finished (millwork, flat-screen TVs, and richly upholstered furniture) and double-paned window quiet. Connected to the hotel is the California Health & Longevity Institute that provides health and lifestyle services from diet and exercise revamps to diagnostic testing. **Pros:** gorgeous spa and many extras like private pool and spa dining, on-site healthful cooking lessons, expansive gym with yoga classes. **Cons:** secluded, corporate park location, blazing hot summers, room windows sealed shut. ✉ *2 Dole Dr., Westlake Village* ☎ *818/575–3000 or 800/819–5053* 🌐 *www.fourseasons.com/westlakevillage* *243 rooms, 27 suites* *In-room: safe, refrigerator, DVD, Internet, Wi-Fi. In-hotel: 3 restaurants, room service, bars, 2 pools, gym, spa, laundry service, Internet terminal, Wi-Fi, parking (paid), some pets allowed, no-smoking rooms* 💳 *AE, D, DC, MC, V.*

WOODLAND HILLS

$$–$$$ **Hilton Woodland Hills.** If you're doing business in the west San Fernando Valley, this location at the center of the congested Warner Center business hub is hopping weekdays. The giant Topanga Westfield Mall (and multiplex) is within sight; franchise restaurants offer alternatives to the hotel's fare. A complimentary shuttle will drive you within a 3-mi radius. Comfortable guest rooms, with a touch of Mediterranean style, have armoires, marble-tile bathrooms, and large work desks. Across the driveway is a full-service health club, use of their pool is available free to hotel guests. **Pros:** business-centric weekdays, decent on-site fitness room, numerous nearby restaurants and shopping. **Cons:** deserted most weekends (cheaper stays), pool next door, uninspired decor in public areas. ✉*6360 Canoga Ave., Woodland Hills* ☎*818/595–1000 or 800/922–2400* 🌐*www.woodlandhills.hilton.com* *295 rooms, 23 suites* *In-room: safe, Internet, Wi-Fi. In-hotel: restaurant, room service, bar, gym, laundry facilities, laundry service, Internet terminal, Wi-Fi, parking (paid), some pets allowed, no-smoking rooms* *AE, D, DC, MC, V.*

4

PASADENA

$$$ **Hilton Pasadena Hotel.** Two blocks south of busy Colorado Boulevard, the Hilton Pasadena is still within walking distance of the city's vast convention center and close to the shops and plentiful restaurant choices of Old Town. A light and airy sandstone lobby says California casual, as do the rooms done in soft gold and tan colors, complete with pillowy beds. Bathrooms are noticeably compact. Business travelers appreciate the Smart Desk with ergonomically correct chair. Note: the rooms with balconies are best. **Pros:** amiable and helpful staff, central downtown Pasadena location. **Cons:** compact bathrooms, typical hotel dining options, small pool. ✉*168 S. Los Robles Ave., Pasadena* ☎*626/577–1000 or 800/445–8667* 🌐*www.hiltonpasadena.com* *285 rooms, 11 suites* *In-room: refrigerator, Internet, Wi-Fi. In-hotel: restaurant, room service, bar, pool, gym, laundry service, Internet terminal, Wi-Fi, parking (paid), some pets allowed, no-smoking rooms* *AE, D, DC, MC, V.*

$$$$ Fodor's Choice ★ **The Langham, Huntington Hotel & Spa.** An azalea-filled Japanese garden and the unusual Picture Bridge, with murals celebrating California's history, are just two of this grande dame's picturesque attributes. Long a mainstay of Pasadena's social history, the hotel first opened in 1907. The Italianate-style main building, Spanish Revival–style cottages, and lanai building sit on 23 acres fronted by the historic horseshoe garden. In 2008 the hotel was bought by Langham Hotels ending its storied, 15-year stand as Ritz-Carlton. Traditional guest rooms are handsome and sometimes oddly sized; all are in shades of gold and blue. Brocade fabrics are found throughout, as are flat-screen TVs and CD players. The hotel's formal restaurant, the Dining Room, can be counted on for a rarefied contemporary dining experience. Treat yourself and order Chef Craig Strong's multicourse tasting menu. **Pros:** new owners promises updates to the spa, cottages, and restaurants while maintaining the property's many charms. **Cons:** set in a suburban neighborhood far

from local shopping and dining. ✉*1401 S. Oak Knoll Ave., Pasadena* ☎*626/568–3900 or 800/591–7481* 🌐*www.pasadena.langhamhotels.com* *342 rooms, 38 suites* *In-room: safe, refrigerator, Internet, Wi-Fi. In-hotel: 2 restaurants, room service, bar, tennis courts, pool, gym, spa, bicycles, laundry service, Internet terminal, Wi-Fi, parking (paid), some pets allowed, no-smoking rooms* *AE, D, DC, MC, V.*

$$ **Westin Pasadena.** In the midst of Pasadena's business district, the Westin looks more office tower than hotel. Inside, comfy couches and a library warm up the first floor. Rooms range from spacious to modest in size, and some come with plantation shutters, picture windows, and window seats. As with all Westins, the fitness-conscious will like the in-room workout equipment and smoke-free environment. The hotel caters to businesspeople on weekdays; nonholiday weekend rates are 30% less. **Pros:** efficient, corporate stay and staff, lower weekend rates, Pasadena shopping and dining close-by. **Cons:** numerous add-on charges like Internet access and expensive in-house dining. ✉*191 N. Los Robles Ave., Pasadena* ☎*626/792–2727 or 800/937–8461* 🌐*www.starwoodhotels.com* *348 rooms, 2 suites* *In-room: safe, ethernet, Wi-Fi. In-hotel: 2 restaurants, room service, bars, pool, gym, concierge, laundry service, Internet terminal, parking (fee), some pets allowed, no-smoking rooms* *AE, D, DC, MC, V.*

SOUTH PASADENA

$$–$$$ **Artists' Inn & Cottage.** This charming 1895 B&B is in a quiet residential neighborhood of Craftsman bungalows, not far from the antiques shops of South Pasadena. Once a chicken farm, the Artists' Inn still retains a country air with more than 100 rosebushes in the garden, wicker furniture on the front porch, and home-cooked breakfasts, and afternoon tea. Some rooms have fireplaces; all have themes relating to a particular period of art (like impressionism) or famous artist (Degas, Van Gogh, O'Keeffe). Close by is a Gold Line Metro stop for easy access to both Pasadena's cultural attractions and Downtown L.A. **Pros:** room rates include parking, Internet access, and full breakfast. **Cons:** must be a B&B-type guest and prefer the modest stays. ✉*1038 Magnolia St., South Pasadena* ☎*626/799–5668 or 888/799–5668* 🌐*www.artistsinns.com* *10 rooms* *In-room: Wi-Fi. In-hotel: Wi-Fi, parking (free), no-smoking rooms* *AE, MC, V* *BP.*

Nightlife and the Arts

WORD OF MOUTH

"If you want nightlife, cab it over to the Hermosa Pier (parking is tough). There are numerous bars, some with live entertainment. One is Cafe Boogaloo, featuring "Blues, American Roots, Zydeco , New Orleans Funk & Soul"."

—Travel_Gato

"Bar Nineteen 12 at the Beverly Hills Hotel offers great people watching and patio seating with views of the LA skyline."

—andrew8

www.fodors.com/community

Updated by Kastle Waserman

THE TURNOVER AMONG L.A.'S NIGHTSPOTS can be enough to make your head spin—it's almost as dizzying as the diversity that's available virtually every night of the week. Hollywood and West Hollywood, where hip-and-happening nightspots liberally dot Sunset and Hollywood boulevards, are the epicenter of L.A. nightlife and both buzz louder than ever. The city is one of the best places in the world for seeing soon-to-be-famous rockers as well as top jazz, blues, and classical performers. Movie theaters are naturally well represented here, but the worlds of dance, theater, opera and art have flourished in the past few years as well.

For a thorough listing of local events, *www.la.com, losangeles.metromix.com,* and *Los Angeles* magazine are all good sources. The Calendar section of the *Los Angeles Times* (🌐*www.theguide.latimes.com*) also lists a wide survey of Los Angeles arts events, especially on Thursday and Sunday, as do the more alternative publications, *LA Weekly* (🌐*www.laweekly.com)* and *Citybeat Los Angeles* (🌐*www.lacitybeat.com),* both free, and issued every Thursday. Call ahead to confirm that what you want to see is ongoing.

THE ARTS

The outdated belief that Los Angeles is a plastic city devoid of real culture continues to wither with each new cutting-edge performance that happens here. Placido Domingo has put the Los Angeles Opera on the map, while the museums, galleries, and theaters in town persist in push the boundaries of expression, showcasing out-of-the-box performance, dance, and visual artists from all around the world.

ART GALLERIES

★ **6150 Wilshire Boulevard.** Seven contemporary galleries (including Acme, Kopeikin, and Roberts & Tilton) fill two floors around a central outdoor courtyard. Outside Chinatown, this may be the best spot for edgy, mainly local artists. ✉*Between Crescent Heights Blvd. and Fairfax Ave., Miracle Mile* .

★ **Angles.** With one room graced by 16-foot skylighted ceilings, this is undoubtedly one of L.A.'s most beautiful gallery spaces. Come for contemporary international artists working in all mediums, like Tom LaDuke, David Bunn, Linda Besemer, and Kevin Appel. ✉*2230 and 2222 Main St., Santa Monica* ☎*310/396–5019*.

★ **Bergamot Station.** A former trolley stop on the old L.A.–Santa Monica Red Line has become a contemporary art complex with more than 30 galleries, 10 shops, and a café, plus the Santa Monica Museum of Art. Even kids are entertained by the funky setting and diversity of art here, though the opening night soirees and liquor-sponsored special events here make it more of an adult wonderland. It's closed Sunday. ✉*2525 Michigan Ave., at 26th St., Santa Monica* ☎*310/315–9502*.

Blum & Poe. Tim Blum and Jeff Poe's big orange box anchors the up-and-coming part of Culver City, where art spaces are elbowing their way in among auto repair shops. Takashi Murakami and Sam Durant are among the high-profile artists on the gallery's roster, but the space is best known for showcasing hot young new talent and catering to an equally fresh and eclectic clientele. ✉*2754 S. La Cienega Blvd. Washington Blvd., Culver City* ☎*310/836–2062.*

Gagosian Gallery. Designed by Richard Meier (who also designed the Getty Center), this light-filled space shows blue-chip modern and contemporary artists such as Francesco Clemente, Andy Warhol, and Jeff Koons. Owner Larry Gagosian (known as "Mr. Go Go" in New York; he owns spaces in NYC and London as well) knows how to throw the kind of big opening bashes that attract fashionistas and famous faces. In fact, Gagosian soirees are often as dynamic as their exhibits. ✉*456 N. Camden Dr., Beverly Hills* ☎*310/271–9400.*

Ghetto Gloss This relaxed gallery hosts some of L.A.'s wildest bashes every time a new show begins. Graffiti art, cartoon-inspired drawings, groovy art books, and group shows with themes like "100 Things by 100 Artists for Under $100" and "The Art of Dogtown" (the opening party featured a skate ramp in the parking lot) make this one of the hippest galleries in town. ✉*2380 Glendale Blvd., Silver Lake* ☎*323/912–0008* 🌐*www.ghettogloss.com.*

Junc. In the heart of Silver Lake's lively Sunset Junction area (hence the name), this tiny gallery offers everything from Japanese Anime–inspired pieces to more technical styles of illustration and sculpture, popular with the art school set. ✉*4017 Sunset Blvd., Silver Lake* ☎*213/814–2640.*

L.A. Louver. Since it opened in 1976—a lifetime ago by L.A. standards—this gallery has shown contemporary local artists in an international context (David Hockney alongside Leon Kossoff, for instance). Awesome sculptures and large-scale paintings shown here attract big crowds on opening nights. ✉*45 N. Venice Blvd., Venice* ☎*310/822–4955.*

La Luz de Jesus. You'll find only the most colorful, quirky (if often macabre) art at this 20-year-old gallery adjacent to equally kitschy gift emporiums Wacko/Soap Plant. Openings usually offer cheap beer and snacks, but people flock to the parties (every first Friday of the month)—to the point that the scene becomes the focus, and the art is incidental. ✉*4633 Hollywood Blvd.* ☎*323/663–0122* 🌐*www.laluzdejesus.com.*

Margo Leavin Gallery. This has been a preeminent L.A. gallery for more than 30 years, exhibiting contemporary American and European painters, sculptors, photographers, and artists working on paper including

TOP 5

- **Avalon,** where Saturday nights bring the best in electronic music turntablists.
- **Downtown L.A. Standard's rooftop bar** for one of the best views in town (people- and scenery-wise).
- **Highways Performance Space,** a must-go for performance art that's two steps ahead.
- **Spaceland** for no-nonsense, up-and-coming rock.
- **Walt Disney Concert Hall,** compelling architecture and equally outstanding performances.

icons such as Andy Warhol and Jasper Johns, and newer faves like light experimentalist Dan Flavin. ✉812 N. Robertson Blvd., West Hollywood ☎310/273–0603.

CONCERTS

MAJOR CONCERT HALLS

Fodor's Choice ★ One of the Music Center's most cherished and impressive music halls, the 3,200-seat **Dorothy Chandler Pavilion** (✉*135 N. Grand Ave., Downtown* ☎*213/972–7211*) remains an elegant space to see performances with its plush red seats and giant gold curtain. It presents an array of music programs and the L.A. Opera's classics from September through June. Music director Plácido Domingo encourages fresh work (in 2006, for instance, he ushered in *Grendel,* a new opera staged by the hypercreative director Julie Taymor) as much as old favorites (the 2007–08 season marked the return of Verdi's *Otello*, which Domingo himself performed when the L.A. Opera debuted there decades earlier. There's also a steady flow of touring ballet and modern ballet companies.

Adjacent to Universal Studios, the 6,250-seat **Gibson Amphitheater** (✉*100 Universal City Plaza, Universal City* ☎*818/622–4440*) holds more than 100 performances a year, including the Radio City Christmas Spectacular, star-studded benefit concerts, and all-star shindigs for local radio station KROQ 106.7.

In Griffith Park, the open-air auditorium known as the **Greek Theater** (✉*2700 N. Vermont Ave., Los Feliz* ☎*323/665–5857*), complete with Doric columns, presents big-name performers in its mainly pop-rock-jazz schedule from June through October.

★ Ever since it opened in 1920, in a park surrounded by mountains, trees, and gardens, the **Hollywood Bowl** (✉*2301 Highland Ave., Hollywood* ☎*323/850–2000* ⊕*www.hollywoodbowl.com*) has been one of the world's largest and most atmospheric outdoor amphitheaters. Its season runs from early July through mid-September; the L.A. Philharmonic spends its summers here. There are performances daily except Monday (and some Sundays); the program ranges from jazz to pop to classical. Concertgoers usually arrive early and bringing picnic suppers (picnic tables are available). Additionally, a moderately priced outdoor grill and a more upscale restaurant are among the dining options operated by the Patina Group. ■TIP→**Be sure to bring a sweater—it gets chilly here in the evening. You might also bring or rent a cushion to apply to the wood seats. Avoid the hassle of parking by taking one of the Park-and-Ride buses, which leave from various locations around town; call the Bowl for information.**

BOWLED OVER

The Hollywood Bowl's illustrious list of performances includes everyone from the Beatles (the first rock group to ever play there) to Judy Garland to Pavarotti to, more recently, the Rolling Stones. Indeed, a show at the Bowl is a grand event and the acts almost always legendary. You pretty much have to be to stand out within the venue's famous arched band shell, which as of 2004, was replaced with a new, acoustically enhanced version.

> **WORD OF MOUTH**
>
> "I took the Walt Disney Concert Hall's free guided tour on my last trip, but we didn't have time this time. I bought our concert tickets about a month before our trip. Our seats were in the "bench" section, which is behind the orchestra. I liked these seats because we get a good view of the orchestra plus we were able to watch the conducter." —yk

The jewel in the crown of Hollywood & Highland is the **Kodak Theatre** (✉ *6801 Hollywood Blvd., Hollywood* ☎ *323/308–6363* 🌐 *www.kodaktheatre.com*). Created as the permanent host of the Academy Awards, the lavish 3,500-seat theater is also used for music concerts and ballets. Seeing a show here is worthwhile just to witness the gorgeous, crimson-and-gold interior, with its box seating and glittering chandeliers.

Nokia Theatre L.A. Live opened its doors in 2007 with a string of performances by the Dixie Chicks and the Eagles, and it's been showcasing equally grand acts ever since. Boasting what its creators call the best sight lines and acoustics of any live music venue in LA—including Staples center across the street—Nokia is part of the 4 million square foot, 2.5 billion L.A. Live project Downtown, which also includes an array of residential, retail, and entertainment spaces. ✉ *777 Chick Hearn Court, Downtown* ☎ *213/763–6030* 🌐 *www.nokiatheatrelalive.com.*

The one-of-a-kind, 6,300-seat ersatz-Arabic **Shrine Auditorium** (✉ *665 W. Jefferson Blvd., Downtown* ☎ *213/748–5116*), built in 1926 as Al Malaikah Temple, hosts touring companies from all over the world, assorted gospel and choral groups, and other musical acts as well as high-profile televised awards shows, including the Latin Grammys and the Golden Globes.

★ It's used mainly for sporting events, but the **Staples Center** (✉ *1111 S. Figueroa St., Downtown* ☎ *213/742–7300* 🌐 *www.staplescenter.com*) also offers blockbuster concerts. Everyone from U2 to Justin Timberlake to Barbra Streisand has brought their shows here. The Lakers, Clippers, and Kings all call Staples home.

Fodor's Choice ★ Built in 2003 as a grand addition to L.A.'s Music Center, the 2,265-seat **Walt Disney Concert Hall** (✉ *111 S. Grand Ave., Downtown* ☎ *323/850–2000*) is now the home of the Los Angeles Philharmonic and the Los Angeles Master Chorale. A sculptural monument of gleaming, curved steel, the theater is part of a complex that includes a public park, gardens, and shops as well as two outdoor amphitheaters for children's and preconcert events. TIP→ **In the main hall, the audience completely surrounds the stage, so it's worth checking the seating chart when buying tickets to gauge your view of the performers.** And the acoustics definitely live up to the hype.

The **Wiltern LG Theater** (✉ *3790 Wilshire Blvd., Mid-Wilshire* ☎ *213/388–1400*), a green terra-cotta, art deco masterpiece constructed in 1930, is a fine place to see pop, rock, jazz, and dance performances. The main space is standing room only, but there are a few seating areas available.

DANCE

The dance scene in Los Angeles has faced its challenges, with lackluster ticket sales at the top of the list. Though there may not be much of an audience here for ballet, forms of more modern dance are quite popular—after all, most music videos are filmed here. You can see many of the industry's choreographers and backup grinders at many of the theaters listed above and at various clubs around town (try the Key Club and its bimonthly "Choreographer's Ball"). The venues listed below offer the most dance-related fare, including ballet and jazz.

TICKET SOURCES

In addition to contacting venues directly, try these sources.

Good Time Tickets (☎ *323/464-7383* 🌐 *www.goodtime-tickets.com*) covers events at museums and small theaters, plus some stadium fare.

Razor Gator (☎ *800/542-4466* 🌐 *www.razorgator.com*). Sells harder-to-get tickets.

Theatre League Alliance L.A (🌐 *www.theatrela.org*). Score discounted theater tickets.

Ticketmaster (☎ *213/480-3232, 213/365-3500 fine arts* 🌐 *www.ticketmaster.com*). Still the all-around top dog.

Cal State L.A.'s Dance Department (✉ *5151 State University Dr., East Los Angeles* ☎ *323/343-4118* 🌐 *www.calstatela.edu/academic/al*) presents several prominent dance events each year. Check Web site for schedule. The **Kodak Theatre** (✉ *6801 Hollywood Blvd., Hollywood* ☎ *323/308-6363*) hosts various ballet performances each year, including *The Nutcracker.* International dance groups often perform at the **REDCAT** (*Roy and Edna Disney Cal Arts Theater* ✉ *631 W. 2nd St., Downtown* ☎ *213/237-2800*), a 260-seat space that showcases performance of all kinds, including avant-garde dance. **Shrine Auditorium** (✉ *665 W. Jefferson Blvd., Downtown* ☎ *213/748-5116*) hosts touring dance companies, such as the Kirov, the Bolshoi, and the American Ballet Theater (ABT). **UCLA Live** has dance performances in Royce Hall and Gloria Kaufman Hall. Check Web site for schedule (🌐 *www.uclalive.org*). Purchase tickets at central ticket office (✉ *325 Westwood Plaza*) or at venue box office (☎ *310/825-4401*).

FILM

Spending two hours at a movie while visiting Los Angeles doesn't have to mean taking time out from sightseeing; in fact seeing a film here is almost like paying tribute to the temple of entertainment. Some of the country's most historic and beautiful theaters are found here, and they host both first-run and revival films. Movie listings are advertised daily in the *Los Angeles Times* Calendar section. Admission to first-run movies is usually about $9.

ART AND REVIVAL HOUSES

The **American Cinemathèque Independent Film Series** (✉ *6712 Hollywood Blvd., Hollywood* ☎ *323/466-3456* 🌐 *americancinematheque.com*) screens classics plus recent independent films, sometimes with question-and-answer sessions with the filmmakers. The main venue is the Lloyd E. Rigler Theater, within the 1922 Egyptian Theater, which combines an exterior of pharaoh sculptures and columns with a modern, high-tech design inside. The Cinemathèque also screens movies at the 1940 **Aero Theater** (✉*1328 Montana Ave., Santa Monica* ☎*323/466–3456*).

GOLDEN MOMENTS

Watching your favorite stars parade down the red carpet on the tube is one thing, but ogling them in person from only a few feet away? As those credit card commercials say, that's priceless. No, really. You don't have to pay a dime to be one of the 300 people who score bleacher seats along L.A.'s famous entry-way, you just have to be lucky enough to be chosen by the **Academy Awards Bleacher Seat Lottery.** Enter during the month of September at 🌐www.oscars.org/bleachers.

Fodor'sChoice ★ Taking the concept of dinner and a movie to a whole new level, **Cinespace** (✉*6356 Hollywood Blvd., Hollywood* ☎*323/817–3456* 🌐*www.cinespace.info*) screens classics and alternative flicks in its digital theater-restaurant. Comfort food is served during the films, which could be documentaries as easily as they could be old-school faves like *Grease.* The movies are often followed by popular club nights. DJ-provided music and a smoking patio that hovers over bustling Hollywood Boulevard attract indie rockers on Tuesday and hip-hop hell-raisers on weekends.

Fodor'sChoice ★ The **Silent Movie Theatre** (✉*611 N. Fairfax Ave., Fairfax District* ☎*323/655–2520* 🌐*www.silentmovietheatre.com*) is a treasure for both pretalkies and nonsilent films (the artier the better). Live musical accompaniment and shorts precede the films. Each show is made to seem like an event in itself, and it's just about the only theater of its kind. The schedule—which also offers occasional DJ and live music performances—varies, but you can be sure to catch silent screenings every Wednesday.

★ **UCLA** has two fine film series. The programs of the **Billy Wilder Theater** (✉*10899 Wilshire Blvd., Westwood* ☎*310/206–8013* 🌐*www.cinema.ucla.edu*) might cover the works of major directors, documentaries, children's films, horror movies—just about anything. The **School of Film & Television** (🌐*www.tft.ucla.edu*) uses **the James Bridges Theater** (✉*Melnitz Hall, Sunset Blvd. and Hilgard Ave., Westwood* ☎*310/206–8365* 🌐*www.tft.ucla.edu/facilities/james-bridges-theater*), and has its own program of newer, avant-garde films. Enter the campus at the northeasternmost entrance. Street parking is available on Loring Avenue (a block east of the campus) after 6 PM, or park for a small fee in Lot 3 (go one entrance south to Wyton Drive to pay at the kiosk before 7, after 7 at the lot itself).

The best of Hollywood classics and kitsch, foreign films, and, occasionally, documentaries are on tap at the **New Beverly Cinema** (✉*7165 Beverly Blvd., Los Angeles* ☎*323/938–4038*), where there's always a double bill. **Nuart** (✉*11272 Santa Monica Blvd., West L.A.* ☎*310/281–8223*) is the best-kept of L.A.'s revival houses, with good seats, an excellent screen, and special midnight shows.

MOVIE PALACES

The **Arclight** (✉*6360 Sunset Blvd., Hollywood* ☎*323/464–4226*) includes as its centerpiece the geodesic Cinerama Dome, the first theater in the United States designed specifically for the large screen and sound system that went with Cinerama. The complex now includes 14 additional screens, a shopping area, and a restaurant and bar. The only theater in L.A. to begin movies with greetings and background commentary by theater staff, the Arclight also designates some screenings as "premium," which lets you reserve the best seats for an extra fee. "Over 21" shows let you bring cocktails into designated screening rooms.

Bridge Cinema De Lux (✉*6081 Center Dr., in the Promenade at Howard Hughes Center, West L.A.* ☎*310/568–3375*) comes by its name honestly, with superwide screens, leather recliners, and top-notch food (from wrap sandwiches to pizza) and drink (martinis are their specialty). Sip a cocktail at the bar or order a meal to take into the theater. Regular ticket prices start at $9.75, with higher prices for Directors' Hall seating (reserved seats and even bigger screens).

Fodor's Choice ★ **Grauman's Chinese Theatre** (✉*6925 Hollywood Blvd., Hollywood* ☎*323/464–6266*), open since 1927, is perhaps the world's best-known theater, the home of the famous concrete walkway marked by movie stars' hand- and footprints and traditional gala premieres. There are additional, smaller screens at the Mann Chinese Six, in the adjoining Hollywood & Highland Complex.

Across the street from Grauman's is the **Pacific's El Capitan** (✉*6838 Hollywood Blvd., Hollywood* ☎*323/467–7674*), an art deco masterpiece meticulously renovated by Disney. First-run movies alternate with Disney revivals, and the theater often presents live stage shows in conjunction with Disney's animated pictures.

At the intersection of Hollywood and Sunset boulevards, the 1923 **Vista Theater** (✉*4473 Sunset Dr., Los Feliz* ☎*323/660–6639*), now showing first-run films, was once Bard's Hollywood Theater, used for vaudeville shows in the '20s. A Spanish-style facade leads to an ornate, Egyptian-style interior.

THEATER

Los Angeles isn't quite the "Broadway of the West," as some have claimed—the scope of theater here doesn't compare to that in New York. Still, the theater scene's growth has been impressive. Small theaters are blossoming all over town, and the larger houses, despite price hikes to as much as $70 for a single ticket, are usually full. Even small productions might boast big names from the entertainment industry.

LA Stage Alliance (🌐*www.lastagealliance.com*) also gives information on what's playing in Los Angeles, albeit with capsules that are either noncommittal or overly enthusiastic. Its LAStageTIX service allows you to buy tickets online the day of the performance at roughly half price.

CLOSE UP

Cheap Thrills

You don't have to be loaded to load up on after-dark entertainment in L.A. From live music to TV show tapings to karaoke, there's plenty of low-cost and free fun to be had.

Audiences Unlimited (✉ *100 Universal City Plaza, Bldg. 153, Universal City* ☎ *818/260–0041* 🌐 *www.tvtickets.com*) helps fill seats for television programs (and sometimes for televised award shows). The free tickets are distributed on a first-come, first-served basis. Shows that may be taping or filming include *Good Morning America* and *Dr. Phil.* Note: You must be 16 or older to attend a television taping.

The Happy Ending bar and restaurant offers free '80's-theme karaoke with "Coreyoke" (a live backing band dressed as Corey Haim, Corey Feldman, and sunglasses-at-night guy Cory Hart) every Monday, plus dirt cheap drink specials that'll take you back to the future.

The popular dive the **Smog Cutter** and its low-cost libations make for a rip-roaring karaoke party. You may have to wait a while for your turn, but at least you don't have to pay.

Order a snack and enjoy **Cinespace's** movies free. Then, stay and soak up the scene before the crowds come (drinks are often free or cheap before 11).

Monday at **Spaceland** spotlights promising and extremely varied (punk, country, alternative) artists with monthlong (and free) residencies, so you have up to four chances to catch them.

5

MAJOR THEATERS

Jason Robards and Nick Nolte got their starts at **Geffen Playhouse** (✉ *10886 Le Conte Ave., Westwood* ☎ *310/208–5454* 🌐 *www.geffenplayhouse.com*), an acoustically superior, 498-seat theater that showcases new plays in summer—primarily musicals and comedies. Many of the productions here are on their way to or from Broadway.

★ In addition to theater performances, lectures, and children's programs, free summer jazz, dance, cabaret, and occasionally Latin and rock concerts take place at the **John Anson Ford Amphitheater** (✉ *2580 Cahuenga Blvd. E, Hollywood* ☎ *323/461–3673* 🌐 *www.fordamphitheater.org*), a 1,300-seat outdoor venue in the Hollywood Hills. Winter shows are typically staged at the smaller indoor theater, **Inside the Ford.**

There are three theaters in the big Downtown complex known as **the Music Center** (✉ *135 N. Grand Ave., Downtown* ☎ *213/972–7211* 🌐 *www.musiccenter.org*). The 2,140-seat **Ahmanson Theatre** (☎ *213/628–2772* 🌐 *www.taperahmanson.com*) presents both classics and new plays; the 3,200-seat **Dorothy Chandler Pavilion** shows a smattering of plays between the more prevalent musical performances; and the 760-seat **Mark Taper Forum** (☎ *213/628–2772* 🌐 *www.taperahmanson.com*) presents new works that often go on to Broadway, such as Tony Kushner's *Caroline, or Change*.

★ The home of the Academy Awards telecast from 1949 to 1959, the **Pantages Theatre** (✉ *6233 Hollywood Blvd., Hollywood* ☎ *323/468–1770*

🌐*www.pantages-theatre.com*) is a massive (2,600-seat) and splendid example of high-style Hollywood art deco, presenting large-scale Broadway musicals such as *The Lion King* and *Wicked.*

The **Ricardo Montalbán Theatre** (⊠*1615 N. Vine St., Hollywood* ☎*323/463–0089* 🌐*ricardomontalbantheatre.info*) has an intimate feeling despite its 1,038-seat capacity. It presents plays, concerts, seminars, and workshops with an emphasis on Latin culture.

The 1,900-seat, art deco **Wilshire Theatre** (⊠*8440 Wilshire Blvd., Beverly Hills* ☎*323/468–1716* 🌐*www.nederlander.com*) presents Broadway musicals and occasional concerts.

SMALLER THEATERS

★ The founders of **Actors' Gang Theater** (⊠*9070 Venice Blvd., Culver City* ☎*310/838–4264* 🌐*www.theactorsgang.com*) include actor Tim Robbins; the fare has included Molière, Eric Bogosian, and international works by traveling companies.

The **Bob Baker Marionette Theater** (⊠*1345 W. 1st St., at Glendale Blvd., Downtown* ☎*213/250–9995* 🌐*www.bobbakermarionettes.com*) has been a staple for L.A. youth since 1963. Kids sit on a carpeted floor and get a close-up view of the intricate puppets; ice cream and juice are served after the shows.

City Garage (⊠*1340½ 4th St. Alley, between the 3rd St. Promenade and 4th St., Santa Monica* ☎*310/319–9939* 🌐*www.citygarage.org*) really *was* a garage for the city and the police department in the 1930s. Since 1987 it has hosted the **Aresis Ensemble,** whose French artistic director, Frédérique Michel, has maintained a largely European orientation in selecting plays and a casually Continental attitude in their execution—don't be surprised by incidental nudity.

Architect Frank Gehry designed the **Edgemar Center for the Arts** (⊠*2437 Main St., Santa Monica* ☎📠*310/399–3666* 🌐*www.edgemarcenter.org*), an industrial-styled complex of two theaters, offices, and classrooms where the nonprofit performance group holds dramatic performances, dance, music, and film events, as well as outreach programs and workshops. It has such supporters as Neil Simon, Jason Alexander, and Kate Capshaw in its corner.

The **Falcon Theatre** (⊠*4252 Riverside Dr., Burbank* ☎*818/955–8101* 🌐*www.falcontheatre.com*) is the brainchild of TV and movie producer-director-writer Garry Marshall (*Laverne & Shirley, Pretty Woman*). The well-appointed theater is a stone's throw from the Warner Bros. lot; you'll often find one of Marshall's cronies looking to have fun on stage again in works like *Arsenic and Old Lace.*

Though not in the most fashionable neck of the woods, the **Fremont Center Theatre** (⊠*1000 Fremont Ave., Pasadena* ☎*626/441–5977* 🌐*www.fremontcentretheatre.com*) has nonetheless turned out its share of critically appreciated revivals and more obscure dramas.

Three performance venues and a coffee bar in one, the **Hudson Theatres** (⊠*6539 Santa Monica Blvd., Hollywood* ☎*323/856–4249* 🌐*www.hudsontheatre.com*) are popular with TV actors longing to tread the boards during their summer vacations. What's more, the resident company, the

Hudson Guild, has a reputation for some of the finest traditional theater in town—with raves for its reinterpretations of the likes of *Twelfth Night* and *Hedda Gabler*—as well as more experimental fare.

Whether putting on classic Chekhov or more obscure current fare, the **Interact Theatre Company** (☎ *818/765–8732* 🌐 *www.interactla.org*) may no longer have a permanent home, but its plays continue to earn nominations and awards from the L.A. Drama Critics Circle, Theatre L.A., *Back Stage West,* and others.

Though relatively new on the scene, the **Kirk Douglas Theatre** (✉ *9820 Washington Blvd., Culver City* ☎ *213/628–2772* 🌐 *www.taperahmanson.com*) has built a strong reputation for well-staged contemporary drama and comedy. It's got solid backing, too, as it's in the same family as the Ahmanson and the Mark Taper Forum.

Pacific Resident Theatre (✉ *703 Venice Blvd., Venice* ☎ *310/822–8392* 🌐 *www.pacificresidenttheatre.com*) has earned 30 L.A. Drama Critics Awards since its first season as an actors' co-op in '85. It homes in on topical dramas and comedies.

5

The **Theatre of NOTE** (✉ *1517 Cahuenga Blvd., north of Sunset Blvd., Hollywood* ☎ *323/856–8611* 🌐 *www.theatreofnote.com*) has made a critical impact with both full-length plays (classic and new) and evenings of one-act works.

Founded in 1962, the nonprofit theater co-op **Theatre West** (✉ *3333 Cahuenga Blvd. W, Los Angeles* ☎ *323/851–7977 or 818/761–2203* 🌐 *www.theatrewest.org*) has produced a lauded body of work. Its plays have gone on to Broadway (*Spoon River Anthology*) and been made into films (*A Bronx Tale*), and stars like the late Carroll O'Connor and Richard Dreyfuss have acted with the company. Its interactive **Storybook Theatre** (for three- to nine-year-olds) is a long-running favorite.

THEATER ENSEMBLES

The **Cornerstone Theater Company** (☎ *213/613–1700* 🌐 *www.cornerstonetheater.org*) doesn't need a home of its own: it integrates drama into locations like city buses and shopping malls. Having hopped through rural communities in 10 states since its founding, the company is now based in L.A., where it covers everything from Shakespeare adaptations to exploratory faith-theme productions.

★ **Circle X** (☎ *213/804–1042* 🌐 *www.circlextheatre.org*) is one of the most lauded and loved acting groups in the city. The traveling troupe continues to win local theater awards thanks to its continuing quest to find and mount exciting new works on a shoestring budget.

NIGHTLIFE

While the ultimate in velvet-roped vampiness and glamour used to be the Sunset Strip, in the past couple of years the glitz has definitely shifted to Hollywood Boulevard and its surrounding streets. The lines are as long as the skirts are short outside the Hollywood club du jour (which changes so fast, it's often hard to keep track). Indeed, competition has become so fierce—and nightclubbers so fickle—that remodeling and renaming former hot spots is de riguer these days. Many of the places listed below were called something else entirely only a year ago.

The Strip still has plenty going for it too with comedy clubs, hard-rock spots, and restaurants. West Hollywood's Santa Monica Boulevard bustles with gay and lesbian bars and clubs. For less conspicuous—and congested—alternatives, check out the events in Downtown L.A.'s performance spaces and galleries. Silver Lake and Echo Park are best for boho bars and live music clubs.

Despite the high energy level of the L.A. nightlife crowd, don't expect to be partying until dawn—this is still an early-to-bed city. Liquor laws require that bars stop serving alcohol at 2 AM, and it's safe to say that by this time, with the exception of a few after-hours venues and coffeehouses (see the "Late Greats" box), most jazz, rock, and disco clubs have closed for the night. Due to the smoking ban, most bars and clubs with a cover charge allow "in and outs"—patrons may leave the premises and return (usually with a hand stamp or paper bracelet). Some newer clubs offer outdoor smoking patios—a great way to enjoy the city's consistently warm evenings.

Note that parking, especially after 7 PM, is at a premium in Hollywood. In fact, it's restricted on virtually every side street along the "hot zone" of West Hollywood (Sunset Boulevard from Fairfax to Doheny). Posted signs indicate the restrictions, but these are naturally harder to notice at night. Paying $5 to $10, and at some venues even $15–$20, for valet or lot parking is often the easiest way to go.

BARS

Despite its well-publicized penchant for hedonism, Los Angeles, unlike New York, Chicago, and San Francisco, has never been much of a saloon town. But Hollywood's renaissance is changing that part of the equation. Thanks to vibrant new drinking and dining spaces along Cahuenga, Las Palmas, and Ivar, Tinseltown finally feels like a lively—somewhat safe—area to stroll at night, a real barhopper zone. In fact, with all the traffic generated by the new additions, it's smart to park in one place and walk or (gasp!) use the subway to explore the area's hipster joints. There's even a trolley that trundles between various bars along the boulevard (*⇨ see the "Holly Trolley" box, below*). But Hollywood Boulevard aside, to quench your thirst in other parts of La-La Land, you'd still better be prepared to do some driving.

HOLLYWOOD

★ The **Beauty Bar** (*✉ 1638 Cahuenga Blvd., Hollywood ☎ 323/464–7676*) offers manicures and makeovers along with the perfect martinis, but the hotties who flock to this retro salon-bar (the little sister of the Beauty Bars in NYC and San Fran) don't really need the cosmetic care—this is where the edgy beautiful people hang.

The dark and groovy **Burgundy Room** (*✉ 1621½ N. Cahuenga Blvd., Hollywood ☎ 323/465–7530*) has been a Hollywood favorite for some time, attracting an unpretentious rock-and-roll crowd most nights.

CLOSE UP

Late Greats

Sleepless in the City of Angels? Here are the best spots for those who like to (body) rock all night:

Avalon. The house, techno, and progressive electro beats keep pumping strong until 4 AM and for those with energy to go even later, the party continues on Saturday nights until 7 AM.

Giant at **Vanguard.** The city's reigning Saturday night super-club also goes until 4 AM and even though the liquor stops flowing at 2 AM, the floor doesn't.

Not the dancing until dawn type, but still a night owl? These late-night eateries always have plenty of post-clubbin' rubbin' as well as grubbin' going on after 2 AM on weekends.

Canter's. The famous Fairfax deli is a mob scene when the bars let out, as much for the sassy waitresses as the sobering properties of their matzo ball soup.

Fred 62. Silver Lake scenesters come here after shows to see and be seen. Expect lots of tattoos and messy tresses.

Swingers. An über-hip late-night scene that's always enhanced by the killer tunes on the jukebox.

5

The name of the game at the **Cabana Club** (✉ *1439 N. Ivar Ave., Hollywood* ☎ *323/463–0005*), as the tabloids say, is canoodling, whether you want to be seen or not (curtains can be drawn for privacy around the cabanas that line this outdoor club). DJs spin everything from lounge to rock.

The **Cat & Fiddle Pub** (✉ *6530 Sunset Blvd., Hollywood* ☎ *323/468–3800*) is a SoCal hacienda-style venue with a touch of England. Happy hours are weekdays 4–7, with drink specials at the bar. You can play darts, check out the memorabilia displays, or loll on the patio, where jazz is played Sunday night 7–11 (free).

The **Green Door** (✉ *1439 Ivar Ave., Hollywood* ☎ *323/463–0008* is one of the most charming newish lounges in Hollywood. With a whimsical vintage decor (gilded lamps and mirrors, and a giant circular velvet couch in its center), a fun dinner menu, and an atmosphere that gets livelier with inventive DJ mixing and dancing later in the evening, you'll find a hip yet amiable crowd behind this door.

Holly's (✉ *1651 Wilcox Ave.* ☎ *323/461–1400*) sits in the space that used to house Cuban hot spot Paladar; now it offer a billowy French atmosphere, complete with light appetizers, stiff drinks, and DJs spinning groovin' sounds. Getting past the doorman can be tough on weekends, but once inside, the vibe is bliss.

L-Scorpion (✉ *6679 Hollywood Blvd., Hollywood* ☎ *323/464–3026*) might be small but it packs a punch, kinda like the bar's specialty: tequila. The cozy, Mexican drinking hole has 120 different kinds of the strong stuff, and some are so deceptively smooth, salt and lime aren't even necessary. Order from the zingy food menu to soak it up.

Film-studio moguls, movie extras, and those longing for a look at a Hollywood watering hole of yesteryear flock to **Musso & Frank Grill** (✉ *6667 Hollywood Blvd., Hollywood* ☎ *323/467–5123*). This former haunt of F. Scott Fitzgerald is the city's oldest restaurant, established in 1919 and still at the same location. The bar serves up the Rob Roys smooth. Stick with them, or if you *must* eat (and "enjoy" the famous attitude of the waiters), go for the steaks.

Another one of those trendy spots way too cool to put a sign out front, the very exclusive **Nacional** (✉ *1645 Wilcox Ave., Hollywood* ☎ *323/962–7712*) always has a line out front, especially on weekends. Owned by the team behind the Ivar, this space has a woody yet highly modern feel with an open-air rooftop patio, fireplaces, and DJs spinning obscure funk and soul.

Dark and sequestered, the **Room** (✉ *1626 N. Cahuenga Blvd., Hollywood* ☎ *323/462–7196*) promises some of the town's hottest DJs every night. The accent is on hip-hop, but Thursday–Saturday, *anything* is fair game. Enter on the alley.

S Bar (✉ *6304 Hollywood Blvd., Hollywood* ☎ *323/957–2279*) is the newest hot spot from L.A. nightlife superpowers SBE (at least at this writing), but unlike the company's other hangs (Hyde, Area) this whimsical bar claims to have an open-door policy. Still, the surreal decor and even more surreal regulars (the cast from *The Hills* love to hang here) fill the tiny room nightly, so get there early if you don't want to wait among hoi polloi.

★ The casually hip **Three Clubs** (✉ *1123 N. Vine St., Hollywood* ☎ *323/462–6441*) is furtively located in a strip mall, beneath the Bargain Clown Mart discount store. The DJs segue through the many faces and phases of rock-and-roll and dance music. With dark-wood paneling, lamp-lighted tables, and even some sofas, you could be in a giant basement rec room from decades past—no fancy dress required, but fashionable looks suggested.

Tiny's KO (✉ *6377 Hollywood Blvd.* ☎ *323/462–9777* 🌐 *www.tinysko.com*), owned by a couple of punk music scenesters, is a quirky gem amid the boulevard's more garish/glitzy dance clubs. Clown and naked lady paintings cover the tiny space, and the jukebox leans toward aggressive sounds.

The **Tropicana Bar** (✉ *7000 Hollywood Blvd., Hollywood* ☎ *323/466–7000*), an outdoor, poolside lounge in the Roosevelt Hotel, had so much buzz the management had to tone it down. After the hotel's revamp in 2005 and the arrival of lightning-rod promoter Amanda Scheer Demme (now gone), the place became a ridiculously fabulous hot spot for celebs and their tantalizing misbehavior. It's a good place to drink with the beautiful people and the occasional celeb. Inside the hotel, the even more exclusive **Teddy's** continues to pack in celebutants trying to avoid the paparazzi.

★ A lovely L.A. tradition is to meet at **Yamashiro** (✉ *1999 N. Sycamore Ave., Hollywood* ☎ *323/466–5125*) for cocktails at sunset. In the elegant restaurant, waitresses glide by in kimonos, and entrées can zoom up to $39; on the terrace, a spectacular hilltop view spreads out before you. **TIP→ Mandatory valet parking is $3.50, but happy-hour drinks are just a bit more than that.**

WEST HOLLYWOOD

★ As at so many other nightspots in this neck of the woods, the popularity and clientele of **Bar Marmont** (✉ *8171 Sunset Blvd., West Hollywood* ☎ *323/650–0575*) bulged—and changed—after word got out it was a favorite of celebrities. Lately, it's gotten a second wind thanks to a strong DJ selection and luscious cocktails. The bar is next to the inimitable hotel Chateau Marmont, which boldface names continue to haunt.

HOLLY TROLLEY

Looking for a way to barhop without driving in Hollywood? Try the "Holly Trolley" (🌐www.ladottransit.com/other/trolley/), which shuttles between designated lots along Hollywood Boulevard. Tokens, available at most local watering holes, are $1 each, and the trolley runs from 6:30 PM to 2:30 AM, Thursday through Saturday.

Half bar, half restaurant, and home to what the owners call "L.A.'s second-best chili" and the equally touted chili burger, **Barney's Beanery** (✉ *8447 Santa Monica Blvd., West Hollywood* ☎ *323/654–2287*) serves more than 200 different beers. Established in 1920, it's second only to Musso & Frank in restaurant longevity in L.A. The funky decor, long bar, two pool tables, and assortment of air hockey, video, and even pinball games keep the relatively hip but unaffected crowd amused and coming back for more.

Decent Chinese food and pretty good drinking are on offer at the **Formosa Cafe** (✉ *7156 Santa Monica Blvd., West Hollywood* ☎ *323/850–9050*), featured in 1997's noir *L.A. Confidential* for being a rare, still-intact remnant of that bygone Hollywood era. Its railroad-car design allows lots of booths, and the walls are a pictorial shrine to the film community, many of whom have frequented the place (it's across from the former Warner Hollywood lot).

Happy Ending (✉ *7038 Sunset Blvd., Hollywood* ☎ *323/469–7038* 🌐 *www.thehappyendingbar.com*) isn't your typical sports bar. TV screens galore, karaoke, and a colorful "drink wheel" (spin it and you can win everything from $2 shots to $10 beer pitchers) help this bar live up to its name in more ways than one.

Get up close and personal with Hollywood hipsters at **Jones** (✉ *7205 Santa Monica Blvd., West Hollywood* ☎ *323/850–1727*). It's too dark and crowded for you to be able to tell, but this is an authentically preserved old showbiz haunt, with secluded booths, scrumptious food, and very loud music.

Parc (✉ *6683 Hollywood Blvd., Hollywood* ☎ *323/465–6200*) is another posh eaterie attracting the celeb set. With simple interior and a less than adventurous tapas-style menu, this one's about the people-watching more than anything else.

Villa (✉ *8623 Melrose Ave., at Huntley Dr., West Hollywood* ☎ *310/289–8623*), formerly Monroe's and before that the historic J. Sloan's, is more exclusive than either of its prior incarnations. You must know someone associated with the bar to enter or even have the valet park your car there. The vibe is luxe but homey—it was designed to look a mansion.

DOGGY DECADENCE

Cocktails and canines collide at this usually monthly gathering where dogs and the humans who love them can mingle and tinkle (it takes place on a Downtown building rooftop complete with grassy area for pups who've had one too many . . . treats that is. See 🌐 *www.skybark.com* for event info.

Winston's (✉ *7746 Santa Monica Blvd., West Hollywood* ☎ *323/654–0105*) is also notable for its star quota (everyone from Britney to Paris frequent the place, and its dark, '20's flaired opulence was featured on HBO's *Entourage* soon after it opened).

★ The **Rainbow Bar & Grill** (✉ *9015 Sunset Blvd., West Hollywood* ☎ *310/278–4232*), in the heart of the Strip and next door to the legendary Roxy, is a landmark in its own right as *the* drinking spot of the '80s hair-metal scene—and it still attracts a music-industry crowd.

To enter **Skybar** (✉ *8440 Sunset Blvd., West Hollywood* ☎ *323/650–8999*), the poolside bar at the Hotel Mondrian, you must have a Mondrian room key, a screen credit, or a spot on the guest list. The view is phenomenal, as is the staying power of its cachet.

★ A classic Hollywood makeover—formerly a nursing home, this spot in the happening part of Sunset Strip got converted into a smart, brash-looking hotel, the **Standard** (✉ *8300 Sunset Blvd., West Hollywood* ☎ *323/650–9090*), for the young, hip, and connected. (Check out the live model in the lobby's fish tank.) The hotel and especially the bar here is popular with those in the biz.

LOS FELIZ, SILVER LAKE, AND ATWATER VILLAGE

A space that's as popular with nonlocals as it is with the neighborhood's bohemian barflys, **4100** (✉ *4100 Sunset Blvd., Silver Lake* ☎ *323/666–4460*) is a great place to meet and be merry. A lively jukebox mixing rock-and-roll and soul, plus seating around the bar, makes it a hip, no-hassle hookup spot.

Akbar (✉ *4356 Sunset Blvd., Silver Lake* ☎ *323/665–6810*) has retained its friendly neighborhood feel, even after an expansion brought a bigger dance floor and sound system. The largely gay crowd tends be artier than the WeHo pretty boy set, and it's also less of a meat market.

Big Foot Lodge (✉ *3172 Los Feliz Blvd., Los Feliz* ☎ *323/662–9227*) has a cheeky outdoors theme, with a life-size, animated Smokey the Bear, but the twentysomething crowd tends toward the rock and rockabilly set. Different DJs each night offer sounds from '80s metal to '60s French pop. If you're feeling campfire nostalgia, try the Toasted Marshmallow, a creamy drink topped with, you guessed it, a flaming marshmallow.

★ **Cha Cha Lounge** (✉ *2375 Glendale Blvd., Silver Lake* ☎ *323/660–7595*), Seattle's coolest rock bar, now aims to repeat its success with this colorful, red-lighted space. Think part tiki hut, part tacky Tijuana party palace. The tabletops pay homage to the lounge's former performers; they've got portraits of Latin drag queens.

A '40s-style bar that was rediscovered during the mid-'90s lounge craze and immortalized in the film *Swingers*, **Dresden Room** (✉ *1760 N.*

Vermont Ave., Los Feliz ☎*323/665–4294*) is still a popular hangout with old-timers and Gen X lounge lizards alike. Marty and Elayne (also seen in the film) are still burning up the joint with inimitable covers of "Staying Alive" and "Livin' La Vida Loca" (nightly, except Sunday, 9 PM–1:30 AM). No cover, but there's a two-drink minimum.

★ The **Echo** (✉*1822 Sunset Blvd., Echo Park* ☎*213/413–8200*) sprang from the people behind the Silver Lake rock joint Spaceland. Most evenings this dark and divey space's tiny dance floor and well-worn booths attract artsy local bands and their followers, but things rev up when DJs spin reggae, rock, and funk. Opened in the club's basement in 2007, **the Echoplex** (✉*1154 Glendale Blvd., Los Angeles*) books bigger national tours and events.

The red-lighted, Chinese-motif **Good Luck Bar** (✉*1514 Hillhurst Ave., Los Feliz* ☎*323/666–3524*) teems with young singles looking to meet someone, and the sexy vibe (helped along with soul tunes and strong spirits) means this place often lives up to its name.

5

★ It got its name thanks to its proximity to Dodger Stadium, but for decades the **Short Stop** (✉*1455 Sunset Blvd., Echo Park* ☎*213/482–4942*) was even better known for its regulars—the LAPD. Under new ownership for the past couple of years, the low-lighted three-room space still has cop memorabilia on the walls, but now it attracts artsy, fashionable locals. There's a great dance room with DJs spinning all sorts of sounds Thursday through Saturday.

It may be in an iffy part of town, but the **Smog Cutter** (✉*864 N. Virgil Ave., Silver Lake* ☎*323/667–9832*) still attracts a fun cross-section of local barflies and Hollywood hipsters. Come for its raucous karaoke nights and cheap drinks.

★ **Tiki Ti** (✉*4427 W. Sunset Blvd., Silver Lake* ☎*323/669–9381*) is one of the most charming drinking huts in the city. You can spend hours just looking at the Polynesian artifacts strewn all about the place, but be careful—time flies in this tiny tropical bar, and the colorful drinks can be so potent that you may have to stay marooned for a while.

COASTAL AND WESTERN LOS ANGELES, SANTA MONICA, AND VENICE

The retro charm of **the Brig** (✉*1515 Abbot Kinney Blvd., Venice* ☎*310/399–7537*) suits the beachy locals just fine, but with DJs spinning cool sounds and stylish drinks (including a tasty blood-orange martini), it has become a destination for commuting clubbers, too.

The **Chez Jay** (✉*1657 Ocean Ave., Santa Monica* ☎*310/395–1741*) saloon, near the Santa Monica Pier, has endured since 1959. With only 10 tables, checkered tablecloths, and sawdust on the floor, it's a shabby but charming setting for inventive seafood fare and regular celebrity sightings.

Circle Bar (✉*2926 Main St., Santa Monica* ☎*310/450–0508*) gets its name from the bar's circular-shaped interior, a setup that helps make it a see-and-be-seen beachside "it" spot. On weekends DJs spin electronic dance beats, hip-hop, and rock for casually dressed twentysomethings.

CLOSE UP

Glam vs. Grit

The scene and the view compete for attention at the Downtown L.A. Standard.

Media spin may make L.A.'s nightlife seem like a blur of glossy bars, hip clubs, power brokers, and poseurs, but the after-dark scene has as much diversity and creativity as frivolity. The city has a special knack for mixing extremes, though; you may run into celebs in a dingy pub or see a rocker in one of the poshest venues.

The heavily promoted swanky scene (where anyone willing to pay for bottle service, usually starting at about $200, is guaranteed a well-placed table and "somebody" status for a night) is thoroughly prowled by the tanned devotees of personal trainers. Places like these are in especially sharp contrast to the unpretentious dive bars, where smoky voices and well-worn glasses evoke Tom Waits rather than the latest starlet. Expect to pay a $15–$20 cover to get into high-end hot spots (add another $20–$50 if you want to bypass the line by tipping the doorman). The more casual hangouts, on the other hand, rarely charge more than $5. Drink prices are similarly varied, with posh clubs asking $10 and above for specialty drinks, and dive bars selling $2 beers and well drinks. But which places are the best in their respective fields? Let this tally of the top gritty dives and glitzy dens be your guide.

For glitz: the Standard (Downtown L.A. and Sunset Strip); Hyde; Area; LAX.

For grit: Burgundy Room; Short Stop; Echo; Smog Cutter; Mr. T's Bowl; the Smell; Silver Lake Lounge.

Thick with nautical mementos, the **Galley** (☒*2442 Main St., Santa Monica* ☎*310/452–1934*) is tiny but recommended for nostalgics who want to recapture Santa Monica circa 1940.

Carved wooden tribal masks and other Indian and Southeast Asian items make **Monsoon** (☒*1212 3rd St. Promenade, Santa Monica* ☎*310/576–9996*) one of the most elegant spots on the always-jumping Promenade. The restaurant serves South Asian cuisine, and there's live music (from so-so to pretty good) in the upstairs bar most nights.

Spacious **Otheroom** (☒*1201 Abbot Kinney Blvd., Venice* ☎*310/396–6230*) may be a recent harbinger of Abbot Kinney's gentrification, but it's still got that laid-back Venice vibe. In fact, it fits into this neighborhood well enough that you'd never guess the original's from Manhattan. There's an impressive selection of microbrews and wines.

MALIBU

If it's surfer boys or girls you're after, **Duke's Barefoot Bar** (☒*21150 Pacific Coast Hwy., Malibu* ☎*310/317–0777*) will be your new favorite hangout. The tiki-decorated oceanside drinking spot—named after famed surf god Duke Kahanamoku—is a casual place, with a patio right near the waves and an adjoining restaurant offering tasty finger foods.

Famous locals (Britney Spears, Mel Gibson) frequent the restaurant side of **Moonshadows** (☒*20356 Pacific Coast Hwy.* ☎*310/456–3010* 🌐*www.moonshadowsmalibu.com*) due to its location, but it's the adjoining Blue Lodge that steals the spotlight with nightly DJs spinning mostly atmospheric electronic grooves.

WEST LOS ANGELES

The Westside's contribution to cocktail culture, **Liquid Kitty** (☒*11780 W. Pico Blvd., West L.A.* ☎*310/473–3707*) is a swanky hangout with DJs (or live lounge jazz Sunday night) and no cover. You can't miss this place: just look for the neon martini glass on the outside.

HERMOSA BEACH

The **Lighthouse Cafe** (☒*30 Pier Ave., Hermosa Beach* ☎*310/376–9833*) has a full bar and free live music weeknights. Music starts at 9 (4 on Friday). A $5–$10 cover is charged on Friday and Saturday; weekend mornings jazz is on offer at 11.

The **Underground** (☒*1332 Hermosa Ave., Hermosa Beach* ☎*310/318–3818*) is a British pub and sports bar offering imported beers and alcohol-absorbing greasy food, plus darts, pool, and DJs spinning dance hits on the weekends.

DOWNTOWN

The look of **Bar 107**(☒*107 W. 4th St., Downtown* ☎*213/625–7382*) is best described as everything but the "kitsch"-en sink (religious art, taxidermy, chandeliers) and the clientele is equally mixed, which makes for a vivacious vibe whether the night's entertainment is deejays, live burlesque, or just the jukebox.

The 1940s-style **Broadway Bar** (☒*830 S. Broadway, Downtown* ☎*213/614–9909*) feels swanky but avoids velvet-rope syndrome. The two-level, chandeliered room is more Rat Pack than brat pack; it's got stiff drinks, a jukebox filled with rock and lounge, and a smoking balcony overlooking the boulevard.

Fodor's Choice ★ The **Downtown L.A. Standard** (✉ *550 S. Flower St., Downtown* ☎ *213/892–8080*) has a groovy lounge with pink sofas and DJs, as well as an all-white restaurant that looks like something out of *2001: A Space Odyssey.* But it's the rooftop bar, with an amazing view of the city's illuminated skyscrapers, a heated swimming pool, and private, podlike water-bed tents, that's worth waiting in line to get into. And wait you probably will, especially on weekends and in summer. Friday and Saturday $20 cover charge after 7 PM.

Edison (✉ *108 W. 2nd St., Downtown* ☎ *213/613–0000* 🌐 *www.edisondowntown.com*) is at the site of a former power plant and amazingly it manages to be classy and sophisticated while still retaining much of the original look. With waitresses in beaded frocks, deco touches, and jazzy sounds, the space is '20's glam meets industrial vamp. To maintain the ambience, there's even a dress code: no sneakers, jeans, or athletic wear.

The old-school vibe of the **Golden Gopher** (✉ *417 W. 8th St., Downtown* ☎ *213/614–8001*) is as much about the location as the venue. Don't be surprised if you're panhandled on your way inside this downtown spot, which manages simultaneously to be swanky (art deco columns, Victorian wallpaper), kitschy (golden gopher-shaped lamps, video games), and divey (there's a small liquor store inside the place for stocking up on your way home).

Redwood Bar (✉ *316 W. 2nd St., Downtown* ☎ *213/680–2600* 🌐 *www.theredwoodbar.com*) has been around since the '40's (JFK was rumored to hang there), but when new owners took over a couple of years ago and remodeled it with a nautical theme, it quickly became known as "the pirate bar" with the hipster set. Fare includes the obligatory fish-and-chips, and drinks are nice and arrrrrr hearty. DJs spin faves in the back room on weekends.

Seven Grand (✉ *515 W. 7th St., 2nd flr., Downtown* ☎ *213/614–0737* 🌐 *www.sevengrand.la*) has a hunting lodge feel with antlered stuffed heads peering down over leather couches and plaid carpets. It feels warm and friendly, especially after everyone's had a few glasses of the specialty here—there are more than 200 kinds of whiskey, many extremely rare. DJs spin everything from rock to country to jazz on various nights.

MID-WILSHIRE AREA

Another dark drinkin' hole where seasoned neighborhood guzzlers, Sex on the Beach–sipping barhoppers, and even a smattering of celebs peacefully coexist is **the Dime** (✉ *442 N. Fairfax Ave., Fairfax District* ☎ *323/651–4421*). This low-key option gets energetic on weekends—and when DJs take over the sound system with a mix of rock and chilled electro beats.

After-work business types frequent **HMS Bounty** (✉ *3357 Wilshire Blvd., Mid-Wilshire* ☎ *213/385–7275*), an elegant old watering hole in the historic Gaylord apartment building. Be sure to check out the brass plates above each booth—they bear the names of Hollywood heavies who once held court here. The reasonably priced drinks are impressive; so is the jukebox.

Molly Malone's (✉*575 S. Fairfax Ave., Fairfax District* ☎*323/935–1577*) is a small, casual pub where the only posturing is in the pro-Irish posters on the wall. The nightly live music tends to the Irish in flavor, but snappy blues and alternative-rock bands shake up the mix; the cover varies from $3 to $7.

EASTERN LOS ANGELES

The people from the Short Stop bar in Echo Park set up **Footsies** (✉*2640 N. Figueroa St., Cypress Park* ☎*323/221–6900*) way off the beaten path. At this cozy joint, hipsters who opted for more affordable housing on L.A.'s outskirts can get liquored up with like-minded artists and professionals. It has a great jukebox, but on weekends, the soundtrack is even more dynamic, as DJs man the decks.

Another bar in an up-and-coming neighborhood, **Chalet** (✉*1630 Colorado Blvd., Eagle Rock* ☎*323/258–8800*) has a woodsy, calm feel. Regulars get toasty by the '70s-style fireplace while sipping brandies. It's a great place for a date, although weekends are a tad too lively for romancing.

PASADENA

It's all about the beer at **Lucky Baldwin's** (✉*17 S. Raymond Ave., Pasadena* ☎*626/795–0652*), an Old Town hangout known for its robust brews and warm British pub atmosphere. Occasional live music, tasty food, and brew-related events add to the sudsy fun.

THE SAN FERNANDO VALLEY

Aura (✉*12215 Ventura Blvd., 2nd flr., Studio City* ☎*818/487–1488*) might be in the back of a minimall, but the club is actually one of the more chic Valley nightlife options, with a throbbing sound system and separate rooms for VIPs. DJs spin a mix of hip-hop and high-energy dance hits.

Melding Hollywood hip and neighborhood nonchalance, **Nobar** (✉*10622 Magnolia Blvd., North Hollywood* ☎*818/753–0545*) is a welcoming watering hole attracting regulars from nearby galleries and theaters.

BLUES

A half-dozen bars and eateries have live blues on weekend nights, in addition to the clubs below.

Babe & Ricky's Inn (✉*4339 Leimert Blvd., Leimert Park* ☎*323/295–9112*) is an old blues favorite. The great jukebox and photo-poster gallery and the barbecue and brew (or wine) will get you in the mood. It's closed Tuesday; covers vary from $4 to $10, and for Monday night's jam (featuring the inimitable Mickey Champion) admission will also get you a fried-chicken dinner, served at 10 PM.

Café Boogaloo (✉*1238 Hermosa Ave., near Pier Ave., Hermosa Beach* ☎*310/318–2324* 🌐*www.boogaloo.com*) has live blues on tap nearly every night, not to mention more than two-dozen microbrews. It's cozy down-to-earth, Louisiana-style restaurant and bar scene is especially popular O.C. locals. The cover ranges from free to $10.

A young crowd, many of them regulars, packs **Harvelle's** (✉*1432 4th St., Santa Monica* ☎*310/395–1676*) on the weekends; come early or be prepared to stand in line. Watch from the back if you want, but down front, you'll be dancing. The cover's $3 weekdays, $5–$10 on weekends; a two-drink minimum is sometimes enforced.

CABARET AND VARIETY

L.A. may be a film-, television-, and music-industry mecca, but under the surface, other more experimental forms of entertainment continue to burgeon and gain attention, most notably a local burlesque revival. Troupes such as the Pussycat Dolls (now a bona fide pop music group and TV show) and the edgier Lucha Va Voom (featuring tattooed rock chicks and gals of all shapes and sizes performing alongside Mexican wrestling matches) regularly take over local theaters and nightclubs. Cabaret crooners aren't limited to loungey locales; many can be found at rock venues and bars on designated evenings.

Beyond Baroque (✉*681 Venice Blvd., Venice* ☎*310/822–3006* 🌐*www.beyondbaroque.org*), in the old Venice Town Hall, is a performance space and bookstore dedicated to the literary arts, with popular poetry and literature readings that have included the likes of Viggo Mortensen and offbeat offerings like a night of "Crap Poetry."

★ With seating for 120, **Highways Performance Space** (✉*1651 18th St., Santa Monica* ☎*310/453–1755 or 310/315–1459*) is one of the primary venues for avant-garde, offbeat, and alternative performance art as well as theater, dance, and comedy programs. It also has two art galleries.

COFFEEHOUSES

★ One of the best reasons to venture off the beaten path is **Sacred Grounds** (✉*464 W. 6th St., San Pedro* ☎*310/514–0800*), a classic beatnik coffeehouse. There's coffee, tea, bagels, pastries, art on the walls, comfortable couches, and music almost every night (poetry on Monday). It opens at 6 AM daily and stays open until the shows are over (midnight weekdays, a little later on weekends). Covers range from free to $5.

A good place to take a break from the nonstop fun you've been having in L.A. and write about it in your journal is the **Un-urban Coffee House** (✉*3301 Pico Blvd., at Urban Ave., Santa Monica* ☎*310/315–0056*). Enjoy a stiff cup of coffee or some luscious chai tea, scarf down the good but inexpensive breakfast or a sandwich, and hear the music or spoken-word performances on Sunday during the day or on weekend evenings. Open mike nights every Friday.

COMEDY AND MAGIC

Note that in addition to the clubs below, a number of nightspots not specializing in comedy have a hot comedy night every week, and there are some comedy events at a passel of places best rounded up in the listings at 🌐*www.LA.com*.

The **Acme Comedy Theater** (✉*135 N. La Brea, Hollywood* ☎*323/525-0202*) is really what its name suggests, the height of zaniness—mainly improv, sketch comedy, or both in the same production. The fare is consistently nutty, including an improvised game show and an improvised '40s-style radio drama.

★ A nightly premiere comedy showcase, **Comedy Store** (✉*8433 Sunset Blvd., West Hollywood* ☎*323/656-6225*) has been going strong for more than two decades, with three stages (with covers ranging from free to $20) to supply the yuks. Famous comedians occasionally make unannounced appearances.

★ More than a quarter century old, **Groundling Theatre** (✉*7307 Melrose Ave., Hollywood* ☎*323/934-9700*) has been a breeding ground for *Saturday Night Live* performers; alumni include Lisa Kudrow and *Curb Your Enthusiasm*'s Cheryl Hines. The primarily sketch and improv comedy shows run Thursday–Sunday, costing $12–$18.50.

Since 1960, **Ice House Comedy Club and Restaurant** (✉*24 N. Mentor Ave., Pasadena* ☎*626/577-1894*) has featured comedians, celebrity impressionists, ventriloquists, and magicians from Las Vegas as well as from TV. Shows take place nightly; reservations are strongly advised on weekends. Covers vary; there's a two-drink minimum.

Richard Pryor got his start at the **Improv** (✉*8162 Melrose Ave., West Hollywood* ☎*323/651-2583*), a renowned establishment showcasing stand-up comedy. Drew Carey's *Totally Improv* is Thursday night on a semiregular basis. Reservations are recommended. Cover is $10–$15, and there's a two-drink minimum.

Improv Olympic West (✉*6366 Hollywood Blvd., Hollywood* ☎*323/962-7560* 🌐*www.iowest.com*) showcases thematic improv and revues among its nightly shows, with covers from free to $10. It's known for Second City comedy troupe's long-form improv called "the Harold."

Fodor's Choice ★ Look for top stand-ups—and frequent celeb residents, like Bob Saget, or unannounced drop-ins, like Chris Rock—at **Laugh Factory** (✉*8001 Sunset Blvd., West Hollywood* ☎*323/656-1336*). The club has shows nightly at 8 PM, plus added shows at 10 and midnight on Friday and Saturday; the cover is $10–$12.

It may be in a low-rent strip mall, but **M-Bar** (✉*1253 N. Vine St., Hollywood* ☎*323/856-0036*) attracts some big names from the comedy world on a regular basis. Actor David Cross and his sitcom pals make appearances here often.

New York's **Upright Citizens Brigade** (✉*5919 Franklin Ave., Hollywood* ☎*323/908-8702*) marched in with a mix of sketch comedy and wild improvisations skewering pop culture. Members of the L.A. Brigade include VH1 commentator Paul Scheer and *Mad TV*'s Andrew Daly.

COUNTRY MUSIC

Boulevard Music (✉*4316 Sepulveda Blvd., Culver City* ☎*310/398-2583*) is, like McCabe's, primarily a musical instruments store, but most weekend nights it hosts live music. Although the music may be of any genre, it's more countrified than anything else. The cover varies from $12 to $20. No booze is served; all ages are okay.

Rustling up fun since the '70s, **Cowboy Palace Saloon** (✉*21635 Devonshire Blvd., Chatsworth* ☎*818/341–0166*) might just be L.A.'s last honky-tonk; if you want to tie up your horse, you can use the hitching post out back. Dance lessons, including the "electric slide," the two-step and many other country styles nightly and music (around 9) are free of charge. There's a weakly enforced two-drink minimum; on Sunday there's a complimentary barbecue.

Viva Cantina (✉*900 Riverside Dr., Burbank* ☎*818/845–2425*) is mainly a family-oriented Mexican restaurant, but the large, ranch-style bar area is more for grown-ups. That's where the country music happens every night, from the best of the locals to the occasional legendary old-timer like Red Simpson. Music starts at 7:30, and there's no cover.

DANCE CLUBS

Though the establishments listed below are predominantly dance clubs as opposed to live music venues, there's often some overlap. A given club can vary wildly in genre from night to night, or even on the same night. ■ TIP→ **Gay and promoter-driven theme nights tend to "float" from venue to venue. Call ahead to make sure you don't end up looking for retro '60s music at an industrial bondage celebration (or vice versa).** Covers vary according to the night and the DJs.

Area (✉*643 N. La Cienaga Blvd., West Hollywood* ☎*310/652–2012*), formerly Prey, owned by nightlife impresarios Sam Nazarian and Brent Bolthouse, is popular with the model, actor, and model-actor crowds. The feel here is light and bright, all the better for ogling the tabloid tarts who frequent the place.

★ As a bar, **Boardner's** (✉*1652 N. Cherokee Ave., Hollywood* ☎*323/462–9621*) has a multidecade history (in the '20s it was a speakeasy), but with the adjoining ballroom, which was added a couple of years ago, it's now a state-of-the-art dance club. DJs may be spinning electronica, funk, or something else depending on the night—at the popular Saturday Goth event "Bar Sinister," patrons must wear black or risk not getting in. The cover here is anywhere from free to $10.

Ivar (✉*6356 Hollywood Blvd., Hollywood* ☎*323/465–4827*) has been attracting the model-actor "discover me" set with weekly hip-hop, electronic, and Top-40. It has two levels and lots of rooms to wander, including an outdoor patio and five bars.

Fais Do-Do (✉*5257 W. Adams Blvd., West L.A.* ☎*323/931–4636*) is all about rotating theme nights—roots-rock, reggae, hip-hop, and blues have all had their times. The sounds primarily come from DJs; there's a liberal sprinkling of bands, but they're not the main draw. The Cajun-California cuisine (paired with beer or wine; no hard drinks) doesn't hurt either. The cover is $3–$15.

The 18-and-over set crowds into **Florentine Gardens** (✉*5951 Hollywood Blvd., Hollywood* ☎*323/464–0706*) on weekends. DJs from local radio stations often take over the turntables, and the crowd is usually made up of kids who drive in from Hollywood's outskirts.

La Cita (✉*336 S. Hill St., Downtown* ☎*213/687–7111*) is scruffy in more ways than one—Thursday and Friday nights, this red-hue Mexican dive comes alive with hipsters working the American Apparel–patented, disheveled-casual look on its tiny dance floor. Sounds range from ironic '80s dance hits to electro to punk and reggae.

The wait outside **LAX** (✉*1714 Las Palmas Ave., Hollywood* ☎*323/464–0171*) can often be as bad as the baggage check-in lines at its namesake. Revered mash-up man DJ AM mans the decks most nights pumping out everything from Journey to Kanye West.

★ The **Ruby** (✉*7070 Hollywood Blvd., Hollywood* ☎*323/467–7070*) is a popular three-room dance venue for young indie-rock and retro-loving twentysomethings. You might find anything from doomy Goth and industrial ("Perversion") to '80s retro ("Beat It") to '60s–'70s Brit pop and soul ("Bang") to trance and techno. Cover charges are $8–$12.

Ritual (✉*1743 N. Cahuenga Blvd., Hollywood* ☎*323/463–0060*) is a restaurant and nightclub attracting scantily clad, sake-sipping cuties and the fellas who chase them. Its red-swathed and gilded look and breezy outdoor patio makes it a fun place to eat (Pacific Rim dishes are the specialty) and party. Various promoters come in during the week, bringing with them DJs spinning hit mixes.

Formerly XES, and now called **Sugar** (✉*1716 N. Cahuenga Blvd., Hollywood* ☎*323/836–0854*), this Hollywood space has gone for a less vampy but no less vivacious vibe since its remodel. Sleek decor, a descent sized dance floor with DJs spinning rock and hip-hop make it a sweet Saturday night destination.

Funk and hip-hop rule at the DJ-driven **Zanzibar** (✉*1301 5th St., Santa Monica* ☎*310/451–2221*), a warm and inviting spot from the people behind now-closed Temple Bar. Sounds ranging from Latin jazz to soul to deep house attract a mix of locals and commuting Hollywood clubsters.

GETTING BEHIND THE VELVET ROPES

Foxy females, fat-walleted businessmen, and tabloid-familiar faces have no problem getting in anywhere. But there's hope for the rest of us, too. Here's how:

- Try popping in early (beating out the fashionably late).
- Go on a weeknight.
- Bring along your most attractive friends.
- Tip the doorman/security guard (at the real swanky nightspots, expect to drop at least $50).
- Be very, very patient. Persistance does pay off.

5

GAY AND LESBIAN CLUBS

Some of the most popular gay and lesbian "clubs" are weekly theme nights at various venues, so read the preceding list of clubs, *LA Weekly* listings, and gay publications such as *Odyssey* in addition to the following recommendations.

CLOSE UP

Spin Doctors

Anyone with a vinyl collection (or these days, a laptop or iPod) can call themselves a DJ, and in slash-happy L.A. (as in model-"slash"-actress) many try to be (as in model-slash-actress-slash-DJ). Lindsay Lohan, Tommy Lee, and Rosanna Arquette are just a few of the celebs who've taken turns behind the wheels of steel at Hollywood clubs, but it's the real turntable wizards who make the dance floor shake in this town. Here, some of L.A.'s best and where to find them.

DJ AM at LAX (Sunday) – Famous for more than being Nicole Richie's ex, this master music masher seamlessly mixes the likes of AC/DC, Hall & Oates, and Kanye West, a disparate combo that makes music fans of all ilks get jiggy.

DJs Them Jeans and Steve Aoki from Dim Mak Records At Cinespace (Tuesday) play all the latest indie rock, but they aren't too cool to throw in commerical hip-hop and old-school gems from the likes of MC Hammer and even (gasp!) Vanilla Ice. Hipster kids eat it up.

DJ Morty at Dragonfly (Sunday) – He's been spinning his web of hip-hop and retro rock in L.A. for decades, and his specialty is the decadent sounds of the '80s. His, like, totally awesome retro mixes really burned up the floor after sharing the stage with the new wave cover band Spazzmatics.

An ethnically mixed gay and straight crowd flocks to **Circus Disco and Arena** (☒*6655 Santa Monica Blvd., Hollywood* ☎*323/462–1291 or 323/462–0714*), two huge, side-by-side discos with techno and rock music, as well as a full bar and patio, open Tuesday, Thursday, and Friday 9–2. Only certain nights are gay-themed. Top local and international DJs spin funk, house, trance, disco, and more until 4 AM on Saturday for a straight crowd. The cover can range from $3 to $20.

The **Factory** (☒*652 La Peer Dr., West Hollywood* ☎*310/659–4551*) churns out dance music for those who like to grind. In the adjoining **Ultra Suede** (☒*661 N. Robertson Blvd., West Hollywood*), there's '80s–'90s pop on Wednesday and Friday. Saturday, the two houses combine for an event called "The Factory." Covers range from $5 to $15.

★ Nowhere is more gregarious than **Here** (☒*696 N. Robertson Blvd., West Hollywood* ☎*310/360–8455*), where there are hot DJs and an even hotter clientele. Though it's usually a boys' hangout, you'll find WeHo's wildest ladies' night at Tuesday's Panty Raid gathering.

Jewel's Catch One (☒*4067 W. Pico Blvd., Mid-City* ☎*323/734–8849*) is a lively hangout for just about anyone, with male and female dancers and lip-synching shows, karaoke, and DJs spinning hip-hop and disco.

The gay bar **MJ's** (☒*2810 Hyperion Ave., Silver Lake* ☎*323/660–1503*) is laid-back enough to attract locals of every persuasion. DJs spin an array of diva disco, electro, and mash-ups.

A long-running gay-gal fave, the **Palms** (☒*8572 Santa Monica Blvd., West Hollywood* ☎*310/652–6188*) continues to thrive thanks to great

DJs spinning dance tunes Wednesday–Sunday. There are also an outdoor patio, pool tables, and an occasional live performance.

Rage (☒*8911 Santa Monica Blvd., West Hollywood* ☎*310/652–7055*) is a longtime favorite of the "gym boy" set, with DJs following a different musical theme every night of the week (alternative rock, house, dance remixes, etc.). The cover is free to $10.

JAZZ

Powerhouse jazz and blues please crowds at the tiny **Baked Potato** (☒*3787 Cahuenga Blvd. W, North Hollywood* ☎*818/980–1615*). The star of the menu is, of course, the baked potato, jumbo and stuffed with everything from steak to vegetables. The music's on every night, with a $10–$20 cover.

After moving to a bigger space in 2005, **Catalina** (☒*6725 W. Sunset Blvd., Hollywood* ☎*323/466–2210*) is hotter than ever, with top-notch jazz bookings ranging from classic Chicago style to Latin-flavored.

Charlie O's Bar & Grill (☒*13725 Victory Blvd., Van Nuys* ☎*818/994–3058*) has some pretty nifty local jazzers playing nightly, plus steak, chops, and ribs on the bill of fare; and there's no cover most nights except Monday $20.

A tasty array of comfort food complements the nightly happy hour and later evening jazz shows at **Jax** (☒*339 N. Brand Blvd., Glendale* ☎*818/500–1604*), as does the cozy, Tiffany-lamped interior. Bookings range from piano-bar ticklers to slightly more boisterous horn blowers. There's no cover or minimum.

Come to **Jazz Bakery** (☒*3233 Helms Ave., Culver City* ☎*310/271–9039*) for world-class jazz nightly at 8 and 9:30, in a quiet, respectful concert-like setting. The cover is $10–$25; parking is free.

You can't eat or drink—but you can see great jazz—at the no-frills **World Stage** (☒*4344 Degnan Blvd., Leimert Park* ☎*323/293–2451*). It's the brainchild of storied drummer Billy Higgins, and some of his big-name friends are known to stop by. The schedule of workshops, jam sessions, and concerts—many featuring young aspiring musicians—changes frequently; so call ahead.

LATIN

There's no ideal label for it, but this section includes venues for samba as well as salsa, rumba, rock *en español,* and even flamenco. A number of other venues offer such music one or more nights a week and information on them can be found in papers like the *LA Weekly,* but it's always wise to call and check.

Fodor's Choice ★ The Cuban food at **El Floridita** (☒*1253 N. Vine St., Hollywood* ☎*323/871–0936*) is anywhere from good to great—and the music (Monday, Friday, and Saturday) is anywhere from very good to through the roof. A frequent guest is the salsa bandleader Johnny Polanco, backed by the sizzling Conjunto Amistad. Watching some of the paying customers who get up to dance alone is worth the price of admission (usually $10, or free with dinner).

L.A.'s top Latin bands all make their way to **Mama Juanas** (☒*3707 Cahuenga Blvd., Studio City* ☎*818/505–8636*), a colorful restaurant and live music venue with salsa, Afro-Cuban grooves, and an all-female group (the Mariachi Divas) on various nights. You can enjoy a spicy meal and follow it up with some spicier moves on its large dance floor.

ROCK AND OTHER LIVE MUSIC

In addition to the venues listed below, many smaller bars book live music, if less frequently or with less publicity.

The landmark formerly known as the Palace is now the **Avalon** (☒*1735 N. Vine St., Hollywood* ☎*323/462–3000*). The multilevel art deco building opposite Capitol Records has a fabulous sound system, four bars, and a balcony. Big-name rock and pop concerts hit the stage during the week, but on weekends the place becomes a dance club, with the most popular night the DJ-dominated Avaland on Saturday. Upstairs, but with a separate entrance, you'll find celeb hub the **Spider Club,** a Moroccan-style room where celebs and their entourages are frequent visitors.

For the sake of pithiness, the **California Institute for Abnormal Arts** (☒*11334 Burbank Ave., North Hollywood* ☎*818/506–6353* ⊕*www.ciabnormalarts.com*) abbreviates its name to CIA. Its nuttiness (bands and multimedia events) is let loose Thursday–Saturday. It's been said that on "weekends it's a giant magnet for every loose screw in town." No alcohol is served.

Slim Jim Phantom, former drummer of the Stray Cats, is the man behind the **Cat Club** (☒*8911 Sunset Blvd., West Hollywood* ☎*310/657–0888*). Bands play nightly, and Mr. Phantom sometimes comes out to play with buds like ex–Guns N' Roses axman Gilby Clarke. There are an upstairs and a back patio, but it's still, to euphemize, "intimate." Covers range from free to $8.

Dark and grungy, **Dragonfly** (☒*6510 Santa Monica Blvd., Hollywood* ☎*323/466–6111*) showcases a mix of live rock and rock hybrids seven nights a week. After the bands on Friday and Saturday, it morphs into a dance club. On Thursday, it's reggae all night. When you need to cool off, there's an outdoor patio with bar. Cover is $5–$15.

About 8 or 10 times a month, the gloriously restored art deco **El Rey Theater** (☒*5515 Wilshire Blvd., Mid-Wilshire* ☎*323/936–6400*) showcases concerts, often by top-name bands on national tours, as well as an assortment of theme nights. Covers are $10–$30.

At the longtime music-industry hangout known as **Genghis Cohen Cantina** (☒*740 N. Fairfax Ave., Hollywood* ☎*323/653–0640*), you can hear hopefuls and veteran performers of the singer-songwriter sort and sample the kosher Chinese cuisine at the same time.

The **House of Blues** (☒*8430 Sunset Blvd., West Hollywood* ☎*323/848–5100*) is a club that functions like a concert venue, hosting popular jazz, rock, and blues performers such as Etta James, Lou Rawls, Joe Cocker, Cheap Trick, Pete Townshend, and the Commodores. ■**TIP→Avoid**

industry idiots who prefer talking to listening by skipping the tables and bar areas for the central open floor. Occasional shows are presented cabaret style and include dinner in the restaurant area upstairs; you can *sort of* see from some of it. Every Sunday there's a gospel brunch.

Every night the **Joint** (☒*8771 W. Pico Blvd., West L.A.* ☎*310/275–2619*) puts on live music from mostly local, mostly so-so rockers. The real reason to come is its "Big Monday" jam with guitar hero Waddy Wachtel and stellar—and we do mean stellar—guest drop-ins. Surprise jammers have included Roger Daltrey, George Clinton, and Keith Richards.

The **Key Club** (☒*9039 Sunset Blvd., West Hollywood* ☎*310/274–5800*) is a flashy, multitier rock club with four bars presenting current artists of all genres (some on national tours, others local aspirants). After the concerts, there's often dancing with DJs spinning techno and house.

Everything from Latin rhythms to electronic music to raging punk sounds can found at the roomy **King King** (☒*6555 Hollywood Blvd., Hollywood* ☎*323/960–9234*). Good acoustics, even better crowd. The entrance from the parking-lot side of the building helps you avoid slack-jawed tourists on the Walk of Fame.

★ The **Knitting Factory** (☒*7021 Hollywood Blvd., Hollywood* ☎*323/463–0204*) is the L.A. offshoot of the Downtown New York club of the same name. The modern, medium-size room seems all the more spacious for its balcony-level seating and sizable stage. Despite its dubious location on Hollywood Boulevard's tourist strip, it's a great set-up for the arty, big-name performers it presents. There's live music almost every night in the main room and in the smaller Alter-Knit Lounge. Covers are free to $40.

Musician-producer Jon Brion (Fiona Apple, Aimee Mann, and others) shows off his ability to play virtually any instrument and any song in the rock lexicon—and beyond—as host of a popular evening of music every Friday at **Largo** (☒ *366 N. La Cienega Blvd., Hollywood* ☎*310/855–0350*). Other nights, low-key rock and singer-songwriter fare is offered at this cozy supper club–bar. And when comedy comes in, about one night a week, it's usually one of the best comedy nights in town, with folks like Margaret Cho. Reservations are required for tables, but bar stools are open.

The funky people behind Santa Monica's Zanzibar and now-closed Temple Bar moved east for their warm, more intimate spot, **Little Temple** (☒*4519 Santa Monica Blvd., Santa Monica* ☎*310/393–6611*). The DJs and live acts focus on soul, Latin, and reggae music.

McCabe's Guitar Shop (☒*3101 Pico Blvd., Santa Monica* ☎*310/828–4497, 310/828–4403 for concert information*) is rootsy-retro-central, where all things earnest and (preferably) acoustic are welcome—chiefly folk, blues, bluegrass, and rock. It *is* a guitar shop (so no liquor license), with a room full of folding chairs for concert-style presentations. Shows on weekends only. Make reservations well in advance.

Enter **Mr. T's Bowl** (☒*5261½ N. Figueroa Ave., Highland Park* ☎*323/256–7561*) through the rear parking lot. It used to be a bowling alley; now, five or six nights a week (but not Monday) it offers some of

L.A.'s weirdest—and most fun—rockers. (Beck played here during his folky phase.) There's a full bar, the cover is usually $3–$5, and food is available.

The **Roxy** (✉ *9009 Sunset Blvd., West Hollywood* ☎ *310/276–2222*), a Sunset Strip fixture for decades, hosts local and touring rock, alternative, blues, and rockabilly bands. Not the comfiest club around, but it's the site of many memorable shows.

When you're not gawking at the many vintage surfboards on the walls and ceiling of **Rusty's Surf Ranch** (✉ *256 Santa Monica Pier, Santa Monica* ☎ *310/393–7386*), you can watch rock-and-roll bands, singer-songwriters, or blues boppers.

Neighborhoody and relaxed, **Silver Lake Lounge** (✉ *2906 Sunset Blvd., Silver Lake* ☎ *323/666–2407*) draws a mixed collegiate and boho crowd. The club is very unmainstream "cool," the booking policy an adventurous mix of local and touring alt-rockers. Bands play three to five nights a week; covers vary but are low.

The **Smell** (✉ *247 S. Main St., Downtown* ☎ *No phone*) may have bands only two or three nights a week (Wednesday, Friday, or Saturday), but they're often choice—in the alternative fringe world, anyway. If they're not playing at the Knitting Factory, Spaceland, or the Silver Lake Lounge, they just might be at the Smell. There's no liquor, the cover's usually $5, and there's also an art gallery. Enter via the back alley.

★ The hottest bands of tomorrow, surprises from yesteryear, and unclassifiable bands of today perform at **Spaceland** (✉ *1717 Silver Lake Blvd., Silver Lake* ☎ *323/661–4380* 🌐 *www.clubspaceland.com*), which has a bar, jukebox, and pool table. Monday is always free, with monthlong gigs by the indie fave du jour. Spaceland has a nice selection of beers and a hip but relaxed interior.

The **Troubadour** (✉ *9081 Santa Monica Blvd., West Hollywood* ☎ *310/276–6168*), one of the best and most comfortable clubs in town, has weathered the test of time since its '60s debut as a folk club. After surviving the '80s heavy-metal scene, this all-ages, wood-panel venue has caught a second (third? fourth?) wind by booking hot alternative rock acts. There's valet parking, but if you don't mind walking up Doheny a block or three, there's usually ample street parking (check the signs carefully).

Actor Johnny Depp sold his share of the infamous **Viper Room** (✉ *8852 Sunset Blvd., West Hollywood* ☎ *310/358–1880*) in 2004, but the place continues to rock with a motley live music lineup (Monday, local radio station Indie 103.1 presents new rock), if a less stellar crowd.

Whisky-A-Go-Go (✉ *8901 Sunset Blvd., West Hollywood* ☎ *310/652–4202*) is the most famous rock-and-roll club on the Strip, where back in the '60s, Johnny Rivers cut hit singles and the Doors, Love, and the Byrds cut their musical eyeteeth. It's still going strong, with up-and-coming alternative, hard rock, and punk bands, though mostly of the unknown variety.

Sports and the Outdoors

WORD OF MOUTH

"A 'must do' would be to rent a bicycle and ride on the Strand as far as your legs can take you. If you start in Manhattan Beach, you can go south, through Hermosa and Redondo. If you head north, you can get all the way to Venice."

—lvk

www.fodors.com/community

Updated by Kastle Waserman

SURFERS AND BODYBUILDERS AT THE BEACH, Jack Nicholson courtside at the Staples Center cheering on the Lakers, blissed-out yoga practitioners, sweat-suited power-walkers pacing through Beverly Hills—these images have established L.A. as a sports-focused city in the public imagination. But all these scenarios are just the tip of the iceberg; from rock climbing to whale-watching, L.A. has an enviable scope of activities. Given the right weather conditions, it's possible to choose between skiing and a trip to the beach. Some days begin overcast but become, after the clouds' late-morning "burn-off," simply glorious. ■ TIP→ **A word to the wise: the air is dry, so bottled water and lip balm can prove invaluable. Also, don't forget sunscreen; even on overcast days the sunburn index can be high.** Check the *Los Angeles Times*' weather page or local AM radio news stations like KFWB 980 and KNX 1070.

BEACHES

L.A.'s beaches are an iconic and integral part of the Southern California lifestyle; getting some sand on the floor of your car is practically a requirement. From downtown, the easiest way to hit the coast is by taking the Santa Monica Freeway (I–10) due west. Once you reach the end of the freeway, I–10 runs into the famous Highway 1. Better known as the Pacific Coast Highway, or PCH, Highway 1 continues north to Sonoma County and south to San Diego. MTA buses run from downtown along Pico, Olympic, Santa Monica, Sunset, and Wilshire boulevards westward to the coast.

Los Angeles County beaches (and state beaches operated by the county) have lifeguards on duty year-round, with expanded forces during the summer. Public parking is usually available, though fees can be as much as $8; in some areas, it's possible to find free street and highway parking. Both restrooms and beach access have been brought up to the standards of the Americans with Disabilities Act. Generally, the northernmost beaches are best for surfing, hiking, and fishing, and the wider and sandier southern beaches are better for tanning and relaxing. ■ TIP→ **Almost all are great for swimming, but beware: pollution in Santa Monica Bay sometimes approaches dangerous levels, particularly after storms.** Call ahead for **beach conditions** (☎ *310/457–9701*) or go to 🌐 *www.watchthewater.com* for specific beach updates. To find beach and park **campsites** and make reservations, try 🌐 *www.reserveamerica.com*, 🌐 *www.recreation.gov*, 🌐 *www.parks.ca.gov*, or 🌐 *beaches.lacounty.gov*. The following beaches are listed in north–south order:

Leo Carrillo State Beach. On the very edge of Ventura County, this narrow beach is better for exploring than for sunning or swimming (watch that strong undertow!). On your own or with a ranger, venture down at low tide to examine the tide pools among the rocks. Sequit Point, a promontory dividing the northwest and southeast halves of the beach, creates secret coves, sea tunnels, and boulders on which you can perch and fish. Generally, anglers stick to the northwest end of the beach; experienced surfers brave the rocks to the southeast. Campgrounds are set back from the beach; call ahead to reserve campsites. ✉ *35000 PCH, Malibu* ☎ *818/880–0350, 800/444–7275 for camping reservations*

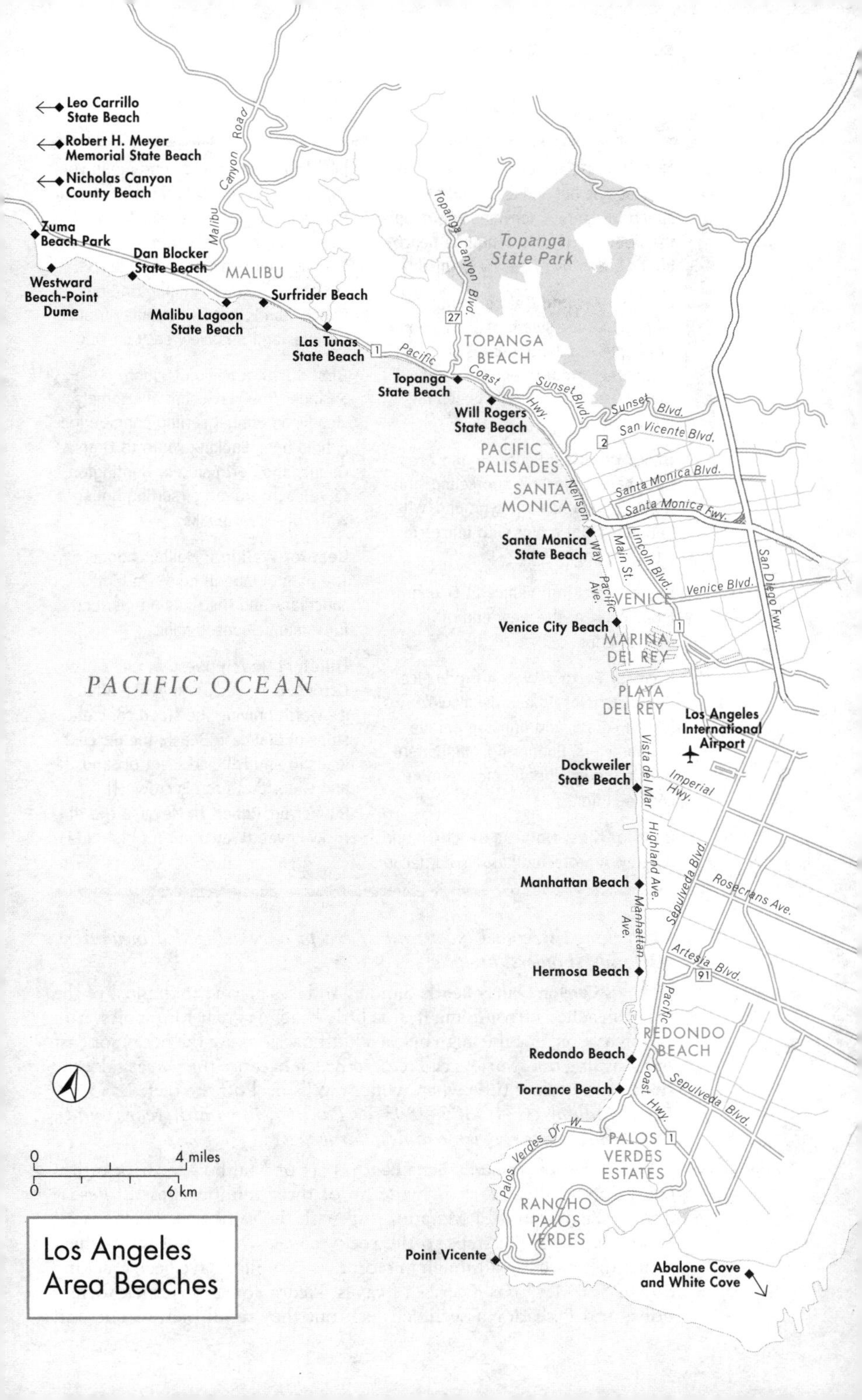

Leo Carrillo State Beach
Robert H. Meyer Memorial State Beach
Nicholas Canyon County Beach
Zuma Beach Park
Westward Beach-Point Dume
Dan Blocker State Beach
Malibu Canyon Road
MALIBU
Malibu Lagoon State Beach
Surfrider Beach
Las Tunas State Beach
Topanga Canyon Blvd.
27
Topanga State Park
TOPANGA BEACH
1
Pacific Coast Hwy.
Topanga State Beach
Will Rogers State Beach
Sunset Blvd.
San Vicente Blvd.
2
PACIFIC PALISADES
SANTA MONICA
Santa Monica Blvd.
Santa Monica Fwy.
Nelson Way
Santa Monica State Beach
Main St.
Lincoln Blvd.
San Diego Fwy.
Pacific Ave.
Venice Blvd.
VENICE
Venice City Beach
MARINA DEL REY
PACIFIC OCEAN
PLAYA DEL REY
Los Angeles International Airport
Vista del Mar
Dockweiler State Beach
Imperial Hwy.
Highland Ave.
Sepulveda Blvd.
Manhattan Beach
Rosecrans Ave.
Manhattan Ave.
Artesia Blvd.
91
Hermosa Beach
Pacific Coast Hwy.
REDONDO BEACH
Redondo Beach
Torrance Beach
Sepulveda Blvd.
Palos Verdes Dr. W.
PALOS VERDES ESTATES
0
4 miles
0
6 km
RANCHO PALOS VERDES
Point Vicente
Abalone Cove and White Cove
Los Angeles Area Beaches

CLOSE UP

L.A.'s Best Beaches

Most Los Angeles beaches are pretty spectacular, but some are better suited for certain activities and people than others. Here's a longtime beach-goer's breakdown, quality by quality.

Best All-Around Beach: Santa Monica. A wide swath of sand, plenty of people-watching, good swimming, great views from the bluffs—other than its surfing (nil), this beach hits the key marks.

Best Activities: Redondo and Zuma. Both have volleyball, snorkeling, and fishing. Zuma has a playground, while Redondo's got a pier with places to eat and shop.

Easiest Parking: Venice at Ocean Front Walk, at the west end of Rose Avenue.

Best for People-Watching: Venice City Beach, for its boardwalk, volleyball courts, and nonstop parade of characters. Runner-up: Manhattan Beach, though the people are more cookie-cutter.

Best for Kids: Mother's Beach/Marina del Rey. A protected lagoon, barbecue pits, and a cool playground mean you can easily make a full day of it. If your kids want to go in the water, though, you should check the water conditions first, as pollution's been on the rise. In Orange County, Huntington State Beach stands out for its family-friendly facilities and relatively easy parking.

Best Surfing: Malibu Lagoon/ Surfrider. The waves are awesomely steady; an annual surfing competition is held here. Looking south to Orange County, the north side of Huntington City Beach is another surfing hot spot with consistent peaks.

Best for Walking: Malibu Lagoon. The natural lagoon here is a bird sanctuary, and the trails are perfect for romantic sunset walks.

Quietest Beach: Western end of Leo Carrillo. If it's seclusion you're after, it's worth braving the steep concrete steps of Staircase Beach; the descent leads to an idyllic crescent of sand and water that's rarely crowded. Runner-up: Robert H. Meyer, a trio of rocky coves. (Watch out for high tide.)

☞ *Parking, lifeguard (year-round, except only as needed in winter), restroom, showers, fire pits.*

Nicholas Canyon County Beach. Sandier and less private than most of the rocky beaches surrounding it, this little beach is great for picnics. You can sit at a picnic table high up on a bluff overlooking the ocean, or cast out a fishing line. Surfers call it Zero Beach because the waves take the shape of a hollow tube when winter swells peel off the reef. ✉ *33904 PCH, Malibu* ☎ *310/305–9503* ☞ *Parking, lifeguard (year-round), restrooms, showers, picnic tables, barbecues.*

Fodor's Choice ★ **Robert H. Meyer Memorial State Beach.** Part of Malibu's most beautiful coastal area, this beach is made up of three minibeaches: El Pescador, La Piedra, and El Matador—all with the same spectacular view. Scramble down the steps to the rocky coves where nude sunbathers sometimes gather—although in recent years, police have been cracking down. "El Mat" has a series of caves, Piedra some nifty rock formations, and Pescador a secluded feel; but they're all picturesque and fairly private. ■ TIP→ **One warning: watch the incoming tide and don't get trapped between those otherwise scenic boulders.** ✉ *32350, 32700, and 32900 PCH, Malibu* ☎ *818/880–0350* ☞ *Parking, 1 roving lifeguard unit, restrooms.*

Zuma Beach Park. Zuma, 2 mi of white sand usually littered with tanning teenagers, has it all: from fishing and diving to swings for the kids to volleyball courts. Beachgoers looking for quiet or privacy should head elsewhere. Stay alert in the water: the surf is rough and inconsistent. ✉ *30050 PCH, Malibu* ☎ *818/880–0350* ☞ *Parking, lifeguard (year-round, except only as needed in winter), restrooms, food concessions, playground.*

TOP 5

- **Angeles National Forest's Gabrielino Trail,** where you can hike along the arroyo seco.
- **Dodger Stadium** for a baseball game.
- **Huntington Library, Art Collections, and Botanical Gardens,** especially the cactus garden with its giant aloes.
- **South Bay Bicycle Trail,** biking and people-watching nonstop.
- **Zuma Beach, Malibu,** for sun, sand, and seafood.

6

Westward Beach–Point Dume. Go tide-pooling, fishing, snorkeling, or bird-watching (prime time is late winter–early spring). Hike to the top of the sandstone cliffs to whale-watch—their migrations can be seen between December and April. Westward is a favorite surfing beach, but the steep surf isn't for novices. ■ TIP→ **Bring your own food, since the nearest concession is a longish hike away.** ✉ *7200 Westward Beach Rd., Malibu* ☎ *310/305–9503* ☞ *Parking, lifeguard (year-round, except only as needed in winter), restrooms, showers.*

Dan Blocker State Beach. Originally owned jointly by the stars of the *Bonanza* TV series, this little stretch of beach was donated to the state after Blocker (who played Hoss) died in 1972. Locals still know this as Corral Beach. Its narrow stretch of fine sand and rocks make it great for walking, light swimming, kayaking, and scuba diving. Because of the limited parking available along PCH, it's rarely crowded. ✉ *25560 PCH, at Corral Canyon Rd., Malibu* ☎ *310/305–9503* ☞ *Parking, lifeguard (year-round, except only as needed in winter), restrooms.*

Malibu Lagoon State Beach/Surfrider Beach. Steady 3- to 5-foot waves make this beach, just west of Malibu Pier, a surfing paradise. The International Surfing Contest is held here in September—the surf's premium around that time. Water runoff from Malibu Canyon forms a natural lagoon that's a sanctuary for 250 species of birds. Unfortunately, the lagoon is often polluted and algae filled. If you're leery of going into the water, you can bird-watch, play volleyball, or take a walk on one of the nature trails, which are perfect for romantic sunset strolls. ✉ *23200 PCH, Malibu* ☎ *310/305–9503* ☞ *Parking, lifeguard (year-round), restrooms, picnic tables.*

Las Tunas State Beach. This small beach known for its groins (metal gates constructed in 1929 to protect against erosion) has good swimming, diving, and fishing conditions, and a rocky coastline. ✉ *19444 PCH,*

Malibu ☎*310/305–9503* ☞*Parking on highway only, lifeguard (year-round, except only as needed in winter).*

Topanga State Beach. The beginning of miles of public beach, Topanga has good surfing at the western end (at the mouth of the canyon). Close to a busy section of the PCH and rather narrow, Topanga is hardly serene; hordes of teenagers zip over Topanga Canyon Boulevard from the Valley. Fishing and swings for children are available. ⊠*18700 block of PCH, Malibu* ☎*818/880–0350* ☞*Parking, lifeguard (year-round, except only as needed in winter), restrooms, food concessions.*

> **WORD OF MOUTH**
>
> "We were in Venice Beach on Christmas Day. People were out and about and there were many rollerskaters/bladers who had gathered just off the beach, skating to disco music on Christmas Day! Only in L.A., I guess. It was a lively atmosphere, but mellow at the same time" —lion

Will Rogers State Beach. This clean, sandy, 3-mi beach, with a dozen volleyball nets, gymnastics equipment, and playground equipment for kids, is an all-around favorite. The surf is gentle, perfect for swimmers and beginning surfers. However, it's best to avoid the place after a storm, when untreated water flows from storm drains into the sea. ⊠*15100 PCH, 2 mi north of Santa Monica Pier, Pacific Palisades* ☎*818/880–0350* ☞*Parking, lifeguard (year-round, except only as needed in winter), restrooms.*

★ **Santa Monica State Beach.** It's the first beach you'll hit after the Santa Monica Freeway (I–10) runs into the PCH, and it's one of L.A.'s best known. Wide and sandy, Santa Monica is *the* place for sunning and socializing: be prepared for a mob scene on summer weekends, when parking becomes an expensive ordeal. Swimming is fine (with the usual poststorm pollution caveat); for surfing, go elsewhere. For a memorable view, climb up the stairway over the PCH to Palisades Park, at the top of the bluffs. Summer-evening concerts are often held here. ⊠*1642 Promenade, PCH at California Incline, Santa Monica* ☎*310/305–9503* ☞*Parking, lifeguard (year-round), restrooms, showers.*

Venice City Beach. The surf and sand of Venice are fine, but the main attraction here is the boardwalk scene, which is a cosmos all its own—with fire-eating street performers, vendors hawking everything from cheap sunglasses and aromatherapy oils, and bicep'ed gym rats lifting weights at legendary Muscle Beach. Go on weekend afternoons for the best people-watching experience. There are also swimming, fishing, surfing, basketball (it's the site of some of L.A.'s most hotly contested pickup games), racquetball, handball, and shuffleboard. You can rent a bike or some in-line skates and hit the Strand bike path. ⊠*1800 Ocean Front Walk, west of Pacific Ave., Venice* ☎*310/399–2775* ☞*Parking, restrooms, food concessions, showers, playground.*

Dockweiler State Beach. The longest (4-mi) strip of beach in the county, Dockweiler has almost all the makings of a perfect beach: RV park, playground, separate bike trail, bonfire pits, mild surf, nice sand. If only the planes from LAX weren't taking off directly overhead and factories weren't puffing out fumes right behind you. But if you don't mind that, you'll find plenty of room to spread out. An additional bonus is the hang-gliding facility (right in front of the water-treatment plant). Contact **Windsports International** (☏*818/367–2430* 🌐*www.windsports.com*); $120 will get you a full lesson with equipment. ✉*8255 Vista del Mar, west end of Imperial Hwy., Playa del Rey* ☏*310/372–2166* ☞*Parking, lifeguard (year-round), restrooms, showers, volleyball.*

Manhattan Beach. A wide, sandy strip with good swimming and rows of volleyball courts, Manhattan Beach is the preferred destination of muscled, tanned young professionals and dedicated bikini-watchers. There are also a separate bike path, a playground, fishing equipment for rent, a bait shop, and a sizable fishing pier. ✉*Manhattan Beach Blvd. and N. Ocean Dr., Manhattan Beach* ☏*310/372–2166* ☞*Parking, lifeguard (year-round), restrooms, food concessions, showers.*

Hermosa Beach. South of Manhattan Beach, Hermosa Beach has all the amenities of its neighbor but it attracts more of an MTV party crowd. Swimming takes a backseat to the volleyball games and parties on the pier and boardwalk. ✉*1201 The Strand, Hermosa Ave. and 33rd St., Hermosa Beach* ☏*310/372–2166* ☞*Parking, lifeguard (year-round), restrooms, food concessions, showers, wheelchair access to pier.*

6

★ **Redondo Beach.** The Redondo Beach Pier marks the starting point of this wide, sandy, busy beach along a heavily developed shoreline community. Restaurants and shops flourish along the pier, excursion boats and privately owned crafts depart from launching ramps, and a reef formed by a sunken ship creates prime fishing and snorkeling conditions. If you're adventurous, you might try to kayak out to the buoys and hobnob with pelicans and sea lions. A series of free rock and jazz concerts takes place at the pier every summer. ✉*Torrance Blvd. at Catalina Ave., Redondo Beach* ☏*310/372–2166* ☞*Parking, lifeguard (year-round), restrooms, food concessions, showers.*

Torrance Beach. This little-known gem of a beach, where the Strand walkway–bicycle path finally comes to an end, has no pier or other loud attractions, just a humble snack shop that's open in the summer. But it's a great place to escape the crowds of Redondo to the north and has a park with great vistas and volleyball. ✉*387 Paseo de la Playa, Torrance* ☏*310/372–2166* ☞*Parking, restrooms, food concessions, showers.*

GARDENS

★ **Descanso Gardens** (✉*1418 Descanso Dr., La Cañada/Flintridge* ☏*818/949–4200* 🌐*www.descansogardens.org*) is a perfect place to come in search of wonderful scents—between the lilacs, the acres of roses, and the forest of California redwoods, pines, and junipers, you can enjoy all sorts of fragrances. Also be sure to check out the 600 varieties of camellias and the Japanese teahouse and garden. On hot days, the lush fern garden is a cool retreat. Classes (yoga and floral arranging, for example), night walks, and activities for families are scheduled throughout the year. The oak-framed main lawn is a lovely setting for summer concerts. A small train ride draws families on weekends. The garden's open daily 9–5; admission is $8.

> **WORD OF MOUTH**
>
> "I suggest a few days in Pasadena to visit the Huntington Gardens and Library, Norton Simon museum, old town, and to go for a hike in the foothills or climb Mt. Hollywood." —POlson

While wandering the 150-acre grounds of the **Huntington Library, Art Collections, and Botanical Gardens** (✉*1151 Oxford Rd., San Marino* ☎*626/405–2100 or 626/405–2141* 🌐*www.huntington.org*), you can truly forget you're in a city. Just over the Pasadena line in San Marino, the former estate of railroad baron Henry Huntington sprawls out in an incredible display of manicured gardening. Among the specialized gardens are a rose garden with 1,200 species from all over the world; a walled Japanese garden with reflecting ponds, a moon bridge, and a bonsai court; and a children's garden of topiary animals, pint-size fountains, and mazes. The stunning desert garden bristles with yellow-spined desert cacti, giant South African aloes, and beds of fiery red and orange succulents. The newest edition is an elaborate Chinese garden and cultural center called Liu Fang Yuan (or Garden of Flowering Fragrance), which includes several hand-carved stone bridges, a natural rock-framed lake, a teahouse, and winding pebbled paths. The Huntington grounds are open Monday, Wednesday, Thursday, and Friday noon–4:30 and weekends 10:30–4:30; entry is $15 for adults on weekdays and $20 on weekends. Admission is free the first Thursday of every month (though reservations are required).

★ At the **Los Angeles County Arboretum** (✉*301 N. Baldwin Ave., Arcadia* ☎*626/821–3222* 🌐*www.arboretum.org*), you can wander from a South Africa landscape to the Australian outback and even through a bit of tropical forest. One highlight is the tropical greenhouse, with carnivorous-looking orchids and a pond full of brilliant Chinese goldfish. The house and stables of the eccentric real-estate pioneer Lucky Baldwin are well preserved and worth a visit. Kids will love the many peacocks and waterfowl that roam the property. The Santa Anita Racetrack is across the street, but you'll seldom see it as you wander these 40 acres. To get there, go east on I–210 just past Pasadena, exit in Arcadia on Baldwin Avenue and go south, and you will soon see the entrance. It's open daily 9–5 and costs $7.

SPORTS

L.A.'s near-perfect climate allows sports enthusiasts the privilege of being outside year-round. The **City of Los Angeles Department of Recreation and Parks** (✉*200 N. Main St., Suite 1350* ☎*866/4LACITY, 213/473–3231* 🌐*www.cityofla.org/rap*) has information on city parks. For information on county parks contact the **Los Angeles County Department of Parks and Recreation** (✉*433 S. Vermont Ave.* ☎*213/738–2961* 🌐*parks.co.la.ca.us*).

Los Angeles is home to some of the greatest franchises in pro basketball and baseball, and the greater L.A. area has two pro teams in each of those sports, as well as hockey. Who knows if L.A.'s quest for a pro football team to replace the Rams and Raiders will succeed—despite years of negotiations with the NFL to bring a team to the Los Angeles Coliseum, a deal seemed unlikely at this writing. In the meantime, there's always the rough-and-tumble arena football of the Avengers, as well as the ferocious college rivalry of USC and UCLA. **Ticketmaster** (☎*213/480–3232* 🌐*www.ticketmaster.com*) sells tickets to most sporting events in town.

BASEBALL

You can watch the **Dodgers** take on their National League rivals while munching on pizza, tacos, or a foot-long "Dodger dog" at one of the game's most comfortable ball parks, **Dodger Stadium** (✉*1000 Elysian Park Ave., exit off I–110, Pasadena Fwy.* ☎*866/363–4377 ticket information* 🌐*www.dodgers.com*). The **Los Angeles Angels of Anaheim** won the World Series in 2002, the first time since the team formed in 1961. For Angels ticket information, contact **Angel Stadium of Anaheim** (✉*2000 Gene Autry Way, Anaheim* ☎*714/663–9000* 🌐*www.angels baseball.com*). Several colleges in the area also have baseball teams worth watching, especially USC, which has been a perennial source of major-league talent.

6

BASKETBALL

COLLEGE

Most of these schools put consistently competitive women's fives, as well as men's, on their respective courts. The Trojans of the **University of Southern California** (☎*213/740–4672* 🌐*usctrojans.cstv.com*) play at **Galen Center** (✉*3400 S. Figueroa St., Downtown* ☎*213/748–6136*). The Bruins of the **University of California at Los Angeles** (☎*310/825–2101* 🌐*uclabruins.collegesports.com*) play at Pauley Pavilion on the UCLA campus. These schools go head to head in Pac 10 competition each year. A lesser-known team that has lately stirred the waters is Malibu's own Waves of **Pepperdine University** (☎*310/506–4000* 🌐*www.pepperdine.edu*). The Titans of **California State University at Fullerton** (*Cal State Fullerton* ✉*800 N. State College Blvd., Fullerton* ☎*714/278–2783* 🌐*www.fullerton.edu*) are experiencing an upswing under coach Bob Burton and made it to the NCAA tournament in 2008. Another local team worth watching is the Lions at **Loyola Marymount University** (✉*2700 LMU Dr., Westchester* ☎*310/338–6095* 🌐*www.lmulions.com*).

PROFESSIONAL

L.A.'s pro basketball teams play at the Staples Center. The **Los Angeles Lakers** (☎*310/426–6000* 🌐*www.nba.com/lakers*) still attract a loyal following that includes celebrity fans like Jack Nicholson, Tyra Banks, and Leonardo DiCaprio. Despite a series of off-the-court conflicts in recent years, the team remains one of the NBA's most successful franchises with 14 NBA championships under its belt. L.A.'s "other" team, the much-maligned but newly revitalized **Clippers** (☎*888/895–8662* 🌐*www.nba.com/clippers*), sells tickets that are generally cheaper and easier to get than those for Lakers games. The **Los Angeles Sparks** (☎*310/426–6031* 🌐*www.wnba.com/sparks*) have built a WNBA dynasty around former USC star Lisa Leslie.

BICYCLING

When you plan to bicycle in the L.A. area, consider the logistics of transportation, rentals, and your chosen terrain. If you plan to get to your bike route via bus, you can do so only if the bus has a rack on its front (if not, you're out of luck). Taking a bike on the subway requires a permit; to apply for one, call the **MTA** (☎*213/922–7023 or 800/266–6883*). The permit's free but is sent to you by mail, so do this well in advance. You can get maps of L.A.'s bike trails and information leaflets on bus bike racks from the MTA or the **Department of Transportation** (☎*213/580–1177*) or through the Web site *www.bicyclela.org.* A word to the wise: don't cruise deep into the national parks and forests by yourself.

For an L.A.–area overview, including maps and useful links, check out **Los Angeles Bike Paths** (🌐*www.labikepaths.com*). For bike-route suggestions or a little company, you can get in touch with the **San Fernando Valley Bicycle Club** (🌐*www.sfvbc.org*). Mountain-biking enthusiasts should visit the **South Bay Mountain Biking Club** (🌐*www.sbmbc.com*); find a date–route rated for your skill level on this Web site, contact the leader for that group, show up with your bike and gear, and you're good to go. Gay and lesbian folks can check in with **Different Spokes Bicycle Club** (🌐*www.differentspokes.com*) for info on recreational rides and events (it has a newsletter, too).

Any L.A.–area yellow pages will yield a bunch of retail bicycle shops where you can rent wheels, pick the brain of a savvy salesperson or customer, or at least pick up the twice-yearly *Bicycling Event Guide.* **MyBikeSite.com** (🌐*www.mybikesite.com*) posts extensive national information, including good coverage of southern California. Also worth a look is the **Los Angeles County Bicycle Coalition** (🌐*www.labikecoalition.org*); though primarily an advocacy group, it also sponsors events.

THE PACIFIC COAST

★ The most famous bike path in the city runs along the Pacific Ocean. The 22-mi concrete route from Will Rogers State Beach down to Torrance Beach, known as the **Strand,** attracts cyclists of all levels. They share the path with joggers, skateboarders, in-line skaters, walkers, and other nonvehicular traffic (although for some stretches, bikes have their own parallel path). Except for a couple of short city-street detours around the Marina del Rey Harbor and the Redondo Beach Pier, the sunny beach scenery is uninterrupted. The ride can be done in a long leisurely afternoon, with plenty of time for stops along the way: rest assured that there's more than enough to see to make the round-trip worthwhile. You can rent a bike at one of many shops along the Strand's middle section between Santa Monica and Venice. (⇨*See Bike Rentals, below.*) Cyclists often refer to the 18.4-mi section south of the Santa Monica Pier as the South Bay Bicycle Trail.

South of the Strand, following the brief and pathless "RAT" (Right After Torrance) beach, is a 23-mi loop with a good sightline of the winding hills and clear ocean views on the relatively untrammeled **Palos Verdes Peninsula.** The trip, which takes at least three hours, is best attempted on a temperate morning when fog isn't obscuring the ocean. Marked bike lanes come and go, so be careful.

OTHER EXCURSIONS

Nod to the brown pelicans in the wetlands as you cruise westward along the **Ballona Creek** path from National and Jefferson boulevards in Culver City; you can hook up with the Strand at the other end. Santa Monica's **San Vicente Boulevard** has a wide, 3-mi cycling lane that parallels the sidewalk. **Balboa Park,** in the San Fernando Valley, is another haven for two-wheelers, although beware after a heavy rain; it'll be flooded. The flat, 3-mi paved path around **Lake Hollywood** is a great place to take in views of the HOLLYWOOD sign. Griffith Park, Malibu Creek State Park, and Topanga State Park are all part of the **Santa Monica Mountains,** which have good mountain-biking paths. Griffith Park also has a flat family-friendly 4.7-mi path that runs along Crystal Springs Drive and Zoo Drive, then turns back along the Los Angeles River and ends on Fletcher Drive near the main entrance.

6

For some solitude and rural terrain, visit **Angeles National Forest,** in the northern reaches of L.A. County. The mostly flat and shaded **Gabrielino Trail** (☎*626/574–5200 forest service*) along the upper Arroyo Seco is a favorite of mountain bikers, runners, birders, and horseback riders. To get there, exit the 210 Freeway at Arroyo Boulevard–Windsor Avenue in Altadena. Drive three-quarters of a mile north and look for the small parking lot just before you reach Ventura Avenue.

BIKE RENTALS

Bike rentals usually cost $6–$10 an hour or $15–$40 a day. You'll likely also need to hand over a photo ID and credit card before cycling off. Double-check the helmet situation with your chosen rental outfitter; some places rent helmets, some only sell, and a couple charge a nominal fee if you're renting a bike for several days.

Perry's has three locations along the Strand: **Perry's Bike & Skate** (✉*2600 Ocean Front Walk, Venice* ☎*310/584–9306*), **Perry's Beach Rentals** (✉*2400 Ocean Front Walk, Venice* ☎*310/452–7609*), and **Perry's Cafe & Sports Rentals** (✉*1200 The Promenade, Santa Monica* ☎*310/485–3975*). Several locations of **Spokes 'N Stuff** (✉*Griffith Park, 4400 Crystal Springs Dr., Los Feliz* ☎*323/653–4099* ✉*Strand, 1715 Ocean Ave., Santa Monica* ☎*310/395–4748* ✉*Strand, 4175 Admiralty Way, Marina del Rey* ☎*310/306–3332*) has a rental shop behind the ranger station in Griffith Park and two rental places on the Strand. **Venice Pier Bike Shop** (✉*21 Washington Blvd., just east of Strand, Venice* ☎*310/301–4011*) rents bikes and other beach-sport stuff.

FISHING

There's plenty of freshwater fishing in the lakes dotting the city and in the Angeles National Forest. A license is required: they're available at many sporting-goods stores. (Out-of-state visitors can get two-day licenses for $18, or one-day licenses for $12.) The **Fish and Game Department** (☎*562/342–7100, 562/594–7268 lake-stocking information* 🌐*www.dfg.ca.gov*) can answer questions about licenses and give advice.

Shore fishing and surf casting are excellent on many of the beaches, and pier fishing is popular because no license is necessary to fish off public piers. The **Santa Monica** and **Malibu** piers have bait-and-tackle shops with everything you'll need.

If you want to break away from the piers, sign up for a boat excursion with one of the local charters, most of which will sell you a fishing license and rent tackle. Most also offer whale-watching excursions. **Del Rey Sport Fishing** (✉*13552 Fiji Way, Dock 52, Marina del Rey* ☎*310/822–3625*) runs excursions for $35 per half day and $50 for three-quarters of a day, with rod rental another $10. **Redondo Sport Fishing Company** (✉*233 N. Harbor Dr., Redondo Beach* ☎*310/372–2111*) has charters starting at $55 for three-quarters of a day and $35 for a half-day. Sea bass, halibut, bonita, yellowtail, and barracuda are the usual catch.

Twenty Second Street Landing (✉*141 W. 22nd St., San Pedro* ☎*310/832–8304*) leads an overnight charter ($150) that lets you stargaze while waiting for a bite. Day charters are $60. **L.A. Harbor Sportfishing** (✉*1150 Nagoya Way, Berth 79 at harbor, San Pedro* ☎*310/547–9916*), which sails some of the area's best charter boats, offers excursions from March through December ranging from half a day ($38) or three-quarters of a day ($45) to two-day runs in summer. Rod rental is $12.

FISHING FINGERS

The most popular and most unusual form of fishing in the L.A. area involves no hooks, bait, or poles. The great grunion runs, which take place from March through July, occur when hundreds of thousands of small silver fish called grunion wash up on Southern California beaches to lay their eggs in the sand. The fish can be picked up by hand while they are briefly stranded on the beach. All that's required is a fishing license and a willingness to get your toes wet. San Pedro's Cabrillo Marine Aquarium (☎*310/548–7562* 🌐*www.cabrilloaq.org*) hosts programs about grunion throughout most of their spawning season. During certain months you're not allowed to touch the grunion; call the Fish and Game Department for details.

FOOTBALL

For a city that lost not one but two NFL teams, there's a lot of football to be seen in the area. The **L.A. Avengers** (☎*213/480–3232 Ticketmaster* 🌐*www.laavengers.com*) are the city's entry into arena football, playing at the **Staples Center** (✉*1111 S. Figueroa St., Downtown* ☎*213/742–7340 box office* 🌐*www.staplescenter.com*). Football fever in L.A., however, still revolves primarily around the college teams.

COLLEGE

The **USC Trojans** (☎*213/740–4672* 🌐*usctrojans.collegesports.com*) play at the **L.A. Memorial Coliseum** (✉*3939 S. Figueroa St., Downtown* ☎*213/748–6136*), both a state and federal historic landmark. After a short-lived threat to decamp to the Rose Bowl in 2007, the Trojans agreed to remain at the venerable field. The **UCLA Bruins** (☎*310/825–2101* 🌐*uclabruins.collegesports.com*) pack 'em in at the **Rose Bowl** (✉*1010 Rose Bowl Dr., Pasadena* ☎*626/449–7673*). Every year, the two teams face off in one of college football's oldest and most exciting rivalries.

GOLF

The City Parks and Recreation Department lists seven public 18-hole courses in Los Angeles, and L.A. County runs some good ones, too. **Rancho Park Golf Course** (✉*10460 W. Pico Blvd., West L.A.* ☎*310/838–7373*) is one of the most heavily played links in the country. It's a beautifully designed course, but the towering pines present an obstacle for those who slice or hook. There's a two-level driving range, a 9-hole pitch 'n' putt, a snack bar, and a pro shop where you can rent clubs.

6

Several good public courses are in the San Fernando Valley. The **Sepulveda Golf Complex** (✉*16821 Burbank Blvd., Encino* ☎*818/995–1170*) has the Balboa course (par 70) and the longer Encino course (par 72), plus a driving range. Five lakes and occasional wildlife spottings make the **Woodley Lakes Golf Course** (✉*6331 Woodley Ave., Van Nuys* ☎*818/780–6886*) fairly scenic. It's flat and thus somewhat forgiving, but the back 9 is more challenging, with only one par 4 under 400 yards.

★ If you want a scenic course, the county-run, par-71 **Los Verdes Golf Course** (✉*7000 W. Los Verdes Dr., Rancho Palos Verdes* ☎*310/377–7370*) has fierce scenery. You get a cliff-top view of the ocean—time it right and you can watch the sun set behind Catalina Island.

Griffith Park has two splendid 18-hole courses along with a challenging 9-hole course. **Harding Municipal Golf Course** and **Wilson Municipal Golf Course** (✉*4900 Griffith Park Dr., Los Feliz* ☎*323/663–2555*) are about 1½ mi inside the park entrance, at Riverside Drive and Los Feliz Boulevard. Bridle paths surround the outer fairways, and the San Gabriel Mountains make a scenic background. The 9-hole **Roosevelt Municipal Golf Course** (✉*2650 N. Vermont Ave., Los Feliz* ☎*323/665–2011*) can be reached through the park's Vermont Avenue entrance.

Sitting on landfill, the **Scholl Canyon Golf Club** (✉*3800 E. Glenoaks Blvd., Glendale* ☎*818/243–4100*) may only be a par 60, but it's fun and challenging, attractive for its top condition as well as its ups and downs and elevated views. You may recall the 9-hole pitch 'n' putt **Los Feliz Municipal Golf Course** (✉*3207 Los Feliz Blvd., Los Feliz* ☎*323/663–7758*) from the movie *Swingers*. The **Holmby Park Pitch 'n' Putt** (✉*601 Club View Dr., near Beverly Glen* ☎*310/276–1604*) is truly cozy: the longest hole is 68 yards.

For those who love to watch the pros in action, the hot golf ticket in town each February is the PGA **Nissan Open** (☎*800/752–6736*). The $6.2 million purse attracts the best golfers in the world to its week of competition at the Riviera Country Club in Pacific Palisades.

HEALTH CLUBS

Don't be fooled by the gossipy environment, pulsating music, and carefully arranged spandex that dominate many top gyms. L.A.'s gym rats take their workouts very seriously, visiting once or twice a day and discussing their body-fat ratios and cardio programs with anyone who asks.

If you belong to national chains, like **24-Hour Fitness** or **Bally's,** you'll find plenty of branches here. If not, they and the many local clubs and chains in the city usually sell daily or weekly memberships. **Meridian** (*✉1950 Century Park E, Century City ☎310/789–1111*) has a full range of cardio classes including aerobic boxing and kickboxing for $20 per day; there are also branches in the Miracle Mile and Beverly–La Brea areas. The state-of-the-art **Crunch Fitness** (*✉8000 Sunset Blvd., West Hollywood ☎323/654–4550*) is popular with celebrities for its expansive facilities. It costs $24 per day; for Chateau Marmont or Standard guests bearing room keys, it's $15 per day, non–hotel guests $25.

Probably the most famous body-pumping facility in the city is **Gold's Gym** (*✉360 Hampton Dr., Venice ☎310/392–6004 ✉1016 N. Cole Ave., Hollywood ☎323/462–7012*). In addition to using the two flagship locations mentioned here, local hulks turn themselves into veritable muscle sculptures at two additional locations in the San Fernando Valley and another in Redondo Beach. For $20 a day or $59 a week, several tons of weights and bodybuilding machines can be yours.

HIKING

"Nobody Walks in L.A." sang the Missing Persons back in the '80s, and it's as true as ever—but people do like to hike. With so many different land- and seascapes to explore, hiking is a major pastime for many Angelenos who crave an escape from city life, heading for the hills en masse on weekends, often with dogs in tow. From almost anywhere in L.A., you should find a fine trail a surprisingly short hop away. ■ **TIP→Remember, the region can be dry and hot at most times of the year, so take plenty of water and liberally apply (and reapply) sunblock.** Hats and sunglasses help with hydration and UV protection.

The coast, the Hollywood Hills, and the parent range of the latter, the Santa Monica Mountains, are convenient getaways. If you're in the Pasadena area, you'll have easy access to the surprisingly wild San Gabriel Mountains of the Angeles Crest National Forest and the gentler San Gabriel Valley. Farther afield, look into some more extensive hikes in the Verdugo or Santa Susana Mountains. ■ **TIP→Don't venture deep into the national parks and forests alone. Griffith Park is one thing; the Angeles National Forest is quite another.** Despite an active park ranger presence there, the Angeles Forest is rugged, parts of it are quite dense, and a person alone and injured could face serious hazards.

For information on hiking locations and scheduled outings in Los Angeles, contact the **Sierra Club** (*✉3435 Wilshire Blvd., Suite 320, Los Angeles ☎213/387–4287 🌐www.sierraclub.org*). Or, check out

Outdoors, the quarterly calendar of events put out by th **Mountains National Recreation Area** (⌧*401 W. Hillcrest D Oaks* ☎*805/370–2301* 🌐*www.nps.gov/samo*).

HOLLYWOOD HILLS

Fodor's Choice ★ One of the best places to begin is **Griffith Park** (⌧*Ranger Stati Crystal Springs Dr., Los Feliz*); pick up a map from the ranger .ation. Many of the paths in the park are not shaded and can be quite steep. A nice, short hike from Canyon Drive, at the southwest end of the park, takes you to **Bronson Caves,** where the *Batman* television show was filmed. ■ TIP→ **Wildfires ravaged much of the park in spring 2007 and made some trails off-limits indefinitely, so it's a good idea to check with the ranger station before planning a hike.**

★ For a walk, run, or bike ride, the **Hollywood Reservoir (aka Lake Hollywood) Trail** is probably one of the best spots in all L.A. The 4-mi flat walk around the reservoir provides great views of hillside mansions (including the spread once owned by Madonna, with its controversial striped retaining wall), the HOLLYWOOD sign, and the reservoir itself. The park is open dawn to dusk. To get there, exit U.S. 101 at Barham Boulevard (near Universal City). Look for Lake Hollywood Drive soon on your right and take it, making sure you stay the course through its tricky turns. Park when you see the gate. The reservoir was built by the god of Los Angeles water, William Mulholland; its dam has a memorable movie cameo in Roman Polanski's *Chinatown.*

The 3-mi **Mt. Lee Trail,** which begins in Hollywood near the junction of Beachwood and Hollyridge drives, climbs 500 feet to L.A.'s most famous landmark, the HOLLYWOOD sign. You can't walk around the sign, but you can get about 100 yards from it, which is pretty good for snapshots.

The stroll in **Franklin Canyon** is just above the northern reaches of Beverly Hills. Less than 2½ mi, it's often used by film crews. Pick up a map from the visitor center (follow Franklin Canyon Drive to Lake Drive, then turn right to find the Franklin Canyon Ranch House). Docent-led walks are also available.

SANTA MONICA MOUNTAINS

The Santa Monica Mountains are an unlikely swath of natural beauty that extend into the city. Although the climate is Mediterranean, the plants suggest more of a prairie, with golden grasses and gnarled live oak. Some of Los Angeles's best-known natural beauty spots, such as Topanga Canyon and Leo Carrillo State Park (with its tide pools and coves), are within the bounds of the Santa Monicas, or you can head farther out of the city to the wilder terrain of Point Mugu State Park.

★ Who knows how many of Will Rogers's famed witticisms came to him while he and his wife hiked or rode horses along the **Inspiration Point Trail** from their ranch, now **Will Rogers State Historic Park** (⌧*1505 Will Rogers State Park Rd., Pacific Palisades* ☎*310/454–8212*). The point is on a detour off the lovely 2-mi loop, which you pick up right by the riding stables beyond the parking lot ($7 per car). On a clear (or even just semiclear) day, the panorama is one of L.A.'s widest and most "wow" inducing, from the peaks of the San Gabriel Mountains in the distant east to the Oz-like cluster of downtown L.A. skyscrapers to Catalina Island looming off the coast to the southwest. If you're looking for a longer trip, the top of the loop meets up with the 65-mi Backbone Trail, which connects to Topanga State Park. And don't forget Will Rogers's sprawling ranch home, which is open for public tours Tuesday through Sunday; no reservations required. **Malibu Creek State Park** (⊠*1925 Las Virgenes Rd., Calabasas* ☎*818/880–0367*) has some of the best hiking in the area, and if you bring a swimsuit, you can take a dip in the rock pool. See the wild country that has doubled as Korea in the *M*A*S*H* TV show and as assorted alien worlds in the original *Star Trek* series.

★ Another way into the Santa Monicas is via the Trippet Ranch entrance to **Topanga State Park** (⊠*20829 Entrada Rd., Malibu* ☎*310/455–2465*), which gives you several options: a ½-mi nature loop, a 7-mi round-trip excursion to the Parker Mesa Overlook (breathtaking on a clear day), or a 10-mi trek to the Will Rogers park. Parking is $4 per vehicle. (Exit U.S. 101 onto Topanga Canyon Boulevard in Woodland Hills and head south until you can turn left onto Entrada; if going north on PCH, turn onto Topanga Canyon Boulevard—a bit past Sunset Boulevard—and go north until you can turn right onto Entrada.)

HOCKEY

The National Hockey League's **L.A. Kings** (☎*213/480–3232 Ticketmaster* 🌐*www.lakings.com*) are sometime playoff contenders (though they rarely make it out of the first round) at the **Staples Center** (⊠*1111 S. Figueroa St., Downtown* ☎*213/742–7340 box office* 🌐*www.staplescenter.com*). The **Anaheim Ducks** (☎*877/945–3946* 🌐*www.mightyducks.com*) push the puck at **Honda Center** (⊠*2695 E. Katella Ave., Anaheim* ☎*714/704–2500*). Long an underdog team, they became the first Southern California team to win the Stanley Cup in 2007. Hockey season runs from October through April.

HORSE RACING AND SHOWS

Santa Anita Race Track (⊠*285 W. Huntington Dr., Arcadia* ☎*626/574–7223* 🌐*www.santaanita.com* 🎟*$5–$20*) is a beautiful facility that has the San Gabriel Mountains for a backdrop. It's still the dominant site for thoroughbred racing from late September to November 1 and from December 26 to late April; the centerpiece of the season is the Breeders' Cup in late October. Seabiscuit tram tours, covering the history of the legendary racehorse, are offered free on weekends from September to November. **Hollywood Park** (⊠*1050 S. Prairie Ave., at Century Blvd., Inglewood* ☎*310/419–1500* 🎟*$7–$10*), next to the Forum, is another favorite venue to see thoroughbreds race. It's open from early November to late December and from late April to mid-July. Several grand-prix jumping competitions and Western riding championships are held throughout the year at the **Los Angeles Equestrian Center** (⊠*480 Riverside Dr., Burbank* ☎*818/563–3252, 818/840–9066 box office* 🌐*www.la-equestriancenter.com*).

HORSEBACK RIDING

For adults and kids 7 and over, **Diamond Bar** (✉*1850 Riverside Dr., just northeast of Griffith Park, Glendale* ☎*818/242–8443*) is a no-frills outfit charging $25 per hour and $20 for each additional hour. The **Los Angeles Horseback Riding** (✉*2623 Old Topanga Rd., Topanga* ☎*818/591–2032* 🌐*www.losangeleshorsebackriding.com*) has guided rides past the giant rock formations of the Santa Monica/Malibu Mountains Conservancy and through countless wildflowers nestled in the area's unique red soil, plus panoramic vistas of Catalina Island and the Pacific Ocean. There are also a variety of full moon rides.

Every day, 8 AM to 5 PM, more than 50 mi of Griffith Park's beautiful bridle trails are open to the public via **Griffith Park Horse Rentals** (✉*480 W. Riverside Dr., Burbank* ☎*818/840–8401*) inside the L.A. Equestrian Center. Rates are $25 for one hour (cash only) and can accommodate riders over 200 pounds for extra charge. The Sunset Dinner Ride is a 1½-hour ride plus a Mexican dinner for $65. At **J.P. Stables** (✉*914 Mariposa St., Burbank* ☎*818/843–9890*), the only limit to your riding time is the endurance of your wallet and your behind; the cost is $25 for the first hour and $20 each additional hour. Hours are 7:30–4:30. Rates at **Sunset Ranch** (✉*3400 N. Beachwood Dr., at Griffith Park's southwestern end* ☎*323/469–5450* 📠*323/461–3061*) are $25 for one hour, $40 for two hours (the maximum). Among the package rides is a Friday-evening dinner ride over the hill into Burbank, where riders dine at a Mexican restaurant (starting at $60, dinner not included).

6

A caveat or two: as docile as the horses may seem, they are not golf carts. Total newbies should stick with the easiest rides. Additionally, novice or not, you're wise to check (or ask the stable folks) that the saddle cinch is tight enough. Many stables have an upper weight limit of around 200–250 pounds. Some of the rental stables offer lessons, or you can go for the package (evaluation, five lessons, and a horsemanship class) offered at the L.A. Equestrian Center by the **Traditional Equitation School** (✉*480 Riverside Dr., Burbank* ☎*818/569–3666* 🌐*www.tes-laec.com*), for $315 (includes evaluation, warm-up, and lesson).

IN-LINE AND ROLLER-SKATING

All of the paths mentioned in Bicycling are also excellent for in-line and roller-skating, though cyclists have the right of way. The **Strand,** specifically the part of it that passes through Venice Beach, is the skating mecca of the area. Distance skaters can hook up with the **Friday Night Skate** (🌐*www.fridaynightskate.org*). Every Friday night at 8:30 (weather permitting), skaters gather at the entrance to the Santa Monica Pier. From here, everyone zips off on a 10-mi route through city streets—you just follow the pack, behind the guy with the boom box strapped to his body.

Papa Jack Skate Park (✉*23415 Civic Center Way, Malibu* ☎*310/456–1441*) is good for in-line and roller-skating and skateboarding. It's open daily; call for hours. To rent in-line skates, try **Boardwalk Skates** (✉*201½ Ocean Front Walk, Venice* ☎*310/450–6634*). You can rent both in-line skates by the day or hour from **Sea Mist Rentals** (✉ *1619 Ocean Front Walk, at Santa Monica Pier, Santa Monica* ☎ *310/395–7076*).

PILATES

Many gyms offer Pilates on their regular class schedules, and studios specializing in this gentle-on-the-joints program operate in just about every neighborhood.

Owner Maria Leone takes a holistic, integrative approach to Pilates at **Body Line Fitness Studio** (✉ *367 Doheny Dr., Beverly Hills* ☎ *310/274–2716* 🌐 *www.bodylinela.com*), which offers private and two-person training sessions and group reformer classes.

Novices love **Pilates Studio City** (✉ *11650 Riverside Dr., Studio City* ☎ *818/509–0914* 🌐 *www.pilatesstudiocity.com*) for its patient instructors, discounted first-time client rates, and wide variety of group classes, from Pilates mat to stretch and conditioning.

POLO

Will Rogers State Historic Park (✉ *1501 Will Rogers State Park Rd., Pacific Palisades* ☎ *310/573–5000*) was donated by Rogers's estate on the condition that the outdoor regulation-size field (now the only one in the nation) be maintained for polo. From April through September, games are played Saturday at 2 PM and Sunday at 10 AM (weather permitting). Parking costs $7 per car.

ROCK CLIMBING

Los Angeles has several excellent indoor facilities, but you came here for the great outdoors, and there's lots of that to be had. In the San Fernando Valley, **Stoney Point** (✉ *Off Topanga Canyon Blvd. south of Hwy. 18 in northern Chatsworth*) is the top choice, both historically—it's where Patagonia founder Yvon Chouinard made his name as a rock climber—and practically, since the 300-foot-high boulders can accommodate all skill levels. If a bit of a journey, **Vasquez Rocks** is pretty surreal and offers good climbing for beginners and the more experienced. The area, named for the 19th-century bandit who hid out among the rocks, is in northeastern L.A. County. For more information, check with the **County Department of Parks and Recreation** (☎ *213/738–2961* 🌐 *www.lacountyparks.org*). Near the **Malibu Creek State Park visitor center** (✉ *1925 Las Virgenes Rd., Calabasas*), the *Planet of the Apes* Wall and the Ghetto Wall make for good climbing, but not for beginners. It's busy on weekends. The cliffs behind beautiful **Point Dume Beach** (✉ *South end of Westward Beach Rd.*) in Malibu are likewise pretty challenging and hopping on weekends. Check out **www.rockclimbing.org** for some opinionated advice on climbing in the L.A. area and beyond.

If you're a total beginner, for your own safety you're best off starting out at an indoor facility; and the best of L.A.'s have engaging routes for advanced climbers, too. One centrally located indoor rock gym is

Rockreation (✉*11866 La Grange Ave., West L.A.* ☎*310/207–7199* 🌐*www.rockreation.com/lahome.html*). It has 9,000 square feet of climbing space, with 24 routes on approximately 20- to 25-foot walls. Belayers (spotters) keep an eye on you and give lessons.

RUNNING

Exposition Park has a scenic course popular with students and downtown workers. The jogging trail circles the Coliseum and Sports Arena, with pull-up bars and other simple workout equipment placed every several hundred yards. **San Vicente Boulevard** in Santa Monica has a wide, grassy median that splits the street for several picturesque miles. The Hollywood Hills' **Runyon Canyon** has a 3-mi loop with a steep section for those seeking a rugged run. The reservoir at **Lake Hollywood,** just east of Cahuenga Boulevard in the Hollywood Hills, is encircled by a 3.3-mi asphalt path with a view of the HOLLYWOOD sign. Within Hollywood's hilly **Griffith Park** are thousands of acres' worth of hilly paths and challenging terrain; **Crystal Springs Drive,** from the main entrance at Los Feliz to the zoo, is a relatively flat 5 mi, and near its midpoint is a ranger station where you can get a park map. **Circle Drive,** around the perimeter of UCLA in Westwood, provides a 2½-mi run through academia. Running along the outer edge of the campus can enlarge the jaunt to just under 4 mi. Near several major hotels, lovely **Beverly Gardens** extends along the north side of Santa Monica Boulevard through Beverly Hills; bracketed by ornate fountains, its leafy paths pass by the Beverly Hills Library and City Hall and through a delightful, block-long cactus garden. Continuing around on Wilshire to Whittier and right onto Elevado, or at the other end up Doheny and left onto Elevado, yields a 3½-mi route. The 22 mi of bike path known as the **Strand,** along the coast from Will Rogers Beach to Torrance Beach, is a great place for a run—especially in the Venice Beach and Santa Monica sections. Beware of cyclists and skaters zipping by at high speeds. If you like races, you'll want to check out **Raceplace** (🌐*www.raceplace.com*) in advance of your trip. For you long-range trail runners, see the Topanga State Park listing above in Hiking. The truly ambitious can check out **50 Trail Runs in Southern California**, by Stan Swartz et al. (Mountaineer Books, 2000).

TOURISM ON THE RUN

Those who like to combine a workout with a bit of sightseeing will want to sign up for Cheryl Anker's Off N' Running Tours (☎310/246–1418), which takes runners and walkers on 3- and 8-mi tours through Santa Monica and Beverly Hills. The $60 tours cater to all fitness levels and include breakfast and a T-shirt. Check out www.offnrunningtours.com.

6

SKIING AND SNOWBOARDING

CROSS-COUNTRY

Ski season in Southern California generally runs from Thanksgiving until Memorial Day. **Idyllwild** (☎*951/659–3259* 🌐*www.idyllwildchamber.com*), near Palm Springs, has excellent cross-country trails.

DOWNHILL

A relatively short drive from downtown L.A. brings you to good snow-skiing and snowboarding. Just north of Pasadena, in the San Gabriel Mountains, there's **Mt. Waterman** (✉ *Angeles Crest Hwy., Star Rte. 2, La Cañada* ☎ *818/952–7676* 🌐 *www.skiwaterman.com*), which reopened in 2008 after new owners took over and made some improvements. It has three lifts and a range of slopes for beginning and advanced skiers. There are no snowmaking facilities, so call ahead to be sure it's open.

East of town, at the San Bernardino County line, is **Mt. Baldy** (☎ *909/981–3344* 🌐 *www.mtbaldy.com*), the largest and steepest ski area in Southern California with 26 runs over 400 acres. Despite rustic facilities and limited snowmaking facilities, it's beloved for its varied and challenging terrain. Take the I–10 or the I–210 over the San Bernardino County line to Mountain Avenue, which you'll take north for 16 mi to Mt. Baldy Road; then continue north. Count on a two-hour drive from downtown L.A.

THE PERFECT MATCH

Soccer sensation David Beckham's decision to jump from Real Madrid to the Los Angeles Galaxy prompted a spike in the team's 2007 ticket sales and a buzz in Hollywood about his arrival along with his wife, former Spice Girl Victoria. Beckham's five-year deal will have him earning up to $50 million a year—or $90 for every second he's on the field—enough to keep the stylish English duo and their kids clothed in Dolce & Gabbana for years to come. An injured knee kept Beckham on the sidelines for much of his first season in L.A., but that didn't seem to hurt his stature among fans.

Big Bear (☎ *909/866–4607 visitor info line, 800/424–4232* 🌐 *www.bigbear.com*), about 100 mi northeast of Los Angeles, is one of the most popular ski retreats on the West Coast, with a full range of accommodations, several ski lifts, night skiing, and one of the largest snowmaking operations in California. To get here, take the I–10 San Bernardino Freeway east past the city of San Bernardino to Highway 30 headed for Highway 330; that goes northeast and becomes Highway 18, which eventually goes around Big Bear Lake. The drive takes at least two hours.

Another ski and snowboard area in the vicinity of Big Bear is **Bear Mountain** (☎ *888/786–6481*), where freestyle terrain tends to attract young thrill-seekers. To get to the lake, take the I–10 San Bernardino Freeway east past the city of San Bernardino to Highway 30. Then connect to Highway 330 going northeast; Highway 330 becomes Highway 18, which circumvents Big Bear Lake. **Snow Valley** (✉ *35100 Hwy. 18, Running Springs* 🌐 *www.snow-valley.com* ☎ *909/867–2751*) has snowmaking capabilities, a kids' snowmobile park, and a designated sledding area. **Mountain High** (✉ *24510 State Hwy. 2, Wrightwood* ☎ *888/754–7878* 🌐 *www.mthigh.com*), as do most of these areas, has lights for night skiing. It's also got a kid-friendly tubing park. The easy-to-navigate facilities and calm vibe at **Snow Summit** (✉ *880 Summit Blvd.* ☎ *909/866–5766*) make it a good spot for beginners, families with small children, and skiers seeking traditional downhill runs without fuss.

SOCCER

The 2005 MLS champions, the **Los Angeles Galaxy** (☎ *877/342–5299* 🌐*www.lagalaxy.com*), play March through September at the new stadium at the **Home Depot Center** (✉*18400 Avalon Blvd., Carson* ☎*877/342–5299* 🌐*www.homedepotcenter.com*).

TENNIS

L.A. Department of Recreation and Parks (✉*3900 W. Chevy Chase Dr., Los Angeles* ☎*818/246–5613* 🌐*www.laparks.org/dos/sports/tennis.htm*) has a complete list of the city's more than 75 public tennis courts. Some are always free, others only weekdays; others charge $5–$10 an hour per court, depending on time of day. Reservations are a must during peak hours at the most popular pay courts; to make them, apply for a reservation card (click on "Permits") at the Web site or call 323/644–3536.

The **Poinsettia Tennis Center** (✉*7341 Willoughby Ave., Hollywood* ☎*323/512–8234*) is a pay-to-play facility with eight lighted courts.

West L.A. has a number of locations with well-maintained, lighted courts: the courts at **Westwood Park Tennis Courts** (✉*1375 Veteran Ave., Westwood* ☎*310/575–8299*) are $8 an hour. The four courts at the **Barrington Recreational Center** (✉*333 Barrington Ave. south of Sunset Blvd., Brentwood*) are always free. And the 14 courts at **Cheviot Hills** (✉*2551 Motor Ave., just south of 20th Century Fox lot* ☎*310/837–5186*) are pay-to-play.

Griffith Park has a dozen lighted courts at the **Griffith-Riverside Pay Tennis Complex** (✉*3401 Riverside Dr., at Los Feliz Blvd., Los Feliz* ☎*323/661–5318*). There are a dozen unlighted courts at Griffith Park's **Griffith-Vermont Pay Tennis Complex** (✉*2715 N. Vermont Ave., Los Feliz* ☎*323/664–3521*).

La Cienega Tennis Center (✉*421 S. La Cienega Blvd., Beverly Hills* ☎*310/550–4767*) has 16 lighted courts available for $10 per hour; you can reserve up to four days in advance if you have a Leisure Services Card ($11 nonresidents; $10 weekends), which can be purchased at the center. Those who don't have the card can call ahead to see how busy it is.

If you're interested in watching the pros, the **Mercedes Benz Cup** (*Formerly the Infiniti Open* ☎*310/825–2101 tickets, 310/824–1010 info* 🌐*mercedes-cup.info*), held in summer at UCLA, usually attracts some of the top-seeded players on the pro tennis circuit.

VOLLEYBALL

The casual beach volleyballer can find pickup games at beaches the length of the coast; more serious players might want to concentrate on the **Santa Monica State Beach** nets or those at **Manhattan Beach** (which has about 200 nets). If you're truly obsessed, contact the **California Beach Volleyball Association** (☎*800/350–2282*) to see about amateur tournaments (grass-court play as well as sand); its California Cup State Championship tourney is held Labor Day weekend.

As for **pro volleyball,** the beach volleyball played by two-person teams, check out the men's and women's tournaments held at city beaches in June, July, and August. The **Association of Volleyball Professionals** (*www.avp.com*) is the best place for information.

WATER SPORTS

BOATING, KAYAKING, AND JET SKIING

Long Beach Windsurf & Kayak Center (*3850 E. Ocean Blvd., near Belmont Pier, Long Beach 562/433–1014*) gives kayaking and stand-up paddleboard lessons starting at $90 for 1½ hours and in-line skating lessons ($45 an hour). For boat and Jet Ski rentals, call **Offshore Water Sports** (*419 E. Shoreline Dr., Rainbow Harbor, Long Beach 562/436–1996*). **Marina Boat Rentals** (*13719 Fiji Way, Marina del Rey 310/574–2822*), behind the El Torito eatery in Fisherman's Village, rents single and double kayaks as well as speedboats, cruisers, and sailboats by the hour or half day for 15% discount. **Malibu Mike's** (*29500 PCH, across from Point Dume, Malibu 310/456–6302*) has kayak rentals and lessons, as well as surf and paddleboard lessons, and kayak tours along the Malibu coast. **Rocky Point Marine Fuels** (*310 Portofino Way, Redondo Beach 310/374–9858*) rents single and double kayaks.

SCUBA DIVING AND SNORKELING

Anyone who can swim can snorkel, but you'll have to show proof of certification to strap on a scuba tank. L.A. is probably not the best place to start learning scuba—the water's rough—but you can get certified at one of the dive centers listed below. Snorkeling and scuba diving require calm waters, and despite its name, the Pacific Ocean does not quite fit the bill. However, there's good diving to be had if you know where to look. Try **Leo Carrillo State Beach** in Malibu; **Abalone Cove, Malaga Cove,** and **Christmas Tree Cove** at Palos Verdes; or, a few minutes farther east, the **Underwater Dive Trail** at White Point, just east of Royal Palms State Beach, which winds by rope through kelp beds, sulfurous hot springs, and underwater coves. Farther afield, there are **Catalina Island,** and the **Channel Islands,** or go down the coast to **Laguna Beach.** Web sites such as *www.ladiver.com* can give you guidance.

If you or your diving partner is injured in a diving-related accident, the 24-hour staff at the **U.S. National Diving Accident Network** (*919/684–8111*) can help you find a doctor trained to treat divers.

All the scuba equipment (and diving lessons) you'll need can be obtained from the following shops. Most rent standard scuba gear packages for $50 and up (some do discounts for multiple days or weekends). That does *not* include basic snorkeling gear (mask, snorkel, booties, fins, and, optional but recommended, gloves), which runs about $20 per day (or which you may be required to buy, for $200–$300). Some shops arrange diving charters to Catalina Island and the Channel Islands. **TIP→Most certification packages include an open-water training trip to**

CLOSE UP

Surf's Up

Nothing captures the laid-back cool of California quite like surfing. It arrived here in the early 1900s, when land developer Henry Huntington staged a surfing demonstration at Redondo Beach to promote the opening of his Redondo–Los Angeles railroad line. Surf clubs began to form up and down the coast, and Hawaiian legends like Duke Kahanamoku and George Freeth fed the frenzy by settling in Southern California. By the late 1950s, it was officially a California way of life, made even more popular by films such as *Gidget* and *Beach Blanket Bingo* and the crooning songs of the Beach Boys. Today, it's still a strong part of the culture, especially in the enclaves of Malibu, Palos Verdes, and Huntington Beach, where you'll find everyone from middle-aged studio executives to local teenagers catching a wave.

Those wanting to sample the surf here should keep a few things in mind before getting wet. First, surfers can be notoriously territorial. Beginners should avoid Palos Verdes and Third Point, at the north end of Malibu Lagoon State Beach, where veterans rule the waves. Once in the water, be as polite and mellow as possible. Give other surfers plenty of space—do *not* cut them off—and avoid swimmers. Beware of rocks and undertows. Surfing calls for caution: that huge piece of flying fiberglass beneath you could kill someone. Also keep in mind that your welcome in the water most likely won't be a shining example of gender equality. Beginning female surfers often get encouragement from local hotshots. A hapless guy, however, should expect a few sneers.

If you're not a strong swimmer, think twice before jumping in; fighting the surf to where the waves break is a strenuous proposition. The best and safest way to learn is by taking a lesson.

Catalina Island, but ask about ancillary costs such as whether the boat trip and equipment are included, for example.

You might use **Pacific Wilderness and Ocean Sports** (✉ *1719 S. Pacific Ave., near Cabrillo Marina, San Pedro* ☎ *310/833–2422* 🌐 *www.pacificwilderness.com*) if you're diving at White Point or Palos Verdes. **Malibu Divers** (✉ *21231 PCH, Malibu* ☎ *310/456–2396* 🌐 *www.malibudivers.com*) may well be on your way to the diving area at Leo Carrillo State Beach, but be warned: its certification classes are so popular that rental gear may be scarce on weekends.

SURFING

A session with **Malibu Ocean Sports** (✉ *295 Heathercliff Rd., # 42,* ☎ *310/456–6302*) will keep you on the sand for at least 30 minutes explaining the basics. Lessons start at $100; if you don't catch a wave, you get your money back. **Surf Academy** (✉ *302 19th St., Hermosa Beach* ☎ *310/372–2790* 🌐 *www.surfacademy.org*) teaches at El Segundo (Dockweiler), Santa Monica, and Manhattan Beach, with lessons starting at $45.

Kanoa Aquatics (✉ *45th St., Manhattan Beach* ☎ *310/308–7264* 🌐 *www.kanoaaquatics.com*) teaches individuals and groups at Manhattan Beach, Venice, Santa Monica, and Malibu. Adult lessons are $110 and include equipment and surf yoga. They also hold highly regarded one- and two-week surf camps for kids ages 5–17.

Learners should never surf in a busy area; look for somewhere less crowded where you'll catch more waves anyway. Good beaches for beginners are Malibu Lagoon State Beach and Huntington City Beach north of the pier, but you should always check conditions, which change throughout the day, before heading into the water. **L.A. County Lifeguards** (☎ *310/457–9701*) has a prerecorded surf-conditions hotline or go to 🌐 *www.watchthewater.com* for beach reports.

SWIMMING

The first-rate **Santa Monica Swim Center** (✉ *2225 16th St., Santa Monica* ☎ *310/458–8700* 🌐 *www.swim.smgov.net*) is open for lap and recreational swims every day (nonresidents pay $5). There's a separate pool for children and families ($12).

Inland swimmers head to the **Rose Bowl Aquatic Center** (✉ *360 N. Arroyo Blvd., Pasadena* ☎ *626/564–0330* 🌐 *www.rosebowlaquatics.com* 🎫 *$10 day pass*) for its Olympic-length lap pool. It's open daily.

WHALE-WATCHING

From December to March or April, California gray whales migrate from northern waters to warmer breeding and birthing waters off the coast of Mexico. To get an up-close look at these magnificent animals as they pass close to shore, hop aboard one of the **whale-watching tours** that depart from Long Beach and San Pedro; prices are $9–$18 per person, and reservations are recommended. **TIP→ Bring binoculars, dress warmly, and be warned that winter seas can be rough.** Contact any of the expedition companies listed under Fishing, *above*; they all have whale-watching outings, too. Or call one of the following tour operators: **Spirit Cruises** (☎ *310/548–8080* 🌐 *www.spiritdinnercruises.com*)

or **Long Beach Sportfishing** (☎*562/432–8993* ⊕*www.longbeachsportfishing.com*).

WINDSURFING

Good windsurfing can be found all along the coast. Reserve in advance for lessons. **Long Beach Windsurf & Kayak Center** (✉*3850 E. Ocean Blvd., near Belmont Pier, Long Beach* ☎*562/433–1014*) provides lessons for $200, including gear and wet suit. At **Captain Kirk's** (✉*525 N. Harbor Blvd., near Slip 93 of L.A. Harbor, San Pedro* ☎*310/833–3397*), you can get a basic beginner's lesson for $225 for three hours, which includes equipment.

YOGA

Los Angeles has nearly as many yoga studios as coffee shops, and most of them are quite good. You'll find schools teaching a variety of styles, including the athletic ashtanga (aka "power yoga"), flowing vinyasa, meditative breathing and stretching classes for senior citizens, pre- and postnatal workouts, and yoga for children; but most schools emphasize one particular style. Some do have more spiritual orientations than others, but this is kept generally low-key. *Yoga Journal* (⊕*www.yogajournal.com*) is an excellent source of information for finding studios as well as yoga retreats and more information.

6

★ Ganga (Frank) White founded **Center for Yoga** (✉*230½ N. Larchmont Blvd., Hancock Park* ☎*323/464–1276*) in 1967. To this day it stays true to his vision of integrating various strands of hatha yoga, such as Iyengar, anusara, ashtanga, and vinyasa. **Golden Bridge** (✉*6322 De Longpre Ave., Hollywood* ☎*323/936–4172* ⊕*www.goldenbridgeyoga.com*) is centered on the teachings of Gurmukh Khalsa, whose approach to kundalini yoga stresses the mind–body connection (yoga for expectant moms is a specialty). **Sacred Movement** (✉*245 S. Main St., Venice* ☎*310/450–7676*) has a meditative feel without being prescriptively spiritual. Kundalini master Yogi Bhajan has made the focus of **Yoga West** (✉*1535 S. Robertson Blvd., Los Angeles* ☎*310/552–4647*) meditation, breathing, and asanas (poses). A large faculty and schedule help make **Yoga Works** (✉*1426 Montana Ave., Santa Monica* ☎*310/393–5150*) live up to its name; friendly staffers will help you choose from among classes in ashtanga, Iyengar, and "Yoga Works Style" (combining elements of these with vinyasa).

Shopping

WORD OF MOUTH

"If your teen likes the kind of stores at malls, but you hate malls, I would suggest the 3rd Street Promenade in Santa Monica. Also fun in Santa Monica is shopping on Main Street and on Montana Avenue."

—dina4

"For the cooler boutiques I love, love, love Montana Avenue in Santa Monica. I also finally visited the Abbot Kinney area in Venice along with Main Street in Santa Monica. I refuse to go to 3rd Street Promenade in SM as it's really crowded and mostly chains."

—skiergirl

www.fodors.com/community

By Stef McDonald, Updated by Kastle Waserman

LOS ANGELES IS KNOWN AS THE CITY OF ANGELS, AND IT REALLY IS HEAVEN FOR SHOPPING. Thanks to L.A. being a sprawling city, the various neighborhoods offer different things for different people. Residents generally split the city in two—by East side (the Hollywood side) and West side (the beach side)—but many enclaves between are peppered with shops you won't want to miss.

The sun-and-sand beach culture and Hollywood stars provide big influences on the shopping scene. Stylists are always on the lookout for the newest trends and looks for the pretty young things they dress, and emerging designers take inspiration from what's being worn on the street. Paparazzi are right there to capture the looks of the stylish starlets the second they're worn, whether they're parading on a red carpet or seen emerging from a hot spot. Together the stylemakers set the cutting-edge pace—what you see here on the racks will be big back home but maybe not for another six months.

"Sunny and 70" is the weather forecast for a good part of the year, and the climate means that most shopping centers are open-air, to allow you to park you car and walk from shop to shop (don't forget to look up to see the palm trees). This foot traffic also means that good eateries open near good shops, and you can always find somewhere delicious to dine and covertly star-watch.

Those new to Los Angeles usually start at Rodeo Drive in Beverly Hills, not far from Hollywood. This tourist hot spot is a destination for window-shopping along the cluster of blocks and can provide a few hours of entertainment—or, if you're looking for a designer logo bag or red-carpet wear, get ready to do some serious spending. Then you can hop in your car and really get your shop on in the city's numerous areas: finding down-and-dirty bargains downtown, hitting funky West Hollywood, kicking back with the laid-back beach vibe of Santa Monica and Venice, or going edgy in Silver Lake/Echo Park/Los Feliz. Let the games begin. . . .

AROUND BEVERLY HILLS

New York City has Fifth Avenue, but L.A. has famed **Rodeo Drive.** The triangle, between Santa Monica and Wilshire boulevards and Beverly Drive, is one of the city's biggest tourist attractions and is lined with shops featuring the biggest names in fashion. You'll see well-coifed, well-heeled ladies toting multiple packages to their Mercedes and paparazzi staking out street corners. While the dress code in L.A. is considerably laid-back, with residents wearing flip-flops year-round, you might find them to be jewel-encrusted on Rodeo. Steep price tags on designer labels make it a "just looking" experience for many residents and tourists alike, but salespeople are used to the ogling and window shopping. In recent years, more midrange shops have opened up on the strip and surrounding blocks. Keep in mind that some stores are by appointment only. **■TIP→There are several well-marked, free (for two hours) parking lots around the core shopping area.**

SHOPPING CENTERS AND MALLS

★ **Beverly Center.** This is one of the more traditional malls you'll find in L.A., with eight levels of stores, including Macy's and Bloomingdale's. Fashion is the biggest draw and there's a little something from everyone, from D&G to H&M, and many shops in the midrange, including Banana Republic, Club Monaco, Coach, and Nine West. Look for accessories at Jacqueline Jarrot and fun fashion at Forever 21. For a terrific view of the city, head to the top-floor terrace and rooftop food court. Next door is Loehmann's, which offers a huge selection of discounted designer wear. ✉*8500 Beverly Blvd., bounded by Beverly, La Cienega, and San Vicente Blvds. and 3rd St., between Beverly Hills and West Hollywood* ☎*310/854–0071.*

TOP 5

- **Abbot Kinney Boulevard,** for fabulous indie boutiques.
- **3rd Street,** between La Cienega and Fairfax, for very chic stores and tasty spots for lunch.
- **Main Street, Santa Monica,** for Sunday shopping after the Farmers' Market.
- **Melrose Avenue and Melrose Place,** for luxury shopping.
- **Sunset Boulevard in Silver Lake,** for edgy finds followed by drinks and dinner.

DEPARTMENT STORES

Barneys New York. This is truly an impressive one-stop shop for high fashion. The Co-op section of this store reliably introduces indie designers before they make it big. Shop for beauty, shoes, and accessories on the first floor, then wind your way up the staircase for couture and Co-op floors for women and men; and keep your eyes peeled for fabulous and/or famous folks eating deli-style lunch at Barney Greengrass on the top floor. ✉*9570 Wilshire Blvd., Beverly Hills* ☎*310/276–4400.*

Neiman Marcus. Luxury shopping at its finest. The couture salon frequently trots out designer trunk shows and most locals go right for the shoe department. ✉*9700 Wilshire Blvd., Beverly Hills* ☎*310/550–5900.*

SPECIALTY STORES

HOME FURNISHINGS AND GIFTS

Del Mano Gallery. One of the best sources for wood turnings, this store also specializes in fine fiber arts, ceramics, jewelry, and art teapots by contemporary American and international artisans. ✉*11981 San Vicente Blvd., Brentwood* ☎*310/476–8508.*

Gearys of Beverly Hills. Since 1930, this has been the ultimate destination for those seeking the most exquisite fine china, crystal, silver, and jewelry, mostly from classic sources like Steuben, Spode, and Royal Crown Derby. (Another location is on Rodeo Drive.) ✉*351 N. Beverly Dr., Beverly Hills* ☎*310/273–4741.*

Le Palais des Thés. Some like it hot; some like it iced. Silver tins lining the walls contain 250 varieties of tea, with each color-coded by the tea's region of origin. Gifts like tea baskets, box sets, and teapots make unique souvenirs. ✉*401 N. Canon Dr., at Brighton Way, Beverly Hills* ☎*310/271–7922.*

Taschen. Philippe Starck designed the space to evoke a cool 1920s Parisian salon—a perfect showcase for the coffee-table books about architecture, travel, culture, and (often racy) photography. A suspended glass-cube gallery space in back shows rotating art and photo exhibits. ✉*354 N. Beverly Dr., Beverly Hills* ☎*310/274–4300.*

MENSWEAR **Anto Distinctive Shirt Maker.** This atelier has been in the custom shirt-making business since the fifties and has an impressive list of clients, from Frank Sinatra to Arnold Schwarzenegger. ✉*268 N. Beverly Dr., Beverly Hills* ☎*310/279–4500.*

Carroll & Co. Dapper is the name of the game at this longstanding, full-service, traditional men's clothing store, which has dressed such icons as Cary Grant and Clark Gable. You'll still find quality goods, excellent service, and styles that endure. (Another branch is in Pasadena.) ✉*425 N. Canon Dr., Beverly Hills* ☎*310/273–9060.*

SHOES **Jimmy Choo.** Find splurge-worthy heels and equally glamorous colorful handbags from the line made famous on *Sex and the City.* ✉*240 N. Rodeo Dr., Beverly Hills* ☎*310/860–9045.*

VINTAGE CLOTHING **Lily et Cie.** Rita Watnick's red-carpet shop is more a museum of Hollywood's golden-era garments than a run-of-the-mill vintage boutique. Oh, you can shop all right, but you might find a price tag marked $100,000 on the selection of one-of-a-kind frocks that date from 1900, from Chanel cocktail dresses to Givenchy evening gowns. ✉*9044 Burton Way, Beverly Hills* ☎*310/724–5757.*

WOMEN'S AND MEN'S CLOTHING **Burberry.** Here's proof that everything old can be new again, as British designer Christopher Bailey made the distinctive plaid—on everything from tot-size kilts to sexy swimwear—a must-have for stylish Angelenos. (Another location is in the Beverly Center mall.) ✉*9560 Wilshire Blvd., Beverly Hills* ☎*310/550–4500.*

Emporio Armani. Sleek suits, separates, and accessories are the draw at this spot that offers Armani cachet for everyday. ✉*9533 Brighton Way, Beverly Hills* ☎*310/271–7790.*

Ron Herman. You might recognize the name from the city's Fred Segal stores. This stand-alone shop is more relaxed but just as plugged-in, with an eclectic mix of local and European designs, and the in-house JET line of weekend wear. ✉*325 N. Beverly Dr., Beverly Hills* ☎*310/550–0910.*

Traffic Men. Those with a taste for luxe without stuffiness come here for Paul Smith, Costume National, or Helmut Lang. Sister store **Traffic Women** (☎*310/659–3438*) has everything from Juicy Jeans to Alexander McQueen. ✉*Beverly Center, 6th fl., 8500 Beverly Blvd., between Beverly Hills and West Hollywood,* ☎*310/659–4313.*

WEST LOS ANGELES

This is L.A.'s errand central, where entertainment executives and industry types do their serious shopping. In general, it's more affordable than Beverly Hills. A nascent art scene is blossoming in Culver City, along the intersection of La Cienega and Washington boulevards and the Santa

Monica Freeway, and down side streets like Comey Avenue. To the west, Westwood is dominated by its largest resident, UCLA.

SHOPPING MALLS

★ **H.D. Buttercup.** The recently renovated and expanded art deco Helms Bakery space is a shopping mecca that's more like a showroom than a traditional store. Manufacturers offer furniture, home decor, gifts, fashion accessories, antiques, books, artwork, bedding and textiles, lighting, candles and soaps, and more. Across the street, a newly opened **Backroom at Buttercup** features outlet prices on remainder stock. ✉*3225 Helms Ave., between Venice and Washington Blvds., Culver City* ☎*310/558-8900.*

Westfield Century City. Known locally as the Century City Mall, this open-air shopping center is set among office buildings on what used to be the backlot of Twentieth Century Fox studios. Find a mix of luxury retailers (Louis Vuitton, Tourneau), mid-range shops (Gap, Zara), department stores (Macy's, Bloomingdale's), and trendy shops (Planet Funk, Una), and Cusp, the hip Neiman Marcus spin-off featuring of-the-moment fashions. ✉*10250 Santa Monica Blvd., Century City* ☎*310/277–3898.*

SPECIALTY STORES

BOOKS **Mystery Bookstore.** There's no mystery behind this store's success. Fan of this genre flock here for a comprehensive selection of new and collectible titles, plus author events and writer workshops. Employees are helpful aficionados of every subgenre. ✉*1036-C Broxton Ave., between Weyburn and Kinross Aves., Westwood* ☎*310/209–0415.*

FOR CHILDREN **Allied Model Trains.** We know both big kids and little ones who light up when visiting this huge shop that celebrates trains old and new. Operating trains choo-choo inside along with model trains, Department 56 Snow Villages, Thomas the Tank Engine, and Playmobil toys. ✉*4371 S. Sepulveda Blvd., Culver City* ☎*310/313–9353.*

Children's Book World. One of the city's largest bookstores is as loved by parents and teachers as it is by kids. The play area and Saturday-morning storytelling series are a huge hit. It's just southwest of Century City. ✉*10580½ W. Pico Blvd., West L.A.* ☎*310/559–2665.*

FOOD ★ **Surfas.** You're very likely to rub elbows with area chefs in their work whites at this spacious and well-organized restaurant supply store that's open to the public. Find aisles of spices (priced wholesale) and jarred delicacies along with all the pots, pans, bowls, and tools you'll need to be your own Top Chef. The adjoining café serves salads, sandwiches, hot specials, gourmet teas, and baked goods. ✉*8777 Washington Blvd., at National Blvd., Culver City* ☎*310/559–4770.*

WOMEN'S CLOTHING **Last Chance.** It looks like a regular boutique, but the price tags show sample-sale prices. Score past-season separates from established and emerging designers Nicole Farhi, Catherine Malandrino, Rebecca Taylor, Twelfth Street by Cynthia Vincent), and lots of premium denim choices (True Religion, Blue Cult), and accessories. The bottom line? Pay less than half on the regular retails prices. ✉*8712 Washington Blvd., between La Cienega and National Blvds., Culver City* ☎*310/287–1919.*

CLOSE UP

The Rodeo Drive Deluxe Tour

Buckle up for the Rodeo tour, which begins at **Via Rodeo,** a cobblestoned one-block section of Rodeo closest to Wilshire Boulevard (at Dayton Way). With its temple dome ceiling and recherché design **Versace** (☒ *248 N. Rodeo Dr., Beverly Hills* ☎ *310/205–3921*) is just the place for a dramatic red-carpet gown, along with bold bags, sunglasses, and menswear. Can't afford that Porsche but would like to live like you could? **Porsche Design** (☒ *236 N. Rodeo Dr., Beverly Hills* ☎ *310/205–0095*) boasts dashboard dial watches, sunglasses, pens, and other indulgent gadgets. Newly opened **Smythson of Bond Street** (☒ *222 N. Rodeo Dr., Beverly Hills* ☎ *310/550–1901*) sells luxurious leather calendars, day planners, wallets, and notebooks (check out ones with "California Wines" and "Film Notes" stamped on their covers). Leaving the V of Via Rodeo, you'll walk the palm tree–lined street and spot all the big names in international fashion—even if you don't recognize the couture collections, you'll recognized their logos. There's **Louis Vuitton** (☒ *295 N. Rodeo Dr., Beverly Hills* ☎ *310/859–0457*) holding court on the corner, plus **Christian Dior** (☒ *309 N. Rodeo Dr., Beverly Hills* ☎ *310/859–4700*) and **Dolce & Gabbana** (☒ *312 and 314 N. Rodeo Dr., Beverly Hills* ☎ *310/888–8701*), which has adjoining men's and women's boutiques and wet bar for celeb clients. Then there's **Yves Saint Laurent** (☒ *326 N. Rodeo Dr., Beverly Hills* ☎ *310/271–4110*), **Tod's** (☒ *333 N. Rodeo Dr., Beverly Hills* ☎ *310/285–0591*), **Fendi** (☒ *355 N. Rodeo Dr., Beverly Hills* ☎ *310/276–8888*), **Michael Kors** (☒ *360 N. Rodeo Dr., Beverly Hills* ☎ *310/777–8862*), **Roberto Cavalli** (☒ *362 N. Rodeo Dr., Beverly Hills* ☎ *310/276–6006*), **Chanel** (☒ *400 N. Rodeo Dr., Beverly Hills* ☎ *310/278–5500*), , and **Giorgio Armani** (☒ *436 N. Rodeo Dr., Beverly Hills* ☎ *310/271–5555*). The Gucci and the Prada "epicenter" offers two very different Italian showcases, both well worth a visit. **Gucci** (☒ *347 N. Rodeo Dr., Beverly Hills* ☎ *310/278–3451*) goes for the stridently modernist aesthetic, with lean, sexy, and mainly black clothing upstairs and cube displays for signature bags downstairs. The Rem Koolhaas–designed **Prada** (☒ *343 N. Rodeo Dr., Beverly Hills* ☎ *310/278–8661*) is so cool it doesn't even have a sign out front, but its 20-foot-wide staircases and funhouse curves offer an inviting way to see the classy clothes, shoes, and bags.

Ba-da-bling! Time for some diamonds? **Cartier** (☒ *370 N. Rodeo Dr., Beverly Hills* ☎ *310/275–4272*) has a bridal collection to sigh for in its chandeliered and respectfully hushed showroom, along with more playful colored stones and an Asian-inspired line. **Tiffany & Co.** (☒ *210 N. Rodeo Dr., Beverly Hills* ☎ *310/273–8880*) has something for everyone, with three floors for its classic and contemporary jewelry and watches, crystal, silver, china, and somewhat-more-accessible sterling silver finds. Bold, contemporary Italian jewelry, watches, and other luxurious necessities are the order of the day at **Bulgari** (☒ *201 N. Rodeo Dr., Beverly Hills* ☎ *310/858–9216*). In business for more than a century, **Van Cleef & Arpels** (☒ *300 N. Rodeo Dr., Beverly Hills* ☎ *310/276–1161*) still designs elegant and distinctive pieces, with lots of pavé floral designs. And perhaps the most locally famous jeweler is **Harry Winston**

(✉ *310 N. Rodeo Dr., Beverly Hills* ☎ *310/271–8554*), *the* source for Oscar-night jewelry loans. The three-level space, with a bronze sculptural facade, velvet-panel walls, private salons, and a rooftop patio, is as glamorous as the gems.

But it's not all about the luxury outfitters here. A few midrange stores are mixed in among the couture designers. The new addition to the block, **Juicy Couture** (✉ *456 N. Rodeo Dr., Beverly Hills 90210* ☎ *310/550–0736*), has made wearing drawstring pants acceptable on Rodeo. **Ralph Lauren** (✉ *444 N. Rodeo Dr., Beverly Hills* ☎ *310/281–7200*) has a greenery-lined corridor with burbling fountains ushers you into ultra-WASPy rooms stocked with preppy clothes galore, and **BCBG Max Azria** (✉ *443 N. Rodeo Dr., Beverly Hills* ☎ *310/275–3024*) offers more affordable designs that attract young celebs: romantic dresses, teeny toppers, halters, and fun accessories. One of the last of the indie clothing stores on Rodeo, **Theodore** (✉ *336 N. Camden, Beverly Hills* ☎ *310/276–0663*) is a haven for the young and perhaps rebellious to find James Perse skinny tees, jeans of all labels, and hoodies aplenty. Upstairs, browse the avant-garde designer wear (Ann Demeulemeester, Jean Paul Gaultier). Next door, Theodore Man has faux-scruffy tees, jeans, and leather jackets for the guys. Though sizes 0 and 2 are the neighborhood norm, **Marina Rinaldi** (✉ *319 N. Rodeo Dr., Beverly Hills* ☎ *310/860–9793*) bucks the trend by carrying stylish, understated (and still pricey) Italian-made clothes in sizes 10 through 22 from the Max Mara line.

7

WINE AND SPIRITS

★ **Wally's.** It may be known as the wine store to the stars, but regular folks also delve into the vast selection of wines and liquor, fine chocolates, imported cheeses, and the impressive assortment of cigars. Saturday-afternoon wine tastings make a visit all the sweeter. ✉*2107 Westwood Blvd., West L.A.* ☎*310/475–0606.*

The Wine House. This beverage warehouse in the shadow of I–405 carries everything from $10 table wines to $500 first-growth Bordeaux—and the right cigars to go with them. The scope of the selection can be daunting, but friendly staffers help neophytes find the perfect bottle at the perfect price. Check the schedule for nightly classes and tastings and also visit the wine bar upstairs. ✉*2311 Cotner Ave., between Pico and Olympic Blvds., West L.A.* ☎*310/479–3731.*

SALES SPIEL

Sample sales abound throughout the year (Billion Dollar Babes and Sassy City Chicks host frequent ones) and the showrooms downtown in the fashion district often open their doors for sales (California Market Center, the New Mart, and Gerry Building, near 9th and California streets). Look at Web site (LA.com, Luckymag.com, DailyCandy.com, and Hautelook.com) and in local publications (the *L.A. Times* and *Los Angeles* magazine) for listings. "Benefit shopping" at sales that support various causes is also popular. Although most are private events, keep your eyes peeled for announcements of public sales.

DOWNTOWN

Downtown L.A. is dotted with ethnic neighborhoods (Olvera Street, Chinatown, Koreatown, Little Tokyo) and several large, open-air shopping venues (the Fashion District, the Flower Market, Grand Central Market, the Toy District, and the Jewelry District). It offers an urban bargain hunter's dream shopping experience if you know precisely what you're looking for (like diamonds and gems from the Jewelry District) or if you're willing to be tempted by unexpected finds (piñatas from Olvera Street, slippers from Chinatown, or lacquered chopsticks from Little Tokyo).

SHOPPING CENTERS AND STREETS

★ **The Fashion District.** Although this 90-block hub of the West Coast fashion industry is mainly a wholesale market, more than 1,000 independent stores sell to the general public (and some wholesalers do so on Saturday, too, when elbow room is scarce). Bonus: bargaining is expected but note that most sales are cash-only and dressing rooms are scarce. **Santee Alley** (between Santee Street and Maple Avenue, from Olympic Boulevard to 11th Street) is known for back-alley deals on knock-offs of designer sunglasses, jewelry, handbags, shoes, and clothing. Be prepared to haggle, and don't lose sight of your wallet. Visit the fashion district's Web site for maps and tips. ✉*Roughly between I–10 and 7th St., San Pedro and Main Sts., Downtown* 🌐*www.fashiondistrict.org.*

Grand Central Market. For almost 100 years, this open-air market has tempted Angelenos with all kinds of produce, fresh meats and seafood,

CLOSE UP

Out-of-the-Ordinary Souvenirs

In a city with so many exceptional shops, it would be a shame to go home with a ho-hum "Hollywood" T-shirt. Some quirky museum gift-shop finds could surprise the folks back home: celebrity-worn clothes at the Hollywood Entertainment Museum; vintage-car models at the Petersen; or a kid-friendly bottle of (fake) tar and bones from the Page Museum. The gift shop at the Fairfax Farmer's Market sells key chains with first names in a Hollywood star, and Ocean Front Walk in Venice is filled with vendors selling tees, hats, and beach towels.

For rare and cool kitsch, go to L.A.'s most off-the-wall gift shops, like Los Feliz's Y-Que for tees with mug shots (Paris, Lindsay, Nicole), plus trucker hats and fake-bling rings. At the L.A. County Coroner's gift shop, **Skeletons in the Closet** (✉ *1104 N. Mission Rd., at Morengo St. 90033* ☎ *323/343–0760*), you can snag coroner toe-tag key chains, a "body bag" garment bag, or a body-outline beach towel. **Samuel French Bookstore** (✉ *11963 Ventura Blvd., Studio City* ☎ *818/762–0535* 🌐 *www.samuelfrench.com*) is known for their scripts and how-to-break-into-acting guides.

Music buffs will appreciate the cheeky fun of eating cornflakes from a "Hollywood Bowl" bowl available at the **Bowl Store** (✉ *2301 N. Highland Ave., Hollywood* ☎ *213/972–3440* 🌐 *www.laphilstore.com* ⏲ *Closed Oct.–June*), next to the outdoor music venue.

7

spices, and fresh tortillas. Burritos, Cuban sandwiches, and kebabs satisfy shoppers on the go. ✉ *317 S. Broadway, between 3rd and 4th Sts., Downtown* ☎ *213/624–2378.*

The Jewelry District. This area resembles a slice of Manhattan, with the crowded sidewalks, diverse aromas, and haggling bargain hunters. Expect to save 50% to 70% off retail for everything from wedding bands to sparkling belt buckles. The more upscale stores are along Hill Street between 6th and 7th streets. (There's a parking structure next door on Broadway.) ✉ *Between Olive St. and Broadway, from 5th to 8th St., Downtown* 🌐 *www.lajd.net.*

Fodor's Choice ★ **Olvera Street.** Historic buildings line this redbrick walkway overhung with grape vines. At dozens of clapboard stalls you can browse south-of-the-border goods—leather sandals, bright woven blankets, devotional candles, and the like—as well as cheap toys and tchotchkes. With the musicians and cafés providing background noise, the area is constantly lively. ✉ *Between Cesar Chavez Ave. and Arcadia St., Downtown.*

The Toy District. This 12-block area of wholesale toy dealers is for the adventurous bargain hunter looking for knock-off versions of popular toys. Find stuffed animals you can buy for loose change or electronic games and gas-powered pocket bikes for bigger bills. Most vendors sell wholesale only, but plenty will also sell to individuals bearing cash. ✉ *Between 3rd and 5th Sts., and Los Angeles and San Pedro Sts., Downtown.*

SPECIALTY STORES

HOME FURNISHINGS AND GIFTS

Museum of Contemporary Art Store. Find Alessi bottle openers, Jonathan Adler vases, Jeff Koons balloon dogs, Comme des Garçons wallets, Loop totes, children's toys, and jewelry, plus tees featuring art from exhibits and art posters and books. Two other branch stores in L.A. have similar contemporary art and design items: **MOCA Store Geffen Contemporary** (☎*213/633–5323*) and **MOCA at the Pacific Design Center** (☎*310/289–5223*), which has a selection of art catalogs and rare art books. ✉*250 S. Grand Ave., Downtown* ☎*213/621–1710.*

HOLLYWOOD

Local shops may be a mixed bag, but at least you can read the stars below your feet as you browse along Hollywood Boulevard. Lingerie and movie memorabilia stores predominate here, but there are numerous options in the retail-hotel-dining-entertainment complex Hollywood & Highland. Hollywood impersonators (Michael Jackson, Marilyn Monroe, and, er, Chewbacca) join break-dancers and other street entertainers in keeping tourists entertained on Hollywood Boulevard's sidewalks near the Kodak Theater, home to the Oscars. Along La Brea Avenue, you'll find plenty of trendy, quirky, and hip merchandise, from records to furniture and clothing.

SHOPPING CENTER

Hollywood & Highland. Dozens of stores, a slew of eateries, and the Kodak Theatre fill this outdoor complex, which mimics cinematic glamour. Find designer shops (Coach, Polo, Ralph Lauren, Louis Vuitton) and chain stores (Victoria's Secret, Planet Funk, Sephora, Virgin Megastore). From the upper levels, there's a camera-perfect view of the famous HOLLYWOOD sign. On the second level, next to the Kodak Theatre, is a **Visitor Information Center** (☎*323/467–6412*) with a multilingual staff, maps, attraction brochures, and information about services. The streets surrounding it provide the setting for the Sunday Hollywood Farmer's Market, where you're likely to spot a celebrity or two picking up fresh produce or stopping to eat breakfast from the food vendors. ✉*Hollywood Blvd. and Highland Ave., Hollywood* ☎*323/817–0220.*

SPECIALTY STORES

BOOKS AND MUSIC

Fodor's Choice ★

Amoeba Records. A playground for music-lovers—this spot is like an overgrown independent record store, with a knowledgeable staff and a "Homegrown" display to highlight local artists. Catch in-store appearances by artists and bands that play sold-out shows at venues down the road several times a week. Find a rich stock of used CDs and DVDs, an impressive cache of rarities and collectibles (like the Beatles' "Butcher" cover), an encyclopedic range of indie releases, and walls filled with posters for sale. ✉*6400 W. Sunset Blvd., at Cahuenga Blvd., Hollywood* ☎*323/245–6400.*

Larry Edmunds Bookshop. After more than 60 years on the boulevard, this cinema and theater bookstore maintains old-school courtesy and charm. Books on movies and about the craft of moviemaking are the main draw, but you'll also find thousands of movie posters (no, really), from *Ain't Misbehavin'* to *Zelig* and countless photographs. ✉*6644 Hollywood Blvd., Hollywood* ☎*323/463–3273.*

FOR CHILDREN **Lost & Found.** The owner, a former stylist, describes this place as "Alice in Wonderland meets Jimi Hendrix." Visit for trippy boys' and girls' clothing (up to size 12) from Asia, Europe, and beyond. ✉*6314 Yucca Ave., Hollywood* ☎*323/856–0921.*

HOME FURNISHINGS **Lost & Found, etc.** For adults who just want to have fun, this colorful auxiliary to the nearby children's store has one-of-a-kind gifts, art, textiles, clothes, and tchotchkes. Choices include brass jewelry from France, African silk batiks, Stella Forest clothing, and other goodies handpicked from around the world. ✉*6320 Yucca St., Hollywood* ☎*323/856–5872.*

TOYS AND GAMES **Hollywood Magic.** A Tinseltown institution since the 1970s, this place draws novices and special-effects experts alike. Prices range from a buck for a gag to $6,000 for a stage illusion. ✉*6614 Hollywood Blvd., Hollywood* ☎*323/464–5610.*

VINTAGE CLOTHING **Jet Rag.** Be prepared to dig for treasure: racks and stacks are filled with everything from worn-in rock tees and bell-bottom jeans to polyester tops and weathered leather jackets. Known for its reasonable prices, Jet Rag takes it one step further on Sunday from 11:30 to dusk with a big parking-lot sale: all items go for $1. ✉*825 N. La Brea Ave., near Hollywood* ☎*323/939–0528.*

LOS FELIZ, SILVER LAKE, AND ECHO PARK

There's a hipster rock-and-roll vibe to this area, which has grown in recent years to add just the slightest shine to its edge. Come for homegrown, funky galleries, vintage shops, and local designers' boutiques. Shopping areas are concentrated along Vermont Avenue and Hollywood Boulevard in Los Feliz; Sunset Boulevard in both Silver Lake (known as Sunset Junction) and Echo Park; and Echo Park Avenue in Echo Park. ■TIP→**Keep in mind that things are spread out enough to necessitate a couple of short car trips, and many shops in these neighborhoods don't open until noon but stay open later, so grab dinner or drinks at one of the area's über-cool spots after shopping.**

SPECIALTY STORES

ANTIQUES **Peter Vanstone, Inc.** Decorators and dealers visit this courteous merchant for his eclectic selection of art, antiques, and furnishings priced anywhere from $5 to $4,000. ✉*2211 Sunset Blvd., Silver Lake* ☎*213/413–5964.*

BOOKS **Secret Headquarters.** This could be the coolest comic-book store on the planet, with a selection to satisfy both the geekiest of collectors and those more interested in artistic and literary finds. Rich wood floors, framed comic book art, and a leather chair near the front window mark the sophisticated setting, which features wall displays neatly organized with new comics and filing cabinets marked DC and Marvel. Along with classics like Superman, you'll find Buffy and Halo offerings. ✉*3817 W. Sunset Blvd., Silver Lake* ☎*323/666–2228.*

Skylight Books. A neighborhood bookshop through and through, Skylight has excellent coverage of L.A. travel, current affairs, children's books, fiction, and film, plus 'zines and journals and a section devoted to urban culture. They play host to book discussion groups and present panels and author readings with hip literati. ✉*1818 N. Vermont Ave., Los Feliz* ☎*323/660–1175.*

CANDY **Zanzabelle.** General stores don't get cooler than this. Find old-fashioned candies (Necco wafers, fresh caramels), handmade Pez dispensers, and penny candies stuffed in vintage boxes decorated with images of Flash Gordon and Bing Crosby. Save room for the locally made ice cream. ✉*2912 Rowena Ave., Silver Lake* ☎*323/663–9900.*

CLOTHING AND ACCESSORIES **Bittersweet Butterfly.** If a shop could represent Valentine's Day, this would be it. This hybrid shop sells frilly lingerie and fresh-cut flowers, along with chocolates and accessories for romantic getaways. Ooh la la. ✉*1406 Micheltorena, Silver Lake* ☎*323/660–4303.*

La La Ling. This shop offers more than your run-of-the-mill clothes for kiddies, with a particularly hip take on tot-sized versions of adult staples (Splendid tees, J Brand jeans) and cutesy tees ("Gucci Coo"), plus stylish slings and diaper bags for moms. ✉*1810 N. Vermont Ave., Los Feliz* ☎*323/664–4400.*

Lake. Styles here are for the sophisticated East Sider: a little edgy and always comfortably chic. Find Mike & Chris hoodies, Earnest Sewn jeans, Fleur Wood separates, and Foley & Corinna bags. Back rooms house apothecary and gift items, including French soaps, John Derian decoupage trinkets, and MarieBelle chocolates. ✉*2910 Rowena Ave., Silver Lake* ☎*323/664–6522.*

Panty Raid. It's all about the fun and functional undergarment here, with an ample selection of favorites, including low-rise thongs from Cosabella and Hanky Panky. The salesgirl is likely to guess a bra size on sight, too. ✉*2378½ Glendale Blvd., Silver Lake* ☎*323/668–1888.*

X-Large. Co-owned by members of the Beastie Boys, X-Large carries baggy, sturdy, urban-edge clothes and accessories in side-by-side shops, one for men and one for women. ✉*1768 N. Vermont Ave., Los Feliz* ☎*323/666–3483.*

COSMETICS **Le Pink & Co.** This small and friendly apothecary-style beauty shop is decorated with vintage perfume bottles. In stock are both old-school cosmetics (root beer lip gloss) and soaps plus current makeup lines like 100% Pure. ✉*3820 West Sunset Blvd., Silver Lake* ☎*323/661–7465.*

★ **Yolk.** Stocked with a little bit of everything you'll want to get or give, this home/gift shop has a spot-on selection of fresh designed goods. Find Voluspa candles, Amenity bedding, Savon soaps, barware and bowls, and a back room with kid stuff that includes organic cotton clothing, bedding, and non-toxic wood toys. Also find handcrafted jewelry by local designers and art on the walls by local artists. ✉*1626 Silver Lake Blvd., Silver Lake* ☎*323/660–4315.*

POP CULTURE **Soap Plant Wacko/La Luz de Jesus Gallery.** This pop-culture supermarket offers a wide range of items, including rows of books on art and design and, uh, "deviant literature." But it's the novelty stock that makes the biggest impression, with Mexican wrestling masks, Marilyn Manson dolls, Napoleon Dynamite band-aids, and novelties such as X-ray specs and hula dancer lamps. The in-store gallery in the back focuses on underground and "lowbrow" art. ✉*4633 Hollywood Blvd., Los Feliz* ☎*323/663–0122 or 323/666–7667.*

Y-Que Trading Post. It's kitsch-central here, where you'll find mostly pop culture tees, including ones with celebrity mug shots, as well as naughty novelties and gag gifts (George Bush toilet paper, Sea Monkeys on Mars). A custom press in the back allows you to choose your own tee design, too. On weekends, crowds of revelers shop here until midnight. ✉*1770 N. Vermont Ave., Los Feliz* ☎*323/664–0021.*

VINTAGE CLOTHING

Flounce Vintage. Scarves, rhinestone baubles, and a great stock of floral dresses and beaded cardigans await in this girlishly sweet store. ✉*1555 Echo Park Ave., Echo Park* ☎*213/481–1975.*

SquaresVille. Vintage and recent recyclables share rack space at this shop with a rockin' vibe. ✉*1800 N. Vermont Ave., Los Feliz* ☎*323/669–8464.*

WINES AND SPIRITS

Silver Lake Wine. Boutique, small-production wineries from 'round the world provide this shop with bottles that fill vertical racks from floor to ceiling. The knowledgeable staff might look unassuming dressed in jeans and tees but they'll steer you to the right wine or spirits for any occasion. You can wet your whistle at tastings on Sunday, Monday, and Thursday. ✉*2395 Glendale Blvd., Silver Lake* ☎*323/662–9024.*

WEST HOLLYWOOD AND MELROSE AVENUE

West Hollywood is prime shopping real estate. And as they say with real estate, it's all about location, location, location. Depending on the street address, West Hollywood has everything from upscale art, design, and antiques store to ladies-who-lunch clothing boutiques to megamusic stores and specialty book vendors. Melrose Avenue, for instance, is part bohemian-punk shopping district (from North Highland to Sweetzer) and part upscale art and design mecca (upper Melrose Avenue and Melrose Place). Discerning locals and celebs haunt the posh boutiques around Sunset Plaza (Sunset Boulevard at Sunset Plaza Drive), on Robertson Boulevard (between Beverly Boulevard and 3rd Street), and along upper Melrose Avenue.

The huge, blue Pacific Design Center, on Melrose at San Vicente Boulevard, is the focal point for this neighborhood's art- and interior design–related stores, including many on nearby Beverly Boulevard. The Beverly–La Brea neighborhood also claims a number of trendy clothing stores. Perched between Beverly Hills and West Hollywood, 3rd Street (between La Cienega and Fairfax) is a magnet for small, friendly designer boutiques. Finally, the Fairfax District, along Fairfax below Melrose, encompasses the flamboyant, historic Farmers Market, at Fairfax Avenue and 3rd Street; the adjacent shopping extravaganza, The Grove; and some excellent galleries around Museum Row at Fairfax Avenue and Wilshire Boulevard.

CLOSE UP

Melrose Place

Marc Jacobs's three boutiques—one for his women's collection (✉ *8400 Melrose Pl.*), one for his men's line (✉ *8409 Melrose Pl.*), and the third (✉ *8410 Melrose Ave.*) for his more affordable Marc by Marc bridge line—established the area on and around this one-block street as a fashion destination. At 8428 Melrose Place, **Bird** had a well-edited selection of coveted imports, such as Repetto ballet flats and Alice Roi clothing. Hair maven **Sally Hershberger** snips shags (her signature cut) at 8440 for a mere $600—if you can even score an appointment. **Santa Maria Novella** (*8411*) offers soaps, tonics, and perfumes from Italy, and **Me & Ro** (*8405*) showcases the line's silver and fine gold jewelry. At the end of the block, at 8460, the Italian label **Marni** exhibits bohemian luxury wear (like cropped furs and chunky bead accents) in a fabulously modernist space. Across the street, **Diane von Furstenberg**'s shop (✉ *8407 Melrose Ave.*) flaunts her classic wrap dresses and resort wear in distinctive geometric prints, while you can find sleek and sophisticated separates at **Theory** (✉ *8428 Melrose Ave.*) and casual European styles at **A.P.C.** (✉ *619 N. Croft Ave.*).

SHOPPING CENTERS

Fodor'sChoice ★ **Farmers Market and The Grove.** The granddaddy of L.A. markets dates to 1935, and the amazing array of clapboard stalls (selling everything from candy to hot sauce, fresh fruit to fresh lamb), wacky regulars, and a United Nations of food choices must be experienced to be appreciated. Employees from the nearby CBS studios mingle with hungover clubbers and elderly locals at dozens of eateries and shops under one huge roof. The "Red Car" trolley shuttles visitors between the Farmers Market and the nearby **Grove,** a wildly popular outdoor mall with an ersatz European feel and a fabulous people-watching scene. Although many of the stores are familiar in any mall (Nordstrom, Abercrombie & Fitch, the Apple Store, American Girl Place), the elaborate setting, with winding tile walkways, a stream, and a fountain, put this shopping center over the top. ✉ *6333 W. 3rd St., at Fairfax Ave., Fairfax District* ☎ *323/933–9211 Farmers Market, 323/900–8080 The Grove.*

SPECIALTY STORES

ANTIQUES

Blackman Cruz. Browse among David Cruz and Adam Blackman's offbeat pieces (like 1940s New York subway signs) as well as fine Continental and Asian furniture from the 18th to the mid-20th century. ✉ *836 N. Highland Ave., near West Hollywood* ☎ *310/657–9228.*

BOOKS AND MUSIC

A Different Light. Frequent signings and readings pull in the locals for books by and about gays, lesbians, bisexuals, and transgendered people. ✉ *8853 Santa Monica Blvd., West Hollywood* ☎ *310/854–6601.*

Bodhi Tree Bookstore. Incense wafts around a huge selection of spiritual (more Buddhist than Christian) books, gifts, music, and videos. Psychic readings, signings, lectures, and workshops are held regularly. Behind the store, Bodhi's used-book shop also sells herbs and teas. ✉ *8585 Melrose Ave., West Hollywood* ☎ *310/659–1733.*

Fodor'sChoice ★ **Book Soup.** One of the best independent bookstores in the country, Book Soup has been serving Angelenos for more than 30 years. Given its Hollywood pedigree, it's especially deep in books about film, music, art, and photography. Fringe benefits include an international newsstand, a bargain-book section, and author readings several times weekly. ✉ *8818 Sunset Blvd., West Hollywood* ☎ *310/659–3110.*

★ **Cook's Library.** Find every cookbook imaginable here, from *The Joy of Cooking* to *The Santa Monica Farmers' Market Cookbook*. The selection is neatly organized by style or cuisine or region. ✉ *8373 W. 3rd St., near West Hollywood* ☎ *323/655–3141.*

Meltdown. The largest comic-book store on the West Coast is a monument to the artistry, wit, and downright weirdness of comics (from Ghost World to Booty Babe). Toys, art books, graphic novels, tees, posters, and a gallery with comic-related art and photography supplement the scores of comic books.

Traveler's Bookcase. A massive collection of travel titles fills this shop, with tabletop books, maps, guides, literatures, and gifts for travelers (notebooks, pens, luggage tags, compact clocks). ✉ *8375 W. 3rd St., near West Hollywood* ☎ *323/655–0575.*

CAMERAS AND ELECTRONICS

Samy's Camera. This is a we'll-meet-or-beat-any-price kind of place, with cameras, video equipment, lighting, and studio equipment, used wares, collectibles, rentals and repairs, and digital imaging services. But locals know the real reason to come back is the knowledgeable staff. Other branches are in Culver City and Pasadena. ✉ *431 S. Fairfax Ave., south of W. 3rd St., Fairfax District* ☎ *323/938–2420.*

FOOD

Algabar. Fine teas and delicacies are showcased at this beautiful and inviting shop that stocks their own tea leaves and others fine and fancy varieties by Mariage Freres. Also find jarred condiments, soy wax candles, and imported perfumes. ✉ *342 S. La Brea Ave. 90036* ☎ *323/954–9720.*

HOME FURNISHINGS AND GIFTS

Moss. For home design that's a notch above luxurious, Moss can't be beat—here, high design is high art. Inside is a "Swarovski Crystal Palace" installation (featuring huge chandeliers by Georg Baldele) around a Maarten Baas sculpture Baby Grand. ✉ *8444 Melrose Ave., West Hollywood* ☎ *323/866–5260*

O.K. An über–gift shop, O.K. stocks the classy (Scandinavian stemware, vintage candelabras) to the goofy (macramé dog collars, bejeweled Pez holders) and specializes in architecture and design books. ✉ *8303 W. 3rd St., near West Hollywood* ☎ *323/653–3501.*

Soolip. As though the desk accoutrements, custom letterpress stationery, and handmade papers from nearly 50 countries weren't enough, this *paperie* also does a brisk business in couture wrapping. The space includes a bungalow with clothing, accessories, furnishings, and gifts, as well as a florist service. ✉ *8646 Melrose Ave., West Hollywood* ☎ *310/360–0545.*

Zipper. This is the one shop you need for those times when you're utterly stumped for a gift. Find bowls and vases that pass for pieces of art, shell boxes, mod office supplies, luxurious soaps, games, and quirky items

CLOSE UP

Farmers' Markets

Chefs by the bushel, parents, kids in strollers, artists, and fixed-income senior citizens mingle and sample their way through the best of Southern California's fresh produce at Los Angeles's farmers' markets. Fruits and vegetables both recognizable and exotic get scooped up by the bag-full and vendors offer grilled corn, plates of crepes, omelets, and Mexican breakfast burritos.

Markets are held every day of the week, but weekends are the most popular. Many have special events like cooking demonstrations, pony rides, or live music to accompany the fresh bounty. Check with the **Southland Farmers' Market Association** (🌐 *www.cafarmersmarkets.org*) for locations, days, and times of the more than 70 local markets. Here are a few of the best. The **Beverly Hills Farmers' Market** (✉ *Civic Center Dr. between Alpine Dr. and Foothill Rd.* ☎ *310/550–4796*), held Sunday 9–1, is the only California market to carry wine (no sampling allowed). The **Chinatown Farmers' Market** (✉ *727 N. Hill St., between Alpine and Ord Sts.* ☎ *213/680–0243*), held Thursday 2–6, specializes in Asian produce. The **West Hollywood Farmers' Market** (✉ *1200 N. Vista St., at Fountain Ave.* ☎ *323/845–6535*), on Monday 9–2, is as busy and cheerful as a street fair, and the **Hollywood Farmer's Market** (✉ *Ivar and Selma Aves.*) is held Sunday 8–6. The greatest of all is the **Santa Monica Wednesday market** (✉ *Arizona Ave. at 2nd St.* ☎ *310/458–8712*). Running from 8:30 to 1:30, it draws all the area's top chefs and amateur foodies alike. Depending on the time of year, you might be tempted by heirloom tomatoes, Chinese long beans, Persian cucumbers, or blood oranges. On Saturday 8:30–1, there's an organic produce market at this same location. Other Santa Monica markets are held Saturday at Pico and Cloverfield boulevards (8–1) and Sunday at Main Street and Ocean Park Boulevard (9:30–1).

like Viewfinders, chocolates, tabletop design books, and jewelry. The back room of kid stuff is also impressive. ✉ *8316 W. 3rd St., near West Hollywood* ☎ *323/951–0620.*

JEWELRY AND ACCESSORIES

C by Karina. This is the place to get statement-making shades, with sunglasses from designers like Tom Ford, plus vintage frames for those looking for more one-of-a-kind glare protection. ✉ *116 S. Robertson, between Beverly Hills and West Hollywood* ☎ *310/777–0231.*

MENSWEAR

Douglas Fir. Comme des Garçons, Paul Smith, Masons, Skaen are among the designers on the racks here, where you'll also find select books, hats, sunglasses, and shaving essentials. ✉ *8311 W. 3rd St., West Hollywood* ☎ *323/651–5445.*

John Varvatos. The celebrated menswear designer's showroom has vaulted, beamed ceilings and a separate VIP room for celebrities. The "L.A. look" of sport coat, jeans, and Converse sneakers is a staple here. ✉ *8800 Melrose Ave., at Robertson Blvd., West Hollywood* ☎ *310/859–2791.*

POP CULTURE

Kidrobot. Underground art is the draw at this toy boutique for grown-ups. Ugly dolls, Dunnys, Ice-Bots, and other limited-edition figures draw collectors and the curious. ✉ *7972 Melrose Ave., near West Hollwyood* ☎ *323/782–1474.*

SHOES

Boot Star. A huge selection of boots here spells heaven to urban cowboys and cowgirls. You'll find everything from calfskin to alligator, turquoise cobra skin to hand-tooled skulls and crossbones, with most boots handmade in Mexico and Texas. Custom sizing is available. ✉ *8493 Sunset Blvd., West Hollywood* ☎ *323/650–0475.*

Sigerson Morrison. The strappy sandals, polished flats, and mod boots from this British designer have inspired many a pedicure. ✉ *8307 W. 3rd St., near West Hollywood* ☎ *323/655–6133.*

Undefeated. Find serious kicks here—for grown-up kids—including old-school Converse, Vans, Adidas, Nike, and Reebok. Other locations are on Main Street in Santa Monica and on Sunset Blvd. in Silver Lake. ✉ *112½ S. La Brea Ave., Beverly–La Brea* ☎ *323/937–6077.*

TRAVEL

★ **Flight 001.** No other shop celebrates the fine art of travel like this one. Start with the totes, duffels, and roll-on bags (Jack Spade, Mandarina Duck, Tumi, Orla Kiely) and then think of everything you need to fill it with, including cashmere throws, pill cases, luggage tags, eye masks, and "No Cootie" travel spray. ✉ *8235 W. 3rd St., West Hollywood* ☎ *323/966–0001.*

VINTAGE CLOTHING

★ **Decades.** Stylists and A-listers come here to scour the racks for dresses for award season. Owner Cameron Silver's stellar selection includes dresses by Pucci and Ossie Clark, and Hermès bags. On the street level, the newly expanded **Decades Two** (☎ *323/655–1960*) resells contemporary designer and couture clothing (often worn once by celeb clientele) and accessories at up to 80% off. ✉ *8214 Melrose Ave., near West Hollywood* ☎ *323/655–0223.*

Resurrection. There's a spot-on selection of high-quality 1960s–'80s vintage wear from the likes of Halston, YSL, and Pucci, as well as vintage Levi's, Gucci accessories, and more—all neatly arranged by color and style. ✉ *8006 Melrose Ave., near West Hollywood* ☎ *323/651–5516.*

The Way We Wore. Overlook the over-the-top vintage store furnishings to find one of the city's best selections of well-cared for and one-of-a-kind items, with a focus on sequins and beads. Upstairs, couture from Halston, Dior, and Chanel can cost up to $20,000. ✉ *334 S. La Brea, Beverly–La Brea* ☎ *323/937–0878.*

WOMEN'S AND MEN'S CLOTHING

Fodor's Choice ★ **American Rag Cie.** Half the store features new clothing from established and emerging labels and of-the-moment denim lines, and the other side is stocked with well-preserved vintage clothing, neatly organized by color and style. Also find shoes and accessories. Adjoining store World Denim Bar stocks jeans galore. Browse the mainly French home furnishings and European CDs in another store annex, **Maison Midi** (☎ *323/935–3157*), which also has a bistro/café with a lively lunch scene. ✉ *150–160 S. La Brea Ave., Beverly–La Brea* ☎ *323/935–3154.*

Fodor's Choice ★ **Fred Segal.** The ivy-covered building and security guards in the parking lot might tip you off that this is *the* place to be. Go during the lunch hour to star-gaze at the super-trendy café. This longtime L.A. fashion landmark is subdivided into miniboutiques that range from couture clothing to skateboard fashions. The entertainment industry's fashion fiends are addicted to the exclusive goods here, some from overseas, others from cult L.A. designers just making their marks. ✉ *8100 Melrose Ave., at Crescent Heights Blvd., near West Hollywood* ☎ *323/651–4129.*

H. Lorenzo. Funky, high-end designer clothes (D-Squared, Junya Watanabe, Jaded by Knight) attract stylists and a young Hollywood crowd, people who don't blink at paying $250 for jeans. Next door, **H. Men** (☎ *310/652–7039*) provides the same hot styles for the guys. ✉ *8660 Sunset Blvd., West Hollywood* ☎ *310/659–1432.*

James Perse. The soft cotton tees (and sweaters and fleece) are quintessentially L.A. Find them here in an immaculate gallery-like space, with sleek white and light wood furnishings. ✉ *8914 Melrose Ave., West Hollywood* ☎ *310/276–7277.*

★ **Kitson.** Stars that want to be seen (and seen shopping) come here to choose from piles of jeans, tops, hoodies, Pucci scarves, sequined Converse, thongs with "naughty" bejeweled across the front, and unusual pampering products. It's pure girly glitz. Across the street, **Kitson Kids** (☎ *310/246–3829*) provides mini-me versions of trends and Kitson Men (✉ *146 N. Robertson* ☎ *310/358–9559*) has walls of jeans, plenty of hoodies, plus cool sneakers and accessories like a sleeping eye mask printed with "PIMP." ✉ *115 S. Robertson Blvd., between Beverly Hills and West Hollywood* ☎ *310/859–2652.*

Fodor's Choice ★ **Maxfield.** Enter the modern concrete structure for one of L.A.'s too-cool-for-school sources for high fashion, with sleek as can be offerings from Balenciaga, Comme des Garçons, Christian Dior, Jill Sander, and Yohji Yamamoto. For serious shoppers (or gawkers) only. ✉ *8825 Melrose Ave., at Robertson Blvd., West Hollywood* ☎ *310/274–8800.*

MILK. Milk bottles and old trunks and suitcases line the shelves at this spacious shop, which has become a destination for new trends. Tees and jeans top the tables and racks feature well-edited picks, from silky dresses and lacy tops to luxe sweaters. Part of the back is devoted to menswear. ✉ *8209 W. 3rd St., near West Hollywood* ☎ *323/951–0330.*

Paul Smith. You can't miss the shocking fuchsia "shoebox" that houses Paul Smith's fantastical collection of clothing, luggage, boots, hats, and objets d'art, where photos and art line the walls above shelves of tomes on pop culture, art, and Hollywood. The clothing vibrates in signature colors like hot pink and mustard yellow and you can find Smith's signature stripes on everything from socks to notebooks. ✉ *8221 Melrose Ave., near West Hollywood* ☎ *323/951–4800.*

Ted Baker. Rich cord, tweed, and velvet suiting and wild striped shirts are showcased here. ✉ *131 N. Robertson Blvd., between Beverly Hills and West Hollywood* ☎ *310/550–7855.*

WOMEN'S CLOTHING

Bleu. Ever dream of getting a fresh look without lifting a finger? The friendly, style-savvy staff will size you up in minutes and deliver just the right edgy basics for day or flirty party frocks for night (with the jewelry, shoes, and undies to match) to your dressing room. ✉ *454*

S. La Brea Ave., Beverly–La Brea ☎*323/939–2228.*

Curve. Chains from the ceiling hold wood bars for hanging garments at this shop that features layers of chiffon, lace, silk, mesh, and leather separates that will take you beyond jeans and a tank. Curve's own line rubs elbows with fresh designers like Inhabit and Michelle Mason. ✉*154 N. Robertson Blvd., between Beverly Hills and West Hollywood* ☎*310/360–8008.*

Hillary Rush. The shopkeeper here is third-generation, and her expertise shows: edgy and sleek separates, the latest skinny jeans, soft tees by local lines L.A. Made and Daftbird plus just the right accessories are spot-on L.A. ✉*8222 W. 3rd St., near West Hollywood* ☎*323/852–0088.*

WORD OF MOUTH

"At 9 AM [in the top farmers' markets], you'll find sous-chefs from the top-end restaurants shopping for that evening's specials. By lunchtime, everyone's there—executives from surrounding office buildings, bodybuilders looking for organic salad fixings, leaflet distributers. . . . You get to walk around in the sun, taking in the produce and the people. It's just really cool." —rjw_lgb_ca

Intermix. The new addition of NY-based Intermix on Robertson is giving already established area boutiques a run for their money. Racks feature looks that are both femme and fierce, with brightly colored options from Vince, Robert Rodriguez, Jill Stuart, Ella Moss, and more. The dress selection is especially notable. ✉*110 N. Robertson Blvd., between Beverly Hills and West Hollywood* ☎*310/860–0113.*

Lisa Kline. For that very Hollywood look that's trendy but grown-up, visit this dependable, celebrity-friendly shop for Foley & Corinna, C&C California, Kooba, and Rachel Pally, and those all-important underpinnings for revealing outfits. Lisa Kline Men and Lisa Kline Kids have also opened on the same strip. ✉*136 S. Robertson Blvd., between Beverly Hills and West Hollywood* ☎*310/246–0907.*

Lotta. True bohemian glamour prevails here, with halters and tunics in bright colors from the shop's line and other hippie-chic designers. Piles of accessories complete the look. Walls and shelves are adorned with magazine tearsheets of celebs wearing the same styles you see on the racks. ✉*7965 Melrose Ave., near West Hollywood* ☎*323/852–0520.*

Madison. This local mini-chain has neatly arranged racks that happen to always hold what is hot right this minute. There are items for everyday, too—Fendi shares shelf space with Uggs. Another location is on Melrose Avenue. ✉*8741 W. 3rd St., near West Hollywood* ☎*310/275–1930.*

Satine. This small shop has a retro feel to it, matched by the selection of clothing by indie designers you won't find elsewhere and more well-known ones (Stella McCartney, Alexander McQueen). A vintage–loving style permeates the air, with a playful touch of little-girl-grown-up. ✉*8117 W. 3rd St., near West Hollywood* ☎*323/655–2142.*

South Willard. Hit this store/design lab, which stocks mostly menswear for the man not shy about wearing well-cut high-style designs from mostly European lines. ✉*8038 W. 3rd St., near West Hollywood* ☎*323/653–6153.*

Trina Turk. Interior designer Kelly Wearstler put her stamp on this beautiful space, with mod furnishings providing a perfect setting for Turk's bohemian-chic line. The place has a resort feel, with mannequins wearing big sunglasses and print scarves. ✉*8008 W. 3rd St., near West Hollywood* ☎*323/651–1382.*

SANTA MONICA AND VENICE

The breezy beachside communities of Santa Monica and Venice are ideal for leisurely shopping. Scads of tourists (and some locals) gravitate to the Third Street Promenade, a popular pedestrians-only strolling–shopping area that is within walking range of the beach and historic Santa Monica Pier. A number of modern furnishings stores are nearby on 4th and 5th streets. Main Street between Pico Boulevard and Rose Avenue offers upscale chain stores, cafés, and some original shops, while Montana Avenue is a great source for distinctive clothing boutiques and child-friendly shopping, especially between 7th and 17th streets. **■ TIP→ Parking in Santa Monica is next to impossible on Wednesday, when some streets are blocked off for the farmers' market, but there are several parking structures with free parking for an hour or two.** In Venice, Abbot Kinney Boulevard is abuzz with mid-century furniture stores, art galleries and boutiques, and cafés.

SHOPPING CENTERS

Brentwood Country Mart. A preservationist has restored this faux country market with its red-barn backdrop and cobblestone courtyards, and it still has an old-school charm. The dozen or so stores include Calypso (for beachy, boho brights), Turpan (for luxury home goods and gifts), Marie Mason Apothecary (for beauty), James Perse (for laid-back cotton knits), and Sugar Paper (for letterpress cards and paper goods), and the recently opened Broken English (for exotic and fine jewelry). Grab a gourmet lunch or baked treat at City Bakery. ✉*225 26th St., at San Vicente Blvd., Santa Monica.*

★ **Third Street Promenade.** Whimsical dinosaur-shaped, ivy-covered fountains and buskers of every stripe set the scene along this pedestrians-only shopping stretch. Stores are mainly the chain variety (Restoration Hardware, Urban Outfitters, Apple), but there are also Quiksilver and Rip Curl outposts for cool surf attire. Movie theaters, bookstores, pubs, and restaurants ensure that virtually every need is covered. ✉*3rd St. between Broadway and Wilshire Blvd.,*

SPECIALTY SHOPS

BOOKS AND MUSIC

Arcana. A treasure trove for artists and filmmakers, this store boasts a serious collection of new and out-of-print books on art, architecture, design, and fashion—with an especially impressive selection on photography. ✉*1229 Third Street Promenade, Santa Monica* ☎*310/458–1499.*

Equator. This bookstore gallery specializes in out-of-print and collectible books, with literature on one wall and another filled with art, design, architecture—and surf culture. Select shelf space is given to local Venice history, plus less obvious choices (circus freaks, bullfighting). The back space now houses collectible records (they sell turntables, too). Monthly exhibits show art from mostly local artists (including one of the owners; the other owner is an author). ✉ *1103 Abbot Kinney Blvd., Venice* ☎ *310/399–5544.*

Hear Music. Pick up a latte in the entryway and take it to a burn-and-print station, where you can make your own compilation, choose your own cover art, and walk away minutes later with a new CD. With its excellent selection of jazz, folk, world, electronica, and alternative music, the store will take you out of your comfort zone. On weekend nights, the burn stations are jammed. ✉ *1429 Third Street Promenade, Santa Monica* ☎ *310/319–9527.*

Hennessey + Ingalls Bookstore. A stop here would make a perfect end to a day at the Getty. In L.A., this is the largest collection of books on graphic design, art, architecture, and photography. ✉ *214 Wilshire Blvd., between 2nd and 3rd Sts., Santa Monica* ☎ *310/458–9074.*

COSMETICS **Palmetto.** This shelves and counters at this longstanding shop are literally crammed with bath, body, and beauty treats from little-known and sought-after lines, with a focus on products that are made with natural ingredients. ✉ *1034 Montana Ave., Santa Monica* ☎ *310/395–6687.*

Vert. A new addition to Abbot Kinney, this lifestyle shop owned by a makeup artist stocks luxury body and beauty products, along with some jewelry and accessories that are "green" (including Stella McCartney's organic line). ✉ *1121 Abbot Kinney Blvd., Venice* ☎ *310/581–6126.*

Strange Invisible Perfumes. A custom-made fragrance by botanical perfumer Alexandra Balahoutis might run you in the thousands, but you can pick up ready-made scents from her exotic line, along with body lotions, washes, and candles in her exquisitely designed shop that is both modern and romantic. ✉ *1138 Abbot Kinney Blvd., Venice* ☎ *800/919–7472.*

FOR CHILDREN ★ **Acorn.** Remember when toys didn't require computer programming—and weren't recalled for containing lead? Ellen West's old-fashioned shop sparks kids' imaginations with dress-up clothes, books, and hand-painted wooden toys: no batteries or plastic allowed. Closed Sunday. ✉ *1220 5th St., near Wilshire Blvd., Santa Monica* ☎ *310/451–5845.*

Every Picture Tells a Story. This well-stocked children's bookstore doubles as an art gallery with framed pieces from classic books, from Dr. Seuss, Maurice Sendak, Charles Schulz, and others hanging on the walls above the shelves of old and new titles. ✉ *1311-C Montana Ave., Santa Monica* ☎ *310/451–2700.*

Jenny Bec's. This children's toy store is jam-packed with everything from puzzles and books to crafts and classics like Slinkies and bubbles, with special sections throughout (for pirates, fairies), with a back baby room. Bonus: colorful gift-wrapping and shipping services. ✉ *927 Montana Ave., Santa Monica* ☎ *310/395–9505.*

HOME FURNISHINGS **Colcha.** This gem-filled Abbot Kinney spot moved to a more spacious location up the block to better showcase its home decor and gifts, with John Derian plates, Burn candles, leather-bound journals, glassware, art books, and furniture. ✉*1416 Abbot Kinney Blvd., Venice* ☎*310/392–3600.*

JEWELRY

Moondance Jewelry Gallery. This accessories shop has cases built into the walls to display its truly bountiful selection of jewelry. There's something for every taste (and price) level, from boho to bling-bling pieces. Trunk shows and special events are given several times a year. ✉*1530 Montana Ave., Santa Monica* ☎*310/395–5516.*

MENSWEAR

Sean. A stop for the stylish guy who doesn't want to look like he's trying too hard: Emile Lafaurie's clean and classic house-line features clothes with just enough polish: button-downs with a narrow cut, boxy painter's jackets, sedate suits. **Station 25**, an in-store shoe boutique, provides the finishing touches. ✉*1107 Montana Ave., Santa Monica* ☎*310/260–5616.*

WOMEN'S AND MEN'S CLOTHING

Fodor's Choice ★

Fred Segal. The West Hollywood branch might draw more celebrities, but this location is larger and decidedly more laid-back. Across-the-street shops in two buildings feature mini-boutiques for everything from the latest denim styles to handbags. The beauty selection at the Apothia mini-boutique is particularly impressive. The Comfort Café and a hair salon provide reprieves from shopping. ✉*500 and 420 Broadway, Santa Monica* ☎*310/458–8100 or 310/394–9814.*

Harmonie. Located on the less-traveled part of Abbot Kinney, this cool, modern store is worth the short drive. One side outfits women, the other men, and there's an impressive selection—Tracey Reese dresses and Development separates for women and Ben Sherman jackets and Drifter tees for men, plus jeans for both. ✉*2800 Abbot Kinney Blvd., Venice* ☎*310/306–5059.*

The Levi's Store. Step into the Fit Locator booth here for a full body scan and printout of your best fit and size. This is the largest Levi's outlet in Southern California, with thousands of jeans in various colors and configurations. Vests, jackets, shirts, and boots break up the sea of denim. ✉*1409 Third Street Promenade, Santa Monica* ☎*310/393–4899.*

Wasteland. This vintage emporium, located one block from the Third Street Promenade, also sells recently recycled items for both women and men in good condition. Find everything from wide-lapelled polyester shirts to last year's Coach bag. Another location is on Melrose Avenue. ✉*1338 4th St., Santa Monica* ☎*310/395–2620.*

ZJ Boarding House. One of the area's best surf, skate, and snow shops has a smaller shop for women next door. Both offer gear and essentials for board sports (from wax to boards and wetsuits) but also an ample selection of apparel from the best lines. ✉*2619 Main St., Santa Monica* ☎*310/392–5646.*

WOMEN'S CLOTHING

Heist. Owner Nilou Ghodsi sends thank-you notes to customers and employs a sales staff that is friendly and helpful but not at all overbearing at this warm, box-shaped boutique that is small but never claustrophobic. A table at the center of the store is surrounded by racks of fetching separates (from beachside Calypso to downtown Paul & Joe) and a loft room upstairs features denim, tees, and sale items. ✉*1104 Abbot Kinney Blvd., Venice* ☎*310/450–6531.*

★ **Planet Blue.** The quintessential Malibu style is found here, with baskets on the floor filled with flip-flops and an abundance of jeans, cute tops, dresses, and accessories. It does hippie-beach-chic best, hands-down. Another location is on Montana Ave. ✉*2940 Main St., Santa Monica* ☎*310/396–1767.*

WORD OF MOUTH

"Two words: Fred Segal. This is the quintessential LA shopping experience. Expensive. Super-trendy. Celebrity sightings. There are two locations, one on Melrose, one on Broadway in Santa Monica."

—julieland

Principessa. A recent renovation of this warm and homey boutique means more space for comfy and oh-so-cool clothes from Mint, La Rok, Twelfth Street by Cynthia Vincent, Collective Clothing, and more. An ample selection of jeans and jewelry, some from local designers, completes the look. The adjoining shop Vamp features deals on its stock, with everything marked $100 or less. ✉*1104 Abbot Kinney Blvd., Venice* ☎*310/450–6531.*

SAN FERNANDO AND SAN GABRIEL VALLEYS

Over "the Hill" and into the San Fernando Valley, Studio City's Ventura Boulevard is the vital artery of Valley shopping. Mimicking Hollywood, stars line this shopping drag, but here they honor past TV shows. Only 20 freeway minutes over another hill east of Hollywood are the San Gabriel Valley communities of Burbank and Pasadena. In Pasadena, the stretch of Colorado Boulevard between Pasadena Avenue and Arroyo Parkway, known as Old Town, is a popular pedestrian shopping mecca, with everything from Crate & Barrel to H&M, and Tiffany's sits a block away from Forever 21. A few blocks east on Colorado, the open-air "urban village" known as Paseo Colorado mixes residential, retail, dining, and entertainment spaces along Colorado Boulevard between Los Robles and Marengo avenues. Enter on Colorado or Marengo for free parking.

SPECIALTY STORES

Storyopolis. This huge children's bookstore features sections for "world of classics" and "land of possibilities"; plenty of seating and a back room art gallery and side room for readings and other events; and a toy room with paint-by-numbers and crafts plus plush toys. ✉*14945 Ventura Blvd., Studio City* ☎*818/509–5600.*

Vroman's Bookstore. Southern California's oldest and largest (27,000 square feet) independent bookseller is justly famous for great service. An attached newsstand, café, and adjacent gift and stationery store boost the total shopping experience. Some 400 author events annually, plus a fab kids' zone complete with play area, make this a truly outstanding spot. ✉*695 E. Colorado Blvd., Pasadena* ☎*626/449–5320.*

MEN'S AND WOMEN'S CLOTHING

It's a Wrap. Looking for castoffs from *Six Feet Under, General Hospital,* or the latest Disney Studios production? The wardrobe departments of movie and TV studios and production companies ship clothes here daily. A "letter of authenticity" accompanies each bargain (that's 35%–95% off retail). Another store is open near Beverly Hills, on S.

CLOSE UP

Flea Markets

Flea markets are a fantastic resource for those who love all things vintage. Flea market culture has a few rules: arrive early (the "great finds" tend to go fast), polite haggling is allowed, and remember that what you see is what you get (no, those Pumas from the '70s don't come in other colors).

Held every Sunday 9–5 in Fairfax High School's parking lot, the **Melrose Trading Post** (✉ *Fairfax Blvd. and Melrose Ave.* ☎ *323/655–7679* ⊕ *www.greenwayarts.org/tradingpost.htm*) is hip, fairly junk-free, and popular with Hollywood denizens and you're likely to find a recycled rock tee or some vinyl to fill your collection. Live music and fresh munchies entertain vintage hunters and collectors. The market benefits Fairfax High's clubs and organizations. Parking is free, but admission is $2.

Huge and hyped, the **Rose Bowl Flea Market** (✉ *1001 Rose Bowl Dr., Pasadena* ☎ *323/560–7469* ⊕ *www.rgcshows.com*), happens on the second Sunday of every month, rain or shine. This extremely popular market attracts more than 2,500 vendors looking for top dollar for their antiques, crafts, and new furniture. It's an especially good source for pop culture odds and ends (like a $100 Partridge Family lunchbox). Admission is $7 from 9 to 3; more expensive special passes will get you in one to three hours ahead of time.

For better bargain hunting and less stress, try the **Pasadena City College Flea Market** (✉ *1570 E. Colorado Blvd., at Hill Ave., Pasadena* ☎ *626/585–7906*), on the first Sunday of each month. With 500 vendors (70 of them selling records), this is a great source for collectibles, furniture, and clothing at prices that won't break the bank. Admission and parking are free 8–3.

Robertson Boulevard. ✉ *3315 W. Magnolia Blvd., at California St., Burbank* ☎ *818/567–7366*.

WOMEN'S CLOTHING

Belle Gray. Everything in actress Lisa Rinna's recently expanded boutique is comfortable but chic, with a range of styles that are casual (their own drawstring sweats and thin tees by Daftbird) and more luxe (cashmere sweaters, Diane von Furstenberg dresses). The new shoe room in back is particularly inviting. ✉ *13812 Ventura Blvd., Sherman Oaks* ☎ *818/789–4021*.

Dari. Bohemian kicked up a notch is what you'll get at this boutique, which offers separates in warm, rich colors from the likes of Philip Lim and Mike & Chris. ✉ *12184 Ventura Blvd., Studio City* ☎ *818/762–3274*.

Elisa B. Elisa's small but well-edited collection of up-and-coming L.A. designers (Wasabi, Adina) and established favorites (Tocca, Tracey Reese) draw women of all ages to this friendly Old Town boutique. ✉ *12 Douglas Alley, Pasadena* ☎ *626/792–4746*.

Faire Frou Frou. It's a lingerie shop first and foremost but the pretty shop also stocks pieces to be worn on the outside, including lace-trimmed chemises, silk camisoles, and bustiers. Find lacy and racy underthings along with more practical-but-still-sexy options from Eres and Eberjey. ✉ *13017-A Ventura Blvd., near Coldwater Canyon Ave., Studio City* ☎ *818/783–4970.*

Playclothes Vintage Fashions. This gigantic off-the-beaten-path shop offers vintage clothing from all eras and an especially impressive selection of accessories found in cases and on display throughout the store. ✉ *11422 Moorpark St., Studio City* ☎ *818/755–9559.*

Stacey Todd. Three Stacey Todd shops occupy this same block: a denim shop for men and women, which displays pairs hanging by belt loops from the wall; a women's shop of sleek and sophisticated separates in neutrals; and a home shop with bath and body luxuries. ✉ *13025-9 Ventura Blvd., Studio City* ☎ *818/981–7567.*

Disneyland Resort and Knott's Berry Farm

WORD OF MOUTH

"Here is a very important tip: Mr Toad's Wild Ride is scary for little kids! Do not take your children on it first thing because then they will refuse to go on any other rides that are inside, like It's a Small World and Pooh's Heffalump Ride. Yeah, I might have done that and ruined what could have been a fun day with my three year old!"

—MonicaRichards

www.fodors.com/community

By Laura Randall, Updated by Kastle Waserman

DISNEYLAND AND KNOTT'S BERRY FARM HAVE BEEN THE ENTERTAINMENT ANCHORS of Anaheim and all of inland Orange County since opening amid orange groves and farmland in the middle of the 20th century. Each is surrounded by hotels, restaurants, and fun-based entertainment options that survive and often thrive in the shadows of these two popular amusement parks. Though they share similar humble beginnings (not to mention quirky founders with revolutionary ideas), the parks today operate in different stratospheres with their own unique personalities and charms.

Disneyland, with its three park-adjacent hotels and downtown promenade, is by far the bigger and shinier powerhouse. Walking down Main Street, U.S.A. with Sleeping Beauty Castle straight ahead, you really will feel like you've landed on one the happiest places on earth. Trolleys cling-clang merrily beside you, little girls skip down the thoroughfare in princess gowns while the sounds of peppy, hummable tunes float through the air. You can't help but let your inner child escape for a few hours, or days. When you need a dose of adulthood, visit Johnny Depp's rock-star pirate, Jack Sparrow, on the new and improved Pirates of the Caribbean ride, or head over to California Adventure for a breathtaking ride on Soarin' Over California or a wine flight and hand-sliced prosciutto at the Wine Country Trattoria.

A 10-minute drive away, Knott's is Disney's louder, somewhat rowdier neighbor. Before even passing through the gate, you'll hear the gleeful screams of people being pulled and suspended and twisted into oblivion on the park's many high-tech thrill rides. Although the park seems to increasingly focus on bigger, better, and faster rides, there's a softer, cornier side as well. This includes the skill-based carnival games that draw cheering crowds, Camp Snoopy's pint-size kiddie rides, and the Western Trails Museum, home to coins and guns from the Old West, menus from the original chicken dinner restaurant, and Mrs. Knott's antique button collection.

WHAT IT COSTS

	¢	$	$$	$$$	$$$$
Restaurants	under $7	$7–$12	$12–$22	$22–$32	over $32
Hotels	under $75	$75–$125	$125–$200	$200–$325	over $325

Restaurant prices are per person for a main course, excluding 8.25% sales tax. Hotel prices are for two people in a standard double room in nonholiday high season on the European Plan (no meals) unless otherwise noted. Taxes (9%–14%) are extra. In listings we always name the facilities available, but we don't specify whether they cost extra. When pricing accommodations, always ask about what's included. Prices are often lower in winter near Disneyland, unless there's a convention in Anaheim, and weekend rates are often rock-bottom at business hotels. It's worth calling around to search for bargains.

GETTING THERE

Disneyland is about a 30-mi drive from either LAX or downtown. From LAX, follow Sepulveda Boulevard south to the I–105 freeway and drive east 16 mi to the I–605 north exit. Exit at the Santa Ana Freeway (I–5) and continue south for 12 mi to the Disneyland Drive exit. Follow signs to the resort. From downtown, follow I–5 south 28 mi and exit at Disneyland Drive. ✉ *1313 Harbor Blvd., Anaheim* ☎ *714/781–4565* 🌐 *www.disneyland.com.*

The **Anaheim Orange County Visitor & Convention Bureau** is a good source for maps and news on the area. ✉ *800 W. Katella Ave., Anaheim* ☎ *714/765–8888* 🌐 *www.anaheimoc.org.*

Disneyland Resort Express offers daily nonstop bus service between LAX, John Wayne Airport, and Anaheim. Reservations are not required. The cost is $32 one-way for adults, $25 for children. ☎ *714/978–8855* 🌐 *www.airportbus.com.*

TOP 5

- **Disneyland** because it really does feel like the happiest place on earth.
- Baseball games at **Angels Stadium of Anaheim**—good clean fun in the sun.
- **Disney's Soarin' Over California** at California Adventure—get a front-row seat for this orange blossom–scented airborne tour.
- The tasting menu at **Napa Rose** in Disney's Grand Californian Hotel.
- **Mystery Lodge**, a unique, visually stunning show about Native American history at Knott's Berry Farm.

TIMING

Beat the crowds and the heat by visiting in winter, spring, or fall. School holidays and the entire spring break window of late March and April can also be mobbed. Ticket booths are on the esplanade between the two parks, but purchasing tickets online ahead of your arrival saves time. To minimize the line waits, get there early and pick up a "Fastpass" near the entrance for popular rides like Space Mountain, Indiana Jones Adventure, and Grizzly River Run. You'll be given a designated time window to return and be able to breeze ahead of those waiting in the regular lines.

Disneyland and Disney's California Adventure are open daily, 365 days a year; hours vary, depending on the season, but typically Disneyland opens at 8 AM and Disney's California Adventure at 10 AM. Guests at Disney hotels and those with a multiple-day Park Hopper pass are often allowed in an hour ahead of the official opening time. Disneyland stays open as late as midnight on weekends and in summer, but it's always a good idea to check the Web site or call ahead.

If you plan to visit for more than a day, you can save money by buying three-, four-, and five-day Park Hopper tickets that grant same-day "hopping" privileges between Disneyland and Disney's California Adventure. You get a discount on the multiple-day passes if you buy online through the Disneyland Web site. A one-day Park Hopper pass costs $94 for anyone 10 or older, $84 for kids ages 3–9. Admission to either park (but not both) is $69 or $59 for kids 3–9; kids 2 and under are free. Don't forget to factor in parking costs; $12 for cars, $17 for RVs.

DISNEYLAND RESORT

26 mi southeast of Los Angeles, via I–5.

The snowcapped Matterhorn, the centerpiece of the Magic Kingdom, punctuates the skyline of **Anaheim.** Since 1955, when Walt Disney chose this once-quiet farming community for the site of his first amusement park, Disneyland has attracted more than 450 million visitors and thousands of workers, and Anaheim has been their host. To understand the symbiotic relationship between Disneyland and Anaheim, you need only look at the $4.2 billion spent in a combined effort by the Walt Disney Company and Anaheim, the latter to revitalize the city's tourist center and run-down areas, the former to expand and renovate the Disney properties into what is known now as **Disneyland Resort.** The resort is a sprawling complex that includes Disney's two amusement parks; three hotels; and Downtown Disney, a shopping, dining, and entertainment promenade. Anaheim's tourist center includes Angel Stadium of Anaheim, home of baseball's World Series Champion Los Angeles Angels of Anaheim; Arrowhead Pond, which hosts concerts and the hockey team the Anaheim Ducks; and the enormous Anaheim Convention Center.

DISNEYLAND

Fodor'sChoice ★

One of the biggest misconceptions people have about **Disneyland** is that they've "been there, done that" if they've visited either Florida's mammoth Walt Disney World or one of the Disney parks overseas. But Disneyland, opened in 1955 and the only one of the kingdoms to be overseen by Walt himself, has a genuine historic feel and occupies a unique place in the Disney legend. There's plenty here that you won't find anywhere else: for example, Storybook Land, with its miniature replicas of animated Disney scenes from classics such as *Pinocchio; Alice in Wonderland*; and the Indiana Jones Adventure ride.

Characters appear for autographs and photos throughout the day; guidebooks at the entrances give times and places. You can also meet some of the animated icons at one of the character meals served at the three Disney hotels (open to the public). Belongings can be stored in lockers just off Main Street; purchases can also be sent to the package pickup desk, at the front of the park. Main Street stays open an hour after the attractions close, so you may want to save your shopping for the end of your visit.

DISNEY LANDS

Neighborhoods for Disneyland are arranged in geographic order.

MAIN STREET, U.S.A.

Walt's hometown of Marceline, Missouri, was the inspiration behind this romanticized image of small-town America, circa 1900. It opens half an hour before the rest of the park, so it's a good place to explore if you're getting an early start to beat the crowds. The sidewalks are lined with a penny arcade and shops that sell everything from tradable pins to Disney-theme clothing and photo supplies. **Main Street Cinema** offers a cool respite from the crowds and six classic Disney animated shorts, including Steamboat Willie. There's rarely a wait to enter. Board the **Disneyland Railroad** here to save on walking; it tours all the lands, plus offers unique views of Splash Mountain and the Grand Canyon and Primeval World dioramas.

> **DID YOU KNOW?**
>
> Walt Disney himself would sometimes stay in an apartment over Main Street's fire station. Now a light always stays on in the apartment's window in his honor.

NEW ORLEANS SQUARE A mini–French Quarter with narrow streets, hidden courtyards, and live street performances, this is home to two iconic attractions and the Cajun-inspired Blue Bayou restaurant. **Pirates of the Caribbean** now features Jack Sparrow and the cursed Captain Barbossa, in a nod to the blockbuster movies of the same name, plus enhanced special effects and battle scenes (complete with cannonball explosions). Nearby **Haunted Mansion** continues to spook guests with its stretching room and "doombuggy" rides (plus there's now an expanded storyline for the beating-heart bride). Its Nightmare Before Christmas holiday overlay is an annual tradition. This is a good area to get a casual bite to eat; the clam chowder in sourdough bread bowls, sold at the French Market Restaurant and Royal Street Veranda, is a popular choice.

FRONTIERLAND Located between Adventureland and Fantasyland, Frontierland transports you to the wild, wild West with its rustic buildings, shooting gallery, mountain range, and foot stompin' dance hall. The marquee attraction, **Big Thunder Mountain Railroad,** is a relatively tame roller coaster ride (no steep descents) that takes the form of a runaway mine car as it rumbles past desert canyons and an old mining town. Tour the Rivers of America on the **Mark Twain Riverboat** in the company of a grizzled old river pilot or circumnavigate the globe on the **Sailing Ship Columbia,** though its operating hours are usually limited to weekends. You can also raft over from here to Pirate's Lair on **Tom Sawyer Island,** which now features pirate-theme caves, treasure hunts, and music along with plenty of caves and hills to climb and explore. If you don't mind tight seating, have a snack at the Golden Horseshoe Restaurant while enjoying the always-entertaining comedy and bluegrass show of Billy Hill and the Hillybillies. Children won't want to miss **Big Thunder Ranch,** a small petting zoo of real pigs, goats, and cows beyond Big Thunder Mountain.

CRITTER COUNTRY Down-home country is the theme in this shady corner of the park, where Winnie the Pooh and Davy Crockett make their homes. Here you'll find **Splash Mountain,** a classic flume ride accompanied by music and appearances by Brer Rabbit and other characters from Song of the South. Don't forget to check out your photo (the camera snaps close-ups of each car just before it plunges into the water) on the way out. The patio of the popular Hungry Bear Restaurant has great views of Tom Sawyer's Island and Davy Crockett's Explorer Canoes.

ADVENTURELAND Modeled after the lands of Africa, Polynesia, and Arabia, this tiny tropical paradise is worth braving the crowds that flock here for the ambience and better-than-average food. Sing along with the animatronic birds and tiki gods in the **Enchanted Tiki Room,** sail the rivers of the world with joke-cracking skippers on **Jungle Cruise,** and climb the Disneyodendron semperflorens (aka always-blooming Disney tree) to

Tarzan's Treehouse, where you'll walk through scenes, some interactive, from the 1999 animated film. Cap off the visit with a wild jeep ride at **Indiana Jones Adventure,** where the special effects and decipherable hieroglyphics distract you while you're waiting in line. The kebabs at Bengal Barbecue and pineapple whip at Tiki Juice Bar are some of the best fast-food options in the park.

> **WORD OF MOUTH**
>
> "There is some good food to be found in Disneyland if you know where to look: New Orleans restaurant for monte cristos, Bengal Barbeque in Adventureland for beef and chicken and asparagus skewers, Dole whips in front of the Tiki Room, bratwursts at the Fantasyland Theater, chocolate honeycombs on Main Street, fritters at the mint julep bar and clam chowder at the veranda in New Orleans Square are some of my favorites." —ReneeS

FANTASYLAND Sleeping Beauty Castle marks the entrance to Fantasyland, a visual wonderland of princesses, spinning teacups, flying elephants, and other classic storybook characters. Rides and shops (such as the princess-theme Once Upon a Time and Gepetto's Toys and Gifts) take precedence over restaurants in this area of the park, but outdoor carts sell everything from churros to turkey legs. Tots love the **King Arthur Carousel, Casey Jr. Circus Train,** and **Storybook Land Canal Boats.** This is also home to **Mr. Toad's Wild Ride, Peter Pan's Flight,** and **Pinocchio's Daring Journey,** classic, movie-theater-dark rides that immerse riders in Disney fairytales and appeal to adults and kids alike. The Abominable Snowman pops up on the **Matterhorn Bobsleds,** a roller coaster that twists and turns you up and around a made-to-scale model of the real Swiss mountain. Anchoring the east end of Fantasyland is **it's a small world,** a smorgasbord of dancing animatronic dolls, cuckoo clock–covered walls, and variations of the song everyone knows by heart.

MICKEY'S TOONTOWN Geared toward small fry, this lopsided cartoonlike downtown, complete with cars and trolleys that invite exploring, is where Mickey, Donald, Goofy, and other classic Disney characters hang their hats. One of the most popular attractions is **Roger Rabbit's Car Toon Spin,** a twisting, turning cab ride through the Toontown of *Who Framed Roger Rabbit?* You can also walk through **Mickey's House** to meet and be photographed with the famous mouse, take a low-key ride on **Gadget's Go Coaster,** or bounce around the fenced-in playground in front of **Goofy's House.**

TOMORROWLAND This popular section of the park underwent a complete refurbishment in 1998 and continues to tinker with its future with the regular addition of new or enhanced rides. The newest attraction, **Finding Nemo's Submarine Voyage** updates the old Submarine Voyage ride with the exploits of Nemo, Dory, Marlin, and other characters from the Pixar film. Try to visit this popular ride early in the day if you can and be prepared for a wait. The interactive **Buzz Lightyear Astro Blasters** lets you zap your neighbors with laser beams and compete for the highest score. Hurtle through the cosmos on **Space Mountain,** refurbished in 2005, and take a shuttle ride on Endor in **Star Wars.** There are also mainstays like the futuristic **Astro Orbiter** rockets, **Innoventions,** a self-

CLOSE UP

Disney Strategies

On your mark, get set . . . a trip to Disneyland Resort gets the adrenaline pumping, but to most enjoy your visit, study these helpful tips. If you're traveling with children, check out the book *Fodor's Disneyland & Southern California with Kids* for more advice.

Buy entry tickets in advance. Many nearby hotels sell park admission tickets; you can also buy them through the Disney Web site. If you book a package deal, such as those offered through AAA, tickets are included, too. The lines at the ticket booths can take more than an hour on busy days, so you'll definitely save time by buying in advance, especially if you're committed to going on a certain day regardless of the weather.

Come midweek. Weekends, especially in summer, are a mob scene. A winter weekday is often the least crowded time to visit.

Plan your times to hit the most popular rides. If you're at the park when the gates open, make a beeline for the top rides before the crowds reach critical mass. Another good time to avoid lines is in the evening, when the hordes thin out somewhat, and during a parade or other show. Save the quieter attractions for midafternoon.

Look into Fastpasses. These passes allow you to reserve your place in line at some of the most crowded attractions (only one at a time). Distribution machines are posted near the entrances of each attraction. Feed in your park admission ticket, and you'll receive a pass with a printed time frame (generally up to 1–1½ hours later) during which you can return to wait in a much shorter line.

Plan your meals to avoid peak mealtime crowds. Start the day with a big breakfast so you won't be too hungry at noon, when restaurants and vendors get swarmed. Wait to have lunch until after 1. If you want to eat at the **Blue Bayou** in New Orleans Square, it's best to make reservations in person as soon as you get to the park. Another (cheaper) option is to bring your own food. There are areas with picnic tables set up for this. And it's always a good idea to bring water and a few nonmeltable snacks with you.

Check the daily events schedule online or at the park entrance. During parades, fireworks, and other special events, sections of the parks clog with crowds. This can work for you or against you. An event could make it difficult to get around a park—but if you plan ahead, you can take advantage of the distraction to hit popular rides. The Web site also lists rides that are closed for repairs or renovations, so you know what to expect before you go.

guided tour of the latest toys of tomorrow, and **Honey, I Shrunk the Audience,** a 3-D film featuring Rick Moranis. Disneyland Monorail and Disneyland Railroad both have stations here. There's also a video arcade and dancing water fountain that makes a perfect playground for kids on hot summer days.

Besides the eight lands, the daily live-action shows and parades are always crowd pleasers. **Fantasmic!** is a musical, fireworks, and laser show in which Mickey and friends wage a spellbinding battle against Disneyland's darker characters; and the daytime and nighttime **Celebrate! A Street Party** features just about every animated Disney character ever drawn. ■TIP→**Arrive early to secure a good view; if there are two shows scheduled for the day, the second one tends to be less crowded. A fireworks display sparks up Friday and Saturday evenings.** Brochures with maps, available at the entrance, list show- and parade times.

DISNEY'S CALIFORNIA ADVENTURE

★ The sprawling 55-acre **Disney's California Adventure,** right next to Disneyland (their entrances face each other), pays tribute to the Golden State with four theme areas. In an effort to attract more crowds, the park began a major five-year overhaul in late 2007 that will infuse more of Walt Disney's spirit throughout the park and add a host of new attractions, including a nighttime water-effects show and a 12-acre section called Cars Land based on the Pixar film. The first new attraction, an interactive adventure ride called Toy Story Mania! and hosted by Woody, Buzz Lightyear, and friends opened at Paradise Pier in 2008. ✉*Disneyland Dr. between Ball Rd. and Katella Ave., Anaheim* ☎*714/781–4565* 🌐*www.disneyland.com* ⏲*Hrs vary.*

DISNEY LANDS

GOLDEN STATE — Celebrate California's history and natural beauty with nature trails, a winery, and a tortilla factory (with free samples). The area of Condor Flats has **Soarin' Over California,** a spectacular simulated hang-glider ride over California terrain, and the **Redwood Creek Challenge Trail,** a challenging trek across net ladders and suspension bridges. **Grizzly River Run** simulates the river rapids of the Sierra Nevadas; be prepared to get soaked. The Wine Country Trattoria is a great place for a relaxing outdoor lunch.

HOLLYWOOD PICTURES BACKLOT — With a main street modeled after Hollywood Boulevard, a fake blue-sky backdrop, and real soundstages, this area celebrates California's most famous industry. **Disney Animation** gives you an insider's look at the work of animators and how they create characters. **Turtle Talk with Crush** lets kids have an unrehearsed talk with computer-animated Crush, a sea turtle from *Finding Nemo*. The Hyperion theater hosts **Aladdin—A Musical Spectacular,** a 45-minute live performance with terrific visual effects. ■TIP→**Plan on getting in line about half an hour in advance: the show is well worth the wait.** On the latest film-inspired ride, **Monsters, Inc. Mike & Sulley to the Rescue,** you climb into taxis and travel the streets of Monstropolis on a mission of safely returning Boo to her bedroom. A major draw for older kids is the looming *Twilight Zone Tower of Terror,* which drops riders 13 floors.

A BUG'S LAND Inspired by the 1998 film *A Bug's Life,* this section skews its attractions to an insect's point of view. Kids can cool off (or get soaked) in the water jets and giant garden hose of **Princess Dot Puddle Park,** spin around in giant takeout Chinese food boxes on **Flik's Flyers,** and hit the bug-shapedå bumper cars on **Tuck and Roll's Drive 'Em Buggies.** The short show *It's Tough to Be a Bug!* gives you a 3-D look at insect life.

PARADISE PIER This section re-creates the glory days of California's seaside piers. If you're looking for thrills, the **California Screamin'** roller coaster takes its riders from 0 to 55 mph in about four seconds and proceeds through scream tunnels, steeply angled drops, and a 360-degree loop. **Mickey's Fun Wheel,** a giant Ferris wheel, provides a good view of the grounds at a more leisurely pace. **Mulholland Madness** is a fun tribute to L.A.'s crazy traffic cycles. There's also carnival games, a fish-theme carousel, and Ariel's Grotto, where future princesses can dine with the mermaid and her friends (reservations a must).

OTHER ATTRACTIONS

Downtown Disney is a 20-acre promenade of dining, shopping, and entertainment that connects the Disneyland Resort hotels and theme parks. Restaurant-nightclubs here include the **House of Blues,** which spices up its Delta-inspired ribs and seafood with various live music acts on an intimate two-story stage. At **Ralph Brennan's Jazz Kitchen** you can dig into New Orleans–style food and music. Sports fans gravitate to **ESPN Zone,** a sports bar–restaurant–entertainment center with American grill food, interactive video games, and 175 video screens telecasting worldwide sports events. There's also an **AMC** multiplex movie theater with stadium-style seating that plays the latest blockbusters and, naturally, a couple of kids' flicks. Promenade shops sell everything from Disney goods to antique jewelry; don't miss **Vault 28,** a hip boutique that sells one-of-kind vintage and couture clothes and accessories from Disney, Betsey Johnson, and other designers. ✉ *Disneyland Dr. between Ball Rd. and Katella Ave., Anaheim* ☎ *714/300–7800* 🌐 *www.disneyland.com* 🎟 *Free* 🕒 *Daily 7* AM*–2* AM*; hrs at shops and restaurants vary.*

Muzeo is a stunning 20,000-square-foot exhibition hall housed in a 1908 Carnegie Library building. It hosts touring art and cultural exhibitions about everything from Imperial Rome to Chicano culture. There's also a small permanent exhibit on Anaheim and north Orange County. ✉ *241 S. Anaheim Blvd., North Anaheim* ☎ *714/778–3301* 🌐 *www.muzeo.org* 🎟 *$10–$13* 🕒 *Daily 10* AM*–5* AM.

Anaheim ICE is the training facility for the Anaheim Ducks hockey team. Practices are open to the public from mid-September to mid-April; call ahead for info. The rink also has public skating sessions, adult and youth hockey games, and lessons. ✉ *300 W. Lincoln Ave., Anaheim* ☎ *714/535–7465* 🌐 *www.anaheimice.com* 🎟 *Free* 🕒 *Daily 7* AM*–2* AM*; public skate times vary.*

GO FOR A TOAST

Unlike Disneyland, which is dry, Disney's California Adventure has restaurants that serve beer and wine. In addition, a small winery here has grapevines growing on the hillside and illustrations showing the transformation from grapes to wine.

Restaurants

Anaheim White House 6
Catal Restaurant & Uva Bar 3
JW's Steakhouse ..1
Luigi's D' Italia ...7
Morton's 4
Mr. Stox 5
Napa Rose 2

Hotels

The Anabella 5
Anaheim Fairfield Inn ... 12
Anaheim Holiday Inn 1
Anaheim Marriott 6
Candy Cane Inn . 13
Desert Palms Hotel 9
Disneyland Hotel ..2
Disney's Grand Californian Hotel & Spa 4
Disney's Paradise Pier Hotel 3
Doubletree Guest Suites 8
Hilton Anaheim . 10
Park Vue Inn ... 11
Sheraton Anaheim Hotel .. 14
Sheraton Park Hotel 7

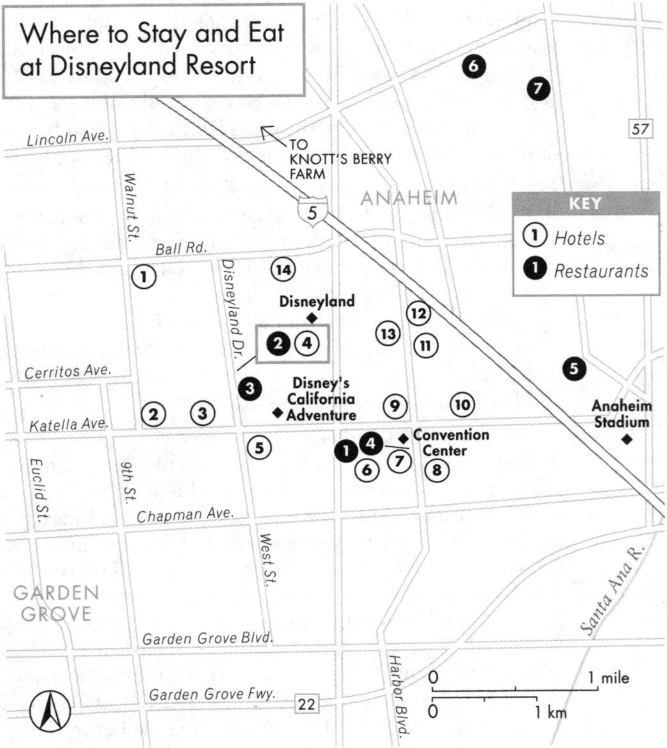

WHERE TO EAT

$$$–$$$$ ITALIAN

✕ **Anaheim White House.** Several small dining rooms are set with crisp linens and candles in this flower-filled 1909 mansion. The northern Italian menu includes steak, rack of lamb, and fresh seafood. Try the Gwen Stefani Ravioli, lobster-filled pasta on a bed of ginger and citrus. A three-course prix-fixe "express" lunch, served weekdays, costs $24. ✉ *887 S. Anaheim Blvd., Anaheim* ☎ *714/772–1381* ▭ *AE, MC, V* ⊙ *No lunch weekends.*

$$–$$$ MEDITERRANEAN

✕ **Catal Restaurant & Uva Bar.** Famed chef Joachim Splichal takes a more casual approach at this bi-level Mediterranean spot—with tapas breaking into the finger-food territory. At the Uva (Spanish for "grape") bar on the ground level you can graze on olives and Spanish ham, choosing from 40 wines by the glass. Upstairs, Catal's menu spans paella, rotisserie chicken, and salads. ✉ *1580 S. Disneyland Dr., Suite 103* ☎ *714/774–4442* ▭ *AE, D, DC, MC, V.*

$–$$ ITALIAN

✕ **Luigi's D'Italia.** Despite the simple surroundings—red vinyl booths and plastic checkered tablecloths—Luigi's serves outstanding Italian cuisine: spaghetti marinara, veal Parmesan, homemade pizza, and all the classics. Kids will feel right at home here; there's even a children's menu. It's an easy five-minute drive from Disneyland, but less crowded and expensive than many restaurants adjacent to the park. ✉ *801 S. State College Blvd., Anaheim* ☎ *714/490–0990* ▭ *AE, D, DC, MC, V.*

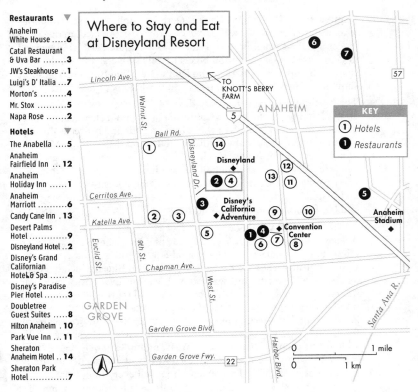

$$$–$$$$ CONTINENTAL **Morton's.** This upscale steak-house chain is a block from the convention center. Besides its usual menu of prime aged beef and seafood, the place features Bar 12*21, which has a plasma TV, extensive martini list, and snack menu featuring mini-cheeseburgers and filet mignon sandwiches. *1895 S. Harbor Blvd., Anaheim 714/621–0101 AE, D, DC, MC, V No lunch.*

$$–$$$$ **Mr. Stox.** Intimate booths and linen tablecloths create a sophisticated, old-school setting at this family-owned restaurant. Prime rib, Maryland crab cakes, and fresh fish specials are excellent; the pasta, bread, and pastries are made in-house; and the wine list is wide-ranging. *1105 E. Katella Ave., Anaheim 714/634–2994 AE, D, DC, MC, V No lunch weekends.*

$$$–$$$$ AMERICAN ★ **Napa Rose.** In sync with its host hotel, Disney's Grand Californian, this restaurant is done in a lovely Arts and Crafts style. The contemporary cuisine here is matched with an extensive wine list (600 bottles on display). For a look into the open kitchen, sit at the counter and watch the chefs as they whip up signature dishes such as Gulf of California rock scallops in a sauce of lemon, lobster, and vanilla and spit-roasted prime rib of pork with ranch-style black beans. A four-course $80 prix-fixe menu changes weekly. *Disney's Grand Californian Hotel, 1600 S. Disneyland Dr. 714/300–7170 AE, D, DC, MC, V.*

WHERE TO STAY

The Anaheim area has more than 50,000 rooms in hotels, family-style inns, and RV parks. **TIP→One handy perk of staying in a Disney hotel: you can charge anything you buy in either park, such as food and souvenirs, to your room, so you don't have to carry around a lot of cash. (This doesn't hold true for Downtown Disney, though.)**

An Anaheim Resort Transit (ART) bus can take you around town for $3. The buses run every 10 minutes during peak times, 20 minutes otherwise. They go between major hotels, Disney attractions, the Anaheim Convention Center, and restaurants and shops. See the ART Web site (*www.rideart.org)* for more information. In addition, many hotels are within walking distance of the Disneyland Resort.

¢–$$ **The Anabella.** This Spanish Mission–style hotel on the convention center campus is a good value. The suites are spacious with granite bathrooms and sleeper sofas. Interior rooms (away from Katella Avenue) are quieter. The hotel's Oasis, with a hot tub and pool, plus an adults-only pool, is a perfect place for relaxing. **Pros:** attentive service; landscaped grounds; pet-friendly rooms. **Cons:** some say the room walls are thin; it's a long walk to Disneyland's main gate. *1030 W. Katella Ave., Anaheim 714/905–1050 or 800/863–4888 714/905–1054 www.anabellahotel.com 308 rooms, 50 suites In-room: safe, refrigerator, Wi-Fi. In-hotel: restaurant, room service, bar, pools, gym, spa, laundry facilities, laundry service, executive floor, parking (paid) AE, D, DC, MC, V.*

$ **Anaheim Fairfield Inn by Marriott.** Attentive service and proximity to Disneyland (a 10-minute walk away) make this high-rise hotel a big draw for families. Most of the spacious rooms come with sleeper sofas as well as beds. In summer keep an eye out for the magician who roams

8

the premises, entertaining adults and kids alike. **Pros:** proximity to Disneyland; close to many restaurants; the lobby offers fruit-infused drinking water and a TV showing Disney movies. **Cons:** small pool abuts the parking lot; lack of green space. ✉*1460 S. Harbor Blvd., Anaheim* ☎*714/772–6777 or 800/228–2800* 📠*714/999–1727* 🌐*www.marriott.com* *467 rooms* *In-room: refrigerator. In-hotel: restaurant, room service, pool, laundry facilities, laundry service, Wi-Fi, parking (free), no-smoking rooms* 💳*AE, D, DC, MC, V.*

¢–$ **Anaheim Holiday Inn.** The warmth of Old California is found in this Holiday Inn, where the walls are furnished with historic photos and water paths snake through the grounds. Rooms are on the small side, but the residential location makes for quiet evenings. **Pros:** attractive pool; friendly, personal service despite the size. **Cons:** confusing layout; it's a 10-minute drive to Disneyland's main entrance and many off-property restaurants. ✉*1240 S. Walnut Ave., Anaheim* ☎*714/535–0300 or 800/824–5459* 📠*714/491–8953* 🌐*www.hianaheim.com* *255 rooms, 28 suites* *In-hotel: restaurant, room service, bar, pool, laundry service, parking (free), no-smoking rooms* 💳*AE, D, DC, MC, V.*

$$–$$$ **Anaheim Marriott.** Rooms at this busy convention hotel are well equipped for business travelers, with desks, two phones, and data ports. Spacious rooms have one king or two double beds; some have balconies. Disneyland is about a 30-minute walk away; shuttles are available. Fodor's readers say you won't find as many small children here as you may at other Disney-area hotels. **Pros:** efficient, attentive service; rooms are spacious. **Cons:** it's a long walk to Disneyland's main gate and off-property restaurants; conventioneers often take over the place. ✉*700 W. Convention Way, Anaheim* ☎*714/750–8000 or 800/228–9290* 📠*714/750–9100* 🌐*www.marriott.com* *1,031 rooms* *In-room: safe, refrigerator, Internet. In-hotel: 2 restaurants, room service, bar, pools, gym, laundry facilities, laundry service, public Internet, public Wi-Fi, parking (paid), no-smoking rooms* 💳*AE, D, DC, MC, V.*

$–$$ ★ **Candy Cane Inn.** One of the Disneyland area's first hotels (deeds were executed Christmas Eve, hence the name), the Candy Cane is one of Anaheim's most relaxing properties. Rooms are spacious and understated, while the palm-fringed pool is especially inviting. Premium rooms have two queen beds, microwaves, and coffeemakers. The hotel is just around the corner from Disneyland's main gate. A free Disneyland shuttle runs every half hour. **Pros:** proximity to Disneyland; friendly service; well-lighted, landscaped property. **Cons:** rooms and lobby are on the small side; all rooms face parking lot. ✉*1747 S. Harbor Blvd., Anaheim* ☎*714/774–5284 or 800/345–7057* 📠*714/772–5462* 🌐*www.candycaneinn.net* *171 rooms* *In-room: refrigerator, Wi-Fi. In-hotel: pool, spa, no elevator, laundry facilities, laundry service, parking (free), no-smoking rooms* 💳*AE, D, DC, MC, V* 🍽*CP.*

$ **Desert Palms Hotel and Suites.** This hotel midway between Disneyland and the convention center is a great value, with some $129 one-bedroom suites that can accommodate a group of four or more. Book well in advance, especially when large conventions are in town. **Pros:** lobby is large and welcoming; central location. **Cons:** drab exterior fronts busy Katella Avenue; small pool gets limited sun. ✉*631 W. Katella*

Ave., Anaheim ☎714/535–1133 or 888/788–0596 🖷714/491–7409 🌐www.desertpalmshotel.com ⇨59 rooms, 128 suites ♨In-room: refrigerator, microwave. In-hotel: pool, laundry facilities, laundry service, parking (free), no-smoking rooms ▭AE, D, DC, MC, V ¶○¶CP.

$$$–$$$$ **Disneyland Hotel.** Not surprisingly, the first of Disney's three hotels is the one most full of Magic Kingdom magic, with Disney-theme memorabilia and Disney music. Check out the Peter Pan–theme pool, with its wooden bridge, 110-foot waterslide, and relaxing whirlpool. The cove pools' sandy shores are great for sunning and playing volleyball. East-facing rooms in Dreams Tower have the best views of the park, while west-facing rooms look over gardens. At Goofy's Kitchen, kids can dine with Disney characters. Room-and-ticket packages are available. **Pros:** Disney theme is everywhere; great kids activities. **Cons:** uninviting lobby; lots of kids means the noise level is high at all hours. *✉1150 Magic Way ☎714/778–6600 🖷714/956–6582 🌐www.disneyland.com ⇨990 rooms, 60 suites ♨In-room: safe, refrigerator, Internet. In-hotel: 5 restaurants, room service, bars, pools, gym, spa, children's programs (ages 5–12), laundry service, airport shuttle, public Wi-Fi, parking (paid), no-smoking rooms ▭AE, D, DC, MC, V.*

$$$$ Fodor's Choice ★ **Disney's Grand Californian Hotel & Spa.** The newest of Disney's Anaheim hotels, this Craftsman-style luxury property has guest rooms with views of the California Adventure park and Downtown Disney. They don't push the Disney brand too heavily; rooms are done in dark woods with amber-shaded lamps and just a small Bambi image on the shower curtain. Restaurants include the Napa Rose dining room and Storytellers Cafe, where Disney characters entertain children at breakfast. Of the three pools, the one shaped like Mickey Mouse is just for kids, plus there's an evening child activity center and portable cribs in every room. Room-and-ticket packages are available. The new Mandara spa has a couple's suite with Balinese-inspired art and textiles. In late 2007 the resort began an expansion project that will add 200 new rooms and 50 Disney Vacation Club villas to the property. **Pros:** large, gorgeous lobby; direct access to California Adventure. **Cons:** the self-parking lot is across the street from the hotel; standard rooms are on the small side. *✉1600 S. Disneyland Dr. ☎714/956–6425 🖷714/300–7701 🌐www.disneyland.com ⇨701 rooms, 44 suites ♨In-room: safe, refrigerator, Internet. In-hotel: 2 restaurants, room service, bars, pools, gym, children's programs (ages 5–12), laundry service, parking (paid), no-smoking rooms ▭AE, D, DC, MC, V.*

$$$–$$$$ **Disney's Paradise Pier Hotel.** The Paradise Pier has many of the same Disney touches as the Disneyland Hotel, but it's a bit quieter and tamer. From here you can walk to Disneyland or pick up a shuttle or monorail. SoCal style manifests itself in seafoam-green guest rooms with lamps shaped like lifeguard stands, and surfboard motifs. A wooden roller coaster–inspired waterslide takes adventurers to a high-speed splashdown. Room-and-ticket packages are available. **Pros:** first-rate concierge; friendly service. **Cons:** small pool area; it's a 15-minute walk to Disneyland despite its location within the Disney resort area. *✉1717 S. Disneyland Dr. ☎714/999–0990 🖷714/776–5763 🌐www.disneyland.com ⇨489 rooms, 45 suites ♨In-room: safe, refrigerator, Internet.*

8

In-hotel: 2 restaurants, room service, bars, pool, gym, children's programs (ages 5–12), laundry service, public Wi-Fi, parking (paid), no-smoking rooms ▭*AE, D, DC, MC, V.*

$–$$ ★ **Doubletree Guest Suites.** This upscale hotel near the Convention Center caters to business travelers and families alike. Rooms have soundproof walls, high-quality linens, large desks, and data ports. The one-bedroom suites have flat-screen TVs and sleeper sofas. There's also a heated pool and spa, fitness center, and video arcade. Disneyland is a 20-minute walk away. **Pros:** huge suites; elegant lobby; within walking distance of a variety of restaurants. **Cons:** some say the hotel seems far-removed from Disneyland; pool area is small. ✉*2085 S. Harbor Blvd., Anaheim* ☎*714/750–3000 or 800/215–7316* 🖷*714/750–3002* *50 rooms, 202 suites* *In-room: refrigerator, microwave. In-hotel: restaurant, pool, spa, laundry facilities, public Wi-Fi, parking (paid), no-smoking rooms* ▭*AE, D, DC, MC, V* *CP.*

$$–$$$ **Hilton Anaheim.** Next to the Anaheim Convention Center, this busy Hilton is one of the largest hotels in Southern California with two restaurants, cocktail lounges, a full-service gym, and its own Starbucks. A shuttle runs to Disneyland, or you can walk there in a few blocks. There's a $14 fee to use the health club. **Pros:** friendly efficient service; Fodor's readers like the large pool area; great kids' programs. **Cons:** its huge size can be daunting; impersonal lobby; bathrooms are on the small side. ✉*777 Convention Way* ☎*714/750–4321 or 800/445–8667* 🖷*714/740–4460* 🌐*www.anaheim.hilton.com* *1,574 rooms, 18 suites* *In-hotel: 2 restaurants, room service, bars, pool, gym, laundry service, public Wi-Fi, parking (paid), no-smoking rooms* ▭*AE, D, DC, MC, V.*

¢–$ **Park Vue Inn.** This bougainvillea-trimmed two-story Spanish-style inn is one of the closest hotels you'll find to Disneyland's main gate. Rooms were renovated in 2007 and most feature two queen beds, desks, and large TVs. **Pros:** easy walk to Disneyland and many restaurants; good value. **Cons:** all rooms face the parking lot; some complain about early-morning street noise. ✉*1570 S. Harbor Blvd., Anaheim* ☎*714/772–3691 or 800/334–7021* 🖷*714/956–4736* 🌐*www.parkvueinn.com* *82 rooms, 12 suites* *In-room: refrigerator. In-hotel: Wi-Fi, pool, gym, spa, laundry facilities, parking (free), no-smoking rooms* ▭*AE, D, DC, MC, V.*

$$–$$$ ★ **Sheraton Anaheim Hotel.** If you're hoping to escape from the commercial atmosphere of the hotels near Disneyland, consider this sprawling replica of a Tudor castle. In the flower- and plant-filled lobby you're welcome to sit by the grand fireplace, watching fish swim around in a pond. Rooms are sizable; some first-floor rooms open onto interior gardens and a pool area. A shuttle to Disneyland is available. **Pros:** large, attractive lobby; game room; spacious rooms with comfortable beds. **Cons:** confusing layout; hotel sits close to a busy freeway and is not within walking distance of Disneyland. ✉*900 S. Disneyland Dr., Anaheim* ☎*714/778–1700 or 800/325–3535* 🖷*714/535–3889* 🌐*www.starwoodhotels.com* *460 rooms, 29 suites* *In-room: refrigerator, Wi-Fi. In-hotel: restaurant, room service, bar, pool, gym, laundry facili-*

ties, laundry service, parking (paid), no-smoking rooms ▭*AE, D, DC, MC, V.*

$$–$$$ **Sheraton Park Hotel at the Anaheim Resort.** Sheraton took over this hotel in 2006 and freshened up the decor in guest rooms and public spaces. The handsome rooms are decorated in rich navy and brown and have private balconies with views of Disneyland or the surrounding area. You can also relax in the nicely landscaped outdoor area or take a dip in the oversize pool. It's about a 15-minute walk to Disneyland. **Pros:** luxury lodging; large fitness center overlooks pool; most rooms have excellent views. **Cons:** impersonal lobby; elevators can be slow when it's busy. ✉*1855 S. Harbor Blvd., Anaheim* ☎*714/750–1811 or 800/716–6199* ℻*714/971–3626* 🌐*www.starwoodhotels.com/sheraton* *483 rooms, 7 suites* *In-room: refrigerator, Wi-Fi. In-hotel: 3 restaurants, room service, bar, pool, gym, laundry facilities, laundry service, parking (paid), no-smoking rooms* ▭*AE, D, DC, MC, V.*

SPORTS

Pro baseball's **Los Angeles Angels of Anaheim** play at **Angel Stadium of Anaheim** (✉*2000 GeneAutry Way, East Anaheim* ☎*714/940–2000* 🌐*www.angelsbaseball.com*). An "Outfield Extravaganza" celebrates great plays on the field, with fireworks and a geyser exploding over a model evoking the California coast. The National Hockey League's **Anaheim Ducks,** winners of the 2007 Stanley Cup, play at **Honda Center** (✉*Formerly Arrowhead Pond, 2695 E. Katella Ave., East Anaheim* ☎*714/704–2400* 🌐*www.mightyducks.com*). Orange County's first National Basketball Association franchise, the **Anaheim Arsenal,** began its first season in 2006. The team plays at the **Anaheim Convention Center Arena** (✉*800 W. Katella Ave., Anaheim* ☎*714/635–2255* 🌐*www.nba.com/dleague/anaheim*). The USA Men's National Volleyball Team recently moved from Colorado to Anaheim. The team practices at **American Sports Centers** (✉*1500 S. Anaheim Blvd., Anaheim* ☎*714/917–3600* 🌐*www.americansportscenters.com/volleyball.htm*).

KNOTT'S BERRY FARM

25 mi south of Los Angeles, via I–5, in Buena Park.

★ The land where the boysenberry was invented (by crossing red raspberry, blackberry, and loganberry bushes) is now occupied by Knott's Berry Farm. In 1934 Cordelia Knott began serving chicken dinners on her wedding china to supplement her family's income. Or so the story goes. The dinners and her boysenberry pies proved more profitable than husband Walter's berry farm, so the two moved first into the restaurant business and then into the entertainment business. The park is now a 160-acre complex with 100-plus rides, dozens of restaurants and shops, and even a brick-by-brick replica of Philadelphia's Independence Hall. Although it has some good attractions for small children, the park is best known for its roster of awesome thrill rides. And, yes, you can still get that boysenberry pie (and jam, juice—you name it). ✉*8039 Beach Blvd., Buena Park* ✣*Between La Palma Ave. and Crescent St., 2 blocks south of Hwy. 91* ☎*714/220–5200* 🌐*www.knotts.com.*

GETTING THERE

Knott's is an easy 10-minute drive from Disneyland or a 30-minute drive from downtown Los Angeles. Take I–5 to Beach Boulevard and head south 3 mi; follow the park entrance signs on the right.

SCARY FARM

In October, Knott's shifts into Scary Farm gear at night. To celebrate Halloween, the attractions take on scary new guises, with prowling costumed cast members out to spook you. They go all out to creep you out, so the Scary Farm is not recommended for kids under 13.

TIMING

The park is open June–mid-Sept., daily 9 AM–midnight; mid-September–May the park usually opens at 10 and closes between 5 and 8 on weekdays, and between 10 and midnight weekends. Call ahead or check Web site to confirm hours. You can see the park in a day, but plan to start early and finish fairly late. Traffic can be heavy, so factor in time for delays.

■ TIP→ **If you think you'll only need a few hours at the main park, you can save money by coming after 4 PM, when admission fees drop to $25.** This deal is offered any day the park is open after 6. A full-day pass for adults is $51.99; Southern California residents pay $41.99 and children 3 and older, up to 48 inches tall, are $22.99. Tickets can be purchased online and printed out ahead of time, to avoid waiting in line.

DISNEY LANDS

BOARDWALK Not-for-the-squeamish thrill rides and skill-based games dominate the scene at **Boardwalk.** Go head over heels on the *Boomerang* roller coaster, then do it again—backward. The **Perilous Plunge,** billed as the world's tallest, steepest, and—thanks to its big splash—wettest thrill ride, sends riders down an almost-vertical chute. The 1950s hot rod–theme **Xcelerator** launches you hydraulically into a super-steep U-turn, topping out at 205 feet. **Supreme Scream** propels you 254 feet in the air, then plunges you straight back down again in three terrifying seconds. Boardwalk is also home to a string of test-your-skill games that are fun to watch whether you're playing or not, and Johnny Rockets, the park's newest restaurant.

CAMP SNOOPY It can get gridlocked on weekends, but small fry love this miniature High Sierra wonderland where the *Peanuts* gang hangs out. They can push and pump their own mini-mining cars on **Huff and Puff,** zip around a pint-size racetrack on **Charlie Brown Speedway,** and hop aboard **Woodstock's Airmail,** a kids' version of the park's Supreme Scream ride. Most of the rides here are geared toward kids only, leaving parents to cheer them on from the sidelines. **Sierra Sidewinder,** a roller coaster that opened near the entrance of Camp Snoopy in spring 2007, is aimed at older children with spinning saucer-type vehicles that go a maximum speed of 37 mph.

FIESTA VILLAGE Over in **Fiesta Village** are two more musts for adrenaline junkies: **Montezooma's Revenge,** a roller coaster that goes from 0 to 55 mph in less than five seconds, and **Jaguar!,** which simulates the motions of a cat stalking its prey, twisting, spiraling, and speeding up and slowing down as it takes you on its stomach-dropping course. There's also **Hat Dance,** a version of the spinning teacups but with sombreros, and a 100-year-old Dentzel Carousel, complete with an antique organ and menagerie of hand-carved animals.

GHOST TOWN Clusters of authentic old buildings relocated from their original mining-town sites mark this section of the park. You can stroll down the street, stop and chat with a blacksmith, pan for gold (for a fee), crack open a geode, check out the chalkboard of a circa-1875 schoolhouse, and ride an original Butterfield stagecoach. Looming over it all is **GhostRider,** Orange County's first wooden roller coaster. Traveling up to 56 mph and reaching 118 feet at its highest point, the park's biggest attraction is riddled with sudden dips and curves, subjecting riders to forces up to three times that of gravity. On the Western-theme **Silver Bullet,** riders are sent to a height of 146 feet and then back down 109 feet. Riders spiral, corkscrew, fly into a cobra roll, and experience overbanked curves. The **Calico Mine** ride descends into a replica of a working gold mine. The **Timber Mountain Log Ride** is a worthwhile flume ride, especially if you're with kids who don't make the height requirements for the flumes at Disneyland. Also found here is the park's newest thrill ride, the **Pony Express,** a roller coaster that lets riders saddle up on packs of "horses" tethered to a platforms that take off on a series of hairpin turns and travel up to 38 mph. Don't miss the **Western Trails Museum,** a dusty old gem full of Old West memorabilia, plus menus from the original chicken restaurant, and Mrs. Knott's antique button collection. **Calico Railroad** departs regularly from Ghost Town station for a round-trip tour of the park (bandit holdups notwithstanding).

WILD WATER WILDERNESS Just like its name implies, this section is home to **Big Foot Rapids,** a splash-fest of white-water river rafting over towering cliffs, cascading waterfalls, and wild rapids. Don't miss the visually stunning show at **Mystery Lodge,** which tells the story of Native Americans in the Pacific Northwest with lights, music, and beautiful images.

8

Knott's Soak City Water Park is directly across from the main park on 13 acres next to Independence Hall. It has a dozen major water rides; the latest is **Pacific Spin,** an oversize waterslide that drops riders 75 feet into a catch pool. There's also a children's pool, 750,000-gallon wave pool, and funhouse. Soak City is open daily after Memorial Day; weekends only after Labor Day.

WHERE TO EAT AND STAY

$$ AMERICAN ✕ **Mrs. Knott's Chicken Dinner Restaurant.** Cordelia Knott's fried chicken and boysenberry pies drew crowds so big that Knott's Berry Farm was built to keep the hungry customers occupied while they waited. The restaurant's current incarnation (outside the park's entrance) still serves crispy fried chicken, along with tangy coleslaw, mashed potatoes, and Mrs. Knott's signature chilled cherry-rhubarb compote. The wait, unfortunately, can be two-plus hours on weekends; another option is to order a bucket of the same tasty chicken from the adjacent takeout counter and have a picnic at the duck pond next to Independence Hall across the street. ✉ *Knott's Berry Farm Marketplace Area, 8039 Beach Blvd., Buena Park* ☎ *714/220–5080* ▭ *AE, D, DC, MC, V.*

$$$$ AMERICAN ✕ **Pirate's Dinner Adventure.** During this interactive pirate-theme dinner show, 150 actors/singers/acrobats (some quite talented) perform on a galleon while you eat a three-course meal. Food—shrimp, roast chicken, salad, mixed veggies, and unlimited soda, beer, and wine— is mediocre and seating is tight, but kids love making a lot of noise to cheer on their favorite pirate, and the action scenes are breathtaking. ✉ *7600 Beach Blvd., Buena Park* ☎ *866/439–2469* ▭ *AE, D, MC, V.*

$–$$ **Knott's Berry Farm Resort Hotel.** Knott's Berry Farm took over this hotel on park grounds from the Radisson chain in 2006 and renovated the rooms and lobby. The second-floor "camp rooms" are decorated in a Camp Snoopy motif and come with telephone bedtime stories. Shuttle service to Disneyland is available. Ask about packages that include entry to Knott's Berry Farm. **Pros:** easy access to Knott's Berry Farm; plenty of kids' activities; basketball court. **Cons:** lobby and hallways can be noisy and chaotic. ✉ *7675 Crescent Ave., Buena Park* ☎ *714/995–1111 or 866/752–2444* 📠 *714/828–8590* 🌐 *www.knottshotel.com* *320 rooms, 16 suites* *In-room: safes, Internet. In-hotel: restaurant, room service, bar, tennis court, pool, gym, laundry facilities, parking (paid), public Wi-Fi* ▭ *AE, D, DC, MC, V.*

Orange County and Catalina Island

WORD OF MOUTH

"Where else on the southern California coast can you find a hotel that is right on the sand, with the ocean rolling right up to the wall below our 1st floor balcony? We could have pitched pennies into the surf below at high tide. The Surf and Sand Hotel in Laguna Beach is 'Hawaii in California.'"

—Melissa5

Updated by Roger Grody

WITH ITS TROPICAL FLOWERS AND PALM TREES, THE STRETCH OF COAST BETWEEN SEAL BEACH AND SAN CLEMENTE IS OFTEN CALLED THE CALIFORNIA RIVIERA. Sure, few of the citrus groves that gave Orange County its name remain, and this region—south and east of Los Angeles—is now ruled by affluent subdivisions, high-tech businesses, theme parks, and shopping malls. But Orange County is still bucolic and refined enough to hold lots of appeal to both outdoor enthusiasts and culture vultures alike.

Exclusive Newport Beach, artsy Laguna, and the surf town of Huntington Beach are the stars, but lesser-known gems on the glistening coast—such as Corona del Mar and Dana Point—are also worth visiting. Offshore, meanwhile, lies gorgeous Catalina Island, a terrific spot for diving, snorkeling, and hiking. And despite a building boom that began in the 1980s, the region is still a place to find wilderness preserves, canyon trails, greenbelt bike paths, and stunning coastline.

You can also get an evocative dose of California history by visiting the 18th-century Mission San Juan Capistrano or enjoying state-of-the-art acoustics at one of America's premier performing arts centers (which, in quintessential OC form, is located next to the massive South Coast Plaza shopping center). Several major bands got started here, including ska-infected No Doubt, metal group Korn, and the punk band Social Distortion. And while local style was long focused on hometown surf-gear companies like Quiksilver and Billabong, the current obsession with chic designers means that Orange County now gets profiled in *Vogue*.

Some of Orange County's towns are now high profile, thanks to TV shows like The O.C., The Hills, Laguna Beach, and The Real Housewives of Orange County. But life here is much more diverse and sophisticated than the McMansion world depicted on TV. Orange County is now far more multicultural than its reputation. A strong Mexican influence contributes to the cuisine and architecture; the largest Vietnamese community outside Asia is that of Westminster's Little Saigon. Though the region has long been a one of California's conservative bastions, it's also becoming more politically diverse. And please don't tell the 3 million locals that they live in a suburb of Los Angeles. Orange County is different, with its own economy, culture, and lifestyle. It's more relaxed, more family oriented, and friendlier. (Not every waiter here is trying to break into the movies.)

ORIENTATION AND PLANNING

GETTING ORIENTED

Like Los Angeles, Orange County stretches over a large area, lacks a singular focal point, and has limited public transportation. Every community in the region has a distinct personality, from the vibrant Vietnamese-influenced Westminster to Huntington Beach, where blond surfer dudes and babes still rule. You'll need a car and a sensible game plan to make the most of your visit. There are many options for lodging throughout the county, but if you can afford it, staying at the beach is always recommended.

The Coast. Orange County's magnificent coastline is lined with a variety of vibrant communities, from unpretentious surf towns like Seal Beach to glamorous oceanfront enclaves like Corona del Mar. All share spectacular Pacific views buffered by generous swaths of protected beachfronts and plenty of recreational opportunities. And after a stunning sunset, both biker bars and romantic bistros await their respective clienteles.

Inland Orange County. Culturally diverse and cosmopolitan, the inland cities of Orange County—offer world-class arts venues, and beguiling ethnic neighborhoods, and great shopping.

Catalina Island. This mountainous island has a charming seaside village ideal for sportsman, artists, and romantics, and a rugged interior as unspoiled as any part of the Golden State.

TOP REASONS TO GO

- **Catalina Island:** Take in the breathtaking views from an unspoiled slice of California.
- **Newport Beach:** Water enthusiasts delight in this sophisticated coastal town's endless yachting and boating options.
- **Huntington Beach:** With more than 50 annual surf competitions, there's always lots of sporty oceanfront action.
- **Laguna Beach:** Come here for SoCal's best stretches of beach, posh resorts, and quirky art scene.
- **Mission San Juan Capistrano:** Offers a fascinating glimpse into California's history.

PLANNING

WHEN TO GO

The sun shines year-round in Orange County, though in early summer there are the "June gloom" days that can easily include May and July, when skies are overcast, particularly before noon. Clear, warm, sunny days are the rule in fall and winter.

GETTING HERE AND AROUND

AIR TRAVEL

The county's main facility is John Wayne Airport Orange County (SNA), which is conveniently located near the intersection of the I–405 and Highway 55 freeways. Nine major domestic airlines and four commuter lines fly there; even if you can't get to John Wayne directly from your departure city, booking a connecting flight is usually a better bet than flying nonstop into the less convenient and far more congested Los Angeles International Airport (LAX). It's a glossy facility, complete with a statue of its namesake, and its relatively small size makes it easy to negotiate. Still, you should leave plenty of time for security checks and parking.

Farther north, Long Beach Airport (LGB) serves four airlines, including its major player, JetBlue. It's smaller and more low-key than John Wayne; it may not have many airport amenities, but parking is generally a snap. It's roughly 20 to 30 minutes by car from Anaheim. *For details on other L.A. County airports, including LAX, see ⇨ the Travel Smart chapter.*

9

AIRPORT TRANSFERS The only transfer service from John Wayne or LAX to Orange County coastal cities is provided by SuperShuttle, which can be expensive. Fares, determined by distance, are for the first person in a party; add $9 for additional persons. You'll pay $18 from John Wayne to Newport Beach and $33 to Laguna Niguel. Fares to the same destinations from LAX are $51 and $63 per person, respectively. The Disneyland Resort Express and Prime Time Airport Shuttle provide transportation from John Wayne and LAX to the Disneyland area of Anaheim. Fares average about $15 per person from John Wayne and $20 from LAX.

Airport and Shuttle Information Disneyland Resort Express (☎ *800/828–6699* 🌐 *www.graylineanaheim.com*). **John Wayne Airport Orange County** (✉ *MacArthur Blvd. at I–405, Santa Ana* ☎ *949/252–5200* 🌐 *www.ocair.com*). **Long Beach Airport** (✉ *4100 Donald Douglas Dr., Long Beach* ☎ *562/570–2600* 🌐 *www.longbeach.gov/airport*). **Prime Time Airport Shuttle** (☎ *800/733–8267* 🌐 *www.primetimeshuttle.com*). **SuperShuttle** (☎ *800/258–3826* 🌐 *www.supershuttle.com*).

BUS TRAVEL

The Orange County Transportation Authority will take you virtually anywhere in the county, but it will take time; OCTA buses go from Knott's Berry Farm and Disneyland to Huntington Beach and Newport Beach. Bus 1 travels along the coast; buses 701 and 721 provide express service to Los Angeles.

Fares for the OCTA local routes are $1.50 per boarding; you can also get a $4 local day pass (valid only on the date of purchase). Day passes can be purchased from bus drivers upon boarding. Express bus fare between Orange County and L.A. is $4.50 a pop, $3 if you have a day pass. The bus-fare boxes take coins and dollar bills, but you must use exact change and pennies are not accepted.

Bus Information **Greyhound** (☎ *800/231–2222* 🌐 *www.greyhound.com*). **Los Angeles MTA** (☎ *800/266–6883* 🌐 *www.metro.net*). **Orange County Transportation Authority (OCTA)** (☎ *714/636–7433* 🌐 *www.octa.net*).

CAR TRAVEL

The San Diego Freeway (I–405), the coastal route, and the Santa Ana Freeway (I–5), the inland route, run north–south through Orange County. South of Laguna I–405 merges into I–5 (called the San Diego Freeway south from this point). A toll road, the 73 Highway, runs 15 mi from Newport Beach to San Juan Capistrano; it costs $4.25–$5.25 (lower rates are for weekends and off-peak hours) and is usually less jammed than the regular freeways. Do your best to avoid all Orange County freeways during rush hours (6–9 AM and 3:30–6:30 PM).

Highways 55 and 91 head west to the ocean and east into the mountains and desert. Highway 91, which goes to inland points, has some express lanes for which drivers pay a toll, ostensibly to avoid the worst of rush-hour traffic. If you have three or more people in your car, though, you can use the Highway 91 express lanes most of the day for free (except 4 PM–6 PM on weekdays, when you pay half-fare). Highway 55 leads to Newport Beach. The Pacific Coast Highway (Highway 1) allows easy access to beach communities and is the most scenic route.

TRAIN TRAVEL

When planning train travel, consider where the train stations are in relation to your ultimate destination. You may need to make extra transportation arrangements once you've arrived in town. From the station in San Juan Capistrano you can walk through the historic part of town.

Amtrak makes daily stops in Orange County at Fullerton, Anaheim, Santa Ana, Irvine, San Juan Capistrano, and San Clemente. Metrolink is a weekday commuter train that runs to and from Los Angeles and Orange County, starting as far south as Oceanside and stopping in Laguna Niguel, Tustin, San Juan Capistrano, San Clemente, Irvine, Santa Ana, Orange, Anaheim, and Fullerton. The Metrolink system is divided into a dozen zones; the fare you pay depends on how many zones you cover. Buy tickets from the vending machines at each station. Ticketing is on an honor system.

Train Information Amtrak (☎ *800/872–7245* 🌐 *www.amtrak.com*). **Metrolink** (☎ *800/371–5465* 🌐 *www.metrolinktrains.com*).

RESTAURANTS

Much like L.A., restaurants in Orange County are generally casual, and you'll rarely see men in jackets and ties. However, at top resort hotel dining rooms, many guests choose to dress up. Of course, there's also a swath of super-casual places along the beachfronts—fish-taco takeout, taquerias, burger joints—that won't mind if you wear flip-flops. Reservations are recommended for the nicest restaurants. Many places don't serve past 11 PM, and locals tend to eat early. Remember that according to California law, smoking is prohibited in all enclosed areas.

WHAT IT COSTS

	¢	$	$$	$$$	$$$$
Restaurants	under $7	$7–$12	$13–$22	$23–$32	over $32
Hotels	under $75	$75–$125	$126–$200	$201–$325	over $325

Restaurant prices are per person for a main course, excluding 8.25% sales tax. Hotel prices are for two people in a standard double room in nonholiday high season on the European Plan (no meals) unless otherwise noted. Taxes (9%–14%) are extra. In listings, we always name the facilities available, but we don't specify whether they cost extra. When pricing accommodations, always ask about what's included.

HOTELS

Along the coast there's been a flurry of luxury resort openings in recent years; Laguna's Montage and Dana Point's St. Regis Monarch Beach resorts elevated expectations and were followed by the renovation of Dana Point's Ritz-Carlton and the debut of The Resort at Pelican Hill on the Newport Coast, among others. As a rule, lodging prices tend to rise the closer the hotels are to the beach. If you're looking for value, consider a hotel that is inland along the I–405 freeway corridor. In most cases, you can take advantage of some of the facilities of the high-end resorts, such as restaurants and spas, even if you aren't an overnight guest.

VISITOR INFORMATION

The Anaheim-Orange County Visitor and Convention Bureau is an excellent resource for both leisure and business travelers and can provide materials on many area attractions. It's located on the main floor of the Anaheim Convention Center. The Orange County Tourism Council's Web site is also a useful source of information.

Contacts **Anaheim-Orange County Visitor and Convention Bureau** (*⊠Anaheim Convention Center, 800 W. Katella Ave., Anaheim ☎714/765-8888 🌐www.anaheimoc.org*). **Orange County Tourism Council** (*🌐www.visitorangecounty.net*).

THE COAST

Running along the Orange County coastline is scenic Pacific Coast Highway (Highway 1, known locally as PCH). Older beachfront settlements, with their modest bungalow-style homes, are joined by posh new gated communities. The pricey land between Newport Beach and Laguna Beach is where Laker Kobe Bryant, novelist Dean Koontz, and a slew of Internet and finance moguls live. Though the coastline is rapidly being filled in, there are still a few stretches of beautiful, protected open land. And at many places along the way you can catch an idealized glimpse of the Southern California lifestyle: surfers hitting the beach, boards under their arms.

HUNTINGTON BEACH

40 mi southeast of Los Angeles, I–5 south to I–605 south to I–405 south to Beach Blvd.

Once a sleepy residential town with little more than a string of rugged surf shops, Huntington Beach has transformed itself into a resort destination. The town's appeal is its broad white-sand beaches with often-towering waves, complemented by a lively pier, shops, and restaurants on Main Street and a growing collection of luxurious resort hotels. A draw for sports fans and partiers of all stripes is the U.S. Open professional surf competition, which brings a festive atmosphere to town each July. Other top sporting events are the AVP Pro Beach Volleyball Tournament in August and the Core Tour Extreme BMX Skate Competition in September. There's even a Surfing Walk of Fame, with plaques set in the sidewalk around the intersection of the PCH and Main Street.

ESSENTIALS

Visitor and Tour Info **Huntington Beach Conference and Visitors Bureau** (*⊠301 Main St., Suite 208, Huntington Beach ☎714/969–3492 or 800/729–6232 🌐www.surfcityusa.com*).

EXPLORING

❹ **Huntington Pier** stretches 1,800 feet out to sea, well past the powerful waves that made Huntington Beach reach for the title of "Surf City U.S.A." A farmers' market is held on Friday; an informal arts fair sets up most weekends. At the end of the pier sits **Ruby's** (*☎714/969–7829 🌐www.rubys.com*), part of a California chain of 1940s-style burger joints.

The **Pierside Pavilion** (✉ *PCH across from Huntington Pier*) has shops, restaurants, bars with live music, and a theater complex. The best surf-gear source is **Huntington Surf and Sport Pierside** (☎ *714/841–4000*), next to the pier, staffed by true surf enthusiasts.

Just up Main Street from the pier, the **International Surfing Museum** pays tribute to the sport's greats with the Surfing Hall of Fame, which has an impressive collection of surfboards and related memorabilia. They've even got the Bolex camera used to shoot the 1966 surfing documentary *The Endless Summer.* ✉ *411 Olive Ave., Huntington Beach* ☎ *714/960–3483* 🌐 *www.surfingmuseum.org* *Free, $1 suggested donation for students, $2 for adults* ⏲ *Year-round weekdays noon–5, weekends 11–6.*

3 ★ **Bolsa Chica Ecological Reserve** beckons wildlife lovers and bird-watchers with an 1,180-acre salt marsh where 321 out of Orange County's 420 bird species—including great blue herons, snowy and great egrets, and brown pelicans—have been spotted in the past decade. Throughout the reserve are trails for bird-watching, including a comfortable 1½-mi loop. Free guided tours depart from the walking bridge the first Saturday of each month at 9 AM. ✉ *Entrance on PCH 1 mi south of Warner Ave., opposite Bolsa Chica State Beach at traffic light* ☎ *714/846–1114* 🌐 *www.bolsachica.org* *Free* ⏲ *Daily dawn–dusk.*

WHERE TO EAT

$$$ SEAFOOD ✕ **Duke's.** Oceanfront vistas and fresh-caught seafood reign supreme at this homage to surfing legend Duke Kahanamoku, which is a prime people-watching spot right at the beginning of the pier. Choose from several fish-of-the-day selections—many Hawaiian—prepared in one of eight ways. Or try the spicy sugar cane shrimp or seven spice ahi tuna. Duke's mai tai is not to be missed. ✉ *317 Pacific Coast Hwy.* ☎ *714/374–6446* ▭ *AE, D, MC, V.*

$–$$ AMERICAN ✕ **Lou's Red Oak BBQ.** You won't find any frills at Lou's Red Oak BBQ—just barbecue pork, grilled linguica, rotisserie chicken, and a lot of beef. Try the tri-tip (either as an entrée or on a toasted bun smothered with garlic butter) or a Hawaiian teriyaki plate to get into the surfing spirit surfing spirit. ✉ *21501 Brookhurst St., Huntington Beach* ☎ *714/965–5200* 🌐 *www.lousbbq.com* ▭ *MC, V.*

$$$ ECLECTIC ✕ **Savannah at the Beach.** At Savannah, which is beneath Duke's restaurant and right on the beach, nostalgic chophouse fare is combined with globally-inspired seafood dishes and modern, spicy takes on Southern specialties. By day this is a casual place where you can sit outside in your flip-flops and almost reach out and touch the passing joggers, volleyball players, and skateboarders. In the evening the ambience is more sophisticated, as are the menu items such as beef Stroganoff, maple-glazed salmon, and blacked red snapper with Creole sauce. ✉ *315 PCH* ☎ *714/374–7273* ▭ *AE, D, DC, MC, V.*

¢–$ AMERICAN ✕ **Sugar Shack Café.** The long lines in front testify to this local favorite, which has been owned by the same family since 1967. Breakfasts, served all day, are standouts, as are the hamburgers, salads, and sandwiches. Streetside sitting is so popular you have to sign a clipboard by the door

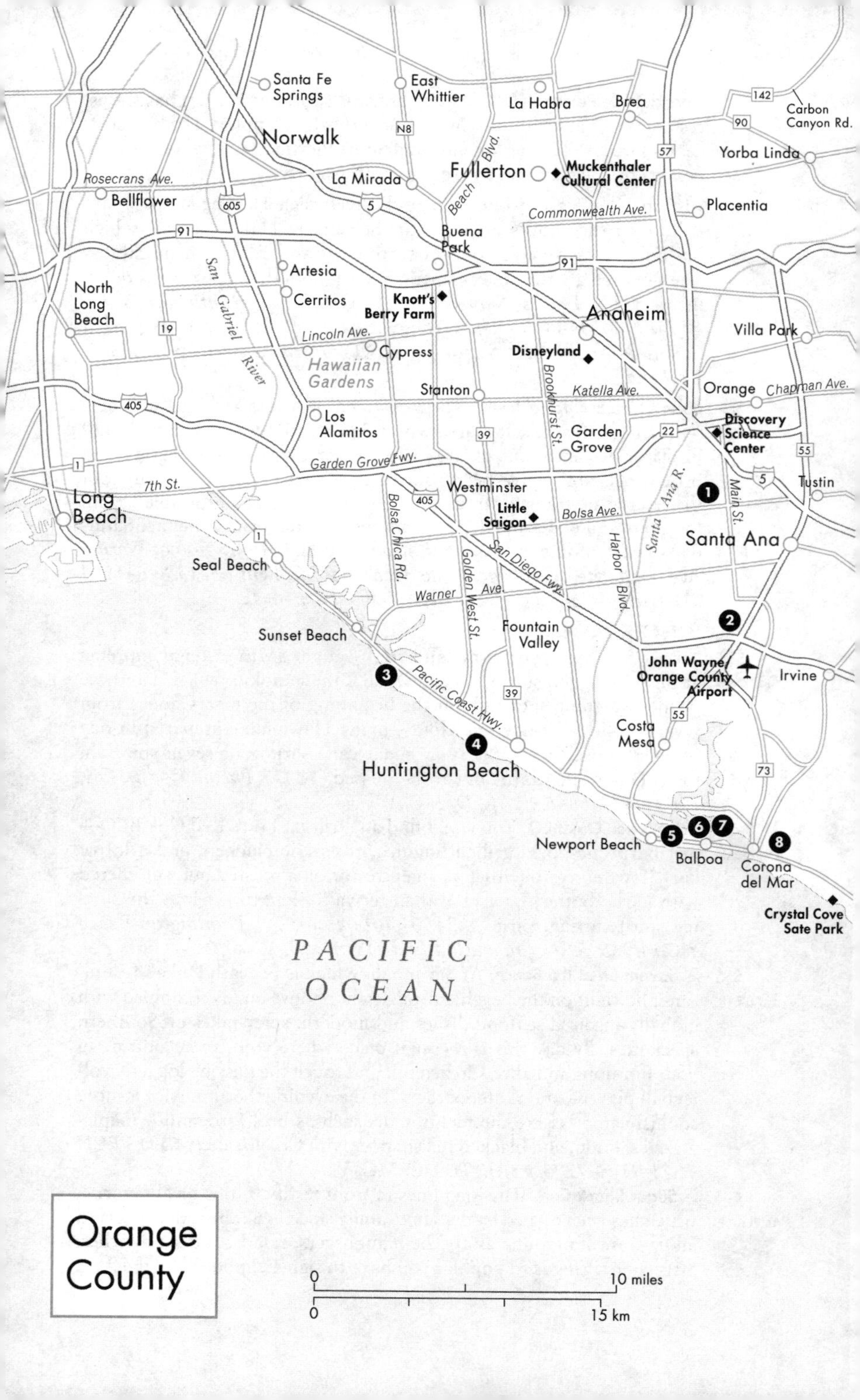
Santa Fe Springs
East Whittier
La Habra
Brea
Carbon Canyon Rd.
142
90
N8
Norwalk
57
Yorba Linda
Fullerton
Muckenthaler Cultural Center
Beach Blvd.
Rosecrans Ave.
La Mirada
Bellflower
605
5
Placentia
Commonwealth Ave.
91
Buena Park
San Gabriel River
Artesia
North Long Beach
Cerritos
Knott's Berry Farm
Anaheim
19
Lincoln Ave.
Villa Park
Cypress
Disneyland
Hawaiian Gardens
Brookhurst St.
Stanton
Katella Ave.
Orange
Chapman Ave.
405
Los Alamitos
Garden Grove
Discovery Science Center
22
39
55
1
Garden Grove Fwy.
7th St.
Westminster
Tustin
Long Beach
Bolsa Chica Rd.
Little Saigon
Bolsa Ave.
Santa Ana R.
Main St.
Santa Ana
Harbor Blvd.
San Diego Fwy.
Seal Beach
Golden West St.
Warner Ave.
Fountain Valley
Sunset Beach
John Wayne/ Orange County Airport
Irvine
Pacific Coast Hwy.
Costa Mesa
Huntington Beach
73
Newport Beach
Balboa
Corona del Mar
Crystal Cove Sate Park
PACIFIC OCEAN
Orange County
0
10 miles
0
15 km

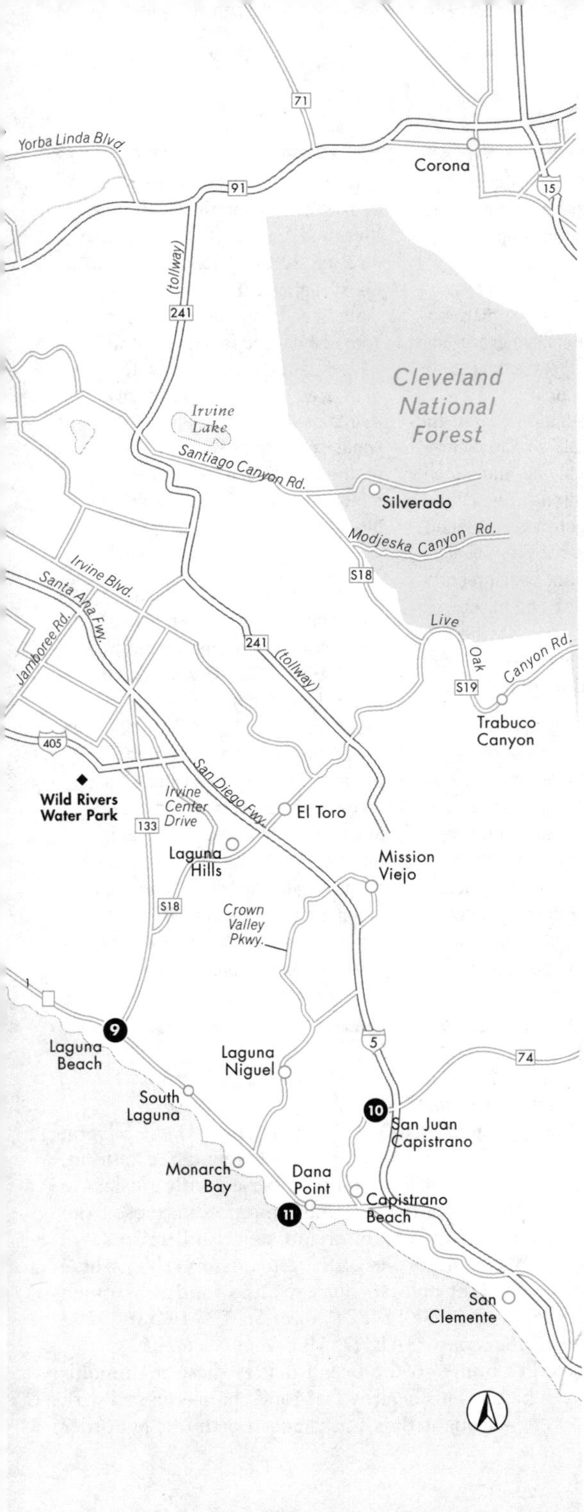

Balboa Pavilion 6
Bolsa Chica Ecological Reserve 3
Bowers Museum of Cultural Art 1
Dana Point 11
Huntington Pier 4
Laguna Beach 9
Newport Harbor 5
Orange County Museum of Art 7
San Juan Capistrano 10
Sherman Library and Gardens 8
South Coast Plaza 2

CLOSE UP

The Great Outdoors

Water sports rule the coast of Orange County. Those inexperienced at riding the waves along the coastline can get a feel for the waves by riding a boogie board at Seal Beach or at the Newport River jetties. Surfing is permitted at most beaches year-round (check local newspapers or talk to lifeguards for conditions), and surfboard-rental stands line the coast. The best waves are usually at San Clemente, Newport Beach, and Huntington Beach. From June through September the ocean temperature tops 70°F and lifeguards patrol almost every beach. Local newspapers print beach reports with wave information and notice of any closures. You can also check local news on surf and water quality through the **Surfrider Foundation** (🌐 *www.surfrider.org*).

Keep a lookout for signs warning of dangerous conditions: undertow, strong currents, and big waves can all be hazardous. Avoid swimming near surfers. When a yellow flag with a black circle is flying (known to locals as "black balling"), it means no hard boards are allowed, but swimming and bodyboarding are permitted.

If you'd like to explore the coastline by bike or on foot, the **Santa Ana Riverbed Trail** hugs the Santa Ana River for 20½ mi between the Pacific Coast Highway (PCH) at Huntington State Beach and Imperial Highway in Yorba Linda. Joggers have an uninterrupted path the whole way. There are entrances, restrooms, and drinking fountains at all crossings. A bike path winds south from Marina del Rey all the way to San Diego with only minor breaks. Most beaches have bike-rental stands.

You'll usually hear the name Irvine linked to soulless suburban sprawl, but balancing that is the **Irvine Ranch Conservancy** (☎ *714/508–4757* 🌐 *www.irvineranchwildlands.org*). These 50,000 protected acres stretch 22 mi from Weir Canyon to the coast, where the reserve meets the Laguna Coast Wilderness Park and Crystal Cove State Park. The Conservancy and its affiliated environmental organizations sponsor many activities, from tough mountain bike rides to leisurely family picnics in regional parks. You'll need advance reservations for any of their docent-led activities.

---

and wait your turn. ✉*213½ Main St.* ☎*714/536–0355* ▭*AE, D, MC, V* ⏲*No dinner; lunch served until 8 on Wed.*

$$ JAPANESE ✕**Tuna Town Sushi Bar and Teppanyaki Grill.** Korn drummer David Silvera, a Huntington Beach resident, owns this Japanese-Hawaiian restaurant. Korn memorabilia is on the walls, which reverberate with music and chatter. Load up on sushi, specialty rolls, and tempura or choose from entrees like sautéed chicken in wasabi cream sauce and miso-sake-marinated butterfish. If you sit at one of the *teppanyaki* table, where the chefs chop and grill right before your eyes, the food is as much of a show as the eclectic clientele. ✉*221 Main St.* ☎*714/536–3194* 🌐*www.tunatownsushibar.com* ▭*AE, D, MC, V* ⏲*No lunch.*

¢ MEXICAN ✕**Wahoo's Fish Taco.** Proximity to the ocean makes these mahimahi-filled tacos taste even better. This healthy fast-food chain—tagged with dozens of surf stickers—brought Baja's fish tacos north of the border to quick success. ✉120 Main St., Huntington Beach ☎714/536–2050 🌐www.wahoos.com 💳MC, V.

WHERE TO STAY

$ **Best Western Regency Inn.** This moderately priced, tidy Tudor-style hotel is near PCH and close to the main drag and its restaurants and shops. Rooms are cookie-cutter, but some have private whirlpools. Forgo an ocean view and you can save a lot of money. Breakfast is included in the room rate. **Pros:** great value; large rooms (some with Jacuzzi tubs); free Internet in lobby; complimentary Continental breakfast. **Cons:** ten-minute drive to beach; unglamorous neighborhood; a bit dated. ✉*19360 Beach Blvd., Huntington Beach* ☎*714/962–4244* 🌐*www.bestwestern.com* *64 rooms* *In-room: refrigerator, Internet. In-hotel: pool, gym, laundry facilities, parking (free), no-smoking rooms* 💳*AE, D, DC, MC, V.*

$$$ **Hilton Waterfront Beach Resort.** Conveniently situated smack dab across the street from the beach and within walking distance of Main Street, this Mediterranean-style Hilton attracts a varied clientele—singles, families, couples, and business travelers. All guest rooms have private balconies; oceanfront rooms boast views of Catalina Island. A heated free-form pool, exotic landscaping, and sand volleyball court add to the resort vibe. **Pros:** within walking distance of several restaurants; excellent Sunday brunch buffet; oceanfront views. **Cons:** no self-parking; noise can be an issue. ✉*21100 PCH, Huntington Beach* ☎*714/845–8000 or 800/822–7873* 🌐*www.waterfrontresort.com* *266 rooms, 24 suites* *In-room: safe, refrigerator, Internet. In-hotel: restaurant, room service, bar, tennis court, pool, gym, parking (paid), no-smoking rooms* 💳*AE, D, DC, MC, V.*

$ **Hotel Huntington Beach.** This eight-story hotel's inland location by the I–405 puts it into the value category for visitors to Huntington Beach and nearby business parks. However, the beach is a hotel-provided short shuttle ride away. Modest motel-style rooms have basic amenities.**Pros:** superb location; shuttle to beach; decent budget option. **Cons:**general decor and rooms in need of update; Internet and business center facilities aren't always reliable. ✉*7667 Center Ave.* ☎*714/891–0123 or 877/891–0123* 🌐*www.hotelhb.com* *224 rooms* *In-room: Wi-Fi. In-hotel: restaurant, bar, pool, gym, Internet terminal, Wi-Fi, parking (free), no-smoking rooms* 💳*AE, D, DC, MC, V.*

$$$$ ★ **Hyatt Regency Huntington Beach Resort and Spa.** The design of this handsome property, which sprawls along the PCH and incorporates courtyards with fountains and firepots, is a nod to California's Mission period. Nearly all of the spacious rooms offer ocean views and private balconies or terraces. Beach-themed artwork by local artists enhances guest rooms and public spaces. This Hyatt aims to create a village atmosphere, with expansive common grounds and an inviting shopping area, and to a large extent it has succeeded. Beach access is via a bridge over the PCH. **Pros:** close to beach; responsive staff; family-friendly. **Cons:** some partial ocean-view rooms are disappointing; pesky resort and daily valet fees. ✉*21500 PCH* ☎*714/698–1234 or 800/554–9288* 🌐*www.huntingtonbeach.hyatt.com* *517 rooms, 57 suites* *In-room: safe, Internet, Wi-Fi. In-hotel: 3 restaurants, bar, gym, spa, water sports,*

9

bicycles, children's programs (ages 3–12), laundry service, Internet terminal, Wi-Fi, parking (free), no-smoking rooms ▭*AE, D, DC, MC, V.*

SPORTS AND THE OUTDOORS

BEACHES **Huntington City Beach** (☎*714/536–5281* 🌐*www.ci.huntington-beach.ca.us*) stretches for 3 mi north and south of the pier from Bolsa Chica State Beach to Huntington State Beach on the south. The beach is most crowded around the pier; amateur and professional surfers brave the waves daily on its north side. As you continue south, **Huntington State Beach** (☎*714/536–1454* 🌐*www.parks.ca.gov/?page_id=643*) parallels Pacific Coast Highway. On the state and city beaches there are changing rooms, concessions, lifeguards, Wi-Fi, and ample parking; the state beach also has barbecue pits. At the northern section of the city, **Bolsa Chica State Beach** (☎*714/846–3460* 🌐*www.parks.ca.gov/?page_id=642*) has barbecue pits and RV campsites and is usually less crowded than its southern neighbors. **Dog Beach** (✉*19000 PCH* ☎*714/841–8644* 🌐*www.dogbeach.org*), just north of the pier, is the rare place that encourages dogs to run and splash sans leash. You might even see a dog surfing with his owner. The beach is open daily 5 AM–10 PM.

SURFING **Corky Carroll's Surf School** (☎*714/969–3959* 🌐*www.surfschool.net*) organizes lessons, weeklong workshops, and surfing trips. You can rent surf- or boogie boards at **Dwight's** (☎*714/536–8083*), one block south of the pier. **Zack's Pier Plaza** (✉*405 PCH at Main St.*) provides surfing lessons for individuals or groups and rents boards, wet suits, and other beach equipment.

SURF'S UP!

Many of the world's most famous surfers are represented on the Surfing Walk of Fame (along Main Street and Pacific Coast Highway in Huntington Beach) including Robert August, the star of Endless Summer, Corky Carroll, a pioneer surfing promoter, and Mark Richard, winner of the most surfing championships. Super-surfers have been selected since 1994 by a committee representing the surfing industry worldwide. Inductions take place during the annual U.S. Open Surfing event held in Huntington Beach in July. (Surfing Walk of Fame ☎714/960–3483 🌐*www.surfingmuseum.org*).

NEWPORT BEACH

6 mi south of Huntington Beach, PCH.

Newport Beach has evolved from a simple seaside village to an icon of chic coastal living. Its ritzy reputation comes from megayachts bobbing in the harbor, boutiques that rival those in Beverly Hills, and spectacular homes overlooking the ocean. Newport is said to have the highest per-capita number of Mercedes-Benzes in the world; inland Newport Beach's concentration of high-rise office buildings, shopping centers, and luxury hotels drive the economy. But on the city's Balboa Peninsula, you can still catch a glimpse of a more innocent, down-to-earth beach town scattered with tackle shops and sailor bars.

ESSENTIALS

Visitor and Tour Info Newport Beach Conference and Visitors Bureau (*✉110 Newport Center Dr., Suite 120, Newport Beach ☎949/719–6100 or 800/942–6278 🌐www.visitnewportbeach.com*).

EXPLORING

6 The **Balboa Pavilion,** on the bay side of the peninsula, was built in 1905 as a bath- and boathouse. Today it houses a restaurant and shops and it serves as a departure point for harbor and whale-watching cruises. Look for it on Main Street, off Balboa Boulevard. Adjacent to the pavilion is the three-car ferry that connects the peninsula to Balboa Island. In the blocks around the pavilion you'll find restaurants, beachside shops, and the small **Fun Zone**—a local kiddie hangout with a Ferris wheel and a nautical museum. On the other side of the narrow peninsula is **Balboa Pier.** On its end is the original branch of Ruby's, a 1940s-esque burger-and-shake joint.

Newport's best beaches are on **Balboa Peninsula,** where many jetties pave the way to ideal swimming areas. The most intense bodysurfing place in Orange County and arguably on the West Coast, known as the **Wedge,** is at the south end of the peninsula. Created by accident in the 1930s when the Federal Works Progress Administration built a jetty to protect Newport Harbor, the break is pure euphoria for highly skilled bodysurfers. ■ **TIP→Since the waves generally break very close to shore and rip currents are strong, lifeguards strongly discourage visitors from attempting it—but it sure is fun to watch an experienced local ride it.**

Shake the sand out of your shoes to head inland to the ritzy **Fashion Island** outdoor mall, a cluster of arcades and courtyards complete with koi pond, fountains and a Venetian-style carousel—plus some awesome ocean views. Although it doesn't have quite the international-designer clout of South Coast Plaza, it has the luxe department store Neiman Marcus and expensive spots like L'Occitane, Kate Spade, Ligne Roset, and Design Within Reach. Chains, restaurants, and the requisite movie theater fill out the rest. *✉410 Newport Center Dr., between Jamboree and MacArthur Blvds., off PCH, Newport Beach ☎949/721–2000 🌐www.shopfashionisland.com.*

5 ★ **Newport Harbor,** which shelters nearly 10,000 small boats, may seduce even those who don't own a yacht. Spend an afternoon exploring the charming avenues and surrounding alleys. Within Newport Harbor are eight small islands, including Balboa and Lido. The houses framing the shore may seem modest, but this is some of the most expensive real estate in the world. Several grassy areas on primarily residential Lido Isle have views of Newport Harbor. In evidence of the upper-crust Orange County mind-set, each is marked PRIVATE COMMUNITY PARK.

Balboa Island is a sliver of terra firma in Newport Harbor whose quaint streets are tightly packed with impossibly charming multimillion-dollar cottages. The island's main drag, Marine Avenue, is lined with equally picturesque cafés and shops. Stop by ice cream parlor **Sugar & Spice** (*✉310 Marine Ave., Balboa Island ☎949/673–8907 🌐www.killer orange.com*) for a Balboa Bar—a slab of vanilla ice cream dipped first in chocolate and then in a topping of your choice such as hard candy or Oreo crumbs. Other parlors serve the concoction, but Sugar & Spice claims to have invented it back in 1945. **Basilic** (✉*217 Marine Ave.* ☎*949/673–0570* 🌐*www.basilicrestaurant.com*), an intimate French-Swiss bistro, adds a touch of elegance to the island with its white linen and flower-topped tables. Head here for foie gras, steak au poivre, and a fine Bordeaux. At **Olive Oil & Beyond** (✉*210 Marine Ave.* ☎*949/566–9380* 🌐*www.oliveoilbeyond.com*), you can sample and purchase premium oils from around the globe. There's also a lineup of unique balsamic vinegars—some flavored with fig or tangerine—and other gourmet goodies.

> **O SOLO MIO IN THE O.C.**
>
> Try a one-hour gondola cruise with the Gondola Company of Newport (☎*949/675–1212* 🌐*www.gondolas.com*). It costs $85 for two and is frequently voted as the best place to take a date in Orange County.

The **Newport Harbor Nautical Museum, in the Balboa Fun Zone (a small, historic amusement park),** has exhibits on the history of the harbor as well as of the Pacific as a whole. There's a fleet of ship models, some dating to 1798; one is made entirely of gold and silver. Another fun display is a virtual deep-sea fishing machine. New exhibits include a touch tank holding local sea creatures and a virtual sailing simulator. ✉*600 E. Bay Ave., Newport Beach* ☎*949/675–8915* 🌐*www.nhnm.org* 🎫*$5 suggested donation* ⏲*Wed. and Thurs. 11–5, Fri. and Sat 11–6, Sun. 11–5, closed Mon. and Tues.*

Newport Pier, which juts out into the ocean near 20th Street, is the heart of Newport's beach community and a popular fishing spot. Street parking is difficult at the pier, so grab the first space you find and be prepared to walk. A stroll along West Ocean Front reveals much of the town's character. On weekday mornings, head for the beach near the pier, where you're likely to encounter dory fishermen hawking their predawn catches, as they've done for generations. On weekends the walk is alive with kids of all ages on in-line skates, skateboards, and bikes dodging pedestrians and whizzing past fast-food joints, shops, and bars.

7 ★ The **Orange County Museum of Art** gathers a collection of modernist paintings and sculpture by California artists and cutting-edge, international contemporary works. Works by such key California artists as Richard Diebenkorn, Ed Ruscha, Robert Irwin, and Chris Burden are included in the collection. The museum also displays some of its digital art, Internet-based art, and sound works in the Orange Lounge, a satellite gallery at South Coast Plaza; free of charge, it's open the same hours as the mall. ✉*850 San Clemente Dr., Newport Beach* ☎*949/759–1122* 🌐*www.ocma.net* 🎫*$12* ⏲*Wed.–Sun. 11–5, Thurs. 11–8.*

Sate your inner clotheshorse at **Trovata.** Located across the street from the laid-back Alta Coffee House, the surf-inspired threads at this upscale boutique channel a Southern California vibe. The creative force behind the Trovata label keeps things young and playful, while designing tastefully simple pieces. ✉*505 31st St., Newport Beach* ☎*949/675–5904* 🌐*www.trovata.com.*

WHERE TO EAT

$$–$$$ AMERICAN

3-Thirty-3. If there's a nightlife "scene" to be had in Newport Beach, this is it. This swank and stylish eatery attracts a convivial crowd—both young and old—for midday, sunset, and late-night dining; a long list of small, shareable plates heightens the camaraderie. Pair a cocktail with Chinese-spiced lollipop lamb chops or chicken satay while you check out the scene, or settle in for a dinner of Kobe flatiron steak or potato-crusted wild salmon. *333 Bayside Dr.* *949/673–8464* *www.3thirty3nb.com* *AE, MC, V.*

$$–$$$ SEAFOOD

Bluewater Grill. On the site of an old sportfishing dock, this popular spot offers seafood from around the globe—from Mississippi catfish to barramundi from Australia. There's a tranquil bay view from either the dining room, which is adorned with early-1900s fishing photos, or the waterfront patio. Favorites include blue-nose sea bass, local Pacific red snapper, and calamari steak for those who miss the abalone that used to be common in the area. There's an emphasis on freshness—the menu changes daily—and wines are reasonably priced. *630 Lido Park Dr., Newport Beach* *949/675–3474* *www.bluewatergrill.com* *AE, D, DC, MC, V.*

$$$ SEAFOOD

The Cannery. This 1920s cannery building still teems with fish, but now they go into dishes on the eclectic Pacific Rim menu rather than being packed into crates. Settle in at the sushi bar, dining room, or patio before choosing between sashimi, bouillabaisse, or oven-roasted Chilean sea bass prepared with a tropical twist. The menu includes a selection of steaks and ribs as well as desserts like bananas Foster and Key lime pie. *3010 Lafayette Rd., Newport Beach* *949/566–0060* *www.cannerynewport.com* *AE, D, DC, MC, V.*

$$$ AMERICAN

Gulfstream. This trendy restaurant has an open kitchen, comfortable booths, and outdoor seating on warm evenings. Especially tasty are the short ribs with mustard barbecue sauce; the most popular item is the ahi tuna burger. Salads, such as a mélange of cabbage, white beans, avocado, corn, and grapes, tend to be healthy and steaks and seafood dishes are simply prepared. It gets noisy near the bar area, so come early or retreat to the patio if you prefer quiet. *850 Avocado Ave.* *949/718–0188* *www.hillstone.com* *AE, MC, V.*

WHERE TO STAY

$$$–$$$$

Balboa Bay Club and Resort. Sharing the same frontage as the private Balboa Bay Club where Humphrey Bogart, Lauren Bacall, and the Reagans hung out, this hotel has one of the best bay views around. There's a yacht-club vibe in the public spaces, especially in the nautical dining room. The spacious rooms, which have either bay or courtyard views, have a beachy decor of rattan furniture, plantation shutters, and tropical-pattern drapes. Duke's Place, a bar named for John Wayne, a former member and club governor, has photos of the star in his mariner-theme films. **Pros**: exquisite bayfront views; comfortable beds; romantic. **Cons**: service is helpful but can be slow; not much within walking distance. *1221 W. Coast Hwy.* *949/645–5000 or 888/445–7153* *www.balboabayclub.com* *150 rooms, 10 suites* *In room: safe, DVD, refrigerator, Wi-Fi. In-hotel: 2 restaurants, room service, bar, gym, spa,* *tennis courts, laundry service, Wi-Fi, some pets allowed, no-smoking rooms* ▭*AE, D, DC, MC, V.*

$$$ **Hyatt Regency Newport Beach.** The best aspect of this grande dame of Newport hotels is its lushly landscaped acres: 26 of them, overlooking the Back Bay. The casually elegant, low-profile architecture, spread over the generous grounds, will appeal to travelers weary of high-rise hotels. When booking your room, suite, or bungalow, let them know your preference of bay, golf course, garden, or pool views. Most rooms have patios or balconies. There's a nine-hole golf course and 16 lighted tennis courts. **Pros:** high-quality linens and bedding; centrally located for shopping. **Cons:** self-parking is far from main property; 10-minute drive to beach. ✉*1107 Jamboree Rd.* ☎*949/729–1234* 🌐*www.newportbeach.hyatt.com* *388 rooms, 11 suites, 4 bungalows* *In-room: safe, refrigerator, Internet. In-hotel: restaurant, room service, bar, golf course, tennis courts, pools, gym, spa, bicycles, laundry service, Wi-Fi, parking (paid), no-smoking rooms* ▭*AE, D, DC, MC, V.*

$$$$ **The Island Hotel.** A suitably stylish hotel in a very chic neighborhood (it's across the street from the Fashion Island shopping center), this 20-story tower caters to luxury seekers by offering weekend golf packages in conjunction with the nearby Pelican Hill golf course. Guest rooms have private balconies (usually with outstanding views), marble bathrooms and original art. The spa does its bit for luxury with a pearl powder facial. The hotel lured Beverly Hills chef Bill Bracken, who now pampers diners at the elegant Palm Terrace with a contemporary menu of seductive small bites and entrées such as potato-encrusted Chilean sea bass. **Pros:** proximity to Fashion Island; 24-hour exercise facilities; first-class spa. **Cons:** steep valet parking prices; some rooms have views of mall; pricey. ✉*690 Newport Center Dr., Newport Beach* ☎*949/759–0808 or 866/554–4620* 🌐*www.theislandhotel.com* *295 rooms, 83 suites* *In-room: safe, DVD, Wi-Fi. In-hotel: 2 restaurants, room service, bar, tennis courts, pool, gym, spa, Internet terminal, Wi-Fi, parking (paid), some pets allowed, no-smoking rooms* ▭*AE, D, DC, MC, V.*

$$$ **Newport Beach Marriott Hotel and Spa.** Here you'll be smack in the moneyed part of town: across from Fashion Island, next to a country club, and with a view toward Newport Harbor. The property recently underwent a $70 million makeover, and it shows. Rooms have that no-fuss contemporary look: dark wood, granite bathroom counters and welcome splashes of color; request one with a balcony or patio that provides a view of the lush gardens or faces the ocean. There are plenty of ways to pamper yourself: indulge in a massage at the full-service Pure Blu spa, cocktails at a poolside cabana, or a rib eye at the hotel's sleek steakhouse. **Pros:** four concierge floors offer enhanced amenities, complimentary breakfast, and snacks; bike rentals; fantastic spa. **Cons:** sprawling floor plan; small bathrooms; car is essential for exploring beyond shopping malls. ✉*900 Newport Center Dr., Newport Beach* ☎*949/640–4000* 🌐*www.marriott.com* *512 rooms, 20 suites* *In-room: Internet, Wi-Fi. In-hotel: restaurant, room service, bar, pools, gym, spa, Wi-Fi, parking (paid), no-smoking rooms* ▭*AE, D, DC, MC, V.*

$ **Newport Dunes Waterfront Resort and Marina.** With more than 100 acres of private beach along Newport's Back Bay, Newport Dunes is one of the poshest RV parks in the world. Although beachfront pull-in premium sites—complete with Wi-Fi and TV plus hookups to water, electricity, and sewer—are considerably larger (and less cramped) than those a few rows back, all sites are immaculately clean. There are a few sites for freestanding tents, as well as a handful of cottages with kitchens and porches that can accommodate up to six guests. At the Village Center you'll find a pool, a spa, and a convenience store, and the upscale Back Bay Bistro. Nonguests are able to access the park for day use to swim, surf or take a nature tour on a Segway. **Pros:** pristine campsites; courteous staff; L'Occitane products in cottage bathrooms. **Cons:** steep valet parking fees; located in busy (read: potentially loud) business district. ✉ *1131 Back Bay Dr.* ☎ *949/729–3863 or 800/765–7661* 🌐 *www.newportdunes.com* *378 RV sites (55 allow tents), 24 cottages* *In-hotel: restaurant, pool, spa, beachfront, bicycles, laundry facilities, Internet terminal, Wi-Fi, parking (paid)* *AE, D, MC, V.*

SPORTS AND THE OUTDOORS

BOAT RENTALS You can tour Lido and Balboa isles by renting kayaks ($15 an hour), sailboats ($45 an hour), small motorboats ($65 an hour), and electric boats ($75–$90 an hour at **Balboa Boat Rentals** (✉ *510 E. Edgewater Ave., Newport Beach* ☎ *949/673–7200* 🌐 *www.boats4rent.com*). You must have a driver's license, and some knowledge of boating is helpful; rented boats must stay in the bay.

BOAT TOURS **Catalina Passenger Service** (✉ *400 Main St., Newport Beach* ☎ *949/673–5245* 🌐 *www.catalinainfo.com*), at the Balboa Pavilion, operates 90-minute daily round-trip passage to Catalina Island for $68. Call first; winter service is often available only on weekends. **Hornblower Cruises & Events** (✉ *2431 West Coast Hwy., Newport Beach* ☎ *949/646–0155 or 888/467–6256* 🌐 *www.hornblower.com*) books three-hour weekend dinner cruises with dancing for $72 Friday, $75 Saturday; the two-hour Sunday brunch cruise is $53.

GOLF **Newport Beach Golf Course** (✉ *3100 Irvine Ave., Newport Beach* ☎ *949/852–8681* 🌐 *www.npbgolf.com*), a par-59 executive course, is lighted for night play. Rates start at $17. Reservations are accepted up to one week in advance, but walk-ins are accommodated when possible.

RUNNING The **Beach Trail** runs along the coast from Huntington Beach to Newport. Paths throughout Upper Newport Back Bay wrap around a marshy area inhabited by lizards, rabbits, and waterfowl. For information on free walking tours in this ecological reserve, call the **Newport Bay Naturalists & Friends** (☎ *949/640–6746* 🌐 *www.newportbay.org*).

SPORTFISHING In addition to a complete tackle shop, **Davey's Locker** (✉ *Balboa Pavilion, 400 Main St., Newport Beach* ☎ *949/673–1434* 🌐 *www.daveyslocker.com*) operates sportfishing trips starting at $40, as well as private charters and, in winter, whale-watching trips for $30.

TENNIS Call the **Recreation Department** (☎ *949/644–3151* 🌐 *recreation.city.newport-beach.ca.us*) to find out about courts throughout Newport Beach, where play is usually free and on a first-come, first-served basis.

CORONA DEL MAR

2 mi south of Newport Beach, via Hwy. 1.

A small jewel on the Pacific Coast, Corona del Mar (known by locals as "CDM") has exceptional beaches that some say resemble their majestic Northern California counterparts. South of CDM is an area referred to as the Newport Coast or Crystal Cove—whatever you call it, it's another dazzling spot on the California Riviera.

WORD OF MOUTH

"We enjoyed eating at the Beachcomber at Crystal Cove State Park. There was a little bit of a wait, but that gave us time to wander a few steps away and see the house used in the filming of Beaches. Silly, maybe, but I enjoyed seeing it." —starrs

ESSENTIALS

Visitor and Tour Info **Newport Beach Conference and Visitors Bureau** (*110 Newport Center Dr., Suite 120, Newport Beach 949/719–6100 or 800/942–6278 www.visitnewportbeach.com*).

EXPLORING

Corona del Mar State Beach (*949/644–3151 www.parks.ca.gov*) is actually made up of two beaches, Little Corona and Big Corona, separated by a cliff. Facilities include fire pits, volleyball courts, food stands, restrooms, and parking. TIP→ **Two colorful reefs (and the fact that it's off-limits to boats) make Corona del Mar great for snorkelers and for beachcombers who prefer privacy.**

Fodor's Choice ★ Midway between Corona del Mar and Laguna, stretching along both sides of Pacific Coast Highway, **Crystal Cove State Park** (*www.crystalcovestatepark.com*) is a favorite of local beachgoers and wilderness trekkers. It encompasses a 3½-mi stretch of unspoiled beach and has some of the best tide-pooling in southern California. Here you can see starfish, crabs, and other sea life on the rocks. The park's 2,400 acres of backcountry are ideal for hiking, horseback riding, and mountain biking, but stay on the trails to preserve the beauty. Environmental camping is allowed in one of the three campgrounds. Bring water, food, and other supplies; there's a pit toilet but no shower. Open fires and pets are forbidden. Parking costs $10. **Crystal Cove Historic District** holds a collection of 46 handmade historic cottages (14 of which are available for overnight rental), decorated and furnished to reflect the 1935–55 beach culture that flourished here. On the sand above the high tide line and on a bluff above the beach, the cottages offer a funky look at beach life 50 years ago. Cottages, which average $174 per night for four people, can be reserved up to six months in advance from **Reserve America** (*800/444–7275 www.reserveamerica.com*). Beach culture flourishes in the Crystal Cove Historic District's restaurant, the **Beachcomber at Crystal Cove Café** (*949/376–6900 www.thebeachcombercafe.com*),whose umbrella-laden deck is just a few steps above the white sand. **The Store** (*949/376–8762*) carries fine art photography works by local plein air artists, as well as jewelry, children's toys, and beach apparel. ☎*949/494–3539* 🌐*www.crystalcovestatepark.com* ⏲*Daily 6–dusk.*

Further adding to Orange County's overwhelming supply of high-end shopping and dining is **Crystal Cove Promenade** (✉*7772–8112 East Coast Hwy., Newport Beach*), which might be described as the toniest strip mall in America. The storefronts of this Mediterranean–inspired center are lined up across the street from Crystal Cove State Park, with the shimmering Pacific waters in plain view. Standouts include Eric Hanan (✉*7916 East Coast Hwy., Newport Beach* ☎*949/494–7222* 🌐*www.erichanan.com),* creator of spectacular custom jewelry, while gems of the edible variety are found at Bluefin *(*✉*7952 East Coast Hwy., Newport Beach* ☎*949/715–7373* 🌐*www.bluefinbyabe.com*), the area's most renowned sushi bar. There is plenty of sidewalk and courtyard seating at this center that is both a regional destination and dog-friendly neighborhood hangout for the lucky locals.

8 **Sherman Library and Gardens,** a 2½-acre botanical garden and library specializing in the history of the Pacific Southwest, makes a good break from the sun and sand. You can wander among cactus gardens, rose gardens, a wheelchair-height touch-and-smell garden, and a tropical conservatory. There's a good gift shop, too. Café Jardin serves lunch on weekdays plus Sunday brunch. ✉*2647 E. PCH, Corona del Mar* ☎*949/673–2261, 949/673–0033 lunch reservations* 🌐*www.slgardens.org* 🎟*$3* ⏲*Daily 10:30–4.*

WHERE TO EAT AND STAY

$–$$ MEDITERRANEAN ✕**Caffe Panini.** For fresh, reasonably priced food and outstanding espresso drinks with an Italian flair, this cozy café packs a lot of punch for your dining dollars. Think straight-from-the-oven breads, pizzas, pastas, and grilled panini like roast beef with onions and provolone cheese. It's a breakfast-time favorite among locals; at dinner, Mediterranean entrées include moussaka and kebabs. ✉*2333 E. Coast Hwy.* ☎*949/675–8101* 🌐*www.mypaninicafe.com* ⏲*Closed Sun.* 💳*AE, D, MC, V.*

$$$ SEAFOOD ✕**Oysters.** Whether you want to dine light (the list of hot and cold appetizers is lengthy) or engage in a full-blown multicourse affair, the vibe is always casual and definitely romantic at this jazz-filled bistro-style establishment. Oysters—you can try them panko crusted, served Rockefeller style, or in a raw sampler—are a definite highlight. Afterward, tuck into seared Hawaiian ahi with spicy soy-chili glaze or a New York steak with mac-and-(blue-)cheese—but be sure to leave room for housemade s'mores. ✉*2515 E. Coast Hwy., Corona del Mar* ☎*949/675–7411* 🌐*www.oystersrestaurant.com* 💳*AE, D, MC, V* ⏲*No lunch.*

$ AMERICAN ✕**Pacific Whey Cafe & Baking Company.** The ovens rarely get a break here; everything is made from scratch daily. Pick up a B.L.T.A. (a BLT with avocado) for a picnic across the street at Crystal Cove State Park. Or stay—at a communal table inside or in the courtyard, which has an ocean view—for the likes of lemon soufflé pancakes or grilled salmon with citrus sauce. ✉*7962 E. Coast Hwy., Crystal Cove Promenade* ☎*949/715–2200* 🌐*www.pacificwhey.com* 💳*AE, MC, V.*

9

$$$$ ★ **The Resort at Pelican Hill.** This new ultra-glam resort, which opened in 2008, allows golfers to stay at Pelican Hill, one of the state's most renowned links with 36 championship holes designed by Tom Fazio. Adjacent to Crystal Cove State Park, the resort has 204 bungalow suites, each a minimum of 847 square feet with Italian limestone fireplaces and marble baths, built into terraced hillsides overlooking the Pacific; the resort's 128 villas are larger than most suburban homes and staffed with butlers 24/7. With its wraparound terraces, the Coliseum Pool (inspired by the Roman landmark), is a spectacular focal point. Soothe sore muscles at a 23,000-square foot spa after a day on the course before enjoying a sunset dinner from the Andrea Ristorante, one of the area's most opulent dining rooms. Kids are treated like VIPs too; Camp Pelican, a separate facility, has all sorts of games and activities for young 'uns, and there are surf lessons, kayaking trips, and nighttime events geared to teens as well. **Pros:** paradise for golfers; a gracious, attentive staff. **Cons:** sky-high prices, even for a swanky resort; common areas can feel cold. ✉*22701 Pelican Hill Rd. S., Newport Coast* ☎*949/467–6800* ⊕*www.pelicanhill.com* *204 bungalows and suites, 128 villas* *In-room: safe, kitchen (some), refrigerator (some), DVD, Wi-Fi. In-hotel: 4 restaurants, room service, bar, golf courses, pools, gym, spa, children's programs (ages 4–17), laundry service, Wi-Fi, parking (free), no-smoking rooms* *AE, D, DC, MC, V.*

$$$ NEW AMERICAN ★ **Sage on the Coast.** Between Newport and Laguna in the Crystal Cove Promenade, chef and owner Rich Mead offers contemporary American cuisine in an expansive stainless-steel and glass setting, set off by a warm fireplace and garden area. The ever-changing menu, which has equal European and Asian influences, may include tropically-inspired Dungeness crab cakes, swordfish with a pinot noir reduction and rib eye with green peppercorn sauce. The grilled beef fillet medallion with portobello mushrooms and gorgonzola is recommended. Mead uses only the finest ingredients, which he sources from local farmers and fishermen. ✉*7862 E. Coast Hwy.* ☎*949/715–7243* ⊕*www.sagerestaurant.com* *AE, DC, MC, V.*

LAGUNA BEACH

9 Fodor's Choice ★

10 mi south of Newport Beach on Hwy. 1; 60 mi south of Los Angeles, I–5 south to Hwy. 133, which turns into Laguna Canyon Rd.

Even the approach tells you that Laguna Beach is exceptional. Driving in along Laguna Canyon Road from the I–405 freeway gives you the chance to cruise through a gorgeous coastal canyon, large stretches of which remain undeveloped *(⇨see the Laguna Coast Wilderness Park in Sports and the Outdoors, below)*. You'll arrive at a glistening wedge of ocean, at the intersection with PCH.

Laguna's welcome mat is legendary. For decades in the mid-20th century a local booster, Eiler Larsen, greeted everyone downtown. (There's now a statue of him on the main drag.) On the corner of Forest and Park avenues you can see a 1930s gate proclaiming, THIS GATE HANGS WELL AND HINDERS NONE, REFRESH AND REST, THEN TRAVEL ON. A gay community has long been established here; until relatively recently, this was quite the exception in conservative Orange County. The Hare Krishnas have a temple where they host a Sunday vegetarian feast, environmentalists rally, artists continue to gravitate here—there seems to be room for everyone.

There's a definite creative slant to this tight-knit community. The California plein air art movement coalesced here in the early 1900s; by 1932 an annual arts festival was established. Art galleries now dot the village streets, and there's usually someone daubing up in Heisler Park, overlooking the beach. The town's main street, Pacific Coast Highway, is referred to as either South Coast or North Coast Highway, depending on the address. From this waterfront, the streets slope up steeply to the residential areas. All along the highway and side streets, you'll find dozens of fine art and crafts galleries, clothing boutiques, jewelry shops, and cafés.

LIFE IMITATING ART

An outdoor amphitheater near the mouth of the canyon hosts the annual **Pageant of the Masters** (☎ *949/494–1145 or 800/487–3378* 🌐 *www.foapom.com*), Laguna's most impressive event. Local participants arrange tableaux vivants, in which live models and carefully orchestrated backgrounds merge in striking mimicry of classical and contemporary paintings. The pageant is part of the **Festival of Arts,** held in July and August; tickets are much in demand, so plan ahead.

ESSENTIALS

Visitor and Tour Info Laguna Beach Visitors Bureau (✉ *252 Broadway, Laguna Beach* ☎ *949/497–9229 or 800/877–1115* 🌐 *www.lagunabeachinfo.org*).

EXPLORING

Laguna's central beach gives you a perfect slice of local life. A stocky 1920s lifeguard tower marks **Main Beach Park,** at the end of Broadway at South Coast Highway. A wooden boardwalk separates the sand from a strip of lawn. Walk along this, or hang out on one of its benches, to watch people bodysurfing, playing sand volleyball, or scrambling around one of two half-basketball courts. The beach also has children's play equipment, picnic areas, restrooms, and showers. Across the street is a historic Spanish Renaissance movie theater.

The **Laguna Art Museum** displays American art, with an emphasis on California artists from all periods. Special exhibits change quarterly. **■ TIP→ The museum, along with galleries throughout the city, stays open 'til 9 for Art Walk on the first Thursday of each month** (🌐 *www.firstthursdaysartwalk.com*). A free shuttle service runs from the museum to galleries and studios. ✉ *307 Cliff Dr., Laguna Beach* ☎ *949/494–8971* 🌐 *www.lagunaartmuseum.org* 🎫 *$10* ⏲ *Daily 11–5.*

WHERE TO EAT

$ VEGETARIAN ✕ **Café Zinc & Market.** Families flock to this small Laguna Beach institution for well-priced breakfast and lunch. Try the signature quiches or poached egg dishes in the morning, or swing by later in the day for healthy salads, quesadillas, lasagna, or one of their pizzettes. The café also has great artisanal cheese and gourmet goodies to go, and your four-legged friends are welcome in the outdoor patio area. ✉ *350*

9

Ocean Ave., Laguna Beach ☎*949/494–6302* 🌐*www.zinccafe.com* ▭*AE, MC, V* ⏲*No dinner.*

$$$ CHINESE ★ **Five Feet.** Others have attempted to mimic this restaurant's innovative blend of Chinese and French cooking styles, but Five Feet remains the leader of the pack. Begin with a smoked albacore salad with miso-Caesar dressing before moving on to beef short ribs with hoisin barbecue sauce, rack of lamb with curry sauce, or the house's signature whole fried catfish. Small plates, such as Montrachet goat cheese wontons with raspberry coulis, are available as well. The setting is pure Laguna: exposed ceiling, open kitchen, high noise level, and brick walls hung with works by local artists. ✉*328 Glenneyre St., Laguna Beach* ☎*949/497–4955* 🌐*www.fivefeetrestaurants.com* ▭*AE, D, DC, MC, V* ⏲*No lunch.*

$$$ FRENCH **French 75.** Locals love this bistro and champagne bar, inspired by Paris supper clubs of the 1940s, for its intimate, opulent feel. It's definitely a change from the usual bright, casual restaurant look; the space has low lighting, dark-wood paneling, and a mural of cherubs spritzing bubbly. The menu focuses on bistro classics like escargots, moules frites and coq au vin with the occasional curveball, like barramundi with salsa verde. One constant: the Callebaut chocolate soufflé. ✉*1464 S. Coast Hwy., Laguna Beach* ☎*949/494–8444* 🌐*www.culinaryadventures.com* ▭*AE, D, DC, MC, V* ⏲*No lunch.*

$$$ JAPANESE **Mosun & Club M.** This is the "it" spot for the young and fabulous sushi-loving crowd, who come to dance, to dine, or to canoodle with a date over cocktails. At this restaurant-cum-nightclub, if its Tuesday night, you're partying with $3 hand rolls; at Sushi Sessions on Thursday and Sunday nights, you can order $5 rolls and $5 sake bombs. The wide-ranging menu offers much more, however: panko-crusted halibut in an Asian-inspired beurre blanc, filet mignon, and soy-glazed salmon. No reservations are accepted on Monday, Wednesday or Friday, but the rest of the week it's wise to call ahead—this is one of Laguna Beach's hottest spots. ✉*680 S. Coast Hwy., Laguna Beach* ☎*949/497–5646* 🌐*www.mosunclubm.com* ✍*Reservations not accepted Mon., Wed., Fri.* ▭*MC, V* ⏲*No lunch.*

$$$ INTERNATIONAL **Sapphire Laguna.** This Laguna Beach establishment is part gourmet pantry (a must-stop for your every picnic need) and part global dining adventure. Iranian-born chef Azmin Ghahreman takes guests on a journey through Europe and Asia with dishes like Malaysian black pepper shrimp, crispy Tasmanian ocean trout with sweet corn risotto cake, and a version of Spanish paella. Nearly a dozen beers from around the world and an extensive, fittingly eclectic wine list rounds out the experience. The dining room is intimate and earthy but infused with local style. Brunch is fast becoming a favorite with locals, as well—enjoy it on the patio in good weather. ✉*The Old Pottery Place, 1200 S. Coast Hwy.* ☎*949/715–9888* 🌐*www.sapphirellc.com* ▭*AE, MC, V.*

¢–$ VEGETARIAN **The Stand.** If an eatery can be called typically Laguna, this is it. Only organic vegan ingredients are used to prepare the salads, burritos with brown rice and hummus, pita sandwiches, and smoothies. There are about 20 outdoor seats where you can eat, read the supplied tracts and newspapers, and maybe argue a point or two. ✉ *238 Thalia St., near PCH* ☎ *949/494–8101* ▭ *AE, D, MC, V* ⏲ *Open 7–7 daily.*

$$$$ AMERICAN ★ **Studio.** In a nod to Laguna's art history, Studio has food that entices the eye as well as the palate. You can't beat the location, on a 50-foot bluff overlooking the Pacific Ocean—every table has an ocean view. And because the restaurant occupies its own Craftsman-style bungalow, it doesn't feel like a hotel dining room. The menu changes daily to reflect the finest seafood and the freshest local ingredients on hand. You might begin with salmon tartare with caviar, avocado, and tarragon cream, or risotto with lobster and truffles before moving on to rack of lamb or pan-seared John Dory with a curry sauce. The wine list here is bursting, with nearly 2,000 labels. ✉ *Montage Hotel, 30801 S. Coast Hwy.* ☎ *949/715–6420* 🌐 *www.studiolagunabeach.com* *Reservations essential* ▭ *AE, D, DC, MC, V* ⏲ *Closed Mon. Labor Day–Memorial Day. No lunch.*

$ MEXICAN **Taco Loco.** This may look like a fast-food taco stand, and the hemp brownies on the menu may make you think the kitchen's *really* laid-back, but the quality of the food here equals that in many higher-price restaurants. Some Mexican standards get a Louisiana twist, like Cajun-spiced seafood tacos. Other favorites include blackened lobster tacos and the mushroom-and-tofu burgers. It stays open late on Friday and Saturday, until 2 AM. ✉ *640 S. Coast Hwy.* ☎ *949/497–1635* ▭ *AE, MC, V.*

$$–$$$ ITALIAN **Ti Amo Ristorante.** An intimate setting, creative Mediterranean cuisine and a celebrity clientele have earned this place favorable notoriety. The several charming dining areas here have tall candles and cozy booths and contribute to the restaurant's legendary sense of romance—there's also a grand fireplace in the main room. You can also request a table in the enclosed garden out back. Try the Linguine ai Frutti di Mare, linguine with shrimp, mussels, clams, calamari, fresh fish in a spicy tomato broth, or the veal Marsala. Service can be slow, but the views are spectacular and the food well worth it. ✉ *31727 S. Coast Hwy., Laguna Beach* ☎ *949/499–5350* 🌐 *www.tiamolagunabeach.com* ▭ *AE, D, DC, MC, V* ⏲ *No lunch.*

9

WHERE TO STAY

$$$ ★ **Hotel Casa del Camino.** This historic Spanish-style hotel was built in 1927 and was once a favorite of Hollywood stars. Its ace in the hole is the large rooftop terrace, with clear ocean views—an ideal spot at sunset. Rooms have warm color schemes; beds have feather duvets to ward off the seaside chill. Those on the highway side of the property are apt to be noisy. K'ya, the hotel's cozy restaurant, has a contemporary menu with French and Asian influences. **Pros**: breathtaking views from rooftop lounge; personable service; close to beach. **Cons**: decor a bit dated; frequent on-site events can make hotel busy and noisy. ✉ *1289 S. Coast Hwy., Laguna Beach* ☎ *949/497–2446 or 888/367–5232* 🌐 *www.casacamino.com* *42 rooms, 7 suites* *In-room: refrigerator (some), DVD (some), Wi-Fi. In-hotel: restaurant, bar, gym, parking (free), some pets allowed, no-smoking rooms* ▭ *AE, D, MC, V.*

$$ **Hotel Laguna.** The oldest hotel in Laguna (opened in 1888) has manicured gardens, beach views, and an ideal location downtown adjacent

to Main Beach. Accommodations take second stage to the outdoor ambience, so expect rooms to be small, short on amenities, and somewhat tired in terms of decor. Among the perks is access to the hotel's private beach, where guests are provided with lounges, umbrellas, and towels and can order lunch or cocktails from the Beach Club menu. **Pros:** fantastic location; lovely views from restaurant; clean rooms. **Cons:** in need of an upgrade; street noise. ✉*425 S. Coast Hwy., Laguna Beach* ☎*949/494–1151 or 800/524–2927* 🌐*www.hotellaguna.com* *63 rooms, 2 mini-suites* *In-room: no a/c, refrigerators (some), DVD, Wi-Fi. In-hotel: 2 restaurants, bar, beachfront, parking (paid), no-smoking rooms* *AE, DC, MC, V* *CP.*

> **WORD OF MOUTH**
>
> "Laguna Beach can be quite affordable as it is at heart an artist community. If you paint or take photos you will feel like a local."
>
> —Kailani

$$ **Inn at Laguna Beach.** On a bluff overlooking the ocean, this inn is steps from Main Beach and the surf. You can walk to the art museum, shops, galleries, and restaurants . . . even the Festival of Arts grounds. Rooms have a beachy feel, and most have full or partial ocean views and balconies. Those on the highway side are apt to be noisy. Proximity to the beach makes this a good hotel for children. Continental breakfast, delivered to the room, is included in the price and Las Brisas, a restaurant famous for its view, is located next door. **Pros:** large rooms, complimentary continental breakfast, oceanfront location. **Cons:** ocean-view rooms are pricey; foot traffic on nearby public walkway can be noisy. ✉*211 N. Coast Hwy., Laguna Beach* ☎*949/497–9722 or 800/544–4479* 🌐*www.innatlagunabeach.com* *70 rooms* *In-room: refrigerator, DVD (some), Wi-Fi. In-hotel: pool, beachfront, Wi-Fi, parking (paid), no-smoking rooms* *AE, D, DC, MC, V.*

$$$$ Fodor's Choice ★ **Montage Resort & Spa.** Laguna's connection to the Californian plein air artists is mined for inspiration at this head-turning, lavish hotel. The Montage uses the local Craftsman style as a touchstone. Shingled buildings ease down a bluff to a sandy cove; inside, works by contemporary and early-20th-century California artists snare your attention. Guest rooms balance ease and refinement; all have ocean views and amenities such as CD/DVD players and extra-deep tubs. Of the restaurants, Studio is the fanciest, with more sweeping Pacific views and a refined contemporary menu. At the 20,000-square foot oceanfront spa and fitness center, you can indulge in a sea-salt scrub, take a yoga class, or hit the lap pool. **Pros:** top-notch service; idyllic coastal location; special programs for all interests, from art to marine biology. **Cons:** pricey; food inconsistent given the prices. ✉*30801 S. Coast Hwy., Laguna Beach* ☎*949/715–6000 or 888/715–6700* 🌐*www.montagelagunabeach.com* *190 rooms, 60 suites* *In-room: safe, DVD, Wi-Fi. In-hotel: 3 restaurants, room service, bars, pools, gym, spa, beachfront, water sports, children's programs (ages 5–12), laundry service, parking (paid), no-smoking rooms* *AE, MC, V.*

$$$$ ★ **Surf & Sand Resort.** One mile south of downtown, this Laguna Beach property has been made over and is now even more fantastic than

longtime locals remember. On an exquisite stretch of beach with thundering waves and gorgeous rocks, this is a getaway for those who want a boutique hotel experience without all the formalities. Expect clean white decor in the rooms, private balconies, slumber-worthy beds within earshot of the ocean, and a small yet full service spa—all within walking distance of downtown Laguna. The seasonal California cuisine at Splashes is top notch. **Pros:** easy beach access; intimate property; new gym facilities. **Cons:** expensive valet parking; surf is quite loud. ✉*1555 S. Coast Hwy., Laguna Beach* ☎*949/497–4477 or 888/869–7569* 🌐*www.surfandsandresort.com* *155 rooms, 13 suites* *In-room: no a/c (some), safe, refrigerator (some), DVD, Internet. In-hotel: restaurant, room service, bar, pool, gym, spa, beachfront, children's programs (ages 5–12), laundry service, parking (paid), no-smoking rooms* 💳*AE, D, DC, MC, V.*

NIGHTLIFE AND THE ARTS

Bounce (✉*1460 S. Coast Hwy., Laguna Beach* ☎*949/494–0056* 🌐*clubbounce.net*) is a popular gay lounge with an upstairs dance floor. The **Laguna Playhouse** (✉*606 Laguna Canyon Rd., Laguna Beach* ☎*949/497–2787* 🌐*www.lagunaplayhouse.com*), dating to the 1920s, mounts a variety of productions, from classics to youth-oriented plays. The **Sandpiper Lounge** (✉*1183 S. Coast Hwy., Laguna Beach* ☎*949/494–4694*), a hole-in-the-wall dancing joint, attracts an eclectic crowd. The **Sawdust Arts Festival** (☎*949/494–3030* 🌐*www.sawdustartfestival.org*), held from late June to late August opposite the Festival of the Arts amphitheater, always hosts musicians and entertainers.

White House (✉*340 S. Coast Hwy., Laguna Beach* ☎*949/494–8088* 🌐*www.whitehouserestaurant.com*), a hip club on the main strip, has nightly entertainment and dancing.

SPORTS AND THE OUTDOORS

BEACHES There are a handful of lovely beaches around town besides the Main Beach. **Aliso Creek County Beach** (☎*949/923–2280* 🌐*www.ocparks.com/alisobeach*), in south Laguna, has a playground, fire pits, parking, food stands, and restrooms. **1,000 Steps Beach,** off South Coast Highway at 9th Street, is a hard-to-find locals' spot with great waves. There aren't really 1,000 steps down (but when you hike back up, it'll certainly feel like it). **Wood's Cove,** off South Coast Highway at Diamond Street, is especially quiet during the week. Big rock formations hide lurking crabs. Climbing the steps to leave, you can see a Tudor-style mansion that was once the home of Bette Davis.

BICYCLES Mountain bikes and helmets can be rented at **Rainbow Bicycle Co.** (✉*485 N. Coast Hwy., Laguna Beach* ☎*949/494–5806* 🌐*www.teamrain.com*).

GOLF **Aliso Creek Inn & Golf Course** (✉*31106 S. Coast Hwy., Laguna Beach* ☎*949/499–1919* 🌐*www.alisocreekinn.com*) offers a 9-hole facility whose stunning views and challenging par-fours elevate it well above most executive courses. Green fees are $26–$35 with discounts for twilight play (after 2 PM in winter or 4 PM during daylight savings time); pull carts cost $3, motorized ones are $14. Reservations are accepted up to 30 days in advance.

HIKING The **Laguna Coast Wilderness Park** (☎*949/923–2235* 🌐*www.lagunacanyon.org*) is spread over 19 acres of fragile coastal territory, including the canyon. The trails are great for hiking and mountain biking and are open daily, weather permitting. Docent-led hikes are given regularly; call for information.

TENNIS Six metered courts, four of which are lighted, can be found at **Laguna Beach High School.** Two lighted courts are available at the **Irvine Bowl Park.** Six unlighted courts are available at **Alta Laguna Park** on a first-come, first-served basis. For locations of all public tennis courts in the city and other information, call the **City of Laguna Beach Community Services Department** (☎*949/497–0716* 🌐*www.lagunabeachcity.net*).

WATER SPORTS Because its entire beach area is a marine preserve, Laguna Beach is ideal for snorkelers. Scuba divers should head to the Marine Life Refuge area, which runs from Seal Rock to Diver's Cove. Rent bodyboards at **Hobie Sports** (✉*294 Forest Ave., Laguna Beach* ☎*949/497–3304* 🌐*www.hobie.com*).

SHOPPING

Coast Highway, Forest and Ocean Avenues, and Glenneyre Street are full of art galleries, fine jewelry stores, and clothing boutiques.

A riot of color, **Art for the Soul** (✉*272 Forest Ave., Laguna Beach* ☎*949/497–8700* 🌐*www.art4thesoul.com*) has hand-painted furniture, crafts, and unusual gifts. **Artisance** (✉*278 Beach St.* ☎*949/494–0687* 🌐*www.artisancelaguna.com*) pulls together posh tableware and decorative odds and ends, from timeless furniture from Didier of Belgium to exquisite French candles by Maison Trudon. Get your sugar fix at the time-warped **Candy Baron** (✉*231 Forest Ave.* ☎*949/497–7508* 🌐*www.thecandybaron.com*), filled with old-fashioned goodies like gumdrops, bull's-eyes, and more than a dozen barrels of saltwater taffy. **La Rue du Chocolat** (✉*Peppertree La., 448 S. Coast Hwy., Suite B, Laguna Beach* ☎*949/494–2372*) dispenses hand-crafted chocolates in flavors like lemon-chile and lavender-peppercorn.

The **Crystal Image** (✉*225 Forest Ave., Laguna Beach* ☎*949/497–3399* 🌐*www.thecrystalimage.com*) has an almost overwhelming trove of rare minerals, meteorites, fossils, jewelry, and art. Perfume bottles and boxes made from minerals are particularly eye-catching. Hit **Fetneh Blake** (✉*427 N. Coast Hwy., Laguna Beach* ☎*949/494–3787*) for pricey, Euro-chic clothes. The emerging designers found here lure Angelenos to make the trek south. Be prepared to be dazzled at **Adam Neeley Fine Art Jewelry** (✉ *353 N. Coast Hwy., Laguna Beach* ☎*949/715–0953*) where young artisan proprietor Adam Neeley creates one-of-a-kind modern pieces. At **Trove** (✉*1233 N. Coast Hwy., Laguna Beach* ☎*949/376–4640* 🌐*www.trovelaguna.com*) you can rummage for estate jewelry, 18th- to 20th-century pieces, and odd, whimsical finds.

ART GALLERIES Most South Village art galleries line up along the South Coast Highway in the 900 to 2000 blocks. **DeRu's Fine Art** (✉*1590 S. Coast Hwy., Laguna Beach* ☎*949/376–3785* 🌐*www.derusfinearts.com*) specializes in California impressionist works by artists such as Edgar Payne, William Wendt, and others. The **Redfern Gallery** (✉*1540 S. Coast Hwy., Laguna Beach* ☎*949/497–3356* 🌐*www.redferngallery.com*) is another top source for California impressionists. You can see more of its collection at the Montage Resort. **Mandarin Fine Art Gallery** (✉ *1294 S. Coast Hwy., Suite C, Laguna Beach* ☎ *949/376–9608* 🌐 *www.mandarinfineart.com*) has stunning contemporary Chinese art.

DANA POINT

11 *10 mi south of Laguna Beach, via PCH.*

Dana Point's claim to fame is its small-boat marina tucked into a dramatic natural harbor and surrounded by high bluffs.

ESSENTIALS

Visitor and Tour Info **Dana Point Chamber of Commerce** (☎ *949/496–1555* 🌐 *danapoint-chamber.com*) offers a useful visitor's guide.

Dana Point Harbor (☎ *949/923–2255* 🌐 *www.danapointharbor.com*) was first described more than 100 years ago by its namesake, Richard Henry Dana, in his book *Two Years Before the Mast.* At the marina are docks for private boats and yachts, marine-oriented shops, restaurants, and boat and bike rentals. In early March the **Dana Point Festival of Whales** (☎ *949/472–7888 or 888/440–4309* 🌐 *www.festivalofwhales.org*) celebrates the passing gray whale migration with concerts, 40-foot-long balloon whales on parade, films, sports competitions, and a weekend street fair.

At the south end of Dana Point, **Doheny State Beach** (☎ *949/496–6172, 714/433–6400 water quality information* 🌐 *www.dohenystatebeach.org*) is one of Southern California's top surfing destinations, but there's a lot more to do within this 61-acre area. Divers and anglers hang out at the beach's western end, and during low tide, the tide pools beckon both young and old. You'll also find five indoor tanks and an interpretive center devoted to the wildlife of the Doheny Marine Refuge. There are food stands and shops, picnic facilities, volleyball courts, and a pier for fishing. The beachfront campground here is one of the most popular in the state with 120 no-hookup sites that rent for $30–$35 per night; essential reservations from Reserve America ☎ *800/444–7275.* **TIP→ Be aware that the waters here periodically do not meet health standards established by California (warning signs are posted if that's the case).**

Two indoor tanks at the **Ocean Institute** contain touchable sea creatures, an accessible man-made tidepool, as well as the complete skeleton of a gray whale. Anchored near the institute is *The Pilgrim,* a full-size replica of the square-rigged vessel on which Richard Henry Dana sailed. You can tour the boat Sunday 10–2:30. Weekend cruises are also available. In addition, marine-mammal exploration cruises are given January through March. ✉ *24200 Dana Point Harbor Dr., Dana Point* ☎ *949/496–2274* 🌐 *www.ocean-institute.org* *$6.50, $35 marine mammal cruises* ⏲ *Weekends 10–3.*

WHERE TO EAT

$$$ FRENCH **Gemmell's.** Accomplished chef Byron Gemmell's moderately priced bistro is a welcome change from the fish houses that dominate this town, particularly around the harbor. In a laid-back but romantic setting, you can begin with escargots or French onion soup before moving

CAMPING AT DOHENY STATE BEACH

Due to its stunning beachfront location, Doheny State Beach is one of the most popular camping sites in the California State Park system. Set on a south-facing beach, where the wave action is ideal for surfing, fishing, and swimming, the park is in two sections, bisected by San Juan Creek. The northern section is reserved for day-use, while campers and their activities fill a long narrow strip of sand beneath the bluffs on the southern section. The campground with 165 sites accommodates tent campers as well as motorhomes and trailers. Some sites are just steps from the beach, while others are big enough for 35-foot-long vehicles. Among these are accessible sites, and hike/bike sites.

Facilities include restrooms, showers, dump station, picnic tables, water, and Wi-Fi. There are no hookups. The park offers a number of activities popular with campers: campfire programs, junior ranger programs, and special events such as summer grunion hunts (schools of grunion swarm on the beach in the moonlight). Reservations are absolutely essential at this park and they should be made the first day they're available, six months in advance from Reserve America (☎ *800/444–7275* 🌐 *www.dohenystatebeach.org*). Even if you have a reservation, it's a good idea to call the park directly at ☎ *714/496–6172* a day or two before you expect to arrive.

on to rack of lamb with thyme demi-glace or roasted duck in a seductive rum-banana liqueur reduction. Finish with a soufflé—either classic chocolate or Grand Marnier. The wine list includes some reasonably priced Bordeaux. The food is rich, but a meal here won't break the bank. ✉ *34471 Golden Lantern St., Dana Point* ☎ *949/234–0063* 🌐 *www.gemmellsrestaurant.com* ✍ *Reservations essential* 💳 *AE, D, DC, MC, V* ⏲ *No dinner Sun.*

$$ ITALIAN ✕ **Luciana's Ristorante.** This intimate family-owned eatery serves simply prepared, tasty Italian food. Try one of the homemade soups or gnocchi classico—Grandma's homemade potato dumplings with marinara sauce. If you don't have a reservation, be prepared to wait at the bar with a glass of one of the many reasonably priced Italian wines, chatting with the predominantly local clientele. ✉ *24312 Del Prado Ave., Dana Point* ☎ *949/661–6500* 🌐 *www.lucianas.com* 💳 *AE, MC, V* ⏲ *No lunch.*

$–$$ AMERICAN ✕ **Turk's.** This neighborhood joint—its detractors might call it a dive—is a remnant of the days when Dana Point was a crusty fishing village, not a posh resort town. You'll find steaks, chicken, fish-and-chips, and seafood at this old school bar and grill, and at great prices. Once owned by Hollywood bit player and strongman Turk Varteresian, Turk's is now run by his daughter Candy. Overhead, clear-bottom aquariums create a nautical feel; the walls are adorned with old pictures of Turk's movie days and various celebrities. It stays open until 2 AM, and has an old-fashioned jukebox. ✉ *34683 Golden Lantern St., Dana Point* ☎ *949/496–9028* 💳 *AE, DC, MC, V.*

$$ AMERICAN ✕ **Wind & Sea.** An unblocked marina view makes this a particularly great place for lunch or a sunset dinner. Among the entrées, the macadamia-

crusted mahimahi and the shrimp-stuffed halibut with lobster sauce stand out. On warm days, patio tables beckon you outside, and looking out on the Pacific might put you in the mood for a retro cocktail like a mai tai. ✉*34699 Golden Lantern St., Dana Point* ☎*949/496–6500* 🌐*www.windandsearestaurants.com* 💳*AE, MC, V.*

WHERE TO STAY

$$$ ★ **Blue Lantern Inn.** Combining New England–style architecture with a Southern California setting, this white-clapboard B&B rests on a bluff overlooking the harbor and ocean. A fire warms the intimate, inviting living area and cozy library, where you can enjoy complimentary hors d'oeuvres and wine or play backgammon every afternoon. Don't miss the sweeping harbor and ocean view from the inn's patio dining area. The spacious Nantucket-style guest rooms also have fireplaces and updated bathrooms with whirlpool tubs. The top-floor Tower Suite has a 180-degree ocean view. Forgot your toothbrush? Don't worry, the staff will take care of you. **Pros:** gas fireplaces; amazing harbor views from room #304; afternoon wine and cheese; breakfast buffet. **Cons:** nearby restaurant can be noisy; understaffed compared to larger resorts. ✉*34343 St. of the Blue Lantern, Dana Point* ☎*949/661–1304 or 800/950–1236* 🌐*www.bluelanterninn.com* *29 rooms* *In-room: refrigerator, Internet. In-hotel: gym, bicycles, Wi-Fi, parking (free), no-smoking rooms* 💳*AE, D, MC, V* *BP.*

$$$$ Fodor's Choice ★ **Ritz-Carlton, Laguna Niguel.** Take Ritz-Carlton's top-tier level of service coupled with an unparalleled view of the Pacific and you're in the lap of complete luxury at this opulent resort. Rooms are well-appointed and spacious; tricked out with oversize plasma TVs, private balconies, and posh marble bathrooms. Splurge for the Club Level where the list of included extra amenities is exhaustingly long. Service is impeccable for all guests, as every need is anticipated. Enjoy the panoramic views at Restaurant 162', where the focus is on California cuisine, or bone up on your wine knowledge at ENO, the property's wine, cheese, and chocolate tasting room. Guests can leisurely stroll through opulent gardens, and down perfectly manicured trails to the pristine white-sand beach. **Pros:** beautiful grounds and views; luxurious bedding; seamless service. **Cons:** some rooms are small for the price; culinary program has room to grow. ✉*1 Ritz-Carlton Dr., Dana Point* ☎*949/240–2000 or 800/240–2000* 🌐*www.ritzcarlton.com* *363 rooms, 30 suites* *In-room: safe, refrigerator (some), DVD, Internet. In-hotel: 3 restaurants, room service, bar, tennis courts, pools, gym, spa, beachfront, children's programs (ages 5–12), laundry service, Wi-Fi, parking (paid), no-smoking rooms* 💳*AE, D, DC, MC, V.*

9

$$$$ **St. Regis Monarch Beach Resort and Spa.** Exclusivity and indulgence carry the day here; you can even have someone unpack for you. The 172-acre grounds include a private beach club, an 18-hole Robert Trent Jones Jr.–designed golf course, and tennis courts across the street. Rooms have views of either the coast or the lush landscaping; such amenities as CD and DVD players and libraries are among the pluses. The premier restaurant is Stonehill Tavern, which serves celebrated San Francisco chef Michael Mina's modern American fare. You can order a tasting trio (three small plates showcasing a key ingredient like duck or bigeye

tuna), or concentrate on entrées such as prime beef with truffle jus or Tasmanian ocean trout with cauliflower puree. Reflecting the legendary services standards of the St. Regis, even pets are offered deluxe packages involving toys and special treats in silver bowls. **Pros:** immaculate rooms; big bathrooms with deep tubs; beautiful I. **Cons:** service can be standoffish; portions can be small at Stonehill Tavern. ✉ *1 Monarch Beach Resort, off Niguel Rd., Dana Point* ☎ *949/234–3200 or 800/722–1543* 🌐 *www.stregismb.com* *325 rooms, 75 suites* *In-room: safe, Internet, Wi-Fi. In-hotel: 6 restaurants, bar, golf course, pools, gym, spa, beachfront, laundry facilities, laundry service, children's programs (ages 5–16), some pets allowed, no-smoking rooms* 💳 *AE, D, DC, MC, V.*

SPORTS AND THE OUTDOORS

Inside Dana Point Harbor, **Swim Beach** has a fishing pier, barbecues, food stands, parking, restrooms, and showers. Rental stands for surfboards, windsurfers, small powerboats, and sailboats can be found near most of the piers.

Dana Wharf Sportfishing & Whale Watching (✉ *34675 Golden Lantern St., Dana Point* ☎ *949/496–5794* 🌐 *www.danawharfsportfishing.com*) runs charters and whale-watching excursions from early December to late April. Tickets cost $29; reservations are required. **Hobie Sports** (✉ *24825 Del Prado, Dana Point* ☎ *949/496–2366* 🌐 *www.hobie.com*) rents surfboards and boogie boards.

On **Capt. Dave's Dolphin & Whale Safari** (✉ *24440 Dana Point Harbor Dr., Dana Point* ☎ *949/488–2828* 🌐 *www.dolphinsafari.com*), you have a good chance of getting a water's-eye view of resident dolphins and migrating whales if you take one of these tours on a 35-foot catamaran. Dave, a marine naturalist–filmmaker, and his wife run the safaris year-round. The endangered blue whale is sometimes seen in summer. Reservations are required for the safaris, which last 2½ hours and cost $55.

SAN JUAN CAPISTRANO

❿ *5 mi north of Dana Point, Hwy. 74, 60 mi north of San Diego, I–5.*

San Juan Capistrano is best known for its historic mission, where the swallows traditionally return each year, migrating from their winter haven in Argentina, but these days they are more likely to choose other local sites for nesting. St. Joseph's Day, March 19, launches a week of fowl festivities. After summering in the arches of the old stone church, the swallows head south on St. John's Day, October 23. Charming antique stores, which range from pricey to cheap, line Camino Capistrano.

If you arrive by train, which is far more romantic and restful than battling freeway traffic you'll be dropped off across from the mission at the San Juan Capistrano depot. With its appealing brick café and preserved Santa Fe cars, the depot retains much of the magic of early American railroads. If driving, park near Ortega and Camino Capistrano, the city's main streets.

ESSENTIALS

Visitor and Tour Info San Juan Capistrano Chamber of Commerce and Visitors Center (*31421 La Matanza St., San Juan Capistrano 949/493–4700 www.sanjuanchamber.com*).

EXPLORING

Fodor's Choice ★ **Mission San Juan Capistrano,** founded in 1776 by Father Junípero Serra, was one of two Roman Catholic outposts between Los Angeles and San Diego. The Great Stone Church, begun in 1797, is the largest structure created by the Spanish in California. Many of the mission's adobe buildings have been preserved to illustrate mission life, with exhibits of an olive millstone, tallow ovens, tanning vats, metalworking furnaces, and the padres' living quarters. The gardens, with their fountains, are a lovely spot in which to wander. The bougainvillea-covered Serra Chapel is believed to be the oldest church still standing in California and is the only building remaining in which Fr. Serra actually led Mass. Mass takes place daily at 7 AM in the chapel. *Camino Capistrano and Ortega Hwy., San Juan Capistrano 949/234–1300 www.missionsjc.com $9 Daily 8:30–5.*

Near Mission San Juan Capistrano is the **San Juan Capistrano Library,** a postmodern structure built in 1983. Architect Michael Graves combined classical and Mission styles to striking effect. Its courtyard has secluded places for reading. *31495 El Camino Real, San Juan Capistrano 949/493–1752 www.sanjuancapistrano.org Mon.–Wed. 10–8, Thurs. 10–6, Sat. 10–5, Sun. noon–5. Closed Fri.*

WHERE TO EAT

$$ AMERICAN **Cedar Creek Inn.** Just across the street from the Mission, this restaurant's location is ideal for visiting families, with a patio perfect for a late lunch or a romantic dinner. The menu is fairly straightforward, dishes are tasty, and portions are substantial—try the chicken salad in papaya shell or a burger at lunch, or splurge on the rack of lamb for dinner. The patio, which has a waterfall and a view of the mission, is irresistible in warm weather. Don't miss the Toll House pie for dessert. *26860 Ortega Hwy., San Juan Capistrano 949/240–2229 www.cedarcreekinn.com AE, MC, V.*

$$$ FRENCH **L'Hirondelle.** Locals have romanced at cozy tables for more than 25 years at this delightful restaurant. Classic Belgian dishes such as escalope of veal with Béarnaise sauce and rabbit with white wine and prune sauce are the hallmark of this French and Belgian restaurant, whose name means "the little swallow" in French. The extensive wine list is matched by an impressive selection of Belgian beers. You can dine in the cozy dining room or on the lovely patio, which is perfect for the superb Sunday brunch. *31631 Camino Capistrano, San Juan Capistrano 949/661–0425 www.lhirondellesjc.com AE, DC, MC, V Closed Mon.*

$–$$ AMERICAN **The Ramos House Cafe.** It may be worth hopping the Amtrak for San Juan Capistrano just for the chance to have breakfast or lunch at one of Orange County's most beloved restaurants. Here's your chance to visit one of Los Rios Historic District's simple, board and batten homes dating back to 1881. This café sits practically on the railroad tracks across

9

from the depot—nab a table on the patio and dig into a hearty breakfast, such as the mountainous wild-mushroom scramble. For lunch, consider the memorable mac-and-cheese or Southern fried chicken. Every item on the menu illustrates chef-owner John Q. Humphreys's creative hand. ✉*31752 Los Rios St., San Juan Capistrano* ☎*949/443–1342* 🌐*www.ramoshouse.com* 💳*AE, D, DC, MC, V* ⏲*Closed Mon. No dinner.*

NIGHTLIFE

Coach House (✉*33157 Camino Capistrano, San Juan Capistrano* ☎*949/496–8930* 🌐*www.thecoachhouse.com*), a roomy, casual club with long tables and a dark-wood bar, draws crowds of varying ages for dinner and entertainment ranging from hip new bands to Dick Dale, the take-no-prisoners king of the surf guitar.

Prayer and misbehavior lie cheek by jowl; across the way from the mission you'll find a line of Harleys in front of the **Swallows Inn** (✉*31786 Camino Capistrano, San Juan Capistrano* ☎*949/493–3188* 🌐*www.swallowsinn.com*). Despite a somewhat tough look, it attracts all kinds—bikers, surfers, Marines from nearby Camp Pendleton, grandparents—for a drink, a casual bite, and some rowdy live music. There's no cover charge.

OFF THE BEATEN PATH

San Clemente. Travelers who shun the throngs in favor of a low-key beach experience—the part of the OC coast that Hollywood doesn't base TV series on—should drive 10 mi south of Dana Point on Pacific Coast Highway to San Clemente. There, 20 square mi of prime bicycling terrain await. Camp Pendleton, the country's largest Marine Corps base, welcomes cyclists to use some of its roads—just don't be surprised to see a troop helicopter taking off right beside you. Surfers favor **San Clemente State Beach** (☎*949/492–3156* 🌐*www.parks.ca.gov.com*), which has camping facilities, RV hookups, and fire rings. San Onofre State Beach, just south of San Clemente, is another surfing destination. Below the bluffs are 3½ mi of sandy beach, where you can swim, fish, and watch wildlife.

INLAND ORANGE COUNTY

If you can tear yourself away from Orange County's lush coast, you'll be rewarded with a variety of cultural attractions inland, from Bowers Museum of Cultural Arts to the wonders of Little Saigon to the concerts and musicals held at the Orange County Performing Arts Center.

SANTA ANA/COSTA MESA

39 mi south of downtown Los Angeles via I–5, I–605, and I–405 to South Coast Plaza.

Ethnically diverse Santa Ana is the region's largest city and the governmental hub of Orange County (the county's administrative offices and courts are here). It adjoins Costa Mesa, the OC's cultural epicenter and home to one of Southern California's toniest and most expensive shopping centers, South Coast Plaza. This designer-dominated mall is connected by sky bridge to the Orange County Performing Arts Center, which has evolved into one of America's premier cultural entertainment complexes. City lines blur here, making it hard to tell exactly where you are, but the bottom line is, this is where you'll catch a glimpse of Orange County's cosmopolitan face.

ESSENTIALS

Visitor and Tour Info Costa Mesa Conference and Visitors Bureau (*Box 5071, Costa Mesa, 92628 714/435–8530 or 866/918–4749 www.travelcostamesa.com*).

EXPLORING

1 Santa Ana's premier cultural asset is the **Bowers Museum of Cultural Art,** which exhibits collections from both the British Museum and Beijing's Palace Museum. Permanent exhibits include Pacific Northwest wood carvings; beadwork of the Plains cultures; clothing, cooking utensils, and silver-adorned saddles used on early California ranches; and California impressionist paintings. Special exhibits such as a show of Egyptian mummies rotate through on a regular basis. A recent $15 million addition accommodates an Asian art gallery and 300-seat auditorium. Enjoy a salad, pasta dish or French-inspired lamb shank beneath abundant skylights at Tangata, the museum's outstanding café. The neighboring **Bowers Kidseum** (*1802 N. Main St.*) has interactive exhibits geared toward kids ages 6–12, in addition to classes, storytelling, and arts-and-crafts workshops. Admission is included in the general museum ticket. *2002 N. Main St., off I–5, Santa Ana 714/567–3600 www.bowers.org $12; permanent exhibits, additional charges for special exhibits, free 1st Sun. every month Tues.–Sun. 10–4.*

With a 108-foot tilting architectural cube beckoning from the I–5 freeway, the **Discovery Science Center** is easy to spot. The hands-on exhibits are for kids from preschool through teens (they especially like the Virtual Volleyball). Children with an interest in dinosaurs will hit the jackpot: there are life-size dinosaur models, a giant walk-through Argentinosaurus, a fossil dig, and online game of Dinosaur Quest. Other fun activities include lying on a bed of nails, climbing a rock wall, and making tidal waves. *2500 N. Main St., Santa Ana 714/542–2823 www.discoverycube.org $12.95 Daily 10–5; closed Thanksgiving and Christmas.*

OFF THE BEATEN PATH

Little Saigon. Little Saigon encompasses much of the city of Westminster, but the heart of the action is around Magnolia and Bolsa streets, where the colorful Asian Garden Mall tempts shoppers with jewelry and gift shops (bargaining on the prices is expected), Asian herbalists, and informal family restaurants. For a snack, try the *pho* (Vietnam's signature beef and noodle soup) at Pho 79. Note that the mall gets extremely crowded on weekends and is total madness around the Chinese New Year. *Bolsa St. between Bushard and Magnolia Sts., Westminster.*

2 ★ If you look at the where-to-buy listings at the bottom of couture ads in glossy magazines, you'll often see, sandwiched between listings of shops in Paris and Beverly Hills, the name of Costa Mesa's most famous landmark, **South Coast Plaza.** This immense complex gets ritzier by the year as international designer boutiques jostle for platinum-card space. The original section has the densest concentration of shops: Gucci,

Armani, Burberry, La Perla, Hermès, Versace, Chloé, and Prada. You'll also find all the familiar mall stores like Victoria's Secret and Banana Republic. Major department stores, including Saks and Bloomingdale's, flank the exterior, and restaurants range from fast-food to haute cuisine (among the most prominent are Charlie Palmer at Bloomingdale's and the acclaimed contemporary bistro Marché Moderne). A pedestrian bridge crosses Bear Street to the second wing, a smaller offshoot with a huge Crate & Barrel. ✉ *3333 S. Bristol St., off I–405, Costa Mesa* ☎ *714/435–2000 or 800/782–8888* 🌐 *www.southcoastplaza.com* ⏲ *Weekdays 10–9, Sat. 10–8, Sun. 11–6:30.*

WHERE TO EAT

$$–$$$ MEDITERRANEAN

✕ **Onotria.** In a soaring space that has the feel of an Italian village piazza, chef and owner Massimo Navarretta celebrates the wine country cuisine of his native Campania and adopted California. You can see Navarretta's own vegetable garden and miniature vineyard through the windows. Begin with velvety *burrata,* a fresh cheese made with mozzarella and cream, paired with blood orange and drizzled with passion fruit syrup, or grilled cuttlefish with caper berries. For hearty entrées, consider a contemporary curry-scented cassoulet with beef and lamb meatballs or pumpkin gnocchi with venison-lingonberry ragoût. The wine list offers innumerable choices for seasoned oenophiles and enthusiastic novices alike. ✉ *2831 Bristol St., Costa Mesa* ☎ *714/641–5952* 🌐 *www.onotria.com* ✍ *Reservations essential* 💳 *AE, D, DC, MC, V* ⏲ *Closed Sun. No lunch Sat.*

$$ AMERICAN

✕ **Plum's Café.** Salmon hash and Plum's famous Dutch baby, a deep-dish skillet-baked pancake, keep the locals coming back to start their days at Oregon transplant Kim Jorgenson's Pacific Northwest-inspired eatery. Coconut French toast and dark chocolate chip pancakes are also popular breakfast picks, especially with kids; lunch and dinner specialties include the Limburgerwith feta and couscous and the filet mignon in a Washington cabernet reduction. Dine at the bar, in the casual dining room, or on the patio. ✉ *369 E. 17th St., Costa Mesa* ☎ *949/722–7586* 🌐 *www.plumscafe.com* 💳 *AE, MC, V.*

¢–$ MEXICAN ★

✕ **Taco Mesa.** If fresh, fast Mexican fare is what you want, this frill-free, small chain of always-packed taquerias serves up huge burritos (try it "wet," bathed in enchilada sauce) and *carnitas pibil* (a specialty from the Yucatan) and makes its salsa fresh daily. Personable service, festive ambience, and healthy menu options have given this joint a state-wide reputation (there are now several branches in the O.C. but this is the original). Try the fresh squeezed juices. ✉ *647 W. 19th St., Costa Mesa* ☎ *949/642–0629* 🌐 *www.tacomesa.net* 💳 *MC, V.*

$$$ MEDITERRANEAN ★

✕ **Zov's Bistro.** There's a well-worn path to both sides of Zov's. The restaurant out front prepares bistro favorites with a deft Middle Eastern spin, such as rack of lamb with pomegranate sauce or a Moroccan-inspired seafood *tagine* (mussels, clams, prawns, and grape leaf-wrapped halibut with couscous). Locals flock to the separate, more modestly priced café and bakery (open for breakfast and lunch) for fresh pastries, *meze* (small plates), or burgers. Both the bistro and the café have patio tables. ✉ *Enderle Center, 17440 E. 17th St., Tustin* ☎ *714/838–8855* 🌐 *www.zovs.com* 💳 *AE, D, DC, MC, V* ⏲ *Closed Sun. No lunch Sat.*

WHERE TO STAY

$$$ **Westin South Coast Plaza.** Ideal for business travelers, this high-rise hotel adjoins the South Coast Plaza complex—within just a few steps, your every retail therapy need can be met. Modern, spacious rooms are outfitted with flat-screen TVs, deliciously comfortable beds with feather duvets, and spalike showers. Tennis aficionados will appreciate the convenience of nearby courts. The hotel is steps from the Orange County Performing Arts Center. **Pros:** contemporary decor; business-friendly; close to shopping, dining, and the arts. **Cons:** spotty concierge service; Internet costs extra. *686 Anton Blvd., Costa Mesa 714/540–2500 or 866/716–8132 www.westin.com 391 rooms, 5 suites In-room: safe, Internet, Wi-Fi. In-hotel: restaurant, room service, pool, tennis courts, Internet terminal, Wi-Fi, laundry, children's programs (ages 3–12), gym, some pets allowed, no-smoking rooms AE, D, DC, MC, V.*

NIGHTLIFE AND THE ARTS

The 500-seat **OC Pavilion** theater opened in 2005; its performance slate ranges from comedians to Kenny G to Kool & The Gang. State-of-the-art acoustics and comfortable, wide seats are pluses at this venue, whose modern facade hides a Renaissance-inspired interior. There are also a jazz lounge and a posh contemporary restaurant. *801 N. Main St., Santa Ana 714/550–0880 www.ocpavilion.com.*

Costa Mesa's role in consumer consumption is matched by its arts venues. The **Orange County Performing Arts Center** (*600 Town Center Dr., east of Bristol St. 714/556–2787 www.ocpac.org*) holds three music venues plus the highly regarded South Coast Repertory Theater. The original 3,000-seat Henry Segerstrom Concert hall offers fine acoustics for opera, ballet, symphony, and musicals. The intimate 250-seat Founders Hall is the place to hear chamber music and occasional jazz concerts. A third venue, the Henry and Renée Segerstrom Concert Hall, is home to the Pacific Symphony and Philharmonic Society of Orange County. This acclaimed César Pelli-designed structure, which was unveiled in 2006, has state-of-the-art sound equipment, a 30-ton organ with 4,322 pipes, and a modern, upscale dining room called Leatherby's Café Rouge. Richard Lippold's enormous *Firebird,* an angular metal sculpture, extends outward from the glass-enclosed lobby of the original Seagerstrom concert hall.

OFF THE BEATEN PATH

Yorba Linda's main claim to fame is the **Richard Nixon Presidential Library and Birthplace,** final resting place of the 37th president and his wife, Pat. Exhibits illustrate the checkered career of Nixon, from heralded leader of the free world to beleaguered resignee. You can listen to the so-called smoking-gun tape from the Watergate days, among other recorded material. Life-size sculptures of foreign world leaders, gifts Nixon received from international heads of state, and a large graffiti-covered section of the Berlin Wall are on display. You can also visit Pat Nixon's tranquil rose garden and the small farmhouse where Richard Nixon was born in 1913. Don't miss the bookstore, selling everything from birdhouses to photos of Nixon with Elvis. *18001 Yorba Linda Blvd., at Imperial Hwy., Yorba Linda 714/993–5075 www.nixonlibraryfoundation.org $9.95 Mon.–Sat. 10–5, Sun. 11–5.*

CATALINA ISLAND

Just 22 mi out from the L.A. coastline, across from Newport Beach and Long Beach, Catalina has virtually unspoiled mountains, canyons, coves, and beaches; best of all, it gives you a glimpse of what undeveloped Southern California once looked like.

Summer, weekends, and holidays, Catalina crawls with thousands of L.A.–area boaters, who tie their vessels at protected moorings in Avalon and other coves. Although Catalina is not known for its beaches, sunbathing and water sports are big draws; divers and snorkelers come for the exceptionally clear water surrounding the island. The main town, Avalon, is a charming, old-fashioned beach community, where yachts bob in the crescent-shaped bay. Wander beyond the main drag and you'll find brightly painted little bungalows fronting the sidewalks, with the occasional golf cart purring down the street.

A large wildfire swept over the hills and through the island's canyons in May 2007, approaching Avalon. Fortunately, it stopped at the edge of town, leaving virtually all visitor venues and services untouched. If you venture into the island's interior, you may still see some evidence of blackened hillsides and charred chaparral, but these scars are fading as rain generates new growth.

Cruise ships sail into Avalon twice a week and smaller boats shuttle between Avalon and Two Harbors, a small isthmus cove on the island's western end. You can also take bus excursions beyond Avalon. Roads are limited and nonresident vehicles prohibited, so hiking (by permit only) and cycling are the only other means of exploring.

Perhaps it's no surprise that Catalina has long been a destination for filmmakers and movie stars. In its earlier past, however, the island also sheltered Russian fur trappers (seeking sea-otter skins), pirates, gold miners, and bootleggers (carrier pigeons were used to communicate with the mainland). In 1919 William Wrigley Jr., the chewing-gum magnate, purchased a controlling interest in the company developing Catalina Island, whose most famous landmark, the Casino, was built in 1929 under his orders. Because he owned the Chicago Cubs baseball team, Wrigley made Catalina the team's spring training site, an arrangement that lasted until 1951.

In 1975 the Santa Catalina Island Conservancy, a nonprofit foundation, acquired about 86% of the island to help preserve the area's natural flora and fauna, including the bald eagle and the Catalina Island fox. These days the conservancy is restoring the rugged interior country with plantings of native grasses and trees. Along the coast you might spot oddities like electric perch, saltwater goldfish, and flying fish.

GETTING HERE AND AROUND

HELICOPTER TRAVEL Island Express helicopters depart hourly from San Pedro and Long Beach (8 AM–dusk). The trip takes about 15 minutes and costs $86 one-way, $164 round-trip (plus tax). Reservations a week in advance are recommended.

FERRY TRAVEL Two companies offer ferry service to Catalina Island. The boats have both indoor and outdoor seating and snack bars. Excessive baggage is

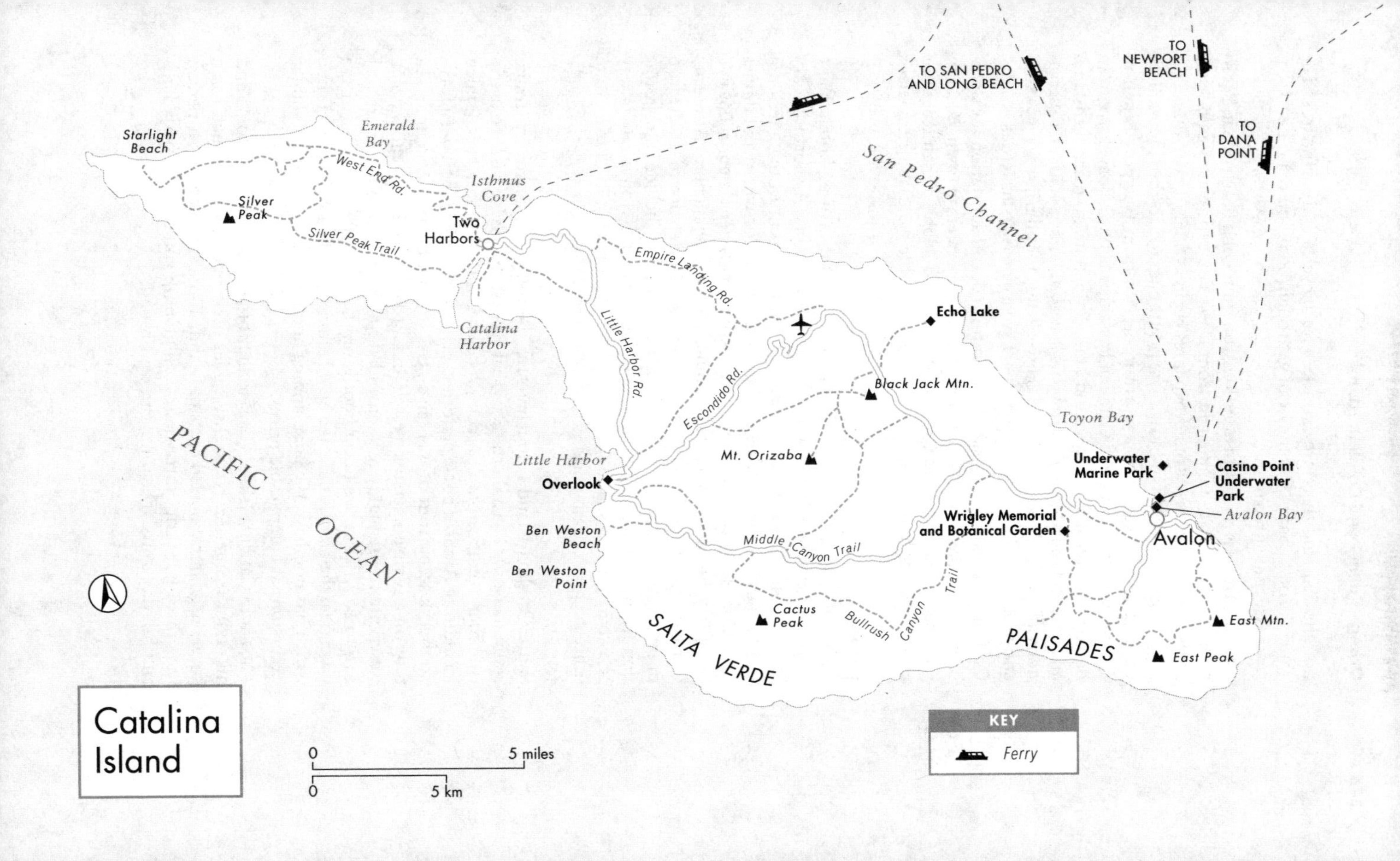
Catalina
Island
TO NEWPORT BEACH
TO SAN PEDRO AND LONG BEACH
TO DANA POINT
San Pedro Channel
Starlight Beach
Emerald Bay
West End Rd.
Isthmus Cove
Silver Peak
Silver Peak Trail
Two Harbors
Empire Landing Rd.
Catalina Harbor
Little Harbor Rd.
Echo Lake
Escondido Rd.
Black Jack Mtn.
Toyon Bay
Mt. Orizaba
Little Harbor
Overlook
Underwater Marine Park
Casino Point Underwater Park
Avalon Bay
Avalon
Wrigley Memorial and Botanical Garden
Ben Weston Beach
Ben Weston Point
Middle Canyon Trail
Cactus Peak
Bullrush Canyon Trail
East Mtn.
East Peak
PALISADES
SALTA VERDE
PACIFIC OCEAN
0
5 miles
0
5 km
KEY
Ferry

not allowed, and there are extra fees for bicycles and surfboards. The waters around Santa Catalina can get rough, so if you're prone to seasickness, come prepared.

Catalina Express makes an hour-long run from Long Beach or San Pedro to Avalon and a 90-minute run from Dana Point to Avalon with some stops at Two Harbors. Round-trip fares begin at $66.50, with discounts for seniors and kids. On busy days, a $10 upgrade to the Commodore Lounge, when available, is worth it. Service from Newport Beach to Avalon is available through Catalina Passenger Service. Boats leave from Balboa Pavilion at 9 AM (in season), take 75 minutes to reach the island, and cost $68 round-trip. Return boats leave Catalina at 4:30 PM. Reservations are advised in summer and on weekends for all trips. ■ TIP→ **Keep an eye out for dolphins, which sometimes swim alongside the ferries.**

GOLF CARTS Golf carts constitute the island's main form of transportation for sightseeing in the area, but they can't be used on the streets in town. You can rent them along Avalon's Crescent Avenue and Pebbly Beach Road for about $40 per hour with a $30 deposit, payable via cash or traveler's checks only.

TIMING

Although Catalina can be seen in a day, several inviting hotels make it worth extending your stay for one or more nights. A short itinerary might include breakfast along the boardwalk, a tour of the interior, a snorkeling excursion at Casino Point, and a romantic waterfront dinner in Avalon. ■ TIP→ **If you plan to stay overnight between Memorial Day and Labor Day, be sure to make reservations before heading here.** After late October, rooms are much easier to find on shorter notice, rates drop dramatically, and many hotels offer packages that include transportation from the mainland and/or sightseeing tours. If you'd rather stay at a charming freestanding cottage or home, contact a local real estate office such as Catalina Island Vacation Rentals.

TOURS

Santa Catalina Island Company runs the following Discovery Tours: a summer-only coastal cruise to Seal Rocks; the *Flying Fish* boat trip (summer evenings only); a comprehensive inland motor tour (which includes an Arabian horse performance); a tour of Skyline Drive; a Casino tour; a scenic tour of Avalon; a glass-bottom-boat tour, an undersea tour on a semisubmersible vessel; and a tour of the Botanical Garden. Reservations are highly recommended for the inland tours. Tours cost $16 to $99. There are ticket booths on the Green Pleasure Pier, at the Casino, in the plaza, and at the boat landing. Catalina Adventure Tours, which has booths at the boat landing and on the pier, arranges similar excursions at comparable prices.

The Santa Catalina Island Conservancy organizes custom ecotours and hikes of the interior. Naturalist guides drive open Jeeps through some gorgeously untrammeled parts of island. Tours start at $98 per person for a three-hour trip (three-person minimum); you can also book half- and full-day tours. The tours run year-round.

ESSENTIALS

Helicopter Contacts **Island Express** (*☎800/228–2566 🌐www.islandexpress.com*).

Ferry Contacts **Catalina Express** (*☎800/481–3470 🌐www.catalinaexpress.com*). **Catalina Passenger Service** (*☎949/673–5245 or 800/830–7744 📠949/673–8340 🌐www.catalinainfo.com*).

Golf Cart Rentals **Island Rentals** (*✉125 Pebbly Beach Rd., Avalon ☎310/510–1456*).

Vacation Rentals **Catalina Island Vacation Rentals, Inc.** (*119 Sumner Ave., Ste. B, Avalon ☎310/510–2276 🌐www.catalinavacations.com*).

Visitor and Tour Info **Catalina Adventure Tours** (*Box 92766, Long Beach 90809 ☎877/510–2888 🌐www.catalinaadventuretours.com*). **Catalina Island Chamber of Commerce & Visitors' Bureau** (*✉#1 Green Pleasure Pier, Avalon ☎310/510–1520 🌐www.catalinachamber.com*).

Santa Catalina Island Company (*Box 737, Long Beach ☎310/510–2800 or 800/626–1496 🌐www.scico.com*). **Santa Catalina Island Conservancy** (*✉125 Claressa Ave. , Avalon ☎310/510–2595 🌐www.catalinaconservancy.org*).

AVALON

A 1- to 2-hr ferry ride from Long Beach, Newport Beach, or San Pedro; a 15-min helicopter ride from Long Beach or San Pedro.

Avalon, Catalina's only real town, extends from the shore of its natural harbor to the surrounding hillsides. Its resident population is about 3,500 but it swells with tourists on summer weekends. Most of the city's activity, however, is centered along the pedestrian mall on Crescent Avenue, and most sights are easily reached on foot. Private cars are restricted and rental cars aren't allowed, but taxis, trams, and shuttles can take you anywhere you need to go. Bicycles and golf carts can be rented from shops along Crescent Avenue.

EXPLORING

A walk along **Crescent Avenue** is a nice way to begin a tour of the town. Vivid art deco tiles adorn the avenue's fountains and planters—fired on the island by the now-defunct Catalina Tile Company, the tiles are a coveted commodity.

Head to the **Green Pleasure Pier,** at the center of Crescent Avenue, for a good vantage point of Avalon. At the top of the hill you'll spot a big white building, the Inn at Mt. Ada, now a top-of-the-line B&B but originally built by William Wrigley Jr. for his wife. On the pier you'll find the Catalina Island Chamber of Commerce, snack stands, the Harbor Patrol, and scads of squawking seagulls.

★ On the northwest point of Avalon Bay (looking to your right from Green Pleasure Pier) is the majestic landmark **Casino.** This circular white structure is one of the finest examples of art deco architecture anywhere. Its Spanish-inspired floors and murals gleam with brilliant blue and green Catalina tiles. In this case, *casino,* the Italian word for "gathering place," has nothing to do with gambling. Rather, Casino life revolves around the magnificent ballroom. The same big-band dances that made the Casino famous in the 1930s and '40s still take place several times a year. The **New Year's Eve dance** (☎*310/510–1520*) is hugely popular and sells out well in advance.

WORD OF MOUTH

"Usually when it is 'June gloom' at the coast, it's gorgeous in Avalon (although the water will still be cold). There are still a lot of fun things to do in the quaint town even if it is for one night. You can rent a golf cart and cruise the island, catch a movie at the casino, have dinner, or just walk around." —tahititams

Santa Catalina Island Company leads tours of the Casino, lasting about 55 minutes, for $16. You can also visit the **Catalina Island Museum,** in the lower level of the Casino, which investigates 7,000 years of island history; or stop at the **Casino Art Gallery** to see works by local artists. First-run movies are screened nightly at the **Avalon Theatre,** noteworthy for its classic 1929 theater pipe organ. ✉*1 Casino Way, Avalon* ☎*310/510–2414 museum, 310/510–0808 art gallery, 310/510–0179 Avalon Theatre* 🌐*www.catalinamuseum.com* 🎫*Museum $5, art gallery free* ⏲*Museum: daily 10–4, closed Thurs. Jan.–mid-Mar. Art gallery: mid-Mar.–Dec., daily 10:30–4; Jan.–mid-Mar., Tues., Sat., and Sun. 10–4.*

In front of the Casino are the crystal-clear waters of the **Casino Point Underwater Park,** a marine preserve protected from watercraft where moray eels, bat rays, spiny lobsters, halibut, and other sea animals cruise around kelp forests and along the sandy bottom. It's a terrific site for scuba diving, with some shallow areas suitable for snorkeling. Scuba and snorkeling equipment can be rented on and near the pier. The shallow waters of **Lover's Cove,** east of the boat landing, are also good for snorkeling.

Two miles south of the bay via Avalon Canyon Road is **Wrigley Memorial and Botanical Garden.** Here you'll find plants native to Southern California, including several that grow only on Catalina Island: Catalina ironwood, wild tomato, and rare Catalina mahogany. The Wrigley family commissioned the garden as well as the monument, which has a grand staircase and a Spanish mausoleum inlaid with colorful Catalina tile. (The mausoleum was never used by the Wrigleys, who are buried in Los Angeles.) Taxi service from Avalon is available, or you can take a tour bus from the downtown Tour Plaza or ferry landing. ✉*Avalon Canyon Rd., Avalon* ☎*310/510–2897* 🎫*$5* ⏲*Daily 8–5.*

WHERE TO EAT

$$$ STEAK ✕**Catalina Country Club.** The beautifully restored California Mission-style structure, which was built in 1921 as a spring training clubhouse for the Chicago Cubs, is now a restaurant with dark wood, white linen, and an air of formality that's unusual on this casual island. This is the place on the island for a special occasion. The menu emphasizes organic and sustainable ingredients; offerings might include scallops in vanilla beurre blanc, filet mignon, and local sand dabs meuniére. The adjacent bar, which connects to the old Cubs locker room and is

filled with memorabilia, is great for an after-dinner drink. ✉ *1 Country Club Dr., Avalon* ☎ *310/510–7404* *Reservations essential* ▭ *AE, D, DC, MC, V.*

¢–$ AMERICAN ✕ **Eric's on the Pier.** This little snack bar has been an Avalon family–run institution since the 1920s. It's a good place to people-watch while munching a breakfast burrito, hot dog, or signature buffalo burger. Most of the action (and seating) is outside, but you can also sit down at a table inside and dine on a bowl of homemade clam chowder in a baked bread bowl or an order of fish-and-chips. ✉ *Green Pier No. 2, Avalon* ☎ *310/510–0894* ▭ *AE, MC, V* ⊗ *Closed Thurs. No dinner Nov.–May.*

$$$ STEAK ✕ **Steve's Steakhouse.** Within spitting distance of the bay and most Catalina hotels, this second-floor steak-centric restaurant keeps hungry diners happy with USDA Choice steaks and slow-cooked baby back ribs, as well as ample seafood such as locally caught swordfish and the popular Avalon-style shrimp. The sultry black-and-blue decor and old-fashioned supper club feel create a romantic, retro atmosphere that's enhanced by the restaurant's stunning harbor views. ✉ *417 Crescent Ave., Avalon* ☎ *310/510–0333* ⊕ *www.stevessteakhouse.com* ▭ *AE, D, MC, V* ⊗ *No lunch Wed. and Thurs.*

¢–$ ECLECTIC ✕ **Umami Café.** This café's culturally diverse fare is perfect for casual dining in the courtyard of the Metropole Market Place or for taking along on a hike or picnic. There's no table service here—just line up and order at the counter—but the use of fresh, high quality ingredients distinguish this little cafe. You'll find falafel, Cobb salad and, in the spirit of the New Orleans-inspired marketplace, Louisiana po-boy sandwiches. There are good options here for vegetarians, kids, and a selection of boutique wines. ✉ *205 Crescent Ave., Avalon* ☎ *310/510–9095* *Reservations not accepted* ▭ *AE, D, DC, MC, V* ⊗ *Closed Sun. in winter. No dinner.*

WHERE THE BUFFALO ROAM?

Zane Grey, the writer who put the Western novel on the map, spent a lot of time on Catalina, and his influence is still evident in a peculiar way. When the movie version of Grey's book *The Vanishing American* was filmed here in 1924, American bison were ferried across from the mainland to give the land that Western plains look. After the moviemakers packed up and left, the buffalo stayed, and a small herd of about 150 of these majestic creatures still remains, grazing the interior and reinforcing the island's image as the last refuge from SoCal's urban sprawl.

WHERE TO STAY

$$$–$$$$ **Aurora Hotel & Spa.** In a town dominated by historic properties, the Aurora is refreshingly contemporary, with a hip attitude more reminiscent of Hollywood than Avalon. Standard rooms are small but appointed with mod chocolate and blue furniture and flat-screen TVs, while suites have Jacuzzi tubs or elaborate showers—the spacious Aurora Suite is a great splurge. There are striking ocean views from the rooftop deck. Unwind after a day of hiking or boat with a Mermaid's Kiss massage—a blend of Swedish, Japanese, and Thai techniques—at the spa. A complimentary Continental breakfast is served and the front desk loans

9

out laptops, binoculars, and GPS units to guests. **Pros:** trendy design; quiet location off main drag yet still close to restaurants. **Cons:** standard rooms are small, even by Catalina standards. ✉ *137 Marilla Ave., Avalon* ☎ *310/510–0454* 🌐 *www.auroracatalina.com* *15 rooms, 3 suites* *In-room: refrigerator, DVD, Internet, Wi-Fi. In-hotel: spa, Wi-Fi, no-smoking rooms* *AE, D, DC, MC, V.*

¢–$ **Hermosa Hotel and Catalina Cottages.** This historical 1890s hotel offers small rooms with shared baths and plenty of charm and character. If you're looking for luxury or amenities, this may not be the place for you. Cottage with basic kitchen facilities and cooking essentials are more spacious and comfortable; you can also request one of the more updated rooms, which have heat, a/c, and private baths. A few suites with private entrances, full kitchens, and private baths sleep six and are ideal for families or groups. The beach is half a block away.**Pros:** quiet enforced after 10 PM; kitchenettes available; reasonably priced. **Cons:** no frills; some shared bathrooms; some rooms lack heating and/or a/c. ✉ *131 Metropole St., Avalon* ☎ *310/510–1010 or 888/684–1313* 🌐 *www.hermosahotel.com* *27 rooms, 19 cottages, 3 suites* *In-room: no a/c (some), no phone, kitchen (some), no TV (some). In-hotel: Wi-Fi, no-smoking rooms* *AE, D, DC, MC, V.*

$$ **Hotel Metropole and Market Place.** This romantic hotel evokes the former look of New Orleans's French Quarter. Some guest rooms have balconies overlooking a flower-filled courtyard holding restaurants and shops; others have ocean views. Many have fireplaces. Room 102, an oceanfront suite with vaulted ceilings and lavish bath, is a pricey indulgence. For a stunning panorama, head for the rooftop deck. **Pros:** family-friendly; outdoor Jacuzzi and sundeck; convenient location. **Cons:** some rooms on small side; nearby grocery store deliveries make some rooms noisy in morning. ✉ *205 Crescent Ave., Avalon* ☎ *310/510–1884 or 800/541–8528* 🌐 *www.hotel-metropole.com* *44 rooms, 8 suites* *In-room: refrigerator, DVD (some), Wi-Fi. In-hotel: room service, no-smoking rooms* *AE, MC, V* *CP.*

$ **Hotel Villa Portofino.** Steps from the beach and the Pleasure Pier, this hotel has a European flair and creates an intimate feel with brick courtyards and walkways. Rooms are decorated in deep jewel tones and suites are named after Italian cities. Some ocean-facing rooms have open balconies, fireplaces, and marble baths. You can sunbathe on the private deck, or ask for beach towels and chairs to take to the cove. **Pros:** romantic; close to beach; incredible sun deck. **Cons:** though quiet in general, ground floor rooms can be noisy; *some rooms are on small side; no elevator.* ✉ *111 Crescent Ave., Avalon* ☎ *310/510–0555 or 800/346–2326* 🌐 *www.hotelvillaportofino.com* *35 rooms* *In room: refrigerator, Wi-Fi. In hotel: restaurant, no-smoking rooms* *AE, D, DC, MC, V* *CP.*

$$$ ★ **Hotel Vista del Mar.** Centrally located on the middle of Main Street, this beautiful property is just steps from the beach, where complimentary towels, chairs, and umbrellas await guests. The 14 rooms and suites are aligned along a lovely glass-covered promenade. Modern Mediterranean decor, nightly milk and cookies, and in-room fireplaces and whirlpool tubs make the hotel a popular spot for honeymooners

and couples seeking a quiet getaway. **Pros:** comfortable king beds; central; modern decor. **Cons:** no restaurant or spa facilities; only two rooms have ocean views or balconies; no elevator. ✉ *417 Crescent Ave., Avalon* ☎ *310/510–1452 or 800/601–3836* 🌐 *www.hotel-vistadelmar.com* *11 rooms, 3 suites* *In-room: refrigerator, DVD, Wi-Fi. In-hotel: Wi-Fi, no-smoking rooms* *AE, D, MC, V* *CP.*

$$$$ Fodor's Choice ★ **Inn on Mt. Ada.** If you stay in the mansion where Wrigley Jr. once lived, you'll enjoy all the comforts of a millionaire's home—at a millionaire's prices. Nightly rates, which start at $400 in summer, include breakfast, lunch, beverages, and snacks (note that the restaurant does not serve dinner), plus use of a golf cart. The guest rooms are traditional and elegant; some have fireplaces and all have water views. The hilltop view of the curve of the bay is spectacular; the Windsor Room, with views of both the ocean and bay, is among the most coveted. Service is gracious and attentive, and a stay at this enchanting property is memorable. **Pros:** timeless charm; shuttle from heliport and dock; first-class service. **Cons:** smallish rooms and bathrooms; pricey. ✉ *398 Wrigley Rd., Avalon* ☎ *310/510–2030 or 800/608–7669* 🌐 *www.innonmtada.com* *6 rooms* *In-room: no a/c, no phone, DVD, Wi-Fi. In-hotel: restaurant, Wi-Fi, no kids under 14, no-smoking rooms* *MC, V* *MAP.*

NIGHTLIFE

El Galleon (✉ *411 Crescent Ave., Avalon* ☎ *310/510–1188*) has microbrews, bar nibbles, and karaoke. **Luau Larry's** (✉ *509 Crescent Ave., Avalon* ☎ *310/510–1919* 🌐 *www.luaularrys.com*), famous for its potent Wiki Wacker cocktail (a concoction of rum, brandy, orange-pineapple juice, and grenadine), comes alive with boisterous tourists and locals on summer weekends.

SPORTS AND THE OUTDOORS

BICYCLING Bike rentals are widely available in Avalon starting at $5 per hour and $12 per day. Look for rentals on Crescent Avenue and Pebbly Beach Road such as **Brown's Bikes** (✉ *107 Pebbly Beach Rd., next to Island Rentals, Avalon* ☎ *310/510–0986* 🖷 *310/510–0747* 🌐 *www.catalinabiking.com*). To bike beyond the paved roads of Avalon, you must buy an annual permit from the Catalina Conservancy. Individual passes cost $65; family passes cost $90. You may not ride on hiking paths.

DIVING AND SNORKELING The Casino Point Underwater Park, with its handful of wrecks, is best suited for diving. Lover's Cove is better for snorkeling (no scuba diving allowed, but you'll share the area with glass-bottom boats). Both are protected marine preserves. **Catalina Divers Supply** (✉ *Green Pleasure Pier, Avalon* ☎ *310/510–0330* 🌐 *www.catalinadiverssupply.com*) rents equipment, runs guided scuba and snorkel tours, gives certification classes, and more. It has an outpost at Casino Point.

HIKING Permits from the **Santa Catalina Island Conservancy** (✉ *125 Claressa Ave., Box 2739, Avalon* ☎ *310/510–2595* 🌐 *www.catalinaconservancy.org*) are required for hiking into Catalina Island's interior. **TIP→ If you plan to backpack overnight, you'll need a camping reservation. The interior is dry and desert-like; bring plenty of water and sunblock.** The permits are free and can be picked up at the main house of the conservancy or at the airport. You don't need a permit for shorter hikes, such as the one

9

from Avalon to the Botanical Garden. The conservancy has maps of the island's east-end hikes, such as Hermit's Gulch Trail. It's possible to hike between Avalon and Two Harbors, starting at the Hogsback Gate, above Avalon, though the 28-mi journey has an elevation gain of 3,000 feet and is not for the weak. ■ TIP→ **For a pleasant 4-mi hike out of Avalon, take Avalon Canyon Road to Wrigley Gardens and follow the trail to Lone Pine. At the top, you'll have an amazing view of the Palisades cliffs and, beyond them, the sea.**

Another hike option is to take the **Airport Shuttle Bus** (☎ *310/510–0143*) from Avalon to the airport for $25 round-trip. The 10-mi hike back to Avalon is mostly downhill, and the bus is an inexpensive way to see the interior of the island.

Travel Smart Los Angeles

WORD OF MOUTH

"Of all the studio tours, Warner Bros. is the best. I've been on them all (and worked on all the lots)–trust me on this. The NBC tour is also great . . . I haven't been on the new double-decker tour buses but have seen them all around town. If you're not comfortable driving in the city then yes, I think this is a good way to cover a lot of ground."

—Erin74

"The Art Deco tour is definitely on our list, along with the Broadway Historic Theatre District tour. There are actually quite a few, some of which need reservations and some which do not. Their website also has links to other tours of cities surrounding L.A."

—Linny1951

www.fodors.com/community

GETTING HERE AND AROUND

Stretching almost 500 square mi and with more than 12 million residents, visitors will need to be prepared to rent a car and fight for space on the freeway (especially at rush hour) to make their way along the array of destinations that span from the carefree beaches of the coastline to the glitz and glamour of Beverly Hills shops, the nightlife of Hollywood, and the film studio action of the Valley. But it's worth it. Nowhere else in the country can you spot celebrities over breakfast, sunbathe on the beach in the afternoon, and head out to the slopes for skiing within hours (if you have that much energy). Anything is possible in Los Angeles. It may be a little pricey compared to other states but residents like to think of it as paying for the nearly constant good weather, so enjoy, and explore!

TIP→Ask the local tourist board about hotel and local transportation packages that include tickets to major museum exhibits or other special events.

> **WORD OF MOUTH**
>
> After your trip, be sure to rate the places you visited and share your experiences and travel tips with us and other Fodorites in Travel Ratings and Talk on www.fodors.com.

AIR TRAVEL

Nonstop flights from New York to Los Angeles take about six hours; with the three-hour time change, you can leave JFK by 8 AM and be in L.A. by 11 AM. Some flights may require a midway stop, making the total excursion between 7½ and 8½ hours. Many of the flights out of Chicago are nonstop with a duration of four hours. Nonstop times are approximately three hours from Dallas, 10 hours from London, and 15 hours from Sydney.

Flights in and out of Los Angeles International Airport (LAX) are seldom delayed because of weather and generally run on time. Because of heavy traffic around the airport (not to mention the city's extended rush hours) and difficult parking, however, you should allow plenty of time to arrive at the airport prior to scheduled departure or arrival times. Some hotels near LAX offer air-travel perks, such as free shuttles to the airport. There are three other nearby airports that serve L.A. County; they're smaller and have more limited services but are worth investigating when booking flights (⇨ *Airports*). For instance, the Long Beach airport is a hub for the low-cost domestic airline jetBlue (which also flies out of Burbank and Ontario), while Southwest has a big presence at the Burbank (Bob Hope), Ontario, and Orange County airports.

Plan to arrive at the airport about two hours before your scheduled departure time for domestic flights and 2½ to 3 hours before international flights. You may need to arrive earlier if you're flying from LAX or during peak air-traffic times.

Airlines and Airports Airline and Airport Links.com (🌐 *www.airlineandairportlinks.com*) has links to many of the world's airlines and airports.

Airline Security Issues Transportation Security Administration (🌐 *www.tsa.gov*) has answers for almost every question that might come up.

AIRPORTS

The major gateway to L.A. is Los Angeles International Airport. Departures are from the upper level, and arrivals are on the lower level. LAX is serviced by more than 85 major airlines and is the fourth-largest airport in the world in terms of passenger traffic. Make the best of long delays or layovers by heading to Encounter, the intergalactic-theme restaurant and cocktail lounge just across the street from Terminals 1 and 2 on the lower level (reservations are recommended for lunch and dinner; ☎*310/215–5151* 🌐*www.encounterlax.com*). For longer delays, several hotels are a five-minute walk or shuttle ride away, including Courtyard Marriott and Radisson. They have spa services and restaurants. Ontario International Airport, about 35 mi east of Los Angeles, serves the San Bernardino–Riverside area with a dozen airlines. Burbank's Bob Hope Airport serves the San Fernando Valley with six airlines. Four airlines use Long Beach Airport. John Wayne/Orange County Airport serves Orange County with 14 airlines, including four commuter carriers.

SECONDARY AIRPORTS

It's generally easier to navigate the secondary airports than to get through sprawling LAX. Bob Hope Airport in Burbank is closest to downtown L.A., and domestic flights to it can be cheaper than flights to LAX—it's definitely worth checking out. From Long Beach Airport it's equally convenient to go north to central Los Angeles or south to Orange County. Flights to Orange County's John Wayne Airport are often more expensive than those to the other secondary airports.

Airport Information **Bob Hope Airport** (*BUR* ☎*818/840–8830* 🌐*www.bobhopeairport.com*). **John Wayne/Orange County Airport** (*SNA* ☎*949/252–5006* 🌐*www.ocair.com*). **Long Beach Airport** (*LGB* ☎*562/570–2600* 🌐*www.lgb.org*). **Los Angeles International Airport** (*LAX* ☎*310/646–5252* 🌐*www.lawa.org or www.airport-la.com*). **Ontario International Airport** (*ONT* ☎*909/937–2700* 🌐*www.lawa.org*).

GROUND TRANSPORTATION

LAX provides free bus service from one terminal to another, and the car-rental companies also have gratis shuttles to their nearby branches. Some hotels, especially those near the airport, provide free airport shuttles for their guests.

Driving. Driving times from LAX to different parts of the city vary considerably: it will take you at least 45 minutes to get downtown, 20 minutes to get to Santa Monica, 30 minutes to Beverly Hills, and 45 minutes to an hour to Van Nuys or Sherman Oaks (the central San Fernando Valley). With traffic, particularly on the 405 freeway, it can take much longer. From Burbank, it's 30 minutes to downtown, 40 minutes to Santa Monica, 45 minutes to Beverly Hills, and 15 minutes to the central San Fernando Valley. The drive from downtown L.A. to the Ontario or Orange County airports takes at least an hour; plan on at least 45 minutes for the drive to Long Beach Airport.

Taxis. Taxis are the most convenient way to get between the city and the airports. It's a $50 flat rate between downtown L.A. and LAX in either direction, plus a $2.50 surcharge. Taxis to and from Ontario Airport run on a meter and can cost up to $60 and $70 depending on traffic; taxis between downtown and Bob Hope Airport are also metered and can cost $40 to $5. From Long Beach Airport to Long Beach hotels, some taxis offer a $24 flat rate; trips to downtown L.A. are metered and cost roughly $65.

Shuttles. For two or three travelers—particularly if you're going a longish distance, for example, to the San Fernando Valley from LAX—shuttle services are economical, $16–$21 per person. However, an individual traveler, depending on the destination, may end up paying more than by cab. Shuttle ride costs are determined by postal codes; fares increase depending on how many postal-code areas you pass. A shuttle ride generally takes longer than a cab ride. These big vans typically circle the airport repeatedly to fill up with passengers. Your travel time will be determined in part by how many other travelers are dropped off before you. At LAX, Prime Time and SuperShuttle allow walk-on shuttle passengers without prior reservations; otherwise, you'll need to make a reservation at least 24 hours in advance for a ride either to or from an airport.

FlyAway buses. In 2006 the Los Angeles World Airports group started a nonstop bus service between Union Station in downtown L.A. and LAX and between Van Nuys and LAX. The ride takes about 45 minutes and costs $6 (cash only). Buses run 24 hours a day: every half hour between 5 AM and 1 AM, then every hour from downtown, or every 15 minutes between 4:45 AM and 9:30 AM from Van Nuys. They've got luggage bays on board. If you're on a domestic flight, you can avoid lines at the airport by checking your luggage and getting your boarding pass before getting on the bus. See the Web site *www.lawa.org/flyaway*.

Public transportation. If you don't have much to carry, are not in a hurry, and know your destination is near a bus or subway stop, consider taking public transit from LAX into L.A. Free shuttles take passengers from the arrivals levels of each terminal to public transit points; shuttle C will take you to parking lot C and MTA bus connections, while shuttle G goes to the Metro Rail Green Line Aviation station. The Green Line trains run every 15–20 minutes until 1 AM. Several bus lines include the airport, but they often don't stick to their schedule. It may take four times as long as it would by car, but the fare is usually $5 or less. From Burbank's airport, meanwhile, you can connect with Metrolink or Amtrak train service for a 20-minute trip to downtown Union Station. The fare is $5.25, but you may have to wait up to an hour between trains. There's no direct public transportation from the Ontario or Long Beach airports into Los Angeles proper.

AIRPORT TRANSFERS

Shuttles **Xpress Shuttle** (☎ *800/427-7483* 🌐 *www.expressshuttle.com*). **Prime Time** (☎ *800/733-8267* 🌐 *www.primetimeshuttle.com*). **SuperShuttle** (☎ *323/775-6600, 310/782-6600, or 800/258-3826* 🌐 *www.supershuttle.com*).

FLIGHTS

Delta and American have the most nonstop and direct flights to Los Angeles International Airport (LAX) from U.S. cities. JetBlue Airways, a low-fare domestic airline, has daily nonstop flights from LAX to New York and Boston, and between Long Beach and Oakland; Ontario; Burbank; Sacramento; Chicago; Salt Lake City; Las Vegas; New York City; Boston; Washington, D.C.; Austin, Texas; and Fort Lauderdale; it also recently added nonstop flights between Burbank and New York and Las Vegas. Low-fare Southwest Airlines serves the LAX, Ontario, Burbank, and Orange County airports.

Major Airlines **Alaska Airlines** (☎ *800/252-7522* 🌐 *www.alaskaair.com*). **American Airlines** (☎ *800/433-7300* 🌐 *www.aa.com*). **Continental Airlines** (☎ *800/523—3273* 🌐 *www.continental.com*). **Delta Airlines** (☎ *800/221-1212* 🌐 *www.delta.com*). **jetBlue** (☎ *800/538-2583* 🌐 *www.jetblue.com*). **Northwest Airlines** (☎ *800/225-2525* 🌐 *www.nwa.com*). **Southwest Airlines** (☎ *800/435-9792* 🌐 *www.southwest.com*). **United Airlines** (☎ *800/864-8331* 🌐 *www.united.com*). **USAirways** (☎ *800/428-4322* 🌐 *www.usairways.com*).

Smaller Airlines **AirTran Airlines** (☎ *800/247-8726* 🌐 *www.airtran.com*). **Hawaiian Airlines** (☎ *800/367-5320* 🌐 *www.hawaiianair.com*).

BUS TRAVEL

TO AND FROM LOS ANGELES

The duration of a bus trip from other parts of California or nearby states can be comparable to the time it takes to take a plane, preflight waiting considered. The only Greyhound terminal is in an industrial area of downtown L.A., off Alameda Street. The waiting room and restrooms are clean, and there are individual pay TVs. The terminal is not close to other transit stations but by taking MTA Bus 58 you can get to Union Station. Taxis are also available at the terminal.

Greyhound has dozens of daily routes serving Los Angeles. It often has promotional fares from other West Coast cities to L.A. You can buy tickets by phone, on the Greyhound Web site, or in person at the terminal. The online purchasing service is called Will Call; you'll need to make the transaction at least two hours before departure.

WITHIN LOS ANGELES

In L.A., unless your car's in the shop, you're probably behind the wheel. Inadequate public-transportation systems have been an L.A. problem for decades. That said, many local trips can be made, with time and patience, by bus. In certain cases, it may be your best option; for example, visiting the Getty Center, going to Universal Studios and/or the adjacent CityWalk, or venturing into downtown. There's also a special Metropolitan Transit Authority (MTA) bus that goes between Union Station and Dodger Stadium for Friday night home games. It doesn't save money, but it can save you time and parking-related stress. For the fastest MTA service, look for the red-and-white Metro Rapid buses; these stop less frequently and are able to extend green lights. At this writing, there were 15 Rapid routes including routes on Wilshire and Vermont boulevards; over the next few years more Rapid routes will be added.

The Metropolitan Transit Authority DASH (Downtown Area Short Hop) minibuses cover six different circular routes in Hollywood, Mid-Wilshire, and the downtown area. The buses stop every two blocks or so. The Santa Monica Municipal Bus Line, also known as the Big Blue Bus, is a pleasant and inexpensive way to move around the Westside, where the MTA lines leave off. There's also an express bus to and from downtown L.A., and a shuttle bus, the Tide Shuttle, which runs between Main Street and the Third Street Promenade and stops at hotels along the way. Culver CityBus Lines run six routes through Culver City. Smoking is never allowed in the L.A. public transportation system.

MTA schedules are available through the information line below, but heavy local traffic can make them unreliable. Service is available at all hours. An MTA bus ride for both standard and Rapid service costs $1.25, plus 25¢ for each transfer between buses or from bus to subway. From 9 PM to 5 AM, the fare goes down to 75¢. At this writing, a one-day pass cost $5, and a weekly pass $17 for unlimited travel on all Metro buses and trains (biweekly and monthly passes are also available), but fare increases were expected beginning in January 2009. Passes are valid from Sunday through Saturday. EZ Transit passes are a long-term option; this $62 monthly pass covers transit on virtually all public transit options throughout the county.

DASH buses make pickups at five-minute intervals. You pay 25¢ every time you get on. Buses generally run weekdays 6 AM–7 PM and Saturday 10 AM–5 PM; a few downtown weekend routes run on Sunday as well. Note: the Downtown Discovery Route (DD) makes a continuous loop among downtown sites; Route E is a shopper's tour with stops in the Broadway, Jewelry, and Fashion districts, as well as at two downtown malls.

The Santa Monica Municipal Bus Line (the Big Blue Bus) costs 75¢, while Big Blue's Tide Shuttle is a quarter. Transfers are free from one Big Blue Bus to another; to MTA or Culver CityBus it's 50¢. The Route 10 (downtown) express bus costs $1.75. Packs of 10 tokens are $7. You can also use a prepaid Metrocard, the Little Blue Card, and get the same discounted rate for multiple rides (70¢ per ride). The Big Blue buses generally run from 5 AM to midnight, while the Tide Shuttle runs Sunday to Thursday from noon until 8 PM and Friday and Saturday from noon to 10 PM.

Culver CityBus is 75¢ and runs 6 AM–midnight. The Santa Monica bus line's Metrocard can be used on this system but not Big Blue Bus tokens. Culver CityBuses also accept MTA tokens but not MTA passes. Children and people over 65 always pay less on all lines.

You can pay your fare in cash on MTA, Santa Monica, and Culver City buses, but you must have exact change. You can buy MTA passes and tokens throughout the city at MTA customer centers and some convenience stores and grocery stores. Metrocards or tokens for the Santa Monica buses can be purchased at local libraries and retailers. Call or check the pertinent bus Web site for the retail location nearest you.

Bus Information **Commute Smart** (☎ *800/266-6883* 🌐 *www.commutesmart.info*). **Culver CityBus Lines** (☎ *310/253-6500* 🌐 *www.culvercity.org*). **DASH** (☎ *213/626-4455 or 310/808-2273* 🌐 *www.ladottransit.com/dash*). **Greyhound** (☎ *213/629-8405 or 800/231-2222* 🌐 *www.greyhound.com*). **Metropolitan Transit Authority (MTA)** (☎ *213/626-4455* 🌐 *www.mta.net*). **Santa Monica Municipal Bus Line** (☎ *310/451-5444* 🌐 *www.bigbluebus.com*).

CAR TRAVEL

Picture L.A. and you might see a hectic mesh of multilane freeways with their hypnotic streams of cars. Once you've joined the multitudes you'll be caught up in the tempos of traffic: frustration, exhilaration, and crushing boredom. "Freeway culture" is one of the city's defining traits.

BASICS

GASOLINE

In L.A., as of this writing, gasoline costs around $2.50 a gallon. Most stations offer both full and self-service stations. There are plenty of stations in all areas; most stay open late, and some are open 24 hours. To find the stations with the lowest gas prices in town, visit 🌐 *www.losangelesgasprices.com*. Prices are updated every 36 hours by a network of volunteer spotters.

> **NAVIGATING LOS ANGELES**
>
> L.A. traffic can be frightful, especially during rush hour, but there are ways to tackle it. Avoid the freeways before 10 AM, and between 5 and 7 PM, if you can. Hit the surface streets at these times, and allow plenty of time to get to your destination. The San Diego Freeway (I–405) at the Hollywood Freeway (U.S. 101) (known as the Sepulveda Pass) is often jammed at all hours, as is the area around downtown where the Harbor Freeway (Rte. 110) meets the Santa Monica Freeway (I–10). The subway system works well, for some destinations. Consider it if you're trying to get between Hollywood or Pasadena and downtown L.A., or to Universal City. It doesn't stop in Beverly Hills, Santa Monica, or most of the beach towns.

NAVIGATING LOS ANGELES

Finding your way by car in Los Angeles can be a piece of cake or a nightmare. If you're used to urban driving, you shouldn't have too much trouble, but if you're unused to driving in big cities, L.A. can be unnerving. The city may be sprawling and traffic clogged, but at least it has evolved with the automobile in mind. Streets are wide and parking garages abound, so it's more driver-friendly than many older big cities. Get a good map and remember a few of the pointers we list here, and you should be able to avoid confusion.

There are plenty of identical or extremely similar street names in L.A. (Beverly Boulevard and Beverly Drive, for example), so be as specific as you can when getting or checking directions. Also, some smaller streets seem to exist intermittently for miles, so unless you have good directions, you should use major streets rather than try for an alternative that is actually blocked by a dead end or detours, like the side streets off Sunset Boulevard.

Expect sudden changes in street-address numbering as streets pass through neighborhoods, then incorporated cities, then back into neighborhoods. This can be most bewildering on Robertson Boulevard, an otherwise useful north–south artery that, by crossing through L.A., West Hollywood, and Beverly Hills, dips in and out of several such numbering shifts in a matter of miles.

In Santa Monica, odd numbers switch over from the north and west sides of streets to the south and east sides.

Try to get clear directions and stick to them. The *Thomas Guide*, a hefty, spiral-bound, super-thorough street guide and directory, is published annually and is available at bookstores, grocery stores, and the like. It's worth the money if you're planning to stay longer than a week and spend the majority of your time navigating the area in your car, but for most visitors the compact L.A. city maps available at auto clubs and retail shops are more manageable and work just fine.

If you get discombobulated while on the freeway, remember the rule of thumb: even-numbered freeways run east and west, odd-numbered freeways run north and south.

PARKING

For some shops and many restaurants and hotels in L.A., valet parking is virtually assumed. The cost is usually $4–$6 and/or an optional tip; keep small bills on hand for the valets.

But there are also some inexpensive and easy garage and lot parking options. For instance, the underground facility at the Hollywood & Highland entertainment and shopping complex, at 6801 Hollywood Boulevard, charges $2 for the first four hours and a maximum of $10 for the day; no validation is required.

In Beverly Hills, the first two hours are free at several lots on or around Rodeo Drive (for a detailed map, visit 🌐 *www.beverlyhills.org*). There's never a parking fee or a long wait to enter and exit at the Westside Pavilion's open-access garage at 10800 Pico Boulevard.

Parking in downtown L.A. can be tough, especially on weekdays, but the garage at the 7+Fig retail complex at Ernst and Young Plaza (725 S. Figueroa St.) is spacious, reasonable, and visitor-friendly. Validation from a shop or restaurant gets you three hours free; otherwise, it's $7 before 9 AM and $8 after 4 PM and on weekends. Staples Center patrons should ask about the discounted rates.

Parking rules are strictly enforced in Los Angeles, so make sure you check for parking signs and pay attention to their rules. Illegally parked cars are ticketed or towed quickly (and the minimum ticket is $35). Parking is generally available in garages or parking lots; some public lots are free all or part of the day; otherwise prices vary from 25¢ (in the public lots) to $2 per half hour or from a few dollars to $30 per day. Downtown and Century City garage rates may be as high as $25 an hour, though prices tend to drop on weekends.

Speaking of posted limits, street parking in L.A. is confusing because of the many and varying restrictions (during the day, only at night, once a week during street-cleaning hours, etc.). When visiting residential areas, be sure to ask your hosts about parking restrictions since signs aren't always easy to find. If you have to park in a restricted space for even the briefest amount of time, put on your emergency blinkers.

Sometimes businesses will offer validated parking if you've parked in an affiliated lot; validation will give you free parking for a certain time period. At a restaurant, for instance, ask for parking validation from the host or hostess. Metered parking is also widely available; meter rates vary from 25¢ for 15 minutes in the most heavily trafficked areas to 25¢ for one hour; have a bunch of change available. In some areas, metered parking is free on weekends or on Sunday. Another bonus: if a meter is out of order (for example, if it is flashing the word *FAIL* where the time remaining would appear), parking is free for the posted time limit.

...hen parking in a large lot or parking garage, note the section or level of your parking space. Stadiums, malls, theme parks, and other venues with giant parking areas post signs, but some garages don't have much in the way of indicators.

ROAD CONDITIONS

Beware of weekday rush-hour traffic, which is heaviest from 7 AM to 10 AM and 3 PM to 7 PM. Both KFWB and KNX have frequent traffic reports; the Los Angeles city Web site and southern California CommuteSmart Web site have real-time traffic information maps, and the California Highway Patrol has a road-conditions line. To encourage carpooling, some crowded freeways reserve an express lane for cars carrying more than one passenger.

Parallel streets can often provide viable alternatives to jam-packed freeways, notably Sepulveda Boulevard for I–405; Venice and Washington boulevards for I–10 from Mid-Wilshire west to the beach; and Ventura Boulevard, Moorpark Street, and/or Riverside Drive for U.S. 101 through the San Fernando Valley. Highway signage is on the whole good but can't substitute for maps and detailed directions.

Fog is generally equated with San Francisco, but the coastline of Southern California does get some pea-soup conditions that are dangerous for drivers. In late 2002, for instance, nearly 200 cars piled up on the Long Beach Freeway due to heavy fog. If you encounter thick fog, slow down, switch on your low beams and fog lights, and watch carefully for the lights of other vehicles. If the fog is extremely heavy, pull over cautiously and wait for it to pass.

Information **California Highway Patrol** (☎ *800/427–7623 for road conditions*). **City of Los Angeles** (🌐 *www.sigalert.com* 🌐 *traffic info.lacity.org*). **CommuteSmart** (🌐 *www.commutesmart.info*).

ROADSIDE EMERGENCIES

For lesser problems on L.A.'s freeways (being out of gas, having a blown tire, needing a tow to the nearest phone), Caltrans (California's Department of Transportation) has instituted the Freeway Service Patrol (FSP) 6:30 AM–7 PM. More than 145 tow trucks patrol the freeways offering free aid to stranded drivers.

If your car breaks down on an interstate, try to pull over onto the shoulder and either wait for the state police to find you or, if you have other passengers who can wait in the car, walk to the nearest emergency roadside phone and call the state police.

When calling for help, note your location according to the small green mileage markers posted along the highway. Other highways are also patrolled but may not have emergency phones or mileage markers.

Emergency Services **Freeway Service Patrol** (☎ *213/922–2957 general information; for breakdowns call 323/982–4900*).

RULES OF THE ROAD

The use of seat belts for all passengers is required in California, as is the use of car seats for children five years old or younger or 60 pounds or less. The speed limit is 25–35 mph on city streets and 65 mph on freeways unless otherwise posted. Turning right on a red light after a complete stop is legal unless otherwise posted. Many streets in downtown L.A. are one-way, and a left turn from one one-way street onto another is okay on a red light after a complete stop. On some major arteries, left turns are illegal during one or both rush hours (watch for signs). Certain carpool lanes, designated by signage and a white diamond, are reserved for cars with more than one passenger. Freeway on-ramps often have stop-and-go signals to regulate the flow of traffic, but cars in high occupancy vehicle (HOV) lanes can pass the signal without stopping.

As of July 2008, California law began requiring that all drivers use hands-free devices when talking on cell phones.

Some towns, including Beverly Hills and Culver City, use photo radar at stoplights to try to reduce speeding (these intersections are always identified with signs). LAX is notorious for handing out tickets to drivers circling its busy terminals; avoid the no-parking zones and keep loading or unloading to a minimum. Also keep in mind that pedestrians always have the right of way in California; not yielding to them, even if they're jaywalkers, may well result in a $100 ticket.

Speeding can earn you a fine of up to $500. It is illegal to drive in California with a blood alcohol content of 0.08% or above (0.01% if you're under 21); the cost of driving while intoxicated can be a $390–$1,000 fine plus 48 hours to six months in jail for first offenders. The police are not easygoing about traffic offenses in general. They don't typically engage in selective enforcement when the flow of traffic exceeds the speed limit, but they'll then focus on the drivers making dicey moves. Parking infractions can result in penalties starting at $30 for a ticket on up to having your vehicle towed and impounded (at an ultimate cost of nearly $200 even if you pay up immediately, more if you don't). In California, radar detectors aren't illegal, but "scanners" (which receive police radio signals) *are*; per the FCC, "jammers" (which interfere with signals) are illegal throughout the United States.

TIMING

It takes about 45 minutes to an hour to drive to Pasadena from Santa Monica, and anywhere from 30 to 45 minutes to get from Santa Monica to downtown.

CAR RENTAL

In Los Angeles, a car is a necessity. When renting one, keep in mind that you'll likely be spending a lot of time in it, and options like a CD player or power windows that might seem unnecessary may make a significant difference in your day-to-day comfort.

Major-chain rates in L.A. begin at $35 a day and $110 a week, plus 8.25% sales tax. Luxury and sport utility vehicles start at $69 a day. Open-top convertibles are a popular choice for L.A. visitors wanting to make the most of the sun. Note that the major agencies offer services for travelers with disabilities, such as hand-controls, for little or no extra cost.

Beverly Hills Budget Car Rental, with six locations, offers the widest range of vehicle rentals, including Hummers, convertibles, minivans, and economy cars. Daydreaming of a restored classic Chevy or the latest Porsche? Beverly Hills Rent-A-Car, a rental facility with branches in Santa Monica, Beverly Hills, Hollywood, and near LAX, rents exotics, classic cars, luxury models, economy cars (including Mini Coopers), vans, and SUVs. Midway Car Rental, with seven offices on the Westside, in the Valley, and in Mid-Wilshire, has the usual, plus some extra-large vans and, in its "executive class," Lexus, BMW, Mercedes, and so on. Possibly the handiest in the lower-price range is Enterprise, with two dozen branches in the area (some have luxury vehicles as well). You can rent an ecofriendly electric or hybrid car through Budget; for more information contact EV Rental Cars.

In California you must be 21 and have a valid credit card, often with $200–$300 available credit on it (regardless of how you'll ultimately pay), to rent a car; rates may be higher if you're under 25. There's no upper age limit.

Automobile Associations U.S.: **American Automobile Association** (*AAA ☎ 315/797–5000 🌐 www.aaa.com*); most contact with the organization is through state and regional members. **National Automobile Club** (*☎ 650/294–7000 🌐 www.thenac.com*); membership is open to California residents only.

Local Agencies **Beverly Hills Budget Car Rental** (*☎ 310/274–9173 or 800/227–7117* www.budgetbeverlyhills.com). **Beverly Hills Rent-A-Car** (☎ *310/337-1400 or 800/479-5996* *www.bhrentacar.com*). **Enterprise** (☎ *800/736-8222* *www.enterprise.com*). **Fox Rent a Car** (☎ *877/387-3682* *www.foxrentacar.com*). **Midway Car Rental** (☎ *888/682-0166* *www.midwaycarrental.com*). **Rent A Wreck** (☎ *800/995-0994* *www.rent-a-wreck.com*). **Town Rent A Car** (☎ *310/973-6815 or 323/934-4780*). **@West Rent a Car** (☎ *310/417-9050 or 877/404-0404* *www.atwestcarrental.com*).

Major Agencies **Alamo** (☎ *800/462-5266* *www.alamo.com*). **Avis** (☎ *800/230-4898* *www.avis.com*). **Budget** (☎ *800/527-0700* *www.budget.com*). **Hertz** (☎ *800/654-3131* *www.hertz.com*). **National Car Rental** (☎ *800/227-7368* *www.nationalcar.com*).

METRO RAIL TRAVEL

Metro Rail covers a limited area of L.A.'s vast expanse, but what there is, is helpful and frequent. The underground Red Line runs from Union Station downtown through Mid-Wilshire, Hollywood, and Universal City on its way to North Hollywood, stopping at the most popular tourist destinations along the way. The light commuter rail Green Line stretches from Redondo Beach to Norwalk, while the partially underground Blue Line goes from downtown to the South Bay (Long Beach/San Pedro). The Green and Blue lines are not often used by visitors, though the Green is gaining popularity as an alternative, albeit time-consuming, way to reach LAX. The monorail-like Gold Line, opened in summer 2003, begins at Union Station and heads northeast to Pasadena and Sierra Madre. The Orange Line, a 14-mi bus corridor connecting the North Hollywood subway station with the western San Fernando Valley, opened in fall 2005.

There's service from about 4:30 AM to 12:30 AM, every 5–15 minutes, depending on time of day and location. Buy a ticket from any station's vending machines (use bus tokens, coins, or $1 or $5 bills). It costs $1.25 plus 25¢ per transfer, or $5 for an all-day pass. The machines print your tickets and make change. (If you have a valid Metro Pass for buses, you don't need a ticket.) Metro Rail operates on the honor system; officers make periodic checks for valid tickets or passes onboard. Bicycles are not allowed during rush hours and then only with permits, but you can store them on a rack (free) or in a locker (fee). The Web site is the best way to get info on Metro Rail. See also "L.A. on the Fast Track" in Chapter 1.

TICKET/PASS	PRICE
Single Fare	$1.25
All-day Pass	$5
Monthly Pass	$52

ZONE	PRICE
A	$1.50
B	$3
C	$4.50

Metro Rail Information **Metropolitan Transit Authority (MTA)** (☎ *800/266-6883 or 213/626-4455* *www.mta.net*).

TAXI AND LIMO TRAVEL

Don't even try to hail a cab on the street in Los Angeles. Instead, phone one of the many taxi companies. The metered rate is $2.45 per mi, plus a $2.65 per-fare charge. Taxi rides from LAX have an additional $2.50 surcharge. Be aware that distances between sights in L.A. are vast, so cab fares add up quickly. On the other end of the price spectrum, limousines come equipped with everything from a full bar and telephone to a hot tub. If you open any L.A.–area yellow pages, the number of limo companies will astound you. Most charge by the hour, with a three-hour minimum.

Limo Companies **ABC Limousine & Sedan Service** (☎ *818/980-6000 or 888/753-7500*). **American Executive** (☎ *800/927-2020*). **Black & White Transportation Services**

(☎ *800/924-1624*). **Chauffeur's Unlimited** (☎ *888/546-6019* 🌐 *www.chaufusa.com*). **Dav El Limousine Co.** (☎ *800/922-0343* 🌐 *www.davel.com*). **Norman Lewis Limousine** (☎ *800/400-9771* 🌐 *www.first-classlimo.com*). **ITS** (☎ *800/487-4255*).

Taxi Companies **Beverly Hills Cab Co.** (☎ *800/273-6611*). **Checker Cab** (☎ *800/300-5007*). **Independent Cab Co.** (☎ *800/521-8294* 🌐 *www.taxi4u.com*). **United Independent Taxi** (☎ *800/411-0303 or 800/822-8294*). **Yellow Cab/LA Taxi Co-Op** (☎ *800/200-1085 or 800/200-0011*).

TRAIN TRAVEL

Union Station in downtown Los Angeles is one of the great American railroad stations. The interior is well kept and includes comfortable seating, a restaurant, and snack bars. As the city's rail hub, it's the place to catch an Amtrak train. Among Amtrak's Southern California routes are 13 daily trips to San Diego and seven to Santa Barbara. Amtrak's luxury *Coast Starlight* travels along the spectacular coastline from Seattle to Los Angeles in just a day and a half (though it's often a little late). The *Sunset Limited* goes to Los Angeles from Florida (via New Orleans and Texas), and the *Southwest Chief* from Chicago. You can make reservations in advance by phone or at the station. As with airlines, you usually get a better deal the farther in advance you book. You must show your ticket and a photo ID before boarding. Smoking is not allowed on Amtrak trains.

Information **Amtrak** (☎ *800/872-7245* 🌐 *www.amtrak.com*). **Union Station** (✉ *800 N. Alameda St.* ☎ *213/683-6979*).

ESSENTIALS

DAY TOURS AND GUIDES

You can explore L.A. from many vantage points and even more topical angles. Not surprisingly, lots of guides include dollops of celebrity history and gossip. Most tours run year-round, and most require advance reservations.

BUS AND VAN TOURS

Guideline Tours gives sightseeing tours all around L.A., including downtown, stars' homes, Universal Studios, and Hollywood. L.A. Tours and Sightseeing has several tours ($45–$109) by van and bus covering various parts of the city, including downtown, Hollywood, and Beverly Hills. The company also operates tours to Disneyland, Universal Studios, Six Flags Magic Mountain, beaches, and stars' homes. Starline Tours of Hollywood ($18–$100) picks up passengers from area hotels and from Grauman's Chinese Theatre. Universal Studios, Knott's Berry Farm, stars' homes, and Disneyland are some of the sights on this popular tour company's agenda.

Fees and Schedules Guideline Tours (☎ *323/461–0156* 🌐 *www.tourslosangeles.com*). **L.A. Tours and Sightseeing** (☎ *323/460–6490* 🌐 *www.latours.net*). **Starline Tours of Hollywood** (☎ *323/463–3333 or 800/959–3131* 🌐 *www.starlinetours.com*).

HELICOPTER TOURS

If you want an aerial tour, lift off with Orbic Helicopters. It offers two 30-minute tours (a general L.A. tour and a scenic shoreline/Westside tour) and a 45-minute tour combining those itineraries. Orbic's been flying its two- and four-passenger helicopters for more than a dozen years, and the pilots each have 16 or more years of flying experience. Flights cost $160 per person ($225 if you book two tours; custom tours are $280 per hour); reserve via credit card and cancel within 24 hours at no charge (no-shows pay full fare).

Fees and Schedules Orbic Helicopters (☎ *818/988-6532* 🌐 *www.orbichelicopters.com*).

PRIVATE GUIDES

L.A. Nighthawks will arrange your nightlife for you. For a rather hefty price (starting at $250 per person for three clubs in three hours), you'll get a limousine, a guide (who ensures you're in a safe environment at all times), and immediate entry into L.A.'s hottest nightspots.

Fees and Schedules L.A. Nighthawks (☎ *310/392–1500*).

SCOOTER TOURS

For an unusual perspective on L.A.'s attractions, you can take a tour of the city via the Segway, the electric scooter and "human transporter" that debuted on city sidewalks in 2003. Tours range from $59 to $89 per person, and there are 15 different areas or themes from which to choose, including the UCLA campus, Santa Monica, and Rodeo Drive. All tours begin with an instruction session, followed by a guided ride, totaling just over two hours.

Fees and Schedules Segway Tours (☎ *310/358–5900* 🌐 *www.segwow.com*).

SPECIAL-INTEREST TOURS

With Architecture Tours L.A., you can zip all over the city in a 1960s Cadillac on a private tour with an architectural historian. Rates start at $68. Architours customizes walking and driving tours for architecture buffs; these can include interior visits with architects, artists, and designers. A three-hour driving tour is $85; a downtown walking tour is $35.

The city of Beverly Hills operates year-round trolley tours that are focused on art and architecture and local sights. They last 40 minutes and run from 11 AM TO 4 PM every Saturday. Tickets cost $5. Soak up the shimmer and glow of classic neon signs from an open double-decker bus on a Neon Art Tour; tours and cruises $55.

The Next Stage also has an innovative take on the city; it takes people by foot, bus, van, train, and helicopter on its tours. Favorites (mostly in the $45–$65 range) include the Insomniac's Tour, a chocolate-covered L.A. tour, and a culinary tour. Take My Mother Please will arrange lively, thematic combination walking and driving tours; for instance, you could explore sights associated with Raymond Chandler's detective novels. Custom tours are also available. Rates start at $350 for up to three people for a half day.

Fees and Schedules **Architecture Tours L.A.** (☎ *323/464–7868* 🌐 *www.architecturetoursla.com*). **Architours** (☎ *323/294–5821* 🌐 *www.architours.com*). **City of Beverly Hills Trolley Tours** (☎ *310/285–2438* 🌐 *www.beverlyhills.org*). **Neon Art Tours** (☎ *213/489–9918 Museum of Neon Art* 🌐 *www.neonmona.org*). **The Next Stage** (☎ *626/577–7880* 🌐 *www.nextstagetours.com*). **Take My Mother Please** (☎ *323/737–2200* 🌐 *www.takemymotherplease.com*).

WALKING TOURS

Red Line Tours offers daily one- and two-hour walking tours of Hollywood behind the scenes and historic and contemporary downtown Los Angeles. Tours, which cost $20, are led by a docent, and include live audio headsets to block out street noise.

The Los Angeles Conservancy's walking tours (each about 2½ hours long at a cost of $10 per person) chiefly cover the downtown area. The Historic Core tour showcases the city's art deco and beaux arts past. A pleasant, self-guided walking tour of Santa Monica is detailed in a brochure available at the Santa Monica Visitors Information Center.

Fees and Schedules **Los Angeles Conservancy** (☎ *213/623–2489* 🌐 *www.laconservancy.org*). **Red Line Tours** (☎ *323/402–1074* 🌐 *www.redlinetours.com*). **Santa Monica Visitors Information Center** (☎ *310/319–6263 or 800/544–5319* 🌐 *www.santamonica.com*).

HEALTH

Air pollution in L.A. may affect sensitive people in different ways. During particularly bad days in summer (the media update pollution levels each day), it's a good idea to plan a day indoors or on a windy beach. The sun can burn even on overcast days, and the dry heat can dehydrate, so wear hats, sunglasses, and sunblock and carry water with you.

Do not fly within 24 hours of scuba diving, or you'll put your lungs at risk by going from a high-pressure environment to a low-pressure one.

HOURS OF OPERATION

Los Angeles is not a city that never sleeps, but through much of the area, business extends well into the evening, especially for the bigger stores and chains and malls. On Monday certain restaurants, nightclubs, and shops (such as outdoor sports–gear rental stores) are closed.

Many L.A. museums are closed on Monday and major holidays. However, a few of the preeminent art museums, including the Norton Simon and Los Angeles County Museum of Art, stay open on Monday. Instead, the Norton Simon is closed Tuesday, the Los Angeles County museum on Wednesday. Most museums close around 5 PM or 6 PM, and most stay open late at least one night a week, often Thursday. Many museums, large and small, have weekly or monthly free days or hours when no admission is charged.

Most stores in Los Angeles are open 10 to 6, although many stay open until 9 PM or later, particularly those in trendy areas such as Melrose Avenue and in Santa Monica. Amoeba Music in East Hollywood, for example, is open until 11 PM most nights. Shops along Melrose, Abbot Kinney Boulevard in Venice, and in Los Feliz often don't get moving until 11 AM or noon. Most shops are open on Sunday at least in the afternoon.

MONEY

Although not inexpensive, costs in Los Angeles tend to be a bit less than in other major cities such as New York and San Francisco. For instance, in a low-key local diner, a cup of coffee might cost a dollar. In high-profile or trendy establishments, though, costs escalate; a cup of coffee in an upscale restaurant can cost as much as $5.

ITEM	AVERAGE COST
Cup of Coffee	$1.75
Glass of Wine	$7
Glass of Beer	$5
Sandwich	$7
15-minute Taxi Ride in Capital City	$12
Museum Admission	$7

Prices throughout this guide are given for adults. Substantially reduced fees are almost always available for children, students, and senior citizens.

CREDIT CARDS

Throughout this guide, the following abbreviations are used: **AE,** American Express; **D,** Discover; **DC,** Diners Club; **MC,** MasterCard; and **V,** Visa.

Reporting Lost Cards **American Express** (☎ *800/992–3404 in U.S.* ⊕ *www.americanexpress.com*). **Diners Club** (☎ *800/234–6377 in U.S.* ⊕ *www.dinersclub.com*). **Discover** (☎ *800/347–2683 in U.S.* ⊕ *www.discovercard.com*). **MasterCard** (☎ *800/622–7747 in U.S.* ⊕ *www.mastercard.com*). **Visa** (☎ *800/847–2911 in U.S.* ⊕ *www.visa.com*).

RESTROOMS

Some restrooms in L.A. are clean as a whistle; others are pigsty awful. You can assume that gas stations along the highways outside of town will have a bathroom available, but this isn't true of every station in L.A. itself. Restrooms in parks are often dirty. Restaurants and bars may have signs that read FOR PATRONS ONLY so that you're obliged to buy something to use the facilities. Better bets for relatively clean, obligation-free restrooms are those in department stores and large chain bookstores.

SAFETY

In L.A., as in any other major American city, street smarts and common sense are your best methods of staying safe. At night, avoid areas that are deserted or unlighted. When driving in unfamiliar areas, plan your route ahead of time rather than figuring it out on the way. Do not respond to people offering cab rides or help with your luggage.

Keep valuables out of sight on the street or, better yet, leave them at home. Men should carry wallets in front pants pockets rather than in back pockets. Do not hang purses or backpacks on the back of chairs or put them on empty neighboring seats. Keep your belongings close; for example, tuck your bag between your feet at a movie theater. Money belts and waist packs peg you as a tourist; if you carry a purse, consider one with a thick strap that can be worn across the body, bandolier-style. When leaving your car, put any valuables out of sight; put all the windows up and lock all doors and the trunk.

The most concentrated homeless population in the city is Downtown, and on some blocks panhandling is common. Hollywood and Santa Monica are other areas where you're most likely to be approached for money or food.

After years in decline, gang-related violent crime has recently been on the rise, prompting aggressive new antigang initiatives. Gang-related street violence is concentrated in certain neighborhoods; South L.A., Compton, and Watts should be avoided, particularly at night.

Of the Metro lines, the Red and Green lines are the safest and are more heavily patrolled. The Blue Line can be sketchy after dark. Avoid riding in empty cars, and move with the crowd when going from the station to the street.

Safety **Transportation Security Administration** (*TSA* 🌐 *www.tsa.gov*).

EARTHQUAKES

Very minor earthquakes occur frequently in Southern California; most of the time they're so slight that you won't notice them at all. If you do feel a stronger tremor, follow basic safety precautions. If you're indoors, take cover in a doorway or under a table or desk—whichever is closest to you. Protect your head with your arms. Stay clear of windows, mirrors, or anything that might fall from the walls. Do not use elevators. If you're in an open space, move away from buildings, trees, and power lines. If you're outdoors near buildings, duck into a doorway. If you're driving, slow down and pull over to the side of the road, avoiding overpasses, bridges, and power lines, and stay inside the car. Expect aftershocks; if you feel a smaller quake following a larger tremor, take cover again.

TAXES

The sales tax in Los Angeles is 8.25%. There's none on most groceries, but there is on newspapers (unless bought from a coin-operated machine) and magazines. The tax on hotel rooms ranges from 13%–15.5%.

TIME

Los Angeles is in the Pacific time zone, two hours behind Chicago, three hours behind New York, eight hours behind London, and 18 hours behind Sydney.

Time Zones 🌐 *www.worldtimezone.com* can help you figure out the correct time anywhere in the world.

TIPPING

The customary tip rate is 15%–20% for waiters and taxi drivers and 10%–15% for hairdressers and barbers. Bellhops and airport baggage handlers receive $1–$2 per bag; parking valets are usually tipped $1–$2. Bartenders are generally tipped $1 per drink. Hotel maids should generally receive $1–$3 per day of the stay. In upscale establishments, they should receive at least 4% of the room rate before taxes, unless the hotel charges a service fee that includes a gratuity. In restaurants, a handy trick for estimating the tip is to move the decimal point one space and the doubling that to get 20%.

VISITOR INFORMATION

L.A. Inc./The Convention and Visitors Bureau (CVB) publishes an annually updated general information packet with suggestions for entertainment, lodging, dining, and a list of special events. There are two L.A. visitor information centers, on Figueroa downtown and on Hollywood Boulevard in Hollywood. The Santa Monica CVB runs two drop-in visitor information centers, one in the Santa Monica Place Shopping Center and another in Palisades Park; both are open daily 10–4.

City and State Contacts **California Office of Tourism** (☎ *916/444–4429 or 800/862–2543* 🌐 *visitcalifornia.com*). **L.A. Inc./The Convention and Visitors Bureau** (☎ *213/624–7300 or 800/228–2452* 🌐 *www.lacvb.com*).

Neighborhood Contacts **Beverly Hills Conference and Visitors Bureau** (☎ *310/248–1000 or 800/345–2210* 🌐 *beverlyhillschamber.com, lovebeverlyhills.org*). **Hollywood Chamber of Commerce Info Center** (☎ *323/469–8311* 🌐 *www.hollywoodchamber.net*). **Long Beach Area Convention and Visitors Bureau** (☎ *562/436–3645* 🌐 *www.visitlongbeach.com*). **Pasadena Convention; Visitors Bureau** (☎ *626/795–9311* 🌐 *www.pasadenacal.com*). **Redondo Beach Visitors Bureau** (☎ *310/374–2171 or 800/282–0333*

FOR INTERNATIONAL TRAVELERS

CURRENCY

The dollar is the basic unit of U.S. currency. It has 100 cents. Coins are the penny (1¢); the nickel (5¢), dime (10¢), quarter (25¢), half-dollar (50¢), and the rare golden $1 coin and rarer silver $1. Bills are denominated $1, $5, $10, $20, $50, and $100, all mostly green and identical in size; designs and background tints vary. A $2 bill exists but is extremely rare.

CUSTOMS

Information U.S. Customs and Border Protection (*www.cbp.gov*).

DRIVING

Driving in the United States is on the right. Speed limits are posted in miles per hour (usually between 55 mph and 70 mph). In small towns and on back roads limits are usually 30 mph to 40 mph. Most states require front-seat passengers to wear seat belts; children should be in the back seat and buckled up. In major cities, rush hours are 7 to 10 AM and 4 to 7 PM. Some freeways have high-occupancy vehicle (HOV) lanes, ordinarily marked with a diamond, for cars carrying two people or more.

Highways are well paved. Interstates—limited-access, multilane highways designated with an "I–" before the number—are fastest. Interstates with three-digit numbers circle urban areas, which may also have other expressways, freeways, and parkways. Limited-access highways sometimes have tolls.

Gas stations are plentiful, except in rural areas. Most stay open late (some 24 hours). Along larger highways, roadside stops with restrooms, fast-food restaurants, and sundries stores are well spaced. State police and tow trucks patrol major highways. If your car breaks down, pull onto the shoulder and wait, or have passengers wait while you walk to a roadside emergency phone (most states). On a cell phone, dial *55.

ELECTRICITY

The U.S. standard is AC, 110 volts/60 cycles. Plugs have two flat pins set parallel to each other.

EMBASSIES

Contacts Australia ☎ *202/797–3000* *www.austemb.org*. **Canada** ☎ *202/682–1740* *www.canadianembassy.org*. **UK** ☎ *202/588–7800* *www.britainusa.com*.

EMERGENCIES

For police, fire, or ambulance, dial 911 (0 in rural areas).

HOLIDAYS

New Year's Day (Jan. 1); Martin Luther King Day (3rd Mon. in Jan.); Presidents' Day (3rd Mon. in Feb.); Memorial Day (last Mon. in May); Independence Day (July 4); Labor Day (1st Mon. in Sept.); Columbus Day (2nd Mon. in Oct.); Thanksgiving Day (4th Thurs. in Nov.); Christmas Eve and Christmas Day (Dec. 24 and 25); and New Year's Eve (Dec. 31).

MAIL

You can buy stamps and send letters and parcels in post offices. Stamp-dispensing machines can occasionally be found in airports, bus and train stations, office buildings, drugstores, convenience stores, and in ATMs. U.S. mailboxes are stout, dark-blue steel bins; pickup schedules are posted inside the bin (pull the handle). Mail parcels over a pound at a post office.

A first-class letter weighing 1 ounce or less costs 44¢; each additional ounce costs 17¢. Postcards cost 28¢. Postcards or 1-ounce airmail letters to most countries cost 98¢; post-cards or 1-ounce letters to Canada or Mexico cost 79¢.

To receive mail on the road, have it sent c/o General Delivery to your destination's main post office. You must pick up mail in person within 30 days with a driver's license or passport for identification.

Contacts DHL ☎ *800/225–5345* 🌐 *www.dhl.com.* **FedEx** ☎ *800/463–3339* 🌐 *www.fedex.com.* **Mail Boxes, Etc./The UPS Store** ☎ *800/789–4623* 🌐 *www.mbe.com.* **USPS** 🌐 *www.usps.com.*

PASSPORTS AND VISAS

Visitor visas aren't necessary for citizens of Australia, Canada, the United Kingdom, or most citizens of EU countries coming for tourism and staying for under 90 days. A visa is $100, and waiting time can be substantial. Apply for a visa at the U.S. consulate in your place of residence.

Visa Information Destination USA (🌐 *www.unitedstatesvisas.gov*).

PHONES

Numbers consist of a three-digit area code and a seven-digit local number. In Los Angeles, the area codes are 424 and (newer) 310. Within many local calling areas, dial just seven digits. In others, dial "1" first and all 10 digits; this is true for calling toll-free numbers—prefixed by "800," "888," "866," and "877." Dial "1" before "900" numbers, too, but know they're very expensive.

For international calls, dial "011," the country code, and the number. For help, dial "0" and ask for an overseas operator. Most phone books list country codes and U.S. area codes. The country code for Australia is 61, for New Zealand 64, for the United Kingdom 44. Calling Canada is the same as calling within the United States (country code: 1).

For operator assistance, dial "0." For directory assistance, call 555–1212 or 411 (free at many public phones). To call "collect" (reverse charges), dial "0" instead of "1" before the 10-digit number.

Instructions are generally posted on pay phones. Usually you insert coins in a slot (usually 25¢–50¢ for local calls) and wait for a steady tone before dialing. On long-distance calls the operator tells you how much to insert; prepaid phone cards, widely available, can be used from any phone. Follow the directions to activate the card, then dial your number.

CELL PHONES

The United States has several GSM (Global System for Mobile Communications) networks, so multiband mobiles from most countries (except for Japan) work here. It's almost impossible to buy just a pay-as-you-go mobile SIM card in the U.S.—needed to avoid roaming charges—but cell phones with pay-as-you-go plans are available for well under $100. AT&T (GoPhone) and Virgin Mobile have the cheapest with national coverage.

Contacts AT&T (☎ *888/333-6651* 🌐 *www.wireless.att.com*). **T-Mobile** (☎ *877/453-1304* 🌐 *www.t-mobile.com*). **Verizon** (☎ *800/922-0204* 🌐 *www.verizon.com*).

www.visitredondo.com). **Santa Monica Convention; Visitors Bureau** (*310/319–6263 or 800/544–5319 www.santamonica.com).* **West Hollywood Convention and Visitors Bureau** (*310/289–2525 or 800/368–6020 www.visitwesthollywood.com).*

ONLINE RESOURCES

There are several community Web sites that will give you a closer look at particular neighborhoods and often include events listings; a few of the best include Venicebeach.com (*www.venicebeach.com*), Santa Monica's LookOut newsletter site (*www.surfsantamonica.com*), and LA Commons guide (*www.lacommons.org*) to Koreatown, Highland Park, and other urban communities.

The Los Angeles Conservancy site (*www.laconservancy.org*) includes info on the preservation of local historic buildings, as well as the latest on its walking tours and self-guided podcast tours of downtown. For information on festivals, exhibitions, performances, and special events, visit the Los Angeles Cultural Affairs Department site (*www.culturela.org*). The city's Department of Recreation and Parks (*www.laparks.com*) posts info on all kinds of sports facilities, parks, and even dog runs. The Sierra Club's Angeles chapter has a good Web site about trails and events in Griffith Park (*angeles.sierraclub.org/griffith*); there's also an excellent downloadable map of the entire park. Through Gallery Guide.org (*www.galleryguide.org*) you can check on upcoming openings, shows, and events in the city's fine-arts community. The Academy of Motion Pictures Arts and Sciences rolls out scads of Academy Awards info at *www.oscars.org*, plus details on other Academy events. Get more celebrity scoops on where stars shop, dine, and play at *www.seeing-stars.com.*

All About Los Angeles **LAVoice.org** (*www.lavoice.org*) is an independent blog with news, observations, and unscripted rants about all things L.A. Check out *www.la.com* for insiders' guides to bars, restaurants, concerts, and other forms of entertainment. An editor's blog opines on everything from new billboards to movie premieres.

L.A. Observed (*www.laobserved.com*) is a must-read for many Angelenos, who want its daily media and political updates. It's also good for L.A. history references and links to other local media sites.

For L.A.–centric gossip, check out **Defamer** (*www.defamer.com*) and **Perez Hilton** (*www.perezhilton.com*); both sites track celebrity sightings and the activities of A-list stars with snarky honesty. Foodies keep tabs on their favorite celebrity chefs via the Web site **Eater Los Angeles** *la.eater.com.*

TV personality Huell Howser's Web site (*www.kcet.com/programsa-z/huells*) revisits unusual L.A. places he has covered on his show, from a *menudo* (tripe stew) factory to a museum for African-American firefighters.

The city of Los Angeles government site (*www.lacity.org*) has various entertainment and cultural links. The Central Library's Web site (*www.lapl.org*) has sections on books set in L.A. and regional history resources.

INDEX

D

Photo Credits: Chapter 1: Experience Los Angeles: 8, Richard Cummins/viestiphoto.com. 9 (left), Liane Cary/age fotostock. 9 (right), Manfred Baumann/age fotostock. 12, Nadine Markova/LACVB. 13 (left), Gary Crabbe/Alamy. 13 (right), Michele & Tom Grimm/LACVB. 14, David Crockett Photography/Alamy. 15 (left), Walter Bibikow/age fotostock. 15 (right), Jon Arnold Images/Alamy. 16 (top left), Ken Ross/viestiphoto.com. 16 (bottom left), Rodolfo Arpia/Alamy. 16 (right), Martin Sasse/laif/Aurora Photos. 17 (top left), Richard Cummins/viestiphoto.com. 17 (bottom left), Wendy Connett/age fotostock. 17 (top right), Kenna Love/LACVB. 17 (bottom right), Corbis. 20, Corbis. Chapter 2: Exploring Los Angeles: 32, Joe Viesti/viestiphoto.com. 77, Allstar Picture Library/Alamy. Chapter 3: Where to Eat: 115, Los Angeles Convention and Visitors Bureau. 140, Angela Hampton Picture Library/Alamy. Chapter 5: Nightlife & the Arts: 228, Die Bildagentur der Fotografen GmbH/Alamy. Chapter 6: Sports & the Outdoors: 263, JingleBeeZ Photo Gallery/Shutterstock. Chapter 7: Shopping: 273, Uripos/eStock Photo.

NOTES